The Family

A Sociological Interpretation

Fifth Edition

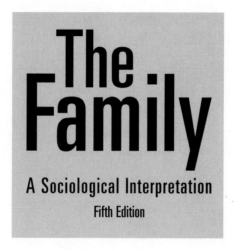

The Family

A Sociological Interpretation

Fifth Edition

BERT N. ADAMS

University of Wisconsin, Madison

HARCOURT BRACE COLLEGE PUBLISHERS

Fort Worth Philadelphia San Diego New York Orlando Austin San Antonio
Toronto Montreal London Sydney Tokyo

Publisher	TED BUCHHOLZ
Acquisition Editor	CHRIS KLEIN
Project Editor	KAREN ANDERSON
Production Manager	JANE TYNDALL PONCETI
Art Director	NICK WELCH

Address for editorial correspondence:
Harcourt Brace College Publishers
301 Commerce St. Suite 3700
Fort Worth, Texas 76102

Address for orders:
Harcourt Brace and Company
6277 Sea Harbor Drive
Orlando, Fl 32887-6777
1-800-782-4479 (outside Florida)
1-800-433-0001 (in Florida)

ISBN: 0-15-501925-2
Library of Congress Catalogue Number: 94-076726

Printed in the United States of America
4 5 6 7 8 9 0 1 2 3 039 0 9 8 7 6 5 4 3 2 1

CONTENTS

PREFACE

This book presents a sociological perspective on the past, present, and future of the family. While emphasizing the U.S. family, we have placed it in a cross-cultural and historical framework to help the reader grasp what is happening to families today. The relevant literature has been reviewed and incorporated, but in a pointed and—we hope—readable fashion. The attempt has been to be interpretive, not encyclopedic.

The continuing advance of family scholarship, changes in the family itself, and the passage of eight years since the fourth edition, has required the almost complete reworking of this text. While virtually no page has been left unchanged, the major alterations include the following:

First, we have changed the titles of chapters 9 and 10 from "Dating" and "Mate Selection" to "Prelude to Pairing Up" and "Choosing a Partner." The reasons for this change are that the term "dating" no longer covers the variety of pairing processes. One aspect of this is seen in the discussion of cohabitation here, rather than in chapter 18 on "Alternatives." As for the chapter on "Choosing a Partner," we have changed the title to recognize the fact that marital choices, friendship choices, and homosexual units involve many of the same selective processes. Of course, for the large majority choosing a partner still means choosing a *marital* partner.

Second, literature by feminist scholars, while already helpful in the mid-1980s, has become increasingly well-developed in the past decade. One result has been to add the term "patriarchy" to the two forms of embeddedness already utilized for explanation in the previous editions. Discussion of patriarchy, drawn from the cross-cultural and historical materials, makes it possible to ask the following question throughout: in what ways and to what extent does patriarchy still describe U.S. families and society today?

Third, gender role literature abounded in the 1970s and early '80s, but has been produced by feminist and other scholars ever more rapidly in the past decade. This has required a complete reworking of chapter 12.

Fourth, the chapter that is completely new is chapter 17, on "Divorce, Death, and Remarriage." As the divorce rate has remained high, the number of studies of divorce and remarriage have outrun all other sub-areas of family study. Thus, the literature on post-divorce adjustments—of both adults and children—has mushroomed, as have studies of step-relationships.

Thus, while keeping much of the outline, this fifth edition is virtually a new book. I hope you will find it exciting.

Any author is obliged to many people. I would like to acknowledge the contributions of Terri Lischka, Dianna Zimmerman, Kirsten Papp, and Judith Ziemann in reviewing literature. Sandra Ramer put the manuscript on discs and

Joel Adams did several tasks on the manuscript. At Harcourt Brace, Chris Klein, as Executive Editor, was encouraging throughout the project, and Karen Anderson was the Project Editor. Others at Harcourt who helped were Nick Welch, as art director, Marco Ruiz, as free lance artist, and Jane Ponceti as production manager.

Bert N. Adams

The Family

A Sociological Interpretation

Fifth Edition

Introduction to Family Study

CHAPTER 1

The family is a central institution in modern society, but one that is always changing. Today's questions concern definitions, activities, and institutionalization. Some believe the family is doing okay in meeting people's needs for love and belonging. Others feel it is thriving, but sick. Still others see it as in serious trouble, either because it is doing too much for the individual, or too little, or doesn't know what it is supposed to do or be. Scientific study of the family spread in the twentieth century, and theorizing about the family has made considerable advances since the early 1970s. Patriarchy, institutional embeddedness, and individual embeddedness, three important concepts in this volume, are introduced and will be treated in considerable detail in Chapters 2 through 5.

This book is about a basic institution in our society, the family. If asked, many U.S. citizens will say that the primary institutions of the community are home, church, and school. However, *institution* is often a vague term, which requires some definitional attention. First, it is assumed to involve some important subsection of social life, such as politics, economics, or religion. Second, it is defined by certain structures, activities, and values. Thus, an institution is an organized aspect of society that is perpetuated by various norms or rules. We live in, experience, alter, and have attitudes toward our institutions. And it is alteration of and attitudes toward the family that give rise to today's confusion regarding it.

Governmental institutions are concerned with social control and mobilization, economic institutions regulate the production and distribution of goods and services, and religious organizations seek to relate us to the supernatural and to ultimate values. Yet, basic to these aspects of society in recent history has been the family—that institution pertaining to sexual relations, marriage, reproduction and childbearing, socialization or child-rearing, and to relating the individual to the other institutions of society.

The key phrase in the previous sentence is in "recent history." Has the family always played those roles, and is it doing so today? Or is it possible that the family described above is both a recent phenomenon and one that is not completely defined by the listed characteristics? To answer this we must examine possible definitions and characteristics. A key concern of this book will be to show how family rules (or the family institution) have changed throughout history. And since most readers have experienced a particular kind of "family," it will be important for us to try to stand far enough back from our experience that we can see it in a much larger contemporary and historical context. John Scanzoni and his co-authors have noted that "the traditional family" is the form against which all other types of relationships are judged (Scanzoni et al., 1989: 13). What this means is that the family described above is often defined as "the best"—clearly a value judgment. So certain rules, structures, and activities may be seen not only as what families are, but as what they should be, as better than alternative ways of organizing intimate life. In fact, there are few institutions about which more value judgments or ideology have been intermingled with description. Maxine Baca-Zinn warns of the ideology-laden nature of family studies: "The sociology of the family has been noted for its absence of a strong tradition of theory and for being heavily normative, moralistic, and mingled with social policy and the social objectives of various action groups" (Baca-Zinn, in Lorber and Farrell, 1991: 121). To this, David Cheal adds that a troublesome problem in writing his book was "the assumption in standard sociological theory that there is a universal core to family life, which can be given an objective definition as *the family*" (Cheal, 1991: 9).

Three questions are being raised today about this "universal core": (1) Has the family's core always been as described above? (2) Does the core description capture the character of the traditional industrial family, or are there aspects, such as love, that are variables instead of defining qualities of family life, and others, such as patriarchy, conflict, and coercion, that should be included? (3) How quickly is this core giving way to a variety of other arrangements of intimate life that may or may not be labelled "family"?

This third question raises the definitional problem once again. How should family be defined in a book like this? Is it better to adhere to the monogamous nuclear family concept (i.e., one female, one male, and some children, living together), so that we can ask questions such as: What is happening to the family? Is the family disappearing? etc. Or should we define "family" as "however people organize their intimate life," so that it continually is redefined by what people do? (see Feature 1.1 below) Or should we give up the concept of "family" entirely as being too laden with ideological baggage, and replace it with some new and uncluttered idea, such as Scanzoni et al.'s SBPR (sexually-based primary relationship) that does not subsume sexuality under marriage (Scanzoni et al., 1989). Though Scanzoni's book is full of insights, they are not really trying to replace "family" with "SBPR," but are simply making clear the separation between sexuality and family today. SBPR may take its place alongside family as a usable concept. For the most part, "family" in this book will be qualified by additional terms, such as "monogamous nuclear," so as to make it more specific, or else will be unmodified, to be explained by the context within which it is being discussed.

There are two ways to tell if institutional norms or rules exist: first, by the answers you get to the question "what is the marriage and family system here?" If an answer predominates that includes characteristics like those listed above, then you can still say that family norm exists—even though much behavior departs from it. Second, you may notice who feels they must explain their behavior or plans and who does not. For example, if you are graduating from college and plan (among other things) to get married and have children, ordinarily you will not have to explain why. However, in most U.S. social circles if you plan to

Feature 1.1 REDEFINING A "FAMILY":

The alternative families bill, introduced at last week's common council meeting, is unprecedented in Wisconsin for extended equal rights to families that don't fit the traditional mold—opening up opportunities in housing, credit, health insurance, membership, and sick leave that were never before available.

The legislation . . . is expanded to include gay or lesbian couples, unmarried heterosexual couples, elderly persons, and disabled persons with live-in attendants under its provisions.

. . . The bill promises to be one of the most controversial that the city has seen in some time.

Chris Karlin, "Redefining a 'family,' Proposal extends rights to gay couples," *Badger Herald*, November 12, 1987.

organize your intimate life some other way, such as raising a child without marrying, or never marrying, or if you plan to live in a homosexual relationship, you may still have to explain your behavior, since it departs from an existing norm. Furthermore, one way to tell when another behavior is an equal alternative, or has replaced the previous one, is when you no longer have to explain why you plan to organize your life that way.

This leads to an insightful discussion by C. C. Harris of what is happening to marriage in the industrialized world. It is, he says, becoming "deinstitutionalized." If marriage "is a prerequisite neither for mating, coresidence, nor child-rearing, and does not regulate sexual access, it ceases to be in any sense the institution of marriage and simply becomes a type of relationship available to partners should they happen to choose it" (Harris, 1983: 209).

Characteristics, expectations, and change—these are the sorts of issues that will confront us throughout this volume. Yet it is impossible to treat the subject matter as simply a focus for scientific study and understanding. We cannot ignore the commentaries and interpretations that abound in both the popular and social science literature. Is the family today still of central importance? Is it dominant? Is it specializing and adapting to the contemporary world? Or is it disintegrating? Let us examine some of these interpretations.

SECTION ONE

WHAT IS HAPPENING TO THE FAMILY?

Doing Okay, Thank You

The family has become a specialist in a world of specialists. Its function is to meet its members' needs for love and belonging. It is well adapted to the modern, industrialized world, being a small, easily mobile unit that can follow the job market without being encumbered with many kin. This depiction of the family as doing fine today is closely linked with the name of Talcott Parsons (1949, 1955) but is also found elsewhere. In a book on transitions, Peter Uhlenberg notes that profound changes occurred in American society between 1870 and 1970, with the following effects on the family:

> *Over this time span, an increasing proportion of women entered marriage, an increasing proportion bore children, and many fewer had their marriage disrupted by death before the child-rearing years were completed. For males, also, the changes over this century did not reduce participation in family roles. More males from the 1930 cohort will be married and living with their first wife at age 30 than was true for the 1870 cohort, and the percentage who never marry among the more recent cohort will be less than half that of the earlier one. . . . An increasing proportion of the population lives out the life course almost wholly within a family context. In speculating on the family of the future, one should not ignore the remarkable stability and adaptability of the American family during the past century of vast social change (Uhlenberg, 1978).*

Mary Jo Bane expands on the theme of family stability in a book entitled *Here to Stay: American Families in the Twentieth Century*. Although more mothers work outside the home, Bane feels that "the quantity and quality of actual mother-child interaction has probably not changed much." Marriage is still exceedingly important in American life, since 90 to 95 percent of Americans (when she wrote) marry at least once. In addition, married men and women are more likely to say that they are very happy than are the various categories of single individuals. Furthermore, when divorce occurs there is a great sense of grief and emptiness on the part of both partners. Even the divorce rate itself, Bane feels, "falls far short of the level that would characterize a society of casual liaisons rather than permanent families" (Bane, 1976: 36). Based on her analysis of numerous studies of the family, Bane concludes as follows:

The facts—as opposed to the myths—about marriage, child-rearing, and family ties in the United States today provide convincing evidence that family commitments are likely to persist in our society. Family ties, it seems clear, are not archaic remnants of a disappearing traditionalism, but persisting manifestations of human needs for stability, continuity, and nonconditional affection (Bane, 1976: 141).

The title of Bane's book makes clear the intent of the argument. Likewise, in 1990, Ed Kain wrote a book entitled *The Myth of Family Decline*, in which he argues along similar lines to Bane. However, he adds that rapid change makes it seem the family is disintegrating when, in fact, it is adapting and adjusting as always. Today, those who are sympathetic with the "traditional industrial family" are more likely to be wringing their hands than glorifying its stability. Yes, the family is amazingly adaptable, and people do need to belong and to be loved, but recent writers are more likely to see this type of family as in decline than as doing okay (see Scanzoni et al., 1989; Stacey, 1990).

Stable and Thriving, but a Sick, Mad Institution

According to R. D. Laing and Jules Henry, the family is very much alive, but it is alive at the expense of the individual. Sociologists of the family speak of its adaptation to its environment. To this, Laing responds: "adaptation to what, to a world gone mad? The family is an institution where normal men exploit women, where normal parents get their children to love and obey them by terrorizing them, and where the essence of good behavior is to buy things, keep moving, and not think or communicate too much. It is a destructive unit that effectively distorts the individual, leading to madness in the midst of a mad society." (Laing, 1969; Laing and Esterson, 1964; Henry, 1963) The family, in other words, may be well adjusted to a distorted and distorting society.

To this "underside" view of the family Jessie Bernard adds an essay on "The Paradox of the Happy Marriage." Wives, she finds, report more dissatisfaction with marriage than do husbands. Yet they report themselves to be happy. If marriage is as unfavorable to women as Bernard believes, why do they say they are happy?

Could it be that women report themselves as happy because they are oversocialized, overculturated, or too closely integrated into the norms of society? . . . Could it be that because married women thus conform and adjust to the demands of marriage, at whatever cost to themselves, they therefore judge themselves to be happy? Are they confusing adjustment with happiness? . . . Some clinicians are now seriously questioning whether the qualities that are associated with marital happiness for women may not themselves be contrary to good mental health. Is it possible that many women are "happily married" because they have poor mental health? (Bernard, 1971: 156–158)

Could it be, Bernard asks in conclusion, "that marriage itself is 'sick.'"

More recent feminist writers have picked up and expanded this theme, arguing that "marital quality" and "patriarchy" are mutually exclusive, and that neither men nor women may be mentally healthy in the "traditional industrial family." This issue will arise again.

In Trouble

A third view holds that the family is in grave danger today. The reasons given to support this view vary: (a) the family is too separate from the rest of society; (b) the family has too little to do; (c) the family has been given too much to do; (d) the family does not know what it is supposed to do.

TOO SEPARATE   The industrial revolution has separated work from life, whereas on the family farm they used to be "of a piece." The family is now separate from the economy; it is the sphere of personal life, divorced from the productive process. This separation has left family members to search for personal identity, to attempt to get their "heads straight": and while this search gives meaning to family life today, it also threatens to blow it apart. All of the concern today with self-assertion and uniqueness, which we will call "individualism" throughout this volume, is a result of this separation. Eli Zaretsky, from whom the above analysis is drawn, feels that this separation is a negative development, leading the family toward uselessness and the factory workers further and further away from changing the conditions of their work (Zaretsky, 1976). Work and family, Zaretsky feels, should be reunited so that the system can be changed. This notion of separation is, of course, found in the work of Parsons and others who feel that the family is doing perfectly all right as a specialist in personal relationships. However, neo-Marxists like Zaretsky and other critics view this separation as destructive. This destructiveness is a result of both the family's uselessness and the individualistic, nonfamilistic values that have arisen.

TOO LITTLE TO DO   The loss of family functions has been a theme in the family literature since the work of W. F. Ogburn in the 1930s (Ogburn, 1933: Chapter 13). One by one, the functions of education, religion, protection, medicine, production, and so on, became separated from the family into distinct institutional spheres. G. Robina Quale, in 1988, phrased it thus: "The elementary conjugal family has been left with little more than the rearing of very young children, the management of income . . . and the relief of tensions through mutual supportiveness and expression of enduring affection and acceptance" (Quale, 1988: 203).

In the hands of Christopher Lasch, this idea has been carried beyond the notion that the family simply evolved into a specialized institution with little to do. According to Lasch's book *Haven in a Heartless World*, the family is a victim of the intentional encroachment of the external world. Government will not leave the family alone, and the helping professions have consciously invaded the family to take over its functions. Nursing homes, social security, child care, and welfare payments, among other developments, have been planned penetrations of the family. This hyperrationality, say the Bergers, "affects the family both from the outside and from within. On the outside there are the professional empires of experts and advice givers of all sorts" (Berger and Berger, 1983: 120). In fact, says Lasch, the family has been so penetrated and undermined by society's leaders and experts that it can no longer perform its specialized role as a "haven in a heartless world" (Lasch, 1977).

The results of this penetration and loss can be seen in the personalities of the family members. The father is no longer a strong, authoritarian role model for his son; he is weak at home and lost in the work place. The mother, once a loving mother and homemaker, now is a confused and harried neurotic, not knowing what to be or how to handle her children. The children are taught to be dependent on their mother, to overevaluate their "unknown" father, and to respond to authority only when it is enforced. They turn their rage against authority upon themselves and seek escape through immediate gratification. Males especially, are taught by their mothers to be angry and murderous, but this anger they turn on themselves in the form of depression, anxiety, impotence, and hypochondria. Far from being a "haven," then, the family has become the basis for the psychopathology of our society, much as Laing and Henry said.

Others besides Ogburn and Lasch have used the analysis of loss of functions in either of two ways: first, it can be argued that family strength and modern individualized industrial life are incompatible, that the family farm and family division of productive labor, when lost, makes this development inevitable. Second, George Gilder and others have used this analysis to argue for the patriarchal industrial family as the ideal, with the authoritarian father and subservient, homemaking mother, and everyone "knowing their place" (Gilder; 1987). Loss, then, means confusion; and we return to the issue of confusion below.

TOO MUCH TO DO   This rather unusual viewpoint starts from many of the same premises as the foregoing. As expressed by Philippe Aries, it holds that, prior to the industrial revolution the family had no domain of its own; rather, the economy, church, politics, and the family were all embedded in each other. Now, however, with the separation of work and other institutions from the family, it has a domain of its own. That domain is under scrutiny and control by the state, which constantly seeks to penetrate it. In reaction, though, the family withdraws even further into itself, becoming the "only place where a person could legitimately escape the inquisitive stare of industrial society" (Aries, 1977). Up to this point, the discussion sounds like a combination of Ogburn, Zaretsky, and Lasch. But what is the result, according to Aries?

> *The family has had a monopoly on emotions, on raising children, and on filling leisure time. This tendency to monopolize its members is the family's way of coping with the decline of the public sector. . . .*

Although people today often claim that the family is undergoing a crisis, this is not, properly speaking, an accurate description of what is happening. Rather, we are witnessing the inability of the family to fulfill all the many functions with which it has been invested, no doubt temporarily, during the past half-century. Moreover, if my analysis is correct, this overexpansion of the family role is a result of the decline of the city and of the urban forms of social intercourse that it provided. The twentieth-century post-industrial world has been unable, so far, either to sustain the forms of social intercourse of the nineteenth century or to offer something in their place. The family has had to take over in an impossible situation; the real roots of the present domestic crisis lie not in our families, but in our cities (Aries, 1977: 234-5).

Thus, to Aries, the result of institutional specialization and separation has been not to leave the family "twiddling its collective thumbs" or with nothing to do, but to lay on the family the *total* burden of leisure and social life. Such a burden is too much for a small, intimate group of individuals; it cannot live up to its demands and often explodes or flies apart.

WHAT TO DO? This is a prevalent view today, closely related to the notion that the family is disintegrating. Commentators who glorify the "traditional industrial model" often see changes as confusions rather than opportunities. From Lundberg and Farnham in 1947 to Gilder in 1987, family conservatives have argued that liberation for the female simply means being lost and confused, and for the male it means obliteration of maleness. Gilder states this view dramatically:

Family breakdown and demoralization can occur with frightening suddenness when government policy destroys the role of the male provider in the family. The alternative to traditional family roles is not a unisex family; it is sexual suicide (Gilder, 1987: 154).

The best summary of the various reasons for family "decline" is found in David Popenoe's book *Disturbing the Nest* (1988).

The obverse side of this is the view of critical and feminist writers, who argue that change does not mean disintegration, and only temporary confusion. Rather, it means new opportunity — for freedom, fulfillment, for both genders to be complete human beings, unfettered by traditional definitions and limitations. What it means is at least a partial escape from the sicknesses of which Laing and others have spoken — partial in the sense that it will not completely erase the negative aspects of an individualized consuming society.

What Is Happening: A Summary

The family is doing fine; it has adjusted to the needs of the modern world. It has adjusted adequately, but it is producing sick individuals for a sick world. The family is in trouble because it is too separate from the economy and the rest of society, because it has too little to do, because it has too much to do, or because it doesn't know what to do. These are some of the sentiments expressed by commentators on the family since the 1970s. They cannot all be correct, although some may be complementary. Of course, those like Parsons who feel the family is functioning as it should be in the world of the '40s and '50s are expressing their values or preferences. Likewise, those who see it as being in grave danger today are expressing their values. Michael Mitterauer and Reinhard Sieder (1982) express this negative comparison and the underlying values very clearly:

> *The egoism and individualism of the small modern family was contrasted with the feeling of responsibility towards relatives in need of help of former times. . . the desire to develop one's own personality in the best way possible with the greater willingness to curb personal feelings for the mutual benefit of the family that formerly prevailed. . . sexual license with the willingness to abstain from sex by marrying late or, indeed, by remaining single. . . . Certain potentially dangerous attitudes are often concealed behind such images of the family—hostility towards democracy, for example, and above all, hostility towards the emancipation of women (Mitterauer and Sieder, 1982: 25–26).*

So, what *is* happening? Fortunately, we have several bodies of material available to help us understand the U. S. family today and to help us attempt to resolve the issues raised by the various writers. First, there are *factual materials*, drawn from empirical studies of various sorts. Sometimes their results reinforce each other, while at other times they appear to be contradictory. Second, there are *interpretations and explanations* of the facts. How, why, and to what extent has the family changed? What is the larger significance of the family's characteristics? How can the differences between research results be reconciled? Several of the best available sociological texts on the family assemble vast amounts of research findings but explicitly avoid taking interpretive positions on the open issues. In fact, the scientific study of the family has, until recently, been long on data and short on interpretation and explanation. Now, however, this situation is being remedied by authors such as those discussed above and by theorists bent on explaining family phenomena. Third, there are *social criticisms or critiques* by such commentators as Lasch, Bane, Stacey, and Barrie Thorne (1983), as well as by Karl Marx and Sigmund Freud and their followers. Finally, there are abundant *suggestions* for family improvement and change that have been articulated by both professionals and nonprofessionals concerned with today's family.

The majority of twentieth-century family texts have focused on either factual materials or suggestions and have been called *sociological* and *functional* texts, respectively. We, however, have determined to emphasize *interpretation* instead, using suggestion and criticism quite selectively and introducing those research studies that seem most useful for understanding the contemporary family. These interpretations should not be accepted as final; you will find yourself agreeing with some and disagreeing with others. Their purpose is to get you to think *sociologically and interpretively* about the family in its historical and cross-cultural context.

SECTION TWO

THE HISTORY OF FAMILY STUDY

Systematic study of the family did not begin until after the middle of the nineteenth century. Until then, interest in the family had been expressed by means of folklore, proverbs, moralisms, and laws. The family's importance in the structure of society was affirmed in much of the early wisdom literature of China, India, and the pre-exilic Hebrews. Its qualities and characteristics were argued in the Western classics from Aristotle to Hegel (Adams and Steinmetz, 1993). But the beginning of the movement toward systematic understanding of the family can be traced roughly to the appearance of Charles Darwin's *Origin of the Species* in 1859. The years from 1860 to the present may be profitably divided into five periods, each characterized by a particular emphasis with respect to the family. Each of the first four periods is approximately thirty years in length, while the last is from 1980 to the present.

1860–1890: Social Darwinism

From 1860 to 1890 numerous writers attempted to apply Darwin's biological evolutionary scheme to the course of human history. Discussions of origins, coupled with notions of evolution and progress, were found in the writings of Lewis Henry Morgan, Friedrich Engels, J. J. Bachofen, Edward Westermarck, and others. Did the family begin in a primitive horde or group marriage? Was marriage originally by capture? How did monogamy arise, and what will be its fate? Such questions interested those influenced by Darwin's theories when they wrote about the family. Their treatises were macrocosmic, or large-scale, and cross-cultural, attempting to devise universally applicable laws of societal development. Their scholarly techniques were often intuitive, sometimes involving the somewhat unscientific approach of drawing a conclusion or developing a theory and then mustering evidence from diverse sources to support it. Yet, despite the inadequacy of some of their methods, the writings of the Darwinists aroused the kind of interest in family and kinship that eventually gave rise to efforts to investigate families empirically in relation to their societies.

During this period there were exceptions to the eclectic, large-scale approach to family analysis, a prime example being the work of Frederic Le Play, a Frenchman. The methods he used to study the families of European working-men foreshadowed later developments in the use of both the interview and participant observation in data collection. He lived in many workingmen's homes and took notes on his observations as he participated in family activity. On this basis, Le Play distinguished three types of families in France: The "unstable," or nuclear, family consisted of husband, wife, and young children. In the "stem" family, one married child stayed in the parental home. The "patriarchal" family included the aging parents and their male, and sometimes their female, offspring and their spouses and children. Thus, Le Play can be viewed as a forerunner of later attempts at scientific study of the family (Le Play, 1870, 1885).

1890–1920: Social Reform

The second period was dominated, especially in America, by an urgent concern with social problems and reform. Industrialization and urbanization had resulted in a heightened awareness of poverty, child labor, illegitimacy, and other problematic or problem-producing aspects of family life. Furthermore, the "accepted" post-Victorian morality diverged in obvious ways from actual behavior. The Chicago school of sociology, with its journal, *The American Journal of Sociology*, founded in 1894, became a mouthpiece for reform. The school's underlying assumptions, not always expressed, were that "we understand both the family and the effects of urban and industrial developments; what we must do is solve the resulting problems and strengthen the family." However, the problem and reform orientation gave rise in the 1900s to another viewpoint, to the effect that "maybe we don't know as much as we need to about the conditions and characteristics of the modern family." Some academics at institutions other than the University of Chicago, such as Ernest Groves at the University of North Carolina, were able to embody both the "reform" and the "research" orientations in their work. However, the new research orientation likewise had its focal point at the University of Chicago.

1920–1950: Scientific Study

The 30 years from 1920 to 1950 are best characterized as the years of proto-scientific study of the family. In the early years of this century, even while reform movements dominated, statistical techniques were being developed and social psychologists such as W. I. Thomas and Charles H. Cooley were focusing on individual personality adjustment. While both Thomas and Cooley were influential, it was under the leadership of Ernest Burgess at Chicago that the study of the family became a major sociological endeavor. Burgess conceived of the family as a "unity of interacting personalities," as he stated in an article published in 1926; through Burgess and his students, the study of the family became more than speculations about origins or pleas for social improvement. With major researches on marital adjustment in the thirties, forties, and fifties, Burgess' various studies fostered efforts to understand the factors involved in choosing a mate in the United States, the forms of interaction between family members, divorce and breakup, the position of the aged, and so on. By 1950, and perhaps earlier, it was proper to speak of a body of scientific facts about the family. Looking at family structures cross-culturally, British social anthropologists were ahead of U.S. sociologists in theorizing about various types of families in the world. Raymond Firth, Meyer Fortes, E. E. Evans-Pritchard, Audrey Richards, and others had distinguished varieties of marriage and kinship systems, and in Chapter 2 we draw upon their insights.

1950–1980: Attention to Family Theory

From 1950 to 1980, research activity continued to accelerate, but in addition, there were renewed efforts to interpret and explain the family and its forms and changes—attempts to go beyond mere description. Harold Christensen, in his *Handbook of Marriage and the Family* (1964), designates this as the period of systematic theory building. This label, however, was a bit presumptuous when Christensen wrote in the early sixties, coming to be more appropriately applied to the 1970s. The 20 years from 1950 to 1970 might best be described as the period of summarization, of conceptual frameworks, of reworking family history, of complaints about the lack of comprehensive theory, and of tentative theoretical attempts. It is instructive to view the 1960s as dominated by conceptual frameworks and the 1970s as oriented toward codification and multivariate quasi-mathematical models. During the 1960s and 1970s, much comparative work continued to be done by Edmund Leach and Jack Goody in Britain, while in the United States the synthesizing and reworking by William J. Goode, Reuben Hill, Ira Reiss, F. Ivan Nye, Wesley Burr, and Bernard Farber sought to bring family sociology into the mainstream of the sociological discipline.

Christensen in 1964 reported seven dominant trends in family study from its beginning: (1) There has been increasing acceptance of the scientific viewpoint. (2) The field has become increasingly respectable within sociology. (3) Increasing attention has been paid to personal adjustment within the family context—a result of Ernest Burgess' influence. (4) Substantive reports or empirical studies have been proliferating. (5) Organization programs concerned with the family have been developed. Of special importance in this connection is the National Council on Family Relations (NCFR), whose official publications are the *Journal of Marriage and the Family*, *Family Relations*, and the *Journal of Family History*. (6) Research methodology has been increasingly refined. (7) Concern over theory building has been growing. These last two trends Christensen (and we) may use to characterize the period from 1950 to 1980.

Let us spend some time on Christensen's methods and theory building trends. Until the 1970s, the theoretical inroads were limited. During that decade, however, the older traditions, such as structure-functionalism, developmentalism, and symbolic interactionism, were supplemented by approaches such as exchange/equity theory and systems theory (Hays, 1977). All of these theories tended to have a status quo conservative ideological bent, since they did not question the presuppositions concerning the "traditional industrial" family model described above.

As important as the macro-theories that prevailed in family sociology in the 1970s were, the developments in the methodology of middle-range theorizing. Theories of mate selection, of socialization outcomes, of family violence, and others drew upon the path-modeling methods brought into Sociology by Dudley Duncan in the 1960s, and upon other sophisticated statistical techniques such as multiple regression. Let us briefly examine these techniques and their theoretical results in the 1970s.

Family concepts and propositions based upon them are organized as variables into cause and effect relationships. Using a limited number of such variables for explanation requires the assumption of *ceteris paribus*, or "other things being equal." There is more to the relationship between variables, however, than their connection. In fact, says Burr,

> *relationships can differ in* direction, shape, *and* amount of time *involved in them. In addition, there is one other characteristic of relationships that . . . has received very little attention elsewhere. This is* variation in the *amount of* influence *that occurs in relationships (Burr, 1979: 10–11).*

The result of the linking of variables is the development of numerous propositions that are linked together into a model that posits the relations between many independent or causal variables and dependent or "affected" variables. As in any area of social theory, the simpler theories of an earlier time become more complex, and Burr and Carl Broderick agree that such "complexification" is necessary to understanding and explanation. As Broderick puts it, "Family theory will increasingly have to deal with complex, multivariate models . . . and with the specification of richer typologies of family structure and developmental sequences (Broderick, 1971: 152). The key word is *specification*, as earlier propositions are qualified according to the conditions under which they are correct.

Let us take an example from the Burr et al. volume on *Contemporary Theories about the Family* (1979): In his chapter, the "Effects of Social Networks on the Family," Gary Lee reviews the literature and derives several propositions concerning the interrelations between socioeconomic status, crises, age, and the exchange of aid between the family and its kin network. Some of his propositions are as follows:

> *Socioeconomic status is positively related to financial aid between related nuclear families but negatively related to the exchange of services; this is due, in part, to the typically greater proximity of the generations in the lower and working strata.*
>
> *In case of crisis, the duration of the crisis is positively related to aid from kin but negatively related to aid from neighbors.*
>
> *The relationship between age and receipt of aid from kin is curvilinear, with the greatest receipt of aid occurring in early adulthood, and, particularly, old age (Lee, 1979: 50-51).*

Notice in this illustration that the author specifies the direction and degree of relationship between variables.

It should be noted that some of the theorists who did not use this model-building approach, such as Farber, are not convinced that it can lead to major breakthroughs. Burr's reaction is that this codification of existing empirical data and theories is not the end of the theory-building process. Rather, such propositional model building, he feels, "should be viewed as a process that occurs at one particular period in the history of science, and much if not all . . . [of it] will subsequently be revised (Burr, 1973: 40).

1980–Present: Family Demography, Feminism, and Critical Theory

Family sociology has gone in two opposing directions since the Burr et al. volumes at the end of the 1970s. Family demographers have moved the frontiers of data collection forward and, in combination with the statistical techniques of the previous 20 years, have given us much better factual information on which to base our interpretations. A significant example is the large national sample longitudinal study of families and households being carried out by James Sweet, Larry Bumpass, and their colleagues at Wisconsin, with the data being analyzed by family researchers across the United States.

In addition to data collection, scholars are improving and summarizing methods at present. In the *Handbook of Marriage and the Family* (1987), Larzelere and Klein summarize several aspects of methods in the mid-1980s. Then in

1990, Draper and Marcos edited a volume on *Family Variables*, covering a wide range of measurement techniques. Still others have noted the importance of qualitative methods and of efforts to study the private realm of family experience (LaRossa and Wolf, 1985; Gubrium and Holstein, 1987).

The other direction of the 1980s and 1990s has seen the revision (of which Burr speaks) being carried out. Feminist and critical scholars have called into question many of the assumptions of the "accepted" traditions noted above. Judith Stacey, David Cheal, Jetse Sprey, Marie Osmond, Barrie Thorne and her colleagues, and others, have raised basic questions about the family past and present. Feminist deconstructionism is actually reanalyzing such "givens" as male and female, causing a rethinking of many of the categories of family theorizing.

It will not be necessary for us to decide in the present volume whether various approaches to theorizing are dead ends, interim stages, or the last word. We will simply draw upon different theories and theorists, utilizing whichever of their interpretations and explanations seem most helpful, and making the reader aware of the open issues raised by the most recent developments. Like the work of Burr and his associates, our purpose in the present volume is to supplement summaries of research results with explanation and interpretation. The setting for the interpretations includes the various types of family *structures* found around the world, the *functions* performed within family and kinship units, and the other internal aspects of *family life*. Family systems and families within the same system vary in terms of their structures, including marital linkages, household members, and residential location vis-à-vis kin. The issue of family functions, or what the family does on behalf of the individual and society, has also been analyzed by scholars. Other aspects of family-kin culture include descent and inheritance, husband-wife authority and relationships, approaches to partner selection, and the cultural emphases in child-rearing. While all of these are important in preparing the reader to understand modern U.S. families, our treatment of families in the United States will focus upon the last three issues: gender relations, partner selection, and child rearing.

SECTION THREE

APPROACHING FAMILY STUDY

Key Concepts

Within the setting of the structural types, functions, and other internal family culture, three basic concepts will be employed to help the reader understand the family against a historical and cross-cultural background. These concepts are *patriarchy*, *institutional embeddedness*, and *individual embeddedness*. The first concept, patriarchy, pertains to unquestioned male authority—in society and in the family. Patriarchy has been institutionalized for millenia, not just in the West, but in much of the world. Judith Stacey, in her book on China (1983), defines patriarchy as "a family and social system in which male power over women and children derives from the social role of fatherhood, and is supported by a political economy in which the family unit retains a significant productive role." Gerda Lerner refers to how resilient and varied the manifestations of patriarchy have been in different times and places (1986: 216). Some of its manifestations include polygyny (or multiple wives), patriliny (or male property control), female domesticity, the double sexual standard, and so on. One of the questions that will demand our attention throughout this book is the extent to which patriarchy is changing, in the family or elsewhere, and what the changes look like. Lerner, for example, argues that changes in the family "do not alter the basic male dominance in the public realm, in institutions and in government" (Lerner, 1986: 216). We shall see.

The other two concepts, institutional and individual embeddedness, mirror the two orientations of family and kinship: toward society and toward the individual. The first idea, that of *institutional* embeddedness, is well expressed by David Schneider:

> *In many primitive and peasant societies a large number of kinds of institutions are organized and built as parts of the kinship system itself. Thus the major social units of the society may be kin groups —lineages perhaps. These same kin groups may be property-owning units, the political units, the religious units, and so on. Thus, whatever a man does in such a society he does as a kinsman of one kind or another.*

In such societies, the other institutions are "embedded" in, or undifferentiated from, the kinship system, so that economic-productive, political, religious, medical, and other activities take place within, and as aspects of, the kinship organization of the society. Thus, the head of the kin line may also be the political ruler, performer of religious ritual, primary educator, and leader of the kin division of labor. A second form of institutional embeddedness is present if a "nuclear" unit (a set of parents and their children) is the seat of multiple societal activities but is emancipated from the larger kin group. One of the key questions toward which this volume is directed concerns the extent to which other institutions have become differentiated from —are no longer embedded in—either the kin groups or the nuclear families of the contemporary United States.

Individual embeddedness, or the relation of the individual to family and kin, is a third major focus of this book. This involves interaction patterns, solidarity, and values. Two questions may be asked to help determine just how embedded the individual is in family or kin group. (1) Who are the people you spend time, or interact, with? If most of the time you spend with other people is with family or kin, this is an indication of the interaction embeddedness of the individual. (2) Who matters to you; what people are most valuable or important in your life? If the answer is almost exclusively kin and family, this indicates the value embeddedness of the individual. So, individual embeddedness has an interactional and a value component. If the alternative to institutional embeddedness is institutional differentiation or specialization, à la Parsons and Zaretsky, the alternative to individual embeddedness is, of course, individualism. Therefore, a third guiding focus in the present volume is the extent to which the individual is still embedded in the family and the family within the kin group in the modern world.

It should be noted that as institutions differentiate or separate from the family, the interactional aspect of individual embeddedness also lessens. For example, if there is no separate educational institution, so that all education takes place within the family or kin group, educational time will be spent interacting with these people. But when education differentiates, so that one goes to college to get an education, educational time is no longer spent with family and kin but with professors and other students. The value aspect of individual embeddedness does not, however, necessarily change as rapidly. You can be in college and out of touch with members of your family, and they can still be the most important people in your life. So individual embeddedness may not change in toto as rapidly as institutional embeddedness in the course of history.

Individual embeddedness and patriarchy are also related in important ways. For twenty years I have written in various editions of this text about the move away from individual embeddedness in families and toward individualism. I treated this as a development affecting all family members and, despite having read Gilman's writing in the early 1900s and the feminist writers of the 1960s and 1970s, did not distinguish such embeddedness by gender. However, the message has finally gotten through to me (and, I hope, to you) that, as Stacey states, "to focus on patriarchy allows us to remove the screen that projects the family as an undifferentiated unity" (Stacey, 1983: 28). One aspect of patriarchy is that females have been more embedded in their families than have males. As Stacey puts it: "Women (in China) were secluded and confined to the innermost compartments of the domestic sphere" (Stacey, 1983: 39).

Another way to put it is that males have had more of an extra-familial existence throughout much of history. Thorne and Yalom, for example, connect the two concepts quite plainly: "Feminists have claimed women's right to break from their embeddedness in the family, to seek full individualism and equality" (Thorne and Yalom, 1982: 18). So patriarchy and the two forms of embeddedness are, in the real world, concepts through which to understand history, and through which to understand today's changes.

This introduction to the three concepts has been both brief and somewhat premature, for the understanding of these concepts requires a level of cross-cultural and definitional sophistication that the reader may not yet have attained. The author, however, feels compelled to introduce these concepts early; they should become increasingly clear as you move through the cross-cultural and historical materials of Chapters 2 through 5. Particularly in Chapter 5, these and other theoretical issues in family study will be confronted directly. It is the author's conviction that explanation and interpretation, however tentative, is preferable to simple fact-gathering. You must judge the outcome for yourself.

Studying the Family

Studying the family in one's own society, it may be well to note, is different in one crucial way from the study of theoretical astrophysics, the classical background of English literature, or the use of path analysis in social research. This difference is that most readers are familiar in their daily lives with, and thus to some extent experts on, the phenomenon we call "the family." This familiarity and expertise in family relations can be both a help and a hindrance to the sociological study of this institution. It is a help because a certain amount of understanding can be assumed. When readers see the word *family*, they still may think of two parents and one or more children who they are rearing. Seeing the term *marriage*, they will think—though perhaps not in these terms—of two individuals of different sexes, legally joined together for the sake of sexual access, procreation, and the sharing of a common residence. *Divorce* they will understand to be the legal separation of these two individuals. When *courtship* is mentioned, the sharing of time and activities with a member of the opposite sex will come to mind, perhaps in terms of dating or going steady.

Yet this very familiarity may likewise stand in the way of an attempt to step back and consider the family either objectively or in terms of generalizations. The majority of families in the United States may or may not closely resemble one's own or the above description. However, even if the reader's family is rather typical, it is important to be aware of the tendency to feel that the way one's own family does things is the only, or at least the best, way. It would be improper to condemn such feelings; it is quite proper to be aware of them.

Our subject is the modern family, its history and change over time, its relation to the society of which it is a part, its formation and dissolution, and its internal relationships. The foundation for this superstructure includes cross-cultural and historical variations in structure, functions, and internal culture. This setting or foundation is the focal point of the next four chapters, beginning in Chapter 2 with structural principles and types and certain other aspects of kin-family culture.

Family Structure and Varieties

CHAPTER 2

The different types of family structures that have existed in various societies are almost innumerable. In this chapter the most important structural principles, and the types produced thereby, are introduced. These principles include marital and blood linkages and residential clustering. In addition, other factors useful for distinguishing family systems are introduced: descent and inheritance, types of nuclear families, and the cultural issues of authority and intimacy. Special attention is given to three problems in family study: (a) the difference between norms or expectations and actual behavior in families; (b) types or typologies and their use; and (c) the incest taboo and its relation to social structure.

FAMILY STRUCTURAL PRINCIPLES

In U.S. society a young male and female decide to marry. Ordinarily, his surname is added to her maiden name, and they affirm that their marriage will be for life. If possible, they move into a dwelling separate from both sets of parents and they begin to plan for the coming of children. Their parents and other kin are interested in them and help them when the need arises, but the young couple is generally expected to be independent, to go it alone. In an introductory textbook written in the Western world, the word *family* is likely to signify what we have just described. Technically, this unit, consisting of a male, a female, and their offspring, is called the monogamous nuclear family, and it is the prevalent and legalized form of family in the contemporary United States. Some students have asked if the term nuclear family has anything to do with nuclear fission or the atomic age. It doesn't. It refers to the fact that this unit is a nucleus within that larger entity we call the kin group. Common residence, which is typical for the monogamous nuclear family, facilitates the sexual access of the married couple, care for the offspring, and a familial division of labor. This division of labor, unwritten but understood as part of the traditional marriage contract, is described by Lenore Weitzman as follows: "1. The husband is head of the household. 2. The husband is responsible for support. 3. The wife is responsible for domestic services. 4. The wife is responsible for child care, the husband for child support" (Weitzman, 1981: 2). A distinction is made in everyday speech between this marital/family unit and one's kin; when people in the United States say, "I want you to meet my family," they ordinarily mean parents, brothers, and sisters—or else (if they are the parents), spouse and children.

   This then, is the type of family with which Americans are most familiar. Yet when actual families are observed both in the United States and cross-culturally, the variations from this pattern are seen to be enormous. These variations are based upon such structural issues as the number of persons of each sex who are allowed to marry; the expected household composition, including both marital units and blood kin; and the pattern of residential clustering of kin. An understanding of these structural principles and of the types of kin-family systems produced by them should give the reader a better sense of the U.S. family system as but one type among many. In addition, we shall try to make it clear that expectations and reality often diverge—that the ways people expect to behave, desire to behave, and say they behave are not necessarily the same as the way they actually behave. The last point, while drawn in this chapter from cross-cultural illustrations, will be seen to be important when husband-wife decision-making, treatment of the aged, the position of the employed wife, and other issues in the U.S. family are confronted. Feature 2.1 notes the gap between traditional norms and behavior in U.S. families. Though it is quite natural for the individual without cross-cultural experience to assume that this is the way marriage "should" be, when marriage in the United States is compared with marriage in other times and places, monogamy is seen to be but one type among others. The other possibilities, all involving more than one member of one or both sexes, are together called by the term *polygamy*, or multiple marriage. The polygamous possibilities are three: two or more females married to one male, for which the term *polygyny*, or "many women," is used; two or more males married to the same female, for which the term *polyandry*, or "many men," is used; and theoretically two or more males married to two or more females, an arrangement called *cenogamy*, or group marriage (Lee, 1979: 701). Therefore, polygyny + polyandry + cenogamy = polygamy, as distinguished from monogamy. The literature often uses polygamy and polygyny as synonymous, the reason being that about 99 percent of the cases of polygamy are, in fact, polygynous.

The frequency with which these four types of marital arrangements occur normatively, that is, as expectations or desires, in various societies is interesting because of the light it sheds on the human experience. In a world sample of 554 societies, Murdock found polygyny to be the norm in 415 of them, monogamy in 135, polyandry in 4, and cenogamy in none (1957: 686). Later, in 1,170 societies described in the *Ethnographic Atlas*, over 80 percent were found to prefer polygyny, 6 percent polyandry, and the rest monogamy. Though polygyny is found throughout the world, Africa is its stronghold. Jack Goody quotes Vernon Dorjahn as reporting that, in Africa, 35 percent of all husbands have more than one wife (Goody, 1973).

A caution is in order regarding the actual prevalence of polygamous marriages in societies that prefer them. A distinction must be made between the normative marital arrangement in a society, or that dictated by its ideology, and the frequency with which specific arrangements occur empirically. In some so-

---

Feature 2.1 **FAMILY VALUES**

In the last 30 years, the "family" has been redefined.

Americans still rear children, still live together, still love and support each other. But fewer households fit the "Leave it to Beaver" mold.

Although the government defines a family as members of a group related by blood or marriage—a husband, wife and biological or adopted children—Americans live in a variety of family-style arrangements.

Unprecedented numbers of single parents, homosexual couples, and grandparents are rearing children. Unmarried couples are living together. Adults facing hard times are returning to their parents' homes. "Sandwich generation" couples are caring for their children and for elderly parents.

Carol Tannehill, "Family Values . . . may be in the eye of the beholder; TV, experts, politicians can't agree," *Wisconsin State Journal*, August 2, 1992

cieties, such as that of the United States, monogamy is required and multiple partners are prohibited. Yet in many, if not all, of the 415 societies in which polygyny is normative, monogamy predominates numerically. Suppose, for example, that in a normatively polygynous society each male married only two females. If the sex ratio (the number of males per 100 females in a population) of the society were approximately 1:1, half the males would have to remain unmarried. James Smith and Phillip Kunz speak to this issue of normative and actual prevalence of polygyny at some length:

> While a significant number of the world's societies have at some time normatively allowed the practice of polygyny, the nearly universal existence of an equal sex ratio has restricted the incidence of polygyny in most human populations. Male infanticide, high male mortality due to warfare, and importation of females from other populations are some factors which may sufficiently imbalance the sex ratio in some populations to allow for polygyny. But even in the absence of such factors, a high rate of natural increase combined with a tendency of women to marry men older than themselves may produce an excess of females in the marriage market (Smith and Kunz, 1976: 465).

Late marriage for males, death in warfare, and importation of females can all increase the prevalence of polygyny in societies that prefer it. However, the overall result is that monogamy predominates numerically in polygynous societies. In fact, Goody's figure of 35 percent polygyny on the part of sub-Saharan African males seems high, since many societies report 20-30 percent, and 35 percent would mean that (with an equal gender ratio) a third of the males would remain unmarried. However, this is somewhat counterbalanced by the fact, noted by Quale, that

> a man in a polygynous society generally adds a second wife only after some years, and a third after some years more. . . . Moreover, a man's younger wives are likely to remarry after his death. Often they do so through husband-succession by a brother, or through widow-inheritance by a brother or by a son of an earlier wife (Quale, 1988: 60).

It is well to note at this juncture that some of the early anthropologists who asked informants how things were done in their society came away with the normative rather than the actual structural arrangements. The resultant difference is comparable to that between the impression visitors from Mars would receive if they accepted our account of what families are like in the United States and their impression if they went into our houses to observe those living there. We shall return again to this normative-actual distinction.

Helen Ware's study of urban Yoruba women in Nigeria describes many of the characteristics of polygyny from the woman's viewpoint. Almost half are living polygynously—primarily the less educated and the non-Christians. Sixty percent say they would be pleased if their husband took another wife because there would be more help in the home and a secondary wife for them to dominate. Almost a quarter of these women were upset at the thought of another wife, fearing jealousy and hatred between co-wives. In fact, says Ira Reiss, "the connection of jealousy to polygyny is made more apparent by the fact that in Africa and elsewhere the word for polygyny and jealousy is often the same.

However, says Ware, three out of four would prefer another wife over the husband having a mistress, because the husband would spend more money on the mistress than on the wife. Despite the fear of jealousy, "twice as many wives mentioned the risk of the children suffering from sharing a father as mentioned the possibility of the wives suffering from sharing a husband" (Ware, 1979: 190). Polygyny may actually increase a wife's power position, not only vis-à-vis junior wives, but also by increasing her freedom from her husband: "the wife in a monogamous marriage is forced to be more yielding than the wives in a polygynous union just because her status as the only wife is constantly under threat" (Ware, 1979: 192).

If these are consequences of polygyny as perceived by the wives, what are its causes—why is it so widespread normatively? Lee has summarized the major theories: (a) unequal sex drives of men and women, with men governed by a stronger drive and one toward sexual variety; (b) a response to lengthy postpartum (post-birth) sex taboos; (c) a high value placed upon large numbers of children; (d) all females are allowed to marry in societies where they outnumber the men; and (e) a high value placed on women's economic contribution to the family (Lee, 1979; Becker, 1981: 47-56). Lee's research and that of others generally indicate that (c) and (e)—economics and reproduction—are the key factors (Lee and Whitbeck, 1990). Economic contribution seems particularly important: "To be rich is to possess several wives; and the more a man has, the more his fortune increases." So goes a saying among the Fang of Gabon in West Africa. "Only the poor and the Christian converts may succumb to the humiliation of monogamy," say the Igbo of Nigeria (Ekechi, 1971: 329). Polygyny is more an economic than a sexual phenomenon, and there is more than a logical-statistical reason why monogamy predominates numerically in societies that ideologically favor polygyny. Most men in a polygynous society are simply too poor to afford more than one wife. The important or high-ranking male takes additional wives to validate his superior status, to aid him in the care of the fields, the raising of cows, or other economic ventures, and to produce offspring. His family must, however, be able to afford the bridewealth, the cost of removing her from family and kin (see Adams, 1994). As Felix Ekechi says, the possession of many wives is an indication of personal success and achievement, as well as a status symbol (1976: 329). Goody, however, argued earlier that "the reasons behind polygyny are sexual and reproductive rather than economic and productive (1973: 189). In any case, polygyny involves some combination of reproduction, production, and sexuality, perhaps being explained by differential importance of the three factors in different societies. Polygyny is normative, therefore, for what it signifies, but it is not behaviorally dominant in the 415 societies that prefer it.

Cassidy and Lee have analyzed the small number of polyandrous societies, and have concluded that two factors seem to cause it: (1) extreme poverty and a harsh environment that only permit low population and marginal subsistence, and (2) a limited role for women in economic production (Cassidy and Lee, 1989). It has also been noted that multiple marriage principles may be at work within the same society.

Among the Abisi of Nigeria, both polygyny and polyandry appear to be practiced. Women marry three men all on the same day—one chosen by the patriline,

FIGURE 2.1   THREE TYPES OF HOUSEHOLD ARRANGEMENTS BASED ON
CONSANGUINEAL TIES

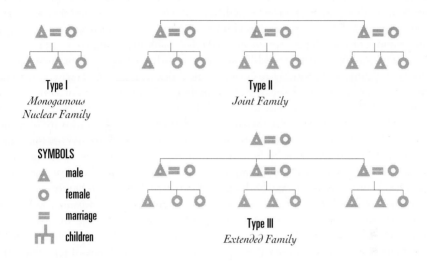

Type I
*Monogamous
Nuclear Family*

Type II
Joint Family

SYMBOLS

△ male
○ female
═ marriage
⊓ children

Type III
Extended Family

one by the woman's parents, and one with whom she is in love. Likewise, the men may get involved in marriages to more than one female (Chalifous, 1980). In Sri Lanka, Nur Yalman finds three forms of marriage occurring together:

> *Polyandry . . . is primarily a strategy of the poor. It is often the only way very poor men can get a wife at all—by sharing one. It is often brothers who do this. Monogamy characterizes the middle strata and goes with nuclear families. The upper stratum and the rich practice polygyny, although some poorer men will try to emulate this if they can, polygyny being a sign of status. . . . (in Fox, 1980: 204–205)*

The issue of multiple norms or ideals will arise again in the discussion of household arrangements.

Household Arrangements

In the United States a couple, following marriage, may live for a time with the parents of one of them. This arrangement is usually temporary, for the desires and expectations of the pair are ordinarily for housing apart from all other kin. The nuclear family is not, however, the normative household unit in all societies. On the contrary, the number of nuclear units may be compounded, as indicated above, by the addition of marital partners and their children in the various forms of polygamy. The household may also be compounded by the addition of consanguineal, or other blood, kin. Perhaps the two best-known examples of consanguineal household extension are the three-generation extended family and the joint family. These may be compared with the monogamous nuclear family by means of Figure 2.1.

Each of the three parts of Figure 2.1 depicts a household type based on blood ties. Type I is, of course, the typical household in the United States, consisting of a parent of each sex and their children. Type II shows a joint family composed of three brothers, their wives, and their children. The best-known example of such a family pattern is the traditional Hindu family of India. Type III depicts the extended, or three-generation extended, family. Here the aging parents live with their sons and the sons' wives and children. Classical China is frequently used as an example of a society in which the extended household pattern was prevalent.

Three qualifications should be added to the discussion of normative household arrangements according to consanguineal ties. First, C. C. Harris notes that the terminology used to describe the Indian family is not as clear-cut as the above discussion would indicate. The term "joint family" often has been used instead of "extended family" to describe the three generations under the authority of a single head (Harris, 1983: 46). Such conceptual inconsistencies are not unusual, and you should not allow them to become stumbling blocks to your understanding, since the arrangements are more important than the terms used to describe them. Second, it will be noted that both the extended and the joint family were diagrammed with the brothers living together and their sisters presumably having married into other such units and having left home. There is no logical reason why the diagram should not have shown sisters living together with their husbands and children, with their brothers having married and moved out. The only reason for depicting these consanguineal arrangements as we have done is a statistical one: the pattern in which brothers live together after marriage is normative in a larger number of societies than is that in which sisters live together.

Third, the important distinction between norms or expectations and actuality or behavioral variety can be profitably reinforced in this connection. In classical China, the ideal in the upper echelons of society was for the aged patriarch to keep his family together and continue to wield authority over them as long as he lived. As in the case of normative polygyny, however, extended-family households were in the minority. Historical data indicate that, in reality, the great majority of pre-Communist Chinese households were rather small, averaging about five persons. The family ideology, especially among the literati, and actual family patterns are again found to be divergent.

A study of an Arab village, reported by Henry Rosenfeld, may illustrate and help to explain the great disparity between normative and actual family structures. Upon entering this community, the researcher asked what sort of family system they had. The uniform response was that they were an extended-family village. Then, rather than stop with the verbal expression of norms, he went from door to door to see the household composition himself. Here is what he found:

- ✦ 17 complete extended families, consisting of grandparents, their sons, and the son's wives and children;
- ✦ 27 partially extended families, one or more brothers having left;
- ✦ 15 joint families with the grandparents deceased;
- ✦ 11 unmarried brothers living alone or with their mothers, their fathers being deceased; and
- ✦ 205 nuclear family households, consisting of a male, a female, and their children.

Are the 205 nuclear families unhappy and longing for the norm or cultural ideal? The answer is simply no. If anything, the tendency is for more of those involved in extended or joint households to desire the nuclear arrangement than vice versa.

What, then, keeps some of the extended and joint families together? The religio-cultural norm of filial piety or obligation to parents is still quite strong and influential. However, the primary reasons for the continuation of extended and joint households appear to be economic. Extended, partially extended, and joint families are most prevalent under two opposing conditions. First, if the family is economically *prosperous*, the aging father may attempt to keep his family together for reasons of prestige and authority and for reasons of economy, that is, to help him do the work. The male offspring, on their part, may be willing to accept this subordinate position during the father's lifetime for the sake of the inheritance that will eventually come their way. At the other extreme, the *poor* are likely to stay together out of economic necessity. They must pool their resources in order to survive. Unquestionably, the overall movement in the village is toward more nuclear households, though the people, when asked, will still express the traditional extended-family ideology (Rosenfeld, 1958).

It is necessary, we are suggesting, to examine not only the cultural ideal but also the variations and the direction of change when studying the family system of any given society. The fact is that different ideals may even be operating within the same culture. Some of Rosenfeld's villagers desire, for very good reasons, to preserve the traditional extended-family household and economic unit, while others, for what they consider to be equally good reasons, prefer the monogamous nuclear family. When we turn to the family in the United States, we shall once again see multiple normative principles at work, and we will then discuss the direction and speed of change.

The monogamous nuclear family, polygamous marriage, and the composite consanguineal unit—these are three basic structural distinctions among marriage-family-household types. One further word regarding these distinctions is instructive. Meyer Nimkoff, as well as several other writers, in making the same general threefold distinction,[1] simply uses the term nuclear family to refer to the monogamous nuclear family. Our purpose in adding the word monogamous is to indicate that there are nuclear units within each of the structural types. The monogamous nuclear family has but one "nucleus," consisting of two parents and their children. In a polygynous family, a man who has three wives is simultaneously a member of three nuclear units, each consisting of himself, a wife, and their children. Likewise, in a composite consanguineal household, multiple nuclear units live under the same roof. The classical Chinese ideal, for example, might comprise four nuclear units: the grandparents and their sons being one nuclear family, and each of the sons and his wife and children being another. Thus, if the term *nuclear family* is used to describe the first structural type, that type is not mutually exclusive of the two composite types. The addition of the marital designation *monogamous* makes the three structural categories mutually exclusive.

Residential Clustering and Location

Besides the typical marital linkages and household units described above, other structural principles differentiate family-kinship systems. One pertains to residential clustering from the perspective of the nuclear family. When a man and woman marry, they may be expected to locate with or near his kin, her kin, both sets of kin, neither set of kin, or they may spend part of their married life near his kin and part near hers. Among the possible arrangements, the ones that occur most frequently may be reduced to five. The single most prevalent residence pattern cross-culturally is that closely related to Figure 2.1: settling with or near the husband's parents following marriage, a practice that is called *patrilocality*. Other common patterns include *matrilocality*, living near the parents and kin of the wife, and *neolocality*, settling apart from both sets of parents. The last is the normative pattern in the contemporary United States. Some young couples in the United States may live for a time with one set of parents or the other, but this arrangement is usually out of necessity; the ideal, or desired, arrangement is a separate, or neolocal, residence not governed by the location of either set of kin. John Rothchild and Susan Wolf in their book *Children of the Counterculture* state this neolocal principle in dramatic fashion:

> . . . *the nuclear family reduces its size, sends grandmother to the old-age home, little Billy to the rehabilitation center, Sally to a northern college, parceling off its people according to the needs of a more professional society. If our children don't leave home to become specialists, they leave home to be treated by them (Rothchild and Wolf, 1976: 203).*

Two other patterns occur in enough societies to be worthy of mention. In one of them, called *bilocality* by Murdock, the newly married couple may choose whether to reside near the husband's or the wife's parents. *Avunculocal* residence, the fifth pattern, signifies that the young couple is expected to live with or near the husband's mother's brother (the husband's maternal uncle) (Murdock, 1949: 15–17).

Other aspects of residential clustering involve not the location of the nuclear family, but of such persons as aging parents, single adults, and so on. The major issue here is the way in which the nuclear family is related structurally to household and kin clusters.

SECTION TWO

SELECTED CULTURAL DISTINCTIONS AND THE USE OF TYPES

Thus far we have introduced the marital, consanguineal, and residential clustering principles that help to shape the various family-kin structures. These principles, and the types of structures produced thereby, give us some sense of the U.S. family within the larger context of societal variations. At this point we shall turn to some additional cultural distinctions that are useful in defining the setting and background of the U.S. family. Rules of descent and inheritance, types of nuclear families, and the culture of authority and intimacy will be discussed.

Descent and Inheritance

Descent and inheritance are closely related, but not synonymous. Descent has to do with the formal manner in which the individual is related to kin. Inheritance involves the property, goods, and obligations that are passed along through specified kin. The three most prevalent types of descent groups are *patrilineal* and *matrilineal* (unilineal) systems and *bilateral*—as practiced in Western societies. All determine property holding and inheritance, as well as performing other functions. As can be seen in Figure 2.2, in the patrilineage each time a female is born, she is part of her father's patrilineage. But the line stops with her; it does not continue through her children. However, when a male child is born the patriline continues through him to his children. What, then, is the role of a woman in a patrilineal system? It is to provide offspring for her husband's line.

In the matrilineage precisely the opposite principle is at work; that is, each time a male is born the line stops with him, whereas each time a female is born the line continues through her to her children. The role of the man is, therefore, to provide offspring for his wife's lineage. Notice another aspect of these unilineal systems. In Figure 2.2 those on both sides of an equals sign are *never* in the same lineage. This means that, compared to blood ties, marital ties are weak. Being in a family system where marriage is the central fact, it is difficult for us to put ourselves inside a system where the wife may be sent back to her kin for not providing children for her husband's lineage. It is also striking that in the patrilineage one's own mother is an outsider: she is part of the lineage into which she was born. It is not that she is not intimately related to her children; she is simply not part of her husband's and children's kin group.

As for inheritance, there are three possibilities in the patrilineage. First, the oldest son may inherit all the property, with the others having to make their own way, though often with some help from the kin line. This is known as *primogeniture*. Or the inheritance may be partible, so that each son is given a separate share. Or the inheritance may be non-partible, so that the sons inherit an "undivided interest" in it. This is most frequent, and occurs in agrarian societies, as described by Harris:

> *If the property concerned is a farm whose economic viability depends on its size, then, in order to inherit, the children of the owner of that farm will have to stay together to work on it (Harris, 1983: 20–21).*

Another aspect of unilineal systems concerns genealogical relationships. While this author was living in Uganda, our neighbor, a Muganda, invited us to the wedding of his brother. At the close of the wedding we were introduced not only to this brother, but to 23 others as well. Noting our surprise, he indicated

FIGURE 2.2   PATRILINEAL AND MATRILINEAL SYSTEMS

Matrilineal System

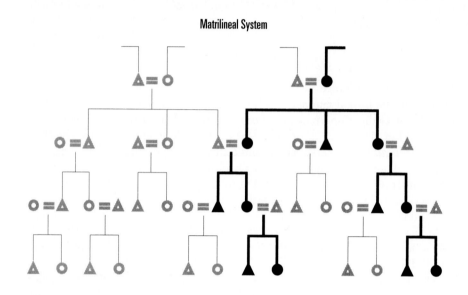

Patrilineal System

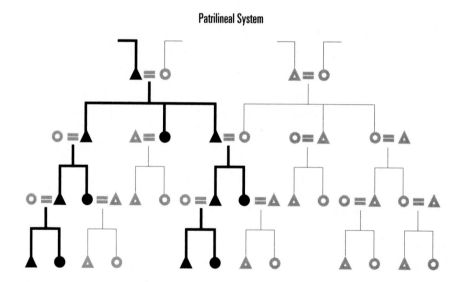

that he also had seven fathers, so the number of brothers should not be all that unusual. What he meant, of course, was that all those of the same sex and generation are related to the next generation the same way. So, instead of a father and six uncles, he had, sociologically speaking, seven fathers. Likewise, instead of three brothers and 20 male cousins on his father's side, he had 23 brothers.

Every system works once you are inside it, and every system has stresses and tensions inherent in it. The tensions in the patrilineage are likely to be between mother-in-law and daughter-in-law, since both are outsiders to the lineage and have low status until it is gained with age. In fact, the daughter-in-law's position in the family is lower than that of her sons and borders on servitude. She can, however, comfort herself with the thought that her son will eventually bring her a daughter-in-law to dominate. The other point of tension in the patrilineage occurs among brothers, since they are due to inherit the family property. The greatest point of tension in the matrilineage occurs between the man and his wife's brother because the man is in fact raising sons that will inherit not from him but from his wife's line. It is well to remember that matrilineage does not mean matriarchy, or women running the show. In fact, the brothers tend to control the property that will eventually pass through the female line. The husband can console himself in the matrilineage with the thought that his sister is raising children for him.

Bilaterality signifies normative equality in affiliation with both the mother's and the father's kin, although in actuality kin ties in a bilateral system tend to be overbalanced in favor of the preferred kin. Inheritance follows the same types of patterns, but is generally more complex than the determination of descent because multiple items tend to be inherited, as we shall see below. The U.S. family is basically bilateral in descent; that is, we trace descent through, and consider ourselves equally related to, both parental kin groups. Only in the practice of adding the husband's family name to the wife's at marriage, does the U.S. family retain a vestige of patrilineal inheritance.

Although descent lines tend to be relatively clear-cut, neither descent nor inheritance ordinarily operates in either-or terms. Patrilineal descent does not mean that an individual is related to her/his father's male kin to the exclusion of interaction, obligation, and intimacy with mother's kin. In fact, intimacy in a patrilineal society is often greater between an individual and her/his maternal kin simply because there are "no strings attached." In the case of inheritance, even more than in the case of descent, involvement with the two kin groups tends to be a matter of degree or kind rather than of exclusiveness. For example, J. B. Christensen reports that, among the Fanti of West Africa, along with membership in a matrilineal clan (matrilineal descent) goes the right of property inheritance, the use of clan land, succession to a position of political authority, and a proper funeral and burial. Thus, the Fanti might easily be considered a matrilineal society; yet, the father's line among the Fanti is also a source of certain types of inheritance. From the patriline, individuals receive their military allegiance, their fathers' deity, and their souls; physically, they regard their fathers as the primary sources of their blood. Christensen concludes that the Fanti are, in fact, characterized by double descent (from our perspective: double inheritance), receiving certain benefits and obligations from each of the two kin lines (1954). While inheritance is not always as equally divided as it is among the Fanti, many *unilineal*, that is, either patrilineal or matrilineal, systems are characterized by a secondary inheritance and by close relationships with members of the opposing kin group or line.

What factors favor unilineal descent in a society, and what factors lead to the disintegration of these systems? According to E. Kathleen Gough, as quoted by Robert Winch, factors favoring unilineal descent

> *include scarcity of land and the heritability of valuable immovable property (build-ings, trees, etc.) and a mode of organization whereby the leaders of the descent group control distribution to its members of the fruits of production. Conversely she found that the rise of a market system, access to jobs, and the opportunity to acquire per-sonal property were factors leading to the disintegration of the descent group (Winch in Burr et al., 1979: 165).*

Several authors have noted that matrilineages are more fragile than patrilin-eages under the pressure of modern urban life, the tendency being to reverse in-heritance rules from the mother's brother to the father (see Nsamenang in Lamb, 1987: 290).

Offspring desiring to inherit property when a parent dies may be obliged to help care for that property while the parent is alive. For this and other socioeco-nomic reasons, it is not surprising that a fairly high correlation exists between residential clustering and descent-inheritance patterns: patrilocality with patri-lineality, matrilocality with matrilineality, and neolocality with bilaterality. These correlations are, however, far from perfect. Under certain conditions, for exam-ple, matrilocal residence may occur in combination with bilateral or patrilineal descent. In order to understand the bases for the relation between residential clustering and descent-inheritance in a particular society, one must understand the overall societal patterns, not just the kinship system, economy, polity, or ge-ography. Our discussion of the Nayar, Afghan, Chinese, and Russian family sys-tems in Chapter 3 should make more apparent both the viability of and strains on systems very different from that of the United States.

Types of Nuclear Families

The diagrammatic presentation of the patrilineal extended family in Figures 2.1 shows that, within this household type, the adult son is simultaneously a mem-ber of two nuclear families. One of these comprises his parents and brothers (as well as sisters who may have married and moved away), and the other consists of his wife and their children. Referring to W. Lloyd Warner's dis-tinction, Murdock asserts: "Every normal adult in every human society belongs to at least two nuclear families—a family of *orientation*, in which he was born and reared, and which includes his father, mother, brothers, and sisters, and a family of *procreation* which he establishes by his marriage and which includes his" spouse and their children (Murdock, 1949: 13). Though use of the words "normal" and "his" may be questionable, whether the members of the nuclear unit are living together or apart is irrelevant to the definition. The sisters who have married and left home (and are therefore omitted from Figure 2.1) are still members of the adult son's family of orientation. The residential compo-nent may be clarified by the use of the term *kin of orientation* to indicate a non-domestic unit. The neolocal U.S. pattern means that the norm is for adults to live with their families of procreation and apart from their families (kin) of orientation.

Family Culture: Authority and Emotions

Societal authority has been dominated by patriarchy, as noted in the Chapter One discussion of Lerner and Stacey. It is not a simple concept, but clearly focusses on the issue of normative male dominance. Bonnie Fox points out that patriarchy is both structured into a society's institutions and a subjective belief held by the genders (Fox, 1988: 177). Lerner traces the history of patriarchy, showing how it moved from the economics of property, to being defined as "right," to public law (Lerner, 1986: 121). This, of course, is one of the guiding concepts for this book, with a key issue being change or non-change in this area. Male authority, or societal acceptance of patriarchy, may be distinguished from decision-making and influence — behavioral issues that may or may not be consistent with the norm.

As for family and kinship, authority, status, and decision-making may be divided into three ideal types: *patriarchy*, or father rule — the most familiar pattern; *matriarchy*, in which the women make the decisions and wield authority in the family; and *equalitarian*, which signifies approximate similarity between the husband and wife in status, authority, and decision-making. In this pattern, equality may be effected either by coming to an agreement on all issues or by dividing areas of influence. In unilineal descent systems, an aged individual in each lineage usually wields great authority, with varying amounts of inequality between husbands and wives within nuclear families. Among the topics that will engage us throughout this volume are the extent to which the typical U.S. family has changed from a patriarchal toward an equalitarian authority pattern, and the relative prevalence of the patriarchal and equalitarian patterns in different segments of the U.S. population.

Intimacy or emotional closeness is not likely to be defined as a family cultural issue in the U.S., since love and intimacy are seen as central characteristics of family life. However, it is important to note that cross-culturally and historically emotional closeness is a variable. That is, in a society where marriage is arranged or is for the purpose of extending the lineage, love may be strong or weak, but it is not the reason for the family's existence, nor is it the "glue" that holds families together. Jane Collier et al. have pointed out that neither our ancestors nor our contemporaries "have been uniformly mean or nonnurturant to family members but . . . we have all been both nice and mean, both generous and ungenerous, to them" (Collier et al. in Thorne and Yalom, 1982: 35). What has happened is that the expectation of emotional closeness has become a norm, meaning that most families fall short both behaviorally and attitudinally. The issue of family emotions, and their variations and effects, will also arise over and over again.

The relation between patriarchy and emotional closeness is an interesting one, since several authors have argued that genuine closeness and patriarchy are mutually exclusive. You may not agree with this generalization; what it means is that strong male dominance makes real closeness and love impossible. These and other issues pertaining to the content or culture of family life will continue to arise along with the structural ones throughout this book.

The Use of Types

We have introduced types of family structures based on marriage, consanguineal ties, and residential clustering, as well as descent-inheritance links, authority patterns, and types of nuclear families. We have indicated that these types are often expressed normatively in a society despite a disparity between norms and empirical behavior. The use of types, even when they depict empirical reality fairly accurately, must be within the bounds of three further qualifications. First, they are *group* identifications. When we speak of North Africa as a patrilineal-patrilocal-patriarchal society with extended family households, for example, it may or may not be true that the majority of specific kin-family units in North Africa actually fit the definition of all these types. Nor can we expect our "type" to necessarily predict the character of Ahmed's or Abdul's family. The type is a construct that is predicated upon common denominators, not upon a specific example within the group or society. However, while we can't guarantee that Abdul's family will fit the construct perfectly, we can expect the families of Abdul and his friends to resemble the constructed type more closely than, say, a number of Bemba families from South-Central Africa.

A second qualification on the use of types is that they are *comparative* constructs: we can say that, compared to the Bemba, Arab families are more likely to have the characteristics that have been defined as patrilineal and patrilocal. If Ahmed has no male offspring, his daughter and her husband may decide to live with him in order to inherit the flocks—thus exhibiting a matrilocal pattern. Although this makes their situation more like that of the Bemba than that of their own people, our constructed type tells us that this is an exceptional situation among the Arabs.

Finally, the best way to think of types is as *reference points* on a continuum. The possible variations in human behavior are infinite. Types should be thought of as nothing more than modal (or in some cases even arbitrary) points on a continuum from one logical possibility to another. Thus, for example, the authority continuum described in the three types—patriarchal, equalitarian, and matriarchal—might look something like this:

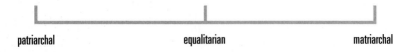

| patriarchal | equalitarian | matriarchal |

Now it would be difficult to find a society in which patriarchal authority means that, in all the family-kin units, females have absolutely no accepted power, either overtly or subtly, to influence decisions and determine policies. In fact, it would be difficult to find societies whose family units would uniformly fit any of the three types. There are, however, noticeable differences among societies, both in their dominant behavior patterns and in the expectations, or norms, that they express regarding structural or behavioral arrangements. These norms and behaviors can be located on an ideal-typical continuum.

In summary, it can be said that types are very useful for distinguishing the gross differences among societies or categories of people, as long as they are seen to be *group* constructs to be used *comparatively* and as points on an ideal-typical *continuum* of either expectations or empirical reality.

FAMILY STRUCTURE AND THE INCEST TABOO

One important feature of family and kinship structure has not yet been mentioned: the incest taboo. This taboo, the prohibition of sexual intercourse and/or marriage between specified kin, is a virtually universal prohibition in human societies, though the specific relationships it covers vary widely. The incest taboo has crucial structural implications for the organization of society. Were brothers and sisters, for example, free to or expected to mate, they could all continue to live in the same household with their parents.

The origin of incest taboos is a subject, says J. Robin Fox, "on which too many words have been wasted already" (Fox, 1962: 128). There are two reasons why discussion of the origin of incest taboos have been unproductive: (a) restrictions against sexual intercourse have not been distinguished from restrictions against marriage; and (b) the post hoc nature of the theories of origins has in most instances resulted either in discussions of motives for avoiding incest or of the advantages of nonincest. A brief description of some of the prevalent theories should make these two points clear.

Two of the theories of incest taboo origins relate almost exclusively to marriage prohibitions. The theory of the biological *ill-effects of inbreeding* is meant to explain why persons in the immediate family are not allowed to mate and produce offspring, but this view has gained few adherents. The notion is that inbreeding is dangerous because it perpetuates deficient genetic traits, such as hemophilia, and that over a period of time all human societies have discovered these effects and have enforced regulations against inbreeding. This theory does not account for the universality of the incest taboo unless one argues for the universal discovery of the harmful effects of inbreeding. In turn, one must assume a universal understanding and sophistication in human societies regarding the reproductive process; an understanding that is simply not in keeping with anthropological evidence. An equally important objection is that there is little evidence that inbreeding is biologically harmful. In fact, inbreeding methods have been used in many animal populations to produce higher-quality specimens. Nor does this theory explain the wide variations from society to society in the categories of kin and family with whom marriage is prohibited. In some cases, marriage with more distant kin is prohibited while marriage with certain kin whom we would define as closer is permitted.

The *structural confusion* theory of incest taboos is nowhere fully spelled out, but it is well illustrated by Kingsley Davis' brief discussion. If brothers and sisters were allowed or expected to marry, he says, jealousy would result if there were two brothers and only one sister in a family. Since the number and sex of siblings is uncontrollable, institutional patterns could not be worked out that would make jealousy a support rather than a menace. Then Davis notes the confusion that would result when children were born of the brother-sister relationship. "The brother would be not only the child's 'father' but also his 'uncle'; the sister would be not only her child's 'mother' but also his 'aunt'" (Davis, 1949: 404).

The words "uncontrollable" and "confusion" are, however, not adequate explanations for incest taboos. Societies have been able to work out the complexities of the six-marriage section system, with its two matrilineal moieties and three patrilineal descent groups (Layard, 1942: 48) and have effected alternatives to primogeniture, or inheritance by the eldest son, in cases where the family has no son. Why, therefore, is it impossible to conceive of structuring brother-sister marriage to account for various occurrences? The oldest son, for example, might be normatively expected to marry the oldest daughter, if there is a daughter. If not, other arrangements could be made. Nor is being a child's mother and aunt simultaneously anything more than a terminological confusion caused by the use of our own culture-bound terms. The great diversity of kinship terminology systems reviewed by Murdock should make it apparent that appropriate terms can be devised for almost any social structural arrangement. Without belaboring the argument, it seems to this author that "impossible structural confusions" hardly explain the ubiquity of incest taboos in human societies.

Prohibitions of sexual intercourse (as differentiated from marriage) with designated kin have been explained by three theories of incest taboos. The first, while it could be applied to marriage taboos as well, seems more closely related to intimate sexual involvement. There is, says Robert Lowie, an *instinct* against inbreeding, a universal revulsion against sexual intimacy with close kin (Lowie, 1920). This theory need detain us but briefly, since it accounts neither for the scattered occurrences of incest despite the taboos nor for the wide variety of kin relationships covered by the taboos. If there were an instinctual revulsion, it would operate quite consistently and naturally from one society to another. Lowie later repudiated this position.

Westermarck proposed to account for the incest taboo as due to the "absence of erotic feelings between persons living very closely together from childhood" (1926: 80). *Lack of interest* is transformed into a positive aversion because of the intimacy resulting from everyday contacts between these close kin. Though there is substantial evidence that close association may dull the sexual appetites even of married persons, this single-factor explanation cannot account for the occurrence of incestuous relations despite the taboos, for the variety of kin relations implicated in the taboo, or for the strength of the sanctions brought against those violating the taboo.

◄ Finally, the theory proposed by Freud states that the opposite of a cooling of interest accounts for incest taboos. The taboos are a result of the *primacy of incestuous love and sex desire*. The child is sexually attracted to the parent of the opposite sex but must repress these feelings due to the consequences that would result if the same-sex parent found out about them. It is in the repression of such feelings that the strong taboo appears, strengthening individuals in their attempts to withstand their own impulses (Freud, 1920: 187, 294). This, of course, sounds most reasonable to Western observers, with their own history of general sex repression and guilt. However, Freud's theory has some of the same difficulties as the other theories in accounting for the variety of prohibitions.

These theories, it must be recalled, have been introduced as accounting for the origin of the incest taboo. Their proponents, except in the case of the instinct and Freudian theories, make no such claim. It appears that Freud's theory is the only one of the five that might be even a partial explanation of origins. Aided by insights gained from observations of lower animals, some writers, including Freud, have advanced the theory that there was a stage in human development during which the strongest and largest male had sexual control over a number of females. Other males, including his offspring, who tried to encroach upon his mating territory had a physical struggle on their hands. The earliest prohibitions of intercourse and mating have grown up around just such impulses and struggles.

Much human history, however, separates these hypothetical early developments from the current motivations for and structural ramifications of incest taboos. More profitable than the hypothetical reconstruction of origins is the attempt to explain the motivations and structures that now embody the incest taboos. Time and again we have noted that a particular single-factor theory cannot seem to account for extensions of the incest taboo, sexually and maritally, beyond the nuclear family. Two interesting articles and Fox's book are pertinent to this issue of structural extensions and motivations. One article, by Frank Young, notes the relation between incest taboos and general considerations of social solidarity. The other article, by Fox, focuses on brother-sister incest prohibitions. Fox's book, *The Red Lamp of Incest*, brings together much that has been known or speculated about the subject (1980). Let us begin with Fox's article.

Using illustrative material from six societies, Fox concludes that both Freud and Westermarck are right regarding brother-sister incest taboos. In those societies (such as the Tallensi, the Pondo, and the Israeli kibbutzim) in which siblings have engaged in much play and other heterosexual activity prior to puberty, the sexual appetite does in fact appear to be dulled and there is little anxiety in adulthood regarding brother-sister incest. Fox calls this the "interaction—aversion—non-temptation—non-anxiety type." In other societies, such as the Chiricahua Apache, siblings are reared in close proximity, but by the age of six or seven close contact between them has ceased. Furthermore, they are not allowed intimate contact with other members of the opposite sex prior to puberty. The result, says Fox, is the "separation—desire—temptation—anxiety type" reaction, which resembles quite closely Freud's idea that temptation plus frustration demands strong prohibitions. Fox summarizes his bipolar theory of motivations as follows: "The more intensive the bodily inter-action between opposite-sex children during sexual immaturity, the more likely the possibility that they will voluntarily abstain from sexual relations with each other after puberty" (Fox, 1962: 148). The reactions will range from disgust and strong taboo when siblings have been separated prior to puberty, to virtual indifference when they have had close prepubertal contact.

Although Fox does not pursue in detail the ramifications of this separation-interaction theory of motivations for incest taboos, he does note the complications that arise when it is applied to parent-offspring taboos. From his discussion, we can discover four possibilities in the relations between parent and child: mother and son in intimate contact or separated, father and daughter intimate or sepa-rated. Ordinarily, mother and child are in frequent and close contact prior to the puberty of the offspring. According to the theory, this should produce in-difference on the offspring's part but temptation and anxiety on the mother's part, since she obviously had no contact at all with the son prior to her own pu-berty (he was not yet born), and they are now in close contact. As Parsons puts it, her "regressive need system," or suppressed erotic impulses, must not be left uncontrolled (1954: 108). On the other hand, the situation with respect to fa-ther and daughter should tend to produce mutual rather than one-way tempta-tion and anxiety. The reason for this mutual temptation is that there is normally greater prepubertal separation-with-proximity between father and daughter, a situation that should increase the sexual desire of both for each other, accord-ing to Fox's theory. The result should be the highest incidence of incest between fathers and daughters, which is indeed the case. The lesser incidence of incest between sons and mothers, according to Fox's view, should be due to the post-pubertal indifference of the son. Furthermore, there should be virtually univer-sal abhorrence of and strong sanction against parent-offspring incest of either kind, since both adult males and females should recognize their susceptibility to this temptation. Of course, if parent-offspring sexual intimacy were provided for by the society's structure, then abhorrence and sanction will not be present.

This last phrase brings us to Young's article and the issue of societal varia-tions in incest taboo extensions. Young simply claims that the incest taboos and sanctions that are developed will be consistent with the lines of solidarity within a society. If the nuclear family is a solidaristic unit, as it seems to be in most so-cieties, Young would argue that sex and mating must be restricted to one pair within the unit, the father and mother. However, if husbands, wives, and chil-dren are discrete units with little solidarity or intimate contact (as was the case in the royal families of ancient Egypt), it is reasonable to assume that they may be positively oriented toward each other as sex and marriage partners (Young, 1967: 599). Separation, then, is a function of nonsolidarity and a primary basis for mate selection across lines of solidarity. It is out-group status that makes marriage possible; in-group status gives rise to the prohibition of incest.

In his book, Fox repeats and elaborates much of the argument from his 1962 article. He adds that another key issue is *equilibration*, or balance. This simply means that the older males must safeguard women against the younger males, who themselves will eventually be the older males. To forbid incest is not enough. It is controlled by natural aversion and inhibition under the pressure of equilibration (Fox, 1980: 165). But before we become esoteric, let us try to summarize and interpret.

Incest Motivation and Structure: An Interpretation

This writer agrees with Parsons that explaining incest involves "a combination of sociological and psychological considerations . . . ; that a theory which attempts to by-pass either of these fields will find itself in difficulties" (Parsons, 1954: 101). It is quite useful to add Young's emphasis upon societal definitions of solidarity, structural divisions, and "we-ness" and "they-ness" to Fox's concept of prepubertal intimacy and postpubertal taboos, in order to explain the cross-cultural variations in marital and sexual prescriptions and prohibitions.

Societies have differing residential arrangements that bring kinsmen into close proximity or keep them apart. In the patrilocal extended family, a grandparent will live with the young child, as will his/her paternal uncle and parallel cousin. (By parallel cousins is meant the children of brothers or of sisters.) In this structural situation parents, siblings, grandparents, paternal uncles, and parallel cousins all live close together. The first question to ask is whether any of these persons are expected to marry in adulthood. If the answer is no, then there are two ways, according to Fox, in which the incest taboo might work. One way is to allow these kin intimacy or even a joking relationship during the prepubertal phase of the child's development, since this will dull the appetite, make strong taboos unnecessary, and keep these relationships within the bounds of the solidary unit. The other is separation with proximity — such as a clear sexual division of labor and leisure — in which case sexual and mating desires must be controlled by a strong incest taboo. If, however, these proximate parallel cousins are expected to marry in adulthood, proximity without intimacy may be utilized to heighten their interest in one another. This third case is exemplified among the Arabs of Kurdistan, where parallel cousin marriage between the children of brothers is both preferred and prevalent (Barth, 1954: 167–169). Of course, a fourth possibility is that marriage is expected to be with someone who has not been proximate during childhood. Such *exogamy*, or marriage outside one's group or community, is characterized both by nonproximity and by the absence of intimacy prior to puberty, thus making the problem of intimacy and the dulling of interest irrelevant.

The application of Young's and Fox's analyses is, in summary, that strong incest taboos are developed to handle situations of postpubertal proximity with mating prohibited, when there was no intimacy prior to the puberty of the adult member or members of the pair. It is the specific structural arrangement in relation to proximity — nonintimacy — temptation that determines the extensions and strength of incest taboos in a given society. Such an explanation draws upon the psychological viewpoints of Freud and Westermarck, as well as upon the structural insights of Parsons, Young, and others.[2]

Though incest taboos are not universally strong, they do seem to be of particular concern in our family system, and Fox tells us why:

FIGURE 2.3   ENDOGAMOUS AND EXOGAMOUS RESTRICTIONS

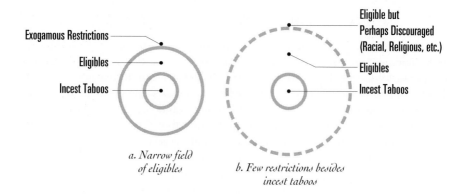

*a. Narrow field
of eligibles*

*b. Few restrictions besides
incest taboos*

> *Much of the concern with incest and incest taboos has been a by-product of the nuclear family obsession. If laws, architecture, and economics force us into nuclear-family living, then all of the burden of the equilibrational conflicts . . . is placed on the shoulders of this compromise institution. The young male has the 'father' on whom to try out his skills of aggression and inhibition, and the mother and sisters are his only objects of sexual possessiveness — at first (Fox, 1980: 203).*

So when the basic unit is the nuclear family, incest taboos will be of great interest and will pertain to that unit.

There are two other reasons why incest taboos are of so much interest in the United States today. First is the increase both in awareness and in the prevalence of incest. Diana Russell, in her powerful book on the incest experiences of girls, states that the sexualization of children, a backlash against gender equality, and other factors help to account for the increase (Russell, 1986). A second major factor is the dramatic increase in step-relations, as a result of more divorces and remarriages. Here the problem is one of definition: is step-sibling sex incest or not? (Beer, 1989: 16, 71f; Ahrons and Rodgers, 1987: 178). Thus, disobeying the taboo will very likely continue to be an important and painful topic in the United States and elsewhere.

Now let us connect the topic of incest taboos back into the more general issues raised earlier in the chapter. Norms of *endogamy*, or marriage within one's group or community, and *exogamy*, or marriage outside one's group, are intertwined with incest taboo extensions, as are the often complex rules of residence and descent.[3] Horst Helle states that the least complex incest taboo may have been between women in a locality grouping and men in that group (Helle, 1988: 349). At the other extreme, it is also possible for rules against incest and endogamy and against exogamy to be so strict and inclusive as to leave the individual with only a single category of persons, such as the mother's brother's daughter, as the preferred marriage partner for the male (see Figure 2.3a). Or it is possible, as in our own society, for endogamous restrictions to cover kin only as far out from the individual as first cousins and for formalized exogamous restrictions to be virtually nonexistent, though there may be pressure not to marry people from certain social categories (see Figure 2.3b). In the latter case, the "field of eligibles" for mating is extremely broad. We shall return to the issue of partner selection in Chapter 10.

How do these rules and the rules governing marriage, authority, and household composition work effectively and coherently in societies that differ from Western industrial society? The answer to this question requires at least a brief description of some family-societal systems that diverge greatly from that of the United States. These illustrations, and the questions they raise and resolve, are the subject matter of Chapter 3.

Family Varieties Exemplified:
Nayar, Afghan, Chinese, Russian

CHAPTER 3

The family systems of the Nayar of South India, the Afghans, the Chinese, and the Russians are discussed and interpreted. The discussion centers on quotations from E. Kathleen Gough, M. Jamil Hanifi, Maurice Freedman and Judith Stacey, and several Russia experts. Four problems in family study are highlighted by these examples: (a) the universality of the nuclear family; (b) the popular question, "How could such a system work?"; (c) the use of historical sources and ideology; and (d) government policy and the family.

The great variety of family possibilities is apparent from the structural and cultural principles discussed in the previous chapter. Family-kin systems do not, however, exist in isolation, but in complex relations with the societies in which they function. These variations and complexities may come alive for readers as they confront specific examples of social systems different from their own.

The family systems of four societies are described at length in the pages that follow. The societies are those of the Nayar, the Afghans, the Chinese, and the Russians. The Nayar are one of several subcastes living in Kerala State, South India, and are sometimes characterized as traditionally practicing group marriage, but more often as polyandrous. A predominantly rural society, the Afghans are located in the mountainous region between Russia and Pakistan. Chinese civilization is an ancient and proud one, traditionally viewed as patrilineal and patriarchal in family structure. Russia, after the revolution of 1917, went through numerous changes, many of which were dictated by government policy. In some ways the family was radically affected by communist policy, while in other ways it remained virtually untouched. Now, of course, Russian policy and polity are changing again. We will consider the family systems of the first two societies in their classical or traditional organization, the Chinese both pre-communist and communist, and the Russian primarily during the communist period. All four should be helpful in answering critical questions about the family.

Whether or not marriage and the family are universal depends upon how one defines the terms. The Nayar are an exceptionally valuable case study, around whom discussion of the family's universality has revolved. A second question, especially troublesome for the beginning study of the family, is, "How could such a system possibly work?" Questioners may be referring to arranged marriage, exogamy, polygyny, or any other pattern that differs greatly from their own. But regardless of the specific aspect that intrigues them, they are likely to see the family as at least strange if not unworkable. The Afghans illustrate polygyny, patrilocality, and patriliny and may aid the reader in perceiving how such a system can "make sense" to the people who practice it. The material on the Chinese family once again points up the ideal-actual, or normative-behavioral distinction, but the reasons for its inclusion in this chapter are also to indicate the problems encountered in using historical materials, and to illustrate the distinction between *nuclear family* institutional and individual embeddedness (in the Chinese) and *kin* embeddedness (in the Afghan). The materials on Russia indicate the way in which governmental policy impinges on the family. While such policy has had a major effect on increasing women's opportunities in the economy and larger society, it has had much less effect on internal relations among family members. We will also note the possible implications of the Russian experience for the women's movement in the United States.

THE NAYAR OF SOUTH INDIA

The nuclear family of father, mother, and their children has been considered by Murdock and others to be virtually universal in human societies, being found without or within the composite marital and consanguineal structures referred to in Chapter 2. However, at least one prime example of a family system without the father as a continuing member has been found: namely, the Nayar of the Malabar coast of India, prior to British rule (before 1792). The best known research on the Nayar is that of Gough; much of the ensuing discussion is drawn from her writings (1959). The use of the past tense indicates that the practices being described have long since been substantially altered.

The Nayar were matrilineal and matrilocal. Between the ages of seven and twelve, or prior to puberty, Nayar girls were ritually married to a male of the appropriate subcaste. After four days of celebration, during which defloration of the bride by the ritual husband was permitted, the husband left the house and had no further obligation to his bride.

> *A bride in turn had only one further obligation to her ritual husband: at his death, she and all her children, by whatever physiological father, must observe death-pollution for him. Death-pollution was otherwise observed only for matrilineal kin.*
>
> *After the ritual marriage, the bridegroom need have no further contact with his ritual wife. If both parties were willing, however, he might enter into a sexual relationship with his ritual bride about the time of her puberty. But he had no priority over other men of the neighborhood group. . . . There appears to have been no limit to the number of wives of appropriate sub-caste whom a Nayar might visit concurrently. It seems, therefore, that a woman customarily had a small but fixed number of husbands from within her neighborhood, that relationships with these men might be of long standing, but that the woman was also free to receive casual visitors of appropriate sub-caste who passed through her neighborhood in the course of military operations.*
>
> *A husband visited his wife after supper at night and left before breakfast next morning. He placed his weapons at the door of his wife's room, and if others came later they were free to sleep on the veranda of the woman's house. Either party to a union might terminate it at any time without formality. A passing guest recompensed a woman with a small cash gift at each visit. But a more regular husband from within the neighborhood had certain customary obligations. At the start of the union, it was common, although not essential, for him to present the woman with a cloth of the kind worn as a skirt. Later he was expected to make small personal gifts to her at the three main festivals of the year. These gifts included a loin-cloth, betel-leaves and arecanuts for chewing, hair-oil and bathing-oil, and certain vegetables. Failure on the part of a husband to make such a gift was a tacit sign that he had ended the relationship. Most importantly, when a woman became pregnant, it was essential for one or more men of*

appropriate sub-caste to acknowledge probable paternity. This they did by providing a fee or a cloth and some vegetables to the low-caste midwife who attended the woman in childbirth. If no man of suitable caste would consent to make this gift, it was assumed that the woman had had relations with a man of lower caste or with a Christian or a Muslim. She must then have been either expelled from her lineage and caste or killed by her matrilineal kinsmen. I am uncertain of the precise fate of the child in such a case, but there is no doubt that he could not be accepted as a member of his lineage and caste.

Although he made regular gifts to her at festivals, in no sense of the term did a man maintain his wife. Her food and regular clothing she obtained from her matrilineal group.

In these circumstances, the exact physiological fatherhood of a child was often uncertain, although of course, paternity was presumed to lie with the man or men who had paid the delivery expenses. But even when physiological paternity was known with reasonable certainty, the genitor had no economic, social, legal, or ritual rights in, nor obligations to, his children after he had once paid the fees of their births. Their guardianship, care, and discipline were entirely the concern of their matrilineal kinsfolk headed by their karanavan [or the oldest male of the group] . . . .

All the children of a woman called all her current husbands by the Sanskrit world acchan, *meaning "lord." They did not extend kinship terms at all to the matrilineal kin of these men. Neither the wife nor her children observed pollution at the death of a visiting husband who was not also the ritual husband of the wife (Gough, 1960: 80).*

The rationale for the Nayar system, so far as it pertained to the fathers, was that they were employed as mercenary troops, often being absent from their village in wars against neighboring kingdoms. The family system, of which they were not expected to be permanent members, meant that their loyalties were not divided between family and military service. The women held land as tenants for a raja or other landlord, to whom they paid rent. The land passed from a mother to her female children, and the matrilineage was buttressed by the absence of the fathers, which prevented them from laying claim to their wives' goods. However, it is not true that males were completely absent from the matrilineal land. Quale points out that a woman's eldest living brother often remained at home to manage the family property, thus minimizing the role of the soldier-husband, who might be lost in battle (Quale, 1988: 3).

Whether the Nayar system is called "cenogamy," since several males and several females appear to have had sexual access to each other simultaneously, or "polyandry," since the women were the permanent residents and entertained several husbands, is relatively unimportant. However, of crucial importance is the absence of the husband(s) as a permanent family member, in conjunction with the necessity of having some male assume legal paternity in order to legitimate the child. This last point—legal paternity—deserves some elaboration. The term *father* may have any of three connotations. It can mean the physiological progenitor of the child; the legal father, or legitimator, of the child, or the socializer of the child—the person with specific responsibilities for passing along family culture. In the case of the Nayar, fatherhood was restricted to legitimation, with no implication of duty as a socializing agent and little direct connection with biological parenthood. There are other societies in which the physiological and social concepts of fatherhood are separated, with the category *father* being more social than physiological (Gough, 1960: 81–83).

Is the Family Universal?

Whether one regards the family as universal depends on one's definition of *marriage* and *family*. The *Notes and Queries* definition of marriage, published in 1951, states that "marriage is a union between a man and a woman such that children born to the woman are recognized legitimate offspring of both parents" (*Notes*, 1951: 24). It can be seen that the family form this definition assumes is the nuclear family, as it was defined earlier. The Nayar are often cited as an exception to the rule that nuclear marriage and the nuclear family are universal, or are found in every human society. We emphasized in the preceding pages that coresidence in marriage is normative, facilitating sexual access, child care, and economic cooperation. The Nayar do not fit this pattern. Nor, as Reiss and others have pointed out, do the Israeli kibbutzim, the matrilocal families of Jamaica, or certain other systems.

When it is claimed that the nuclear family is not universal, is this the same as saying that the family is not universal? The responses of Gough and Reiss to this question are negative. The problem is that, for cross-cultural purposes, the nuclear family cannot be thought of as synonymous with family. Therefore, Gough suggests that marriage be defined as follows: "Marriage is a relationship established between a woman and one or more other persons, which provides that a child born to the woman under circumstances not prohibited by the rules of the relationship, is accorded full birth-status rights common to normal members of his society or social stratum" (Gough, 2960: 90). For her, then, the key is not the idea of mating and common residence, but the legitimation of offspring.

Reiss notes that Murdock postulated the nuclear family—functioning for socialization, reproduction, economic cooperation, and sex relations—as universal. Citing evidence, Reiss states that in some societies the family system does not perform these four tasks. He posits this definition of the family: "The family institution is a small kinship-structured group with the key function of nurturant socialization of the newborn" (Reiss, 1965: 449). In short, Gough and Reiss are saying that, cross-culturally, marriage should be viewed as an institutionalized means of legitimating offspring, while the family is the institutionalized means of raising them.

While these definitions provide valuable insights (we shall return in Chapter 5 to the issue of family functions), their principal effect is to relocate the argument regarding the universality of the family away from the nuclear unit. The difficulty with this relocation is that the posing of definitions of family that might be universally valid has no logical limit. One might reasonably state that the family is "a unit involving two or more persons who share an intimate sexual relationship and a common residence," and in so doing one would include the homosexual unit. Thus, in 1971, Andrew Weigert and Darwin Thomas again tackled the issue of defining the family. Viewing the family as a "conditional universe," they concluded that its minimum necessary structure is "self-plus-infant," a unit that, obviously, can take many forms. We must not, they asserted, base a universal concept like *family* on posited biological or social links that may be broken by culture or technology. Neither marriage nor *parturition* (childbirth) are the ultimate dyadic links that perpetuate society; rather, it is perpetuated by any individual plus a growing infant (Weigert and Thomas, 1971: 188–194).

The point is that one's decision regarding the universality of marriage or the family may be strictly a matter of how one personally defines it, with the debate becoming endless. Harris states this very clearly: "questions concerning 'the universality of marriage' are questions with no precise meaning. They are questions whose answer depends as much on sorting out what we mean by marriage, as it does upon going and looking" (Harris, 1983: 18). Of greater value, it would seem, is the issue of whether or not the *nuclear* family is universal, since the addition of this restriction provides a common denominator for discussion. Cross-cultural indications are that such a unit is not a universal phenomenon, though it is of central importance in a book that focuses primarily upon the family in the modern industrial world. Furthermore, as Weigert and Thomas note, the proper task is empirical: to document and analyze the types of families that exist throughout the world and not to be overly concerned with the issue of whether or not the family per se exists in all societies.

SECTION TWO

AFGHAN FAMILY AND KINSHIP

Afghan society presents a notable contrast to both the Nayar and the U.S. family in the centrality of its kinship organization and in the extent of both institutional and individual embeddedness in the kinship system. The cultural traditions originated among pastoral nomads who roamed central Asia centuries before the rise of Islam. With the spread of Islam and settled agriculture, most of the older family traditions came to be gradually accepted as part of Islamic life. Afghan society is well described by M. Jamil Hanifi, and we will quote a length. The tradition, says Hanifi,

> *which penetrates the entire Afghan social structure, emphasizes the importance of the individual's complete loyalty to his family and gives the familial unit a vital role in social, economic, and political matters. . . . A person learns from earliest childhood to defer to the opinions of the family elders and to place family well-being before all personal wishes and desires (1978: 48).*

While using the word "family," Hanifi makes it clear he is not talking about the nuclear unit consisting of husband, wife, and their unmarried children. Rather, the basic unit is the patrilineal extended family, described earlier. It includes parents, children, aunts, uncles, and cousins. Hanifi describes the traditional household as follows:

> . . . *a man and his wife or wives, unmarried children, and married sons and their wives and children. Additional members may include a man's unmarried, widowed, or divorced sisters, his parents, childless and elderly aunts and uncles, patrilateral first cousins (or children of brothers), and his brother's orphaned children. . . .*
>
> *The extended family is patrilocal. On marriage, a son customarily brings his wife into his father's house (1978: 49).*

If it is too crowded, additional houses or rooms may be built. The result is that families from the same patrilineage cluster together in particular sections of towns and villages.

The extended family is the predominant economic unit in Afghan village and rural society, sharing production, consumption, and reproduction. It shares what is produced, and has almost complete authority over its members. A man is in charge of his wife, children, and their dependents, and responsible for their good conduct. In fact, within the extended family the contrast between males and females is emphasized in every possible way.

> *The mutual separateness and dependence of men and women are factors that hold the household together. Neither men nor women can live outside the household because of the strict division of labor. Since most of the women in the household are related only through marriage to the rest of the members, they are bound to one another by their relationships to men. It is the husband/son who bridges the gap between mother-in-law and daughter-in-law and the brothers who bind the wives together (1978: 51).*

Age, or generation, is also important, with seniority granting authority and prestige. However, the sex distinction overrides all others, so that "even though Afghan mothers command their small children, male and female, adult sons command their mothers."

As is so often true in corporate lineage systems, husbands and wives do not look for friendship or companionship within marriage. The relationship is basically one of economic cooperation and sexual intimacy, for the sake of procreation. The criterion of a successful marriage is the existence of healthy sons.

Marriage is a time of great grief for the bride's mother, since the bride will be moving away to live with her husband's kin, and no attempt is made to conceal the pain. The bride must learn to get along with her mother-in-law more than with her husband. "A bride comes into a household as a relative stranger, and the establishment of rapport with her mother-in-law, under whose direction she will work, is a critical factor in her acceptance into the household."

> *The Islamic incest rules operate as follows: Those prohibited to a man are his lineal descendants and ascendants, his parents' sisters, his own sisters, his nieces, and grandnieces, his father's wives and widows, their stepdaughters, his wife's mother and son's wife, and his living wife's sisters. Beyond this, it is quite common for a man to marry his patrilateral and matrilateral cross-cousins (1978: 57).*

Boys usually marry between ages 16 and 22, and girls three to four years earlier. Like the extended household, polygyny is preferred. However, as Rosenfeld found in the Arab village, reported in Chapter 2, the numerically dominant household unit of Afghan society is the monogamous nuclear family. This is due to both economic and mortality factors.

A man may divorce his wife by saying any words of dismissal before two witnesses. A woman who has been thus "honorably" divorced experiences no social disgrace. In addition, a woman desiring a divorce may leave her husband and return to the household of her nearest living male relative. Though Islamic law does not recognize such a divorce, the community may accept it if her reasons seem satisfactory.

The Workability and Value of Normative Practices

Patriliny with patrilocality, polygyny, cousin marriage, and a great division between the genders seems to work fairly well among the Afghans. Is the point of our discussion, you might ask, the relativist notion that one way of organizing a society and its family system is as satisfactory to its members as another, provided the arrangement is normative or expected? This would be an incorrect interpretation of our Afghan example and of the discussion of norms in general. The mother is genuinely unhappy when her daughter marries and leaves. There is real tension between mother-in-law and daughter-in-law; and polygynous wives are not necessarily "one big happy family." William Stephens, writing not about the Afghans, but about a number of polygynous societies, states that there is often jealously among polygynous wives. "In most known cases at least some co-wives seem to suffer rather intensely from jealousy, and a good many of the polygynous families are strife-torn" (Stephens, 1963: 63).

Stephens' comment indicates that the distinction between workability-acceptance and value-satisfaction should be kept in mind. It might be said that any system that is accepted as normative by a particular people is workable, whether it is polygyny, head-hunting, or the extended family. This is not, however, the same as saying that everyone who accepts a particular system as normative, or "the-way-things-are-supposed-to-be," is consequently happy and satisfied with his or her position in it. Nor is it the same as saying that one system makes for about as many problems as another. The discontent fostered by a given arrangement is one of the seeds of social change, of the rethinking by each new generation of the society's familial and other structural arrangements. It is discontent with lineages and extended families that gives rise to the "nuclear family revolution" in many developing countries of the world, and it is discontent with the monogamous nuclear family that gives rise to staying single, permanent cohabitation, communes, and other alternatives in the modern industrial world. Many different kinds of systems can and have worked reasonably well, historically and cross-culturally; our task is to *understand* their rationale and workability, not to conclude that all systems are equally "good" in some absolute sense or equally satisfying to their constituents. When we confront such issues as divorce or cohabitation in U.S. society, the question "How can a specific system work?" will once again arise.

THE CHINESE FAMILY IN HISTORICAL PERSPECTIVE

Many writers have referred to the society of pre-communist China as one dominated by family and kinship organization. The large family unit with the aging patriarch ruling the household has sometimes been pictured as typical of classical China. This patriarchy has two major ideal-typical foci. First is male control of both production and reproduction (Harris, 1983: 179). Stacey describes it thusly:

> the ideal family structure was an extended joint household in which all married sons, their wives, and their progeny lived with the unmarried siblings under the guidance of the patriarch who was served and assisted by his wife and whatever concubines and servants he possessed (Stacey, 1983: 31).

The eldest male was ideally the head of the family's economy. The second important characteristic was individual embeddedness, described by Stacey as follows: "Confucianism subordinated the needs, interests, and desires of the individual to those of the family group. . . . Eberhard claims that the Chinese language included no words for 'individual,' 'individualism,' or 'freedom' prior to China's contact with the West" (Stacey, 1983: 33). Of course, as noted in Chapter One, in such a system the patriarch—and males in general—have more freedom to act as individuals than do females or children.

Recently, scholars have recognized that two factors altered Chinese social structure away from the ideal. First, classical China had a strong state organization and a complex agrarian economy that counteracted to some degree the power of the kin patriarch. Second, in terms of numbers, pre-communist China was not characterized primarily by the large landed lineage, but by the nuclear family households of the peasants. Distinguishing them from the wealthy patriarchies, Stacey states that "poorer families brought to the revolutionary situation a history of less discrimination of their members by sex and age. They brought, too, a history of family structure in which the husband/wife relationship was stronger" (1983: 58). These considerations allow us to ask what it means for a kinship system to be central to a society's functioning. In his insightful account of pre-communist China, Maurice Freedman clarifies some of the dimensions of family and kinship and the complex relation between them and the politico-economic realities of the larger society, and we will quote him at length.

The first point to make is that China was not a kin-centered society to the same extent that the Afghans were. One reason is that the Chinese state machinery was well developed. Thus, even among high-status Chinese it would be proper to ask whether the patrilineage dominated the state, the state dominated the patrilineage, whether the two institutions were in a power balance, or whether they simply reinforced each other. Let us assume, says Freedman, that the problem is to decide what strength or potency lay in kinship relations as a whole. We may take China as it was in the last hundred years of its existence as an imperial state. The question resolves itself into an analysis of how the solidarities and values of kinship were enmeshed in a political and economic order which required of individuals that they owe allegiance to a state and participate, despite the dominance of agriculture, in a wide-ranging economic system.

From the point of view of the state, a man's obligations to it were in fact both qualified and mediated by his kinship relations. They were qualified in the sense that obligations springing from filial piety and mourning duties were held to modify duties owed to the state. An official who lost a parent was supposed to retire during the mourning. People related to one another in close bonds of kinship were so far regarded by the written law to require solidarity among them that the Code provided that certain relatives might legitimately conceal the offenses of one another (except in cases of high treason and rebellion), either escaping punishment altogether or suffering a penalty reduced in accordance with the closeness of the relationship; and that it was an offense generally for close kinsmen to lay even just accusations against one another. There was built into the system the principle that close patrilineal kinship set up special rights and duties standing apart from the rights and duties between man and the state. . . .

In the eyes of the state, then, a man stood posed against it in a network of primary kinship duties. But the state also regarded kinship units as part of its system of general control, so that a man's duties to it were mediated through his membership in these units. The family is the clearest case. The Confucian emphasis on complex families and the legal power vested in the head of a family to prevent its premature breakup are aspects of a total political system in which some authority is delegated from the administrative system to what, in a metaphorical sense, we may call natural units. The Confucian moralizing about the family, the stress put upon filial piety and the need for solidarity among brothers, the underlining of the importance of domestic harmony—these reflect a political view in which units standing at the base of the social pyramid are expected to control themselves in the interest of the state.

But the family is not the only case. It was morally right for men to align themselves on the basis of their common patrilineal descent and to form lineages. Lineage organization implied ancestor worship, a Confucian value of high order. It implied the promotion of schools and mutual help; in these the state could take pleasure. It implied, finally, an organization which could be used by the state for political and fiscal control. And at once we can see the dilemma faced by the state when it tried to make use of the lineage and encouraged its prosperity. To be of use to the state, the lineage must be organized and strong; but strength might grow to the point at which what was once a useful adjunct of government now became a threat to it. Where the lineages grew in numbers and riches they fought with other lineages. This was objectionable enough, but clearly what frightened the central administration more than anything else was the tendency for patrilineal organization to snowball. A lineage was justified by a genealogy; people began to produce longer and wider genealogies to justify more extensive groups, going so far—and this "excess" excited very great official indignation—that attempts were sometimes made to group together in one organization all the lineages in one area bearing a common surname. It is important to realize that *genealogical rearrangement and the grouping together of lineages makes perfect sense, given the logic of the patrilineal system, and that the objections raised by officialdom, although they might be couched in terms condemning the falsification of genealogies, were essentially political. That is to say, strong nuclei of local power were being created which constituted a threat to state authority.*

From the political point of view, then, kinship organization entailed a balance of forces with the state. . . .

On the role of kinship in economic life we have no systematic and large body of information on which to rely, but we can make a general argument. If we start from the assumption that kinship relations and values predominate in the conduct of economic affairs, we must expect that enterprise will take the form of what is often called the family business. Now, of course, there is plenty of evidence to show that Chinese economic enterprise has tended strongly to be organized so that people associating their capital, or capital and labor, are related by kinship or affinity. But what is the real significance of this fact? Is it that the moral imperatives of kinship impel people to seek out kinsmen with whom to work? The answer is no. Given the nature of the capital market, given a legal system which offers little protection to business, given the tendency to rely on people with whom there is some preceding tie, we should expect that kinsmen would be associating with one another in economic activities. What is really involved is that these activities are made to rest on highly personalized relationships and that a man's circle of relatives is likely to contain the greater number of individuals apt for selection. It is important to remember that, outside the family, the kinsman has few specific economic claims, that he can be approached as a landlord or creditor, and that in general we must not look to see preference being shown to a kinsman in economic matters on the grounds simply that he is a kinsman.

We have so far been concerned with the question of how far the family in "premodern" China can be said to have been the basic unit of society. The argument has taken the form that family and kinship together provided one method of balancing the power of the state and that kinship was not in principle basic to economic life. If we confined our attention to the family in the strictest sense of the term, we might be able, by noting how much of the ordinary individual's life is lived within it, to assert that we were dealing with something fundamental. But in doing this we would be ignoring the whole range of wider institutions without which the family can in fact have little meaning.

One way to summarize Freedman's major points is to say that while much economic, educational, and even political activity took place in the large lineages, it would be incorrect to conclude that the other institutions of society were totally embedded in kin and family. Let us turn now to the inner structure and content of pre-communist family life, looking at both relationships and tensions inherent in it. It is generally acknowledged, says Freedman, that the average size of the traditional Chinese family was no more than five or six. Of greater importance currently would seem to be the question of

why it was that some families were very large and others very small, with many gradations between these extremes. Let us go back to the political point that the state looked to the family as the first unit of social control. The ideal family from this point of view was one in which large numbers of kinsmen and their wives were held under the control of a patriarch imbued with the Confucian values of propriety and order. Some families came close to this model, several generations living under one roof. They were powerful families. We may consider the power they wielded in terms both of their control of economic resources and of their command over other people. They were rich. They owned much land and other capital resources. By renting land and lending money they could exert influence over other people. They could afford to educate their sons and equip them for membership in the bureaucratic elite. They often (perhaps usually) entered into the life of this elite, making use of these ties to control both less fortunate families and their own subordinate members. Such a family may be looked upon as a large politico-economic corporation with much power vested in its chief member. But this corporation could not grow indefinitely in membership, for with the death of its senior generation it split along the lines laid down by the constitution of the next generation, every son having a right to an individualized share of his father's estate on that man's death. However, despite the partition which took place every generation, high status families were able to remain large. The passing of the senior generation was likely to take place at a point when the men in the next generation were themselves old enough to have descendants sufficient for complex families of their own. At this level of society, fertility was relatively high, the chances of survival were higher, adoption was easy, the age of marriage was low, and plural marriage was possible.

At the other end of the social scale the family was, so to speak, scarcely Confucian. Poverty and powerlessness produced, instead of a strong patriarch, a weak father. He could rally no support from outside to dominate his sons. He had few resources to withhold from them. In fact, he might well have only one son growing to maturity. If, however, he had two or more sons reaching manhood, only one would be likely to stay with him, and perhaps even this one would leave him too. Demography, economics, and the power situation at this level of society ensured that families of simple structure were a constant feature of the landscape.

Changes in social status promoted changes in family structure. Upward social mobility was partly a matter of increasing the complexity of the family, both because changing demographic, economic, and power conditions entailed complexity and because the ideal Confucian family was a model towards which people strove when they were moving upwards. And we should note that downward social mobility brought with it a corresponding decline in complexity.

The relations between the sexes and between the generations were dependent on differences in family structure. It will be convenient to start from a feature of Chinese family life which has always attracted the attention of outsiders: the unhappy position of the daughter-in-law. She may be looked upon from three points of view: as a woman, as a member of the family by incorporation, and as a member of a junior generation. It needs no stressing that being a woman was a disadvantage. Every aspect of her society and its values left the Chinese woman in no doubt on that score (Freedman, 1961–62: 328).

The woman's disadvantage in China and elsewhere was often justified by an ideology that said women were inherently inferior. An interesting editorial by a modern Indian woman shows her mixed reaction to this traditional ideology (see Feature 3.1).

Feature 3.1 GIRLS ARE MORE AFFECTIONATE

I am the proud mother of two daughters. The first time, I was thrilled with the beautiful bundle and shrugged off such remarks, "Alas! a girl!" But the second time, much as I tried, I couldn't reconcile myself to the fact.

I was not bothered about the expenses or about who will do my Karma, thus assuring me of a Heavenly Abode. Nor had I any inhibitions about the superiority of the male. What frightened me was the immense responsibility—how to shelter my two little girls from this horrible male world? . . . In spite of the modern girl's education, her very femininity makes her vulnerable. . . . There is always a deep bond between the mother and daughter. Being women they naturally sympathize with each other. . . .

Every educated woman should cleanse herself of all conservative ideas that her family and society have fed her, about the inferiority of girls. A mother fears for her daughter—her frightening insecurity, her physical and emotional vulnerability in this male world, her utter dependency on the male, more so in our Indian society. The mother dreads to see her child go through all that she had. . . .

Padma Prabhakar, "Girls are more affectionate," *Indian Express*, Hyderabad, August 15, 1986, 7.

Her marriage, continues Freedman, cut her off economically and as a legal person from her own family and transferred the rights in and over her to the family receiving her. In this new family she was at once a stranger and a member—the former because she was new and the latter in that, henceforth, the rights and duties in respect to her would lie with her husband's people. From the day of her marriage she must begin to think of her interests as being inevitably involved in those of her husband and the members of his family. She had no secure base outside this family from which to operate, because, while she might try to bring in support from her family of birth to moderate oppression, she could not rely on it. To a large extent physically, and in all degrees legally, she was locked within her husband's gates. Her husband's mother was her point of contact with the new senior generation to preside over her—whence the tears, for she had to be disciplined into a new role in a new family. In fact, however, the difficulties faced by the daughter-in-law were only one aspect of a broader configuration of difficulties. These difficulties are referred to by both Stacey and Freedman. Stacey speaks of the success of the joint household being based on fraternal solidarity, which was threatened by marital intimacy (1983: 53). Sex segregation was carried to such symbolic lengths, says Stacey, that "husbands and wives were admonished not to hang their clothes on the same rack" (1983: 39). Women were troublemakers, Freedman adds,

partly because they were strangers. Her mother-in-law represented for the wife the fe-
male half of the family into which she was firmly thrust if her husband refused to
come to her aid. Mother-in-law, daughter-in-law, and unmarried daughters formed a
battlefield on which any one daughter-in-law must fight for herself and, later, for her
children (Freedman, 1961-62: 328-329).

Such female antagonisms, real and imagined, were blamed for the failures and
problems of the joint family, thereby excusing the males.

If the married brothers did stand together it was because they were posed
against their father, "and this father was a strong figure whose power rested on
the economic resources he controlled and the command he could exert on the
world outside the family" (Freedman, 1961–62: 329). This helps to explain the
apparent contradictions in father-son relations reported by David Ho. There is,
he says, psychological distance rather than closeness in "the very relationship
that is structurally the most important, namely, the father-son relationship"
(Ho, 1987: 241). Children are supposed to be respectful, obedient, and devoted
to fathers, while in actuality they may be distant from, fearful of, even antagonistic toward them. Authority often results in distance rather than closeness,
and classical China is no exception.

> *In a [Chinese] family of low status and simple structure the elemental relation-*
> *ships of father and son, brother and brother, and husband and wife formed a different*
> *pattern. The father's control was weak and the brothers highly individualized among*
> *themselves. Each brother stood close to his wife, so that while the wife might be made*
> *miserable by poverty and hard work, at the lower levels of society she had greater*
> *strength as an individual. Here she was far less likely to need to cope with other ma-*
> *ture women in the house.*
>
> *From this summary analysis we may conclude that the probability of tension be-*
> *tween the generations and the sexes increased with a rise in social status, and we may*
> *look forward from this point to the attempts made in modern times to remedy what*
> *seemed to be the difficulties and injustices of the Chinese family system" (Freedman,*
> *1961-62: 329).*

The reform attempts, as Freedman summarizes them, actually involved change
in the structure of the high-status family, making it more similar to the historical
form of the low-status Chinese family just described. That is, much effort was
expended in the first half of the twentieth century (and was continued under the
Communist regime) to weaken the control of the powerful lineages, thereby increasing the status and power of women and children in relations with men. Yet
Stacey asserts very clearly that, judged by feminist standards, "the family revolution in China, as in Russia, appeared to be a failure. One can readily identify a
persistently strong patriarchal basis to family and social life in both post-revolu-
tionary societies" (Stacey, 1983: 4). We will say more about Russia later, but
what about the revolution in China? Land reform broke up the large patriarchal
feudal estates, and promised women equal rights to land. However, "the centrality of the family economy and the dominance of patriarchal values effectively
prevented most women from realizing any direct benefits of this sort" (Stacey,
1983: 130). Despite the ideology of equality and anti-patriarchy, it is clear that a

goal of the Socialist revolution was not the destruction of the family. The Chinese Communists, says Stacey, "directly appealed to family sentiment to establish a new moral economy, but one still based on family, still patriarchal. . . . Communist family policy always exhibited a delicate compromise between feminist and restorationist tendencies" (Stacey, 1983: 157, 181), so that while the large lineage was attacked, the family per se was not.

> *The more we look at this picture the more familiar it will seem to us, for it contains features from the Western experience of family life. For most of the inhabitants of an industrialized society the family is a small residential group from which many of the major activities of life are excluded. The factory, the office, and the school separate the members of one family for many hours of the day and provide them with different ranges of relationships and interests. What they unite for as a family is a restricted number of activities of consumption, child care, amusement, and emotional exchange. True, if we are to believe what we are told, the Chinese family in the commune has gone further in reducing the minimal functions we associate with family life, but it has not necessarily departed in principle from a pattern which we know to be intrinsic to the modern form of society.*
>
> *It would appear that the form taken by the family in recent years is essentially the same as that which we have seen to have characterized the greater part of the Chinese population before any of the modern trends began. That is to say, the family is either a unit of parents and their immature children, or it includes, in addition to those people, the parents or surviving parent of the husband or the wife (of the former rather than of the latter). The "solution" produced by the Communists is in reality an old one, and in arriving at it the Communists were continuing a process of change which had started many years earlier at the higher levels of Chinese society. In fact, it could be argued that just as the Communists worked on peasant hunger for land to bind the mass of the people to them in the early days of land reform, so they commanded the allegiance of many people by playing on the stresses inherent in complex family organization. The resentment of the wife and the son, and the strains between the sexes and the generations, were material on which politics could work to create opinion favorable to its general aims (Freedman, 1961–62: 333–334).*

According to Freedman, then, classical China was characterized by a balance of power between strong patrilineages and state authority. The vast majority of the population, however, lived on the land in nuclear family units, free from the complexities of highly developed patrilineal organization.

Much of the historical literature on China has, of course, focused on the life of high-status people. The nucleation and weak kin linkages of the poorer segments of the population have hardly been noticed. The primary political trend has been to weaken the powerful intermediate lineage structures, thereby providing state leaders with more immediate access to and control over the nuclear units.[1]

To summarize thus far: (1) pre-communist China was ideologically patriarchal in the extreme, but only the wealthy lived out the ideology and institutions were not completely embedded in the family-kin group; (2) Chinese families today are not all that different from those in the rest of the "modernized" world; and (3) changes have been toward the characteristics that previously were those of the poor.

More needs to be said about China since the revolution. The family survived the revolution, not against the wishes of the Communist leadership, but rather in accordance with their desire to see it persist. The "period of collectivization was marked by a conservative pro-family ideological context. . . . [It] strengthened networks of cooperating male kin" (Stacey, 1983: 209, 211). Moreover, adds Stacey, "the collectives did not release peasant women from, nor remunerate them for, the arduous burdens of domestic labor and child care" (1983: 207). Both patrilocal marriage and the continuing gender division of labor reinforced patriarchy, in its manifestation of what Stacey calls the new democratic patriarchy. True, the double standard and individual embeddedness of pre-communist Chinese women were more extreme, but Stacey makes a telling comparison: "the party was so committed to sustaining private conjugal family life that it found the protosocialist, protofeminist communities of sisters less tolerable than patriarchal 'feudal remnants,' such as purchase of brides, dowry, ancestor worship, or wife beating" (Stacey, 1983: 189). In addition, there are still many intergenerational shared households in China, though not the patrilineal extended households of the past. An interesting interpretation of change proposed by Stacey is that the profound improvements in women's status "are as much generational as they are an indication of flagging male privilege. Young women have gained influence and respect largely at the expense of older women" (Stacey, 1983: 226).

A final issue concerning family change in China concerns the one-child-per-couple policy. That this has been effective is seen in the fact that the rate of childbearing in China declined more than 60 percent from 1970 to 1980. Part of this was accounted for by restricting marriage before the age of 23 (now no longer in effect). In a few decades this will have an effect on population size (Coale, 1989: 833–850).

In summary, our historical materials have made us aware of two dangers, which we will note again in Chapter 4. One is that they may deal with high-status people's lives, to the exclusion of the common people. The other is that they may treat ideology (in this case Confucianism) as empirical reality. Stacey and Freedman have helped us with these problems. The complexity of agrarian China was such that, on the one hand, the nuclear family was more important to the functioning of society than we found it to be among the Nayar, but, on the other hand, kin group and society could not be considered virtually synonymous as we found them to be among the Afghans.

SECTION FOUR

THE FAMILY IN RUSSIA

We are fortunate to have a new book on Russian and U.S. families. Edited by James W. Maddock, M. Janice Hogan, Anatolyi I. Antonov, and Mikhail S. Matskovsky, it is entitled: *Families Before and After Perestroika* (1993). Based especially on materials from the late 1980s, and including impressions as late as

1991, this source will be helpful, but will hardly exhaust the dramatic changes taking place in Russia at present. As Olson and Matskovsky state: "Even in the few years since we began planning for this book, Soviet culture has undergone a revolutionary transformation" (1993: 30).

To understand the Russian family since the 1917 revolution, one must start with classic Marxist theory, since Russia was ideologically Marxist for over 70 years. Marx himself said little about the family, but his colleague, Engels, gave us a clear statement regarding the future of the family under communism (Engels, 1942). The two major forces of history are production and reproduction; that is, economy and family. Prior to the emergence of private property, there was communal ownership of property and equality between the sexes. But with individual control over property came the domestic slavery of the female within the family, so that the males controlled both production and reproduction, property and women. The family has gone through the polygamous stage down to monogamy. But the ideological theme of Engels and Marx is one of liberation, not subjection. With the final revolution there will again be communism, or communal ownership of property, and the monogamous family will be reduced to desired, random, naturalistic contacts between the sexes, thereby liberating the female. Zaretsky explains very clearly that Engels felt the conflict between men and women would be resolved by women being integrated into the industrial proletariat. Engels, says Zaretsky, believed "that male supremacy will 'vanish automatically' along with its original cause — private property. . . . He assumes that under socialism the functions currently performed by the family will be socialized," leaving contact between the sexes to be random and spontaneous" (Zaretsky, 1976: 96). Thus, with the communist revolution the monogamous family will simply wither away.

Vladimir Lenin, the father of the Russian revolution, added that one way to control the impulses that give rise to marriage and family is through "revolutionary sublimation." By this he meant the giving of one's passions and energies to the revolution instead of to sexuality. He himself, incidentally, had no children. Thus, the classic theorists of Russian communism saw the necessary and inevitable abolition of the family, in order that oppression might disappear.

However, one cannot understand what is happening in the Russian family today simply by reading statements by the theorists. Under Josef Stalin the study of the family, like other areas of social research, became taboo. In 1956, however, P. I. Kushner published his study of Russian peasant life, and the field of family studies received its greatest impetus in 1964 with the publication of Anatoli Kharchev's *Marriage and Family in the USSR* (Kushner, 1956; Kharchev, 1964). Since then both Russians and non-Russians have commented on, and in some cases researched, various aspects of Russian families.

To the extent that we can, let us examine changes in Russian families since the Bolshevik takeover of 1917. Zaretsky described the immediate postrevolutionary changes in the following way:

> *In the early years of the revolution the Bolsheviks promulgated the most advanced pro-gramme in European and American feminism; abolition of ecclesiastical marriage; women's right to property, legal abortion, and contraception; marriage and divorce*

codes based upon the equality of men and women; recognition of de facto marriage; and equal rights for illegitimate children. They regarded these measures as part of the bourgeois (or capitalist) phase of their revolution, recognizing that these rights were purely formal. Real equality would come through the entry of women into the labour force and thereby into political life (Zaretsky, 1976: 98).

The party, however, spent most of its postrevolutionary effort on equal opportunity, wages, fines, length of the working day, the form of the state, ownership of land, industrialization, and the development of an industrial proletariat. As Kent Geiger says in his book *The Family in Soviet Russia*: "The party did not and could not afford specific attention to questions of the everyday life of the working masses" (1968: 77). The economic revolution would resolve the oppressions of intimate relationships and everyday life as a by-product of change in the public sphere.[2]

What, then, has happened since those postrevolutionary attempts to put into practice the theory of Engels and Lenin? Gary Lee Bowen catalogued the evolution of Soviet family policy over 65 years. The early postrevolutionary attempts were followed during Stalin's rule by conservative moves to give social cohesion priority over social mobility and equality for women. Following Stalin's death in 1953, attempts were made at compromise legislation, aimed at liberalizing the laws again, and providing more state aid to families. The policy ten years ago was a hybrid, emphasizing both motherhood and employment for women. Marriages were relatively weak, divorce rates high, and fertility low (Bowen, 1983: 299–313). See Feature 3.2 on this.

Feature 3.2 **FAMILY PROBLEMS BESETTING SOVIETS**

The Soviet Union is in the grip of a democratic and social revolution that is breaking up families, lowering the birthrate, and contributing to alcoholism, juvenile delinquency, and crime. . . .

"Today's young family is full of conflict, unstable, and with few children," the demographer, Viktor Perevedentsev, a senior researcher with the Soviet Academy of Sciences, said in an interview. . . .

Under the pressures of a nation-wide shift in values and ways of life, he said, more than one-third of these families break up. In the cities of European Russia, the divorce rate has risen to 50 percent.

The problems stem from an extensive rural-urban shift of nearly 2 million people a year that some sociologists say is transforming the country's social structure as none of the wars or internal conflicts of this century have changed it. . . .

Seth Mydans, "Family problems besetting Soviets," N. Y. Times News Service, August 25, 1985.

Let us be more specific, focusing on three areas: changing laws on abortion and divorce, child-rearing, and women's employment and status. In the 1920s, the Bolshevik party determined that a woman had a right to a legal abortion, thus giving her control over her body so that equality with men could be realized. In 1936, however, Stalin effected a law making abortion illegal and invoked severe punishment for any doctor who performed an abortion. The reason for this law was Stalin's perception that Russia needed more people. How did he justify the change ideologically? He said that, having achieved the happy life in Russia, abortion was no longer necessary. In other words, he argued, easy abortion was an interim phase until Russian society "arrived." Women, however, had become accustomed to abortions on demand and continued to get them, though they were often unsanitary and always expensive. Finally, in 1953, abortion was again made legal, a result, as much as anything, of the government's incapability of changing people's behavior.

A second instructive case is that of divorce laws. After the revolution, divorce was free and easily obtainable. The ease is well illustrated by "postcard divorce": a woman could write on a postcard "I divorce Ivan" and send it to the Central Registry; when it arrived the divorce was final. Children, however, were not taken over by the state, and the women continued to raise them. Thus, instead of raising women's status, easy divorce left many women to raise children alone. Also those women most in need of alimony were least likely to get it. In 1936 the law was changed so that in order to get a divorce you had to pay a fine. The result of this law was only a small reduction in marital breakup, for rather, the rates of desertion, separation, and illegitimacy increased. Again in 1965, divorce laws were relaxed. Thus, in the case of both abortion and divorce laws, the tightening of the 1930s hardly had the desired effect and they were eventually relaxed.

Divorce rates increased through the 1960s and 1970s, and seemed to level off in the 1980s at about 40 percent (Olson and Matskovsky, 1993: 26). Goode argues that divorce rates in Eastern Europe (and Russia) very likely rose because of:

> *(1) the continuing violation of socialist ideals, (2) the harshness of political and economic life . . ., (3) a widespread and growing feeling that the individual could not trust either the state or other persons, and (4) a general difficulty in achieving what most viewed as a 'normal' family life created a feeling of deprivation and malaise (Goode, 1993: 155).*

Shlapentokh adds that there are family "fundamentalists" in Russia who are demanding that male supremacy be reinstated, and that women have the wisdom to take second place to their husbands, and sacrifice for their children (Shlapentokh, 1991: 277). This leads to the discussion of children and women in Russia.

We noted that children were not taken over by the state following a divorce. A portion of the Marxist ideology was that there should be state children's homes so that men and women would be equally free to pursue opportunities for employment. Yet only a few such homes were established: far too few to handle the numbers of children. Furthermore, an exposè by Kotoshchikova called into question the ideology that children are better cared for by the state than by the family. She saw a beautiful child on the beach at the Black Sea who didn't talk and found that the child had been raised in an institutional setting. Koto-shchikova wrote a series of articles for the *Literary Gazette* in which she showed that state-raised children didn't do as well on a number of social and intellectual indicators as children raised by their parents. The debate regarding boarding schools and communal upbringing versus parental childrearing raged during the Khrushchev era but now has subsided. According to Fisher and Khotin, "there is now general consensus that children are better off with their parents and in the family circle" (Fisher and Khotin, 1977: 373). This sentiment is bolstered by statements such as the following by Urlanis, a renowned demographer: "Nurseries were a necessity in their own time, but now we are wealthy enough not to have to deprive a child of its mother's affection" (Urlanis, 1971: 11). Notice that Urlanis says "mother's," not "parents' affection." And while help from the father would be appreciated, Boss and Gurko report that "women sometimes express greater dissatisfaction with the lack of sufficient help in childrearing from their husbands' *parents* than from their husbands" (Boss and Gurko, 1933: Chapter 2, p. 31).

The focal point of the Russian revolutionary ideology as it pertains to the family involves the status of women. By 1926, 51 percent of the Soviet work force were women. A portion of this influx of women involved movement into the professions, especially medicine. The following comparison between the Americans and Soviets in the early 1970s is instructive (Rueschemeyer, 1981: 16):

TABLE 3.1   WOMEN IN SELECTED PROFESSIONS, IN PERCENT

Country	Lawyers	Physicians	Dentists
U.S.	3.5	6.5	2.1
U.S.S.R.	36.0	75.0	83.0

Most women, however, "became office workers, domestics, or factory operatives. . . . this encouraged the consignment of female employment to the lower-paid and less unionized sectors of the economy: the services where labor was similar to that performed within the home" (Zaretsky, 1976: 114). So while there are more women in Russia going into the professions and into technical fields than in the United States, there is still a sex-division of occupations. Janet Schwartz's data indicate this clearly:

- ✦ 73% of teachers are women
- ✦ 99% of nurses are women
- ✦ 85% of social welfare workers are women
- ✦ 91% of sales clerks are women
- ✦ 95% of office workers are women
- ✦ but only 13% of business or enterprise heads are women, and only 2% of Russian Academy of Science positions are held by women (Schwartz, 1979).

There is, furthermore, a difference in earnings according to sex. Michael Swafford describes his survey data as painting a "picture which is altogether familiar. In the U.S.S.R., as elsewhere, women's earnings fall significantly below men's. In the republic capital surveyed, women brought home only 65 percent as much as men, and other evidence suggests that this estimate was applicable to the entire Soviet Union during the sixties" (Swafford, 1978: 669).

One recent trend in Russia has been to couple economic difficulties with the traditional patriarchal ideology in order to get women to leave their employment and return home. The Maddock et al. volume speaks about this several times. Nor has women's employment resulted in an equal sharing of household responsibilities by the genders. Women still do three times as many hours of housework as do men (Sacks, 1977: 805), and Boss and Gurko note the similarity of the U.S. and Russia on this score:

> *Regardless of political ideology over the past 75 years, our cultures have come to expect women to be responsible for marriage and family life, as well as to be income earners in the outside world. No such dual role expectations have been placed upon men (Boss and Gurko, 1993: 65).*

An interesting twist was found in a recent study of young families by Gurko. She finds that "a young husband is often 'prevented' from doing housework by the presence of older parents who directly or indirectly discourage him from helping, even though many wives are also employed and/or studying in high education institutions" (Boss and Gurko, 1993: 45). Sergei Golod, in his important book on *Family Stability*, argues that a major problem is that marital stability requires autonomy and equality, and Russian families fall far short of these (Golod, 1984). In short, then, work and family by gender are related as follows: while women have had a virtually equal opportunity to be employed outside the home, (1) they have not gotten many of the prestigious positions, (2) have not received equal pay, (3) are now being encouraged to "return home," and (4) have never received much help from husbands at home.

One other element in Russian gender relations concerns the relative strength of Russian women, compared to men. Goode, following du Plessix Gray, argues that Russian women feel they are stronger than their men. "Whether husbands or lovers, their men could not adequately lead them, protect them, or even support them, and actually added to their burdens, rather than lightening them" (Goode, 1993: 134). This, says Goode, is an ironic parallel to lower class men and women in the West, especially among African-Americans.

Several additional aspects of Russian family life deserve mention. Economic problems have weakened the social support programs for the elderly, so that they are increasingly thrown back on their own family's resources. Multigenerational families still characterize many Russian households (Olson and Matskovsky, 1993: 29), and these households are ordinarily flats or apartments. As for sexuality, a recent national poll showed that over half thought information on sexuality should come from school courses or educational literature, while another study at the same time indicated that adolescents' primary source of such information was peers (Maddock and Kon, 1993: 117). Finally, while

homosexuality is still more hidden in Russia than in the United States, estimates are that the level of prevalence is about the same—five to ten percent.
Signs that homosexuality is "coming out" in Russia include a gay-lesbian newspaper in Moscow, and a 1990 conference in Estonia on the living conditions of
sexual minorities in Europe and Russia (Maddock and Kon, 1993: 120, 122).

Even as I write this, policy changes are taking place in Russia. Let me list
a few: (1) a law passed in 1990 "allows every family currently living in a state-
owned flat to purchase [it] . . . and to use it thereafter as their own private property" (Detzner and Sinelnikow, 1993: 141). (2) Trying to offset the low level of
fertility, the Moscow City Council in 1991, passed legislation to provide a subsidy to families with three or more children. Whether this will offset the economic difficulties remains to be seen. (3) A proposed change would be to
re-define "family" to include both legal and de facto marriages, thus including
cohabitants and homosexuals as well in various family coverages. Anatolyi
Antonov, however, argues that all recent and current changes are simply necessary reactions to poverty, not long-term efforts to bolster family well-being
(Maddock and Hogan, 1993: 229–230).

Public Policy and Private Life: A Note on Women's Movements

In her book *Here to Stay*, Bane argues that there are often tensions between the
larger world of public policy and the private world of the family. These tensions, she feels,

> *are to some extent resolvable by a public stance that emphasizes the rights of individ-
> uals and leaves family roles to be worked out privately. For example, the most work-
> able approach to sexual equality is probably to enforce the political and economic
> rights of women, and to rely on families to work through the power shifts and chang-
> ing division of labor that political and economic equality imply (Bane, 1976: 141).*

If, however, the Soviet Communists' experience is instructive for such concerns, it would indicate that major changes in the public sector may have little,
if any, effect upon the private world of the family. The Russian focus was on
economic development, and for this they needed women in the labor force. But
they ignored the role of men in the home. Policy never focused directly on home
roles. Sacks, in commenting on the statements of prominent Russian males like
Urlanis and Litvyakov in favor of "motherly obligation," notes that there is a
women's movement in Russia that is demanding that men assume an equal
share of housework. But, he says, time-budget data make it eminently clear
which ideals are reflected in practice. "The data," he feels, "do not support the
hypothesis that an egalitarian ideology has had a direct effect on family behavior" (Sacks, 1977: 393). It is quite possible, this suggests, for a movement for
equal employment or equal pay or equal political participation to assume that
such changes will somehow automatically alter the intimate relations between
the sexes. Such an assumption is at least questionable. We will return to this
issue when we discuss gender roles in the United States in Chapter 11.

SUMMARY OF CHAPTERS 2 AND 3

Some of the major principles by which family and kinship structures may be distinguished include marriage patterns, consanguineal ties, and location of residence. In addition, descent and inheritance patterns differ from society to society. Among the most significant types found cross-culturally according to these principles are: (a) monogamous, polygynous, and polyandrous marriages; (b) monogamous nuclear, joint, and extended households; (c) patrilocality, matrilocality, and neolocality; (d) patrilineal, matrilineal, and bilateral descent and inheritance; and (e) patriarchal, matriarchal, and equalitarian authority. Such types are, of course, group constructs that are useful for comparisons but are in reality simply abstractions and points on a complex continuum of societal expectations and empirical reality.

The married person is simultaneously a member of two nuclear families, that into which one was born, called the family of orientation, and that which one establishes by means of marriage and parenthood, called the family of procreation. Authority and intimacy are two important elements of family culture—perhaps negatively related. The incest taboo, which designates certain categories of kin as unavailable for sexual intercourse or mating, is a virtually universal aspect of human societies, though there are substantial differences from one society to another in the specific relations falling under the taboo. Even sibling and parent-child mating have been considered legitimate in certain societies.

Four societies were used to exemplify some of the problems in cross-cultural family study. The Nayar of South India, a quasi-polyandrous people, were the focal point for discussing the universality of the family. These people appear to have traditionally lacked the husband as a permanent member of the household. Thus, if the question concerns whether the nuclear family, with father, mother, and child as permanent members, is universal, the answer is probably no. If, however, *family* is redefined as a mechanism for bearing and rearing offspring, it is very likely universal.

Western observers understand their own family system and consider it "natural." but how, they might ask, can a totally kin-embedded system work—one that includes polygyny, extended households, and patri- or matrilateral cousin marriage as attributes? Among the Afghans it seems to function fairly satisfactorily; for one thing, the majority of household units are monogamous rather than polygynous. In addition, polygyny itself does not seem displeasing to the Afghan females, or co-wives. This does not mean that polygyny does not cause problems. Instances of jealousy between co-wives are reported in the literature. Rather, the point is that any system can function, once established, although it may include within it the seeds of discontent and eventual destruction.

Classical China was considered for many years to have consisted of a series of large family-kin households. Freedman's discussion illustrates the difficulties in using historical sources, in speaking of family-kin "importance," and in determining the direction of changes over time. In the case of China, the problem is that many authors have written about the high-status family as if it were typical. Likewise, many have written about Confucian ideology as if it was behaviorally dominant. The recent trend in China toward greater nucleation of families has actually been a movement toward the small household that characterized the poorer masses during the classical period. The kin-lineage system was important to classical China in the sense that among the wealthy it acted as a political balance against the forces of centralized state authority and as a major unit of agrarian economic production. Today the nuclear unit is the seat of agricultural production, but industrialization is, in China as elsewhere, weakening even this form of economic embeddedness in the family. Patriarchy continues even today in the small Chinese family.

Russia after the Bolshevik or Communist revolution lived under a government that ideologically favored liberation and gender equality. This government tackled the problem primarily at the level of employment opportunities and has altered its laws from time to time in response either to its leader's demands or to how the people were behaving. While the effect has been to increase opportunity for both sexes to be employed, analyses have called into question whether such change in the public sphere necessarily has much effect on the intimate relations between the sexes in the family. New data are attempting to cope with the potentially dramatic changes today.

Our introduction to cross-cultural family varieties should have accomplished two things: it should have made us aware of the great variety of workable family systems around the world, and it should have raised several important issues to which we shall return throughout this volume. Let us turn now to the historical antecedents of the U.S. family system.

Antecedents of the Modern U.S. Family

CHAPTER 4

Precolonial influences on the family in the United States include a new emphasis on privacy, the appearance of a strong repressive sex code, and the notion of the sanctity of marriage; increased awareness of women's low status in the family; and the development of the romantic love concept. The sex code and the sanctity concept were in direct conflict with the looser norms of the early Middle Ages. Prior to and during the colonial period, other institutions were to a great extent embedded in the nuclear family, not the kin group, although an increasing number of specialized functionaries were operating outside the family unit. In the colonies, romantic love began to be linked with mate selection. There was a substantial gap between sexual norms and behavior. The family was characterized by patriarchal economic-

legal authority. During the period from about 1800 to the present, certain aspects of the family in the United States (such as household composition, personal choice of a mate, and residential mobility) changed but little, while others (such as women's status, sex codes, and institutional embeddedness) underwent substantial alteration.

PRECOLONIAL INFLUENCES

Until recently, attempts to investigate and understand the antecedents of the modern family have confronted the difficulties referred to in our discussion of the Chinese family. The vast majority of historical sources have been descriptive of the high-status family or have been written from a normative perspective; that is, they tell how people *should* have behaved instead of how they *did* behave. Now, however, a flurry of historical research activity, utilizing census records, parish registers, tax records, and legal political documents, has begun to dispel the cloud of uncertainty that blocks our understanding of the behavior of "average" families in precolonial and colonial days.[1]

These historical studies have, of course, not resolved all the issues they have raised. There are several reasons for this. First, historians and historical sociologists have ordinarily worked from data for a particular town or area at a particular point in its history. This limits the generalizability of their results, which often run counter to the conclusions reached by other scholars who have studied other times and places. Second, working even with the same data does not necessarily lead different historians to the same conclusions or interpretations. David Rothman, for example, in presenting an alternative interpretation to that of John Demos of child-rearing in the colonies, states that

> *many historians have experienced that middle-of-the-night panic when contemplating how thin a line separates their work from fiction. But on this score the study of childhood seems especially nerve-wracking, threatening to turn us all into novelists (Rothman, 1971: 181).*

Third, the farther back into history one wishes to delve, the more tenuous one's conclusions are likely to be. Lutz Berhner notes that only after 1800 were there attempts to describe working-class family life accurately. In general, he concludes, the farther back in time one goes, the higher up the social ladder one must look to find people who are literate and about whom adequate source material for family study survives (Berhner, 1973). Finally, as Glen Elder points out and attempts to remedy in his own work, there have been more cross-sectional analyses than links built between the family and other historical trends and events. In particular, the family historians have tended to ignore the major events that may have had dramatic effects upon the family. Using a cohort-historical approach, Elder is seeking to locate individuals and families within their historical context. This is a difficult task for the historian (Elder, 1978: 56).

Thus, we enter upon a discussion of the modern family's antecedents with enthusiasm for the "new family history," but also with caution. It is tempting, furthermore, to begin by dwelling at length on such early antecedents as the family of the ancient Hebrews, the Greeks, the Romans, and the early Christians. Our discussion, however, will be restricted to a few of the more important characteristics and developments during and following the medieval period, with detailed accounts left to other sources.

During the early Middle Ages, the nuclear family and its kin-community were highly embedded in each other in terms of individuals. That is, the nuclear family had little existence either structurally or attitudinally apart from the kin-friend-neighbor milieu in which the individual functioned. The nuclear family seldom operated as a separate entity, and it did not arouse the strong feelings of allegiance among its members that it does today. Mitterauer and Sieder describe the indistinctness of the nuclear family in an interesting fashion:

> When we go back into history, we discover . . . that in the late Middle Ages, and even in early modern times, the German language had no word for the group of parents and children that we understand as "family." . . . The pater was originally the master of the household, . . . the person who had authority over wife, children, slaves and other persons belonging to the household, who collectively composed the familia (Mitterauer and Sieder, 1982: 6).

Among those of high status the lineages were strong, but these extended family forms were found only in portions of the noble, patrician, and rich merchant classes. Additionally, in certain areas, such as central France, there were large kin-based agricultural communities in the early Middle Ages (Mitterauer and Sieder, 1982: 39–40; Parish and Schwartz, 1972: 155). Thus, there were lineages and extended families among certain of the high-status rural and urban dwellers.

Into the 18th century, it took five or six children to ensure population replacement. After that, the rate of premature deaths began to drop (Quale, 1988: 18). There has been some debate whether less care and emotional tie to children caused the high death rate, or whether the high death rate caused parents to invest less in each child. Abraham Stahl concludes from historical sources that the latter is the more likely explanation. That is, apparent indifference was a reaction to the likelihood of the child's death, and children were actually welcomed as a very good thing, contingent on their survival (Stahl, 1991: 81-82). Children as young as seven were active participants in the economy, often being indentured out as "small people" to work for others (McCracken, 1983).

Another aspect of the transactional nature of aristocratic family relations was that, as Zaretsky says,

> marriage was arranged according to the family's rather than the individual's interest. Love and sexual life were sought outside marriage and mostly by men. Arranged marriages necessitated the double standard, mistresses, and illegitimacy (Zaretsky, 1976: 37).

Among the lower strata individual embeddedness simply meant that family and nonfamily, kin and nonkin, were not easily distinguished; nor was it felt necessary to distinguish them. The flow of kin, friends, children, and nuclear family members into and out of the home meant that nuclear family members had virtually no privacy from one another or from other members of the social network and that affective feelings flowed fairly freely through their broader network.

In the early medieval Church, religious ordination was considered a sacrament, but not marriage; the family was not a holy union but a concession to the weakness of the flesh. Thus, sex in the family was only slightly more acceptable to the religious leaders of the day than was sex outside the family. Such normative negativism regarding sex in general was counterposed against a relatively accepting attitude on the part of the average individual. Mitterauer and Sieder comment on the relationship between what we would now call sexual licence and the value of children:

> *Sex before and outside marriage was quite common and was looked upon to some extent as natural and understandable. The cause lay in the very conditions of the family as an economic unit: the overriding importance to the peasant family of having children imposed on the wife the social duty of bearing children. . . . In some areas it was therefore quite usual for a young farmer to test his future wife's fecundity before marriage. If she became pregnant there was nothing to stand in the way of a wedding (Mitterauer and Sieder, 1982: 124).*

The nuclear family was simply embedded interactionally—sexually and otherwise—in its wider social network.

A second possible form of embeddedness involves the relationships between the family or kin group and other societal institutions. In a society such as that of the Afghans in which almost all economic, religious, political, and other functions are performed as aspects of kinship organization, one can speak of total institutional embeddedness in the kin group. However, in medieval Europe this was clearly not the case. There were separate functionaries or specialists set aside in political, religious, and economic institutions. Yet still there was a great amount of embeddedness of these and other social institutions in the kin-friend network. Education took place, for the masses, in the home with kin and friends. Religion had its separate location, but its reinforcement was often left to the family unit. In the early Middle Ages the economy could hardly be called either nuclear family-dominated or kin-lineage-dominated. It was, rather, male-dominated, and this domination ordinarily occurred within a kin-lineage system among the higher strata of European society and within a nuclear-social network system among the lower strata. Generally speaking, then, in the early medieval period the nuclear family was not a clearly distinguished societal entity in its relation either to the individual or to the other institutions of society.

The changes that had occurred by the late Middle Ages in Europe had a profound effect on the family in the American colonies. Underlying many of the other changes was the developing concept of the privacy and sanctity of the nuclear family. In earlier centuries, sociability had meant that the home was open to kin and friends almost as much as to spouse and children. Rooms had not been set aside for specialized functions; family and nonfamily members had

interacted in various circumstances. The concept of *privacy*, to which we will return later, was twofold. It meant the separation of the family from the outside
world and the separation—if they so desired—of family members from one another. This developing separation (far from complete in the Middle Ages) was
accompanied by the glorification of family life and the appearance of the moral
notion of marriage as a sacrament. Monogamy was already the legalized form of
marriage, with important economic motives behind such legalization. Now
came a distinction in the sex code that said that, although sex within marriage
was blessed by the Church, outside of marriage it was a sin. Devoutly religious
people still frequently felt considerable guilt about sex even within marriage,
but the distinction between sex inside the nuclear family and sex outside the nuclear family was now clear. One important long-term effect of this new emphasis on the nuclear family unit was to reduce the individual embeddedness of the
nuclear unit in its social network; another was to alter the institutional embeddedness, in terms of functions performed, away from the network and toward
the nuclear family. John Demos reinforces this in responding to the popular belief that extended families predominated until a century or so ago. The simple
nuclear unit, he says, "has always been with us, admitting only of limited add-
ons (a servant, an apprentice, an aging grandparent or two) in particular times
and places" (Demos, 1986: 5).

One aspect of the change toward the privacy and sanctity—in short, the
self-consciousness—of the nuclear family during the late Middle Ages had to do
with household composition. Lineage systems, with their patriarchal extended
or stem family households, had been prevalent in the early Middle Ages, but by
the eleventh century these systems had begun to decline in France. Even among
the upper classes the extended family household, consisting of aging parents,
their sons and sometimes their daughters, and their sons' wives and children,
had weakened during the thirteenth century. The stem family, in which one offspring, often the eldest male, continues in the household so as to inherit most of
the immovable property, persisted in France, England, and much of the rest of
Western Europe throughout the Middle Ages. Quale, for example, notes that
by the end of the 13th century primogeniture—or inheritance by the eldest
male—"was being practiced in several areas of western Europe. . . ." (Quale,
1988: 181). However, by the 17th century even this household type—a result of
agriculture-based economy, long-term landownership or tenantship, illiteracy,
and regional traditions—had been far outnumbered by nuclear family units
(Matthaei, 1982: 18). The other exception to the nuclear unit, besides the stem
family, is reported by Laslett to have been the well-to-do household that included nonfamily members, especially servants. These servants, often teenage
girls, ordinarily entered domestic service as a distinct phase of their own life cycles (Laslett, 1977). The result of the predominance of nuclear households,
then, is that by the time British and French colonies were established in the
"New World," it was unusual to find households containing more than two generations in the countries from which their colonists came. Neolocality, or movement out of the parental home at marriage, was the rule. As the nuclear family
became more distinct, a new type of emotional bond also emerged, and strong

emotional bonds within families began to be the norm (Herlihy, 1983: 117). "In short," says James Henretta, "the England from which the settlers of Dedham came was at the end of a . . . process of transition which had largely destroyed the earlier peasant society" (1973: 193).

The stem family, it should be added, did not automatically provide large numbers of urban migrants during the late Middle Ages, because its fertility was often low and its child mortality high. However, the predominance of nuclear family households by the beginning of the seventeenth century meant that a mobile labor force would be available when the industrial revolution occurred nearly two centuries later.

Two points need to be made about women's status during the medieval period. First, if a woman had no brothers, she and her husband were likely to inherit family property. However, in the more likely event that she had brothers, she could offer little economic incentive to an eligible man of her own status. Emily Coleman reports the outcome of this situation:

> At the same time, her very status — without the economic inducement of land — would offer positive motivation to a man in a lower social position. In other words, a man would marry up for psychological reasons or with the conscious intention of improving the status of his progeny; a woman would marry down due to the force of economic circumstances (1973:12).

Thus, due to the woman's lack of economic control and the man's dominance and status striving, the class structure was gradually transformed.

The second point concerning women's status has to do with its change during the course of the Middle Ages. One aspect of this change was that

> by the end of the 15th century there was an obvious incongruity between the increasing recognition of the individuality of each human being and the continuing lack of recognition of the individuality of both women and young sons (Quale, 1988: 187).

What Quale means is that only white males and eldest sons were beginning to be less embedded in their families. Another important part of the change in women's status resulted from the increasing self-consciousness of the nuclear family and the concomitant change from institutional embeddedness in the social network to embeddedness of functions in the nuclear family. This made the husband's dominance over his wife more obvious. In the sixteenth century, the wife's position was such that "any acts she performs without the authority of her husband or the law are null and void" (Aries, 356). Some have argued, as does Aries, that changes during the Middle Ages actually served to worsen the woman's position. The present writer would argue that what nucleation and male individuation did was to make increasingly evident the subordinate position that women had traditionally held. This awareness, along with other factors, eventually gave rise to the women's rights movement of the nineteenth century. However, the normatively patriarchal pattern of the family's legal-authority structure was carried over into American colonies and will be referred to again.

Another factor that influenced the family in the American colonies was the development of the concept of romantic love as distinct from other forms of love. In the upper strata of society in the early Middle Ages, parents commonly arranged the marriages of their offspring to members of appropriate kin groups. During this period, codes of etiquette and chivalry became highly developed in the courts of European nobles. These codes were dramatized in the games at which the valiant did battle for the favor of a particular female.

Chivalry and arranged marriage were not, however, sufficient to produce the idea of romantic love as something different from the ordinary love resulting from sharing and companionship. As long as male sexual experimentation outside of marriage was relatively easy to accomplish (due to the fuzziness of nuclear family boundaries), romantic love was not distinguishable as a separate entity. However, with the strengthening of the nuclear unit and the clear normative demarcation between sex with one's spouse and with all others, the arrangement of marriages in the upper strata began to be accompanied by heightened frustration. Romantic love, ordinarily occurring after marriage and with a person other than one's own spouse, was often unrequited or frustrated and involved idealization and strong emotion. In late medieval Europe among those of high status, romantic love came to be a technique of rebellion against familial control of mating. In short, the historical factors most immediately responsible for the development of romantic love as something unique or different from ordinary love included the practice of arranging marriages, the courtly games and etiquette codes, and the increasing separation of the nuclear family—sexually and otherwise—from other societal groups, in accordance with the official morality. During this period, romantic love was distinguishable primarily in the upper strata and had little direct relation with either marriage or the selection of a mate.[2]

We have been speaking of the upper strata of the late Middle Ages. Among those in the upper strata, marriage was planned as a link between two important lineages (and, later, households). Mating among the masses, it should be noted, was frequently a matter of choice and had a strong emotional element. Here, then, is an instance of what Freedman refers to in discussing the Chinese family. A characteristic of the common people, seldom written about by the literati of the time—specifically, personal choice of a mate—came to be a goal for people at all levels of society. There were, however, a few differences between personal choice and love among the masses of medieval Europe and the romantic love concept of the twentieth century. Affectional ties were not the sole basis for most marriages and could not be described by the romantic notions of "love at first sight," frustration, or idealization. Marriage was likely to be between two people who had known each other for years, and it was often based on economic considerations as well as emotional attraction.

Between 1550 and 1750, the rate of pregnancies prior to marriage ranged from 10 percent to 30 percent of English marriages, judging from the number of births within 8 months of marriage. However, there were heavy penalties for a birth out of wedlock, since "the economic burden of child support fell upon her community" (D'Emilio and Freedman, 1988: 5). Thus, the live births do not account for possible abortions. Despite these figures, there was an increase in the rate of illegitimacy between the 16th and 19th centuries. This increase, and the changing *relational* basis for it, is further evidence for the spread of romantic love in European society. Edward Shorter observes that the explosion of bastardy during these centuries may be seen

> *as the supplanting of peasant-bundling and master-servant exploitation by hit-and-run and true-love illegitimacy as the predominant types. This transition came about because popular premarital sexuality shifted from manipulative to expressive, thus elevating the number of conceptions, and because inconstancy crept into the couples' intentions toward each other (Shorter, 1973: 55).*

These changes, especially the change from master-servant illegitimacy to "hit-and-run," had only begun prior to the seventeenth century, and the prevalence of the "true-love" type was still three centuries away. Thus we shall return to this issue later. Suffice it to say, however, that the beginnings of romantic love as the predominant basis for both mate selection and illegitimacy occurred in the late Middle Ages in European society.

In summary, it can be said that the upper strata of the late Middle Ages were characterized by planned marriages and an increased recognition of extramarital romance; while, among the majority, marriage was by choice but was based on a set of complex factors that did not yet include romantic love as a definable type. Normative sanctity, the beginnings of privacy, the increasing demarcation between familial and extrafamilial sex, increasing institutional embeddedness in the nuclear family rather than in the social network, and patriarchy—these are some of the late medieval influences that most affected the family in the New World.

SECTION TWO

FAMILY LIFE IN THE U.S. COLONIES: 1611–1800[3]

Family life in the U.S. colonies was shaped partly by the European traditions of the settlers and partly by the challenges of conquering and exploiting the western hemisphere. The Europeans were little affected by the traditions of the Native Americans, preferring to "Europeanize" or, more often, to kill them. (This, of course, is the sordid world-wide history of European colonization, with some local variations.)

In the pre-U.S. territory there were, as among Rosenfeld's Arab villagers, two sets of norms at work. The norms of the official religio-political morality stressed the sanctity of the nuclear family and its position as separate from the social network, while the norms of the common people retained many elements of the individual embeddedness in which the nuclear family was little distinguished—sexually and otherwise—from its social milieu. However, the mobility that characterized the conquering by Europeans of the North American continent served to weaken network ties as nuclear units moved from place to place, and thus prepared the way for the ascendancy of the nuclear family during the

Victorian era of the 1800s. Primogeniture was practiced in certain of the colonies, especially in the South. However, many northern colonies did not have such a practice, and by dividing the family property more or less equally among the heirs, these estates dwindled in size over the generations. The result was that some of the children pushed westward, only to find themselves isolated from the eastern markets (Matthaei, 1982: 25).

Although romantic love was already a popular theme of the literati of Europe, it was not yet directly or consistently linked to courtship and mate selection. Two factors in the early history of the colonies began to effect this connection. First, the colonists were overwhelmingly from the lower strata of European society. This background meant that they brought with them a tradition of personal choice in marriage, though parents with an eye out for an economically advantageous arrangement for their son or daughter ordinarily influenced the choice. Yet in general, parental influence had to be exerted by subtle means, since choice was the rule.

The second factor that began to link romance to mate selection was the shortage of European women in the colonies, especially on the expanding frontier. To put it in economic terms: when any commodity is in short supply, the desire for it becomes more compelling. The feeling is likely to be: "I've got to have that (one)!" When that feeling is projected toward a human being of the opposite sex, the internal reaction is not very different from that of the medieval courtier to the unavailable lady. The internal pain of the courting male (or males) was in fact the emotional response that had already been labeled by the literati and the upper strata as romance or romantic love. It ordinarily settled upon one love object, and was a forerunner of the idea that one can love only one person at a time. Literature, both fiction and nonfiction, describing the plight of the competing males publicized this approach to mate selection.[4] Thus the combination of a tradition of choice, the shortage of females, and the increasing emphasis upon the nuclear family apart from its milieu began to link romantic love and mate selection in the American colonies. This link was in contrast to the previous situation, in which such love was simply a sort of free-floating emotion that could strike at any time, under any conditions, but most often after and outside of marriage. While long-term acquaintance and economic consideration kept romantic love from becoming the sole basis for marriage in the colonies, romantic-love choice as *the* precondition for marriage was well on its way.

Another aspect of mate selection concerns early racial and ethnic restrictions. In Massachusetts, where the majority of blacks were free, whites were forbidden in 1705 from either marrying or having intercourse with them (which, of course, does not mean that such did not occur). In 1786 in Massachusetts, marriage with Native Americans was also forbidden. Both of these laws were repealed in 1843, though it was well over a century later before such laws were struck down in the South (Quale, 1988: 287). And despite such laws in the colonies in the 1700s, Robert Wells argues that racial and ethnic blending occurred at levels never approached in England (1922: 85–102).

A corollary of the increasing connection between love and mate selection appears to have been a rise in concern for affection *within* marriage. D'Emilio

and Freedman describe this corollary thus: "love was becoming a more respectable basis for marriage choice, encouraging a new view of marriage in
which the affections of husband and wife were as important as their economic
and reproductive obligations to each other" (1988: 41). In an intriguing study
based on Massachusetts divorce records from the 1700s, Nancy Cott discovered that in 1765, for the first time there began to be divorce cases in which loss
of affection was mentioned as one of the complaints (Cott, 1976: 32).

Not only did the seventeenth and eighteenth centuries see an increasing
link between romantic love and mate selection in the colonies, but they very
probably saw a parallel rise in the hit-and-run sex relationship, based on expressive needs and romantic feelings. Such hit-and-run sex was, in turn, accompanied by a dramatic rise in illegitimacy, which came to be treated as more
an economic than a moral problem. Illegitimacy "also reflected the increasing
vulnerability of women, who could not assume that pregnancy would lead to
marriage" (D'Emilio and Freedman, 1988: 49, 52).

Perhaps the best-known feature of official colonial morality was its ethic of
severe sexual repression. One reason this was of great importance to religious
and community leaders was, in all probability, the great gulf that separated official morality from common practice. Premarital sex and pregnancy occurred
increasingly among the populace (Demos, 1986: 6), but the official attempts to
curb such practices, attempts that had become noticeable in late medieval Europe, were continued in the colonies. In New England premarital sexual relations were punishable by public denunciation, and extramarital sex often meant
dismissal from the church. Being thus excluded was intended to make one a social as well as a spiritual outcast, since the church was both a social and a religious organization. Yet the fact that only a small proportion of the population
belonged to the church very likely made dismissal less than completely effective. Furthermore, "selective enforcement led to the prosecution of more women
than men, and to lesser penalties for free, white, and wealthier individuals"
(D'Emilio and Freedman, 1988: 38).

Although the official norms are generally acknowledged to have been severe and repressive, it is extremely difficult to discern their direct effect on
common behavior. In fact, as the historian Charles Francis Adams points out,
no one knows with certainty whether or not the harsh code, the public and
sometimes severe punishment, and the penance leading to reinstatement acted
as deterrents even among the devoutly religious. It is possible that the combination of "forbidden fruit" with the emotional satisfactions that must have
accompanied the completion of penance and reinstatement encouraged the behavior that the code purported to control. Be that as it may, it should be added
that while it has become popular to speak of the preoccupation with sex in the
present-day United States, the colonists were apparently also engrossed in the
subject, although the official stress among colonial spokesmen was upon repression. We shall return to this topic in upcoming pages.

Moving now from courtship, sex codes, and sex behavior to the colonial
family itself, we can see much internal similarity between that family and the
common European family. While we might assume that there were many child
brides in colonial days, that is, that people married at an early age, the norm

was, in fact, 28 years for men and 23 for women in a Connecticut community studied by John Faragher (1976: 17). This is later than the average age at marriage in the United States throughout the twentieth century.

The husband was the actual and legal head of the family, dominating the normative decision-making processes.[5] A content analysis of colonial literature revealed about three references to overt male power over decisions for every reference to overt female power. In addition, Herman Lantz et al. found numerous sources noting the use of subtle power by the female, which they saw as "a reaction to or a way of dealing with male authority" (1968: 419). Such subtle influence on the part of the female is precisely what one might expect in a system that is legally and normatively patriarchal (Oliker, 1989: 7). The female gave up legal title to any resources she brought into marriage; they became resources at her husband's disposal. As the eighteenth century wore on, however, some variations in property-holding by sex began to appear, with certain colonies giving women somewhat more control over property. Likewise, accounts of female attorneys and married women in business become increasingly frequent in the last quarter of the eighteenth century—an involvement that has not been fully recognized (Lantz et al, 1973: 586). Nevertheless, the wife's usual lot in the colonial family was to bear and care for the couple's children and, under difficult conditions, to supervise the household. An excerpt from one written record in a family Bible from this period reads as follows:

> *She had sixteen children. When the first child was a year and a half old the second child was born. The baby was but four days old when the older child died. Five times did that mother's heart bear a similar cruel loss when she had a baby in her arms; therefore when she had been married but nine years she had one living child; and five little graves bore the record of her sorrow (Calhoun, 1945: 106).*

The mother's domestic, reproductive, and socializing (child-rearing) role was one of physical hardship, drudgery, and normative subjection to her husband; it is hardly surprising that she took great pride in those of her offspring who survived to adulthood.

A single illustration from a family Bible is not enough, however. The decline in the rate of population growth during colonial days was a function of both an increase in childhood mortality and a decrease in fertility. In Andover, Massachusetts, for example, Henretta reports a drop in the average numbers of births per marriage from 7.6 in 1700 to 4.2 in the 1770s (1973: 198).

How, then, did colonial family size compare with that of later periods? Studies by Demos, Greven, Wells, Lockridge, Norton, and Higgs and Stettler show a range from 4.64 children per family to 7 to 8 per family. Rudy Seward, in summarizing these studies, notes that, being longitudinal, they give a much larger number of children than the census, which is cross-sectional. He therefore concludes that the number of children per family has been exaggerated, and that the actual number was very likely not too different from that for the first half of the twentieth century (Seward, 1973: 62). It seems to this author that these writers are in danger of confusing the three key factors that affect family size: that is, number of births, childhood mortality, and number of survivors to adulthood.

In the seventeenth century, the birth rate was high and mortality and survival were moderate. In the eighteenth century, the age when women married was higher, the birthrate decreased, the mortality rate rose, and survivorship dropped to a low level (Greven, 1970). It is this level, then, that compares favorably with that of today, a time when the birthrate and mortality rate among children are both at all-time lows.

Some authors have come close to arguing that colonial and pre-colonial couples had many children because they were economic assets and because many would die early. Thus a decline in early mortality was a key factor in family limitation later on. Recent authors like J. A. Banks and Scott and Sally Allen McNall have spoken directly to this issue. Banks says:

> *The assumption that . . . a decline in mortality was a most important factor in family limitation . . . presupposes some unspecified comparisons with what are referred to as "traditional" or "pre-modern" societies, in which parents are presumed to have followed "a strategy" of high fertility to compensate for the high mortality of their offspring; that is, children in such societies are assumed to be regarded by their parents as fairly immediate economic assets above all else (1981: 120).*

But this view places in their minds and motivations ideas which are clear to us only in retrospect, and comparisons which they could not have made. The McNalls clarify this:

> *Although children did help on the farm, they were not a principle economic asset. A couple did not have more children in order to expand their farming operations. Family size seems to have been determined less by economic factors than by individual decisions — or the failure to make such a decision (1983: 19-20).*

The child's position in the colonial family has been characterized as one dominated by the three R's of repression, religion, and respect, although one might add that religion was often primarily used to increase the other two. Children's basic tendencies were considered to be sinful; it was their parents' task to set them straight. The idea that children need firm discipline and guidance included the use of extreme forms of physical punishment (Sather, 1989: 737). Legally, the child was no better off than the wife. The father's role was primarily one of moral oversight and moral teaching (Lamb, 1987: 5). In addition, however, the "father was entitled to his child's services, and he could demand that the child work for him without pay. If the child worked for an outsider, the father was entitled to his earnings" (Kay, 1965: 6). In fact, the family's role as economic producer "caused it to take on or send off members according to its need for labor. Hence, the household was not necessarily coterminous with the nuclear family" (Matthaei, 1982: 20).

Discipline, while stern, also included the first expressions of a new concept of children. Up to this point they had been viewed as small adults; in the colonial family, however, playfulness and mischief were sometimes dismissed with the assertion that "boys will be boys," an expression of the belief that children are somehow different from adults and should be treated differently. But for the most part, childishness merely served to increase parental concern about the youngster's wantonness and sinfulness. Not only were children expected to be submissive, but they were to contribute their fair share to the family economy, whether with the crops, the flocks, or the household. Adult roles were learned by the young from parents and persons like them, including older brothers and sisters. As small adults, when children were "off duty" they were allowed a substantial amount of freedom to roam and govern themselves. In short, children's lives were dominated by their roles in the family division of labor and by a repressive discipline, though they often found—or were given—time to escape temporarily into mischief and fun.

In discussing child-rearing in Plymouth Colony, Demos's *A Little Commonwealth* reports indulgence of the infant during the first year of life, with the second year characterized by rapid weaning, the arrival of a sibling, and harsh and restrictive discipline. Demos notes, as we have, that children's willfulness had to be curbed, their spirits broken, and their autonomy limited. As Demos moves beyond this to an interpretation of the relation of child-rearing to adult personality in Plymouth Colony, his conclusions, as Rothman noted, become open to alternative views. Yet the character of Puritan discipline seems clear (Demos, 1970; Demos, 1973; Rothman, 1973). Straightforward, harsh, and buttressed by legal and moral authority, that discipline appears to have become weaker as the seventeenth and eighteenth centuries went by. Oscar and Mary Handlin, in particular, note that the mobility of late colonial society was such as to begin the undermining of parental authority (Handlin and Handlin, 1971: 18). We shall return to this subject in the next section.

Earlier the drudgery of the housewife's role and the normative subjection of the wife to her husband were mentioned. In his study of Wethersfield, Connecticut, during the seventeenth century, Faragher reports an interesting switch when people got older. For those who reached age 30 between 1640 and 1700, men's life expectancy was 59 and women's was 66.[6]

Among those who outlived their spouses, widowers under 50 years of age were more likely to remarry (84 percent), while only 31 percent of *all* widows remarried. The remarried widowers lived longer than those who remained single, whereas women who remained single lived longer than remarried widows. Faragher feels that this rather striking finding is perhaps due to the social roles played by older people. A widower, he notes, very much needed a wife's labor on the family farm. In addition, there was a negative image of old men, especially single old men, as dabbling in the "sins of youth" (we would call this the "dirty old man" image). Widows, however, could share administration with the eldest son, and they were valued by church and community. The nurturant role available to elderly women had no counterpart for men. Furthermore, says Matthaei, while

> *some such women were maintained in private homemaking by their extended families or by charity, others turned to self-support by working for income. Work for income took one of two forms. Some women undertook "homemaking for income," a special category of work for the market which resembled homemaking and, as such, usually excluded men. Others were propelled by their family responsibilities to take up men's work, properly speaking, as heads of family businesses (Matthaei, 1982: 73).*

Definitions of older people, Faragher concludes, "resulted most directly from the concentration of productive work within the institution of the family. . . . In old age women's work could transcend the family, men's could not" (Faragher, 1976: 19-27). It is important to note, however, that old women in the colonies were more often widows than spinsters, since only a small fraction of these women had never married (Allen, 1989: 23).

The notion of "productive work within the family" brings us to the relation of the family unit to the external world, the world of the other colonial institutions. This relation bore a great resemblance to that of the late medieval European family. Partial embeddedness of the various institutions in the nuclear family, not in the kin-friend network, characterized the colonies. The economy focused on family subsistence farms, from 70 to 90 percent of the colonial population being in such agricultural units. The colonists built homes, made furniture and clothing, and raised food. There were trade centers where individuals could take their surpluses and exchange them for what they lacked, and where certain specialists, such as the blacksmith, had their shops; but for the most part the family was an economically self-sufficient unit. Religion, while having separate functionaries and, usually, a separate meeting place, was frequently employed for socialization or disciplinary purposes in the home. In fact, families that did not employ religion within the home, very often ignored the religious organization and its leaders as well. Recreation, when the colonists found time for it, tended to be home- or church-based, involving the entire family unit in many instances. The educational process was even more home-based than was recreation: it involved training in homemaking and motherhood for daughters and the learning of farm work or an apprenticeship in some trade for sons. Formal education outside the home, even for males, was not universal, and it did not last many years for those who received it. Protection in the colonies demanded cooperation among various family units for mutual defense. The most common type of health care was the "home remedy." Demos describes this very well:

> The family in pre-modern times was indeed a hive of instrumental activity: of production (e.g., the family farm), of schooling, of worship, of medical practice, and of care for all sorts of "dependents" (orphans, elderly people, the insane, even criminals). And the transition to modern times has, for certain, reduced this range dramatically. Public schools, hospitals, asylums, and prisons now stand in the place of the family at many points (Demos, 1986: 17–18).

In short, the nuclear family was functionally central to the economy of colonial society; the male family head held property, and the family, as the unit of production, joined in a well-defined division of labor. Other institutions—religious, recreational, educational, protective, and medical—were all embedded in the nuclear family to a substantial degree. That is, the activities that characterized these institutions generally either took place within the home or involved the family unit as a whole. Only in the political sphere was there almost no direct tie between the institutional activity and the nuclear family unit.

The question of functional centrality, or institutional embeddedness, that came up in the discussion of the Afghan and Chinese families arises again in observing the American colonial family. Two questions implied in the various discussions of institutional embeddedness are often left unanswered. They are (a) Is it the kin group or the nuclear family that is thought of as central to the functioning of a particular society? and (b) Is this family-kin unit essentially political or economic in its centrality? Freedman speaks of the masses in classical China, for example, as nuclear family units on the land, with a balance of political power afforded by certain influential lineages. In colonial America, as in China, we find large numbers of economically important nuclear units working the land, but we do not find the politically strong kin units that were present in the Chinese upper classes. Thus the institutional centrality of the colonial family system may be thought of as lying somewhere between the virtually total institutional embeddedness in the kin group of small, kin-based societies, such as the Afghans, and the institutional differentiation of the family in modern industrial society, which is the focus of this book. That is, institutional embeddedness in the colonial family may not be thought of as total or absolute.

An important concomitant of the colonial type of institutional embeddedness in the nuclear family was the increasing concern in the colonies with keeping family units intact. The growing demarcation between the nuclear family and its social network and the importance of the family, economically and otherwise, were such that divorce laws came to be strict and narrowly delimited, with adultery (particularly on the woman's part) being the single most prevalent, and often the only legal, ground for divorce. Although an intolerable family situation could be escaped by desertion (perhaps by "heading for the frontier"), the norms and sanctions were such that this was apparently a less frequent occurrence than legalized divorce is in contemporary U.S. society.[7]

Having considered institutional embeddedness and differentiation in the colonial nuclear family at some length, we must now briefly mention individual embeddedness. The colonial period was characterized by nuclear family households, often supplemented by one or a few additional kin or nonkin. These "extra" household members, however, followed no traditional pattern, but were idiosyncratic results of specific needs. The "official" morality of the day viewed the nuclear family as of central importance, and this unit was still moving toward its period of greatest ascendancy: the Victorian era of the nineteenth century. However, the high level of residential mobility and neolocality and the frontier and achievement mentalities were simultaneously laying the foundation for a later emphasis on individualism. By the end of the colonial era, the individual was still fairly well embedded in the nuclear family, interactionally and attitudinally, but one could already perceive the beginnings of the coming struggle between family and individualistic values, about which more must be said later. And, we should add, patriarchy meant that in the colonies as well as in most times and places, the adult male was less embedded (or immersed) in the family than were adult females and children.

The last two issues discussed, divorce and the lack of individual embeddedness in the kin network, are both referred to in Cott's study of Massachusetts divorce records. Cott finds 229 petitions for divorce between 1692 and 1786, an average of about 2.5 per year. These findings indicate that divorce was anything but typical. However, the grounds were a little broader than we indicated above; they included not only adultery but wife beating and unwillingness to play the appropriate marital role. "Petitioners' and witnesses' statements repeatedly made it clear that marriage was seen as a relationship in which the husband agreed to provide food, clothing, and shelter for his wife, and she agreed to return frugal management and obedient service" (Cott, 1976: 30). Breakdown in fulfilling such role demands was involved in many of these eighteenth-century divorces. Cott's accounts of divorce testimony reinforce what we have said about the separation between family and kin. It is assumed that petitioners called upon those persons best acquainted with themselves and their marriages, it seems that kin were less important in the social network than some have thought. In fact, in more than half the cases the most frequent witnesses were nonkin neighbors. The next largest group consisted of professionals such as doctors, midwives, and justices of the peace, and only 11 percent of the cases involved testimony by resident or nonresident kin. It is at least possible, Cott cautions, that kin avoided testifying in order not to get involved in conjugal-family conflict (Cott, 1976: 27).

One aspect of the struggle between family and individual values involves the issue of privacy introduced above. David Flaherty's thorough treatment of *Privacy in Colonial New England* notes that during this period there was a great increase in family privacy from the community and some increase in the privacy of family members from each other.

> *The newest houses had more individual rooms and sometimes even hallways. The construction of larger homes and increased partitioning made more and more privacy available in family life. Houses protected colonial families well from external observation. The layout of towns, the plentifulness of land, an agricultural way of life, low population density, and architectural improvements created a hospitable environment for privacy (Flaherty, 1972: 44).*

Despite the increased dispersion of dwellings on family farms and colonial movement to the "suburbs" of large towns like Boston, and despite the increasing size and differentiation of houses architecturally, Flaherty does not overstate the amount of privacy in the colonies. Rather, he says, the colonists were willing to sacrifice some privacy in order to escape the loneliness and boredom that was often a part of the agricultural way of life. "In fact the loneliness of working hours meant that many colonists spent available leisure time in intimate social relationships" within the community, rather than retreating into the family to escape a crowded and anonymous urban world. And as for privacy *within* the family, or between family members, Flaherty reminds us that

> *greater privacy within the family awaited much higher standards of living, the reduction of family size, central heating, labor-saving devices that did away with domestic servants, and many other developments and appurtenances of modernized society (1972: 72, 84).*

Thus, while the colonial courts protected privacy only indirectly, the claim to privacy as a *legal* right developed slowly and later in Western history, a result of crowding and of the separation of other institutions from the family.

During the colonial period these major changes took place: (a) romantic love moved ever closer to being the prime basis for mate selection; (b) family size, in particular the number of children surviving to adulthood, diminished as a result of both fewer births and higher mortality rates; (c) institutional embeddedness, divorce laws, and individual embeddedness all shifted toward a greater focus on the nuclear family's sanctity, societal importance, and inviolability or privacy. Henretta very succinctly puts this increased institutional and individual embeddedness in the nuclear family, rather than in kin and community:

> *The decline in community was paralleled and to some extent offset by the rise of the family. During the eighteenth century the basic social unit took on more of the tasks of socialization and acculturalization. . . . It was the family, likewise, which became the prime economic institution in the society (1973: 209).*

In addition, the seeds were planted for a later individualism, including the privacy of family members from each other. Two areas of family life saw only the beginnings of change during the colonial period: the Revolutionary War opened new opportunities for women, and residential mobility and neolocality began to weaken parents' control over their offspring. In both areas, it was only at the end of the eighteenth century that small signs of the weakening of patriarchy, or father-husband dominance, became very evident. A final factor that deserves mention is that attitudes toward sex became considerably stricter during the colonial period, and this increase in strictness seems to have had the effect of reducing *extra*marital intercourse. Whether it had the same effect on *pre*marital intercourse, however, seems more problematic and less likely.

SECTION THREE

CHANGES IN THE U.S. FAMILY: 1800–1993

Many discussions of changes in the family since colonial days have been plagued by one or more of the following problems. The first difficulty, which has been clarified and to a great extent corrected by recent writers, is the tendency of many historical accounts of the colonial family to present an idealized, or normative, conception of earlier days. The picture of a series of family units living happily in a kinship network on adjoining farms, with little or no sexual promiscuity or other internal difficulty, was labeled by Goode as the "classical extended family of Western nostalgia" (1956: 3). It is, of course, impossible to discuss changes that have occurred unless one can first piece together a basically accurate picture of the past.[8]

A second problem has been that the issue of change was, until recently, consistently posed in terms of the effect of industrialization on the family. While the complexities of causation are recognized today, the tendency to treat the family as the dependent variable is still present. Robert Lazar, for example, writing in 1978, says: "In this effort to describe the general relationship between family and society . . . society is taken as the independent variable and family as the dependent variable" (Lazar, 1978: 3). However, Judith Stacey argues that

> *contemporary revisionist scholarship on the family and modernization has thoroughly undermined unidirectional or deterministic models of family change. . . . However, the effort to demonstrate the family's role as a causal agent cannot yet be judged a success (Stacey, 1983: 7).*

David Cheal adds that, while at one time industrialization was treated as the cause of the nuclear family, recent studies "suggest that in some places nuclear family living in fact preceded industrialization" (Cheal, 1991: 86). In other words, industrialization → family change is too simple. The capitalist market economy, the political ideology of the time, urbanization, the knowledge explosion, communication growth, agricultural productivity, and other changes not completely subsumed under the "industrialization" label may be related to the family in complex ways. It has been argued, for example, that neolocality and the development of nuclear family privacy vis-à-vis its social network may have been preconditions for many of the economic-technological changes that characterized the industrial revolution (Habakkuk, 1955: 1–2). Be that as it may, the posing of the issue as one existing between the family and industrialization simply ignores a whole series of related technological and ideological developments that may have been associated with family change not directly connected with or caused by the industrial revolution itself.

The third difficulty with much theorizing about historical changes in the family is that, in one source or another, as many as 15 different features of the family—such as husband-wife power relations, sex codes, romantic love, courtship, women's status, and divorce—have been linked to industrialization. The results of choosing certain aspects of the family and ignoring others have been three divergent conclusions regarding the family and change: (a) industrialization caused change X or changes XYZ to occur in the family; (b) since no change occurred in feature A or features ABC of the family, the industrial revolution apparently had no effect; and (c) characteristics LMN of the family's structure were the causes of certain changes that occurred in the economy. (The last is the least frequent interpretation.) The argument over change has raged, but has been persistently contaminated by *idealizing the colonial or pre-industrial family; by oversimplifying causes and effects; by ignoring important developments* other than industrialization; or by the *selective use of family features* on the part of the researcher or writer.

An attempt can be made to avoid such pitfalls by asking at the outset, "What changes have and have not occurred in the American family since colonial days?"

TABLE 4.1   APPROXIMATE DEGRESS OF CHANGE IN U.S. FAMILY FEATURES FROM 1800 TO THE PRESENT

Family Feature		Degree of Change
Personal choice of mate	1	Little or no change
Romantic love in mate selection	1	Slight change
Nuclear household composition	2	
Residential mobility	3	
Premarital sexual behavior (probably curvilinear)	1	Moderate change
Husband-wife power norms and behavior	2	
Marital breakup	2	
Individual embeddedness in the nuclear family (probably curvilinear)	2	
Women's status	2,3	
Fertility	2	
Courtship patterns	1	Major change
Premarital sex norms	1	
Husband-wife roles and adjustments	2	
Socialization of children (child-rearing)	2	
Divorce laws	2,3	
Institutional embeddedness in the nuclear family	3	
Marital happiness	2	Unknown

The numbers indicate the categories into which the various family features are divided in the subsequent discussion. Category 1 concerns family formation and premarital relationships. Category 2 pertains to family unit characteristics, or internal relationships. Category 3 involves relationships between the family and the external world.

instead of the more difficult question, "What effect did the industrial revolution and the Western nuclear family have upon one another?" Subsequently, the issue of whether certain changes were in fact related to the industrial revolution will be raised. A second strategy for avoiding the pitfalls inherent in discussing change is to compare current conditions to those that existed at the end of the previous period, that is, 1800, instead of talking in a vague manner about the contemporary family and the "colonial" family. The American family of 1630 was "colonial," and so was that of 1770, and we have just indicated some of the kinds of changes that occurred between those two points in time. As well as the sources will allow, we are therefore comparing the U.S. family in 1800 with that of today. Several excellent sources that have appeared since 1960 discuss changes and stabilities,[9] from them and from the author's own investigation, the preliminary list shown in Table 4.1 was devised. The various family features listed in the table can be subsumed under three general headings:

1. *family formation*, or premarital relationships and mate selection;
2. unit characteristics, or *internal* family relationships; and
3. relations with the *external* world of social network, community, institutions, and society.

FAMILY FORMATION   The formation of nuclear family units in the United States involves personal choice, romantic love, the mechanisms of courtship, and the issues of premarital sexual norms and behavior. As indicated earlier, personal choice of a mate was already typical of the colonists upon their arrival in the New World. Then, as now, there were extremely small numbers of high-status families attempting to keep direct control over mating, but even the arranged marriage of the small number of U.S. elites has never been the prepu-bertal linkage that has characterized some societies. For the most part, mate se-lection in the United States has been controlled by residential patterns and value systems, with personal choice as the norm. Daniel Smith, for example, notes that the decline in parental involvement in mate selection in Hingham, Massachusetts, which began in the eighteenth century, has continued to the present. In fact, in 1850, 48.2 percent of Hingham marriages were between two Hingham residents, and this number had declined to 25.8 percent by 1950 (Smith, 1973: 426). The change with respect to romantic love was that it was becoming more and more common as the basis for mate selection. Lantz, in his study of magazine articles written between 1791 and 1825, reports that by 1825 the motivations for marriage were already beginning to be focused on romantic love (Lantz et al., 1973: 479). This focus was accompanied by significant alter-ations in courtship behavior. *Dating* (unchaperoned heterosexual activity and experience) was not even a part of nineteenth-century vocabulary. Until the early 1900s, courtship had centered in the social gathering or the home, with the couple having little unchaperoned time and lacking the freedom, trans-portation, and places to go that eventually gave rise to dating as the form of courtship in the United States. In addition, both sexes are free today to make direct appeals for each other's attention and interest.

Along with the appearance of dating and eventually cohabitation as focal points of U.S. courtship, major changes occurred in the sexual codes governing premarital behavior. Much has been made of the colonial practice of bundling and its possible implications for premarital sexual intercourse. Flaherty de-scribes *bundling* thus: "A courting couple was permitted to share a bed for the night, provided they took such measures as remaining fully clothed or keeping a board between them. . . . There have been suggestions that bundling was al-most a universal custom among the lower and middle classes between 1750 and 1780" (Flaherty, 1972: 78; also Stiles, 1934).

Historians such as Adams have noted how the officially strict norms and sanctions may have increased rather than limited premarital sex. The crucial el-ement in premarital sex norms and behavior, however, is the rise and fall of the nineteenth-century Victorian era, with its great stress on the nuclear family and sexual continence outside of marriage, especially for the female. One effect of the Victorian era's emphasis on female continence was to strengthen the double standard. As late as the 1830s, as noted by D'Emilio and Freedman, literature on sexuality "continued to draw upon the older image of the voluptuous woman and the necessity that she achieve orgasm in order to conceive . . . (1988: 46). But as men increasingly left the home to work they saw themselves losing con-trol over women. Thus, they divided women into "good" and "bad," so that once a sex object had been degraded into the "bad" category, erotic feelings could have free play. The perverseness of this system was such that, since sex rela-tions degraded a woman, a man might choose as his wife a woman who did not arouse sexual desire in him, says Bryan Strong (1972: 463–4). However, along with the increasingly apparent double standard of sexual morality, an opposing development was occurring. The "free love" network sought to guarantee relationships through love and sexuality more than marriage, and became a small but vigorous counterculture (Spurlock, 1988: 765–779; D'Emilio and Freedman, 1988: 120). Another important aspect of nineteenth-century sexual behavior was homosexuality. D'Emilio and Freedman mention several well-known nineteenth-century homosexuals of both genders. However, they also note that increasing negativism about homosexuality was going hand-in-hand at the end of the century with its increasing availability. While its treatment as a perversion was becoming dominant, the possibilities of same-sex love were expanding. "Wage labor, the ability to live apart from families, and the sociability of the separate sexual spheres had fostered romantic, spiritual, homoerotic, and sexual unions" (D'Emilio and Freedman, 1988: 129).

Another change was that the hit-and-run premarital intercourse and illegitimacy of the eighteenth century gave way in the nineteenth-century to what Shorter calls "true-love illegitimacy," with a concomitant reduction in illegitimacy rate. As Shorter puts it, the stabilization of nineteenth-century society, and the greater integration of the lower and working classes into it, removed the transient quality from many romantic relationships. Legitimation of offspring increased greatly during the last third of the nineteenth century, "a sign that couples who coalesced briefly for intercourse were staying together with connubial intent" (Shorter, 1973: 58). Hit-and-run intercourse, we should add, is again on the rise at the present time, though resulting in pregnancy somewhat less often than in previous centuries. The increasing strictness of the official norms from colonial days through the mid-1800s, followed by a wholesale questioning of this position during the twentieth century, seems to have had the result of decreasing slightly the incidence of premarital sex by the mid-1800s and increasing its prevalence again in this century beyond its incidence in colonial days. Although we can only tentatively conclude that premarital sexual behavior followed this curvilinear pattern with noticeable twentieth-century rises in the 1920s and since 1965, we do know that society has moved toward an overt and often positive attitude in dealing with sexual matters. In particular, this has meant a more favorable attitude toward female sexuality and a substantial movement away from the double standard. Sex education, sex research, popular literature, motion pictures, and other media have brought about the frank and public consideration of all types of sexual practices; a drastic departure even from the treatment of sex in the early 1900s. The white settlers and their colonial progeny did not ignore sexual matters. However, the emphasis among moral leaders is no longer exclusively on denunciation, control, and guilt but has moved toward freedom, permissiveness, and debate.

INTERNAL FAMILY RELATIONSHIPS Internally, the family has generally undergone moderate-to-great changes over the past two centuries. Perhaps the least change has occurred in the actual structural composition of the household (see Graham, 1983: 262–78). Well before the colonists came to America, the European household had taken on a nuclear character. The majority of nuclear families lived apart from the other members of their social network, this being an aspect of the privacy motif referred to above. The two changes that did occur in household composition between the seventeenth and twentieth centuries were (1) a decrease in the proportions of extremely large households, although the modal category stayed between four and five (Seward, 1974: 133); and (2) an increase in the likelihood that both parents would live to see all their children marry and leave home. This was true of fewer than half of couples in 1900, but the figure has risen gradually ever since (Quale, 1988: 290).

Several authors have noted a substantial decline in the birth rate during the nineteenth century. In fact, it dropped by 30 percent between 1800 and 1860 (Juster and Vinovskis, 1987: 194-196). Several authors state that a major reason for this reduction was a shift toward rational planning of reproductive behavior (Gordon, 1976; Juster and Vinovskis, 1987).

Much has been written about greater permissiveness in child-rearing and about the decline in parental authority. It seems, however, that the major changes in socialization center on the division of labor in the family and a more continuous, developmental concern on the part of parents. How did this "more continuous concern" emerge? Banks explains it well:

> When child mortality declined, for whatever reason, the pain of parents may be inferred to have declined also, so that they needed no longer to moderate their affection to the same degree as their grandparents and great grandparents had been obliged to do. Hence, declining child mortality rates in the later eighteenth century made children worth taking seriously: when they were more likely to survive to [adulthood], there was more point in taking pains with their early training and education (1981: 128).

Furthermore, the preparation of the child for adulthood no longer meant simply inheriting the family name; capitalism changed that preparation. Unlike the former family economy, "the child's future work could no longer be simply determined by the father, through the bequeathing of property, apprenticeship and the arrangement of marriage" (Matthaei, 1982: 107). In fact, an important nineteenth-century change was from the father as moral teacher to breadwinner, and to the mother as the primary socializer (Lamb, 1987: 5). The mother's grave responsibility came to be seen as involving the child's preparation for individual decision-making and an independent adult life (Demos, 1986: 10). This is seen in Julie Matthaei's quote from Mrs. Coxe's 1842 book, *The Claims of the Country on American Females:*

> To American Mothers . . . is then committed, in a special manner, the solemn responsibility of watching over the hearts and minds of our youthful citizens who are soon to take their places in the public arena, and to give form and individuality to our national character (1982: 113).

As for parental authority, the family is no longer the basic economic producing unit, a fact that frees the child from the kind of patriarchal authority that could be asserted over someone in a clearly defined and inferior economic role.[10] Yet the child's role in the colonial family's division of labor, buttressed by moral training in absolutes and a tendency to perceive the child as a small adult, included a substantial permissive or self-directive element. That is, colonial children, when "off duty" or free of responsibility were often on their own with internalized absolutes left to suffice. Today, parents lack strong economic-labor authority and are less likely to be buttressed by absolutes, but they tend, as noted above, to be more consciously and continuously concerned with the child as a developing person; that is, with achievement and other aspects of socialization. Rothman makes the clearest statement of the modern child's freedom-from-patriarchy-without-autonomy. "In the middle classes," he states, "parental authority may have maintained itself through a shift in tactics. The manipulation of the child, rather than his outright coercion, became more prevalent in Jacksonian America." Rothman speaks at greater length concerning child-rearing in the nineteenth century:

> *The normative literature of the period insisted that strict obedience be the ultimate goal of parental training, but now authors had a wider variety of fresh strategies to recommend before resorting to the rod. Although they counselled greater displays of affection than their eighteenth-century counterparts, they were no less insistent on denying the child autonomy.*

Typical interpretations, says Rothman, have viewed age-grading and affectional display as evidence of increasing concern for child welfare and freedom. But there is another side to it:

> *Age-grading may have been part of an effort to lockstep the child into rigid and predetermined modes of behavior. The change looked not to his benefit, but to the rationalization of childhood so that behavior would become more predictable and manageable (1973: 188–189).*

Thus only a portion of the apparent greater permissiveness is due to reduced parental authority; the remainder is based on a heightened parental awareness of and concern about individual personality and child-rearing in toto.

A few more words on age-grading and the child's contribution to the family might be helpful. In the nineteenth century, the urban family could expect an economic contribution from its children, even as children contributed to the division of labor on the farm. Today, if children work they usually spend their money for leisure or save it for themselves. Timely action in the nineteenth century, say John Modell, Frank Furstenberg, and Theodore Hershberg, meant helping the family in trouble—doing something "timely"—while today timeliness connotes "timing" or staying on schedule (Modell et al., 1976: 30). Tamara Hareven deals at some length with scheduling or age-grading, relating it to the "discovery" of childhood and adolescence:

> *Middle-class families were the first to follow a clear timing sequence for their children's entry into, and exit from, school, and to promulgate an orderly career pattern that led from choosing an occupation to leaving the parental household, marrying, and forming the new family. Orderly progression along the life course and structured transitions from one stage to the next were related to the "discovery" of childhood, and, subsequently, adolescence as distinct stages of life (Hareven, 1977: 67).*

Child-rearing, then, is a matter of weakened formal or traditional parental authority, a greater use of indirect persuasion, a constant oversight of the child's development, and a greater concern for individual personality development (this final point going counter to part of Rothman's interpretation). We shall return to child-rearing in Chapter 8.

The curvilinear change in individual embeddedness posited in Figure 4.1 is closely related to the socialization issues just discussed. In the late medieval period, the nuclear family began to be distinguished from its social network. Emphasis on the nuclear family, at the expense of the kin-friend network, continued through the colonial period and culminated in the Victorian era of the mid-1800s. Already, however, a new emphasis on the individual was increasing; it was embodied in the various conceptions of home architecture that made possible the privacy of family members from one another. Likewise, the U.S. courts were beginning to counterpose the concept of individual privacy to the corporate privacy of marriage. For example, in *Eisenstadt v. Baird*, the court contended:

> It is true that in Griswold *the right of privacy in question inhered in the marital relationship. Yet the marital couple is not an independent entity with a mind and heart of its own, but an association of two individuals each with a separate intellectual and emotional makeup. If the right of privacy means anything, it is the right of the* individual, *married or single, to be free from unwarranted government intrusion . . . (see* Farber, 1981: 125).

Thus, the move from the Victorian era into the Progressive era at the turn of the twentieth century was characterized by a decrease in nuclear family values and an increase in concern for individuals and their needs for adjustment, understanding, personality development, and uniqueness. James Spickard portrays an individualistic social system as "one in which individuals and individual activity are the focus of social life" (Spickard, 1988: 326). However, as Stacey reminded

FIGURE 4.1   CHANGES IN INDIVIDUAL EMBEDDEDNESS FROM COLONIAL DAYS TO THE PRESENT

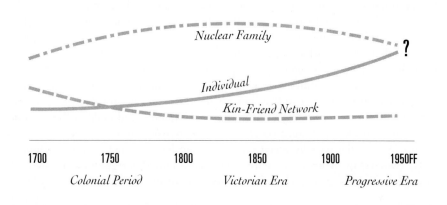

1700	1750	1800	1850	1900	1950FF
	Colonial Period		*Victorian Era*		*Progressive Era*

us in her book on China, we must not automatically assume that men's and women's experiences of individual embeddedness were identical. The man had always been less embedded in the family than the woman, and his extra-familial occupational role increased his individuality. Francesca Cancian puts it well when she notes the emergence in the nineteenth-century of the split between feminine love and masculine self-development (1987: 15). In other words, the gap in individual embeddedness by gender became wider in the nineteenth-century, and is becoming less today as women's opportunities for self-development increase. Precisely where we are today in nuclear embeddedness versus individualism cannot be determined until later in this book, but it is a question that the reader should keep in mind (see Figure 4.1).[11]

Husband-wife power relationships in the family are extremely difficult to ascertain for two primary reasons. For one thing, as Lantz et al. observe, legal and normative authority may be circumvented or overridden by subtle means of influence. Furthermore, there is the nagging question in the study of power anywhere, not just in the family, of whether *not* doing a task or making a decision means that the individual lacks power in that area or whether it means he or she has delegated power or authority to the one doing the task. We do know that wives may have substantial influence in a normatively patriarchal family system. We also know that in the modern couple seeking to make decisions democratically, the husband may, because of his achievements or the resources he controls, find himself with veto power in many key decision-making situations. Despite these facts, it seems likely that some change has occurred in husband-wife power behavior, allowing an increase in the *direct* and *acceptable* influence of the wife. Lantz's two studies show that this change was already under way at the beginning of the present period, his data indicating more female power in the marital relationship during 1794–1825 than during 1741–91 (Lantz et al., 1968: 1973).

Firmer ground is reached in looking at changes in power norms or expectations rather than behavior. Patriarchy, or husband-dominance, was the general expectation in the colonial family; today this norm is competing with the norm of conscious equalitarianism and democracy in the home. The reason for speaking of moderate rather than great change in this area is that *conscious* power equality in the family is increasingly characteristic, not of the entire U.S. family population, but of one major segment: those "white-collar" or middle-class families that are financially fairly well off. Besides that, even in the middle class it is verbalized more often than acted upon.

Another change affecting the family has to do with the position of women in society[12] and the concomitant alteration of husbands' and wives' roles. As late as 1850, in many states a wife had no legal control over personal property; all her belongings were legally at her husband's disposal. However, the democratic ideal, plus the growing awareness that women could make a living in an urban, industrializing society, resulted in the expansion of women's rights movements. Within the past hundred years, women have gained legally and politically; ownership of property within marriage and the right to vote are two examples of these gains. They have gained educationally as well. In colonial days even a grade-school education was thought unnecessary for a girl. A century later the distinction was drawn at the secondary school level. High school—and in high-status families, college—was deemed valuable for men, but impractical for women. The twentieth century ushered in the period of "coeducation," with almost half of today's American college graduates being women. They have likewise gained substantially in the economic sphere: sixty percent of the married women in the United States hold jobs, and the divergence in salaries for men and women doing the same work is beginning to diminish. One must be cautious not to overstate women's gains in the United States. For one thing, as Zaretsky notes, while the rise of industry largely freed women from traditional patriarchal constraints, the expansion of personal life created a new basis for their oppression—the responsibility for maintaining a private refuge for the work-weary male (Zaretsky, 1976: 10). Rather than emptying the home and family of their content and eliminating homemaking, this separation allowed for the emergence of family life as a distinct sphere of social relationships, a sphere assigned specifically to women (Matthaei, 1982: 106).

Thus, industrialization removed the husband from the home to play his major economic providing role elsewhere, thereby giving him economic control over the domestic unit in a way not possible in agrarian society. While close to 50 percent of single women were in the labor force in the nineteenth century, the domestic captivity of the wife, then, is considerable in the nuclear, industrial family. For another thing, even now, job-holding by women usually has *supplemental* connotations economically, since a wife tends to make less money than her husband, and more income means more spent for consumer goods. In addition, job discrimination against females is still strong, both in terms of bars to advancement and in terms of virtual exclusion from many professional and business fields. In fact, after World War II, the glorification of wifehood and motherhood by the mass media undid to some extent the former gains of the feminists. Thus the woman today is in a difficult position: her rise in status has been accompanied by the tendency to play down her traditional role—people may speak of being "just a housewife." And yet this remains a dominant life goal for many women due to the influence of tradition and the systematic, yet subtle, discrimination that they confront in society. Many positive changes in women's status are yet to come.

The change in the status of women in society is related to the changes in courtship practices discussed above, as well as to changes in husband and wife roles and adjustments. The basic movement has been away from predestined economic and familial roles toward an open, free-choice approach to being a man or a woman. In colonial days, a man was expected to run the economic machinery of the family and to be a stern and able disciplinarian; a woman was expected to marry, work on the farm, raise children, and provide for her husband's needs. In the nineteenth century, under the influence of Victorian glorification of the family, the husband and wife often fell far short of the kind of exclusive intimacy extolled by the moralists of that day. However, just as individualism was spreading even while the nuclear family was being extolled, so the biological interpretation of male sexuality was spreading even while the religious solution for that urge was being expounded (Bayles, 1981: 95). With sex viewed as sinful, especially for the female, the married couple faced strains in their intimate life, and manifested a surface or "pseudo" mutuality. This caused the wife to turn to her children for gratification (Strong, 1973: 461). A result was a kind of watchfulness, the "smothering mother" syndrome still referred to in the popular press. However, even pseudomutuality and smothering do not capture the essence of the wife-mother position in the nineteenth-century family. During that same period, as families became smaller and longevity greater, couples found that their lives after their children left home had become a major part of their life cycles (Wells, 12973: 93). This, when combined with the other two characteristics of the period, placed an added burden on the wife, whose psychological existence was more completely tied to family and children than was the husband's. This had a particularly negative effect on the older woman as the anonymous urban environment took from her the "community nurturant" role as described above by Faragher.

The elderly simply did not retire from their occupations, since it was not compulsory and there was no Social Security at the turn of this century. In 1900, seventy percent of the men over 65 years of age were still employed (Dahlin, 1980: 104). There was hardly an empty-nest stage, or a stage after the last child left home, since often all the children did *not* leave home, or the parents would have already died. A majority of older Americans lived with at least one of their grown children in 1900, but since there were not that many old people, only about one out of 16 U.S. households had three generations present (Smith, 1979: 285–298; Chudacoff and Hareven, 1976: 69–83). Widows, more often than elderly couples, lived with adult offspring, and were more prone to take in boarders than non-widows. A major change in the past 100 years has been the greater likelihood of the one-person household. This increase, however, has been twice as great for the elderly as for young or middle-aged adults (Wall, 1989: 372).

In the 19th century the young adult felt some resentment of the presence of an elderly parent. There was ambiguity of status, especially on the part of males. They were, as Hareven notes in her factory study:

> *full-fledged workers in the factory while still being a "son" at home. . . . Young sons and daughters found themselves in a generational squeeze, having to stay at home and support aging parents at a point in their lives when they were ready to move in search of jobs elsewhere or leave home and get married and form independent families (Hareven, 1982: 188).*

There was, in other words, substantial restriction upon personal freedom and preferences.

Regarding male and female roles, options today have multiplied and traditional norms are questioned. How should a father behave toward his children: as disciplinarian, provider, or buddy? How much of himself should a man invest in activities that are internal to the family and how much in community and occupational affairs?[13] Should a woman be a homemaker and mother, or should she be a professional, or just employed, or involved with various forms of community service? The crucial element in all the various role decisions men and women must make is communication because of the weakness of traditional expectations and lack of predetermination. This, of course, heightens the importance of adjustments between men and women; each couple must work out its own role definitions, though equality of choice between the sexes is still far from complete—and the possibility that the man should stay home and the woman go out seldom arises. The intricacies of these role options and the adjustments required are one of the major foci of this book, particularly of Chapters 11 and 12.

The notion of family adjustments brings us to one of the more intriguing dimensions of the "classical extended family of Western nostalgia." It is often assumed that the family in colonial days was a happy, close-knit unit in which conflict and indecision were far overshadowed by stability and tradition. Yet, as we have indicated, the colonial family was kept together by various legal and traditional mechanisms for the sake of economic and other functions that the nuclear unit performed. Thus, personal happiness might vary greatly from one family unit to another. It is not that unhappiness did not result in the breakup of some colonial family units; it is rather that some units very likely stayed together despite unhappiness, for the sake of their other functions. The twentieth-century American family, by contrast, lacks many of the cultural or normative supports for the unit that characterized an earlier day and finds itself held together primarily by the quality of internal relationships. Under such circumstances, happiness, satisfaction, or adjustment becomes the overt goal of the married couple. It is impossible to determine how happy colonial couples were. However, it seems quite possible that the actual "happiness quotient" or level of happiness of marriages existing today is higher than it was in colonial days for two reasons: first, more unhappy marriages weed themselves out today; second, and a function of the first, many married couples work hard at happiness today, since there is so little else holding marriages together. Whether or not this is correct, it would be a mistake to refer nostalgically to the "happy traditional colonial family."

The prevalence of marital breakup is one of the more frequently used indicators of the purported "decay" of the American family. The three factors most influencing the divorce rate the past two centuries are, according to Martin Schultz: changing women's status, urbanization, and changing divorce laws (1990: 108). We do know that the number of legal grounds for divorce increased substantially in the nineteenth century and that this increase was followed in the first half of the twentieth century by a rise in the divorce rate. However, it is difficult to determine the extent of the increase in all forms of family breakup since colonial days. For one thing, family units in colonial days that might eventually have been disrupted by desertion were often broken up by the premature death of one spouse or the other. For another thing, part of the rise in the divorce rate is nothing more than an increase in the tendency to legalize marital separation. Thus, while the divorce rate has risen, the rates of premature family breakup by death, desertion, and separation have declined. In short, the change in the laws governing divorce has been greater than the change in total rates of premature marital breakup. Yet the strictness of the norms and laws and the concern of the colonists to keep families together for the sake of their economic and other functions meant that husband-wife relations had to be worse in colonial days than today before a couple would *voluntarily* separate. We will spend much more time on divorce in Chapter 17.

FAMILY AND THE EXTERNAL WORLD   In the relations between the nuclear family and the external world, which include the already discussed position of women, there is a close connection between individual embeddedness, the dimensions of the household, and the amount of residential mobility. One of the reasons for the increasing separation of the nuclear unit from its social milieu in terms of values and household composition, is the residential mobility of families. This mobility is not, however, so much a difference between colonial days and the present as it is a pervasive characteristic of U.S. history. Thernstrom and Knight describe mobility in the nineteenth century in somewhat dramatic fashion:

> *If American city-dwellers were as restless and footloose as our evidence suggests, how was any cultural continuity—or even the appearance of it—maintained? . . . American society in the period considered here was more like a procession than a stable social order. How did this social order cohere at all? (in Hareven, 1971: 40; see also Landale, 1989: 365–386).*

The history of white colonization and colonial expansion on the American frontier is, in fact, the history of residential mobility. Henretta asserts very simply that "the structure of the colonial American family . . . facilitated geographical mobility and economic expansion," and he notes the rapid decrease over the seventeenth and eighteenth centuries in the proportion of sons who inherited land—immovable property—from their fathers (Henretta, 1973: 203). We may grant that a substantially larger proportion of colonial persons inherited farms or settled on land near their kin, but this is balanced to some extent by the large numbers of working-class persons who, in the nineteenth and twentieth centuries, have clustered together in the same cities with their kin. The number of multiple moves by any one family unit in modern society may have increased, but this is a characteristic of a minority of the population—primarily certain professional and executive persons and their families. Furthermore, twentieth-century mobility is neither uniformly unaffected by the location of kin and friends, nor does it entail virtual isolation from kin and former friends as mobility often did in colonial days. Too much has been made of the modern family's pursuit of industrial and managerial work opportunities; the overall picture is more one of slightly greater freedom to choose one's residential relationship to kin and of somewhat greater frequency of residential movement.

The European and colonial U.S. family systems were already basically different in terms of institutional embeddedness from such societies as the Afghan, in which the family-kin network and social organization were almost synonymous. In the colonies, legal and political institutions were quite separate from kinship and family ties; and economic, religious, and educational institutions had special functionaries as well as strong ties to the nuclear family. Nevertheless, great changes in embeddedness have occurred since colonial days (see Demos, 1986: 18). The industrial revolution, centered in the development of the factory system, directly affected one of these changes by transferring the *economic-productive* function from the family unit and the home to a separate location, to which one or more family members go to work to provide for their family's economic needs. Families were forced off the farms by debts, or went to the cities for opportunities, but regardless of the cause, the rural-urban transition deserves the label "revolution." Here are the percents of the labor force in agriculture at various points in U.S. history: In 1800, fully 84 percent of the work force was in agriculture, in 1840 it was 63 percent, by 1870 it had dropped to 52 percent, and by 1970 the percentage was down to 5 (Bushman, 1981: 56). In 200 years we had gone from 95 percent to 5 percent on the farm. Families tried to get plots of ground to farm in town, so as to supplement their incomes and keep some of the rural way of life. But the family as a unit ceased to be both producer and consumer, becoming merely a consumer. Yet in the capitalist market economy, that "consuming" role is extremely important and the business community of today continues to be cognizant of the value of having nuclear families to sell to.

Other activities that were handled by the family in an immediate and often rudimentary fashion have undergone expansion and spatial separation. *Recreation*, once a family activity at home or church and an individual pursuit around the home, has become increasingly specialized along age lines and centered in various locations other than the home. The *protective* function has ceased to be a cooperative-familial responsibility, being instead the concern of the police, fire department, and other community specialists. *Health care* has become the responsibility of the doctor, the drug store, and the hospital, with the family as coordinating agency.

Except for economic productivity, the *educational* function is perhaps the most dramatic example of expansion and specialization. Today the law makes it difficult, except under unusual circumstances, for parents to keep their children at home to educate them. At five or six years of age the child is removed from the home for 30 to 40 hours a week. Simultaneously, however, parents supervise and give continuing attention to their children's development.

The *religious* function, once of great importance to socialization and discipline, has seen its roots in the home become weakened, with its activity restricted to specific times and places apart from the home. The lessening of the carry-over between the religious institution and the home makes it possible for commentators to note a fourfold increase in church membership since colonial days and, at the same time, to refer to the increasing secularization of society. All these developments may be referred to as institutional differentiation or the weakening of institutional embeddedness in the nuclear family; we have avoided the often used term *loss of family functions* (Ogburn, 1933: Chapter 13). The term, although in common usage since the 1930s, has overtones that might cause some to think of the contemporary family as "twiddling its collective thumbs" for want of responsibilities or activities. This, however, is an incorrect representation on two counts. First, the family is still very much involved in the coordinating of physical care and of socialization. Second, while much family unit interaction occurs in the interstices of other societal institutions (as Freedman puts it), there is an increasingly overt and central involvement of the family unit in meeting the psychological needs of its members. To some degree, says Demos, "the image of 'the family as refuge' remains with us today. Many people still look to the home for buffering, or at least for relief, against the demands and pressures of society at large" (Demos, 1986: 35). And in the 1990s, it is increasingly difficult for families to play even the buffering role successfully.

SUMMARY AND CONCLUSIONS

The most striking changes in family formation or premarital conditions since colonial days have been in courtship and sex codes, with an increasing link between romantic love and mate selection. The major change—in reality, a complex of changes—in relations between the nuclear family and the larger society is in the expansion and parceling out of certain traditional functions to other agencies and locations. By far the most numerous large-scale changes have occurred within the family itself. These have included an increase in the number of role options and definitions open to both sexes, with a concomitant multiplying of the number of necessary adjustments and a loosening of divorce laws, making it easier to dissolve a given family unit.

What precipitated the changes in the family that have occurred during the past two centuries? Shorter, in his book *The Making of the Modern Family*, argues that the family itself brought about the changes.

> *We may think of the family in traditional society as a ship held fast at its moorings. From every side great cables run down to bind it to the dock. The ship sails nowhere and is part of the harbor.*
>
> *Now, in the Bad Old Days—let us say the sixteenth and seventeenth centuries— the family too was held firmly in the matrix of a larger social order. One set of ties bound it to the surrounding kin, the network of aunts and uncles, cousins and nieces who dotted the old regime's social landscape. Another set fastened it to the wider community, and gaping holes in the shield of privacy permitted others to enter the household freely and, if necessary, preserve order. A final set of ties held this elementary family to generations past and future. Awareness of ancestral traditions and ways of doing business would be present in people's minds as they went about their day. Because they knew that the purpose of life was preparing coming generations to do as past ones had done, they would have clear rules for shaping relations within the family, for deciding what was essential and what was not.*
>
> *In its journey into the modern world the family has broken all these ties. It has separated from the surrounding community, guarded now by high walls of privacy. It has cast off its connections with distant kin, and has changed fundamentally even its*

relationship to close relatives. And it has parted from the lineage, that chain of gener-
ations stretching across time: whereas once people had been able to answer questions
such as "who am I" by pointing to those who had gone before and would come after, in
the twentieth century they would have other replies.

. . . How was it that the family managed to slip its moorings at the traditional
dock?

For many years now, one group has thought that the hawsers were cut by roving
gangs of "mass men," bent on pillaging the established order of things. Other writers,
however, have said that the tides sweeping through the harbor became irresistible, and
by their sheer force alone parted the cables. I shall argue in this book that it was the
ship's own crew —Mom, Dad, and the kids — who severed the cables by gleefully reach-
ing down and sawing through them so that the solitary voyage could commence
(Shorter, 1975: 3-4).

Thus, says Shorter, it was not mass men or radicals nor the tides, presumably of
industrial capitalism, that set the nuclear family adrift, but the family itself. In
East Africa it was possible to witness such conscious decisions to sever lineage
obligations in favor of keeping one's urban income for oneself and one's family,
though such decisions were often painful. But Shorter's analysis and my own
Uganda experience are not really consistent. When my colleagues at Makerere
University in Uganda spoke of whether to maintain kin obligations or keep
their individually earned income, it was because the second was a known possibility. It makes no sense to speak of the crew cutting loose from the dock without the individual occupation/income alternative already available as a possible
course to chart. Thus, while Shorter's analogy is useful, his explanation is
faulty: the family did not cut loose until the tide of industrial capitalism had
swept through the harbor.

That does not mean, of course, that many family changes did not predate
the industrial revolution. What it does mean is that some developments between
1800 and 1992 can be directly related to the industrial revolution. Most important, of course, is the influence of industrialization upon institutional embeddedness, especially the economic-productive function. Industrialization also
seems to have had some effect on the status of women and husband-wife roles
and adjustments, though these were also influenced by democratic ideology.
Otherwise, it becomes extremely difficult to perceive direct linkages between
the family and industrialization.[14]

The "new family history" has made it increasingly possible to paint with
broad strokes the characteristics of the colonial family and to compare it with
the family today. This historical reconstruction is not complete, and historians
will continue to illumine additional facets of the colonial and the nineteenth-
century family experience. Of particular concern in attempting to generalize
about "the colonial U.S. family" is the knowledge that much of what has been
discovered about the family in Dedham, Plymouth, and Hingham may very
well not hold for the French Canadians of Lowell (Early, 1982: 188–199) or for
Richmond, Virginia, or Charleston, South Carolina. It is generally understood
that in the South there were more kin-based landholdings and strong lineages,

which were more dominant politically and economically than were such units in the North. This difference, it might be added, did not stop with colonial days but continued into the present period. Much, however, remains to be done in investigating the Southern family system and comparing it with those of New England and the frontier.

Historical comparisons have also been foreshortened by time as well as place. Starting with the colonial era, we have picked up on the literature regarding the Victorian era and 1900, and compared it to today. Omitted has been the important work being done on twentieth-century history, especially that concerning the Depression years, found in the work of Glen Elder.[15] This work will be introduced in the chapters on various aspects of the family, as they arise.

In discussing classical China, Freedman spoke of two organizing principles: that of high-status people and that of the masses. Rosenfeld likewise found two cultural ideals at work in the Arab village he studied: the traditional and the modern. The same issue must now be raised regarding our depiction of changes in the American family since colonial days; when we speak of "sex codes" or "husband-wife power codes," the question arises, "Whose codes?" Are they everyone's codes, or are they the codes of one important group within the society? The answer might be inferred from the previously made comment that "conscious power equality in the family is increasingly characteristic, not of the entire U.S. family population but of one major segment: those 'white-collar' or middle-class families that are financially well off." This equality is the norm of those who dominate American culture; that is, the upper middle and upper classes. The term *dominate* is used here in much the same sense as in the discussion of polygyny. It does not mean numerical *pre*dominance; rather, it refers to that cultural style that, due to the key position of its proponents in government, education, and the mass media, receives the widest dissemination among the populace as a whole. In a society such as the United States, there are active subcultural principles as well as the dominant ones. Chapter 6 is devoted to the delineation of the various subcultural principles at work in the United States and the historic interrelations among them. Furthermore, we must keep our eyes open for conflicting norms even among the middle classes, and for inconsistencies as well as integration within the family system. As Rothman asserts, it is "at least as appropriate to search for discontinuities as for neat matches" (1973: 189). Our discussion of change has led us to consider the family's loss of functions, the effect of gender role changes on patriarchy, and the lessening of institutional and individual embeddedness in the family. These issues and other important theoretical problems already introduced will be discussed in Chapter 5.

Family in a Differentiated Society:
Toward a Theoretical Perspective

CHAPTER 5 *Using Durkheim's view of societal integration, we attempt to clarify the family varieties and changes described in the previous four chapters. Feminist theory is used to explain patriarchy, and to clarify the inherent conservatism of much family theory/ideology. Five continua are presented to deal cross-culturally with family formation, socialization, marital roles, and the two forms of embeddedness, so that the character, direction, and speed of change in U.S. families may be better understood. Problems with functional analysis are explained, followed by an introduction to exchange and systems theory. Finally, a postscript notes inconsistencies and varieties in U.S. families.*

DIFFERENTIATION AND THE FAMILY: EXTENSIONS AND CLARIFICATIONS

In the late nineteenth and early twentieth centuries, Emile Durkheim (1858–1917) presented a view of society and the direction of social change that, while incorrect in some of its particulars and conservative in its ideology, helps bring together much of what has been said in the first four chapters. Durkheim's major emphasis throughout his writing is the nature of societal integration, or what it is that ties people together in society. Historically and cross-culturally, many societies, such as the Afghans, have been composed of relatively self-sufficient or institutionally embedded family-kin units, each carrying out about the same activities as any other. These self-sufficient and similar units do not, out of necessity, have to either stay in close contact with other family/kin units or perish. "On the contrary, since they do not need each other, as each contains within himself all that social life consists of, he can go and carry it elsewhere" (Durkheim, 1964: 151). What, then, is it that links persons together in larger communities within such societies and keeps family units from wandering freely and self-sufficiently on their own? For Durkheim, the answer lies in the society's norms or expectations and interpersonal bonds or "we-feelings." That is, the embedded or undifferentiated society is held together by shared understanding of acceptable behavior, serious punishment of the unacceptable, awareness of the ways in which "our" behavior differs from and is better than that of other societies, and the development of feelings of belonging or connectedness to other members of the larger community and society. Both strong norms and strong bonds are necessary to societal integration in a society in which the family-kin units do not actually need each other. This, says Durkheim, is "mechanical solidarity."

Societies in the modern world are very different from such undifferentiated societies. They are characterized by an ever-expanding division of labor, which we have been calling differentiation or specialization. The individual family-kin units are no longer identical and self-sufficient; rather, there is "organic solidarity" between them. They are linked together like the parts of an organism such as the human body, each with certain functions or tasks to perform and each very much dependent upon the others for survival. In the modern, organically solidary society, my family and I simply cannot survive without the food, clothing, shelter, and protection grown, sewn, built, or provided by others. In other words, as institutions separate (or "dis-embed") themselves from the family, the family does less and less of what is needed to survive, and is more and more dependent on the larger society.

While these ideas from Durkheim are of interest in themselves, a certain amount of extension is necessary before they begin to illuminate the internal nature of the family. Durkheim's efforts were directed largely toward understanding society, and how it is held together. Only periodically did he turn his attention to what goes on within the family-kin units. However, a few hints can be pieced together from the following references. In the *mechanically solidary* or undifferentiated society, "the farmer's life does not extend outside the familial circle. Economic activity, having no consequences outside the family, is sufficiently regulated by the family, and the family itself thus serves as occupational group." But in the *organically solidary* society, in which the family-kin units are no longer self-sufficient, "the family, in losing the unity and indivisibility of former times, has lost with one stroke a great part of its efficacy. As it is today broken up with each generation, man passes a notable part of his existence far from all domestic influence" (Durkheim, 1964, ed.: 17). This transformation is elsewhere described in this way:

> The family, in truth, is for a long time a veritable social segment. . . . Instead of remaining an autonomous society alongside of the great society, it becomes more and more involved in the system of social organs. It even becomes one of the organs, charged with special functions. . . . It is, indeed, a law without exception that the more the social structure is by nature segmental, the more families form great, compact, undivided masses, gathering up in themselves (Durkheim, 1964, ed.: 210, 292).

The family, says Durkheim, comes to be more and more a specialist among specialists, depending upon other such units and upon a differentiated economy for survival. Yet all this has only hinted at the nature of the family-kin units themselves. As society changes from mechanical (or norm-bond) solidarity to organic (division of labor and need) solidarity, what happens to its subunits, i.e., families and kin?

Durkheim's clearest statement on this is found in his first published article, a review of A. Schaeffle's *Bau und Leben*:

> As the family is the germ from which society is born, we should be able to find society there in an abridged form. And in fact, it has its tissues and organs. The family . . . has protective and defensive institutions. . . . It has an economic structure, an industry, and an intellectual life. The family is thus a sort of complete, social organism, which was once self-sufficient and the whole of society (Durkheim, 1885: 84-101).

So when society is tied together by strong norms and bonds, or mechanically, its family-kin units are tied together organically, or like organisms. Cross-cultural study has led anthropologists and other social scientists to conclude that, no matter how simple a society is in terms of technology and division of labor, there is role differentiation *within* families on at least two bases: age and sex.[1] Males and females, adults and children, are assigned different roles, tasks, authority, and privileges in the institutionally embedded (mechanically solidary) society (Zelditch, 1955: 307-342; Quale, 1988: 113).

This differentiation is centered in the family-kin unit, although each of these units is relatively similar to every other. The care and detail with which the family-kin division of labor is spelled out is most appreciated by one familiar with literature on societies such as the Afghans (see Stephens, 1963: Chapter 6). As noted above, in ideal-typical language, we are suggesting that in a society integrated by mechanical solidarity, the subunits, that is, the family-kin groups, will tend to be internally integrated by age and sex differentiation. The strength of the family members' bonds or feelings toward one another is not as important to the family's internal functioning as is their *need* for each other and the strength of the norms and bonds *between* families. Also, whether the nuclear family can be easily dissolved is dependent upon the relative importance of the economic and other functions of this unit as compared to the kin group. If a larger kin unit, such as a patriline, is the chief unit of economic production and other functions, the marital relationship may be somewhat tenuous. If, however, the nuclear unit is the seat of many institutional functions, but is not greatly embedded in a larger kin unit (as was generally true in the colonies of the New World), divorce may be difficult to obtain due to the nuclear family's perceived importance.

When the division of labor and other institutions cease to be primarily embedded in either kin or family units, and begin to involve specialists going elsewhere to perform their occupational and other functions, a change in the internal nature of the family-kin unit occurs as well (Harris, 1983: 185). To put it categorically, as society moves from mechanical to organic solidarity, its family-kin units move from organic to mechanical solidarity (see Vannoy, 1991: 252). That is, the family division of labor becomes less distinct and is predicated more on choice than tradition, with relations within the family increasingly based on strong norms and (especially) bonds. Harris states this very simply: "as social relations have become more impersonal and anonymous, so familial relations have become more intimate and affectional" (Harris, 1983: 150). And Collier et al. note that love or affection are not necessarily inherent characteristics of family life, but perhaps represent a very recent expectation (Collier, 1982: 28, 38). The family in the specialized society is kept together more by the development of behavioral expectations and by strong affection than by either its members' need for one another or society's need for stable family units. Thus, if affectional bonds are weak, the unit may dissolve.

The modern, industrial family has become, as Lasch's cliche might have it, a refuge from a segmented (or differentiated) and impersonal urban life. It is ideally characterized by affection, companionship, and norms or rules of behavior (see Vannoy, 1991: 252, 266). The word *ideally* is used advisedly, for several qualifications must now be added to the foregoing analysis. Collier et al. state clearly that while love may be the goal, real family life is a mixture. We and our ancestors have been "both nice and mean, both generous and ungenerous. . . . The American construct of The Family, after all, is complex enough to comprise some key contradictions." For example, unqualified love is located in the same place that violence is most tolerated—the family (Collier et al., 1983: 35).

Second, notice that Durkheim's mechanically and organically solidary societies have been left vague throughout, both structurally and temporally. One reason for this vagueness is that the kind of historical discussion contained in the preceding pages is both ideal-typical and highly condensed. One passes over much history—the strengthening of the kin group in agrarian societies, its subsequent gradual weakening in favor of the nuclear family, and the slow separation of political, economic, religious, and other specialists from the family—if one refers only to the notion of a historical change from mechanical to organic solidarity. Durkheim is comparing only two ideal types: the institutionally embedded society and the modern industrial society. Freedman described a classical Chinese system in which kin groups were buffers between state and family. The colonial American family was partially differentiated and partially embedded. Other authors referred to later in the chapter will speak of the patriarchal and modern industrial family or of the change of the family from an institution to a companionship. The difficulty with all such ideal-typical summaries lies in their tendency to compare polar opposites and thus to overestimate the changes that have occurred. However, the changes that have been the subject of Chapters 3 and 4 might best be defined by a series of six types, ranging from total institutional embeddedness in the family to total differentiation and specialization (see Figure 5.1).

In *Type 1*, the division of labor is encompassed by the nuclear family, with interaction including other members of the hunting-gathering band. Economic, political, and other specialists are nonexistent. Rather, a family member, perhaps the father, performs whatever religious rituals there are, makes political decisions as necessary, and leads the family's economic division of labor. *Type 2* also has few separate functionaries in institutions other than the family. However, with agriculture or herding, corporate kin groups tend to develop, with individuals and institutions embedded in them; for example, the Afghan. *Type 3* is found in the classical China depicted by Freedman. Here the nuclear family is somewhat less embedded in the kin group, but kin provide a balance of power vis-à-vis the now-separated political and religious functionaries. In this type, the marriage tie may be less binding than the blood tie; the same is true for Type 2. *Type 4* is exemplified by the colonial American family described in Chapter 4. The kin group is no longer central to economic and other functions, nor does it play the role of political buffer. However, much economic, educational, and other activity still involves the nuclear family as a unit or else takes place within the home. It should be pointed out that there were a few Type 3 kin groups in the American colonies, especially in the South, and that the typical pre-communist Chinese family was very similar to Type 4. Thus, the difference is not that Type 3 is Chinese and Type 4 colonial American, but rather that Type 3 is high status and Type 4 is low status. The difference between the Chinese and the American examples arises from the fact that, with a long agrarian history, Chinese society had more—and more powerful—units of Type 3 than did the New World colonies. It is further noteworthy that Types 1, 2, and 4 are somewhat curvilinear in terms of institutional and individual embeddedness. The nuclear family is basic in the simplest hunting and gathering bands and again in the early stages of industrialization, with the kin group most prominent in agricultural and pastoral societies.[2] *Type 5* is modern, industrial society, with the family unit still playing a substantial role in education, recreation, and religion, as it tries to give general direction to the socialization process, but seldom acting *as a unit* in economic production. In addition, women may or may not engage in occupational employment; there is tension between the family unit's

FIGURE 5.1   TYPES OF RELATIONSHIPS AMONG FAMILY, KIN GROUP,
AND OTHER INSTITUTIONS

Type 1: Individuals and institutions embedded in
nuclear family; age and sex division of labor
in family (Durkheim's mechanically solidary
society: e.g., hunting-gathering band)

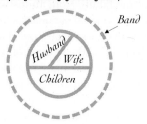

Type 2: Individuals and institutions embedded in kin
group; age and sex division of labor in kin
group (typical of agricultural and pastoral
societies: e.g., the Afghans)

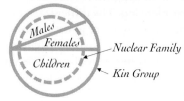

Type 3: Some institutional differentiation; kin group as
buffer between state and family (e.g., high-
status classical China)

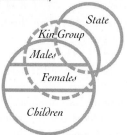

Type 4: Some institutional differentiation, including
economic; individual embedded in nuclear
family (e.g., colonial
America)

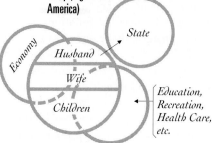

Type 5: Little institutional embeddedness; individual
embeddedness variable (modern, industrial
society: e.g., contemporary U.S.
and Russia)

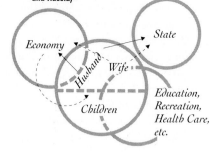

Type 6: Complete institutional differentiation; family
serves the individual (Durkheim's organically
solidary society

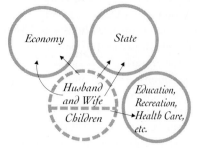

importance and that of the individual in terms of individual embeddedness. *Type 6* is basically hypothetical, although certain systems (for example, the kibbutz in Israel) have attempted to establish a differentiation closely resembling this one. The historical confusion arises when an analysis such as that of the colonial and modern family is viewed as describing a change form Type 1 to Type 6, whereas in reality the change is from Type 4 to Type 5. Thus, a necessary clarification of the ideal-typical discussions of Durkheim, Freedman, and others involves the further specification of the structural and temporal units of analysis.[3]

Another important point regarding the six types in Figure 5.1 is that, on a worldwide basis, there is a predominant trend from Types 1 and 2 toward type 5. This has been noted by many authors, among them Goode, Zelditch, and Murray Straus, not merely as a process but as a process *desired* by the world's people. "Modernization," including the move away from extended families and lineages toward the nuclear family, "is a worldwide aspiration and, barring a planetary catastrophe, it is unlikely to be halted" (Straus, 1971: 71).

The issue of whether or not such a goal is worthy, or *good* for people, is another matter. Suffice it to say that, while it may be easy for one who knows the modern industrial world from the inside to criticize its economic and familial structures and tensions, it is extremely difficult to convince the people of the developing nations that they should not want to "nuclearize" their families and industrialize their economy.[4]

S E C T I O N   T W O

PATRIARCHY AND FEMINISM

Patriarchy is male dominance both in the home and in the larger society; Harris calls it "the control of both production and reproduction by males" (1983: 179). Gerda Lerner's book *The Creation of Patriarchy* explains in great detail the history of how the patriarchal family was institutionalized, and how it moved from private practice to public law. Lerner states that the patriarchal family "mirrored the archaic state in its mixture of paternalism and unquestioned (male) authority," and goes back to the Mesopotamian civilizations of 2000 B.C. (Lerner, 1986: 122). Of course, Stacey might argue that it can be traced even further back in the history of China.

But Lerner is even more interested in patriarchy's persistence than in its inception. The dependence of the state on the patriarchal family for order in the public domain was recognized in Mesopotamia, and "has been constantly reinforced both in ideology and practice over . . . three millennia" (Lerner, 1986: 122). This resilience and the varieties of patriarchy throughout history are well described by Lerner:

> *Oriental patriarchy encompassed polygamy and female enclosure in harems. Patriarchy in classical antiquity and its European development was based upon monogamy,*

but in all its forms a double sexual standard, which disadvantages women, was part of the system. In modern industrial states, such as in the United States, property relations within the family develop along more egalitarian lines than those in which the father holds absolute power; yet the economic and sexual power relations do not necessarily change. . . . Changes within the family do not alter the basic male dominance in the public realm, in institutions and in government (Lerner, 1986: 216).

While Lerner notes its variety and persistence, others have commented on the way in which patriarchy may have been strengthened by the industrial division of labor, by the "exclusion of women from the labour process" (Harris, 1983: 199; Quale, 1988: 140). When the household is linked to production only through the wage labor of the male, patriarchy is strengthened. As further changes (lower fertility, shorter hours) reduce the public/private dichotomy, the conditions for patriarchy are weakened, but subordination may continue due to unchanging norms and socialization (Harris, 1983: 200). It is at this point that struggle and conflict over male authority become intense.

But is patriarchy innate or learned? On this question hangs the theoretical/ideological debate. If it is innate, destroying it goes against nature; if it is learned it can be unlearned and changed. Pre-twentieth-century white male Europeans argued, for the most part, that it is innate. That is, patriarchy exists because males are larger, stronger, more emotionally stable, and more intellectually capable (see Comte, 1842: 504, 505; Darwin, 1871: 565; Spencer, 1893: 177).

We can, however, find the same argument in this century. Robin Fox, in his book on *Kinship and Marriage*, states as Principle 3: "The men usually exercise control" (Fox, 1967: 31). He then goes on, somewhat condescendingly, to say why:

By and large it is overwhelmingly true and for very good reasons. One does not need to recapitulate the evolutionary history of man to see why. For the greater part of human history, women were getting on with their highly specialized task of bearing and rearing the children. It was the men who hunted the game, fought the enemies, and made the decisions. This is, I am convinced, rooted in primate nature, and while social conditions in the very recent past of some advanced societies have given women the opportunity to have a say in things, I still think that most women would agree with this contention (Fox, 1967: 31-32).

George Gilder, the theoretician for the U.S. administration during the 1980s, states that the "woman's place is in the home," where she is "uniquely in charge of the central activities of human life." Her liberation, then, "entails a profound dislocation" (Gilder, 1987: 173, 176). This is the basic conservative argument: patriarchy is both widespread and natural—"What is, is good." We will come across this premise again in the discussion of functionalism below.

It is, however, noteworthy that not all European male thinkers saw such gender differences as natural. As we noted in footnote 1, Durkheim assumed more gender equality in strength in the past, before women's lives became homebound and sedentary. Likewise, Jean Jacques Rousseau, writing in the 1700s, states that the sexes' manner of life had been virtually the same, but with settled agriculture the women became more sedentary. "In other words, for Rousseau gender differences were originally non-existent or slight, but they became greater as a result of cultural developments, such as the establishment of family households" (Adams and Steinmetz, 1993: 80). And John Stuart Mill argues that public life raises women's status, in their own eyes and that of males. Involvement in public life seems, according to Mill, not to go against nature (Mill, 1859: 389). Finally, Engels argued that originally there was matriarchy, but the patriarchal revolution was the world historic defeat of the female sex (Engels, 1884).

That patriarchy is widespread is undeniable. Yet Engels has questioned whether it was historically prior, and twentieth-century feminists have raised basic questions about patriarchy and gender differences. A good place to start is with the often overlooked Charlotte Perkins Gilman, writing in the first quarter of this century (Nies, 1977: 125-145). In 1898, a year before Thorstein Veblen coined the phrase "conspicuous consumption," Gilman spoke of "the consuming female—priestess of the temple of consumption, who creates a market for all that is luxurious and enervating" (Gilman, 1898). This, she says, encourages ruthless competition on her behalf, and fosters the U.S. male's savage individualism. Gilman speaks of specialization, not just the division of labor of which Durkheim speaks, but between men and women. This has driven a wedge between men and women and is neither natural nor healthy. In the animal kingdom, females as well as males have always hunted food. The result of this dichotomy between woman's home and man's public life has caused certain aspects of the female personality—the sexual and maternal—to overdevelop, while her contribution to the larger community has atrophied. Living in a small, dark place (the home) has narrowed the woman, who in turn narrows the man. What Gilman is speaking of is the way in which the male and female personalities have been "narrowed" by the dichotomies of modern life. No longer complete humans, they are narrowed into male or female humans.

In *The Home* she pushes the argument further. Child care and homemaking should be professionalized: common meals and professional child care would be healthy for everyone. As she says:

> *The mother is not ashamed to depend on the doctor if the child is ill, . . . on the teacher when the child is in school. Why should she so passionately refuse to depend on equally skilled assistance for the first five years of her babies' lives—those years when statistics remorselessly expose her incapacity? (Gilman, 1903: 340).*

Her third book, *The Man-Made World*, answers that question. A male-centered culture has made women that way. However, she does not argue that there are no inborn gender differences except child-bearing. Feminist theory continues to debate *alpha* bias—men and women are very different, and *beta* bias—there are no differences that have not been culturally determined. Gilman's answer is that while most personality differences are culturally induced, the domesticating of women has deprived society of women's qualities of cooperation and life-orientation, and has allowed for domination by male characteristics of competition and destruction. The point on which males and females are equal is in their ability to contribute to the modern world. Thus, the public-private gender distinction is unnatural, and the world is worse off for the loss of female abilities.

Though Gilman is given little attention by many current feminists, she has raised many of the key theoretical issues. The invisibility of female work caused by separate and unequal gender spheres has increased women's understanding of patriarchy (Stacey, 1990: 8), and of oppression in the family. Qualitative or subjective methods may, therefore, be needed to tap those insights (Klein and Jurich, 1992: 62). The reason for this is that even the concepts and phrases used on social science surveys are laden with male bias.

This brings us to the issue of post-modernism and deconstructionism. A major premise is that society is so permeated by the male-patriarchal perspective that the effort must be made to deconstruct (or take apart) our concepts and theories. Is there such a thing as "marriage," or—as Bernard said—are *his* marriage and *her* marriage two different phenomena? If so, we must deconstruct the marriage concept. We should also deconstruct maleness/masculinity and femaleness/femininity to try to determine the few aspects that are a result of hormonal or hereditary differences, and the large numbers of characteristics that are determined by socialization and that may be mixed in varying proportions. "Modern" theories—such as exchange and functionalism—with their concepts and categories are so dominated by patriarchal thinking, that they demand deconstruction—a difficult task still in mid-stream (Cheal, 1991; Okin, 1989; Lorber and Farrell, 1991).

A major point of criticism for feminists has been the very structure glorified and treated as natural by Gilder and others: the breadwinner/homemaker monogamous nuclear family. This conventional household has made women dependent, and treats as deviant or abnormal the great variety of family/household forms that actually exist (Agassi, 1991: 316). Boss and Thorne note that enshrining this nuclear family perpetuates the patriarchal ideology, while feminism is trying to make visible and legitimize a range of family structures. Rather than normal and deviant, feminist theory proposes pluralism: varieties of ways to organize intimate life (Cheal, 1991). Boss and Thorne summarize this well: "Feminist scholars have helped make speakable the experiences of domination, conflict, and violence that are silenced by romanticized views of 'the normal family'" (Boss and Thorne, 1989: 83). Throughout this theory chapter, and throughout the book, we must be on guard against the conservative patriarchal assumptions that underlie much of the research we will quote. That is one reason feminism has been introduced this early in the present chapter.

The questions of family change and/or disintegration raised in Chapter 1 cannot be answered on the basis of the discussion thus far. In fact, much effort in this book will be spent on determining the direction and speed of change within the family system of the United States. To this end, several continua, on which current characteristics and directions of change may be located, are presented in Section 3.

FAMILY SYSTEM CHARACTERISTICS: FIVE CONTINUA

In Chapter 4, the various aspects of the family in American history were grouped together under three headings: family formation, internal family relations, and the family and the external world, or other institutions. Internal family relations can be further broken down into socialization, marital roles, and individual embeddedness; all of these aspects, with their logical extremes, are illustrated by the five continua of Figure 5.2.

Looking at the continua one at a time, it is possible, as indicated in Chapter 2, to conceive of a society in which marital arrangements are made by the parents and incestuous and exogamous prohibitions leave the individual with only one category of persons within which to find a mate. Or the prohibitions may be fewer, resulting in a wider range of marital possibilities, but with the parents still working out the pairings. Restricted choice, as in colonial America, is characterized by individuals choosing their own mates, but with religious and racial status, residential immobility in some cases, or other restrictions severely limiting the range within which the choice operates. Quale argues that personal "attraction rather than familial arrangement did not begin to receive serious consideration as a primary basis for marriage until the eighteenth century" (Quale, 1988: 189). One way open choice functions in India at present is through Matrimonial Ads, as seen in Feature 5.1. The notion of open choice, or universal availability, is that all members of the opposite sex in one's society are potentially available to one for mating. They are, furthermore, permanently available, so that an unsatisfactory relationship can be terminated and a new one begun at any time. This is where Farber feels the U.S. family is rapidly heading in terms of mate selection (Farber, 1964: 106-109). The logical end of this continuum also involves universal, permanent availability, but without the legalization of either marriage or divorce. This we have labeled "random liaisons," as we did in our Chapter 3 discussion of classical Marxist theory. The issue here, as far as the modern family is concerned, is whether current mate selection is more accurately described by the term *restricted choice* or by the term *universal, permanent availability*. And this omits, of course, the members of society who either do not "mate," or who choose someone of their own sex (although many of the factors found in Chapter 10 might very well operate in the latter case).

The socialization continuum has, at one extreme, the society in which culture is redefined by each succeeding generation only enough to be consistent with small technological advances in which the family and kin group control the learning process, and thus in which the individual is likely to find crucial positive identification with other family-kin group members.[5] At the other extreme is the hypothetical society in which each generation completely rethinks and reworks its culture—that is, in which *socialization*, or the passing along of culture,

FIGURE 5.2   FIVE IDEAL-TYPICAL CONTINUA ON WHICH TO LOCATE FAMILY
CHARACTERISTICS AND CHANGES

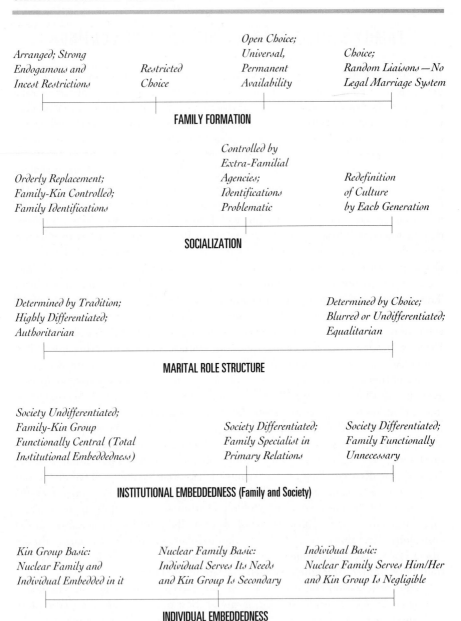

*Arranged; Strong
Endogamous and
Incest Restrictions*
    *Restricted
    Choice*
        *Open Choice;
        Universal,
        Permanent
        Availability*
            *Choice;
            Random Liaisons — No
            Legal Marriage System*

FAMILY FORMATION

*Orderly Replacement;
Family-Kin Controlled;
Family Identifications*
        *Controlled by
        Extra-Familial
        Agencies;
        Identifications
        Problematic*
            *Redefinition
            of Culture
            by Each Generation*

SOCIALIZATION

*Determined by Tradition;
Highly Differentiated;
Authoritarian*
                *Determined by Choice;
                Blurred or Undifferentiated;
                Equalitarian*

MARITAL ROLE STRUCTURE

*Society Undifferentiated;
Family-Kin Group
Functionally Central (Total
Institutional Embeddedness)*
        *Society Differentiated;
        Family Specialist in
        Primary Relations*
            *Society Differentiated;
            Family Functionally
            Unnecessary*

INSTITUTIONAL EMBEDDEDNESS (Family and Society)

*Kin Group Basic:
Nuclear Family and
Individual Embedded in it*
    *Nuclear Family Basic:
    Individual Serves Its Needs
    and Kin Group Is Secondary*
        *Individual Basic:
        Nuclear Family Serves Him/Her
        and Kin Group Is Negligible*

INDIVIDUAL EMBEDDEDNESS

does not take place. Somewhere in the middle would be the society characterized by some redefinition, in which extrafamilial agencies control much socialization so that identification with a family member is as problematic as identification with a football coach, a movie star, a teacher, or any other significant member of one's society. How closely, we might ask, does the extrafamilial socialization model fit the contemporary United States?

Family roles may be traditionally determined so that the society includes only one definition of what it means to be a father, a mother, or a son or daughter of a certain age. In this case, there are no role-definition options open to the individual. Such a society, as noted earlier, tends to have as part of its traditional definition of family roles a carefully worked out division of labor with an authoritarian, usually patriarchal, control of resources and decisions. At the opposite pole, is the society in which definition of the husband, wife, father, or mother role is determined by choice. The choices are such that the members of the family unit may share equally in decision-making and control of resources if they wish; they may divide economic, socialization, and affective roles in any way they see fit since tradition dictates no predetermined family division of labor. The question concerning family roles that will engage us throughout this work is the extent to which there is freedom of choice in the contemporary U.S. family.

The fourth continuum is really a reduction of certain aspects of Figure 5.1. The extremes are the undifferentiated society, with all functions totally embedded in the family (Type 1) or kin group (Type 2), and the totally differentiated society, whose family system is therefore functionally unnecessary (Type 6). In between are Freedman's classical Chinese family, the colonial U.S. family, and the modern industrial family, specializing in primary relations. To what extent, we might ask, do major functions now take place outside the home and involve subsegments of the family? Or must we divide the family along gender lines, noting that during much of this century the male carried out extra-familial functions, and the female carried out those still left to the family? This issue will arise in the next section of the chapter, as well as later.

The final continuum is related in many ways to the preceding four. Yet the multidimensional nature of the "individual embeddedness" concept requires repetition of a portion of our earlier discussion. There are two stages, or types, of individual embeddedness, each with an interactional and a value element. *Kin-group embeddedness* means that the kin group is the primary milieu for social interaction and is valued more highly than either the nuclear family or the individual. The nuclear family in this situation has little existence apart from, or privacy within, its kin group; and kin solidarity takes precedence over that among nuclear family members. To put it briefly, both the individual, and his or her nuclear family, operate within and serve the needs of the kin group. A second form of individual embeddedness is found if the kin group and its community are weak but the individual is still expected to operate primarily within, and to serve the needs of, the *nuclear family*. "He is the black sheep of the family"; "He has disgraced us": such antiquated expressions indicate that "the family" is actually considered more important than individuals and their needs. However, if the family is viewed as basically serving the needs of the individual and as concerned with its members' unique welfare and if both family and kin interaction is less important than extrafamilial activity and involvement, one cannot speak of individual embeddedness, but of *individualism* and independence. The Bergers describe this as "increasing emphasis on the individual over against every collective entity, including the family itself, which had been the historical matrix of modern nuclear family individuation" (Berger and Berger, 1983: 120). "Where did we fail him (or her)?" "What makes for achievement?" Such questions bespeak an individualistic orientation within society. It is generally acknowledged that the culture of the contemporary United States is not characterized by kin-group dominance, with the nuclear family and individual highly embedded in the kin group (see Figure 1 in Chapter 4). A difficult question however (and one that will occupy discussion throughout this book), is whether the correct representation of the present-day United States depicts the family as serving the individual's needs and helping him or her to operate as a unique individual and to maximize potentialities. Or, as Lynne Halem poses the question: "Has the emerging ethic of individualism and personal happiness undermined commitment to the family and society?" (Halem, 1980: 289; see also Harris, 1983, 219). A major sub-issue emerges from our discussion of patriarchy, both in this chapter and Chapter 3. Women have been more embedded in their families than have men, due to men's dominance and extra-familial involvements. How much is that changing toward women having the same opportunities for individualism as men? Looking at this continuum as a logical system and recalling the ideal types of Figure 5.1, we should note that the simplest hunting and gathering band is characterized by nuclear family embeddedness, with the more complex agricultural and pastoral societies closer to the left-hand end of the continuum than either the band or modern industrial society.

Many of the issues raised by these five continua will arise again and again in the chapters on socialization, mate selection, husband-wife interaction, kinship, aging, crises, and family dissolution. However, we must first expand on the issue of family functions referred to.

⚓ FAMILY FUNCTIONS: UNIVERSAL AND CHANGING

The concept of function is multidimensional, having at least three distinct meanings. These meanings may be exemplified by the following statements:

- ✦ The family is functional for society in several ways.
- ✦ The functions of the family have changed.
- ✦ The family functions in the following manner.

In the first statement, the term *functional* has to do with the *good* or *benefit*, perpetuation, or integration of society, and is related to the conservative ideology discussed earlier. The idea of universal family functions, such as reproduction and socialization, is closely related to the issue of the family's universality, referred to in Chapter 3. This idea concerns the way in which the family furthers certain goals of the society in which it is operating. The second use of the idea of family functions has to do with *tasks* performed, or needs met, so that when we speak of the functional centrality of the family we are saying that the central tasks of a given society are performed within the family setting.[6] The third statement, which changes *function* from a noun to a verb, is simply concerned with describing how the family actually *operates*. The kinship system in the United States, we might say, functions for affective ties and a certain amount of obligation. Or one can speak of certain parts of the family system as functioning, that is, operating, in an inconsistent fashion. For example, the norm that says Americans should be independent is inconsistent with the one that says they should honor their aging parents; the way in which these norms are reconciled is the way society functions, or operates, at that point.

The first of the three uses of *function* is not a major concern of this book, though it will be discussed briefly in the next few pages. The question of changing family tasks is a basic issue in this chapter and, like the structural questions, continues to be raised in subsequent chapters. Finally, the large mass of materials describing socialization, dating, husband-wife relations, and other aspects of the family simply depicts the way in which a particular family system—that of the United States—operates.

Universal Family Functions

One strand of theoretical, or explanatory, writing about the family generalizes the question of family functions in the following manner. There are certain goals that any society must accomplish in order to continue existing. It must reproduce individuals to replace the dying; it must protect its boundaries; it must motivate persons to take positions of leadership; it must solve the economic problem of physical survival; and so on (Aberle et al., 1950: 100–111). Among these necessary functions are some assumed by certain writers to be performed by the family in every society; these are called *universal family functions*, or functions that the family has always carried out everywhere. Davis speaks of reproduction, maintenance, placement, and socialization as universal family functions. Murdock says the universal functions are reproduction, socialization, economic cooperation, and sexual relations. Reiss claims there is but one universal function of the family: the "nurturant" socialization of the newborn. Other functions are often, but not always, performed by the family or kin group (Reiss, 1965: 443-453). A particular author's *definition* of the family is, of course, closely related to the functions he or she sees it as carrying out. Thus, a close link exists between the discussion in Chapter 3 of the universality of the nuclear family and the idea of universal family functions.

A distillation of a list of family functions devised by Goode yields three functions which can be viewed form the standpoint either of the family itself or of the family-in-society. First, there is the *reproductive* function, which is dependent upon age at marriage, fertility, and other factors. From society's perspective, this might be called the *replacement* function. That is, for a society to survive, new members must be produced to replace those who are dying off; this occurs within families. The second function is *status placement*, which means the determination of one's life chances within one's society. From the standpoint of society, this is the integrative or *maintenance* function. It simply means that family background has historically and cross-culturally been a major determinant of one's career achievement or status in society. Third, the family, as Reiss indicates, performs the *socialization* or child-rearing function. In the family, the individual learns what to do and what not to do in order to get along in society, in order to be consistent with its demands and expectations. Thus, from society's standpoint, this is the *social control* function: a result of the family's embodying and imparting the society's culture.

Goode rightly cautions the reader against assuming that the three functions he lists are universals in the sense of being constants (Goode, 1959: Chapter 7). Though the discussion of "universals" is valuable as a point for debate, Goode feels that such functions should be thought of as *variables*, with the family system of a given society meeting more or less of a specific need. For example, in some societies one's life chance are predicated almost entirely upon the family unit into which one is born. In other societies, such as that in the United States, the possibility of individual achievement means that the family might be better described as the base, or beginning point, defining certain limits upon status. A careful review of the literature might result in the conclusion that in the United States, about 50 percent of status placement is determined by family background. Or, the reader might conclude that in one society 90 percent of socialization occurs within the family and kin group, while in another society the figure is less than 50 percent. As Morgan says: "While we may argue that all families perform the socialization function the converse is not necessarily true, i.e., that all socialization is performed by families" (Morgan, 1975: 57). Once family functions are treated as variables, we may even go so far as to ask: what happens to the family if child-bearing and child-rearing occur elsewhere? Must we either say that the family no longer exists, or else re-define the unit where they take place as "family?" Treatments of the Swedish family show it leading in moving away from the legalized monogamous nuclear family; yet they do not show the anti-family sentiment sometimes expressed in the United States, nor dramatic internal changes in the family (Trost, 1980: 7–23; Popenoe, 1987: 18). Thus, the so-called universal functions may profitably be transformed into variables for the sake of historical and cross-cultural comparison.[7]

Farber goes even further in criticizing the notion of universal family functions. When you start by saying, "Here are the things which must be done for society to survive, and these are the things which the family does for its society," you are defining the goals of a society, as well as talking about tasks. In speaking of the family as doing certain things for the benefit of society or as furthering societal ends and integration, two value judgments must be made. First, we must ask whether the family is doing a good or a poor job of performing its functions in a given society, thereby drawing a judgment regarding its quality of performance. Also, we are likely to make the subtle judgment that equilibrium is better than change, that stability is better than alteration of society and culture (Farber, 1964: 23–28). Morgan states this point unequivocally: "any statement listing the functions of the family is a theoretical and ideological statement rather than a simple empirical statement" (Morgan, 1975: 20). So when you read in subsequent pages about the functions of the U.S. family, keep in mind that we are not describing how well a set of universal functions is being performed, but are merely noting the changing ways in which the family (and its members) operates (functions) internally and in relation to other institutions.

The Family and Its Changing Functions

Leaving aside the attempt to discover universal family functions, let us discuss how family functions have changed, and where we are today. In the 1930s, W. F. Ogburn described the family's loss of functions. Industrialization and urbanization had resulted in the transferral of one traditional family function after another to specialized institutional settings. The economic producing function had been transferred to the factory and office; the educational function had been moved to the schoolroom; the religious function had been left almost entirely to the church or synagogue; the recreation function had gone to the theater and stadium; the medical function had been transferred to the doctor's office and the hospital. In most cases, family members went to these places individually, not as a family unit. The result was that the family had been left to provide affection and understanding, but little else, for its members (Ogburn, 1933: chapter 13; see also Popenoe, 1988: 25).

Ogburn's main concern was with the traditional family functions, and his point was that activities that used to take place within the home or involve the whole family began to take place elsewhere and engage family segments. The problem with Ogburn's term "loss of family functions" is that in the hands of his misinterpreters it has come to mean that the family now has virtually nothing to do. The actual process, however, has been one in which activities that were performed in a simple or rudimentary fashion within the family (e.g., medical treatment) have expanded to the point where the home can no longer encompass them. The process has in fact been one of *expansion* and *removal* more than loss. Mitterauer and Sieder speak at some length to this issue:

> *In spite of these losses of function, which have affected its very core, the family has not surrendered all of its functions. Those that have been relinquished . . . were all calculated to ensure the survival of members of the group, to secure their existence and to counter the threats of nature. But . . . new activities developed that were not directly concerned with survival but rather enhanced the quality of life (1982: 83).*

The family may no longer be an economic producing unit, but its function as consumer has been heightened. And while the knowledge explosion and specialization have made it virtually impossible for a given family to encompass the educational needs of its offspring, the family still gives direction to its children's lives (positively or negatively). Vannoy-Hiller and Philliber state that one function is now primary: "while the economic, replacement, and socialization functions of the family have declined, the need for the family to provide emotional support to its members has increased" (Vannoy-Hiller and Philliber, 1989: 86). Quale states this combination of consuming/socializing/affection providing somewhat negatively: "The elementary conjugal family has been left with little more than the rearing of very young children, the management of income . . . and the relief of tensions through mutual supportiveness and expression of enduring affection and acceptance" (Quale, 1988: 203). And Sweet and Bumpass make a prediction regarding the family's role:

> *That the family is adaptive, and that family relationships continue to play a very important role in the lives of Americans, are incontrovertible. At the same time, it seems likely that the relative dominance of these relationships in competition with other adult roles is likely to continue to dwindle over the foreseeable future (Sweet and Bumpass, 1987: 401).*

So, according to these recent authors, the family plays an important but perhaps dwindling role as socializer and provider of affection, and is a major consumer of the goods of the market. And, as Collier et al. reminded us, U.S. families often do a poor job of providing unconditional affection.

The concept of the family's lost and remaining functions requires two more qualifications. First, we must not lose sight of the issues raised by the feminists earlier in this chapter. Socialization/affection/consumer: these functions seem to be performed primarily by women in the industrial capitalist family. Thus, a question to keep in mind is whether women playing a greater role in economic production (job-holding) is matched by men playing an increased role in the so-called family functions listed above? Or has women's greater economic op-portunity given them, for the most part, the chance to be both secondary eco-nomic provider and "family functionary?" This is another question that will arise over and over.

Second, some social analysts, especially during the years when industrial-ization and urbanization were being decried as resulting in social disorganiza-tion, expressed the fear (or the view) that the loss of traditional functions would mean the disintegration of the family as we know it. No longer the economic, educational, and religious center of society, the family has lost its reason for being. In rejoinder, the suggestion has been made that, concomitant with the specialization of society, the family has become a specialist in gratifying people's psychological needs — needs for understanding, affection, and happiness. But, it might be argued, what about the high rate of divorce? Does this not indicate that all is not well with the family? In answering these questions, first note that to say that the family, ideally, is a focus for primary relations is also to indicate where its problems will arise. The demand to gratify people's needs for love, companionship, and emotional release is a heavy burden for any social group to bear. This pressure is even greater since neolocality and decreased family size have reduced the numbers of persons sharing intense day-to-day relations. It should not, therefore, be surprising to find that those who do not achieve satis-factory relations within the family are likely to break ties and try again, espe-cially if the economy's need for families as producers does not necessitate keeping them together. The rate of divorce, in other words, may be viewed as either a problem or a solution to a problem, depending on one's perspective.

A further word about divorce is in order: Ogburn and others note that in a society in which the family is functionally central or is the prime economic pro-ducing and socializing unit, there is apt to be great concern for keeping the in-dividual family unit intact. Thus, in the nuclear embedded, functionally central family, sex is controlled (if possible), divorce is difficult to obtain, and mate se-lection is primarily in the hands of the adult generation. However, when func-tions are expanded out of the family unit, the cultural mechanisms for maintaining the boundaries of any given family unit are weakened. This weak-ening is part of the family's recent history.

Besides functionalism, several other theories have been utilized in recent analyses of the family, and we will briefly examine two of them: exchange the-ory and systems theory.

SECTION FIVE

EXCHANGE THEORY AND SYSTEMS THEORY

Exchange theory received its greatest impetus from the work of Thibaut and Kel-ley and George Homans (Thibaut and Kelley, 1959; Homans, 1961). Operating primarily within an economics framework, the theory assumes that individuals will seek relationships in which the outcomes are most favorable for them. Later, Nye, saying that he would like to call it "maximum profit" theory, listed the five most general propositions as follows:

1. Human beings seek rewards and avoid costs to maximize their Goodness of Outcomes (profits).
2. Costs being equal, individuals will choose the alternative which supplies or is expected to supply the most rewards.
3. Rewards being equal, individuals will choose the alternative which exacts the fewest costs.
4. Immediate outcomes being equal, individuals will choose those alternatives which promise better long-term outcomes.
5. Long-term outcomes being perceived as equal, individuals will choose alternatives providing better immediate outcomes (Nye, 1978; Nye, 1980).

Thus, rewards – costs = profit, and people want to maximize profit. Nor, however, does a human relationship occur in a vacuum; there are alternative relationships available, and the "comparison level of alternatives" is the method whereby the individual determines which of two relationships is more profitable (Thibaut and Kelley, 1959).

One variation on this theory is equity or reciprocity theory, which changes the focus from *individual* profit to *relational* equity or balance. Since each of the parties to a relationship is seeking to maximize profits, the result is ordinarily an equitable outcome. However, the equity approach often adds a further element: "Not only do I want to maximize my profits, I want to maximize yours." Critics of equity theory are likely to react as does Isabel Sawhill:

> *The people marching through the economist's household are an enviable group: they are motivated by love and caring and rarely by hate or fear. . . . Why is it that marriage sometimes leads to positive and sometimes to negative caring among family members (Sawhill, 1977: 121).*

Especially in its "maximum profit" version, exchange theory does not need to fall into Sawhill's "Pollyanna" trap; for, as Nye points out, its assumptions must include the "ability and willingness to *inflict costs* (Nye, 1978: 230). "If you hurt me, I will hurt you."

An area to which exchange theory has been applied for several years is that of family power. The resource theory of power says that the family member who provides the most resources will have the most power. I can, in other words, "exchange" a large income and high status for power in relation to my spouse. Warner et al. argue that resource theory can even be used cross-culturally. Wives have more power in nuclear families than in extended households, because they are more critical to the family's well-being, and because they are less easily replaced (Warner et al., 1986: 121–128). Likewise, couple members may bring different resources to a relationship and exchange them: attractiveness for status, for example. Such relational tradeoffs are involved in Elaine and

William Walster's equity treatment of love relationships. Equity principles, they feel "do seem to determine whom we select as a date or a mate in the first place; how we get along, day-to-day and thereafter; and how likely we are to stay together" (Walster and Walster, 1978: 149). Much of the development of a relationship, say the Walsters, is a result of the balance of attributes and qualities that two people bring to it.

Nye feels very strongly that exchange theory in its various forms is applicable to many areas of family life to which it has not yet been applied directly. And Gerald Mcdonald states that consideration of culturally prescribed norms, or structural exchanges, will expand exchange theory and make it more encompassing and comprehensive with regard to social reality (McDonald, 1981). This theory has been criticized by some because: (a) Exchanges may become very complicated, and even unconscious or irrelevant. (b) "Nonrational factors such as love, jealousy, self-esteem, personal needs . . . commitment, and investments become so important that most of the profit-oriented bargaining and consideration of alternatives gets lost in the shuffle" (Holman and Burr, 1980: 732). (c) A further criticism is that exchange theory is based on capitalist exchange for profit, and thus ignores both the unprofitable exchange and the feminist issue of oppression that results in behaving in such a way that your punishment is maximized instead of profit. (d) Finally, it seems inadequate to handle self-sacrifice, though the exchange theorist would say that feeling good is your reward. Despite these important cautions, this perspective will appear in our discussions of mate selection, marital power, and at a few other points.

Systems theory derives from traditions of biological systems, machine technology, and modern computer systems. Focusing on the activities of groups of people, this theory concerns itself with both individual needs and structures. Klein and Jurich state that "systems theory seems to have largely displaced an earlier holistic approach, structure-functionalism, in sociology as well as in the rest of family science" (Klein and Jurich, 1992). The *structure-functionalism* that it has replaced is the notion that structures are totally explained by what they do, and that there are universal family and other functions. Recently, Montgomery and Fewer have published *Family Systems and Beyond*, a new and comprehensive treatment of this perspective (Montgomery and Fewer, 1988).

There are open systems, whose boundaries are permeable, like Lasch's "penetrated" family described in Chapter 1, and there are closed family systems, like Zaretsky's and Parsons's separated, isolated units. Gardner argues that openness and closedness may even vary over the life cycle of the same family, in accordance with changes in the family's structure and dynamics. Whether it is open or closed, says Gardner, "depends, in large part, on the presence and/or age of children" (Gardner, 1990: 88).

Though systems approaches had been available already, it was in David Kantor and William Lehr's book *Inside the Family* that the terminology and propositions were developed on which to base an entire school of theorizing about the family (Kantor and Lehr, 1975). Based on many hours of family observation, the authors devised categories with which to analyze actual family behaviors. Among these categories are space, time, and energy. The dimensions of family *space* include bounding, linking, and centering. Bounding simply means the extent to which families are separate from or connected to the outside world. Overbounded families may lack the kinds of "reality checks" that are made possible by contact with nonfamily members. Underbounded families may be in danger of breakup in a society where marital stability is a function of member commitment. Privacy vis-à-vis the world is an issue in bounding. Likewise, linking refers to the distance and connection between family members. The issue of privacy *within* the family is one element of Kantor and Lehr's idea of linking. *Centering* means the way in which family members coordinate or do not coordinate their activities. Do they meet at a prescribed time for dinner, or does everyone get his or her own meal? How do they coordinate a trip to the grocery store, putting the car in the shop, a music lesson, and housecleaning? Again, families can be highly centered, uncentered, or (usually) somewhere in between.

Family *time*, to Kantor and Lehr, involves orienting, clocking, and synchronizing. *Orienting* means whether the family focuses primarily on the past (for example, an elderly couple), the present, or the future (such as a couple in graduate school). Montgomery and Fewer note three basic time orientations, with respect to feedback. The homeostatic family minimizes the effect of incoming information that challenges its culture, thereby holding onto the past. The balanced-growth family strikes a balance between change and continuity. And the "random" family system is unpredictable, always ready for change, and focuses on the future with little consideration of the past (Montgomery and Fewer, 1988: 156-157).

"Clocking" has to do with the sequence, frequency, and duration of family events. Broderick, in his text, notes some of the kinds of questions raised by the clocking dimension of Kantor and Lehr's analysis:

> *"Why are you never on time?" "Where did you learn to wolf down your food?" "Will you please settle down; you make me nervous with your pacing back and forth." "Once I don't mind, but to call your mother three times in one day is just too much"* (Broderick, 1984: 252).

A couple must decide how often, for how long, and when to make love. They must decide how much television to watch. In fact, much of family life involves clocking. The *synchronizing* dimension is the time equivalent to the centering of space. If I am to pick you up downtown this afternoon we must coordinate not only the spatial dimension—Park and Broadway—but the time dimension—4:45 p.m.

The dimensions of family *energy* are fueling, investing, and mobilizing. The first two concern how we get and how to spend energy, with concern for some return of profit on the investment, while the third refers to the way we balance our energy expenditures in terms of our various commitments and priorities. At this point, systems analysis comes very close to exchange. In a relationship, for example, one may feel that one is investing much and getting little in return (it is nonequitable). Recreation may in some families be a matter of fueling; that is, as in the Puritan work ethic, you "re-create" in order to work. Or recreation may be an investment of energy, as the family expends in a pleasurable fashion the energy stored up from other sources.

Systems theory comes closest to the language of computer analysis when it is applied to family communication. There are communication linkages that involve feedback, and feedback maintains family homeostasis or order, as the family members react to each other's communication (see Montgomery and Fewer, 1988: 156f). Family transactions and communication are more amenable to systems analysis, and in the hands of Kantor and Lehr, Broderick, and others, this theoretical framework is now being applied to many aspects of internal family life. And through concern with openness and boundaries it can be utilized for dealing with at least some aspects of the relation between the family and other systems (institutions) in society as well. There is, of course, the danger of the twin conservative bias in systems theory: (a) it may treat the typical system as normal, and may overlook the fact that the atypical may be healthy and "functioning" (see deChesney, 1986: 293–300), and (b) it has a difficult time recognizing that families are not a single system, but are "his" and "her" systems, often functioning by his rules and to his advantage. When we employ a systems framework in dealing with marital communication, we must be on guard against these dangers.

In Section Two we introduced feminist theory, and in sections Four and Five we have discussed functional, exchange, and systems theories. Feminism reminds us that even the language of function/exchange/system is ideology-laden, presenting a picture of consensus, when reality may be oppression or inequality and struggle. In fact, our own inclination toward feminist principles will cause us to use its arguments throughout much of the book. However, as noted above, the other three theories will be useful from time to time. In addition, in Chapters 7 through 14 we will employ a life course framework, taking the individual from birth through old age. In closing this chapter we will add a postscript on inconsistency and varieties.

SECTION SIX

POSTSCRIPT

Systems theory can easily lead us into a false sense of family integration and functioning. However, many of us know from experience that there are *inconsistent aspects and fragmentary changes* in families. That is, they are not, by any means, entirely coherent. Our brief description of the family in recent history, in Chapter 4, shows that various aspects of the U.S. family system have not changed at the same rate of speed; nor, as Rothman pointed out, are they necessarily consistent with one another at a given point in time; nor are they well integrated into the larger society (Rothman, 1973: 189). The basis for the formation and persistence of family units today is love; yet, as Collier et al. note, the family is also where violence is most tolerated. As ties of economic dependence have become weaker, family relationships have become de-institutionalized, says Popenoe (1988: 809). In other words, we value individual self-sufficiency and family units, but as the former becomes stronger, the latter become weaker. Perhaps the greatest point of conflict in U.S. society is between patriarchy and women's liberation, with important societal leaders and writers on each side of this struggle. Also, the individualistic value of independence and achievement and the familial value of honoring one's parents are at odds, especially when the parents reach old age. Husband-wife roles overlap with, but are not identical to, the roles of men and women. Thus, societal and family expectations for the genders may be out of sync.

Finally, a contradiction between the family and legal system is found in the fact that married couples pay more in federal income taxes than two single workers earning the same amount, and the more equal the couple-members' paychecks, the greater the difference in tax payments. And this is despite our legal system's supposed support for monogamy and the nuclear family. (On this point, see Feature 5.2.) It is not necessary to enumerate all the areas of contradiction and stress at this point, but look for such discrepancies in the remainder of the book. And we will return to inconsistencies in Chapter 19.

A corollary of the realities of inconsistency and stress is that there are in fact *subcultural varieties* within the contemporary United States. Society is not based on the kind of consensual model that says that the middle-class style of life is pervasive in the sense that all social change is in that direction since all people strive to be middle-class. Rather, the upper middle-class style is *dominant*

Feature 5.2   THE "MARRIAGE TAX"

The state of Indiana soon may put its stamp of approval on the growing practice among working class couples to split at year's end to try to avoid the "marriage tax" built into the federal tax code.

Since 1969, married couples have complained—to no avail—that they pay more in federal income taxes than two single workers earning the same amount. The more equal the two paychecks, the heavier the tax.

So an increasing number of working husbands and wives are divorcing at the end of the year and filing federal income tax returns as single people. Sometimes they quickly remarry, often they just continue to live together.

This week, a bill passed the Indiana House and went to the Senate that offers the hope—however faint—that Hoosier couples might evade the marriage tax while also avoiding divorce.

The proposed answer is a one-day separation. . . .

Under the proposed law, couples could get the quickie separations by merely going to the nearest trial-level court and paying a $10 fee. No lawyer would be required. . . .

"Indiana Tries to Beat IRS 'Marriage Tax,'" *The Capital Times*, 16 March, 1979, p. 26.

in the sense that upper middle class people are most able to enact their norms into law and to disseminate their views on what is right, proper, and expected behavior—whether in the family or elsewhere. This dominance is not even necessarily a numerical *pre*dominance, but is due to the key positions of the upper middle class in government, education, and mass communications. However, there are subcultural varieties with their own ideals and expectations; as Rosenfeld, Freedman, and Stacey pointed out, the influence of cultural ideals is not necessarily unidirectional. History and diversity must, in short, be taken seriously. A part of this seriousness involves consideration of the inconsistencies alluded to above; another part involves the consideration of divergent principles. Do ethnic, racial, religious, and socioeconomic categories signify major cultural and social cleavages, or only minor differences? The concern of Chapter 6 will be to outline briefly the key varieties of cultural principles found in the United States and to indicate where their problems lie and in what areas changes are taking place.

Family Subcultures and Subsocieties in the United States

CHAPTER 6

In this chapter we describe middle-, working-, and lower-class models of family behavior. Ethnic and racial subcultures are then introduced and the key problems facing them are noted. For the European ethnic groups, the problem has been to keep cultural heritage alive in a society that tends to assimilate its parts. For Hispanics, the problem has involved both discrimination and maintenance of rituals. We will focus on issues of "machismo" and rituals among Chicanos, or Mexican-Americans. For blacks, or African-Americans, the problems have been inability to achieve economic equality and inability to be accepted into the dominant society. While subcultures are introduced in this chapter, they will appear throughout the book.

The United States is a society characterized by Western, urban, industrial culture. Within that society certain familial attitudes and practices were, until recently, so common as to be considered virtually cultural universals. Among these were monogamy, legal marriage, legal dissolution of marriage prior to remarriage, joint residence of spouses and their dependent children, and responsibility of parents for the care and rearing of their children. Legal and social sanctions of various sorts still tend to restrict deviation from such practices, but gradually they have become less universal both as norms and behavior. A policy issue is still whether these and other dominant culture forms should be legally supported so as to restrict variation.

There is, however, an order of variation that, as Ruth Cavan puts it, "is subordinate to the basic culture and gives a quasi-organization to aggregates of people who accept the basic culture but are distinctive in the ways in which they implement it, or in less fundamental phases of culture" (Cavan, 1964: 536). Thus, within the basic culture, there may be great variation in the acceptance or rejection of birth control, husband-wife role relationships, the socialization of children, the importance of kin, and other aspects of family life. These variations tend to divide the society into subcategories of persons whose intensity of interaction with one another is greater than it is with those whose culture differs substantially. Nevertheless, the congruence between subcultures (particular configurations of attitudes and behaviors) and subsocieties (networks of interacting persons) is not perfect. "The subcultural system of the United States," says Cavan,

> is a composite of social classes and of ethnic-religious and racial groups. They are combined into a vertical hierarchy according to general principles of relative status and along a horizontal spacing according to the degree of mutual acceptability. When groups are unacceptable to each other, they tend to form parallel social-class systems (1964: 541).

This "horizontal spacing" is, in fact, the division of society into subsocieties, whose cultures may in some instances be virtually identical. On the other hand, persons within a society may be characterized by great cultural diversity.

SECTION ONE

MIDDLE-CLASS, WORKING-CLASS, AND LOWER-CLASS FAMILY MODELS

Much has been said already about the middle-class family in the United States. The changes between colonial days and the present are, for the most part, comparisons of the colonial family with the modern, middle-class type. While this approach is valid due to the dominance of middle-class forms today, historically it is only partially correct. The reason is that the modern urban middle-class, working-class, and lower-class family systems can all be traced back to colonial days, with certain similarities and certain divergencies. Thus, beginning with the middle-class model, we shall attempt to clarify the historical processes and connections.

During colonial days, the vast majority of Anglo-American families lived at or near the subsistence level. They were agricultural, following the cultural patterns described in Chapter 4. With the industrial revolution began a whole complex of developments that eventuated in the formation of the urban middle, working, and lower classes, the first becoming dominant. The move from agriculture and the farm to industry and the cities was spearheaded by a small number of creative Anglo-American Protestants who embodied the individualism-work-success motif idealized, but not ordinarily realized, by the eighteenth-century colonists. Along with the industrialists, large numbers of people came to the city to work in the factories. However, the nineteenth and twentieth centuries did not belong simply to the wealthy industrialists and their workers; this was also the period of the emergence of the middle class. Beginning as a small number of independent businessmen, the middle class grew with the differentiation and expansion of government, education, and legal and medical services, and with the vast increase in commercial and office personnel in the industrial complex. These persons—professionals, managers, salesmen, and clerks—are occupationally typical of that category known as the middle class. Economically, these are persons who, along with their families, have risen above the subsistence level, enabling them to turn their attention to self-respect, experience and personality needs, and child development. It was the women within this group of predominantly white Anglo-American Protestants urbanites who found the time and the rationale for the nineteenth-century women's rights movements. This push for gender equality has continued to have substantial impact upon relationships within the family as well as outside it.

What then, are the basic aspects of the *middle-class family style* as it developed during the nineteenth and early twentieth centuries? The first aspect is that economic and work values are central, including, if need be, residential mobility in pursuit of opportunity. Corporate executives are the extreme example of such values, with the emphasis on success being, in its effect on family life, in some ways comparable to the effects of job insecurity on the working class (Voydanoff, 1980: 490). Such values are somewhat more typical of professional and managerial families (often referred to as the upper middle class) than of sales and clerical families but are often used to characterize the entire middle class. Secondly, husband-wife relations are predicated on happiness, communication, and mutual gratification. Even in the sexual sphere, in which formerly only the husband sought pleasure, the stress on equality and mutual needs has resulted in a concern for mutual satisfaction. Love is expected to be fundamental, not only to the selection of one's mate, but to the household as well. With emphasis both on success and on marital happiness, a point of inconsistency appears. Anne Locksley reports that more educated people have felt greater inadequacy and unhappiness in their marriages in the past, but are happier at present, than the less educated. This indicates the greater value placed by the middle classes on verbalization and conflict resolution (Locksley, 1982: 437; see also Krokoff et al., 1988: 216-217). However, in its extreme form, this success-happiness syndrome among executives may have a negative effect upon marriage. Patricia Voydanoff notes that:

> *personal traits needed for a happy family life are not necessarily compatible with those needed to become a successful executive. . . . The husband and wife may grow apart psychologically and develop different interests as the husband grows in his career (1980: 491).*

Of course, writing a decade later, Voydanoff might have said "the husband and wife grow apart psychologically and develop different interests" as both grow in their careers. From the feminist perspective, we might describe middle-class gender relations as subtle instead of overt patriarchy. This means the male still has greater opportunities in society and, except in a small number of "role sharing" relationships (see Chapter 12), more influence in the home.

The third aspect of middle-class family style is that socialization of children tries to emphasize sheltering during their younger days. Though the media and entertainments make it increasingly difficult, the effort is made to insulate children from the adult world's problems. In addition, children are taught that they must get along with other people and that they should learn to do things for themselves. They are expected to internalize the value of deferred gratification, or putting off immediate goals and pleasures for the sake of greater goals in the future, for example, postponing marriage for the sake of a college education. Getting along, initiative, independence, deferred gratification—these are, after all, the values that middle-class parents believe have gotten them where they are.

This middle-class configuration is oriented toward success and respectability as defined by the official societal values. The intensity of emotional ties among family members is great, and punishment may center there. Children learn to identify with their parents more as general symbols of success than in terms of the specific occupational or other roles they play. And a recent middle-class development has been off-spring either staying home longer, or returning home for varying periods of time after reaching adulthood. Martha Riche explains this as follows: young adults from affluent homes take longer to leave because it will take them longer to replicate their parents' living standards (Riche, 1987: 42). Middle-class families differ at many points from the typical colonial farm family; three keys to this divergence are the fact that the husband's or both parents' economic role is "white collar," or nonmanual, that the role is played outside the home, and that the family's focus of attention is no longer subsistence or survival. The first point of divergence between middle-class and colonial families, that is, nonmanual versus manual work, also distinguishes the middle class from the urban working and lower classes. During the nineteenth century, large numbers of unneeded farm laborers moved into the cities in quest of work. Some found it in the growing industries, as foremen, skilled craftsmen, and assembly-line workers. Such members of the urban working class are likely to believe that the middle class does not do "real" work and to value physical rather than intellectual modes of expression. Because occupational advancement is limited, they tend to redefine the success goals of U.S. society in achievable terms. Owning their own home, an automobile, and other possessions—especially possessions related to leisure pursuits—and education for their children are important to the working class.

The *working-class family model* is the most direct descendant of the colonial type at several points, but the change from rural to urban has caused substantial alterations: (a) Segregation of roles between husbands and wives is quite similar in the modern working-class and colonial families (Smith and Fisher, 1982: 77–88). Sex is still often seen as the husband's pleasure and the wife's duty. The husband expects to take little hand in household tasks and child-rearing, since these are "women's work." (b) A second point of similarity between the colonial family and that of the modern, urban working class is in socialization. The primary concern of the parents is to teach their children order, obedience, honesty, respect for adults, and limits; within this framework, the children are given considerable freedom. This freedom is not the kind of supervised independence training that characterizes the middle class, but is a freedom from adult supervision for periods of time.

Changes or differences between colonial and modern working-class families include the following: (c) The husband, in both cases, perceives himself as patriarch, or as dominant, having delegated household and child-rearing responsibilities to the wife. However, when his economic provision for his family is somewhat limited and his economic role is played outside the home, the husband finds himself less able to assert consistent and *acceptable* authority within the home. In fact, says Stacey, "the male family wage was a late and ephemeral achievement of only the most fortunate sections of the modern industrial working class. Most working-class men never secured its patriarchal domestic privileges" (Stacey, 1990: 254). Thus, the husband's actual status in the home is likely to be lower in the urban working-class family than it was in the colonial farm family. That status, however, depends on traits of character as well as economic well-being, so that our generalization accounts only partially for the lower status of working-class husbands. (d) Another aspect of the economic picture concerns women's employment. Studies of working-class women conducted since 1950 "show not only high levels of actual employment but considerable interest in working for pay among women who are home full time" (Gerstel and Gross, 1987: 291). What this means is that many working-class women are working not out of necessity, but by choice. Stacey, however, notes the effect of what she calls "post-industrial structuring" on the employment of formerly working-class women:

> *Driven by decline in real family income, by desires for social achievement and independence, and by an awareness that committed male breadwinners are in scarce supply, such women have flocked to expanding jobs in service, clerical, and new industrial occupations (Stacey, 1990: 257).*

However, these jobs have often been low paying and vulnerable. (e) Much urban manual work does not provide those who do it with a sense of inherent worth, although the differences between their attitudes and those of the farmer tilling the soil have probably been overdrawn. It seems that the shorter work week makes it possible for members of the urban working class to pursue leisure activities with the money provided by stable employment. This working-class notion might be expressed simply as "first we work and then we live." Kin and friend groups, neighbors, and informal work and recreational groups provide much of the social interaction that gives meaning to their lives (Allen, 1989: 33). This also has some similarity to the colonial pattern, though the specific leisure activities have changed.

Deferred gratification and success striving are more characteristic of the middle-class family than of the working-class family, though the major difference here is that in the middle class the striving is by the parents themselves, while in the working class it is often expressed by the hope that the children will "get somewhere."

The *lower class* is felt by some observers to be simply the lower reaches of the working class, since, like the working class, its occupations are manual. What distinguishes the lower class is minimal education, few skills to "sell" in the economic market, and a living standard at the poverty level. The members of the lower class are individuals who have never really made it in the industrial world, though they live in an urban, rather than a rural, environment. Surrounded by affluence, they perceive the cards as stacked against them in their struggle for survival. Economic marginality is at the heart of their lifestyle, which often includes the following characteristics: (a) Lower-class individuals have low but often realistic economic and family aspirations, and thus may strive for immediate gratification. Not only do they see their occupational opportunities as limited, they also see their prospects for marriage as less promising than others (Farber, 1990: 61-62). (b) Their nuclear families include various non-normative characteristics, such as teenage births, early marriage, residential movement, and especially non-marriage or marital breakup (Popenoe, 1988: 288). Of course, these characteristics are not necessarily indications of instability. In colonial times the legal system, social sanctions, and the family unit's functions often held economically marginal families together, although some separated. Perhaps of note today is the number of poor families that do stay together despite weak cultural supports. (c) Their child-rearing tends to vary from great love and value to harsh and erratic, with the latter stemming from either lack of time, energy, or money to spend on children, or else from the frustrations and tensions of the parents' lives. (d) Welfare is an important issue for the poor and for the society in general. Most poor Americans are white, and only about one-third of the poor receive public assistance of any kind. However, marital breakup and assistance are related, with the single female household head most likely to receive assistance (O'Hare, 1986: 22–25; Rank, 1987: 15–20). And, as Feature 6.1 shows, the ranks of the poor are anything but stable. (e) The urban poor express higher levels of perceived health and happiness than the rural poor, when variables of sex, age, race, etc., are controlled. The lowest level of happiness is expressed by single rural men without children (Amato and Zuo, 1992: 229–240). This is not unrelated to the colonial farm/urban poor comparisons we have tried to make.

In many of its characteristics the lower class is unquestionably a logical extension of the working class. Both working- and lower-class families differ from the middle class in that, when they are residentially mobile, they tend to move "within the same area to find better housing; long-range moves to new cities are relatively rare" (Woolsey, 1977: 142). The working-class husband may have some trouble exerting authority; the lower-class husband is apt to have even more trouble. Working-class breadwinners may not find great satisfaction in their work, but this is more likely to be true of the unskilled lower-class workers than of the skilled working-class crafts people. It may, in fact, be that the lower class simply consists of those who, due to multiple problems and minimal preparation, can't and don't make it rather than of those who lack aspirations. Be that as it may, the urban middle, working, and lower classes are sufficiently different to be distinguishable as modal types, or as points on the socio-economic status continuum.

Here, then, are three models of family life today. There is a fourth: the small numbers of extremely wealthy, upper-class families. These families still have a considerable stake in their children making the "right" marriages so that their advantage may be perpetuated. Suzanne Keller describes well the "in-grown" nature of upper-class life. Such families, she says,

---

Feature 6.1 **THE CHANGING POOR**

In *Years of Poverty, Years of Plenty*, (ISR Publication, 1984) Greg Duncan and coauthors Richard Coe and Martha Hill challenge many current assumptions about poor people—that they are chronically poor, that most live in large cities, and that, for many, welfare destroys the incentive to improve their status.

Duncan paints a more variable picture of the poor. Each year many faces are new, and many disappear. The number of people below the poverty line may remain about the same, but there is tremendous annual turnover in the ranks.

Duncan bases his view on ISR's monumental Panel Study of Income Dynamics, which for sixteen years has tracked the fortunes of a representative group of five thousand American families. He finds that a high percentage of the people who comprise the yearly Census Bureau poverty statistics are not consistently poor. Rather, their financial fortunes fall and rise, pushing them into and out of poverty. Divorce, remarriage, and other changes in the family unit . . . account for much of the change in economic status.

Ann Reuter, "Myths of Poverty," *The Research News*, Ann Arbor: Institute for Social Research, The University of Michigan, July-September, 1984, p. 18.

must reverse the general goal of modern parenting, which is to prepare children to leave the nest so as to make their way in the world as independent, self-reliant, and success-ful individuals. By contrast, upper-class families must stress quite opposite virtues and do all they can to keep their children bound to the family, ready to deny themselves for the collective welfare and to subordinate personal desires to family duties. . . . In the fortune-building generation there is generally a single-minded focus on the primary accumulation of needed resources, later followed by the assiduous inculcation of desired values and goals into several generations of young (Keller, 1991: 159).

Most still go to prestigious Eastern prep schools and universities, and sons still go into their father's businesses or professions. Also, kin ties tend to be stronger than in the middle class, resembling those of the lower strata, but for different reasons. As Rosenfeld's study indicated in Chapter 2, the upper strata perpetu-ate close kin ties for the sake of inheritance and power, the lower classes for the sake of survival. Paul Blumberg and P. W. Paul make the following comment about upper-class exclusiveness:

Although tremendous forces have shaken American society in the past generation, the upper class has maintained itself remarkably intact, and, having done so, it is perhaps the most untouched group in American life. It is significant, for example, that despite the civil rights tidal wave which engulfed the country in the 1960s, it is the upper-class territory of school, neighborhood, club, and blue book which remains the most racially segregated turf in America (Blumberg and Paul, 1975: 75; see also Schuby, 1975: 243–255).

Of the four models of family life today, one stresses personality, respectabil-ity, success, and quasi-equality; another stresses role segregation, order and freedom, and the social network; the third stresses survival; the last one, per-petuation and societal domination. But how are such cultural themes or config-urations related to specific societal categories within the U.S. population? We have already indicated the relationship between the various social class styles of family life. But what of the ethnic and racial divisions of U.S. society?

SECTION TWO

THE ETHNIC SUBCULTURE AND SUBSOCIETY

European Ethnics

Throughout the previous discussion, the terms *subculture* and *subsociety* have been employed, and the terms *ethnic group* and *minority* have been avoided. Yet, because the latter terms are descriptive of many elements in American society, some un-derstanding of them is essential. Useful definitions can be found in Tamotsu Shibutani and Kian Kwan's book *Ethnic Stratification*, in which *minority* groups are described as the "underprivileged in a system of ethnic stratification," and as

"people of low standing—people who receive unequal treatment and who therefore come to regard themselves as objects of discrimination" (Shibutani and
Kwan, 1965: 35). An *ethnic* group, say the authors, "consists of those who conceive of themselves as being alike by virtue of their common ancestry, real or fic-
titious, and who are so regarded by others" (Shibutani and Kwan, 1965: 47).
Thus, a minority may or may not be an ethnic group, depending upon whether or
not there is a sense of ancestral identity, and an ethnic group may or may not be
a minority, depending upon whether or not it is discriminated against in society.

Historically, the groups in America that have been most often defined as
ethnic are the non-Protestant European immigrants—including Irish, Polish,
and Italian Catholics and Jewish people—though the latter are hard to distinguish analytically from a religious subculture. According to most observers, the
history of such groups in America is that of a movement from ethnic minority
status to ethnic group to quasi-ethnic group. Speaking of their patriarchal family system, for example, Cavan asserts that "this type of family organization has
faded under the strain of urban-industrial life and the acculturation of immigrants and their children into the prevailing patterns of Anglo-American culture" (Cavan, 1964: 549).

But what is "this type of family organization"? What is the historical ethnic
model Cavan sees as having faded? Oscar Handlin, drawing especially upon
data on the Irish in the nineteenth century, has posited a characterization somewhat as follows. Their premigration homes were primarily peasant villages,
where they had patrilineal, patriarchal, extended families, with the agricultural
economy embedded in the nuclear unit. In the New World, they confronted
both social and economic stresses. The social stresses included an urban life involving density, poor sanitation, disorganized ghettos, and the impingement of
other religions, and the results were mental illness, disease, and criminality.
The economic stresses included a lack of skills, low wages or unemployment,
women and child labor, a longing for the soil, and a lack of social or geographic
mobility. The effects of these stressor conditions on the family, according to
Handlin, were the weakening or breakdown of paternal authority, the isolation
of the nuclear family from the lineage and extended family, family instability
and breakup, and eventual assimilation by the dominant society (Handlin,
1941; Handlin, 1951).

When the data of other writers, such as Zane Miller, Moses Rischin,
Rudolph Vecoli, and Virginia McLaughlin, are compared with Handlin's model,
it becomes clear that there were variations from ethnic group to ethnic group,
from city to city, and from region to region. The Germans, Jews, and Irish in
Cincinnati, described by Miller, were not victims of ghetto life or of the impingement of other religions. These groups were able to effect a greater amount
of upward mobility than that depicted by Handlin, and were able to avoid the
kind of assimilation posited by Cavan and Handlin (Miller, 1968).

Laurence Glasco presents an interesting comparison of Irish, German, and
native-born whites in Buffalo, New York, in 1855. He finds that the family life
cycles of the three groups were quite similar, as was home ownership. There
were, however, expectable differences in their occupations. Those who were

native-born were primarily white-collar workers and entrepreneurs, while the immigrants were mostly unskilled laborers, with the exception of some German craftsmen in the construction industry. The most intriguing aspect of Glasco's study, however, is that teenage immigrant girls very often lived and worked for several years in the homes of native-born families. Their brothers, on the other hand, remained at home and then either boarded with families of the same nationality or married and settled in ethnically homogeneous neighborhoods. The implications of this sex difference for acculturation are enormous, says Glasco, because in "the second generation it would be [the girls] who taught and translated such behavior to their children" (Glasco, 1975: 363).

Myfanwy Morgan and Hilda Golden's study of Irish and Canadian immigrants to Holyoke, Massachusetts, in 1880 makes an important point regarding household size. The fact that it was, on the average, one person larger than for the native born (5.5 to 4.5) is not due to the presence of extended kin, but rather to higher fertility. In fact, 78 percent of the immigrant households in Holyoke were nuclear families (Morgan and Golden, 1979: 59-68).

An interesting recent article by Vosburgh and Juliani studies Irish and Italian Catholic intermarriages in the U.S. They find differences in attitudes toward women's roles, divorce, and ideal family size—differences that do not disappear when socioeconomic status is controlled. Thus, intermarriage does not seem to end "ethnicity"; rather it results in negotiation and/or disruption (Vosburgh and Juliani, 1990: 269–286). Even among ethnic Catholics, assimilation is only up to a point.

Rischin, writing about the New York Jews during the period 1870–1914, notes first of all that, as traders, they had a tradition of urban residence. In coming to New York City, they found no problem with religious pluralism—or the impingement of other religions—and, given their urban tradition, they had low rates of disease and criminality. Furthermore, they did not lack the skills necessary to compete in an urban environment, and although they were assimilated economically, they were able to remain separate socially (Rischin, 1963). Corroborating this depiction from the nineteenth century, Cherlin and Carin Celebuski report on general surveys done in the 1970s. They find that the differences between Jewish and non-Jewish families are more modest than some popular writing suggests. However, with respect to child-rearing, Jews do seem to follow a strategy particularly well suited to enhancing their children's achievement (Cherlin and Celebuski, 1983: 903–910).

Returning to the historical portrait, E. E. LeMasters adds that one mechanism for survival and, we might add, success among both Jews and Italians in the city was

> *a process of doubling up—new arrivals moved in with relatives already established; mothers held outside jobs; older brothers and sisters helped younger children to get a start. This system of mutual aid seems to be extremely functional for low-income families. Resources are shared until each family can care for its own (LeMasters, 1974: 104).*

Thus, the family did not necessarily become either internally fragmented or isolated from its extended network of kin and friends. Herman Lantz and Mary

O'Hara, in studying documents and letters left by Jewish settlers in the eighteenth century, note that they might have assimilated completely to the dominant culture and society, but that they chose not to. The authors hypothesize that instead of complete assimilation the "Jews tried to retain those components of their heritage, especially the institution of the family, that might provide maximum security in periods of crisis whenever they arose (Lantz and O'Hara, 1977: 255–156). The Italians, as described by Vecoli and McLaughlin, were, like the Jews, not peasant farmers but came from the smaller cities of Italy. While the family was subjected to economic stresses, these did not result in the undermining of the father's authority or in the breakdown of the family or its kin ties. As McLaughlin puts it:

> *Although the Italian family had its share of poverty and unemployment, it did not develop a characteristic frequently associated today with the lower-class life—a female-headed family system. In fact, there is little evidence of family disorganization among Buffalo's Italians (McLaughlin, 1973: 125).*

Notice the not-so-subtle use of patriarchal language by McLaughlin and others: "undermining the father's authority" + "female-headed family" = "family disorganization." Their point is that patriarchy was able, in an attenuated fashion, to survive lower-class life. In their recent article on Italian American families, Squier and Quadagno note that for most of the first two generations after immigration there was quasi-patriarchy in the family, with the mother playing a strong social and emotional leadership role (Squier and Quadagno, 1988: 124). Other aspects of U.S. Italian family life are that Italian parents use swift, physical punishment with their children, while emphasizing love and affection with them (Johnson, 1978: 34–41). In addition, Johnson finds, even today, a strong tie with aging parents, to the point of including them in activities and households.

Squier and Quadagno report two writers who have disagreed on Italian American assimilation: Tricarico notes a rejection of Italian culture and ethnicity by the first generation immigrants, with a return to certain elements by third- and fourth-generation Italian Americans, while Roche finds a drop in ethnic characteristics with each succeeding generation (Squier and Quadagno, 1988: 133). This disagreement brings us to Will Herberg's view of ethnic assimilation.

Herberg, in his book *Protestant-Catholic-Jew*, describes a complex and incomplete process of assimilation through which Catholic and Jewish immigrants have passed—a process that differs somewhat from that described by both Tricarico and Roche. The first generation, which arrived after 1840, attempted to hold on to the ways of their homeland and became an enclave within the new society. Language, family forms, and belief systems were retained, and awareness of differences was intensified by the tendency of these groups to cluster together residentially, especially in the growing urban centers along the East Coast. The result was considerable persecution of and discrimination against these groups by the Anglo-American Protestants among whom they settled.

As the members of the second generation moved out into the school system and the peer culture, the conflict of old and new was no longer only intergroup, but became intergenerational and intrafamilial as well. "Frequently, though not always, the man of the second generation attempted to resolve his dilemma by forsaking the ethnic group in which he found himself" (Herberg, 1960: 28). The struggle for incorporation into the American social, economic, and political systems was long and hard, but it was successful because of the second generation's ability to assume the dominant cultural forms and language, and because of the willingness of its members to aid one another educationally and otherwise. Mutual aid and a mutual rejection of many key aspects of the old culture occurred simultaneously.

Herberg notes that a further change occurred after 1920. At this point the stream of immigrants ceased, and the third generation appeared. This generation

> *became American in a sense that had been, by and large, impossible for the immigrants and their children. That problem, at least, was solved; but its solution paradoxically rendered more acute the perennial problem of "belonging" and self-identification.*

Herberg then goes on to describe how this problem was resolved:

> *They wished to belong to a group. But what group could they belong to? The old-line ethnic group, with its foreign language and culture, was not for them; they were Americans. But the old family religion, the old ethnic religion, could serve where language and culture could not.*

With modifications, this religion could be made to serve the American value system and still be used for identification, confirming

> *the tie that bound them to their forebears, whom they now no longer had any reason to reject, whom indeed, for the sake of a "heritage," they now wanted to "remember" (Herberg, 1960: 30–31).*

In the Jewish community today you will find elements of both familism and individualism. As Brodbar-Nemzer says: U.S. "Jews continue to commit themselves to the institution of the family, both on behavioral and social-psychological levels" (Brodbar-Nemzer, 1988: 82). This is theoretically interesting because U.S. Jews are socio-economically and geographically located where changes in (weakening of) families most often occur (Goldscheider, 1986). I was once told by several Jewish scholars that the reason for Jewish familism despite success today is not unique family characteristics, but a long history of persecutions, making strong families rational, or "functional" for survival.

As far as family is concerned, the problem for third and subsequent generations of European ethnics—both Catholics and Jews—has been two-fold. On the one hand, many of the ritual practices by which the ethnic-religious ties had been reaffirmed have been emptied of their former significance and lack a meaningful content. On the other hand, the dominant value system continues to beat away at the remaining features of the old system, for example, birth control among Catholics. A lingering sense of ethnic solidarity and identity remains, but there are few points—with the exception of continuing strong kin ties—at which the family culture of these ethnic groups does not resemble that of either the middle-class or lower-class model described above. What, then, is the central problem for these groups at the present time? They have desired economic and some cultural assimilation—and have found it possible. But therein, as Lantz and O'Hara point out, lies the dilemma. With vast opportunities for economic, political, and social freedom may come eventual assimilation into American culture and loss of identity. This dilemma has never been completely resolved (Lantz and O'Hare, 1977: 255–260). The key problem of the ethnic subcultures has been *to keep alive any of their ethnic subcultural characteristics in a society in which they have achieved success and integration.*

Hispanics in the U.S.

Having dealt with the issue of assimilation among the Jewish and Catholic immigrants from Europe, let us now consider an increasingly important category of religio-ethnics: Hispanic Americans. In keeping with their growing numbers in the United States the literature on Chicanos (Mexican-Americans), Puerto Ricans, and other Hispanics is growing rapidly. The primary focus of this section will be "la familia Chicana," or Mexican families. In terms of households, the nuclear family is the norm. However, whether in New Mexico, California, or northern U.S. cities, this household is embedded in an extended kin group. While poorer Chicanos may live in extended households, the norm is to live separate but close, if possible (on households, see Sena-Rivera, 1979; Katsche, 1983; Tienda and Angel, 1982). Rosina Becerra notes that "Mexican-American families are significantly larger than all other ethnic or racial families. The mean number of persons in Mexican American families is 4.15, compared with 3.88 persons in all Hispanic families and 3.23 persons in all U.S. families" (Becerra, 1988: 151).

Besides family size, what makes the situation of Chicanos different from other Hispanics is their proximity to their homeland and to first generation immigrants. This reinforces traditional ways and slows acculturation (Becerra, 1988: 146). The key issues in literature on Chicano families are: (1) gender roles; (2) *machismo*, or stereotypic maleness; and (3) family rituals.[1] The first two may be discussed together. Machismo is often seen as pathological and as breeding violence. However, Alfredo Mirande and others assert that it is also associated with honor, respect, and stability. This relates to gender roles as follows:

> *Complementing the concept of male dominance is the concept of sex and age subordination, which holds that females are subordinate to males and the young to the old. In this schema, females are viewed as submissive, naive, and somewhat childlike. Elders are viewed as wise, knowledgeable, and deserving of respect (Becerra, 1988: 149; see also Jaramillo and Zapata, 1987: 727–735).*

Whether one emphasizes honor/respect/stability or power and violence, the Mexican-American (and Hispanic) tradition is one of overt patriarchy. From the chapter thus far, it would not seem an overstatement to say that patriarchal culture is stronger among Hispanics than among other U.S. ethnics.

This picture of gender roles may be inadequate for Mexican-Americans today. According to Mirande, patriarchy simply does not describe Chicano families:

> Recent literature suggests that the dominant pattern of decision-making in the Chicano family is not male-dominated and authoritarian, as is commonly assumed, but egalitarian. Husband and wife share not only in decisions but in household tasks and childcare. Sharp sex role segregation appears to be the exception rather than the rule among Chicano couples (Mirande, 1979: 478).

A most instructive addition to the discussion of gender roles comes from an article by Richard Harris, where he notes younger Chicano couples are more like Anglos than are those of the older generation, who cling to strong familism and gender distinctions (Harris, 1980: 173–193). It is, therefore, possible that a portion of what Mirande reports is a result of the same assimilation process Herberg describes for the Europeans. Another important factor affecting egalitarianism is whether or not the wife is employed; if she is, the couple are more likely to lean toward equalitarian roles in household chores, childcare, and so on (Ibarra, 1982: 169-178). Finally, what Mirande calls egalitarianism is more likely the subtle patriarchy we noted when we discussed middle-class gender roles earlier. An increase in female influence and freedom does not mean egalitarianism. A good summary comment regarding gender and machismo is found in Norma Williams' book on tradition and change. In both professional and working-class Chicano families:

> The stereotypical role of the husband and father as having total control was exaggerated in earlier research . . . . At the same time, an egalitarian relationship between husband and wife, which some researchers have claimed exists, is not supported by the data I have collected. Husbands continue to wield greater power than their wives (Williams, 1990: 138).

The other major issue concerns family rituals, and Williams' book treats this subject comprehensively (1990). The women have been the major socializers of their children's religion and culture. The compadrazgo (or god-parenthood) was traditionally a way to develop a link with close friends. Today, it may be friends or relatives, with godparent obligations sharply reduced (Williams, 1990: 44). As for weddings and funerals, there have also been major changes. The wedding used to include a lengthy reception, and food preparation by the women. Today, length of receptions is reduced, and employed women often hire someone for food preparation. Funerals have been reduced even more. The printed death announcement has virtually disappeared; funeral homes are used, and the all-night wake is gone. Women are still the chief mourners, but not as prominently (Williams, 1990: 55–56). As we noted in discussing European ethnics, many successful Mexican-Americans sustain traditional ceremonies, but with the religious meaning almost gone. However, even the changed rituals help to keep ethnicity alive.

An important aspect of Williams' book concerns class differences. In the working class, expectations are still that the man should "provide," and that the woman should care for household and children. Those working-class women who seek change do not seek equality, but a separate though subordinate identity. They still see ethnicity as a more compelling issue than gender. Professional women emphasize either communication or separateness. They have the sense of separate identity that working-class women are striving for (Williams, 1990: 92, 116, 122). These successful women are the archetypical "super-moms," still doing most of the child care and domestic work. For them, gender has begun to exceed ethnicity in importance (on Hispanic affluence, see O'Hare, 1990: 40–43). And as for socialization, Williams notes that the double-standard for raising boys and girls is far less than before, with the rigid controls on daughters having been relaxed (Williams, 1990: 134). Williams' conclusion is that ethnicity, while losing some of its traditional significance and content, still gives rise to a strong sense of community. "Impulse," "narcissism," "self-gratification"—all related to individualism—are still not characteristic even of the successful Mexican Americans (Williams, 1990: 146).

Rates of intermarriage between Chicanos and others form an interesting pattern. Among Mexican Americans in Los Angeles, Robert Schoen and Lawrence Cohen report that generation is more important than occupation in predicting a higher rate. In other words, the recent generation is more likely to intermarry, and this is a more significant predictor than occupational level (Schoen and Cohen, 1980: 359). However, Douglas Gurak and Joseph Fitzpatrick, studying Hispanic groups in New York City, find a somewhat different pattern. First, they report that rates of exogamy (or intermarriage) range from 63 percent for Cubans to 29.5 percent for Puerto Ricans. The key explanatory variable is group size: the smaller the group, the more likely the intermarriage—a phenomenon discussed again in Chapter 10. In fact, group size is so important that the influx of Puerto Ricans to New York City in the past 25 years has resulted in the rate of intermarriage dropping from about 30 percent in 1959 to 21 percent in 1975 (Gurak and Fitzpatrick, 1982: 921–934). Thus, later generations and more successful members of the Hispanic groups are more likely to intermarry but the effect of these factors is overridden by a rapid growth in numbers, causing there to be more potential mates from one's ethnic background.

As for children, Chicano and Puerto Rican fertility rates are higher than that of whites and blacks in the United States. However, unlike the case of other aspects of family life, generation is not the key variable affecting fertility. In fact, if the younger generation of Puerto Ricans perceive themselves as a minority, they tend to have higher fertility. So assimilation reduces fertility, but not minority status (Staples and Mirande, 1980: 897; and Cooney et al., 1981: 1094–1113). As for treatment of children, it is noteworthy that the rate of child abuse among Chicanos is lower than for either whites or blacks (Garbarino and Ebata, 1983: 773–783).

The conclusions regarding Chicanos and other Hispanic groups are somewhat complex. There are still indications of patriarchy and machismo, though success results in a more separate identity for females. Rituals continue, but in an attenuated and transformed fashion. Endogamy is more likely the larger the group and the older the individuals. Children are highly valued, and the numbers remain high for the younger generation if they perceive themselves as out-siders in the United States. Finally, the same problem facing European eth-nics—that of cultural assimilation—faces Hispanics. However, it is nowhere near as pronounced, since Hispanics are at present an ethnic minority, while the European ethnics are just that: ethnic groups.

SECTION THREE

RACIAL GROUPS: AFRICAN-AMERICAN FAMILIES

The everyday division of racial categories—into brown, black, yellow, red, and white peoples—fits quite well into the scholarly discussions of race in America, in which African-Americans, Orientals, and Native-Americans have typically been distinguished from White Americans. While much that has been said about religious and ethnic groups applies to these so-called racial categories as well, there are also some points of divergence both in history and today. Not only do racial minorities differ from the European ethnics, they differ from each other. The Asian Americans, says William O'Hare, "are the fastest growing and most affluent minority market in the United States" (O'Hare, 1990: 26). They are urbanized, and 74 percent live in married couple households, as compared to 72 percent of whites and 43 percent of blacks. Thanks to the current work of Masako Ishii-Kuntz and others, we will very likely have a complete sub-section on U.S. Asians in the next edition of this text, as well as on Native Americans.[2] However, because of their numerical and structural importance in U.S. society, this section will focus on U.S. blacks, or African-Americans.[3]

Seldom has there been a subject within social science literature into which more value judgments have been allowed to creep. From the turn of this cen-tury until the present, writers (both black and white) have had extreme diffi-culty in discussing the African-American without bias and prejudice, conscious or unconscious. The literature, while markedly improved by recent research, must still be handled with great caution.[4] It would be most valuable to begin by isolating the various areas of misconception and disagreement, first concerning history and then concerning the contemporary scene, and subsequently to in-troduce the research data that deal with those issues. Therefore, the discussion of black families and their family culture will be divided into historical issues and current issues.

History of the African-American

African history involves great kingships and a multiplicity of small societies. The history of most African-Americans begins with the slavery experience, but Robert Staples reminds us of an important point:

> *One aspect of black family life frequently ignored during the slave era is the free black family. This group, which numbered about one-half million, was primarily composed*

of the descendants of the original black indentured servants and the mulatto offspring of slaveholders. For this minority of black families, the assimilation and accultura- tion process was, relatively, less difficult. They imitated the white world as closely as possible. Because they had opportunities for education, owning property, and skilled occupations, their family life was quite stable. . . . It is among this group that the early black middle-class was formed (Staples, 1988: 306).

For most, the history of life in the Western Hemisphere begins in exploita- tion and cruelty. It begins in West Africa with the killing and capture of large numbers of men and women, the transporting of the captured to the New World, and their enslavement—usually as agricultural laborers—in a strange land. Their African heritage faded[5] during the period of indentured servanthood, es- pecially under the influence of legalized and nonterminable slavery. The planta- tion system and slavery were not dying institutions, says Robert Fogel and Stanley Engerman, but were profitable right up to the time of the Civil War (Fogel and Engerman, 1974). But with "emancipation" came the weakening of the plantation system that had been crucial to the existence of slavery.

The preceding paragraph is clearly not a full coverage of the 200-250 years it summarizes. We are concerned here with the effects of the occurrences of those years. What happened to the African-American during this period? We must answer by spelling out three versions of the story. The first, that of Fogel and Engerman, says that the plantation and slave system was stable, profitable, and very much a going concern at the time of the war. Slaves were fairly well treated, according to whipping records and other documents, and slave breed- ing was not very widespread. Most slave families were made up of quite stable units (Fogel and Engerman, 1974). This account simply concludes that slavery was not that cruel an institution, and slave life was stable and reasonably good.

A second version, dramatically different, is exemplified by the concentra- tion camp analogy so many commentators have adopted (Elkins, 1963, was one of the first). During World War II, some inmates of the Nazi prison camps be- came childishly silly. Their relations with other inmates became unstable; they became pathological liars and dishonest in all their dealings. In effect, they regressed to childhood. Eventually, they identified with and imitated their cap- tors, coming to view other inmates through Gestapo eyes and sometimes out- doing the Gestapo in cruelty to fellow prisoners.

What caused this type of behavior? The Gestapo used terror and torture, intimidation, isolation, and secrecy. Prisoners were rewarded for compliance with the Gestapo, and, above all, there was a "complete break with the outside world" (Elkins, 1963: 104). In a similar manner, says Stanley Elkins, slaves identified with their masters, who disciplined, taught respect, and held com- plete control over the life of the slave. The master was also the only person with whom identification might occur. Under these conditions, personal relations among the slaves, including those within the family, were extremely tenuous. But didn't the culture brought from Africa act as a stabilizing influence on rela- tionships? The negative answer to this question has been arrived at by two dif- ferent logical paths. Melville Herskovitz's response is that the characteristics of the slave family—female centeredness, common-law marriage, illegitimacy, and weak ties—can be traced back to the polygynous family of West Africa. In other words, the culture the blacks brought with them increased, rather than diminished, the instability of marital relationships during slavery (Herskovitz, 1941). A more prevalent argument is that posed by E. Franklin Frazier: The culture brought from Africa had no stabilizing influence on relationships because that culture was virtually obliterated by experience in the New World. The "rare and isolated instances of survivals associated with the Negro family only indicate how completely the African social organization was wiped out by slavery" (Frazier, 1957: 11–12). The enslaved people were moved randomly from place to place, without any concern for tribal or national groupings. This, plus the conditions described by Elkins, served (over several generations) to destroy most vestiges of African culture.[6]

Because internal stability had been provided (so the argument goes) by the white system and not by the slaves' own relationships, and because the slaves had previously had little or no freedom to govern their own destinies, the results of emancipation could only be disastrous.

> *When the invading armies disrupted the plantation organization, thousands of Negroes were set adrift and began to wander footloose about the country. Not only were the sentimental and habitual ties between spouses severed but even Negro women often abandoned their children. Among the demoralized elements in the newly emancipated Negroes promiscuous sexual relationships and frequent changing of spouses became the rule* (Frazier, 1957: 313).

Such a description, without an offsetting account of the undemoralized elements, leaves the reader to infer that this pattern was typical. And Frazier's picture of postwar anarchy is echoed by Bernard, who writes that

> *in 1865, desertions were innumerable. . . . When the Negroes were moving around to test their freedom, many of them seized the opportunity to desert their wives and children. . . . The young and strong deserted the aged, the feeble, the children, leaving them to shift for themselves* (Bernard, 1966: 110).

This is a second view of the historical process: cultural obliteration, suppression, and enforced order under slavery, and anarchy upon emancipation.

There is, however, a third possible perspective on the same era—one that may be pieced together with the help of a different analogy and a few alternative influences. Helmut Schelsky writes at length, not about the concentration camp, but about the family in post-World War II Germany. He begins by tearing down a stereotype:

> *In general, such times of disorder and distress are considered to be a cause for the disruption and weakening of the family; it is astonishing, therefore, that we must designate the effect of the difficult social experiences which I have mentioned as a* heightening of the stability of the German family. *With the collapse of political and economic order and in the face of the immediate peril to which almost everyone was subjected, marriage and the family were considered to be the natural point of stability*

and protection. . . . The family was often knitted together in the struggle for mere ex-
istence, where it was a matter of thriving or perishing, to such a degree that the per-
sonal tensions, the bored indifference of the usual marital "co-existence," gave way to
a conscious and heightened sense of belonging together (Schelsky, 1954: 331–332).

The family was felt by the German people to be the last element of stability in a
disintegrating world. "Therefore," Schelsky asserts.

the displaced farmer or the "declassed" official . . . lives with clear consciousness and
decisiveness "only for the family," an expression which I heard often enough in the
families I investigated (1954: 332).

Solidarity between husbands and wives and between old and young is evi-
denced in the minimization of tensions and in the astonishingly slight amount of
child neglect. When the rest of the society crumbled, the German people retreated into the family and lived for it. In addition, the balance of power and
importance swung away from male authoritarianism, causing most German
families to take on an equalitarian character.

Before pursuing the possible use of Schelsky's account as an analogue to
the postslavery family among African-Americans, let us return to the family in
Africa. Did the social systems of West Africa, whence blacks were brought to
America, act as a foundation for common-law marriages, weak relationships,
and illegitimacy in the New World, as Herskovits claims? African history was
one of family and lineage stability, but this stability, as well as African culture,
was greatly shaken by the movement of Africans to America as slaves. Yet it is
generally agreed that African culture was not completely wiped out by slavery
(Staples and Mirande 1980: 890). What was most certainly not disrupted were
the basic humanity and mutual concern, often expressed in extended kin ties,
which were functions of that African heritage (see Wetherall, 1981: 294–308).
Slavery was harsh and totalitarian, but it did not result in a continuous shut-
tling of blacks across the South. There was enough residential stability to permit the development of large-scale kin ties, and reasonably stable marriages.[7]
Furthermore, with emancipation, not all blacks began to wander, footloose, on
the countryside. In fact, the majority stayed close to where they had been as
slaves, with the migrations to the great cities of the South and North beginning
gradually over the next generation. Thus, with emancipation and the destruction of the Southern way of life, large numbers of African-Americans retreated
into their family and kin units, attempting to further survival and to find economic and social stability within them. Migrations, first urbanward and then
northward, ordinarily involved family units, not footloose individuals. Whole
kin groups often moved, one family at a time and over several decades, to a single location where economic opportunity was reported to be greater.

It should be added at this point that the present author feels that the issue
of "cultural survivals" is not the key to the debate between the two analogies.
How much obliteration of African culture took place is of historical interest in
itself, and it is important today to U.S. blacks' search for ethnic identity and
cultural roots, as embodied in Alex Haley's dramatic account (Haley, 1974; see

Feature 6.2). However, it is more important to the debate to reconstruct, through continuing historical research, the nineteenth century black family in the United States.

Which picture of African-American history is correct? Was slavery a relatively humane system, with stability and strong family ties characterizing the slave scene? Did the African-American succumb to the "concentration camp influence," with its dehumanization, weakening of peer relationships, and the

Feature 6.2 ROOTS

My earliest memory is of Grandma, Cousin Georgia, Aunt Plus, Aunt Liz, and Aunt Til talking on our front porch in Henning, Tennessee. At dusk, these wrinkled, graying old ladies would sit in rocking chairs and talk, about slaves, massas, and plantations—pieces and patches of family history, passed down across the generations by word of mouth. "Old-timey stuff," Mama would exclaim. She wanted no part of it.

The furthest-back person Grandma and the others ever mentioned was "the African." They would tell how he was brought here on a ship to a place called "Naplis" and sold as a slave in Virginia. There he mated with another slave, and had a little girl named Kizzy. . . .

When other slaves addressed him as Toby—the name given him by his massa—the African would strenuously reject it, insisting that his name was "Kin-tay."

Kin-tay often told Kizzy stories about himself. He said that he had been near his village in Africa, chopping wood to make a drum, when he had been set upon by four men, overwhelmed, and kidnapped into slavery. When Kizzy grew up and became a mother, she told her son these stories, and he in turn would tell *his* children. His granddaughter became my grandmother, and she pumped that saga into me as if it were plasma, until I knew by rote the story of the African, and the subsequent generational wending of our family through cotton and tobacco plantations into the Civil War and freedom.

Could this account possibly be documented for a book? During 1962, between other assignments, I began to follow the story's trail. . . .

This book has taken me ten years and more. Why have I called it *Roots*? Because it not only tells the story of a family, my own, but also symbolizes the history of millions of American blacks of African descent. I intend my book to be a buoy for black self-esteem—and a reminder of the universal truth that we are all descendents of the same Creator.

Alex Haley, "My Search for Roots," first published in *Reader's Digest*, copyright 1974 by Reader's Digest Association, Inc., from the book *Roots* by Alex Haley. Reprinted by permission of Doubleday and Co., Inc.

opportunity it gave the "emancipated" to sever all ties and renounce all responsibility? Or did slavery result in a post-war world in which the African-American drew upon a basic fund of humanity and upon mutual support—often within the family—in the struggle for stability and survival in the crumbling social system? An obvious possibility is that there is some truth to the implications of all three scenarios. The slave system may have been stable but cruel nonetheless, with weak ties becoming weaker and stronger ties stronger in the postslavery period. This, however, evades the issue of whether the pattern of stability or of disorganization was dominant in the late 1800s. Fortunately, several pieces of historical research now speak to this issue.

We begin with Henry Walker's assertion that "blacks and whites experienced similar rates of marriage and marital disruption until recently" (Walker, 1988: 102). Staples adds that data show "that 90 percent of all black children were born in wedlock by the year 1917" (Staples, 1988: 306). The issue, however, is not just one of numerical dominance of two-parent families among blacks; it is also comparative. Crandall Shifflett finds in Louisa County, Virginia, that in 1880, households were 46% nuclear for blacks and 47% for whites—and other types of households were also equally prevalent by race (Shifflett, 1975: 240–245). William Harris's study of black Atlanta in the same year shows a difference, however. Using samples of some 500 white and black households, he discovers that among those with children age 15 and under, 33 percent of the black and 15 percent of the white households were one-parent, and this parent was almost always the mother. This, he says, cannot be explained by different mortality rates by race, since few of the black single parents were widows (Harris, 1976: 322). But it might be explained by economic opportunity. Landale and Tolnay note that even in 1910 urban illiteracy and poverty resulted in a lower motivation and opportunity to marry, and these were more characteristic of Southern blacks than whites (Landale and Tolnay, 1991: 33–45). Thus, marriage, divorce, and two-parent household rates seem to have been fairly similar by race in the period following the Civil War. Such differences that existed were the result of conditions in certain specific locations.

Another point of post-Civil War similarity between whites and blacks was fertility. For rural blacks it dropped from 7.3 to 2.8 children per mother between 1880 and 1940. This trend is similar for Southern whites, with literacy and urban influence resulting in fewer children (Tolnay, 1983: 314–332). Daniel Smith reports an interesting turn-of-the-century racial difference in sexual practices. Though he notes the preponderance of male-headed African-American households, he finds that Southern blacks practiced premarital intercourse and accepted pre- (not non-) marital births (Smith, 1980). However, D'Emilio and Freedman state that "race progress" was associated with the values of chastity and fidelity, and with attempts to establish stable families, as noted above (D'Emilio and Freedman, 1988: 105).

Perhaps the most interesting aspect of black family life after the Civil War is gender roles. As for employment, Staples reports that in 1900, "41 percent of black women were in the labor force, compared with 16 percent of white women"

(Staples, 1988: 307). In the same year, according to Matthaei, the figures for *married* women were 22.7 and 3.2 percent, respectively (Matthaei, 1982: 133). Patricia Collins notes that black women, even before enslavement, combined work and family without seeing a conflict between the two (Collins, 1990: 50). That the male was a regular member of the household until well into this century is clear from our earlier discussion. However, the two-parent household seems from slavery on to have been less patriarchal and more egalitarian than its white counterpart. Bonnie Dill notes an interesting contradiction regarding black women in the United States: they have been described (stereotyped) as assertive and domineering during a time when "femininity" stressed sweetness and demureness. Now, however, the women's movement is trying to accomplish for all women what has been true of black women for a century or more: independence, autonomy, labor force participation, and so forth (Dill, 1979: 554–555). This insight is reminiscent of the movement in China toward a family life that once characterized mainly the lower classes. Recent literature argues, though, that quasi-egalitarianism does not mean matriarchy, but rather a greater sharing of economic provision and decision-making (Demos, 1986: 59; Staples, 1988: 313). The *matricentric* (or female-centered) black family is a more recent phenomenon, resulting from neither the African past, slavery, nor the post-Civil War period. It results from the continuing denial of a family wage to the black male, and from the combined effects of institutional racism (Collins, 1990: 53; Gutman, 1975: 208).

In summary then, the black family was much more likely to be nuclear in 1880 than in 1980. Furstenberg, Hershberg, and Modell raise an interesting issue regarding these findings and the misinterpretation of black history in the United States. Just because most black families were nuclear after the Civil War, this should not be taken

> *to imply that the institution of slavery was not brutalizing and dehumanizing. Yet, one must not convert a sense of moral outrage into a monolithic interpretation of the black experience. Once we recognize that the matrifocal black family is a product of economic discrimination, poverty, and disease we cease to blame the distant past for problems which have their origins in more recent times. It was, and still is, much easier to lament the sins of one's forefathers than to confront the injustices of more contemporary socioeconomic systems (Furstenberg et al., 1975: 232–233).*

Their data, they feel, "provide no evidence for believing that Philadelphia's blacks value anything distinct from what poverty and death often denied them: to raise their children in stable continuous families" (Furstenberg et al., 1975: 231–232).

This, however, has already brought us to the modern period. The particular conclusion the reader draws about slavery and postslavery white and black society is bound to influence conclusions concerning black families today. Keeping this in mind, let us seek to unravel the tangled strands of contemporary debate and research.

The African-American Family Today

Until the mid-1960s, there were two tendencies among students of the American family: one was to ignore the contemporary black family altogether; the other was to treat it as a social problem. The classic statement of the latter approach is expressed by Frazier. "The mass migration of Negroes to the cities of the North resulted in considerable family disorganization." Life for urban Negroes, he feels, is casual, precarious, and fragmentary.

> *It lacks continuity and its roots do not go deeper than the contingencies of daily living. . . . Without the direction provided by family traditions and the discipline of parents, large numbers of Negro children grow up without aims and ambitions (Frazier, 1957: 636).*

Frazier's characterization of the Negro family gained wide attention when it was repeated and programmed by Daniel P. Moynihan:

> *The evidence — not final, but powerfully persuasive — is that the Negro family in the urban ghettos is crumbling. . . . In a word, a national effort towards the problem of Negro Americans must be directed towards the question of family structure. The object should be to strengthen the Negro family so as to enable it to raise and support its members as do other families (Moynihan, 1965: abstract and 47).*

As for the matricentric, or matriarchal, nature of the family, Moynihan claimed that the Negro community has been forced into a pattern "which, because it is so out of line with the rest of the American society, seriously retards the progress of the group as a whole, and imposes a crushing burden on the Negro male and, in consequence, on a great many Negro women as well" (Moynihan, 1965: 29). The household headed by a mother or grandmother is defined as a problem, since no adult male is present, and as problem-producing, since the absence of an adult male makes achievement by the younger generation even more problematic. As Moynihan puts it: "White children without fathers at least perceive all about them the pattern of men working. Negro children without fathers flounder—and fail" (1965: 35). This characterization thus becomes complete: African-Americans developed weak family ties during slavery; even these were loosened by emancipation. They then began the long process of trying to internalize the ways of the dominant society (including the concept of stable marriage), but clustering together in urban ghettos and rural areas arrested the process. Further, acculturation appears to have become reversed, so that instability and weakness of relationships are once again becoming more prevalent.

What was the response to Moynihan's "tangle of pathology" characterization of the black family? The first response to appear, especially in Andrew Billingsley's book *Black Families in White America*, was: it is not that disorganized, not that unstable, not that pathological. How can a people survive under oppression? One way is "to adapt the most basic of its institutions, the family, to meet the often conflicting demands placed on it" (Billingsley, 1968: 21). Disagreeing directly with Moynihan and others, Billingsley states:

> *We do not view the Negro family as a causal nexus in a "tangle of pathology" which feeds on itself. Rather, we view the Negro family in theoretical perspective as a subsys-*

tem of the larger society. It is, in our view, an absorbing, adaptive, and amazingly re-
silient mechanism for the socialization of its children and the civilization of its society
(Billingsley, 1968: 33).

Is it disorganized and unstable? Frazier admitted that, while there is considerable family disorganization in the lower class, "there is a core of stable families
even in this class" (Frazier, 1957: 324). To this, Billingsley added that the large
numbers of stable black working-class families never make the news and are seldom mentioned in social science reports. The majority of "poor Negroes live in
nuclear families headed by men who work hard every day and are still unable to
earn enough to pull their families out of poverty" (Billingsley, 1968: 137, 139).

So is the black family in the United States matricentric or matrifocal—that
is, focussed on the women? Clearly, it may be more so than the white family,
but female-headedness, according to these authors, is neither typical nor pathological. The essence of this response, then, was that black families are very
much like white families, though with the added burden of institutionalized discrimination and prejudice to deal with. The "pathology" view arose because of
two factors: the confusion of social class with race, and the value orientations or
ideologies of primarily white researchers and writers.

One of the problems with the characterizations "pathological" and "similar"
is semantic and statistical. The use of terms like *many* or *a large portion*, when not
based on research, was often left for the reader to interpret ideologically. Does
"many" mean "typically or generally?" After all, black families cover a wide
spectrum of structures and behaviors, as do white families. So let us look at the
last 25 years by beginning with class differences. (We should note here that several black family issues will be left to the chapter where that topic is discussed—socialization, mate selection, happiness, kinship, the elderly—although
we may mention them briefly. It is neither advisable nor possible to cover them
all in this introduction).

One important effect of the 1980s in the United States was to increase the
distance between socioeconomic haves and have nots. As one report puts it:
"the income gap between the wealthiest two-fifths of U.S. society (where blacks
are few in number) and the poorest two-fifths (where most of the black population is found) is now *wider than at any time since 1947* (Center, 1986: 150). Only
seven percent of all black families fall into the wealthiest one-fifth. In 1988, says
Judith Waldrop, 13 percent of black families had annual incomes of $50,000 or
more (Waldrop, 1990: 33). Like other affluent Americans, these families are
often dual income and highly educated.

When Frazier first wrote about the *Black Bourgeoisie* in 1957, he noted their
strenuous efforts to be seen as middle-class and not as "Negro." The work ethic
and other indications of "respectability" were central features of life for successful blacks. However, an interesting point of disagreement in the literature concerns whether affluent African-Americans reject the rest of the black community,
or whether they identify with and seek to help the less successful. Is the greater
economic distance making for a greater social distance as well? Like many such
debates, the answer is probably "for some yes, and for some no." Several authors
have noted that during the 1960s "Negroes" became "Afro-Americans," and a

minority began to become an *ethnic* minority. Billingsley notes that this change was occurring in his own lifetime. In the 1940s, he says, we were still ambivalent about our heritage. We treated African students with disdain and white students with adulation. Even after World War II we still felt a twinge of inferiority regarding our African heritage. "Yet the image is changing radically and rapidly" (Billingsley, 1968: 39). Much more recently, Broman et al. report a strong sense of racial group identification among highly educated U.S. blacks (1988: 146–158). Afrocentric emphasis is continuing to increase such African-American ethnicity, though not for all blacks.

When we turn from the affluent to the majority of African-Americans, we find an important problem regarding education, occupation, and income. First, getting an education has always been difficult. However, the Goldscheiders note that "education is not the only, or perhaps even the major, link in the chain that has blocked the intergenerational mobility of blacks; their opportunity to translate their education into income in the racially segregated occupational structure has been severely restricted as well" (Goldscheider and Goldscheider, 1991: 506).[8] According to Charles Willie, working-class blacks accept the success goals of society, but find the means for achieving those goals blocked. Yet many still seek to prepare their children for achievement, and they continue to work hard and provide for their families.

It is not surprising that the majority of recent literature on black Americans focuses on the poor, since nearly half of all black families fall in the bottom one-fifth of the U.S. population in terms of income. This is the research that has emphasized (perhaps overemphasized) sexual activity, teen pregnancy and childbirth, and female-headed households. Martin Whyte reports that blacks begin sexual activity earlier, and are more likely to become premaritally pregnant. However, he does not find any racial difference in the overall prevalence of premarital sexual activity or in cohabitation (Whyte, 1990: 85).

Low socioeconomic status, one-parent family, and ghetto residence make a premarital birth three times as likely for blacks as their opposites (Bumpass and McLanahan, 1989: 279). To this Edelman adds that American teenagers who are poor and lack basic academic skills are six times more likely to become pregnant, regardless of race. Of course, a larger proportion of blacks are in this situation than whites (Edelman, 1987: 55). A few years ago Zelnik et al. noted that "premaritally pregnant blacks are more likely than whites to carry the pregnancy to term, are less likely in that case to marry during the course of the pregnancy, and, as a result, are more likely than whites to have an illegitimate live birth from a premarital conception" (1981: 175). Does anything reduce or delay the likelihood of pregnancy for such young people? Scott and Perry note the importance for the poor of a positive relation with parents. They add an important point:

> *The physically absent father who visits, nurtures, and provides material and emotional support effectively influences the pregnancy age even from a distance. Moreover, the earlier the father's influence begins, and the longer it lasts, the greater are the additive effects on the delaying of daughter's first pregnancy (Scott and Perry, 1990: 14).*

To this Eggebeen et al. add that the younger the mother is, the less likely it is that there is a co-resident male (father) in the home (1990: 219–223). Presumably this would also include the lack of a non-resident, but nurturing, male. Finally, even educated adolescent blacks have more exposure to premarital childbearing than do educated whites—and exposure may make for more acceptance (St. John and Rowe, 1990).

In addition to the racial comparisons noted above, Edelman points out some most important recent changes. Black teens are having fewer rather than more babies: 172,000 in 1970, and 137,000 in 1983. How, then, can the rate of out-of-wedlock births be going up? "The cause among black teenagers is a drop in marriage rates, not an increase in birth rates. Among white teens the cause is more babies coupled with a decrease in marriage among those who become pregnant" (recall Zelnik) (Edelman, 1987: 4–5; see also Hofferth, 1985: 93). In addition, fertility rates among married black women are decreasing, resulting in a rise in the proportion of black babies born out-of-wedlock. Garfinkel and McLanahan add to Edelman's point thus: whites marry and increasingly divorce, whereas blacks are increasingly likely never to marry at all (Garfinkel and McLanahan, 1986: 47, 54).

One of the issues concerning unwed motherhood is marital opportunity. First, there is a sex ratio problem, with more black women than men, and with more black men than white men institutionalized. South and Lloyd, for example, report that in 1980 there were 93 marriageable white men for every 100 unmarried white females, and 72.6 marriageable black men for every 100 black unmarried females (South and Lloyd, 1992: 247–264). Also, marriage is still a test of the provider role for men, and African-American women find both education and occupation more available to them than do men (Schoen and Kluegel, 1988: 895; Tucker and Taylor, 1989: 664). Collins summarizes the factors that reduce the number of two-parent households among blacks: (1) lack of suitable marital partners; (2) decline in marriages of black professional and managerial women to men in other segments of the labor market; and (3) the choice of both heterosexuals and lesbians to head their own households (Collins, 1990: 61).

Coupling the out-of-wedlock birth with the lower marital opportunity for African-American women brings us to the single female-headed family. In 1988, two-thirds of black children in such families were officially in poverty, compared to 17 percent of black children of two-parent families. Actual income in 1983 was $24,000 for black two-parent families, and $9,000 for the single-mother household (Eggebeen and Lichter, 1991: 801–817); Garfinkel and McLanahan, 1986: 22). While the majority of these women work, it is also among single parents that the highest level of welfare need is found. Much of the strength reported in black women's lives has been treated negatively by white literature. What is needed, says Collins, is "an Afrocentric feminist analysis of motherhood that debunks . . . the white-male-created 'matriarch' or the black-male perpetuated 'superstrong black mother'" (Collins, 1990: 117). It is simply true that African-American females have had to play multiple roles, and have done it for decades, not so much because of innate strength, but because of both tradition and necessity.

This brings us to the U.S. black male today. Staples states most strongly the negative view of both the male and the black family. He says that the "last 30 years have culminated in the gradual disintegration of the black nuclear family. . . . The crisis of the black family is, in reality, the crisis of the black male" (Staples, 1988; 320–321; Staples, 1987, 284). However, he does not suggest starting in the family to remedy the crisis; it is, after all, the legacy of institutional racism. The male role of provider has also been affected by automation and by a general reduction in the unskilled blue-collar jobs they have often been forced to take (Bowman, 1988: 76). McLoyd, for example, notes that black families headed by a person 24 or younger lost 47 percent of the real income between 1973 and 1986. She also notes that labor force participation of black men dropped from 84 percent in 1940 to 67 percent in 1980 (McLoyd, 1990).

The phenomena about which Collins, Edelman, Staples, and others speak are, of course, not generalizable to all U.S. blacks. Yet the very fact that it is interpreted as a substantial and growing situation means it deserves our attention. Much of the literature slips easily into the language of problem, pathology, and disintegration—the language of value judgment. So this brings us to some important interpretive issues regarding African-American families and culture today.

Quite a few writers have noted the difficulties faced by children raised in single-parent families. However, it is difficult to disentangle the issue of family structure from that of poverty. The "deficit model" often treats single parenthood as almost automatically negative in its effects on family members, especially children (Marotz-Baden, 1979: 5–14). Several authors have dealt critically with the structural-determinant argument, with the most persuasive research being that of Reginald Clark among poor blacks in Chicago. Clark found that what matters is not so much who the adults are in the home, but how family members treat each other, how time is used, whether they use both support and control in socialization, whether they are fatalistic, and whether the offspring becomes the family "expert" in something. In other words, it is quality of family life more than the family's composition or even status that determines how the children do. David Demo recently agreed with Clark: "Children's well-being depends much more on enduring parental support and satisfying family relationships than it does on a particular family structure" (Clark, 1983; Demo, 1992: 114). So family culture is more important than structure. However, these authors do not say that the offspring would not be better off with two parents than with one—only that dispositions and relationships are more important.

The last several pages have expressed three views of the black family. One is that it is different from the white, and different equals worse. That is the pathological view. Another is that if the appropriate socioeconomic and family variables are controlled, the differences disappear. Poor black and white families are the same, as are middle-class black and white families. Edelman calls this the "social class view" (Edelman, 1987: 8–9). Scattered through the preceding is a third—and most recent—way of seeing black families. This says that black families are not the same, but different does not equal worse. This "cultural variance" view is that different is just different, not better or worse.

Staples comments that Billingsley, though sympathetic, does not penetrate black families, but sees even their strengths through middle-class eyes. Instead, divergences in sexual behavior, the value of children, and kin ties may be looked at positively. Sexual permissiveness should not be downplayed, but should be seen as reflecting the absence of a double standard of sexual conduct among blacks. Blacks can thus avoid the gender role conflicts that plague the white community. Sexual behavior is natural, but so is having children. In the black community, children are a value in themselves, regardless of marriage. Joyce Ladner asserts that a child has a right to exist, that motherhood is the fulfillment of womanhood, and thus that neither childhood nor motherhood should be degraded by artificial legal statuses (Ladner, 1971). Recently, Jacobsen and Bigner, using a "Value of Children" scale, found that black single parents reported feeling more certain than whites that children provide pluses. They found that few other differences exist, "other than the overall negative parental valuing that white single parents reported" (Jacobsen and Bigner, 1991: 311). The valuing of children by the black community does not mean, however, that marriage is devalued. Kenrick Thompson reports that black adolescents express a stronger belief than whites that having children promotes marital success, personal security, and approval from others (Thompson, 1980: 133). Ladner goes on to state that not only does different not equal worse, but that the white community is currently learning about both sexuality and the value of children from blacks. And, as we noted earlier, the same holds for learning about cohabitation from the poor. Maxine Baca Zinn states this point very clearly: "with respect to single-parent families, teenage childbirth, working mothers and a host of other behaviors, black families serve as barometers of social change and as forerunners of adaptive patterns that will be progressively experienced by the more privileged sectors of American society" (Baca-Zinn, 1990: 79).

As for women's roles and kin ties, Ladner has stated that black women are realistic about resources and opportunities. They are not "emasculating" but attempt to be self-reliant. (Any "emasculating" has been done by white society.) And as for kin ties, McAdoo notes that shared child rearing and economic support from the larger network are long-term characteristics of African-American life (McAdoo, 1978: 775-776). The research of Shimkin et al. notes the strength of black extended families in Mississippi and Chicago. Black extended ties are not based on female dominance and are important to both survival and social mobility. Blacks in such networks, they feel, can be deservedly critical of the shortcomings of the white middle-class model and the dominant legal system.

White people may feel keenly that marital instabilities and the acceptance of human frailties are signs of black failure. Black folks feel as keenly the inadequacies of white care for "father and mother, brother and sister." White favoritism among children, and white indifference to the needs of distant kin are even more profound weaknesses" (Shimkin et al., 1978: 184).

Thus, value ethnocentrism should be a two-way street, and, as the authors state in their introduction, it is time for cultural pluralism to be recognized by society's legal structures.

The better recognition of black family values, institutions, and customary law should serve as the basis of appropriate legislative actions, for example, in the rectification of currently biased laws on adoption and fosterage (Shimkin et al., 1978: 184).

Other authors have tried to account for the uniqueness of black culture, some by tracing African roots, some by noting the greater and more lasting prejudice and discrimination faced by blacks than by the European ethnic groups. But the basis for uniqueness is not the key issue confronting the spokespeople for this view of the black family. This is the key issue: Is the unique black family culture a passing phase, or will it make a continuing contribution to the U.S. experience? Is ethnic minority status and the resulting view of the black family as unique merely a phase through which blacks must pass on the way to societal equality and success in middle-class terms, or is it a permanent part of the cultural pluralism of the United States? Shimkin clearly manifests the dilemma confronting those holding the "uniqueness" position:

As more urbanized blacks ascend the ladder of success the tendency will of course be toward a more viable nuclear household. That appears to be a concomitant of much of urban life and is probably inevitable. But younger blacks, in particular, should always remember that what they are leaving is not something to be ashamed of. It is not something that is reflective of some deficiency in their culture. And it should not be disparaged (Shimkin, 1974: 125).

Is it true that, even for blacks, the process that has led to ethnic minority status will eventually lead to ethnic status? If so, this may mean that, as in the case of the ethnic groups discussed earlier, the problem for blacks will become one of keeping any of their unique culture intact in a society that—at least culturally—tends to incorporate its ethnic groups. Is "nuclearization" and individualism the inevitable price that the black family system will eventually pay for self-esteem and success? Ladner would very likely say no, or at least that in the interim the larger society will learn much from the black experience and model. McAdoo also argues that black kin ties are not an interim survival mechanism but that "the extended family pattern continues to be a viable cultural component for the emotional well-being of blacks at all economic levels, even when middle-class status has been maintained over several generations" (McAdoo, 1979: 775). Only the future itself will answer these questions.

Our concern in the preceding pages has been with three versions of black family culture at present: (1) pathology (or deviant), (2) similarity (or equivalent), and (3) variant. There are, of course, many similarities between white and black families of the same social level. There are also differences. It is certainly not surprising to find poverty and unemployment among African-American men, and poverty and single parenthood among women. After all, the conservative policies of the 1980s were guaranteed to drive the most vulnerable—unskilled black males—out of the work force. And it might not be out of place to use the language of problem, even "crisis" (Staples), to describe this increasing aspect of U.S. African-American life. As for the other differences, whether they are defined as deviant or variant is still likely to depend on the values or ideology of the observer.

An insightful recent article refers to the "Dreams and Aspirations of Black Families" (Huttman, 1991: 147–158). A basic summary would seem to be that African-Americans have the same goals for their families as white families, but they have obstacles which are often too great to overcome. And there are distinct class differences in goals, with the middle-class family wanting a ranch house and a lawn, while the homeless dream of getting *into* the drug-ridden projects that others are fighting to flee. Both reality and goals are as varied for blacks as for whites, but the black community is continuing to struggle with the legacy and fact of white racism—and whether the late 1990s will see a change for the better remains to be seen.

Fertility and the U.S. Family

CHAPTER 7

Trends in the United States since colonial days have been toward lower fertility. People want fewer children, and the actual number of children is closer to what people want than previously. Four issues in unplanned fertility include: (a) nonmarital pregnancy, (b) nonmarital births, (c) ill-timed births, and (d) unwanted births. The revolution in fertility control is based on technological methods and changing values. The two current contraceptive values are complete control and unobtrusive control. Major methods today include the pill, the diaphragm, and sterilization, with abortion as a highly debated "backup."

The majority of people, at some time in their lives, play the social and biological role of parent. There are privileges and costs to parenthood. It used to be that many of the privileges or advantages to parenthood were economic. Today, however, most of the privileges are psychological (for example, being involved in the life of a growing person), while the costs are economic and in terms of foregone opportunities.

Being a parent occupies a smaller and smaller portion of the married years, as longevity increases and the number of children decreases. Now in fact, the majority of a couple's years are spent together after the last child leaves home. The parent role, then, is less dominant in terms of time than it used to be, although it still occupies the time and energy of many people for at least two decades.

Changes in fertility control have been revolutionary, not just evolutionary, and those changes will be examined following discussion of historical trends and unplanned fertility.

SECTION ONE

TRENDS IN U.S. FERTILITY

The number of births per family has dropped dramatically over the course of U.S. history. From a high of eight children per mother in colonial days, fertility dropped to two per mother by the 1920s.[1] Figure 7.1 shows fertility figured according to the crude birth rate, which is the number of births in a given year, divided by the total population at mid-year, times 1,000. You will notice that, for reasons of separation because of war, the crude birth rate dropped during the 1860s, again during the late 1910s, and again during the 1940s. However, one of the lowest points reached in U.S. history was during the Depression years, when the economic situation was such that many couples severely restricted fertility. It is noteworthy, however, that even before the Depression, during the prosperity of the 1920s, the rate was falling rapidly. There are several issues worth raising about U.S. fertility trends.

(1) According to D'Emilio and Freedman, "between the 1830s and 1870s information about contraceptive devices circulated widely," including books on the subject (D'Emilio and Freedman, 1988: 59). However, Linda Gordon reports that, unlike 20th century feminists, 19th century feminists did not support *birth control*. The reason, she says, is that 19th century feminists were concerned to temper individualism with women's nurturing tendencies, while today the central issue is women's control over their lives (though individualism and nurturance are still secondary concerns) (Gordon, 1982: 46; Gordon, 1976).

(2) In 1900, *fertility* for U.S. white women stood at 3.54, half what it was a century earlier. However, that same year almost half of the couples in which the husband was business or professional had two or fewer children, and just ten years later that figure was almost two-thirds (D'Emilio and Freedman, 1988:

FIGURE 7.1   Estimated Crude Birth Rate, United States, 1855–1992

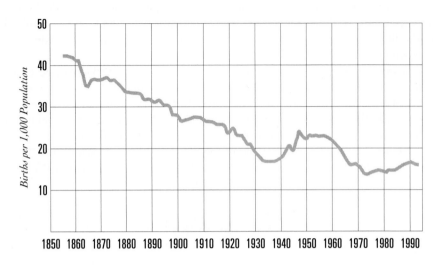

SOURCES: U.S. Bureau of the Census and National Bureau of Vital Statistics, various publications.

174). So why was there a two-century-long decline in U.S. fertility? There is, of course, no simple explanation. It must presumably involve the fact that during the 19th and 20th centuries industrialization and the "individuation" of occupations was changing children from economic assets into liabilities. Research shows that immigrant, farm, and urban lower-class fertility rates have declined more slowly than that of native borns and higher status groups (Graham, 1983; Wilcox and Golden, 1982; Laidig et al., 1981). However, as Larry Bumpass points out, "no simple relationship has been found between any measure of urbanization, literacy, or industrialization and the *onset* of fertility decline" (Bumpass, 1979: 374).

(3) Besides fertility decline and contraception, the third issue regarding trends has to do with the *rise* in fertility between 1946 and 1960. It was expected that—as after other wars—after World War II there would be a temporary rise in the birth rate, as couples were reunited. What was not expected, however, was that the higher level (more than one additional child per family, on the average) would continue for some 15 years. How is the "baby boom" to be explained? First, it was a change in *timing:* couples were marrying earlier and having their children earlier, meaning that the fertility rate looked higher than it was due to the condensing or "squeezing together" of the child-rearing period.[2] There was, however, some actual rise in the fertility rate, and this was accounted for by a *reduction* in the numbers of very small families. That is, whereas during the Depression numerous families had either zero children or one child, during the 1950s almost no married couples had less than two. Just

how dramatic this difference is can be seen in the fact that 40 percent of those married women who were in the fecund years during the 1930s had either zero children or one child, as compared with only 14 percent during the 1950s. Another way to look at the baby boom is to say that it was not a return to large families. In fact, the proportion of families with more than four children in the 1930s and the 1950s was virtually the same.

(4) The final general issue about fertility trends is the small rise during the 1980s. This *boomlet*, of course, is explained by the number of "baby boomers" passing through the childbearing years at that time. Perhaps more pertinent is to explain why the rise was as small as it was, from around 13 per thousand population in the 1970s to 16.6 in 1990 (see Figure 7.1). This means that, while a larger proportion of U.S. population was of childbearing age, there was no apparent rise in number of children per fecund woman.

We turn now from trends in U.S. fertility to current subcategorical differences. We noted earlier that immigrant, lower-class, and farm families traditionally were larger. At present, *class* measures—income, education, occupation—are all slightly inversely related to fertility, e.g., the more income, the fewer children. The effect of education, however, seems entirely accounted for by the fact that those with more education marry later—thereby producing fewer children. However, Grindstaff et al. recently noted that education postpones first birth, but may not reduce total fertility at all (1991: 324–339).

One category of poor women is those on welfare. The policy generalization has been that women on welfare produce more children to get more welfare money. In an intriguing study between 1980 and 1983 of almost 2,800 households, Mark Rank found that even after standardizing for age, children, race, marital status, and education, fertility rates for those on welfare are lower. Furthermore, Rank finds, "the longer a woman remains on welfare, the less likely she is to give birth" (1989: 301). Clearly, much remains to be learned about the relation of class and fertility.

As for *race*, though there has been a substantial reduction in black and Hispanic fertility over the past century, theirs is still higher than for whites and Asian-Americans. However, college educated black women have lower fertility than white women of any educational level. Many of the issues concerning race were raised in Chapter 6, and still others will be discussed below.

A single reference to fertility by *religion* is in order. Catholics have long been known to have higher fertility than Jews and Protestants in the United States. An important reason for this has been the Catholic church's opposition to artificial methods of birth control. However, that difference is currently shrinking, though the fertility rate of Catholics is still somewhat higher. An interesting recent article by Teachman and Schollaert adds timing to total fertility for whites by religion. The authors find that Catholics marry later, and are thus older at first birth. However, "although being Catholic delays marriage, once married, it speeds birth timing" (Teachman and Schollaert, 1991: 157). In other words Catholics start later, but produce children longer and closer together, the result being that they end up with slightly higher fertility.

ISSUES IN UNPLANNED FERTILITY

It is generally acknowledged that in colonial days the tendency was for two people to accept the number of children they had, without planning in advance how large a family they desired. But what about today? Is it now true that people start with a blueprint for family size and follow it? If not, of what does their unplanned factor consist? In dealing with the unplanned factor we will deal with nonmarital pregnancy, nonmarital births, ill-timed births, and unwanted births.

Nonmarital Pregnancy

The age of sexual maturity has been dropping by four to six months every decade since 1900. Thus, a portion of prevalence of premarital pregnancy has to do with the earlier and earlier age at which the risk is present in sexual activity (Caplow et al., 1982: 170).

Just how widespread is premarital pregnancy? In the 1960s, about 22 percent of all marriages involved a pregnant bride, and for teenage marriages the figure was 50 percent. This figure declined somewhat in the 1970s as a result of education, knowledge and availability of birth control devices, and legalized abortion. Now it is estimated that "some one million teenagers become pregnant each year in this country, 80 percent of them unmarried at the time and some 30,000 under the age of 15." If current patterns continue, 40 percent of all 14-year-olds will become pregnant before their 20th birthday (Davis, 1989: 23). "In fact, the United States leads most of the industrialized world in the incidence of pregnancy among teenagers 15 to 19 years of age (Davis, 1989: 21). In relation to risk, however, the rate of pregnancies among teenagers has remained relatively constant for two decades.

While previously married adult women do become pregnant from time to time, this is generally considered an issue for teenagers. Davis states the case very clearly:

> *Until recently, teenage pregnancy was viewed as either a black problem or not a problem at all. In fact, thirty years ago the teenage birth rate was higher than it is today. But it was not considered a problem because, unlike now, the majority of these births occurred within the context of marriage (Davis, 1989: 20).*

Now however, the pregnant teenage female and male are much less likely to marry. In Chapter 6 we indicated the value placed on children in the black community. Ladner and others have asked what right the white community has to say that a child born outside of marriage is "illegitimate'; does that not mean the child has no right to exist? This difference in the relative value placed on marriage in the white and black communities is quite apparent in the fact that, in the 1960s, 60 percent of white girls who became pregnant outside of wedlock married the biological father, as compared to 18 percent of black girls. However, say Nathanson and Becker,

> *there is no indication . . . that parents of adolescent black girls are any more enthusiastic than white parents about either premature sexuality or out-of-wedlock pregnancy; if anything, the contrary is the case (Nathanson and Becker, 1986: 521).*

On the one hand, it might be argued that giving the child a legal father is a good thing to do; on the other hand, it is possible that by marrying "in order to legitimize the child" a couple are "short-circuiting" the mate selection process. The result may simply be that a couple whose relationship would have been terminated if allowed to run its course instead finish the process *after* a pregnancy-induced marriage. Charles Hill et al., for example, speak of premarital breakups as "preventors of divorce" (Hill et al., 1976: 166). There is, of course, at least some truth to the idea that marriages in which the bride is pregnant are less likely to last, and this issue will be discussed further in Chapter 17 on divorce.

More must be said at this point about the use of contraceptives by teenagers. First, while premarital pregnancy was included under the heading "Unplanned Fertility," it is sometimes the case that a couple will purposely expose the girl to pregnancy risk, perhaps in order to escape an unhappy parental home by hoping to force a marriage or simply by having to take on adult roles. In a study of 13,000 high school sophomores, over 25 percent indicated they might or would consider having a child outside marriage. By ethnicity, the percents were 41 for black, 29 for hispanics, and 23 for non-hispanic white. The reasons given for willingness were (1) non-conformity, (2) educational costs, and (3) depression, for whites or hispanics (Abrahamsen et al., 1988: 13–18).

Let us examine contraceptive use more generally. First, where does contraceptive information come from? It is seldom sought from a clinic in isolation, i.e., by the young woman alone. Black teens are more likely to be accompanied by their mother than whites, while whites are more likely to be accompanied by a girlfriend or boyfriend. Nathanson and Becker were somewhat surprised to find how big the role played by family often is, though those who involve family do not also seek help from peers, and vice versa (Nathanson and Becker, 1986: 519–520).

As for usage, Edward Herold and Marilyn Goodwin studied 355 sexually active women between 13 and 20 years of age, asking them about contraceptive usage. Here is what they found:

28% used nothing	*20% used the pill*
26% used the condom	*5% used other methods*
21% used withdrawal	*(rhythm, foam, diaphragm, etc.)*

Only 31 percent said they used some form of protection every time they had sex (Herold and Goodwin, 1981: 248).

But why, one might ask, don't all teenagers use contraception all the time if they in fact want to avoid pregnancy? The two problems have to do with *access* and *self-concept*. Contraceptive devices are still not as available to teenagers as they are to the rest of the population. Though some teenage contraceptive clinics have been established, most localities do not have such clinics available. Besides, as Bumpass points out, "the attitudes of private physicians and pharmacists may still constitute significant barriers to contraceptive access for a large portion of the teenage population" (Bumpass, 1979: 382).

The other issue, self-concept, means that in order to be "on the pill," a girl has to admit to herself that she is sexually active. Herold and Goodwin asked those who do not contracept regularly why they did not. Several gave more than one reason, and the major responses were:

didn't expect sexual intercourse to occur	*44%*
intercourse was safe during that time period	*32%*
just didn't think about getting pregnant	*27%*
afraid to see a physician about contraception	*27%*
afraid parents would discover the contraceptives	*26%*

(Herold and Goodwin, 1981: 250. See also Shah and Zelnik, 1981: 339–348; Jorgenson et al., 1980: 141–155).

Nonmarital Births

In 1940 there were 100,000 births in the United States outside of marriage, in 1973 this figure was 400,000, and by 1980 the figure reached one million. Part of this is due to the fact that during that period the number of fecund women almost doubled. But rates are more instructive than such raw numbers: in 1950, five percent of all births were non-marital, in 1973 it was 13 percent, and by 1980 it was close to 20 percent. But if the rate is not figured as nomarital births divided by all births, but as nomarital births divided by fecund women (or women capable of becoming pregnant), a surprising fact emerges. Computed the second way, the rate of nonmarital births has risen only very slightly since 1960, with the non-marital birth:all birth percent having risen due to the decline in all births (see Figure 7.1). In other words, the rate of nonmarital births has barely risen in relation to fecundity, since fewer fecund women are having children.[3]

Thus far, we have used "nonmarital," not premarital. Wineberg points out that in the 1985 *Current Population Survey*, 62 percent of non-marital births for white women were to never married, and 84 percent for blacks. In other words, the other 38 percent and 16 percent, respectively, were to previously (and in few cases currently) married women (Wineberg, 1990: 256–260). One reason why the percent for whites is so much higher is that whites are still likely to marry and increasingly likely to divorce, while blacks are less likely to marry at all, than formerly.

What is important about pre- or never-married births is not only that they are still the vast majority of nomarital births. Such women, says Wineberg, are younger, less educated, have fewer resources, receive inadequate prenatal care, and are more likely to be in poverty (Wineberg, 1990). In short, they are more "at risk" than the formerly married. And, as Bumpass and McLanahan point out, women—more especially black women—from high risk backgrounds are three times more likely than those from low risk backgrounds to have a premarital birth (Bumpass and McLanahan, 1989: 279–286). Conservative legislators have for years tried to link welfare and "high risk" to forced sterilization. Now, as can be seen in Feature 7.1, they are trying to link it to a new contraceptive device (despite Rank's findings, reported earlier).

Several other points regarding teenage pregnancies are of interest. First, an equitable distribution of income is negatively related to the cumulative birthrate for those under 18—and the United States is the least equitable and has the highest such rate (Jones et al., 1985: 53–63). Second, children of teen mothers are more likely to become teen mothers themselves (Furstenberg et al., 1990: 54–61). Third, birth control knowledge does not seem to reduce the likelihood of a nonmarital birth, but self-discipline and responsibility do (Hanson et al., 1987: 250–251). This is reminiscent of Clark's point about family culture being important to teenage success among ghetto families. Finally, there is a relation between teen childbearing and high school graduation, say Upchurch and McCarthy,

> *but not in the way that most previous studies have assumed. Because we were able to examine the childbearing/schooling association in detail, we conclude that the effect exists not because young mothers are more likely to drop out of school, but because among those who drop out, for whatever reason, those with children are less likely to return to school and graduate (Upchurch and McCarthy, 1990: 231).*

Ill-timed and Unwanted Births

Ill-timed and unwanted births often involve married, rather than unmarried, couples. Some children are wanted, but "not just now," while others are over and above the number the couple had planned ever to have. The former are failures

Feature 7.1 THE NORPLANT DEBATE

Norplant—its capsules are as effective as the pill but last for up to five years. The only serious drawback: couples still need latex condoms to avoid sexually transmitted diseases . . . .

Politicians say they've turned to Norplant out of desperation. Last year Walter Graham, a state senator in Mississippi, proposed that his state require the contraceptive for women with at least four children who want any kind of government support. . . . Graham thinks it will eventually be approved. . . .

Given (the cost), Norplant is increasingly viewed as a contraceptive for women on public assistance. That has helped to revive a long-dormant debate over who should control the fertility of poor women. . . .

(Since 1983), Norplant was approved in 23 countries, including Indonesia, Thailand, and Colombia.

The United States is the only country where coercion has emerged as a serious issue.

"The Norplant Debate," *Newsweek*, February 15, 1993, 37–41.

in timing; the latter were unwanted as well as unplanned. The two National Fertility Studies of Norman Ryder and Charles Westoff asked questions about whether the woman had given birth to a child she wanted to have later, but the birth simply occurred too soon, and also about whether she had given birth to a child after she had the number of children she wanted and thought she was through bearing children (Westoff and Ryder, 1977). Two-fifths of the women in the National Study indicated that they had experienced an ill-timed birth, while, among those women who had had all the children they wanted, one-third reported having a child after they thought they were through. This means, then, that almost three-fourths of women who had completed their child-bearing plans had experienced either a timing or a number failure, with mistiming being more than twice as common as unwanted births (Hofferth, 1983: 533–545; Williams, 1991: 212–215). According to Williams' analysis of the National Survey of Family Growth, the percent unwanted went from 14 in 1973 to 7.7 in 1982 and 10 in 1988. As for ill-timed, the percents were 24, 24, and 25. The differences by race are almost all in unwanted rather than mistimed, with blacks much more likely to have had a child they didn't want (Williams, 1991: 212–215). This is an indication that blacks do not simply welcome any and all births, but that they incorporate the child once it is born.

Such failures, whether in timing or numbers, affect the family economically, in terms of sex-role demands, and in other ways. The result is that unplanned fertility increases the likelihood of marital stress and even disruption. It should also be added that, while unwanted does not mean unloved, the incidence of child abuse and other negative interactions between parent and child is higher when the child was unplanned. Furthermore, the risk of abuse increases with each subsequent unplanned birth: 1.7 times with one child, 2.8 times with two unplanned, 4.6 times with three (Zuravin, 1991: 155–161). This leads to an important question: how can a supposedly technologically and attitudinally "enlightened" population such as that of the United States have such a high rate of contraceptive failure? The answer involves two factors: level of technical efficacy and exposure to risk.

Certain contraceptive methods have a much higher level of technical efficacy than others. Sterilization is, of course, close to 100 percent effective. But among the other methods, the condom and the diaphragm and jelly are considerably less effective than the pill (and the Norplant). Yet none of these methods except sterilization is totally effective; they all have a failure rate, however small.

Exposure to risk involves two elements: first, exposure is greatest if contraception is simply skipped, if the couple "take a chance." But even with constant vigilance the risk is not reduced to zero. In fact, with .95 efficacy (e.g., the condom or diaphragm) an exposure to risk through intercourse four or five times a week will result in only 37 percent of couples using those methods escaping pregnancy over a 15-year period. In other words, high technical efficacy plus high exposure to risk equals a high rate of failure. In this regard, it is noteworthy that, despite the rise in marriage age and the spacing of children, most women have their last wanted child by their early thirties. This leaves them, unless they use sterilization, facing at least 15 years of exposure to the risk of an unwanted birth. The important point to remember is that continued exposure to risk results in substantial contraceptive failure despite an improving technology.

THE REVOLUTION IN FERTILITY CONTROL

Nimkoff wrote in 1960 about "Biological Discoveries and the Future of the Family" (Nimkoff, 1962: 121–127). One of the discoveries he said was imminent was a pill that women could take to avoid having children. In July of that same year such a pill was licensed, setting in motion the contraceptive revolution. Prior to the introduction of the pill, more than three-quarters of all fertility control was by one of three methods: the condom, the diaphragm, or rhythm, which means avoiding intercourse during a portion of the menstrual cycle. By 1970 two-thirds of all women had tried the pill, with half of all women and two-thirds of younger women still using it. Other prevalent methods, besides continued use of the three traditional ones, included the intrauterine device (IUD)—now nearly defunct—and sterilization. Some people use abortion as a "backup" strategy.

Side effects from pill use, including psychological depression, physical discomfort, and fear of cancer were reported by some women during the early years of its dissemination. These effects were reported more often by older women, and though tests have proved inconclusive, the fear of cancer has resulted in fewer older than younger women now using the pill, as noted above, and in some doctors' recommendation that the pill be used for a limited number of years. It is well to note that the revolution in contraception brought on by the pill is far from over. We have already mentioned Norplant, while Atkinson et al. comment on pregnancy vaccines, the male pill, and RU38438, a French development that blocks the action of progesterone (Atkinson et al., 1986: 19–26).

The revolution in contraception is far more than technological; it is not just a matter of a new method becoming predominant in a short period of time. Rather, the pill has introduced new contraceptive expectations and values. The first is: "We should be able to control fertility *completely*." It used to be that couples accepted the very real possibility of contraceptive failure, of unwanted births. In fact, when asked, young wives might even answer the question "How many children do you expect to have?" with a higher figure than the question "How many children do you want?" Now, however, we expect perfect contraception, and the increase in both sterilization and abortion can be seen as at least in part an outgrowth of this expectation (McLaughlin and Micklin, 1983: 47–55). The second new value brought about by the pill is: "Fertility control should be *unobtrusive*." That is, contraception should not intrude upon the sex act or in any way lessen the couple's enjoyment of it. The condom and diaphragm are obtrusive; the pill and IUD are not. The IUD, a device that is inserted into the uterus and left until the woman desires to become pregnant, has been found in a small number of cases to result in infection or even a perforated uterus. It may also fall out, resulting in an unwanted pregnancy. With these discoveries, most couples have ceased to use it and have returned to one of the other methods. There is considerable feeling on the part of feminist groups that a contraceptive method that makes intercourse comfortable for the male but results in health risks for the female is decidedly patriarchal or male biased. One tongue-in-cheek response is found in Feature 7.2. Due to such negative reactions, very few current contraceptors use the IUD.

Sterilization is the fastest growing contraceptive method among couples who have had all the children they want. In 1965 one member of 12 percent of such couples had been sterilized, by 1970 the percent was 18, only 3 years later it had risen to 29 percent, and by 1982 it was 41 percent of contracepting couples (39 percent of married couples) (Bumpass, 1987: 347; Mosher, 1987: 42–43). Bumpass states that over three-fourths of those who do not want more children will eventually sterilize (Bumpass, 1987). Of interest is the fact that this is not a female phenomenon; rather, the sterilized are about half women (through hysterectomies or tubal ligation), and half men (through vasectomies).

What is impressive about the rapid rise in contraceptive sterilization is that only a few decades ago it was thought to be both dangerous and a negative condition reserved for criminals and other "social outcasts." As Bumpass notes, until 1969, the official manual of the American College of Obstetricians and Gynecologists suggested that for a woman to be sterilized she should be 25 years old with 5 living children, 30 years old with 4 children, or 35 years old with 3 children. Now, however, with improved operating techniques and with the unobtrusive value mentioned above, sterilization has become the major method of birth control for couples in which the woman is 25 or older.[4] In 1990, $95 million was spent in the United States to provide contraceptive sterilization, 93 percent of it by the federal government (Gold and Daley, 1991: 204–211).

Abortion is best viewed as a backup or safety net in the sense that it is now employed by some women in the case of contraceptive failure. In other words, the pill and sterilization are preventive measures for an unwanted birth; abortion is a "cure." In the early 1970s the attitude toward legalized abortion was already becoming more positive in certain social categories, so that the Supreme Court ruling of 1973 was not a totally abrupt turnabout. In January of that year the Court ruled that, until the end of three months, abortion was an issue strictly between a pregnant woman and her doctor. During the next three months, the Court ruled that abortion was permissible for the "preservation and protection of maternal health." The ruling likewise permitted states to prohibit abortion during the final trimester. Attitudes were changing prior to 1973, we have said. However, they were still very much divided, as can be seen from the following: in 1968 abortion on demand or "for any reason" was opposed by 84 percent of the U.S. population; in 1974 the percentage had dropped to 59. The drive for abortion rights, says Gordon, was a response to (1) teen sexual activity, (2) an increase in two-earner and single-parent families, that "spurred the demand for abortion among married women for whom contraception had failed," and (3) the underdevelopment of contraception (Gordon, 1982: 49).

Various attitudes toward abortion revolve around such issues as the number of months pregnant, where the abortion occurs, and the reasons for it. These attitudes range from total opposition at any time, under any conditions, for any reason, to approval at any time, under any conditions, for any reason that the mother desires. Most people, of course, range between these positions, with some pro-abortionists tending to oppose it after six months of pregnancy and

Feature 7.2   **MEN! A NEW BREAKTHROUGH IN CONTRACEPTION**

The newest development in male contraception was unveiled recently at the American Women's Surgical Symposium held at the Ann Arbor Medical Center. Dr. Sophia Merkin of the Merkin Clinic announced the preliminary findings of a study conducted on 763 unsuspecting graduate students at a large midwest university. In her report, Dr. Merkin stated that the device—the IPD—was a breakthrough in male contraception. It will be marketed under the trade name "Umbrelly."

The IPD (Intra-penile Device) resembles a tiny folded umbrella which is inserted through the head of the penis and pushed into the scrotum with a plunger-like instrument. Occasionaly there is perforation of the scrotum, but this is disregarded, since it is known that the male has few nerve endings in this area of his body. The underside of the umbrella contains a spermicidal jelly, hence the name, "umbrelly."

Experiments on a thousand white whales from the continental shelf (whose sexual apparatus is said to be closest to man's) proved the Umbrelly to be 100 percent effective in preventing production of sperm, and eminently satisfactory to the female whale since it doesn't interfere with her rutting pleasure.

Dr. Merkin declared the Umbrelly to be statistically safe for the human male. She reported that of 763 male graduate students tested with the device, only 2 died of scrotal infection, only 20 experienced swelling of the tissues, 3 developed cancer of the testicles, and 13 were too depressed to have an erection. She stated that common complaints ranged from cramping to acute abdominal pain. She emphasized that these symptoms were merely indications that the man's body had not yet adjusted to the device, but would probably disappear within a year.

One complication caused by the IPD and briefly mentioned by Dr. Merkin was the incidence of massive scrotal infection necessitating the surgical removal of the testicles. "But this is a rare case," said Dr. Merkin, "too rare to be statistically important." She and other distinguished members of the Women's College of Surgeons agreed that the benefits far outweighed the risk to any individual man.

Belita H. Cowan, reprinted from *The Match*, in *Free For All*, 13 April 1977, p. 2.

with some anti-abortionists willing to allow it if the mother's health is in danger.

By the late 1980s, the anti-abortion movement had succeeded in cutting back both public and private support for family planning clinics, and state legislators (especially male) were "seeking to apply child abuse laws to the fetus to protect it from an offending mother" (Faludi, 1991: 418, 423). And, as Faludi points out, part of the male opposition to abortion is due to the greater control this gives women over their own lives — in other words, the lessening of male (patriarchal) control.

Just how widespread is abortion at present, and how rapidly has it spread? Abortion has a long history both cross-culturally and in the United States. D'Emilio and Freedman note that estimates are "that between 1800 and 1830, one abortion occurred for every 25 to 30 live births. By the 1850s, the proportion had increased to as many as one abortion per every five or six live births" (D'Emilio and Freedman, 1988: 65). However, by 1900 it had become illegal in virtually every state. Between 1940 and 1965 the rate appears to have dropped even further, having picked up again since that time, with the greatest increases coming between 1970 an 1980. This rise in rate is seen most dramatically in the fact that from 1978 through 1981 over one-quarter of all U.S. pregnancies ended in a legal abortion. From 1980 to 1987 the abortion rate fell by six percent (Faludi, 1991: 403). One further issue concerns illegal abortions: no one knows for sure how many illegal abortions occurred in 1966, when there were only 6,000 legal ones, though one estimate is that perhaps 70 percent of current legal abortions would have previously occurred illegally.

Looking at some of the socio-demographic determinants of abortion, Powell-Griner and Trent find that abortions are more likely among metropolitan women, pregnant women with at least 12 years of education, women with no previous live births, and white unmarried women (Powell-Griner and Trent, 1987: 559). As far as notifying the husband is concerned, over 90 percent do at least minimally notify him. However, one reason for not telling is fear of abuse, and another is that the pregnancy was the result of an extra-marital affair. Again, both telling and not telling can be because of patriarchy or male control (Plutzer and Ryan, 1987: 183–189; Smith and Kronauge, 1990: 585–598).

Whether one agrees with the trend in legal abortions or strongly opposes it, it seems clear that the widespread values of complete fertility control and women's liberation from patriarchy have set a climate where abortion is viewed by many as a reasonable alternative to an unwanted pregnancy.

SECTION FOUR

SUMMARY AND CONCLUSIONS

Half of the reduction in fertility since 1957 is due to a reduction in contraceptive failure. The other half is a result of reduced fertility desires. It used to be that our values had built into them expectations (or rationalizations) of child-bearing for women. Now, however, child-bearing can be considered one among several rational choices couples can make. As Sweet and Bumpass say, parenthood has changed from an ascribed to an achieved status; it is truly an option. Accidental pregnancies are simply much less tolerable (Sweet and Bumpass, 1987: 396; see also Francoeur, 1984: 89–105). Roles other than that of mother may be opted for, since there is a fairly good chance of avoiding motherhood if one so desires. Nock comments that women's values about male-female relationships and about women in society are affecting women's fertility. For growing numbers of women, Nock says, "the role of mother is being rede-fined in ways quite similar to the traditional role of father—financial support of children" (Nock, 1987: 373). While this may overstate the change, the fact is that it is now possible that a woman may have *fewer* children than she says she desires. For as other interests and careers intrude on the time and energy of a couple, they may postpone and eventually omit child-bearing. Another way to see the contraceptive revolution is that, for the first time, something must be done besides having intercourse in order to *get* pregnant, rather than to *avoid* getting pregnant. That is, previously one had to put on the condom or put in the diaphragm to avoid pregnancy, while today one has to stop taking the pill in order to become pregnant. That is *quite* a change.

It may be inferred from the reference to "other interests and careers" that fertility and women's careers are inversely related, so that as fertility goes down, the number of women employed goes up, or vice versa. This is not, how-ever, the case. From 1940 until 1960 both fertility and the proportion of married mothers employed rose. They are related to different values: the former to the complete control value of which we have been speaking, and the latter to the value of increased opportunity for women. The issue of employed wives and mothers will be further explored in Chapter 12.

The Socialization Process

CHAPTER 8

Socialization is the process through which the individual incorporates the attitudes and behaviors considered appropriate by any group or society. It involves self-concept (identity formation), which includes conscience development and the twin problems of identification and ego struggle—all of which are related to intrapersonal and interpersonal adjustment. There are differences in socialization, not only between societies, but also between the sexes and among the classes and subcultural groups of a given society. The socialization process is the means whereby similarities and differences are perpetuated. Rapid social change and emphasis on peer activity have gone along with changing fads in child rearing advice. In adolescence the struggle intensifies as the individual balances involvement with parents and peer group while moving toward autonomy and adult roles.

SOCIALIZATION: CROSS-CULTURAL CONTENT AND PRINCIPLES

Cross-cultural Content

Every individual comes into the world with certain physical, emotional, and intellectual characteristics, that is, with a defined heredity. However, the infant has, at birth, the capacity to become a Chinese Communist, a Nigerian, or an American; and what that person does become depends greatly upon his or her socialization. This view, held by many social psychologists and anthropologists today, was well expressed by Margaret Mead:

> *We are forced to conclude that human nature is almost unbelievably malleable, responding accurately and contrastingly to contrasting cultural conditions. The differences between individuals who are members of different cultures, like the differences between individuals within a culture, are almost entirely to be laid to differences in conditioning, especially during early childhood, and the form of this conditioning is culturally determined (Mead, 1950: 191).*

Socialization (Mead's "conditioning") may be defined as *the process by which one learns or is taught how to behave in any group or society.* It is learning the culture, or ways, of a group; the process encompasses both the teachers and the learners, the socializing agents and the socialized. While the early years of childhood are stressed in much of the literature on socialization, the process actually continues throughout life, as a person changes roles and confronts new expectations (Brim and Wheeler, 1966). In fact, the process flows both ways, as when immigrant parents learn the new culture from their children or middle-aged women learn "feminist and liberation" principles from their daughters (Morgan, 1975: 41–42; see also Peters, 1985: 921–933). During childhood, however, much of the individual's culture becomes fixed or internalized, as anyone who has moved from one society to another after childhood can attest.

Biological makeup is, according to Matthaei and others, not enough to turn us into human beings: "An individual who acts according to instinct in society is not considered human. Even activities we consider to be biologically based such as eating or sexual intercourse are ruled by ideas rather than instinct" (Matthaei, 1982: 2). Our biological inheritance *permits* and *requires* socialization, but also *limits* it. No culture can demand that the individual run faster, lift more, or solve harder problems than is humanly possible. But within the bounds of these limitations, the potentialities are almost limitless. My bias, in other words, is that the vast majority of gender, racial, and societal differences is fixed after we enter this world, not before (see Feature 8.1). The "chicken girl," Isabel, is trying to be a chicken. She cannot fly or peck well because of her biological limitations, but she is trying to do what her "socializing agents" have taught her to do. Furthermore, it will be very difficult at this stage for her to catch up and be a completely normal human being.

We tend to be unaware of much of our own socialization process, simply taking it for granted that our beliefs are "good" and that we know "the way" things should be done. Yet there are extreme differences between our "ways" and those of other cultures, involving even aspects of our attitudes and behavior that we may consider to be inherently "human." Economic competitiveness is not universal. Aggressive behavior may be rewarded in one cultural setting, passivity and amiability in another. Mead's summary of the differences between the Arapesh and Mungdugumor of New Guinea illustrates the variability in cultural styles:

We found the Arapesh—both men and women—displaying a personality that, out of our historically limited preoccupations, we would call maternal in its parental aspects, and feminine in its sexual aspects. We found men, as well as women, trained to be cooperative, unaggressive, responsive to the needs and demands of others. We found no idea that sex was a powerful driving force either for men or for women. In marked contrast to these attitudes, we found among the Mungdugumor that both men and women developed as ruthless, aggressive, positively sexed individuals, with the maternal cherishing aspects of personality at a minimum. Both men and women approximated to a personality type that we in our culture would find only in an undisciplined and very violent male (Mead, 1950: 190).

The setting for such cultural differences may be diagrammed as in Figure 8.1. Within the limits set by human endowment, each culture tends to reinforce certain attributes, while rejecting or punishing others. The result is that a particular type of personality comes to be dominant. Harris describes clearly the relation between personality and culture in socialization:

If "personality" is defined in terms of individual emotional structure, and "culture" as a totality of categories, values, and expectations, then the family may be seen as the

---

Feature 8.1   GIRL, 9, CLUCKS, FLAPS HER ARMS AFTER EIGHT YEARS IN CHICKEN COOP

The psychiatrist treating a girl who spent eight of her nine years in a chicken coop is seeking aid from the wife of Portugal's President Ramalho Eanes.

   The dark-haired, severely retarded girl, Isabel Queresma, flaps her arms like a chicken and, unable to talk, makes chicken-like noises.

   Her teeth and jaw protrude in a beak-like profile. She has a cataract on an eye that doctors say may have been caused by repeated hen pecks.

   The girl is currently in a Lisbon institution for retarded children but has not progressed. . . .

   Isabel used to be left inside the coop by her . . . mother. . . . Isabel survived on a diet of corn and cabbage.

The Capital Times, July 1, 1980.

FIGURE 8.1   CULTURAL POSSIBILITIES AND LIMITATIONS

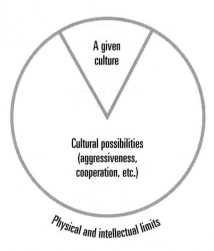

site of the process which simultaneously generates the former while transmitting the latter. The new entrant to the culture both learns to feel certain emotions and to associate them with cultural meanings (Harris, 1983: 158).

Societies do differ, however, in the amount of variability (the size of the wedge-shaped section of Figure 8.1) they allow. Some, like the Mungdugumor, reward and value a very narrow range of personality types, so that only a small number of individuals diverge from the very specific cultural ideal. Such a society is called *homogeneous* with respect to its culture. Other societies—the United States, for example—not only include several subcultural styles, but also reward a wider range of cultural possibilities, making these societies more *heterogeneous* in this respect. In addition, a given member of a heterogeneous society may be more strongly affected than a member of a homogeneous society by the pressures of conflicting cultural principles, such as expectations of cooperativeness and competitiveness, of honesty and success. There are, then, differences between societies, both in the range of acceptable socialization patterns and in the range of alternatives offered the individual.

A particular pattern of socialization and culture also determines who will be the deviant in a society. Though it is impossible to know with certainty, Mead assumes and other writers concur that the range of hereditary types, or innate dispositions, is virtually the same from one society to another. Yet each culture tends to cultivate and value a specific portion of the range of possibilities. Thus, there may be a fundamental discrepancy between an individual's innate disposition and the kind of personality rewarded by the society into which he or she is born. Under these conditions, the socialization process may never bring that person to the point of conforming to society's expectations. Thus in the past, the Cheyenne Indian boy who by his own nature was shy, fearful, and nonaggressive and who never overcame these tendencies may never have reached the cultural ideal of courage and bravery. If he failed to "measure up" during puberty, when he was required to demonstrate his ability to be a brave, he may have been forced to become a transvestite, taking on both the appearance and social role of a Cheyenne woman (Grinnell, 1923). But the same boy might have been incorporated with relative ease into Arapesh culture. One reason for cultural deviance is, of course, that socialization is an imperfect process in two ways. First, as indicated by the Cheyenne example, it does not result in molding every individual to the cultural ideal; second, individuals are not *completely* socialized and, consequently, act upon their society as well as being acted upon by its socializing agents.

Without dwelling further upon the great diversities of socialization and cultural patterns in different societies, it is time to introduce a few of the key terms that will be helpful in understanding socialization in the United States.

Definitions and Principles of Socialization

Socialization is the process by which the individual learns to control his or her biological drives, is taught what behavior is acceptable and what is unacceptable, and develops an identity, or self-concept. At least three relatively comprehensive theories have been advanced to explain various aspects of this process. These are *psychoanalytic* theory, *learning* theory, and *role-symbolic interaction* theory. Though the theories are sometimes viewed as contradictory, they are better seen as emphasizing different components of the human experience. Psychoanalytic theory stresses the importance of biological endowment and drives, as well as unconscious processes. Learning theory stresses responses to stimuli and mental or psychological processes. Role theory and symbolic interaction theory stress sociological processes or the importance of the socializing agents.[1] This discussion will focus on role theory and symbolic interaction theory, though each of the three types will contribute to the discussion at certain points.

Socialization involves identity or self-concept clarification. Identity means a sense of the categories or groups to which one belongs and some conception of the kind of person one is. Important portions of self-concept development include the conscience, ego struggle, and identification. In their book *Children of the Counterculture*, Rothchild and Wolf give a rather picturesque account of *conscience* in their own children as members of "straight" society:

> *One phrase we never heard in a commune was: "You know better than that." We had already developed in Chauncey and Bernsie a kind of Mythical You, some other little person who lives inside them and does everything right. This is the person who "knows better," who "should be ashamed," to whom we say "I am surprised at you" (Rothchild and Wolf, 1976: 200).*

Guilt is, then, the self-punishment you administer when you do what might have been punished by others if they had seen you do it. Culture and socialization, of course, play a big part in accounting for differences in conscience and guilt about specific acts, whether they be masturbating, lying, head-hunting, or walking on the grave of one's ancestors.

The issue of identity is about selection, self-actualization, and choice. According to Pat Caplan, the theorists who brought identity onto "the agenda of the anguished liberal West saw it as roughly equalling individuality, a reality to be struggled for, and to which we will refer below as "ego struggle" (Caplan, 1987: 37). One of these theorists, Erik Erikson, sees socialization patterns as based on a coexistence between permissiveness and strictness. According to Tamar Rapoport, Erikson's subcategories include obligations, control, experimentation, rights, and responsibility (Rapoport, 1988: 160). While these are important issues, McGoldrick warns that most male theoreticians—Freud, Erikson, Piaget, Kohlberg—stress individual instead of relational issues, and thereby ignore female development. Another assumption came close to holding motherhood responsible for whatever happened (McGoldrick et al., 1989: 203, 211).

Ego Struggle, Identification, and Attachment

We have heard it said, perhaps in school, that every individual is unique. *Ego struggle* is the process whereby the growing individual seeks to discover and assert that uniqueness. *Identification* pertains to the "more or less lasting influence one person exerts on the behavior of another" (Winch, 1962: 142). A growing girl is likely to learn that she behaves certain ways as a female and that she must eventually be a wife, lover, mother, jobholder, from significant other people—especially her own mother—she sees playing those roles. Jerome Kagan speaks of the "child's belief that he shares basic qualities with a parental model," and Suzanne Steinmetz, drawing on Robert Sears et al., defines identification as "the mechanism by which the child's behaving like the parents or perceiving the similarity between self and parents becomes intrinsically rewarding" (Kagan, 1977: 35; Steinmetz, 1979: 125). Identification is not a single variable but involves either personal or positional influence or both. A role model is someone in a particular position, such as that of father or husband, from whom one learns how to behave when one assumes that same position. However, one may reject or not even know about the specifics of certain roles that one's father plays and still identify with his character or success, that is, personally rather than positionally.

Attachment goes beyond identification and includes all the various aspects of connectedness with significant others, such as parents. Strong attachment, especially to the mother, is exhibited by most children at least through the third year. After that, the child may begin to be increasingly comfortable with alternate or subordinate attachment-figures, such as a relative or teacher. John Bowlby, in his major work on attachment, reviews what is known about imprinting or attachment in humans thus:

i. In human infants social responses of every kind are first elicited by a wide array of stimuli and are later elicited by a much narrower array, confined after some months to stimuli arising from one or a few particular individuals.

ii. There is evidence of a marked bias to respond socially to certain kinds of stimuli more than to others.

iii. The more experience of social interaction an infant has with a person the stronger his attachment to that person becomes.

iv. The fact that learning to discriminate different faces commonly follows periods of intensive staring and listening suggests that exposure learning may be playing a part.

v. In most infants attachment behavior to a preferred figure develops during the first year of life. . . .

vi. After about six months, and markedly so after eight or nine months, babies are more likely to respond to strange figures with fear responses . . . than they are when they are younger.

vii. Once a child has become strongly attached to a particular figure, he tends to prefer that figure to all others, and such preference tends to persist despite separation (Bowlby, 1969: 222–223).

While Bowlby's work is full of insights, it also treats attachment in a somewhat more either-or, or mutually exclusive, fashion that reality is. The notion, for example, that there is preference for a single figure ignores the possibility of equal attachment toward several, of changing attachments, and of important degrees of attachment. In addition, Rohner's discussion of the "warmth" dimension adds to our understanding of both personality and attachment. Rohner notes what happens to children who perceive of themselves as either rejected or accepted. "Seriously rejected children," says Rohner, "have not learned how to give love because they have not known loving parents" (or adults) "after whom they may model their own behavior, and even though they crave affection they have difficulty giving or accepting it" (Rohner, 1986: 83, 171). This ties together issues of both identification and attachment.

Personality Integration

Personality integration also has two sides. The first is *intrapersonal*, or psychological, adjustment, which involves the reconciling of the individual's preferred self-concept, or how you wish you were, with the actual self-concept, or the way you perceive yourself to be. You may see yourself as a great lover and athlete, but you may be afraid of the opposite sex and unable to catch a ball. In this case you have a "reconciling" problem on your hands, though it is not the kind of conscious process that you can either analyze or manipulate.

The second aspect of personality integration, *interpersonal* adjustment, involves reconciling how one acts with how others think one ought to act. For example, a man may see himself as nonaggressive and friendly and he may live in accordance with this preferred self-concept, but his family may chide him for lack of assertiveness and for not getting ahead. In such a case there is a problem between one's preferred self-concept and the demands of others. Fortunate, it would seem, are those persons for whom what they think they ought to be, what they perceive themselves to be, and what others expect of them all coincide.

With these issues and principles in mind, let us now turn to the specific historical-cultural context with which we are most concerned: socialization in the United States.

SOCIALIZATION IN THE UNITED STATES

The Principles Applied

We must begin by bringing together two points that were made in distinguishing between homogeneous and heterogeneous societies in general. First, the nuclear family of the modern industrial world places a great socializing burden upon parents. How did "nuclear family embeddedness" come to characterize intimate life in the industrial world? Harris notes that Richard Sennett locates the mechanism producing the closed, intense nuclear family:

> *It is a self-defeating search for self-respect, born out of status deprivation in a culture which makes each person feel individually responsible for what happens to them, and identifies self with the badges of achievement (Harris, 1983: 171).*

Sennett, according to Harris, is saying that the lack of true meaning in what one does, coupled with emphasis on individual achievement, puts pressure not only on the nuclear family, but on socialization for the children's future.

In an extended household, such as the joint family of India, there may be multiple adult role models with whom the growing child can identify. Among the Nayar, the biological father may have had no role in socialization whatsoever, the responsibility being borne by the women and certain aging males of the matrilineal kindred. It is not universally true, therefore, that one's parents are the prime significant others, *but it is true in the United States*. James Walters and Nick Stinnett state it thus:

> *From the literature it would appear that in Western Society we think of the responsibility of rearing children as resting with their parents. The disadvantage of localizing this responsibility is that it places extensive responsibility on parents who may be inadequate (Walters and Stinnett, 1971: 130).*

There is some debate, we should add, on how important the father is in U.S. socialization at present. Is it parenting or mothering that is important to the growing child? We will return to this below.

Parental cruciality in the United States must, however, be weighed off against a second conclusion concerning *heterogeneous* modern industrial society. Modernization, Thomas and Weigert find, leads to decreased conformity to *authoritative* significant others, in particular to parents and religious leaders. Conformity to nonauthoritative significant others, such as peer group members, does not show this relationship to modernization (Thomas and Weigert, 1971: 843–844). Thus we find that parents are the most influential significant others in industrial societies such as the United States, but that they have a more difficult time making their authority and influence "stick" than do the significant others, whoever they might be, in preindustrial societies. One study compares youths in the United States with those in Colombia, in terms of their learning of work roles. While U.S. kids discuss work plans more with their parents (especially mothers), they pick nonfamily role models more often than Colombian young people (Laska and Micklin, 1981: 187–204).

Another important issue in socialization concerns the dualistic concepts we use to describe reality. Right/left, over/under, abstract/concrete, sameness/difference, male/female, heterosexual/homosexual—these and other dichotomies guide our thinking, and carry the ideological overtones of good/bad or better/worse (see Rhode, 1990: 15). We noted this earlier in the discussion of racial and ethnic differences, when they are interpreted as deviant or problematic. It is such dualistic thinking that feminists have attacked, since much of it has been used to subordinate females, to treat them as not just different but less. A most interesting research spinoff from gender dichotomization is the study by Prager and Bailey. They find in their small sample that androgynous (non-gender-dichotomous) respondents are the most mature and have the highest level of ego development (Prager and Bailey, 1985: 534). This is another issue that will be discussed later.

So with these issues—nuclear familism, heterogeneity, and dualism—in mind, what can be said about the history of socialization in the United States? The colonial United States, it may be recalled, was "nuclearized" but not "industrialized," and was less heterogeneous than the present-day United States. The colonial nuclear family had achieved a substantial degree of privacy with respect to its social network. Interrelations were fairly intense (in the sense in which that term was used above). That is, children saw their parents at work, at play, at worship, under conditions of discipline, fun, and relaxation. The family was the hub of many societal functions; where this is so, we have postulated that positive identification within the family unit is extremely likely. Not only did children see their parents carrying out the various aspects of their roles, but there were few alternative role models for them to emulate. Thus, even when children had rankled under their own socialization, perhaps at the hands of a stern disciplinarian, they were likely to follow a similar pattern with their children later in life. Though they might have thought as they were being punished, "If I live through this I'll never treat my kids this way," when they became fathers they did in fact behave as their father did, because that is "the way fathers are." Furthermore, the other models available to them, perhaps uncles or older siblings, were more likely to reinforce than to negate the model presented by the fathers.[2]

What about a social setting in which nonfamilial socialization and divergent subculture patterns vie with the family for influence in socialization, and in which a parent plays their basic economic role outside the family? The proposition most appropriate to this situation states that the less central the nuclear family is to the functioning of the society, the more likely it is that one will establish one's major identifications outside that unit. The pattern in the contemporary United States is not quite as simple as this proposition might indicate. The growing individual is most certainly confronted with multiple role-model possibilities. He or she is unlikely to know precisely what father or mother does when they are away from home, but a boy may think he knows what the football coach or the movie actor does. An interesting recent study of adolescence shows how ambivalent attitudes toward marriage parallel those portrayed on television (Signorielli, 1991: 121–149). Socialization, then, involves both family and non-family influences.

As for the parents, the son is aware of his father's home behavior, but not of his economic or extra-home role. Likewise, daughters are more likely to know what a homemaker-mother does than a mother who is employed. However, intensity of interaction—frequently greater than in the colonial family, due to the smaller size of families today—virtually offsets the influence of competing agents of socialization outside the home. Therefore, one small change from the colonial family to today's family is weaker identification with parents' role behaviors, that is, positional identification.

Even this difference must be qualified, however. The foregoing discussion focused on positional identification, making the point that the range of possible role identifications between children and parents is more limited today, since many facets of the parental role are played away from the home. Forms of personal identification between child and parent, however, are quite prevalent today. The son or daughter may identify with a general characteristic of mother or father, such as success, or an aspect of the parent's character, such as honesty. Yet on the whole the proposition still holds: the modeling of day-to-day behavior after members of the nuclear family is more problematic today than was the case in colonial times. In fact, precisely where individuals will find their role models and whether or not they will reinforce one another is problematic.

This leads to an interesting point of speculation: If finding adequate sources of identification is currently more difficult than it was in the colonial family, can we conclude that ego struggle is therefore easier? Once again, the conclusion is not quite that simple. Colonial children, we have said, were given time free from supervision. Yet, in both of these instances, the intensity of the role models was such that the socializing agents were confident that the growing individuals would internalize their group's standards and eventually cease to dabble in alternatives. In other words, children might have perceived themselves as having substantial freedom, not realizing that the lack of clear-cut alternatives and the intensity of relations with significant others prevented ego struggle from ever really becoming an issue.

Ego struggle *is* an issue in the modern industrial world; but it is not necessarily an easy one. Parents are often quite successful in altering the child's unique development. They may in some instances dominate a child for the satisfaction of having someone to dominate. You may have seen cartoons in which the father, having "taken a beating" from his superiors at work, finds occasion to spank or scold his son upon arriving home. Or, as noted above, parents may demand excessive achievement on the child's part in order to compensate for their own mediocre accomplishments, thus helping to solve their own identity problems. Ambitions that were thwarted in the father's youth, in athletics for example, may be achieved through offspring. Or—and this is a criticism often leveled at the middle-class mother—the parent may be so devoted to the child and so attentive to every need as to overprotect the child and thus thwart the development of his or her unique potentialities. Thus, it would be an oversimplification to say that ego struggle was the greater problem in the colonial family and that in the present-day family identification is the greater problem. Due to a lack of awareness of adequate alternatives, ego struggle was not recognized as a problem in the colonial family, although it was at least indirectly noted by the ministers of the day in their preaching against "the sins of the flesh." Nor is it true that parents today limit themselves to simply presenting alternatives and teaching their children how to think critically in order to make their own behavioral decisions. On the contrary, parents are still quite concerned to pass along their culture to their offspring, but awareness of alternatives limits their ability to do so. The result is that identification is more problematic today than it was in the colonial family; ego struggle is more possible today, but is kept problematic by the conscious awareness of alternatives weighed against the indoctrinating efforts of parents and other socializing agents.

Intrapersonal and interpersonal adjustment, when placed in a historical context, are quite closely related to the questions of identification and ego struggle just discussed. In colonial days, the behavioral standards of one's parents and other ancestral models were generally internalized and reinforced by one's experiences. When individuals did encounter divergent expectations, it was assumed that they would behave according to their internalized standards, that is, their preferred self-concept based on strong identifications. In contemporary society, however, as noted in Chapter 5, parents have learned by their own experiences that, in order to be successful members of society, they and their children must be adaptable and flexible. In addition, most of the old behavioral absolutes have been called into question on what are assumed to be rational bases.

Writing a generation ago, David Reisman et al. argued that the individual in U.S. society has changed from an inner-directed person, whose behavior is based on a preferred self-concept drawn from ancestral models, to an other-directed person, whose behavior is based on conforming to the expectations of his or her peers (Reisman et al., 1950). Reisman did not mean, as some interpreted him, that people today worry about what others think while formerly they did not. Instead the issue is: Who are the others whose opinions and expectations influence us? In an earlier day the family and certain members of the ascending generation (often persons no longer alive) tended to dominate; today, as we have said, authoritarian significant others such as parents, while still important, are less dominant models than was formerly the case. This, in turn, increases the influence of whatever group the individual is part of at the moment.

Reisman's ideas are intuitively appealing but have been somewhat difficult to test empirically. Furthermore, we cannot assume that nothing important has changed in forty years. And, of course, a key issue throughout this book has to do with the extent to which individualism (and the ego struggle that fosters it) has made inroads into the other-directedness which is also part of today's scene. To what extent have women's liberation and other attempts to further individual potentialities cut into both male-dominated familism and other-directedness? Our conclusions lean toward the answer: "Not as much as we might like to believe." Inner-directedness and other-directness should not be thought of in either-or terms; nor should individualism. Self, peers, and parents/ancestors are the three orientations of the central players in these three conceptualizations, and while the move from inner- to other-directedness to individualism makes sense historically, it is well to remind ourselves again that much historical analysis has been male-focused. The process for females has kept them more embedded in ancestral models (inner-directed), and less individualistic than males. That is an issue feminism is confronting, and to which we will return below.

The comparison of colonial days with the present again leaves out much intervening history. In addition, it ignores the effects of specific historical events, as well as periodic vacillation in the advice given to parents. In Chapter 4 we referred to some of the data on child-rearing between 1800 and the present. Elder's important work *Children of the Great Depression* demonstrates the effects of a specific period of recent history. Economic deprivation during the Depression, he finds, had an effect on the acquisitive values of offspring. Depression adolescents tended to become more traditional or conservative than those of earlier or later eras and postponed marriage, parenthood, and purchases (Elder, 1974, and subsequent articles). Let us now look at the approaches to child rearing over the course of U.S. history, as seen through the eyes of the "advice-givers."

Advising Parents on Child Development

The passing of family culture from one generation to the next is most easily accomplished in a society that looks to ancestral models for authority, wisdom, and guidance. In the United States of the 1970s, however, Dr. Benjamin Spock, *Parents Magazine*, and other experts became successful in "displacing grandmother as the authority on child development" (Geboy, 1981: 205–210). Spock, with his collaborator Michael Rothenberg, has tried to keep up with current changes, as can be seen in Feature 8.2.

Looking to peers or contemporaries for guidance is, of course a form of other-directedness. The result is that instead of receiving accumulated and relatively unchanged advice, the U.S. parent gets advice that fluctuates with the latest fad. Lynn Bloom, for example, notes that in the early 1800s the emphasis was on the child's sinfulness, and the need to break the child's will "for his own good." After the Civil War, there was increased concern with the child's tenderness and need to develop fully. By the twentieth century, John Watson and others were trying to convince parents of *their* inadequacies and to produce happy and independent children (Bloom, 1976; Watson, 1928). Using a shorter time span, Wolfenstein showed how, in 1890, the dominant viewpoint was to indulge the child; by 1920, scheduling and a certain aloofness predominated; and, by 1945, indulgent mothering was once again recommended (Wolfenstein, 1953: 120–130). Are the fads bad for the offspring? An interesting insight can be gained into that question from a paper by Allen Williams, Frank Bean, and Russell Curtis on parental constraints. Neither permissiveness nor restrictiveness, the authors find, results in maladjusted offspring—unless either orientation becomes extreme. That is, the orientation does not seem to matter so much as that it be "in moderation" (Williams et al., 1970: 283–290).

The swing of the pendulum historically in advice to parents has actually been between two viewpoints regarding the nature and development of the child. These viewpoints are often labelled the "traditional" and "developmental," or, from the child's standpoint, conformity and autonomy (Rossi and Rossi, 1990: 149). The traditional view, which has some roots in Puritan ideology, reached its greatest strength during the Victorian era in Great Britain; this view sees the necessity of curbing the child's impulses. Children are not as wise as their parents, so the reasonable form of socialization should stress nuclear family values and obedience and reserve on the child's part. A typical reaction to the offspring who deviates from the family's expectations used to be: "He is the black sheep *of the family.*" The developmental view, expounded by Freud, Watson, John Dewey, and many others recently, presents the idea that children should be allowed to develop their own potentialities at their own speed and in their own way, thus maximizing creativity and uniqueness. The latter approach, of course, fits well this society's emphasis upon newness, creativity, change, and individualism. A typical reaction to an offspring's deviance is: "Where did we go wrong?" or "Where did we fail *him* or *her*?" In fact, the traditional and developmental emphases in socialization are closely related to individual embeddedness in the nuclear family and individual non-embeddedness—or individualism, respectively. It is not surprising that the overall long-range trend has been—al-

Feature 8.2   **DR. SPOCK'S NEW ADVICE**

There is . . . a detailed list of the "unprecedented strains on American families today" and an exhortation to parents to become politically active and to rear children "to become kind, cooperative, feeling people . . . who will not let their jobs distort their lives. . . ."

It also breaks new ground with discussions of psycho-social developments such as step-family dynamics, homosexuality and open adoptions, with medical updates on AIDS, immunizations, headaches and choking. . . . Here are some new entries in Dr. Spock's venerable book:

Quality time: "The idea of quality time in itself is fine. But I'm concerned that a few . . . parents take it as an obligation . . . long after patience and enjoyment have run out."

Homosexuality: "If you think your adolescent may be homosexual or lesbian, the first thing to do is to get your fears and anxieties under control."

Passive smoke: "Children who live with smokers are more subject to bronchitis, pneumonia, chronic cough and middle ear infections. They have higher than average cholesterol levels in their blood."

Mary Maushard (*Baltimore Sun*), "Spock updates famed baby book," *The Capital Times*, March 3, 1992, 3b.

though there have been fluctuations—toward the developmental, or individual-istic, position. It cannot, however, be concluded that individualism has simply won in U.S. society, but rather that the two views are currently vying for as-cendancy, especially for females.

Gender Differences in Socialization

According to Juanne Clarke, gender or sex identity is based on "(I) the chro-mosomes, (II) the hormone balance, (III) the internal genitalia, (IV) the exter-nal genitalia, (V) the gonads, and (VI) the sex of assignment and subsequent socialization" (Clarke, 1978: 224). Some feel that the first five differences de-termine male and female personalities. Others believe the sixth, socialization, accounts for most of what have been traditionally considered male and female personalities. Although definitions of views of masculinity and femininity have changed in certain particulars over the course of U.S. history, the patterns deemed "culturally appropriate" for boys and girls have generally included the following elements. *Physically*, males should be taller and more muscular and should have facial and body hair. Females, in order to be "feminine," should have an attractive face and body, should be smaller, and should have little ex-traneous facial and body hair. *Behaviorally*, says Shere Hite,

> *Women are not supposed to fight back or take revenge, even psychologically. They are supposed to be "nice" and "loving" no matter what—an almost victim-like psychol-ogy—and to turn the other cheek. While boys are taught in schoolyards to fight back, to compete in athletics, to use a team for support, and so on, girls are taught to be com-passionate and understanding. . . . We (girls) are taught to always question our mo-tives, to give the other person "the benefit of the doubt" (Hite, 1987: 110).*

To this Deborah Tannen adds that boys "tend to play outside, in large groups that are hierarchically structured. . . . Girls, on the other hand, play in small groups or in pairs; the center of a girl's social life is a best friend" (Tannen, 1990: 43). Thus, maleness and femaleness, or manhood and womanhood, are, says Matthaei, "first and foremost ideas, conceptions which females and males strive to realize in their actions" (Matthaei, 1982: 6).

These models, interestingly enough, are reinforced in the picture books that preschool children have been expected to look at (though this orientation is beginning to change). The storybook characters, whether children or adults, have traditionally reinforced the sex-role definitions of males as creative and curious and of females as neat and passive. Attempts to alter these stereotypes during the 1970s resulted in more girls appearing in 1970s books, but with only minor changes in their activities or settings (Kolbe and Lavoie, 1981: 369–374). By the end of the 1980s increasing numbers of children's books were showing women in careers and in various other active roles.

The other way the traditional gender stereotypes have been reinforced is through language. Tannen states this dramatically: "Even if they grow up in the same neighborhood, on the same block, or in the same house, girls and boys grow up in different worlds of words. Others talk to them differently and expect and accept different ways of talking from them" (Tannen, 1990: 43). Talk is what holds girls together, while for boys it is activity. And as Warren Farrell once said: girls ask questions and boys answer them; and girls ask questions even when they know the answer, and boys answer them even when they don't. We will return to communication in Chapter 13.

Various writers and researchers have considered the ways in which these sex-role definitions are implemented in socialization. Some note that physical punishment is used much less frequently with girls than with boys. This links with the fact that the life conditions of girls involve "less physical violence" than is true of boys, while at the same time women have stronger internalized moral standards. Also, more expressiveness is used with and by girls than boys. The genders, say Gill et al., consistently differ in expressiveness and relational orientation, with men less relational. They add that "perhaps because we live in a male-dominant society, the term 'feminine' seems to connote deference to males, emotionality, and lack of assertiveness" (Gill et al., 1987: 396).

Researchers and writers have found that the traditional feminine model still inhibits women from achieving, even instills a fear of success in them. In U.S. society femininity and competitive achievement continue to be viewed as desirable, but mutually exclusive ends (Major, 1979: 63–70). Referring to socialization patterns, Lois Hoffman offers an explanation for the inhibitions of achievement in women:

> *Since girls as compared to boys have less encouragement for independence, more parental protectiveness, less pressure for establishing an identity separate from the mother, and less mother-child conflict which highlights this separation, they engage in less independent exploration of their environments. As a result they develop neither adequate skills nor confidence but continue to be dependent upon others (Hoffman, 1972: 170).*

More recently, Cancian has noted that the family's traditional restriction of freedom, especially for women, is giving way to narcissism (individualism) for both genders (Cancian, 1987: 8). Yet this change is not complete, and the socialization of girls continues to keep them more embedded in family life than boys.

All these writers would agree with Mead that such sex differences are not innate, but are a result of the differential socialization of boys and girls. Despite the increased sex-role awareness of some segments of the population, differential treatment permeates our economic system, the mass media, the school system, and virtually all other institutional structures. Lueptow argues that scholarly reactions in the 1970s overstated public acceptance of and involvement in changing gender roles Lueptow (1984: 287). Werner and LaRussa note that even at Cal-Berkeley, often considered to be on the forefront of change, men and women are still perceived as being fundamentally different from each other (Werner and LaRussa, 1985: 1098). This despite activism and even legislation emphasizing androgyny or the blurring of gender roles. Many in the United States still feel that sex-role differences are a matter of inborn temperament, of the gonads and the hormones, not just of socialization. Others are simply not prepared to support the movement of women into certain types of social roles, feeling that women are needed "in the home and with the children." We saw this view even in recent statements emanating from Russia.

Are the traditional sex-stereotyped models healthy for personality development or not? Much of the current discussion of socialization practices in the United States is related to this question. Featherhead, for example, finds that subjects "high in masculinity" are lower in depression and higher in self-esteem than "feminine" subjects (Featherhead, 1985: 498). Earlier, Weitzman had concluded her article on sex roles in picture books by arguing that rigid sex-role distinctions may be harmful to the normal personality development of boys as well as girls (Weitzman, 1972: 1149–1150). Prager and Bailey's small-sample study agrees with Weitzman: "psychological androgyny is associated with developmental maturity in adulthood and seems to rest in a foundation of successful coping with developmental issues from the early part of the life-span" (Prager and Bailey, 1985: 534). Discussion of the benefits of freedom from rigid sex-role modeling brings us to the verge of the entire feminist-humanist issue, the issue of women's *and* men's liberation, to which we return in Chapters 12 and 18. But for the time being, we close with the reminder that the recent emphasis on freedom for women has not been effective, thus far, in removing all the psychological barriers caused by socialization to the achievement of many otherwise motivated and able young women. And efforts to "liberate" men have only begun.

Socialization and Social Class

We have already noted differences in life style between the affluent mass of United States society—the middle class—and members of the lower class, who must strive to maintain an economic subsistence level. Mention was also made of the working class, the large aggregate of manual workers who have stable employment and a standard of living that includes many of the luxuries of the affluent. This section compares the classes in terms of socialization.

Available evidence from studies conducted the last 60 years or so indicates some of the more important differences between middle, working, and lower class socialization (see Table 8.1). Many studies have found middle-class parents to be more emotionally warm and expressive toward their children, showing pleasure in them and generally bolstering their feelings of confidence. However, Tim Biblarz notes that while black parents, including working-class, are more authoritarian than white, they also give greater amounts of affection and support (Biblarz, 1992: 159). The reason for giving them lots of love at home, says Biblarz, is because the parents know their children will be facing a hostile environment (on this, see Marie Peters, 1988: 228–241). Thus, there is some question about class differences in warmth and affection for children.

If instead of warmth we focus on parental supportiveness, we find a class distinction in the case of fathers. Caplow et al. express it thus: "There are some class differences in norms about child care. Working-class respondents were more likely to see child care as entirely the wife's responsibility" (Caplow et al., 1982: 152). However, this statement does not hold for most working-class

TABLE 8.1   SOCIAL CLASS DIFFERENCES IN SOCIALIZATION

1. The higher the social class, the greater the parental demonstration of warmth.
2. The higher the social class, the greater the supportive role played by the father.
3. The higher the social class, the greater the emphasis on autonomy, and the less the emphasis on conformity.
4. The higher the social class, the greater the use of reasoning and discussion and the less the use of commands.
5. The higher the social class, the more likely is discipline to be related to motives and intent and the less likely it is to be related to overt acts and their consequences.
6. The higher the social class, the more likely is the use of shame and guilt and the less likely is the use of physical punishment in disciplining.
7. The higher the social class, the greater the use of personal appeals and the less the use of positional appeals.
8. The higher the social class, the greater the tolerance for children's impulses.
9. The higher the social class, the greater the emphasis on achievement.

SOURCES: The primary sources are Gecas, 1979: 365–404; and Biblarz, 1992. Others are Bronfenbrenner, 1958: 400–425; Gecas and Nye, 1974: 740–749; Alwin, 1989: 327–346. Many references can be found in Gecas and in Biblarz.

couples. Besides, both middle- and working-class couples prescribe a greater role for females than for males in child care. The support the middle-class father offers his children takes many forms: discussing events and goals, helping with homework, teaching skills, as well as complimenting and encouraging his child. There is, however, a middle-class bias in the conclusions regarding warmth and support in the family. If, as some feel, lower- and working-class families are more embedded in their kin and social network than are middle-class, then the lower-class child may not experience less emotional warmth; rather, the sources of warmth may simply be a grandparent, aunt, or friends—not just parents.

The third statement in Table 8.1 is that higher status families emphasize autonomy and lower status emphasize conformity. This can be traced to the work of Melvin Kohn in the 1950s and 1960s (Kohn, 1959: 337–351; Kohn, 1969). Kohn's insight was that the work environment carried over into the home setting, so that parents who had to conform and be subordinate at work taught their children to conform and be subordinate. More recently Duane Alwin and Tim Biblarz have studied and expanded on Kohn's ideas (Alwin, 1989: 327–346; Biblarz, 1992). Biblarz finds that parents who *perceive* their paid work to be simple place greater importance on their children's obedience to rules (Biblarz, 1992: 116). And within class, fathers seem to value conformity in their children more than do mothers.

In middle-class families, a great deal of emphasis is placed upon the development and use of verbal skills. Lower-class parents are less likely to live and work in the realm of ideas or to give substantial attention to explanation, reasoning, and understanding of motives. This holds for interaction with children and also between husband and wife. In the lower-class family, lack of both verbal skills and time combine to increase the use of commands and physical response. It takes not only inclination but *time* to reason and discuss; and while the middle-class parent may have fewer children to deal with, dual employment is beginning to eat away at the "time available" class difference.

A key area in which the foregoing class difference appears is child discipline. In the first place, the basis for discipline in the middle class tends to hinge
on the question of behavioral intent, while in the lower class it is predicated
upon behavioral consequences. The middle-class parent is concerned with the
motives of the child rather than strictly with the negatively defined outcomes of
specific behavior (Gecas and Nye, 1974: 748). By way of illustration, let us suppose that a six-year-old boy turns over his glass of milk. An immediate attempt
is made by the middle-class parent to assess his intent. Did he spill the milk because he was trying to cut up his own food? If so, encourage him. Did he turn
it over because he was trying to hit his sister or was he angry at having beans
for supper? Then he must be scolded or punished. The decision regarding behavioral intent must be made almost spontaneously; therefore, it is possible that
the parents may make a mistaken assessment. The lower-class parent, when
faced with the same situation, defines this behavior by the six-year-old as punishable, since it is disruptive of routine and damaging to furniture, as well as indicative of lack of control.

A less well supported generalization in Table 8.1 is number 6. Several
earlier studies found that middle-class parents employ shame and guilt, often
coupled with a threat of love withdrawal, in disciplining, while lower- and
working-class parents more frequently use physical punishment (Walters and
Stinnett, 1971). Likewise, Biblarz finds that parents who are dissatisfied with
their jobs and who value conformity in their children are also more likely to use
physical punishment (Biblarz, 1992: 197–198). However, Murray Straus found
no such differences (1971: 662), and Bruce Brown, looking at discipline of children in public places, also found no class difference:

> *Parents view their children's misbehavior in public places as an 'emergency situation'
> and respond with those techniques which are believed to produce the quickest results,
> i.e., restrictive techniques such as hitting and yelling (Brown, 1979: 67–71).*

Finally, Howard Erlanger noted that the difference is not only unclear in the
literature, but the reasons for the lack of clarity include the issues of frequency, intensity, and kind of physical punishment. Physical punishment could
be a slap or a beating, and it could happen regularly or once in a while. Until
the research specifies these factors, definitive differences are not likely to be
forthcoming (Erlanger, 1974: 84). So we should keep in mind that generalization 6 is unconfirmed.

The next generalization involves personal and positional appeals. This distinction can easily be made by giving two answers to the child's question: "But
why must I do it?" Personal appeal would be, "Because I need your help," while
positional appeal would be, "Because I am your mother." Again, as you can see,
there is a connection between this and generalization 4 in Table 8.1, that is, the
use of reasoning versus commands.

The last two differences in socialization to be discussed are middle-class parents' greater tolerance of children's impulses and spontaneous outbursts, and
their greater demand for responsible independence. Lower-class parents are
likely to punish impulsive behavior when it occurs, but their style of socialization

and discipline is not an effective deterrent and, in fact, may foster the behavior it aims to control. Thus, it is not surprising to find Walters and Stinnett reporting that, while upper-middle-class mothers are confident of their child-rearing methods, lower-class mothers

> *were the least confident of their methods, evidenced the least amount of responsibility for the behavior of their children, and while they saw their children as needing close parental control, felt that they were unable to influence behavior outcomes of their children (Walters and Stinnett, 1971: 102).*

An important distinction is captured by the term *responsible independence*. By this is meant self-reliance, learning how to do things for yourself—but always within the bounds of your parents' value system. The middle-class parent is excited when his or her little girl learns to tie her shoes at age four, to make her bed and put her clothes away, to set up a stand and sell lemonade. All these are signs of responsible or, to use Farber's term, "sponsored" independence. For the lower-class parent, a crucial element in socialization might be called freedom or "unsponsored independence" (Farber, 1964: 362–378). To overstate it, children are simply turned out with the expectation that they will return home when they are hungry, sleepy, or injured. This approach on the part of lower-class parents, incidentally, is one of the historical connections between the modern subsistence-level urban family and the U.S. subsistence farm of the past. In both instances, as noted in Chapter 6, when children were not carrying out family responsibilities, they were generally unsupervised. The major difference is in the proportion of free time available. Agrarian family economic endeavor and division of labor ordinarily left growing individuals with only a little time to themselves. Urban lower-class life leaves the child with far less family responsibility and, thus, with much more time to spend in unsponsored independence, or staying out of the way.

Many of the distinctions we have made in the foregoing discussion have been between the middle and lower classes in order to present these distinctions as dramatically as possible. There are some ways in which the working classes (here defined as those families in which the husband is a stably employed manual worker with some skill) are not merely a midpoint between the other two but present a unique combination of attributes. For example, Tim Biblarz notes the relation between statements 3 and 9 in Table 8.1 by class. Higher status families have high expectations for their children's achievement and a low valuation of conformity, because it may lessen the child's adaptability. Among the lower classes there are realistically low expectations for their children, with a high valuation of conformity, since this may help protect their children. However, Biblarz says,

> *Among lower-middle-class and working-class families . . . parents may have relatively high expectations . . . and high valuation for conformity. Their position above the margin of sustenance may lead them to view mobility for their children as possible, hence the high expectations, but they may see conformity as a means to that end (Biblarz, 1992: 121).*

Some studies, of course, have used working and lower class almost inter-changeably, while others have used *working* class for both. But the evidence, to the extent that it can be differentiated, points to the following distinctions. If middle-class socialization is best characterized by independence, interchange, and affection, and lower-class socialization by freedom and discipline, working-class socialization is oriented toward *respectability*—a concern with limits, neat-ness, and achievement and control–values once thought to be strictly middle class. In addition, the mother is likely to want her husband to help and be sup-portive, though it may not always be possible to get him to play that role. We will say more about marital and parental roles in Chapter 12.

Although the differences between middle-class, lower-class, and working-class socialization appear to have remained over the 55 to 60 year period during which the studies have been carried out, the gap between middle- and working-class styles appears to be narrowing. To some extent, this may be a function of the rise in the standard of living among the stable segments of the working class. Or it could be due to the fact that the working-class parent is making more use of middle-class techniques and sources of information, thus reducing the cul-tural differences between them. These sources include child-care manuals and magazines, to which we referred above. Some have even coined the term *mid-dle mass* to incorporate the skilled and stable elements of the working class and the less affluent segments of the middle class, for example, salespeople and clerks. Yet recent studies such as Biblarz continue to produce sufficient differ-ences to justify the retention of middle-class, working-class, and lower-class models.

Other Variables and Socialization

While gender and class are extremely important determinants of child-rearing, other variables should be mentioned. *Race* was reported above when we as-serted that blacks may be concerned with conformity, while giving affection. Biblarz notes that families who face unique "dangers," whether residential or racial, "strongly attempt to control and protect their children." This finding stands in sharp contrast to those who have argued that such subgroups of par-ents have "pathological" or "psychologically deficient" styles of parenting (Biblarz, 1992: 201).

Religion is interesting in its relation to both class and socialization. Parents who value conformity are also likely to hold fundamentalist or absolutist reli-gious beliefs (both Protestant and Catholic). Biblarz notes that those working at jobs they find "simple" also seek absolutes in religion (Biblarz, 1992: 117). We might state that they are looking for simple religious answers as well. And the effect of this religious factor is independent of class, though correlated. However, lest we oversimplify religion's relation to child-rearing, we should let Letha Scanzoni remind us of the variety of approaches to religious life. Reli-gion, she says,

> can serve as a repressive force that legitimizes the status quo, stifles questioning, keeps
> categories of persons "in their place," and forces conformity to a family model that

fails to deal with today's realities. Or religion can provide a stimulus and support for individuals and families (however defined) . . . ." (Scanzoni, 1988, 141).

The effect of dual *employment* has been noted in passing above. One result is the sheer amount of time parents spend with their children. Despite discussions of "quality time" (see Feature 8.2), parents simply have less time to provide comfort and affection when both are employed. But Greenberger and Goldberg report little evidence that investment in work occurs at the expense of investment in children. They do find a gender difference, however. Women's work commitment is negatively associated with their commitment to parenting, while for men commitment to work and parenting seem to vary together (Greenberger and Goldberg, 1989: 22–35).

Another effect of women's employment is that daughters of early-employed mothers rate themselves as less feminine (Tolman et al., 1989: 942–949). This, of course, was seen as positive by some quoted in the "Gender" section above. Finally, Garfinkel and McLanahan report that the effects of mother's employment on young children is neutral to positive, though it is negative for adolescents. It is possible, then, that the effect is a result not of the need for parental attention for the child's early development, but the need for later supervision (Garfinkel and McLanahan, 1986: 37).

A final issue concerns *homosexual* parenting. P. J. Falk raises an interesting question: Since mothering is important and if child care is best done by women, why are lesbian mothers so criticized by society (Falk, 1989). Baber and Allen answer this question by noting that in a patriarchal society women without a male partner violate the context for motherhood in U.S. society. Mothering, they say, "is good only as long as a man or the patriarchal state supervises it" (Baber and Allen, 1992). Schwartz Gottman adds that none of the "studies on children of lesbian mothers and gay fathers reported negative effects on children relative to their sexual orientation" (Gottman, 1990: 186). Childrearing issues relate more to society's rejection of homosexuality than to children's problems, says Gottman. Here, as in the case of fertility, we have a situation where the deeper issue is one of male control and the values (ideology) surrounding it.

SECTION THREE

ADOLESCENCE

An adolescent is an individual defined by his or her society as too old to be a child and too young to be an adult. The answer to the question "What is adolescence?" has been stated in physiological, emotional, intellectual, and cultural terms. To some, adolescence is fundamentally the period of *incipient physiological maturity*. Rapid growth, glandular activity, and surface bodily changes give adolescence its unique character. For others, adolescence is primarily *emotional*. It is the period of emotional intensity, internal stress, and ambivalence during which former interpersonal commitments are tested. Still others see adolescence as basically *intellectual*, involving idealism and the questioning of the value systems and behavior of the older generation. This questioning makes it a period of uncertainty and frustration, since adolescents perceive the world's problems as insurmountable and the adult world as divided and unsure of itself. Finally, there are some who define adolescence *culturally*, as a period of fads and cultural limbo following physical maturation and preceding adult status. How do these four definitions fit the data on adolescence? The answer to this question must await the completion of our discussion.

Adolescence as a period of physical maturation has, of course, always existed; adolescence as defined in terms of emotions, intellect, and culture is a phenomenon of recent centuries. "Verbal distinctions between childhood and youth, practically nonexistent in the seventeenth century and still rare in the eighteenth, became much more common after 1800" (Kett, 1973: 98). As recently as the early 1800s, the young, vigorous, expanding United States could give its young social tasks and roles. For, as Kett says, "in a stable agrarian society, the range of occupational and religious choices open to young people was so narrow as to preclude a period of doubt and indecision" (1973: 97). Speaking of the emergence of an adolescent period, Mitterauer and Sieder propose that

> *the social shape of the phase between physical maturity and the assumption of adult status in modern Western and Central Europe depends, above all, on the degree to which the young person in this phase of life is integrated in the production of goods and rendering of services, or the degree to which he is subject to a specific process of socialization outside the sphere of production—at school, for example—in order to qualify him for his future occupation (Mitterauer and Sieder, 1982: 96).*

Demos adds further explanation thus:

> *To some extent, modern adolescence expressed an altered balance of social circumstance—the decline of apprenticeship, the growth of mass public education, the development of new living situations for young people exiting from their families of origin. But there was also an inner-life aspect—the growth of "identity-diffusion" in the face of ever-widening life-choices (Demos, 1986: 13).*

Not only is adolescence a product of recent history, but it is also culturebound. This period of time, says Mead, is "not necessarily a period of stress and strain . . . these familiar and unlovely symptoms flow from cultural anxieties" (Mead, 1958: 347). That is, the problems by which the period is defined are aspects of Western civilization and not of all youth, and physiological changes alone cannot account for either intracultural or cross-cultural variations.

But what of the adolescent period in the United States; what are its boundaries? Neither sociological nor physiological criteria are entirely unambiguous or satisfactory in defining its scope. The beginning of adolescence may, without great distortion, be considered synonymous with the onset of puberty. Yet one must decide which physiological changes to treat as most basic. While the appearance of pubic hair or the growth of the female's breasts might be used, a frequently employed index of the onset of puberty is first ejaculation by the male and first menses for the female. Even such an unambiguous criterion as the last, which ordinarily occurs about the twelfth year of life, was found a generation ago by Alfred Kinsey et al. to range from age 9 to age 25 (Kinsey et al., 1953: 123). Furthermore, the age at first menses not only varies in a population, but it "has been getting earlier during the last hundred years by four to six months per decade" (Laslett, 1973: 29).

Adolescence may be subdivided into two categories. Hugh Klein suggests calling them "adolescents" and "youth," with the latter being those who go to college and further postpone adulthood (Klein, 1990: 446–471). Many others have simply distinguished "early" and "late" adolescence. Let us, then, spend a few minutes on early adolescence.

Early adolescence is generally considered to be the period from puberty to high school, or about ages 12 to 15. The parents' well-being has been found to be related to advanced cognitive skills on the part of their early adolescent offspring, while early physical development was negatively related to parental well-being, at least for some parents (Silverberg and Steinberg, 1990: 658–666). In another interesting study, Nelson and Keith found a major difference in gender role attitudes of daughters depending on whether their mother worked: daughters of employed mothers "held less traditional sex role attitudes than did daughters of women who were not employed . . . . The happier the father was with his wife's employment, the more nontraditional was the daughter" (Nelson and Keith, 1990: 196). As for the early teens' stress and adaptation, the school helps to buffer problems at home and elsewhere. However, early hassles and stresses are predictive of increased hassles, suggesting that, once begun, they may become self-sustaining (DuBois et al., 1992: 542–557). The problem with the school as buffer is noted by Baumrind, who comments that unfavorable youth development has increased as a result of (1) the unravelling of the social fabric of families and schools, (2) exclusion of adolescents from adult life and (3) the permanent alteration of women's roles (Baumrind, 1991: 113). In summary, neither parents nor children may be quite prepared for the changes that occur in early adolescence, and societal changes have lessened that preparation.

Late adolescence might be considered to begin when the young person achieves his or her first adult status, such as being licensed to drive. But how does one determine when the entire adolescent period ends and adulthood begins? For certain high-status families in American society it might be the "debut," coming anywhere between age 17 and age 22. For the masses, however, possible criteria might include graduation from high school, graduation from college, entering military service, beginning one's first full-time job, moving out of the parental home, and marriage. All these factors cannot coincide, and there is no ceremony marking the assumption of full adult status. Therefore, the passage from adolescence into adulthood is more a gradual occurrence than an abrupt or clearly demarcated transition. If two or three factors, such as college graduation, marriage, and the first full-time job do coincide, the end of adolescence may be fairly clear-cut. However, the increase in 18- to 24-year-olds staying at home or returning home again points out the difficulty with boundaries, since the end of adolescence has much to do with adult independence (Riche, 1990: 24–30). Thus, adolescence continues to be something of a vague concept in its empirical referent; perhaps the very ambiguity of its duration and nature increases the difficulties of the period.

Adolescence as a process can be thought of as the movement from dependence upon and control by parents and other adults through a period of intensive peer group activity and influence and, finally, to the assumption of adult roles. The familial aspect of this process involves the twin issues discussed earlier: identification and ego struggle. We will present the discussion under two headings—emancipation and parents and peers—realizing that they are in fact part of a single process.

Emancipation

There are actually three aspects to autonomy or emancipation: emotional, behavioral, and value. Many young people neither seek nor achieve the third, since as adults they mirror their parents values. However, the first two are important, and occur both at various times and to varying degrees. One study finds that autonomy does not increase with age, but rather simply is accomplished to different degrees by different young people at different ages (Enright et al., 1980: 529–545).

Differences in level of independence are not distributed randomly within the American population, but are related both to parental styles and to such factors as gender and socioeconomic class. The three styles of parenting are *autocratic, democratic,* and *permissive,* with adolescents reporting the democratic style to be most prevalent (Kelly and Goodwin, 1983: 567–571). Autocratic parents decide everything, democratic parents negotiate with their teenagers, and permissive parents let their children decide for themselves. As you might surmise from Table 8.1, the democratic style is most often found in the middle- and upper-middle-class family, while autocratic and sometimes permissive styles are more often working- and lower-class.

Males develop greater autonomy under autocratic fathers and mothers, while females become more autonomous when their fathers are permissive and their mothers democratic (Enright, 1980). These outcomes may be a result of the male being in a "tug-of-war" with his parents which produces the stereotypic male competitiveness, while the female is *not* being treated independently.

DeWayne Moore and Lucy Fischer also note a difference between boys and girls in this process. Males have more difficulty achieving emancipation while renegotiating relations with their parents into a positive adult-adult relationship. And females, Fischer reports, develop a "holding on/letting go": relation with their parents (Moore, 1987: 306; Fischer, 1986: 16). Girls, in other words, may go through the emancipation process while continuing to be somewhat embedded in their families. An interesting research by Lloyd Lueptow finds, however, a general liberalization of adolescent—especially female—values concerning independence and freedom. But females still tend to be oriented toward service and altruistic adult roles, while males are still oriented toward status, money, etc. (Lueptow, 1980: 48–59). Thus, traditionally, the middle-class male seems to have been oriented toward sponsored independence and the middle-class female inclined toward semi-embedded independence, but this is slowly changing.

Parents and Peers

A part of the emancipation process involves the peer group, or members of the adolescent age group to which attachment becomes stronger over time. McGoldrick et al. state that "adolescent girls typically concentrate a lot of attention at this phase on boys, and orient their behavior around male approval," perhaps due to a continuing emphasis on getting a mate (McGoldrick et al., 1989: 215). This may be changing toward greater same-sex orientation for females, but very slowly.

In 1986 Hans Sebald reported that seeking advice from peers rose and from parents fell between 1963 and 1976, and turned back slightly after 1976 (Sebald, 1986: 5–13). His interpretation is that the late 1960s and early 1970s was a period of substantial disjuncture between youth and parents, while the 1980s saw some swing back toward conservative (traditional) attitudes. A further interesting point is that after 1975 over a quarter of Sebald's respondents stated that advice came from "myself"—an indicator of the individualism of that period. One study reports adolescents as perceiving their relations with parents as less *rewarding* than with peers (Wright and Keple, 1981: 559–570). One reason for this is that peer interaction is more enjoyable, and less confining and controlling, than that with parents (Larson, 1983: 739–750). So attachments to parents remain strong, while those to peers increase in importance.

What values and behaviors do adolescents learn from parents, and which ones from peers? Parents are much more influential on educational plans than are peers, while peers have more influence on drinking behavior. An interesting recent study shows that two-thirds of 619 college freshmen drank first with peers, and parents did not notice. Furthermore, students who started earlier drank more often and in higher quantities, while those who drank with their parents first or whose drinking was noted by their parents drank less (Lo and Globetti, 1991: 20–29). In fact, in several areas young people pick up norms from parents and behaviors from age-mates (Davies and Kandel, 1980: 373–374; Biddle et al., 1980: 1057–1079; Smith, 1981: 85–93). An area in which parents are most influential is religion, where symbolism, modelling, and "relationships with others who share the same beliefs and the same group identity" all foster parent-child continuity (Stack, 1988: 227).

In an important paper that brings together much of the literature on intergenerational cultural continuity, Lillian Troll and Vern Bengtson report that similarity in parent and offspring values is most noticeable in the religious and political areas, and least in sex-role and lifestyle attitudes. They go on to present the following proposition:

> *Friends or peers may serve as a moderating influence on family transmission in some areas . . . which are particularly salient issues for their cohort. However, parental*

influences seem strong in achievement, work, and educational orientations. Moreover, in general, peer and parent influences appear complementary rather than oppositional (Troll and Bengtson, 1979: 146).

Just how different, then, are the values and attitudes of parents and youth? Two decades ago Bengtson and J. A. Kuypers reported what they label the "generational stake." When asked about their values and attitudes, parents and youth showed substantial disagreement. However, the youths exaggerated the differences, while the parents exaggerated the similarities. This is the generational stake, with the young people trying hard to assert their uniqueness (ego struggle) and the parents trying to convince themselves and others that they have done a good job of socializing their children (Bengtson and Kuypers, 1971: 249–260; also Acock and Bengtson, 1980: 501–515). In the late 1980s Demo et al. reported that adolescents and their parents have independent but overlapping perceptions of their relationships (Demo et al., 1987: 713). Closer to Bengtson and Kuypers is the finding of Callan and Noller that adolescents rate family members as more anxious, less involved, and less dominant than do their parents. While adolescents "overestimate negative features of families, parents overestimate socially desirable traits" (Callan and Noller, 1986: 820).

We have spoken of attachment and influence in relation to parents and peers, and will close this section with a word about youth society. Historically, as in the case of the child, the treatment of the adolescent as a distinct kind of person is a fairly recent phenomenon. In industrial society growing individuals are not needed in economic production. They are age-segregated in school and community, and left to define activity patterns within the peer group. These patterns, however, ordinarily reflect what youth perceive to be the most basic, if unverbalized, values of the adult world. Popularity and material good, such as cars, may be central to adolescent society, but perhaps this is because these are seen by young people to be of great importance to the adult world as well.

Adolescents are not wanted as economic contributors, but their sex powers are developed and active. They begin to drive at one age, drink at another, and vote at another. In the last resort, it is the peer group where the relation between these factors must be hammered out. So while adolescents may not have a separate culture, in many ways they are a society separate from both the world of childhood and that of adults. As parents increasingly remove themselves from the home (through work or divorce), and as young people's experiences increasingly take place outside the home, their social separation from family becomes greater (Baumrind, 1991: 113; Goldscheider and Waite, 1991: 21). This, recall, is precisely the problem that has historically plagued racial minorities in the United States: being a subsociety more than a subculture. However, the analogy between adolescents and minorities is actually of little help. The major difference is that adolescents are constantly being incorporated into the adult world and new youngsters are constantly entering the adolescent age group, while the racial minority is kept socially separate throughout the lifetime of the individual. Adolescents are, in short, more accurately described as a partially distinct society than as a distinct culture.

At this point we shall go beyond the research and literature on adolescence to express an *opinion* on what adolescents need from their parents: Having read about the adolescent today, having watched young people grow up in my home, and having spent several decades in school as student and professor, my impression is that adolescents need three things from their parents:

1. real responsibilities, either in the home or the community, to make them feel that they are essential *now;*
2. to be recognized as the family "expert" in something (though this does not have to be good grades or a letter in sports. It could be having helped to improve the community in some way or simply having held a job.); and
3. most important, to know that acceptance and love are *not* based on either of the other two, but *unconditional.*

These three are as difficult to accomplish as they are important.

SECTION FOUR

SOCIALIZATION AND ADOLESCENCE: SUMMARY AND CONCLUSIONS

We close the discussion of adolescence by returning to the question raised at the beginning of Section Three. How can the adolescent period in the United States best be characterized? Is it primarily the period of incipient physiological maturity, of emotional intensity and upheaval, of intellectual questioning, or of postponement-segregation-cultural limbo?

Since the first is a uniform human occurrence—while adolescence appears to be variable—physiological changes do not seem useful in defining the peculiar character of adolescence in U.S. society. In order to come to grips with the other three parts of the question, we must now recall the discussion of ego struggle and identification. It may be true that in colonial days identification was easy and ego struggle difficult; however, it must not be inferred from that statement that the opposite is the case today. Contemporary children are not presented with clear and intense role models, nor do they always receive support in their ego struggle from the key socializing agents. They are thus prepared for life as other-directed individualists who can adapt to many social and organizational settings, but who have not gained a clear picture of the kind of people they are.

This is of course an overdrawn characterization of the pitfalls in U.S. socialization. It does, however, suggest that the process can cause the individual trouble with both identification and ego struggle. Put simply, it is difficult for the individual to develop into a mature adult with a clear self-concept.[3] A tentative

FIGURE 8.2   THE APPROXIMATE LOCATION OF SOCIALIZATION IN THE CONTEMPORARY UNITED STATES ON THE SOCIALIZATION CONTINUUM

Orderly Replacement;
Family-Kin Controlled;
Family Identifications

Controlled by
Extra-Familial Agencies;
Identifications
Problematic

Redefinition
of Culture by
Each Generation

Contemporary U.S.
Socialization

answer to the definitional problem regarding adolescence would therefore be as follows. If we consider adolescence to be a period of intellectual questioning and idealism, then in our society there have never been more than a few adolescents—a few young people who ever overtly questioned the dominant or parental pattern, even if they were not really committed to it. Thus, the *postponement* of adult status following physiological maturity, when accompanied by social *segregation* and *ill-defined* roles, is enough to cause the kind of stress usually thought to characterize adolescence. Postponement is sufficient to define the adolescent period as it has been known for the past century in the United States.

How do the conclusions of Chapter 8 relate to the socialization continuum presented in Chapter 5? The passing of culture from parents to children is somewhat problematic, but not to the extent that socialization has been taken over by extrafamilial agencies, such as the schools and the mass media. Rather, many of these agencies should be viewed as extensions of parental influence and others as in competition with parents. In either case, because parents are concerned about the possibility of losing control of their children's development, they try very hard to control their behavior and influence their values. Although socialization is an extremely complex and multifaceted process, we might summarize by reproducing the continuum and indicating approximately where the author feels socialization in the contemporary United States is located (see Figure 8.2). The reader should, of course, feel free to relocate this complex of factors wherever he or she believes the facts would warrant.

One further aspect of the young person's emancipation, or movement out of the family of orientation, involves pairing relations with peers. Therefore, in Chapters 9 and 10 we turn our attention to going out, sex, and choosing a partner in the United States.

Prelude to Pairing Up

CHAPTER 9

Courtship, dating, "going out," cohabitation —the process of pairing up has passed through several phases in recent U.S. history, and is still changing. Dating and cohabitation, twentieth century phenomena, are important and difficult. They are important functionally for adolescents, as well as being problematic. Premarital sex has changed from being normatively condemned to being an acceptable behavior for most in the United States. The revolution in these areas has been mainly a female revolution. A recently noticed phenomenon is dating violence, especially "date rape."

By the time you finish this book, you will have read about many areas of intimate life in which recent change has been dramatic: marital roles, divorce and remarriage, and the subject of these next two chapters—pairing or choosing a partner. I have used the title to this chapter instead of "Dating" to indicate just how much variety there is in the preparation for forming pairs at present in the United States. Courtship was once the accepted term, but it is unlikely you will hear one of your peers declare: "I am going courting tonight." Even dating, the twentieth century phenomenon, is but one of several aspects of the pairing process. The term "pairing" itself is used instead of "mate selection" to recognize that same-sex pairs exist, and deserve to be discussed. However, selecting a marriage partner and establishing a family of procreation is still one of life's crucial tasks for the great majority in the United States.

Historically and cross-culturally, three clearly definable approaches to mate selection and the heterosexual contacts that precede it can be discerned; each of these approaches is closely linked to one of the types of individual embeddedness. The first, *arranged marriage*, is found most frequently in those societies in which the individual and the nuclear family are embedded in the larger kinship group. In such societies marriages are arranged primarily for the purpose of fostering or strengthening the appropriate kin linkages and have definite economic overtones. Concern with domestic or individual happiness is strictly secondary.

The second and third approaches to mate selection are both based on individual choice, and differ from each other in degree rather than in kind. Nevertheless, it is in this quantitative difference that dating as a basis for heterosexual relationships appeared. *Restricted choice* occurs when the domestic unit is considered all-important, and when the preferences of the individuals involved are believed to be the most adequate basis for establishing a sound unit. However, historically such preferences have been restricted by several influences. One of these restrictive influences is the overt and expected intervention of parents in numerous ways, including the chaperoning of the heterosexual activity of teenagers. A second is the residential stability of large numbers of the population, so that choice is made among persons with whom one has been acquainted most or all of one's life. A third restriction is the length of time during which premarital relationships occur. The "courtship" period itself is quite brief, so that when a young person begins to court a member of the opposite sex, it is assumed that he or she has "serious intentions." Thus, restricted choice takes place under the considerable influence of significant others, that is, under conditions of nuclear family embeddedness, often within the bounds of lengthy acquaintance and usually within the scope of a few months or years.

Open choice, of which there is no pure example in the world at present, would best characterize a situation where marriage or pairing is totally subservient to individual needs and desires. This is exemplified in Farber's ideal-typical model of universal and permanent availability. According to this idea, all members of the opposite sex are potentially available to me for mating, with no "artificial" restrictions. Furthermore, they are permanently available, so that if my first attempt to find a satisfying relationship fails, I am free to sever my ties and try again, for my individual needs and happiness are all-important.

The closest approximation to the open choice basis for mate selection is a result of historical developments within the United States. Prior to the twentieth century, most courtships resembled fairly closely the "restricted choice" alternative. Most young people lived at home until an early marriage. Though mate choice was individual, adult expectations were that heterosexual contacts would occur under the watchful eye of parents, and ruses were often used by the young to escape surveillance. Yet the seeds of change were present in the nineteenth century. Industrialization and mobility were increasing, and higher education, a development that postponed adulthood, was expanding. Particularly with the spread of coeducation during the first 20 years of this century, increasing numbers of young people spent several unmarried years living away from home and parental supervision. While coeducational colleges were expected to assume a position *in loco parentis*, college adolescents had much less difficulty than those living at home in arranging rendezvous free from adult supervision. During the early years of this century, then, the relations between the sexes prior to marriage began to resemble what Reiss calls a participant-run system (Reiss, 1968).

Concurrent with the spread of coeducation in the United States, the growth of cities and advances in technology increased the number and types of places for urban entertainment and improved the means for getting to them. Movies, nightclubs, theaters, sporting events—these and other places became increasingly available to the unchaperoned young couple, whose participation in such activities came to be known as "dating." At first, dating was considered a form of recreation that had little direct relation to courtship or mate selection. The same opportunities were available to high-school-age people, but their young age plus the fact that they lived at home meant that it would be several more years before dating would be prevalent and acceptable at the high school level. Yet from this beginning under the influence of postponed adulthood, individual mobility, and urban entertainment, dating came to be a ubiquitous and multipurpose aspect of premarital relationships in the United States.

Dating slowly took on a world-wide significance. Very much as escaping from the extended lineage into the nuclear family is defined as a demonstration of modernity in many parts of the world, so dating has come to symbolize modernity for many young people. After all, dating indicates that parents no longer control their offspring's life, including their choice of a partner.

SECTION ONE

PRELUDE TO PAIRING: NATURE AND FUNCTIONS

The Pairing Continuum

Geoffrey Gorer, an English anthropologist, described American dating practices as a competitive game in which each side makes points; he concludes that "the ideal date is one in which both partners are so popular, so skilled, and so

self-assured that the result is a draw" (Gorer, 1969: 114). One of the first sociological descriptions of dating produced in the United States, that of Willard
Waller, is consistent both with Gorer's comments and with the early history of
dating as a recreational pursuit. Waller's account of the "Rating and Dating
Complex" was based on research done at Pennsylvania State in the early 1930s
(Waller, 1937: 727–734). Dating, says Waller, is a "dalliance" relationship, a
recreational activity; the qualities rated highly in a date—campus leadership,
money, a car, and good clothes—are not the same as the personality- and char-
acter-based qualities desired in a mate.

Since Waller's article appeared in 1937, his distinction between courtship
and dating, the former serious and the latter not, has apparently become increasingly inappropriate, if it ever was. Michael Gordon, for example, reports a
lot of group or communal "dating" in the nineteenth century, and he argues that
Waller's rating-dating phenomenon was a brief interlude that is virtually nonexistent today (Gordon, 1981: 67–76). Dating itself has been supplemented by
two further developments: (1) the heterosexual group often precedes the beginning of coupling or pairing, while (2) cohabitation now often occurs between "dating" and marriage. Three points are worth making regarding
cohabitation. First, it was a lower class phenomenon for a long time, and has
only recently become widespread in the middle class. Second, cohabitation may
be a non-marriage instead of a pre-marriage, though the latter is still more
prevalent in the middle class. And third, cohabitation was treated in Chapter 18
of the previous edition of this text as an alternative; it is now incorporated as a
frequent and accepted final stage of pairing up. At the end of this section, we
will focus on cohabitation.

It seems justifiable, therefore, to talk about the "Pairing Continuum," meaning that it covers a wide range of experiences, with dating still a major portion
for many adolescents. Given the fact that mean age at marriage in the United
States is now between 23 and 25 years of age, and that the pairing process begins for most between the ages 12 and 14, most adolescents now spend at least
ten years in the pairing process. And we have decided to use the phrase "pairing
up" rather than courtship, dating, or "going out," since the first seems *passe*, the
second does not encompass the process, and the third is less than "catchy."

Prelude to Pairing: General Functions

In the United States this period of time is neither strictly for recreational purposes nor just for choosing a partner. There are at least five complex functions
that the system of heterosexual contacts performs for the individual in society. (a)
Dating is a form of *recreation*, as Waller said. "It provides entertainment for the individuals involved and is a source of immediate enjoyment" (Skipper and Nass,
1966: 412). (b) It is a form of *socialization*. It gives individuals an opportunity to
learn about members of the opposite sex at close range, to develop techniques
of interaction, to play roles, to learn effective functioning, and to define their
self-concept as they observe others' reactions to them as persons (Rusbult et al.,
1986: 744–753). (c) It meets *ego needs*. The young person—like all people—needs

understanding, serious conversation, and to be considered important. For some young people, a portion of the meeting of ego needs involves sexuality, and more will be said about this below. It may also involve learning both the positives and negatives involved in competition with another person while developing a more intimate relationship with them (Laner, 1986: 275). In addition, it may give the individual a feeling of support and belonging that may be lacking from their family (Hoelter and Harper, 1987: 136). A satisfactory prelude may help young people over the rocky period of independence struggle and postponement of adulthood that is called adolescence. (d) The pairing process functions as a means of *status placement*. This function is performed strictly by the family or kin unit in many societies, so that the unit into which an individual is born determines the category of persons into which he or she will marry as well as his or her adult status. In the United States, where personal choice is basic to pairing, it is possible for certain persons to be rated highly desirable and in this way to raise their status within the peer group. Thus, the pairing process helps to control the operation of free choice by sorting out prospective mates according to their "status value." (e) Finally dating functions for the *selection of a marriage partner*. This, after all, is the end result of at least one relationship for most individuals. Most young people do not begin each relationship by asking, "Would I marry this person?" Yet somewhere in the course of the prelude period this latent question may be answered affirmatively. Choosing a partner is, therefore, both the cause and the final effect of the pairing continuum.

Prelude to Pairing: Stages and Specific Functions

The prelude period may be thought of as a succession of gradual changes in seriousness, including such identifiable stages as groups and casual dating, going steady, cohabitation, engagement, and marriage or pairing. The five general functions listed above are not *all* performed at *all* stages of *all* relationships.

Besides the more general functions performed by the pairing continuum, there are several functions, or purposes, that are more specific to a particular stage of the continuum. *Group dating* existed in the nineteenth century, and now, says David Knox, there is again a change away from paired dates to going out in groups (Knox, 1980: 145–150). An opinion on why this is happening is in order. One argument is that a large group decreases the anxiety that goes along with pairing. However, anxiety would seem no greater today than in the recent past, so this seems a less than adequate explanation. Another possibility is that it is a result of sexual liberalism, of the fact that the issue of sex can arise early, even on a first date. Thus, to avoid confronting the issue, a group may go out together. Another possible or partial explanation for the group phenomenon at an early stage of the pairing continuum is that the areas of common interest between males and females have increased as a result of women's liberation. It used to be that recreationally, men did "men's things" with other men and women did "women's activities" with other women, and they went out together for a narrow range of common interests. As the areas of overlap have increased, so has the possibility of doing things together in heterosexual groups. In any case, this is a phase of pairing for adolescents at various ages.

Another stage of special interest is *going steady*, a stage that ordinarily embodies the transition from a recreational to a serious relationship, and may or may not include cohabiting. Looking at reasons for going steady among college students, the author found avoidance of the anxiety of having someone to do things with—or "date security"—a secondary motive. The dominant reasons were love (seriousness) and ego needs. A minority, some ten percent, of the male students also indicated that a reason for going steady is to guarantee a sexual outlet, a subject to be discussed in Section 3 of this chapter.

There are also differences in needs met by the pairing continuum for different categories of adolescents. Early daters, for example, are different in several ways from late starters. They date more frequently, are more likely to be sexually active, and also develop "steady" relationships relatively early (Thornton, 1990: 239). Not surprisingly, early, middle, and late adolescents diverge in views of the process and its functions. Roscoe et al. distinguish between 6th graders, 11th graders, and college students:

> *Findings indicate that early and middle adolescents tended to perceive reasons for dating from an egocentric and immediate gratification orientation, while late adolescents placed greater emphasis on aspects of reciprocity in a relationship. Regarding factors for partner selection, early adolescents tended to weight the person's superficial features and their approval by others more heavily. Late adolescents were more concerned with potential partners' future plans. Results suggest that with maturity and increased dating experience, adolescents become more realistic and independent in their perceptions of dating and dating partners (Roscoe, 1987: 60).*

Not surprisingly, then, early daters do not see seriousness and future plans as central to that stage of the process.

There are differences in late adolescence by gender. Recalling what we reported above regarding some males going steady for the sake of sexual access, Mayolin finds the following: "women are more likely to see dating as a screening device or precursor to matrimony, whereas for men dating is seen as an outlet for romance and recreation" (Mayolin, 1989: 99). Thus, while various functions are performed at various stages of the pairing continuum, they differ by age, gender, and even by when the pairing (dating) process began.

Thus far we have reviewed the general functions and stages of the dating continuum, and the prevalence of, functions of, and reasons for going steady. A generation ago, Clyde McDaniel attempted to synthesize several previous analyses of the dating process, giving particular emphasis to the changing role played by the female. Drawing upon Winch's work, McDaniel claimed that the possible roles played by females during dating are assertive, receptive, or some combination of the two. Assertive daters are achievement-oriented, competitive, autonomous, dominant, and hostile. Receptive daters are deferential, succorant (eager to help), prone to vicariousness (gaining pleasure from others' achievements), and anxious.

> *Girls, in the early stage of courtship, are inexperienced and unsophisticated with regard to appropriate role behavior. They are assertive initially because they view their right to act as aggressors in social interaction as identical with boys' right to act as aggressors. In heterosexual interaction on dates, however, they are made aware of their inappropriate role behavior through negative reinforcement from boys. In this way, they learn that receptivity is more frequently approved than assertiveness (McDaniel, 1969: 100).*

Waller's and Gorer's descriptions of dating as a competitive recreational activity seem to McDaniel to fit quite well the early stage of dating, in which there is assertiveness on the part of both couple members. However, socialization into "appropriate" roles occurs, and in the later or more serious stages the female plays a more "acceptable," receptive role.

McDaniel's interesting analysis does an injustice to previous research, especially Lowrie's and Waller's, because it tries to fit the differing views onto a single, nonhistorical continuum. However, it does raise certain intriguing questions. In closing, he reiterates his description of the "cycle wherein girls learn through trial and error to become receptive." It may not be overstating the case, McDaniel feels, to assert that "if they do not become receptive, they never get married" (McDaniel, 1969). One cannot help wondering whether McDaniel's closing assertion might not have been more correct in an earlier period of U.S. history than it is today. In the colonial and Victorian eras of role separation and normative patriarchy, the female who could not learn to be receptive may have had great difficulty in finding a partner. Today, however, substantial change in the status of women and a blurring or loosening of role specifications make one question the extent to which female receptivity is a *necessary* condition for marriage. It is at least possible that the emphases of women's liberation, freedom and equality, are hastening the day when women—premaritally as well as maritally—will no longer find it *necessary* to play a receptive role. An insightful indication of some change away from female "receptivity" is found in Sheila Korman's research on non-traditional dating behaviors. She finds feminist college females likely to initiate dates and to pay for their share of the expenses. Korman goes on to say that this may be an indication that dating is not becoming obsolete, but is simply being transformed into a more egalitarian process (Korman, 1983: 576, 580).

While McDaniel's assertions may not be as true today as they were in the late 1960s, they do raise an interesting issue about which I will express an *opinion*. Recall his assertion that the assertive female will never get married. This, of course, concerns the relation between personality and role playing. It is quite possible that a female who is assertive may in fact be forced to play a more receptive role than "comes naturally" in order to find a mate. Likewise, a male may have to "role play" assertiveness, even when that is not comfortable for him. The likely effect of such role playing would seem to be that after marriage his and her "real" personalities may manifest themselves, with conflict and marital breakup as the possible result of discovering that your partner is not the kind of person you thought you married. This, of course, deserves further research. It is worth repeating, however, that McDaniel's interesting insight into receptivity and assertiveness by gender is certainly not as true as it once was—but how much it has changed needs attention.

The process of love and breakup was investigated recently by Zick Rubin, Letitia Peplau, and Charles Hill, who found that the woman's emotions are better predictors of how the relationship is going than are the man's. They also found intercourse and cohabitation to be totally unrelated to the likelihood of breakup. They found the women somewhat more likely (51 percent to 42 percent) to initiate the breakup, with the men hit harder by the breakup. Though unable to isolate psychological reasons for these differences, they stated the following sociological reason: women have less power in the marriage market than men, and thus they have to be more careful about their choice. Also, women are socialized to be more expressive, and are thus probably more careful in evaluating their relationships while they are in process (Rubin et al., 1981: 821–835).

The prelude to pairing involves stages from casual and group "going out" to pairing. Many relationships terminate at an early stage due to loss of interest, an alternative attraction, or some other reason. In the next chapter we will examine at length the key factors in this weeding out or filtering out process that leads to choosing a partner. But now we will look at a late stage of many relationships: cohabitation.

Cohabitation

Cohabitation, or the nonlegalized heterosexual domestic unit, is the final stage of the pairing process for many couples. It is at present still more often a premarriage or a postmarriage than a nonmarriage.

How prevalent is cohabitation? According to U.S. Census Bureau figures, in 1970 there were 654,000 cohabiting couples, double that number by 1978, and by 1981 the figure was 1.8 million couples (Cherlin, 1981: 12; Spanier, 1983: 277–288). By the time the NSFH data were collected in 1987–88, the number of cohabiting units existing was over 2 million (Bumpass and Sweet, 1987: 261). To show the increase among never-marrieds, Gwartney-Gibbs found that in one Oregon county 13 percent of those filing for a marriage license in 1970 were cohabiting, while by 1980 the figure was 53 percent (Gwartney-Gibbs, 1986: 423–434). Rates of cohabitation, Bumpass and Sweet find, are higher among women, whites, and those who lived in a single-parent family while growing up, as well as non-high-school graduates (Bumpass and Sweet, 1989: 615). This last point reminds us that, despite the publicity, cohabiting is not primarily a college student phenomenon. Traditionally, both in this country and elsewhere, common law co-residence was fairly widespread among the very poor. However, in recent times, says Cherlin, "living together has become more common among two different groups of urban young adults: a better-educated group who tend to cohabit prior to marrying, and a less-well-educated group whose relationships are more likely to include at least one previously married partner" (Cherlin, 1981: 13). Almost 75 percent of cohabitors have no children in the home, although in absolute numbers cohabitors with children have increased dramatically since 1977 (Glick and Spanier, 1980: 20).

Not surprisingly, cohabitors are generally more liberal and even more androgynous in attitudes than noncohabitors, which fit with the findings regarding religious orientation. As less conventional people, they are more willing to engage in a variety of nontraditional living styles (Macklin, 1980: 405–423). However, E. M. Markowski and H. J. Johnson find two groups of cohabitors: those who do it for growth and self-fulfillment, and those who participate for selfish or rebellious reasons. Yet they find no differences in the personalities of the two groups—only in their attitudes toward cohabitation (Markowski and Johnson, 1980: 115–120). So why do students cohabit, or not cohabit? Lucy Jen Huang-Hickrod and Wilbert Leonard reported the reasons given by 2,000 Illinois students for cohabiting as follows: convenience, testing out compatibility, love, hope for establishing a more permanent relationship, and economic reasons. These same students listed the following reasons for not cohabiting: parental disapproval, partner disapproval, conscience, and pregnancy fears. In another study, cohabitors reported a great deal of pressure from parents either to marry or end the relationship (Huang-Hickrod and Leonard, 1990: 281–300; Risman et al., 1991, 77–83). A major change in the last decade is that in the late 1970s the majority of cohabitors did not marry each other, while by the NSFH survey in 1987 about 60 percent of first cohabitations resulted in marriage (Newcomb, 1979: 597–603; Bumpass and Sweet, 1989: 615).

In the section below on the "Problematic Aspects of the Pairing Continuum" we will discuss problems of cohabitation. However, it is well to note now that cohabitors tend to express a higher level of satisfaction with their relationships than noncohabitors do with theirs. They report more intimacy, more time together, and fewer problems (Risman et al., 1981: 77–83). But how does cohabitation—as a *premarriage*—relate to both choosing a partner and, in the case of marriage, staying together? Bob Lewis and Graham Spanier present the following general proposition: "The better acquainted a couple are before marriage, the higher the marital quality" (Lewis and Spanier, 1979: 275). "Some writers argue," says Cherlin, "that cohabitation will enhance personal growth, lead to a better choice of marriage partners, and lower the divorce rate" (Cherlin, 1981: 17). This argument is, incidentally, used by many students themselves: "I saw my parents (brother, aunt, and so on) get a divorce, so I want to know all I can about the other person so as to make the best choice possible, and perhaps avoid a divorce." Mort Perlmutter argues that it *could* act as a screening and learning device, but does not because most cohabitors are *playing* at marriage, not "prepping for marriage." Cherlin, however, takes the negative argument a little further: as a model for marriage, he says, what it teaches is not to make careful and lasting choices, but rather that a relationship can be ended if either party is dissatisfied. This individualistic ethic, he feels, carries over to marriage. Cherlin then states that "unmarried adults who do not cohabit may have a more traditional view of the sanctity of the marriage bond, and they may bring this traditional attitude to their marriages" (Cherlin, 1981: 17). One of the more interesting studies that speaks to this issue is Roy Watson's, with a sample not restricted to college students. He finds during the early years of marriage that noncohabitors rank higher than cohabitors in their mean scores on marital adjustment tests. He puts forward two explanations for this and favors the second. First, noncohabitors may be in the honeymoon phase of living together, while cohabitors completed that phase while living together. Second, the two groups have differing views of marriage in relation to courtship. For noncohabitors, marriage is a liberating moment: publicly establishing a household. Cohabitors, however, view marriage as restricting, representing the taking on of more confining responsibilities (Watson, 1983: 139–147). Whether such differences in adjustment last beyond the first years of marriage is not tapped by Watson's study. However, no topic concerning cohabitation aroused more research interest during the 1980s than its relation to marital stability. Thomson and Colella report from the NSFH data that cohabitors perceive a greater likelihood of divorce later on (perhaps for the reasons Cherlin gave above). They also find that longer cohabitations are in fact associated with a higher likelihood of divorce (Thomson and Colella, 1992: 259–267). Working with the same data, DeMaris and Rao also find cohabitors who marry more likely to divorce (DeMaris and Rao, 1992: 178–190). Looking at the first ten years after marriage, Teachman and Polonko also report cohabitants more likely than noncohabitants to have dissolved their marriages (Teachman and Polonko, 1990: 207–220). One qualification on this, however, is that Bennett et al. find that differences in dissolution rates decrease as marital duration increases. In other words, the biggest differences in divorce rates are during the first few years of marriage (Bennett, et al, 1988: 136). A new trend is reported by Robert Schoen, who finds the rates of marital dissolution fell for the youngest two cohorts of cohabitors (specifically those born 1948–1952 and 1953–1957), as compared to earlier cohabitors (Schoen, 1992: 284). Perhaps as cohabitation becomes more acceptable it also attracts more conventional young people. Notice that Schoen is not saying that cohabitors do not still divorce with greater frequency than noncohabitors, only that their rate of divorce is less than it was.

The final issue regarding cohabitation concerns the law. The Marvin vs. Marvin decision, involving a property distribution between actor Lee Marvin and Michel Triola-Marvin, his "cohabitor," indicates an attempt by the law to recognize and keep pace with changing societal behavior (Myricki, 1980: 210–215; Beck, 1978–79: 685–702). Several additional states have followed suit in recognizing cohabitation or *de facto* marriage as nearly equivalent to the legalized form of monogamy, while a few states have rejected it. Informal, oral, and nonmarital agreement have now been accepted as legally binding in several states. What is more important is that the legal system is trying to grapple with an issue arising from a change in behavior—and those legal ramifications are not yet completely resolved.

Cohabitation is obviously a spreading phenomenon. During a period when the age at marriage is rising, it is a stage of the pairing process for many young people. Whether it is good or poor preparation for a traditional marriage is not altogether clear: it may teach one to make a careful choice or it may teach one that breakup is fine if one is dissatisfied. And it is true that 25 percent of cohabiting households have children present. Finally, the law is beginning to take seriously the economic and other complexities of this growing practice.

PROBLEMATIC ASPECTS OF THE PAIRING CONTINUUM

You may have surmised by this point that I regard the continuum from casual to cohabitation as the pairing process par excellence. This conclusion does not, however, necessarily follow from the foregoing discussion of the stages and nature of the prelude to pairing in the United States. On the other hand, the process is hardly as fraught with danger as one would be led to believe from the tongue-in-check Feature 9.1.

Parental Influence

Parents naturally take an interest in the dating behavior of their sons and daughters. In 1981, 60 percent of the women and 40 percent of the men in an undergraduate class stated that their parents had sought to influence who they date (Knox and Wilson, 1981: 255–258). A finding of long-standing is that parents get involved in their daughters' relationships more than in their sons', and that mothers are more involved than fathers. This means that the greatest amount of attempted influence is on daughters by mothers. While most parents feel compelled to speak out on the subject, the reaction of young people to the intrusion varies from acceptance to resentment and conflict.

Another interesting study looks at the way the adolescents influence their parents by either withholding information or providing selective information about their partner (Leslie et al., 1986: 57–66). However, little disapproval by parents is found. The reason is because the adolescents are going to a university where most of the students are from the same religious and other backgrounds,

---

Feature 9.1 **THE DATING GAME**

The next century will be a time of many informational breakthroughs . . . . By this time, sex and dating will be so dangerous (owing to the numerous rampant communicable diseases and personality disorders) that they will be attempted only by the kind of thrill seekers who now do things like bungee jumping (and) sky surfing . . . . By the year 2020, in fact, "casual dating" will be a popular arena sport. People too terrified to pursue something so hazardous themselves will witness actual live human beings who, for big money stakes, will eat dinner with and then perhaps (if dinner goes well) become intimate with people they are attracted to but basically know nothing about.

Merrill Markoe, "The Dating Game," *Time*, Fall 1992, 53.

so that parents' perceived need to monitor is minimized. In any case, this is one aspect of current practices in which the choice falls short of being "open," and is a cross between restricted and open, between adult-influenced and youth- or participant-run.

It may be argued that since parental approval of the partner selected seems to be positively related to success in marriage for the offspring, such intrusion is therefore vindicated. Yet great parental insight is but one possible explanation for the relative success of parentally approved marriages. Another plausible explanation might be that when parents disapprove of a marriage, they tend to cause trouble for the young couple afterward, increasing the likelihood of its dissolution. Whichever interpretation one accepts, it must be concluded that, with a participant-run pairing system and weak cultural supports for parental intrusion, this will remain a problematic aspect of courtship in the United States.

Intergroup or Heterogeneous Relationships

Dating somebody of a different background from one's own is a problem primarily in relation to the issue of parental intrusion, as well as that of kin and friends. If young people were entirely free from group constraints, the difficulties posed by interclass, interreligious, and interracial relationships would very likely be minimal. Either they would avoid such relationships because they had internalized negative stereotypes concerning the differences represented, or else would engage in heterogeneous "asking out" with no thought of there being problems involved. (Note that we are speaking here of heterogeneous dating, not partner choice.) Parents or other significant persons, in arguing against heterogeneous dating, may be motivated by a sincere belief that such relations are problem-producing if they culminate in partner choice. Yet in this last phrase lies a part of the problem: while these "others" are focusing on the possibility of marriage, the young people involved may be seeking enjoyment and experience, with little or no thought of making a choice. Thus, the fact that the pairing continuum serves for both socialization and choosing a partner may become the basis for misunderstanding. A second issue in intergroup "going out" may be a basic value disagreement between the generations or between persons in the same social network. Members of the older generation who consider group values to be very important may be considered by younger people to be snobbish or bigoted. Such differences, the young people may feel, "simply don't matter any more." The key point regarding heterogeneity is what it signifies, that is, divergent values and norms; any trouble in intergroup dating is likely to be caused by disagreements concerning the importance of these divergences. This issue must be raised again when choosing a partner is discussed in Chapter 10.

Physical and Social Issues

In a society where marriage is arranged by parents and kin, physical attractiveness may be valued but still not be central to the pairing process. However, in a participant-run system both physical attractiveness and social skills may be important to pairing. For every individual who achieves high status in the peer group, another is devalued because they lack those qualities. Physical appearance and maturation may be important at the beginning of the pairing process, but does not cease to be so as more is learned about the other person (see Gargiulo et al., 1987: 730–737).

Socially, awkwardness and conversational discomfort are the opposite side of the coin of the prelude period as part of socialization. One learns during the pairing process how to interact with members of the opposite sex and how to play various roles. But if the participants run the system, as they do in the United States, a premium is placed upon social and conversational abilities at the outset; those deficient in these areas may have difficulty both in starting a relationship and in handling themselves thereafter. Ideally, the prelude period should afford opportunities for socialization, for developing social skills; it may not, however, enhance the development of individuals who flounder in the attempt to make a good impression. This is a theme played upon in the mass media: fashion magazines and teen magazines are good examples (Evans et al., 1991: 99–120). These publications demonstrate quite well how the pairing continuum may overemphasize the superficial aspects of looks and social skill. Early efforts at pairing may simply serve in some cases to accentuate tendencies already present for the smooth to become more so, and for the awkward to become more anxious and less adept at handling social situations. (On anxiety and attachment, see Simpson et al., 1992: 434–446). One finding is that there is a strong relationship among college women between high self-esteem and frequency of going out. It could be that having high self-esteem makes one appealing to be with, or that going out frequently raises one's self-esteem. But regardless of the causal connection, the relationship is clearly explained at least in part by the physical and social issues noted above.

Violence During the Prelude to Pairing

Besides sexuality, violence and cohabitation are the two topics concerning the pairing process that have received the most attention in the past decade. Some fifteen years ago, James Makepeace introduced the subject of dating violence to the readers of sociological journals (Makepeace, 1981: 97–102, and other papers). Since then, work has appeared in both the popular and scholarly press on aggression, violence, and rape among adolescents (see Feature 9.2).

In one interesting college student study, women reported having used aggression against their partners more often than men did, and in a substantial number of cases the aggressors reported having seen aggression between their parents. They noted that

> *previous authors have suggested that the lesser likelihood of severe consequences resulting from female-to-male aggression increases the likelihood that women will engage in such aggressive behavior. The report of women's . . . low-level aggressive behaviors such as pushing, grabbing, and slapping, within continuing romantic relationships in the current study is consistent with the idea that couples discount the severity of the woman's aggression (Riggs et al., 1990: 70; also Breslin et al., 1990: 247–258).*

While experience with violence in the family is a precursor to dating violence in some cases, it does not appear to be explained by the factors most
closely related to violence between spouses. DeMaris reports the following, in
his attempt to use the spouse violence model on pairing violence:

> *three factors have been found to be significant predictors of marital violence: social*
> *class, the balance of resources between the partners, and experience with violence in the*
> *family of orientation. Taken together, these factors do not provide a very powerful*
> *model of courtship violence, at least among the particular sample of college men and*
> *women (DeMaris, 1987: 291–305).*

The assumption that violence is somehow a lower-class phenomenon is not supported by data from Lune and Gwartney-Gibbs, who find that violence is more
frequent among those from high-income families, whites, and cohabitors than
among others (Lune and Gwartney-Gibbs, 1985: 51).

Violence during the pairing process is not only related to a history of family
violence. It is also related to the following factors: (1) a previous history of
dating violence on the part of the individual (Deal and Wampler, 1986: 469).
(2) Stress and support from the male peer group seem to increase the likelihood
of violence by males (DeKeseredy, 1990: 236–243). (3) Finally, it is connected to
relationship control, with males (in a patriarchal world) not surprisingly more
likely to try to control. There is, however, a difference in this relationship:
"women inflict aggression as a way to get control while men who already have
control, structurally, inflict aggression to maintain control" (Stets and Pirog-
Good, 1990A: 387). Stets and Pirog-Good add that there is some evidence that
dating aggression continues after marriage (Stets and Pirog-Good, 1990B: 387).

We noted above that minor aggression may in fact be more frequent on the
part of females during the pairing process. However, Feature 9.2 and a study by

---

Feature 9.2 DATE RAPE

If a woman goes out on a date with a man, and he then forces her to
have sex, is that rape? The dictionary says it is, and so does the law . . . .
Yet for many people, including most juries and even some women,
criminal rape is *only* sexual violation by a stranger . . . .

When a friend or acquaintance rapes, the victim tends to blame
herself. "It made me question myself more," says Devon. "I had to ask,
'what does this say about my judgment of people, about my behavior?'
People are accusatory because I didn't fight him off. I feel guilty, but
there's nothing I could have done" . . . .

Only one in about 10 rapes is reported at all, but the ratio is even
lower when the rapist is an acquaintance.

Dr. Joyce Brothers, "Date Rape," *Parade Magazine*, September 27, 1987, 4.

Feltey et al. make it clear that sexual violence or rape is almost exclusively inflicted by males (Feltey et al., 1991: 229–250). Rape is, of course, a crime of violence, to be explained in part by the weak and threatened ego of the perpetrator. It is, however, also a sexual crime of violence, meaning that the male has chosen that method of expressing his aggression—as distinct from assault with a deadly weapon, for example. Thus, another portion of the explanation for the prevalence of rape along with "sexual revolution" may be the feeling on the part of males that they are losing patriarchal control and that they are unable to get their share of sexual activity by appealing to the interest of the female (Morgan, 1975: 199). This leads us to the discussion of sexuality during the prelude to pairing. First, however, let us review our discussion of the pairing continuum. The pairing process is both functional and problematic. Most of what has been said holds for young people at all levels of the socioeconomic ladder. Lower-class and working-class pairing processes do, however, diverge at a few points. The pairing activity of lower-class young people is governed by lesser financial resources and is oriented toward sex and marriage more immediately and directly than is that of the middle class. One reason for this is that only a small portion of lower-class young people postpone marriage in order to attend college. Thus, the pairing continuum of the lower class is foreshortened by a generally earlier age at marriage than that of the middle class. The chapter on marital dissolution will return to the issue of early marriage and its relation to marital permanence.

SECTION THREE

SEXUAL RELATIONS DURING THE PRELUDE TO PAIRING

The forerunners of current discussion of sex in the modern industrial world are ethnographic reports of anthropologists who studied a wide variety of preindustrial societies.[1] All societies, it seems, control sexual behavior in some manner; the two most universal forms of control appear to be the incest taboo and marriage. In addition, accounts of such practices as premarital sex, extramarital sex, masturbation, and homosexuality indicate that these activities may be encouraged, permitted, ignored, condemned, or suppressed, depending upon the society and its norms. Furthermore, there are variations in the degree of correspondence between verbalized norms and typical behavior. However, as Zelnik et al. point out, traditional patriarchal societies which characteristically enforce restrictive, punitive codes against youth and women typically have little sex or illicit reproduction among their young women (Zelnik et al., 1981: 182).

Among the sex practices mentioned above, the one that has received most widespread cross-cultural acceptance is premarital intercourse. After analyzing a large sample of societies, Murdock stated that "premarital license prevails in 70 percent of our cases. In the rest, the taboo falls primarily upon females and appears to be largely a precaution against child-bearing out of wedlock rather than a moral requirement (Murdock, 1949: 265). The arrangements in the majority of societies that permit premarital sex include safeguards against exploitation of the female, and equal and legitimate status for children born out of wedlock. In other words, where premarital sex is accepted as a part of a society's culture, few stressful and guilt-producing features are attached to it. The greater problems occur in those societies that officially prohibit premarital sex, since it is extremely difficult to enforce the prohibition and many social leaders do not consider the prohibition important enough to enforce.[2]

Extramarital sex, unlike sex before marriage, is *not* permitted by a majority of societies. Many factors concerning the stability and integration of societies and their family systems are related to the control of extramarital sex. We therefore introduce our discussion of premarital sex with the statement that the sex practices of a culture are usually consistent with its other characteristics. In the U.S. culture change has occurred rapidly, and at present norms in the area of sexuality are becoming more consistent with other elements of its culture. However, as you are probably aware, some inconsistences still exist in the area of sexuality, including the continuing stigma attached to births out of wedlock while premarital sexuality has become more acceptable.

Prelude to Pairing and Sexuality in the U.S.

The sexual double standard has existed for a long time in the United States. At the turn of this century the high incidence of intercourse among unmarried middle-class men pointed to a major area of tension. "Large numbers of middle-class men were participating in sexual activities not shared by women of the same class who, overwhelmingly, entered marriage without the experience of coitus" (D'Emilio and Freedman, 1988: 181). And during the period between the world wars the double standard continued. D'Emilio and Freedman will speak at some length:

> *female sexual expression continued to be deeply attached to the emotion of love and to commitment in a relationship. For a young man, sex might be an expression of love, but it could also be justified for its own sake, as a symbol of conquest, or as a badge of prestige to be sported among one's fellows. Class differences also played an important role in the maintenance of the double standard. By pursuing sex with working-class girls, middle-class males could expect chastity from their peers without relinquishing access to intercourse themselves (D'Emilio and Freedman, 1988: 265).*

The massive research on sex in the United States carried out by Alfred Kinsey and his associates burst upon the public following World War II (Kinsey et al., 1948; 1953). Because the research noted the prevalence of many types of sexual practices and the discrepancy between the expressed and behavioral morality of the middle classes, it was perceived as a threat by many persons. Researchers attacked its methodology, editorialists rejected its conclusions, and moral leaders accused its authors of undermining the moral fiber of the nation

TABLE 9.1   PREMARITAL SEXUAL ATTITUDE AND BEHAVIOR

Study and Year	BEHAVIOR No Premarital Intercourse (Virgins)		ATTITUDE Premarital Sex Immoral (Abstinence)	
	Males	Females	Males	Females
Ehrmann (1957)	33%	86%	32%	86%
Reiss (1965)	—	—	28	55
Robinson/Jedlicka (1965)	35	71	33	70
Simon and Gagnon (1967)	43	67	28	55
Robinson/Jedlicka (1970)	35	63	14	34
DeLamater (1973)	25	40	5	11
Robinson/Jedlicka (1975)	26	43	20	21
Levin/Levin (1975)	—	10	—	—
Robinson/Jedlicka (1980)	23	36	17	25

SOURCES: Ehrmann, 1959; Reiss, 1967; Robinson and Jedlicka, 1982; Simon and Gagnon, 1968; DeLamater and MacCorquodale, 1979; Levin and Levin in Stein, 1976.

(Himmelhoch and Fava, 1955). While the same criticisms would apply to much other sociological research, the significant fact is that the Kinsey studies were felt to deserve extensive critical attention. They were correctly viewed as heralding a new day of openness and frankness regarding sexual matters; the result has been a flood of studies examining sex, which continues unabated to the present.[3]

By drawing upon the findings of Ehrmann, Reiss, and many recent researchers, changes can be traced over time in sexual attitudes and behavior during the prelude period. One area of change concerns the *double standard*, which says premarital sex is acceptable for a man but not for a woman. In the 1960s, for example, Reiss spoke of millions of males engaged in reducing the number of virgins while holding a deep desire for a virgin mate. Also, a basic middle-class distinction between men and women in the 1950s, according to Ehrmann, was that women base their indulgence in premarital intercourse on love and males on eroticism. To elaborate, most women indicated to Ehrmann that they had engaged in intercourse only with the man whom they eventually married. Being "respectable," they seldom engaged in what the official morality would label as promiscuous or random sexuality. Thus, 30 years ago sex was viewed as an expression of love on the part of the middle-class female and as an erotic release on the part of the male, who nevertheless desired a virgin bride. This led to Ehrmann's conclusion that, in the middle class, the degree of physical intimacy varies inversely with the intensity of affection among males and directly with the intensity of affection among females (Ehrmann, 1959: 338).

Ehrmann also concluded that attitudes cause behavior, and Reiss followed Ehrmann's lead in 1965 by asking only about attitudes. However, the research of the 1970s raised many questions concerning Ehrmann's findings. Table 9.1 presents some of the studies reporting premarital sexual attitudes and behavior.

First, it is obvious why Ehrmann concluded that attitudes cause or determine behavior. After all, his percentages for virginity and favoring abstinence
were virtually identical. But look at the percentages for John DeLamater's
study at Wisconsin. There are actually fewer who have engaged in intercourse
than who no longer see it as a moral issue. In other words, attitudes have outrun behavior toward a liberal stance, which presumably means that some of the
liberals have simply had no opportunity to act upon their liberalism.

Second, women have obviously been the focal point of the changes reported
in Table 9.1. When percentages change from 86 to 10 in 20 years or so, it seems
to deserve the label "revolution." Do these figures mean the old sexual double
standard has now disappeared? The answer to this question is rather complex.
Clearly, the table indicates that most of the gender differences in attitudes and
behavior are gone. Martin Whyte adds that in four marriage cohorts, the percentages of women who had had sexual partners prior to their husband were:

> *1965–1969: 17%*
> *1970–1974: 31%*
> *1975–1979: 41%*
> *1980–1984: 51% (Whyte, 1990: 27)*

It is not too difficult to predict a further rise since the mid-1980s, based on these
percentages. However, the Hendricks, writing in 1992, assert that college males
are currently more permissive and instrumental; and the norm is still for males
to initiate sexual activity and for females to set limits (Hendrick and Hendrick,
1992: 138). Wilson and Medora's research with 641 college students breaks up
sexual behaviors into a variety of categories, and finds some areas in which
there are no gender differences, and some in which there still are:

> *Significant differences were found between males' and females' attitudes toward premar-
> ital sex when the couple is casually acquainted, and attitudes toward extramarital sex,
> oral-genital sex, and anal sex. However, significant differences were not found between
> males' and females' attitudes toward premarital sex when the couple is in love . . . (or)
> engaged, . . . (or) toward masturbation, homosexuality, and sexual fantasizing
> (Wilson and Medora, 1990: 615).*

Their conclusion is that while attitudes continue to converge, there are still differences. Females are more likely to connect sex with seriousness, and this is
not captured by Table 9.1.

The third issue raised by Table 9.1 concerns the extremely low female virginity figure reported by the Levins in *Redbook*. Their percentage is for women
25 years of age and younger, nine-tenths of whom were married at the time of
the survey. They were asked if they had ever engaged in premarital intercourse
prior to marriage, and 90 percent said yes. Almost all the other research in
Table 9.1 was done with college samples, most of whom were as yet unmarried.
When the question "Have you ever engaged in sexual intercourse?" is asked of
the unmarried, it must always be interpreted: "Have you ever engaged in sexual
intercourse *up to now*?" Thus, if you really want to find out what proportion of a

population will *ever* engage in sex prior to marriage, the only truly appropriate time to collect your data is after marriage, since only married persons can describe the entire prelude to pairing period.[4]

A final clarification concerns social-class differences in premarital sexuality. Most of the studies reported in Table 9.1 involve middle-class or college samples only. Besides the change in middle-class female attitudes and behavior, the other major change has been toward similar sexual behaviors in the middle, working, and lower classes. And the "meeting ground" has been the standards traditionally associated with the lower social strata. This lifestyle stresses individual self-development and the gratifying of personal desires and is sufficiently tolerant of premarital intercourse to have overcome the traditional verbalized and internalized norms against sex before marriage.\

· Four further issues concerning sex during the pairing period deserve our attention: (1) timing and life course; (2) influences on sexual attitudes and behavior; (3) effects of AIDS; and (4) subsequent effects of sexual activity. Several recent researchers have examined timing and behavior. Phinney et al. found, not too surprisingly, that "early-maturing girls are more likely to engage in dating and sexual intercourse at earlier ages than are their late-maturing peers" (Phinney et al., 1990: 328). Another expectable result is that early sexual experience predisposes an individual to more later on (Koyle et al., 1989: 461–476). Likewise, as we reported above, early daters have earlier and more frequent sexual experience (Thornton, 1990: 239). One study shows that blacks have earlier sexual experience than whites. However, black males in predominantly white high school classes are much less likely to have engaged in sex than are blacks in predominantly black classrooms — a most interesting contextual effect (Furstenberg, 1987: 511–518).

. The second point concerns where adolescents get their sexual attitudes. Some 25 years ago, Ira Reiss reported that permissive sexual standards come from the peer group, and conservative standards come from parents and religion. Recently, this proposition has been found to be too simple. One study finds that mothers' attitudes influence children's attitudes more than their behavior, and mothers' religiosity also has an influence (Thornton and Camburn, 1987: 337). Moore et al. add that parent-adolescent communication does not by itself discourage early sexual experience. It has that effect only for the daughters of parents with traditional values (Moore et al., 1986: 781). What this suggests is that parents have less effect on their sons, and the parents attitudes themselves may vary greatly. A third study of family effects finds that having both parents at home, mother having a college education, and weekly church attendance all are associated with a delay in the timing of first intercourse. One additional influence is an older sibling's behavior, with sexual activity leading to earlier activity on the part of the younger sibling (Haurin and Mott, 1990: 537–557).

Two decades ago, Reiss reported a large difference in premarital sexuality as a result of religious affiliation, with Protestants most liberal and Catholics most conservative. Now, the rate for Protestants is still highest, but the rate for all religious groups has increased, and the gap between them has been reduced. The result is that religiosity, as measured by attendance at services, is now more important than the group you belong to, with the high attenders being more conservative (Bell and Courtney, 1980: 353–357; Singh, 1980: 387–393). Finally, Reiss and Miller report that among adults of the same (middle) age, those who are married and have teenage offspring tend to be more restrictive concerning premarital sexuality (Reiss and Miller, 1979: 83). This, of course, may simply be an indication that it is easier for parents to be (or seem) liberal when they do not have teenagers of their own who "just might get pregnant." In general, then, Reiss's findings continue to have some validity, with closeness to parents and religiosity biasing one toward conservative standards and strong peer group influence encouraging one toward liberal sexual standards.

The third issue—and one receiving increasing attention—is the relation between AIDS and sexual behavior. A logical hypothesis would seem to be that the threat of AIDS reduces the number of sexual partners and the initiation of sexual activity. A "Digest" report in *Family Planning Perspectives* reports that about "one-third of sexually experienced, unmarried American women have changed their sexual behavior in response to the threat of AIDS; the most common change is limiting their number of sexual partners to one man" (Digest, September/October 1991: 234). Another study, by Roscoe and Kruger, reported that despite being knowledgeable about AIDS, only about one-third had changed their behavior (1990: 39). Still another found some reduction in initiation of intercourse, but also a decrease in regular use of condoms. In other words, despite knowing about AIDS, they were hardly working to prevent its transmission (Maticka-Tyndale, 1991: 31–49). And Hobart's study in Canada reports the most ironic finding: those "who know the most AIDS victims and so are most aware of the spread of the disease and rate the seriousness of the AIDS threat most highly are the respondents who rate sex with briefly known partners as *least* risky and are *least* inclined to use condoms in sexual encounters with briefly known partners" (Hobart, 1992: 429–430).

The overall results to this point are, therefore, (1) that much is known about AIDS, at least at a general level; (2) that a minority of women have restricted their behavior as a result of this knowledge; and (3) that many of the most sexually active are both knowledgeable and taking risks. Of course, such a recent phenomenon is bound to go through more changes in the immediate future.

. The final issue concerns the effects of premarital sexual activity in the future. Miller and Heaton's analysis of the National Survey of Family Growth finds that those who begin sexual activity early are more likely both to delay marriage after childbirth (if birth occurs first), and to give birth soon after marriage (if marriage occurs first) (Miller and Heaton, 1991: 719–732). Another study using the same data reports that women who hold traditional attitudes about marriage are less likely both to engage in premarital sex and to divorce later on (Kahn and London, 1991: 845–855). Finally, all respondents except females who had engaged in homosexual contact rejected opposite-sex partners with homosexual experience. The most rejecting were heterosexual females of males with prior homosexual experience (Williams and Jacoby, 1989: 495).

So sexuality is still withheld until marriage by some young people in the United States. However, they are no longer in the majority, and seem to be fighting a battle against the liberalizing activities of those around them. A comment by Ira Reiss would be a good way to end this section:

> *In short, when we assert that sexuality usually contains pleasure and disclosure characteristics, it becomes apparent why sexuality is everywhere viewed as important. This plainly follows if you assume as I do that almost all humans value physical pleasure and the psychic release and intimacy potential of self-disclosure (Reiss, 1986: 35).*

That sexual activity does not always lead to a high level of disclosure is an issue we will raise in Chapter 10. And whether the revolution we have described is viewed positively or negatively is as likely to be based on the individual's values as it is on empirical evidence that it is either good or bad for the individual.

Feature 9.3 BITNET'S INTERCHAT . . .

I thought you might be interested in the operation of a largely college-based approach to dating and mate selection that has emerged in recent years: BITNET'S Interchat Relay Network and similar systems.

"Relay" is essentially a computer version of CB radio. Instead of communicating verbally, users communicate visually via words and symbols on a computer screen. Because they cannot see or hear each other, people often use keyboard symbols to supplement the written word. Thus, for example, :-) is a smile . . . . They also exchange detailed biographical data . . . in what are known as IDs which are sent via electronic mail.

People typically begin chatting on a public channel with up to about a dozen other people and if any two or more wish to talk privately they can switch to a vacant channel. Users can also temporarily identify special interest channels devoted to a sport, type of music, or other topic. (Only one channel has been permanently assigned by convention, that being the gay channel.)

Users frequently assert that personality and similarity of interests are more important on Relay, because physical attractiveness cannot be observed. Not surprising, people who are shy in face-to-face interaction, or who are physically disabled, are often attracted to the system.

I have interviewed a number of people who met on Relay and are now cohabitating, engaged or married . . . .

Romantic relationships typically progress from casual chatting to long conversations on the system, then the exchange of letters and photographs, telephone conversations, then to face-to-face meetings.

I suspect that this approach to dating and mate selection will become increasingly widespread.

David J. Hanson, Professor

SECTION FOUR

CONCLUSIONS

The prelude to pairing involves a continuum that ranges from casual and group relationships to eventual pairing. An important but non-exclusive aspect of this continuum is dating, which in some cases reinforces family culture and in some cases expresses the participant-run and individualistic nature of the continuum. This pairing process performs certain important functions for the adolescent, and is also problematic.

Two important points: first concerns the use of the words "prelude" and "pairing." We have not used the term "dating" because it does not incorporate all the current elements in the process, especially cohabitation. (For another exception, see Feature 9.3.) In addition, we have used the term "pairing" and in the next chapter we will speak of "choosing a partner" to recognize the fact that some pairs are nonmarital (rather than premarital) cohabitants, and others are homosexual. Both of these exist with enough frequency to make it valid to avoid the label "premarital," even though it is a premarital process for all but perhaps 20 percent (half nonmarital cohabitors and half homosexual pairs). Again, this issue will be noted in the next chapter.

The prelude to pairing and choosing a partner are, in fact, a single process. However, in this chapter we have focused on the characteristics of the process or stages, while in the next chapter we emphasize the factors leading to the choice itself. The result of the pairing continuum is still marriage for most persons in the United States, and much research has been done to determine the factors governing this choice. Chapter 10 examines these factors.

Choosing a Partner in the United States

CHAPTER 10

Societies of the Western world, unlike many other societies, have institutionalized romantic love as the basis for mate selection. Love does not, however, occur in a vacuum. Among the conditions that limit love and marital choice are: incest taboo, propinquity, and various subsocietal categories, such as race and religion. Factors that enhance love and increase the likelihood of pairing are: physical attractiveness, shared interests and values, similar personalities, rapport, and empathy. Choosing a partner is a process that cannot be completely reduced to a series of variables. The process we have discussed is useful for understanding many instances of either homosexual or friendship relations as well as marriage. An important example of nonuniversal availability in U.S. mate selection is racial intermarriage; a consideration of this closes the chapter.

Love is an innate disposition, a complex emotion, that—like humor, anger, hate, fear, and jealousy—is a universal potentiality in human beings.[1] As universal potentialities, emotions that manifest themselves behaviorally may pose a threat to the structures and solidarities of societies. The behavioral manifestation of anger may be injury or murder, and, while societies permit anger, they take drastic measures against injury and murder in an attempt to control the disruptive aspects of the emotion. Fear—when expressed in either immobility or flight—can dissolve social solidarity. Therefore, a society must devise means to control fear; for example, magic may be used to allay anxiety and increase courage. The emotional attraction of one person for another, which we call love, has as its behavioral manifestation sexual relations. However, sexual relations are defined in human societies as integrally related to procreation and mating. Thus it is that three strong controls have been placed upon love in order to avoid or channel its behavioral manifestation. The most universal of these controls involves the *incest taboo*, which is based, as described in Chapter 2, on the great potentiality for the development of love among immediate kin and on the equally great desire in most human societies for mating to occur exogamously with respect to this category of kin. The second control, which is sometimes imposed when sexual relations are defined as strictly a matter of procreation, is the *prohibition of homosexuality*. However, I say "sometimes" because there are many instances when homosexuality has been fairly widespread despite the procreational model for marriage. We will return briefly to the issue of homosexual pairing at the end of this chapter and again in Chapter 18. Of primary interest in this chapter is the third control, that over *choice of a marriage partner*. This differs from incest prohibitions in the extent to which it controls not only the sexual manifestation of love, but the development of the emotion as well. Harris generalizes the control over marital choice as follows:

> *we find in all societies either that marriage is hedged around by rules specifying which categories of people are eligible mates for the members of different groups or, at least, that the groups which constitute society make strenuous efforts to control or influence their children's choice of marriage partner (Harris, 1983: 18).*

Why should a society attempt to control the nonincestuous development of love between members of the opposite sex? The most obvious answer, if the above argument is correct, must be that the members of that society are convinced that giving love free reign would be detrimental to structures and solidarities. By the expression "giving love free reign," we mean allowing heterosexual love to be the only basis for mating and procreation. A further question arises: In what kind of society would social structures and solidarities be threatened if love were permitted to operate as the sole basis for mate selection? This would obviously be detrimental in a society whose basic functions are performed by and embedded in kin groups. Thus, arranged marriages are more likely to be found in extended kin societies, and romantic love is less likely to be used as a criterion for mate selection in such societies (Lee and Stone, 1980: 319–326). If economic productivity, political authority, inheritance, residential location, and religious symbols are controlled by the lineage or kin group, it is imperative that the marriage linkages of its offspring be arranged, or at least limited. Individuals and nuclear families are embedded in the kin group which controls mate choice in order to guarantee the appropriate continuation of solidarities and functions. The "free reign" of romantic love is minimized by such mechanisms as child marriage, stringent definition of eligibles, and isolation from potential mates (Goode, 1959: 43–44).

Romantic love is not unique to the Western world. Given the opportunity, it can "break out" in any society.[2] Variation from one society to another in the prevalence and desirability of love is thus not a matter of emotional capabilities, but of definition and control. Love is an inadequate basis for mating and sex relations in the kin-centered society and is therefore defined negatively and controlled by the kin group. A love relationship may develop between mates, but this is not the basis for, nor even a necessary concomitant of, their marriage. "Kinfolk or immediate family," says Goode,

> can disregard the question of who marries whom, only if a marriage is not seen as a link between kin lines, only if no property, power, lineage honor, totemic relationships, and the like are believed to flow from the kin lines through the spouses to their offspring. Universally, however, these are believed to follow kin lines (1959: 43).

The logical alternative to kin control of mating would be found in a society in which kin lines are totally unimportant and solidarities and functions are individual-based, with the domestic unit—if it exists—serving individual needs. In such a society, which can be observed nowhere in the empirical world, entirely free choice could be permitted; this choice would in all likelihood be based strictly upon emotional attraction. Such a scheme is related to Farber's "universal availability" conceptualization.

Between the two polar alternatives described above, that is, complete kin control and completely free choice, can be found several degrees of restriction upon love and mating. In the colonial U.S. family, for example—in which the nuclear family dominated many functions and vied with the kin group for solidarity—choice was individual but greatly restricted by nuclear family and kin influences. In the contemporary U.S. family, in which individual values and functions compete with both nuclear family and kin solidarity, mate selection is by choice, based on love; but family and kin still use various methods, often successful, to influence the process.

Love is, therefore, an emotional potential that is controlled to varying degrees by different societies. The amount of control varies directly with the degree to which institutional functions and individuals are embedded in the kin group. But when the mate selection process is participant-run, it is highly correlated with romantic love as a selection criterion. Other conditions for individual choice include, according to Quale, commercialization, centralization, and suprafamilial mode of registering births, and "late marriage for women as well as for men, combined with a variety of experience great enough to give both sexes sufficient grounds on which to base a reasonable choice" (Quale, 1988: 193). Thus, in modern U.S. society, love has been institutionalized as the basis for individual choice of a mate, but even in this society diverse means are employed by family and kin to restrict the opportunity for love to develop.

Normatively, then, people in the United States will cite love as the reason for their marriage. Love may cause marriage, but what is love? What causes it? How is it controlled in U.S. society? The first question has seldom been answered directly. A novelist may view love viscerally and sexually, giving descriptions of the attraction one human being holds for another. Poets may ennoble love through the use of adjectives and hyperbole, as they "count the ways" in which they are drawn to the ones they love. Sociologist Robert Winch reduces love to a twofold definition, more causal than descriptive, which sees love as resulting from the person's (a) having certain attributes highly prized by me and (b) meeting specific personal or psychological needs that I have (Winch, 1958). Goode is perhaps most realistic when, having attempted a definition of his own, he admits that verbal definitions of the emotion called love "are notoriously open to attack" (Goode, 1959: 41). It is better perhaps to refer to the experience without attempting an inclusive and conclusive definition, such as one might give for fear or anger, and to assume that most readers are sufficiently familiar with the phenomenon to provide their own intuitive perception of its meaning. Thus, we shall move on to a consideration of controls upon and causes of love in the United States, an approach that will very likely lead closer to an understanding of love than would expending further effort trying to define it.

SECTION ONE

PARTNER SELECTION IN THE UNITED STATES[3]

Theories of mate selection in the United States abound (Surra, 1990: 844–865). The discussion that follows will bring together the best evidence from these theories and the research that has tested them. Organization of the discussion will center on three concepts developed by George Levinger to summarize factors that cause marital cohesiveness or dissolution: *barriers, attractions,* and *alternative attractions* (Levinger, 1965:19–28). By barriers, Levinger meant those factors, such as the belief that marriage is for life, that might keep a couple from divorcing despite a low level of attraction to the marriage. We will expand the term *barriers* to include not only barriers to getting out of a relationship, but barriers to beginning a relationship. With the help of these concepts, we will attempt to treat mate selection as a process, as a series of stages through which a relationship passes on the way to marriage or pairing.

Orientation to Marriage

The process discussed concerns the choosing of a specific person as a partner, but first consider the attractiveness of marriage itself. An individual may be more or less prone to marry at any given time. Surra and Huston, for example, note that orientation to marriage may be totally conscious: "Some couples decide to marry only after considerable thoughtful debate about matrimony's good and bad points and their suitability for marriage, while others . . . seem to 'fall into' marriage (Surra and Huston, 1987: 93). Bernard Murstein calls the level of desire to marry an "enhancer" or "suppressor" variable (Murstein, 1967: 293). Along the same line, Sindberg et al. find that a highly significant variable, "which rarely has been emphasized in the literature, is the conscious and overtly expressed desire to marry" (Sindberg et al., 1972: 612). As mentioned in Chapter 7, an impetus toward an early marriage may be the desire to escape an unhappy home. At the other extreme, having passed the typical marriage age and watching the available people "pairing up" may also increase orientation to marriage. Dan Lichter, for example, finds "striking evidence that assortative mating declines with age at marriage. . . . Although nonmarriage is an option increasingly taken by older women, a demographic alternative (is) . . . to redefine the 'field of eligibles' in the mate selection process" (Lichter, 1990: 809). In other words, as you get older you cannot be as "choosy" about the characteristics of potential mates, since so many have already paired up. In addition, Luther Otto notes the way in which educational, occupational, and marital opportunities and interests intertwine to affect marital timing (Otto, 1979: 119). The educational and occupational opportunities may of course operate in combination with alternatives to traditional marriage to reduce the strength of orientation toward marriage. Cherlin, for example, reports that, with the exception of younger blacks, women who plan to work outside the home tend to postpone marriage longer than those without such plans (Cherlin, 1980: 355–365). Employment does not only delay marriage, however. Faludi reports the following: "The more women are paid, the less eager they are to marry. A 1982 study of three thousand singles found that women earning high incomes were almost twice as likely to *want* to remain unwed as women earning low incomes" (Faludi, 1991: 16). Lichter et al. report the same finding: female marriage rates are highest in local areas that provide the fewest economic alternatives to marriage (Lichter et al., 1991: 843–867). Another negative effect on orientation toward marriage is having lived away from the family in which you grew up. Goldscheider and Waite state it thus: "the experience of non-family living early in the transition to adulthood does appear to result in a decrease in the probability of subsequent marriage for women" (Goldscheider and Waite, 1987: 514).

Ivan Nye and Felix Berardo note that when a couple have decided they are right for each other marriage will probably occur. Then, in a footnote, they state the following:

"Probably" [is used] because an occasional person places a higher value on single than married status. Such a person would remain single even though "in love" or having rationally decided that he has found the person best suited to him as a spouse (Nye and Berardo, 1973: 123).

A fairly complete catalog of pushes and pulls toward marriage and singlehood is found in Peter Stein's book *Single*. Pushes into marriage include pressure from parents, the need to leave home, and loneliness. Pulls toward marriage include desire for a family, example of peers, and emotional attachment to the partner. Pushes toward singlehood include feeling trapped in a relationship, isolation, and limited availability. Finally, pulls toward singlehood include sexual availability, exciting lifestyle, freedom, and self-sufficiency (Stein, 1976: 65–66). So some factors may speed up, intensify, or short-circuit the mate selection process, while others may retard it. Keeping in mind attraction or nonattraction to marriage itself, we turn now to the factors influencing the choice of a specific mate.

Barriers to Beginning

Even if we consider, with Farber, that everyone of the opposite sex is in fact available to us for pairing, there are certain factors that limit the field of eligible people.

INCEST TABOO   The first of these is the *incest taboo*, referred to at some length in Chapter 2. Here we will simply note that in the United States, as in the great majority of societies, this taboo involves parents and siblings, as well as other close kin of ascending generations, such as aunts, uncles, and grandparents. First cousins are also ordinarily excluded from marriage, though examples of cousin marriage are reported from time to time. No distinction is made in the United States between cousins on the mother's side and those on the father's side of the family.

PROPINQUITY   One seldom marries a person one has not seen, met, and interacted with; and one is more likely to interact with a person located nearby than with a person located at a distance. These self-evident facts introduce a second limiting condition upon mate selection—*propinquity*, or proximity. This obvious factor in mate selection was first described in detail by James H. S. Bossard in 1932. Investigating five thousand marriages in Philadelphia, Bossard discovered that one-third of the couples applying for marriage licenses lived within five blocks of each other, and more than half lived twenty or fewer blocks apart (Bossard, 1932:19–24).

Subsequently, other researchers reported the same results: the closer to each other two persons live, the more likely they are to get married. Many writers interpreted the findings as another manifestation of homogamy. That is, people of the same social and cultural group tend to live close together. Thus they interact more frequently, and, therefore, they marry each other. In 1958, Alvin Katz and Reuben Hill reviewed and summarized the research on propinquity by means of three propositions. (a) *Marriage is normative*, or follows subcultural lines. This, of course, embodies the homogamy interpretation of many previous writers. (b) Within the normative field of eligibles, *the probability of marriage varies directly with the probability of interaction*. Many of us have heard stories about couples who correspond by letter for years and marry at their first meeting. These are the exceptions that prove the rule that the possibility of frequent interaction is the logical precondition for dating and marriage. (c) *The probability of interaction is lessened by intervening opportunities for interaction*. This might be called the density factor; it becomes apparent when we compare the likelihood that two persons on adjoining farms one-half mile apart will interact and become well-acquainted with the likelihood that two residents of dormitories or apartment buildings one-half mile apart will become acquainted (Katz and Hill, 1958: 27–35).

The locational character of any given individual's life may not be stable. He or she may move from place to place, thus complicating the operation of propinquity. Thus, for example, we can say that a man attending the University of Pennsylvania is more likely to marry a woman attending the University of Pennsylvania than one attending the University of Florida, unless he resided near the Floridian at an earlier stage of their lives. Residential movement does not void the effect of propinquity but merely complicates it.

A reduction in the importance of propinquity is reported by Martin King Whyte: In the prewar generation, distance between woman and first husband's residence when they started dating was three miles; in the baby boom generation it was four miles, and for women marrying since 1965 it was five miles. "So there is some evidence for the view that propinquity is a somewhat less binding constraint than in the past, but still the fact that half of all recent brides lived less than five miles away from their future husbands when they started to date is notable" (Whyte, 1990: 35). One reason for the lessening importance of residential distance is that resources may offset distance. Resources, or being able to afford to travel, can bring you into proximity with many you would not otherwise meet, and interaction is easier once you are there. Finally, William Catton notes that since people of the same racial, religious, ethnic, and social categories tend to cluster together residentially, one effect of propinquity as a barrier to beginning is to limit the likelihood of intermarriage between such categories (though this limiting function is greater for certain categories, such as race, than for others) (Catton, 1964: 529). We will return to the issue of categorical homogamy below.

Early Attraction

Once the incest taboo and nonpropinquity have been established as barriers to contact or as limits on the field of eligible people, we can turn to the bases for early attraction. Murstein calls this the "stimulus" phase, Hendrick and Hendrick call it the "awareness" period, and Levinger, Senn, and Jorgensen call it the "encounter" phase of the mate selection process (Murstein, 1980: 777–792; Hendrick and Hendrick, 1992: 150; Levinger et al., 1970: 427–443). Early attraction between the sexes may, of course, be based on many of the same factors as any other form of friendship. Thus, valued public behaviors, such as gregariousness and poise, or similar interests and abilities may stimulate early attraction. Nevertheless, regardless of sexual preference, the most likely stimulus is physical appearance and attractiveness. As the Hendricks say, there is "a very strong tendency to prefer highly attractive others, regardless of one's own physical attractiveness. People want to be associated with beautiful people" (Hendrick and Hendrick, 1992: 42). Goodwin finds that this is a more important factor for males than for females (Goodwin, 1990: 501–513). Unfortunately, little has been done on the precise physical characteristics seen as attractive or what sorts of public behaviors appeal to what sorts of opposite-sex individuals. It is worth noting that simply having a good time during early contacts can increase mutual interest.

One further factor was proposed by Anselm Strauss many years ago as a possible contributor to early attraction. We carry around in our minds, Strauss felt, an image of the ideal mate for us. This image includes both physical and personality features and we compare those with whom we come in contact with that image (Strauss, 1946: 204–210). Richard Udry, however, has argued that the ideal mate image is not a basis for attraction or mate selection, but rather this image changes "in response to new relationships into which the person enters" (Udry, 1965: 477–482). While the image of the mate one wants may or may not change, the evidence on ideal mate image is sufficiently skimpy to omit it from the major factors in early attraction (on the "Fantasy" Mate, see Feature 10.1). Those factors, we have said, are physical attractiveness, certain valued behaviors, and perhaps similar interests.

Homogamy in Mate Selection

An important limiting factor in U.S. mate selection is in reality a complex of social structural categories. When availability allows, the person chosen as a mate is often from the same general social background as oneself. The reason for saying "when availability allows" is that group size is inversely related to exogamy, or marrying outside the group (Blau et al., 1982: 45-62). Brym et al. report that in Canada, Jewish "outmarriage" varies with the number of Jews in each

---

Feature 10.1   "FANTASY" MATE

Do most people marry a "fantasy" mate instead of a real person?

Yes, declared Dr. Marilyn Skully, a consulting psychologist at Mercy College in Detroit. She said she believes "we decide we're in love with someone and make him or her over in our minds to fit the image we want to see. We may not even be acquainted with the real person. . . .

"Sometimes the real person emerges, thus disappointing the other's expectations. Other times the couple never communicates. Trouble can result either way. Other people can live together for 30 years and never reveal themselves to each other—what irritates them, what makes them happy. It's incredible what they don't know about each other."

Dr. Skully said that a marriage originally based on a "fantasy" often crops up in psychotherapy sessions.

"'Fantasy' Mate is Cause of Many Marital Breakups," *Jet Magazine*, 10 October 1974, p. 25.

province (Brym et al., 1985: 108). More generally, then, if there are few members of your race, or religion, or from your region of the country close by, it is likely you will marry someone of another race, religion, or region. But if someone is a WASP (White Anglo-Saxon Protestant), for example, the chances are pretty good he or she will marry another WASP. "Education, IQ, race, religion, income, family background, height, and many other traits are . . . strongly positively sorted," says Gary Becker (1981: 222).

The categories of U.S. society that have received the most research attention with respect to their limitation of partner choice are race, religion, ethnic or nationality group, social class, and more recently education and age. One terminological clarification is in order. *Homogamy* and *heterogamy*—the marriage of people who are alike and the marriage of people who are different—are simply opposite sides of the same coin. The same holds for *endogamy* and *exogamy* or *intermarriage*—marriage within one's group and marriage outside one's group. The terms endogamy and homogamy are used almost interchangeably in the literature; their relationship can be seen in the fact that if the rate of religious endogamy is 90 percent, then the rate of religious intermarriage is 10 percent. For the most part, we will use *homogamy* and *intermarriage*, the two terms most prevalent in the literature.

Studies of *racial* homogamy, or marriage within the same racial group, have generally divided the population into white and black and—if included in the study—Native American, Chicano, and Oriental. The norms restricting racial intermarriage have been extremely stringent; this issue will be dealt with at length in the last section of the chapter. Most investigations of *religious* intermarriage have been based on the three-fold division into Protestants, Catholics, and Jews, although a few have further subdivided Protestants into either liberal or conservative denominations or into the largest denominational groupings, (such as Presbyterians, Methodists, Baptists, Lutherans, and Episcopalians) and Jews into Orthodox, Conservative, and Reformed. *Ethnic* or nationality categories are difficult to distinguish definitively from both racial and religious categories. Chicanos, for example, are actually an ethnic group, but are often treated as a racial category. Also, the members of many nationality groups are almost all of the same religion; for example, the vast majority of Italians are Roman Catholic, while Scandinavians are largely Lutheran. The United States comprises numerous ethnic groups, including Irish, Hispanics, Italians, Japanese, Chinese, Filipinos, Hungarians, Norwegians, Germans, Poles, and English. In some studies of ethnic homogamy, such national aggregates have been combined into more inclusive groupings, such as southeastern European, northwestern European, and so on. It is apparent that the possibilities of confusion, both within the ethnic category and between the ethnic category and race or religion, are substantial; studies of ethnic homogamy must, therefore, be interpreted cautiously.

Social class, or status grouping, is the only one of the four structural designations that the individuals themselves are unlikely to make. The individual may say: "I am a white Irish Catholic," but is less likely to add: "I am upper middle class," or "I am working class." Thus, while an observer will recognize that there are actual differences in education, income, and occupation within U.S. society, and that these differences have behavioral manifestations, it may be argued that social class designations are artifacts of the investigator. Some studies of social class homogamy have divided the population into only two categories, middle class and working class, or—according to occupation—white collar and blue collar. Others have dichotomized each of these categories into upper and lower, while still others have used as many as six or seven class divisions. Of course, the rate of intermarriage reported is bound to fluctuate as a result of the number of categories employed, it might be well to indicate the possible interpretations of social class homogamy that seem viable. According to Bruce Eckland, *class endogamy*, the term he uses for homogamy, may be explained by: (a) similar values, which reflect within-class cultural similarity; (b) residential segregation along class lines (noted in the discussion of propinquity); (c) the close relation between class and ethnicity-race; (d) family pressure to marry one's "own kind"; and (e) educational advantages or disadvantages that cause class differences to persist (Eckland, 1968: 79). These five explanations show once again the relationships between the four categories we have discussed so far: race, religion, ethnicity, and class. Therefore, keeping in mind the cautions concerning category overlap and the arbitrary nature of the number of subdivisions within each of them, let us turn to homogamy rates and trends.

The general tendency in U.S. society is for categorical homogamy between partners to persist but lessen gradually over time. Though racial intermarriage has been legal in all States since 1967, Sweet and Bumpass note that it "remains very rare—five percent of all marriages—although it has increased markedly over the last decade" (Sweet and Bumpass, 1987: 50). Scott South adds that African-Americans and Hispanics are more willing than whites to marry someone of another race (South, 1991: 928–940). So racial homogamy is still clearly the rule (see the last section of this chapter for more). But while black-white intermarriage has been especially slow to increase, the same cannot be said for intermarriage between Japanese-Americans and whites. A weakening of Japanese-American cultural distinctiveness and the desire on the part of Japanese-American females to escape the traditional submissive gender role may have been factors contributing to the rise in outmarriage from 30 percent in the 1950s to 50 percent in the 1970s (Tinker, 1973: 49–66; Kikamura and Kitano, 1987: 67–81).

Religious homogamy in the 1970s was reported at between 80 and 90 percent when the population was divided into just Protestant/Catholic/Jew. Using a larger number of denominations, the Rossis report a "secular trend toward religious intermarriage . . . from the low incidence among parents of older respondents to more recent marriages of young respondents who show close to 31 percent . . ." (Rossi and Rossi, 1990: 149). Larson and Munro find that religious intermarriage is more prevalent in Canada than in the United States, with one-third of U.S. marriages and 54 percent of Canadian marriages being across religious lines. They also note that for Canadian Jews it is 28 percent, for Catholics 44 percent, and for Protestants 58 percent (Larson and Munro, 1990:

239–250). Norval Glenn reported that in 1980 the rate in the United States was 15–20 percent, substantially less than that reported above (Glenn, 1982: 555–566). Whatever the rate is at present, there is general agreement that it is rising more rapidly than in the area of race. The usual argument is that religious intermarriage increases as the importance of the religious subdivisions in U.S. life decreases. Several recent studies have related religious homogamy or heterogamy to marital satisfaction. These studies we will examine in Chapter 13.

If six to ten of the most populous nationality groupings are examined, the homogamy rate is fairly close to that for religion when the same number of categories is used. However, the great variation in ethnic intermarriage is seen in Gurak and Fitzpatrick's study of New York Hispanics. The range is from 29.5 percent for Puerto Ricans to 63.4 percent for Cubans (Gurak and Fitzpatrick, 1982: 921–934). One reason for this is the larger numbers of Puerto Ricans in New York, making homogamy more possible. Social class homogamy differs from 75–80 percent when two classes are used to 50 percent or less when six or seven classes are used. This is the one category where intermarriage rates do not seem to be increasing at present.

Social class is ordinarily divided according to occupation, but other factors such as education and income would be equally usable. Rob Mare recently looked at education and found that over five decades marriage between those with differing amounts of education has actually diminished. He states that barriers to marriage between people with unequal amounts of schooling have increased since the 1930s (Mare, 1991: 15–32). A second issue pertaining to class is the fact that women have generally "married up" or on their own class level. This means that women whose education and occupation place them at the top find it difficult to marry at all (see Feature 10.2). While Farrell's article makes

---

Feature 10.2   MEN AS SUCCESS OBJECTS

Since many women now earn substantial incomes, doesn't this relieve the pressure on men to be a wallet? No. Why? Because successful women do exactly what less-successful women do — "marry up," that is, marry a man whose income is greater than her own. According to statistics, if a woman cannot marry up or marry someone with a higher wage-earning potential, she does not marry at all. Therefore, a man often reflexively backs away from a woman he's attracted to when he discovers she's more successful than he is. . . . She may sleep with him, or live with him, but not marry him unless she spots "potential." Thus, of top female executives, 85 percent don't get married; the remaining 15 percent almost all marry up.

Warren Farrell, "Men as Success Objects," *Utne Reader*, May/June, 1991, 83.

it sound like women are rejecting less successful men, it is at least as likely that it is the men doing the rejecting: meaning that men don't want to be married to women "at the top," rather, they want to be at the top themselves.

The final issue in homogamy concerns age. Like education, this is a variable in which homogamy is becoming greater at present. Using data from the 1900, 1960, and 1980 censuses, Atkinson and Glass find that the percentages of marriages in which the spouses were four or less years apart in age were 37 percent, 63 percent, and 70 percent, respectively (Atkinson and Glass, 1985: 685–691). Lichter adds that the older a woman is when she marries, the greater the discrepancy between her age and that of her spouse. This, of course, is due to the reduction in the "field of eligibles" noted earlier (Lichter, 1990: 809).

The influence of social categories on pairing in the United States can be summarized by indicating the significance of four terms: consciousness, availability, visibility, and salience. The question, "To what social categories do you belong?" is not always, and perhaps *not* even usually, verbalized or *consciously applied* to one's partners. Yet limitation does occur, if not as a conscious process, then as a result of feeling more "at home" with a partner of similar background or as a result of the residential segregation imposed by parents' choice of location. The mention of residential segregation leads to the second issue in homogamy, that of *availability*. As noted above, the more members of your group (religious, ethnic, etc.) are around, the more likely you will select one of them as a partner. Nonavailability is, of course, related to the propinquity factor discussed earlier.

A third influence upon the operation of background categories in limiting mate selection is *visibility*. Recognition of the influence of the visibility factor makes it easy to see why religious intermarriage is more frequent than racial intermarriage. However, even more important is the fourth and final influence upon homogamy—*salience*. Two persons of different races who say, "Sure, we are of different races, but what difference does it make?" may very well get married. But an interracial couple who say, "We are strongly attracted, but, conditions being what they are, our racial difference would be bound to cause our children and us lots of heartaches," are demonstrating that their racial differences is salient to them, or is made so by others. The salience or nonsalience of each of the four social categories could be illustrated in a similar way by asking: "Does their difference in background matter to the couple, or doesn't it?" If it matters, it may not stand in the way of going out for enjoyment or experience, but it may very well stop them from marrying. The role of salience might be diagramed as follows:

Farber makes a good point when he says that "intermarriage is occurring not only because of a breakdown in parental control over mate selection, but also because the traditional social categories for endogamy are themselves becoming vague and diffuse" (Farber, 1964: 152). This decrease in salience is particularly noticeable in college populations, but does not hold for racial barriers to the extent that it does for the other three social categories. The question of salience or nonsalience is really one of values, of what matters to the individual. An individual who values highly a particular aspect of his or her background or a particular characteristic of his or her group is unlikely to compromise it for the sake of marriage.

We should note in closing that the reason for treating homogamy separately is not only that it is so important but that we could legitimately have put it with either "barriers to beginning" or "deeper attraction." According to Kerckhoff and Davis, for example, race, religion, and social class are likely to limit people's choices before they begin going out, though this limitation may be unconscious or may be determined by either residential location or parental influence (Kerckhoff and Davis, 1962: 295–303). It is quite possible, however, that the social categories of a dating partner may not even be known at the outset, though this situation is unlikely for race. But as a couple become attracted at a deeper level, the discovery that they are from different backgrounds may cool or even terminate the relationship, if finding a mate of the same categories as oneself *matters*. So, homogamic concerns may arise at several points in the mate selection process.

Deeper Attraction

√ COMMUNICATION AND SELF-DISCLOSURE   Much of the cause for a relationship's moving or not moving to the level of deeper attraction is a result of communication. Of course, disclosure through communication may have a positive or negative effect on the relationship, depending upon each couple member's reaction to what is disclosed. In an interesting paper, Timothy Stephen sought to determine whether disclosure led to weeding out those relationships in which the individuals disagreed on important issues, or whether attraction led couple members to modify each other's beliefs. His finding was that both are true, but at different stages. That is, there is an initial filtering process by which couples who differ on too many things simply call it quits. However, "as time passes couples in the study became more alike in their thinking" (Stephen, 1985: 960). So communication leads to both weeding out couples who disagree and causing couples who are attracted to become more alike. This, in turn, leads to rapport, or being able to put yourself in the other person's shoes. Zick Rubin makes the processual nature of self-disclosure clear in his discussion of commitment and intimacy:

> *The development of intimacy and of commitment are closely linked, spiraling processes. When one person reveals himself to another, it has subtle effects on the way each of them defines the relationship. Bit by bit the partners open themselves to one another, and step by step they construct their mutual bond. The process only rarely*

*moves ahead in great leaps. . . . And inasmuch as no one can ever disclose himself to-
tally to another person, continuing acts of self-revelation remain an important part of
the developmental process (Rubin, 1973: 180–181).*

Traditional gender roles would lead one to believe that females would disclose more than would males (strong, silent?). So Rubin et al. checked this out
in a college sample and found almost 60 percent of *both* sexes indicating that
they have tried to disclose themselves completely to their partner. They did,
however, find that members of equalitarian couples disclose more than more
traditional couples, and—not surprisingly—that disclosure is greater the longer
the relationship has lasted (Rubin et al., 1980: 305–317).

Sexual intimacy is one of those elements in self-disclosure that can lead to a
major change or "great leap" in the relationship. Depending on whether the couple members find themselves adjusted or maladjusted sexually, the effect can be
either positive or negative. It is important to note, however, that while sexual involvement is a major step in *physical* self-disclosure, it does not *necessarily* have a
direct effect on other aspects of psychological, personality, and value disclosure—in fact, sexuality may not lead to other forms of intimacy. These tend to be
the more gradual, incremental processes described by Rubin (1973).

VALUE CONSENSUS   A crucial aspect of self-disclosure as it leads to deeper
attraction is value consensus or co-orientation, that is, the similar orientation of
couple members toward beliefs, ideas, and goals noted by Stephen (1985).
Likewise, Levinger, Senn, and Jorgensen note that disclosure may result in the
discovery of co-orientation, a value concept; and the second stage of Murstein's
mate selection theory involves values (Levinger et al., 1970: 427–443; Murstein,
1967: 75–88).

Eckland, in his review of mate selection theories, qualifies the way in which
value similarity serves to deepen attraction. "Apparently," he says, "our *perception*
that other persons share with us the same or similar value orientations and beliefs facilitates considerably our attraction to them" (Eckland, 1968: 80). In
other words, perception is more important than reality. Of course, there is no
real distinction between disclosure and value consensus, since the former is the
process leading to the latter condition. And Eloise Snyder agrees with Stephen's
causal finding when she asserts that, among 561 students, similarity of attitudes
among marital pairs appears to be "the result of the adjustive interaction shared
by the couple and not necessarily an affinity present at the outset of the relationship" (Snyder, 1971: 373–395). In other words, consensus may increase attraction, but it is also at least possible that attraction may increase consensus.

SIMILARITY AND COMPLEMENTARITY   Besides similar values, through the
sorting-out process other similarities between couple members may increase
their attraction to each other. Several researchers have found similar physical
attractiveness contributing to the deepening of a relationship, with differences
in attractiveness resulting in termination. The Hendricks put it thus: "there is
a tendency for people of similar appearance to select each other as romantic
partners and as friends" (Hendrick and Hendrick, 1992: 41). Other similarities
that seem to deepen attraction include economic background (homogamy),

self-esteem, and other personality characteristics (Hendrick and Hendrick, 1992: 33; Caspi and Herbener, 1990: 258). Thus, it seems that in many ways "birds of a feather flock together."

There is, however, a second aphorism that has also come down through the centuries: "opposites attract." This concept is essential to Robert Winch's argument that love, and therefore mate selection, is attributable to need complementarity. The reader will recall that Winch's definition of love included attraction to another who shows promise of meeting one's psychological needs. He explicates this idea throughout his book *Mate-Selection*, detailing at length that the way needs are gratified is by finding a partner whose personality characteristics are the opposite of, but complementary to, one's own (Winch, 1958). If one is basically a submissive person, he or she will seek as a partner someone who will dominate them. If one is a "nurturant" person (need to have things done for them), the partner they choose will be a succorant, or receptive, person (that is, someone who is gratified by doing things for others). Winch's intensive study of 25 married student couples at Northwestern University revealed the presence of these and other complementary need patterns, which Winch assumed to have been a key factor in their selection of each other as partners. What is attractive about this theory is its fascinating simplicity and its intuitive reasonableness. The problem it presents is the inconclusive nature of the evidence. Winch and his students are among the few who have been able to compile any evidence that complementary psychological undercurrents are operative in the mate selection process. On the other hand, research by Murstein and others discloses a random relation between complementarity and mate selection (Murstein 1961: 194–197). That is, for every couple characterized by a particular form of complementarity, another couple can be found whose members share the same general personality traits. In a study of 47 married and 50 engaged couples, Udry noted a tendency to project one's own traits onto the partner. Furthermore, he found no evidence of general complementarity in mate selection, though some asymmetrical specific complementarity was discovered (Udry, 1963: 281–289). Winch's traits are too broad, Udry feels, to be useful as predictors of mate choice.

As is usually the case when an argument is based on polar types, such as personality similarity or complementarity, the truth is never that simple. Murstein, for example, notes that those cases where complementarity is operative are those in which

> one or both of the partners are strongly insufficient in some area, and an attempt is made to find a partner whose personality makeup is as different as possible from the unacceptable or unfulfilled aspects of oneself (Murstein, 1967: 304).

Augustus Napier, though reporting the similarities listed earlier, finds that couples are characterized by a complex mix of similarity and complementarity. As he puts it: "You are like me, you remind me of myself, but you are also strange and different" (Napier, 1971: 393).

Winch, it should be noted, never said that complementarity is the only factor governing mate selection in the United States. He does feel, and Kerckhoff and Davis agree, that it operates to weed out bad bets after homogamic considerations have already greatly limited the field of eligibles. He has even suggested that perhaps complementarity should be supplemented by the concept of role compatibility, to which we shall turn below (Winch, 1967: 756–762).

While complementarity is an intriguing idea, the data are both old and nondefinitive. So we will leave it out of Figure 10.1; perhaps it is time for someone to turn their attention to this personality issue again.

✓ *ROLE COMPATIBILITY*   The third part of Murstein's "stimulus-value-role" theory of mate selection is what he calls "role compatibility" (Murstein, 1967: 125–127, 186–199). This concerns the playing of various roles in ways that are satisfying to one's partner. These roles might include interaction with a relative, eating a meal, going to church, changing a tire, watching a movie, or engaging in sexuality; but there are numerous situations, including cohabitation, in which members of a couple may have the opportunity to observe each other. If the couple members like each other's role behavior, this reaction can be a major impetus toward seriousness and pairing.

Chapter 12 will discuss the possibility of role conflicts in marriage, but it is instructive at this point to note that one study of attraction indicates that males are more attracted to women who manifest the sex-stereotypic female traits, while women students are more attracted to androgynous, or nonstereotypic, males (Kulik and Harackiewics, 1979: 443–452). This may mean that it is difficult at present for males and females to be equally satisfied with the role behaviors of their partners. And, as we said in discussing McDaniel in Chapter 9, how much males have changed toward acceptance of female assertiveness since 1980 remains to be discovered.

The discussion of deeper attraction has been subdivided into four sets of factors: communication and self-disclosure, value consensus, similarity or complementarity, and role compatibility. It should be apparent that all of these — and homogamy as well — are actually a matter of self-disclosure, and part of a single process. In fact, we might over-generalize a bit by concluding that favorable response to self-disclosure results in deeper attraction, while unfavorable response to self-disclosure results in relationship termination. There is another factor that can result in relationship termination, which will be discussed briefly at this point.

Alternative Attraction

Relationships do not necessarily occur one at a time. An individual may be interested in more than one person simultaneously. At any time from early attraction into marriage or pairing an alternative attraction may develop, one that may become stronger than the original relationship. In such a case, the termination of the original relationship is likely. The alternative, we should note, is not always another human being. It could be going to school, taking a new job, or even the single lifestyle itself. In any case, a relationship is constantly weighed against alternatives: sometimes it survives, and sometimes it does not.

Barriers to Breakup

At this point we move beyond the immediate attractions of the relationships itself to another level.

> *Instead of falling prey to an alternative attraction, a given relationship may be moved toward marriage by the conscious or unconscious feeling that this person is "right for me." This may in fact be the surface expression of the unexpressed feeling that he or she is "the best I can get," after a more or less lengthy period of comparing alternatives. There are several possible reasons why one might conclude that a partner is "right for me." If relative physical unattractiveness is coupled with a mutual acceptance and attraction between two people, they may feel that the "bargain" is good for both (Adams, 1979: 265).*

Lillian Troll, Sheila Miller, and Robert Atchley state the same idea thus: "Since in our society marriage is the product of personal choice, and since presumably those who decide to marry feel that the person they choose is the *best match they can get*, marriage must logically begin at the point of maximal fit" (Troll et al., 1979: 56). (Italics added). Another barrier to breakup occurs when the relationship begins to take on a life of its own. This has been described various ways by different authors. Murstein speaks of the "conveyor belt" influences that make compatibility a less salient consideration once the courtship progresses to the point where the network of friends and relations begins to regard the man and woman as a couple (Murstein, 1974: 231–234). Lewis calls the last stage of his mate selection process "dyad crystallization," but more directly applicable at this point are Charles Bolton's idea of "pair commitment" and the Levinger, Senn, and Jorgensen notion of pair "communality" (Lewis, 1973: Bolton, 1961: 234–240). Bolton describes this as a relation-centered basis for continuation, while Levinger, Senn, and Jorgensen speak of the buildup of a joint enterprise (Levinger et al., 1970). In other words, the relationship itself, at some point, becomes more than the sum total of the categories, personalities, and values of the two people who constitute the couple. The two begin to work actively for the relationship's perpetuation, and, according to Bolton, a series of "escalators" move the relationship on toward marriage. These include finding a part of one's identity in being "Tom's girl" or "Jane's guy" and formal engagement—a very late and obvious escalator toward marriage. The fact that the relationship begins to have a life of its own is noted by Mark Krain, who reports that, in the later stages of dating, closeness to other friends lessens, and those friends see the two individuals as a couple (Krain, 1977: 121).

Not only is there a positive interest in perpetuation, but Ivan Nye has pointed out that the obverse side of the coin is the cost of breaking a long-term relationship. Such a breakup necessitates contending with the expectations of significant others, having to create alternative relationships, and especially, if one partner continues to want the relationship, hurting, embarrassing, and disappointing the other (Adams, 1979: 263).

When these barriers to breakup occur, they can be considered the final phase of the pairing process, the next step being marriage itself. In Figure 10.1 the process is presented in diagrammatic form.

FIGURE 10.1   THE MATE SELECTION PROCESS IN THE UNITED STATES

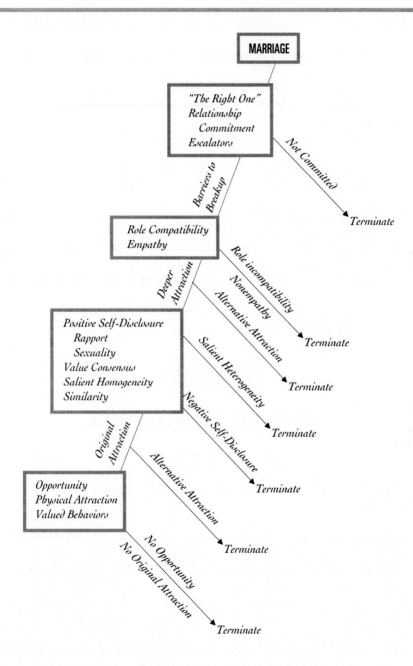

Perlman and Fehr summarize the process of relationship development from casual to close. In their list of changes, you will see several of the factors included in our discussion, especially from the "Barriers to Breakup" stage:

1. Interaction in terms of frequency, duration, and number of settings in which it occurs.
2. Individuals gain knowledge of the innermost being of their partner, the breadth and depth of knowledge expands, and partners develop personal communication codes.
3. Individuals become more skilled at mapping and anticipating their partner's views and behaviors.
4. Partners increase their investment in the relationship.
5. Interdependence and sense of "we-ness" experienced by the partners increases.
6. Partners come to feel that their separate interests are inextricably tied to the well-being and outcome of their relationship.
7. The extent of positive affect (liking or loving) and the sense of caring, commitment, and trust increase.
8. Attachment develops so partners try to restore proximity if they are separated.
9. Partners see the relationship as irreplaceable, or at least special (Perlman and Fehr, 1987: 31).

SECTION TWO

CRITIQUE AND CAUTIONARY NOTES

Though the description of the pairing process may be generally correct for many in the United States, there are bound to be variations. Farber has indicated the differing importance of the factors we have been discussing as follows: Individuals today, he says, seek personal happiness, adjustment, and freedom within the family setting. Now, Farber adds, in a society in which the trend is also toward permanent availability (so that if things don't work out the couple may split up and try again), one mate selection factor-complex stands out. Mutual enjoyment and general goal similarity take precedence in the selection process over both background homogamy and complementarity. If, he says, the most salient aspect of marriage were its permanence, we would be much more careful than we are to filter out background factors and to determine deeper psychological compatibility. Complementarity may be needed and desired under traditional conditions, or under conditions of permanent mating; however, under conditions of availability, interests and congeniality of goals appear to override both complementarity and categorical distinctions in the U.S. selection process. Permanent availability, therefore, implies that the basic interests of people may change, as may their goals, in the course of their lifetimes;

since these interests and goals were the prime bases for the marriage, it may be voided by such changes. Farber feels that what may happen is that a marriage already consummated on the basis of interests and certain shared goals may be severely tested if social categories and needs are found to be incompatible. Feature 10.3 notes the extreme version of permanent availability: planning premaritally for an eventual divorce.

Here, then, is one attempt to compare the importance of the pairing factors. The author cannot, however, accept Farber's interpretation in its entirety. For one thing, while the movement toward universal and permanent availability is apparent, it does not seem to have progressed quite as far as Farber assumes it has. Within the racial categories, the three general religious divisions, and the major social classes, homogamy is still the rule.

Other cautions about the model (Figure 10.1) are necessary. First, Rodney Cate and James Koval have questioned the sequential models of mate selection: Murstein's, Lewis's, Kerckhoff and Davis's, and presumably ours. They claim that intimacy (self-disclosure) need not be present any time in a relationship, and that external forces (escalators?) often move a couple to marriage (Cate and Koval, 1983: 507–514). Thus, rather than relationships passing through all the stages outlined, it is possible that some only go certain distances before culminating in marriage. However, despite Cate and Koval's critique of processual models, they and others such as Surra and Murstein continue to work with the factors in pairing.

Feature 10.3 **LOVE AND PRE-NUPTIAL PACTS**

NEW YORK (AP) — Hearts and flowers may be the traditional way of professing love on Valentine's Day, but for about 200 people who attended a seminar on love, marriage and money Saturday, the main concern was hearts and dollars.

The participants, 70 percent of them couples married or planning to marry, listened attentively as a six-member panel of divorce lawyers, career consultants and corporate managers told them how to mix love and money.

Among the panel members was Marvin Mitchelson, noted "palimony" divorce lawyer. He told the group he considered pre-nuptial contracts "very unromantic" but said it's "safer" to have such written agreements in view of the rising divorce rates.

New York City divorce attorney Bernard Clair urged the group to discuss the possibility of a marital breakup at the beginning of relationships instead of waiting to the end.

"A writing (agreement) need not detract from your love," Clair said. "In the 1980s, it may be the best way to express it."

Wisconsin State Journal, Sunday, February 15, 1981, p. 1.

As noted earlier, age may either speed up or slow down the process described in Figure 10.1. If one is marrying either to escape singlehood or to escape one's parents, or if one is past the typical marriage age, the feelings that a particular partner is "the best I can get" may be heightened relative to other factors in the mate selection process. You simply may not feel that you can afford to be all that concerned about value consensus, empathy, or role compatibility.

We must note Bernard's distinction between *parallel* and *interactional* marriages (Bernard, 1964). In a parallel marriage the wife goes her way and has her friends, and the husband has his. They are not, very simply, each other's best friend. An interactional marriage is one in which the couple members are each other's best friend and closest companion. Kerckhoff relates these marriage types to mate selection as follows:

> *Value consensus, personality fit, and so on may well be important in mate selection where the expected marital pattern is interaction. But there is no reason to believe that these factors should affect the choice of a spouse in the same way when the expected marital pattern is parallel (Kerckhoff, 1974).*

We might, therefore, suggest that while our pairing process is meant to be applicable to U.S. society, it is quite possible that the disclosure-value-role variables that are so central to the foregoing discussion are more characteristic of the middle classes than of the working classes, and especially of the lower classes. In other words, according to the above cautions, the model presented in Figure 10.1 should hold best for modern, industrial middle-class individuals in their early twenties and should be less accurate in certain particulars for any deviation from these categories.

Finally, we have used the words "pairing," "choosing a partner," and "mate selection" almost interchangeably in the foregoing discussion. The reason for talking mostly of "pairing" or "partners" is that we recognize some do not marry, either because they cohabit or because they choose a partner of their own gender. The fact is much of what we have said holds for these other two as well as many friendships. Blumstein and Schwartz studied homosexual as well as marital pairings. Women's homosociality has strong roots in the 19th century (Smith-Rosenberg, 1975; D'Emilio and Freedman, 1988: 120f), and the process of "merger" between lesbians includes a sense of shared identity, very much like that described in the last part of the previous section (Baber and Allen, 1992: 45f). Differences between friendship, non-marital cohabiting, homosexuality and marital choice include the fact that the first does not include sexuality, the second is not legalized, and the third is still often secret or private. But any of the last three may include preparation for parenting, though only the last is directly related. Our point is simply that the pairing process is not distinctively different according to either the type of pair or its legal status.

Let us now attempt to place the pairing process in the United States on the family formation continuum proposed in Chapter 5 (see Figure 10.2). As always, the interpretation is tentative and subject to the reader's reinterpretation and relocation.

FIGURE 10.2   MATE SELECTION OR FAMILY FORMATION IN THE CONTEMPORARY
UNITED STATES IN RELATION TO THE FAMILY FORMATION CONTINUUM

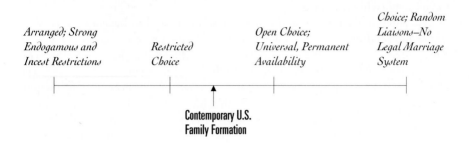

One aspect of mate selection on which the evidence is clear is the continuing, though lessening, tendency for marriage to occur between persons of a generally similar social background. Prime among homogamous considerations is race; a discussion of black-white intermarriage closes this chapter.

SECTION THREE

RACIAL HOMOGAMY: A CASE IN NONUNIVERSAL AVAILABILITY

For most white persons in the United States, the field of eligibles simply does not include members of the black race; also, the field of eligibles for most black persons does not include whites. While the issue of racial homogamy includes Orientals and others, the following discussion concentrates on the norms, laws, and motives (and their respective behavioral manifestations) governing intermarriage between whites and blacks in the United States.

Norms Governing Black-White Intermarriage

The question of norms, or expectations, regarding marriage by race has focused historically in the antiamalgamation doctrine, which says that the various races were meant to be separate. How far back does this idea go, legally and otherwise? "In Massachusetts, where slaves were few and some blacks were already free, whites were forbidden in 1705 either to marry blacks or to have intercourse with them. In 1786 whites were also forbidden to marry Indians. Both laws were repealed in 1843 (Quale, 1988: 287). However, such laws were still in force in many parts of the United States as late as 1967. For many years whites in the United States argued more strongly and publicly against black-white intermarriage than did blacks. They based their objections on notions of the inherent inferiority of black people, frequently bolstered by religious pronouncements concerning the curse of Canaan (translated by some ministers as a curse on black people). The lower one's social position, the greater one's *expressed* opposition to intermarriage was likely to be. Educated whites also demonstrated substantial prejudice, but were better able to hide it. In some cases, because these whites felt less threatened by intermarriage, they were able to talk a more liberal line.

As noted in Chapter 6, in the last generation there has been a necessary increase in racial pride among blacks. Bell et al., for example report the way in which Afrocentric cultural consciousness has reduced the likelihood of interracial heterosexual relations (Bell et al., 1990: 162–189). This emphasis on racial identity and heritage among blacks has resulted in there being conspicuous pressures toward homogamy, among both whites and blacks, as well as opposing pressures toward intermarriage from liberal elements of the population trying to manifest their lack of concern for the racial barrier. Which pressures are greater?

Changes in U.S. antimiscegenation laws, that is, laws forbidding interracial mating, were dramatic in the 1960s. As late as 1960, 29 states, mostly Southern and Western, still had such laws, and in 1966 there were 17 such states. In 1967, antimiscegenation laws were declared unconstitutional by the Supreme Court. Has this decision had any direct effect upon intermarriage rates? The answer seems to be: probably not in and of itself, nor will it have any effect as long as the norms against intermarriage remain strong.

Black-White Intermarriage: How Many and Who?

In the 1960s an attorney claimed there were one million racially intermarried persons in the U.S., of whom 810,000 were either passing or didn't even know they were of different races. The concept of not knowing suggests that the person or his or her mate may have an unknown black ancestor, and this, in turn, is based on the indefensible and outdated idea of black or white "blood." Thus, it is only appropriate to discuss rates of intermarriage in terms of overt numbers, not to be concerned with "passing" as whites or "not knowing."

Historically, the rate of intermarriage was extremely low in the Southern United States, and a little higher in Northern cities like Boston and New York. In Boston, for example, the period of maximum racial intermarriage appears to have been 1850–1900. From the 1900–1904 period to the 1914–18 period, racial intermarriage declined from 14 to 5 per 100 marriages involving blacks (Heer, 1966: 267). From 1916 through 1937, black-white marriages in New York State, exclusive of New York City varied from 1.7 to 4.8 percent of all marriages involving blacks. The equivalent for whites would, of course, be even lower. Between the two World Wars the rate of intermarriage in Boston averaged 3.9 per 100 black marriages and 0.12 per 100 white marriages, with a slight, but perceptible, decline over that period (Cavan, 1969: 204–205).

Thus we have good historical figures on which to base a comparison with the present time. David Heer reports a 26 percent increase in the number of black-white marriages during the 1960s, with the 66 percent rise in the North and West offsetting a 35 percent decline in the South (Heer, 1974: 246–258). Monahan finds an even greater percentage increase between 1963 and 1970 than does Heer. Of all marriages in the United States, Monahan finds three-fourths of one percent racially mixed, primarily because the vast majority are white-white marriages. In the 35 states for which Monahan found adequate data, the percent of all black marriages that were racially mixed was 1.4 from 1963 to 1966, and 2.6 from 1967 to 1970 (Monahan, 1976: 225). These figures represent more than an 80 percent rise since the Supreme Court ruling. Yet "percentage rise" can be quite misleading. After all, for blacks 97 percent of all marriages were racially homogamous in 1970, and for whites it was still 99 percent. Even with a similar percentage jump since 1970, the current rates of intermarriage are no more than 4 percent for whites and 6–7 percent for blacks.

The second aspect of black-white intermarriage does not concern how many but *who*. Who are the intermarriers? Before the Supreme Court decision about four out of every five intermarriages involved a black male and a white female, and during the 1960s Heer found a 62 percent increase in such inter-marriages, as compared to a 9 percent decline in those involving a white hus-band and a black wife. Monahan found only two states, Louisiana and Alabama, in which more intermarriages involved a black female and a white male than a black male and a white female (Heer, 1974: 258; Monahan, 1976: 225). Re-cently, Tucker and Mitchell-Kernan found the same thing in Los Angeles. That is, more interracial pairs were black male/white female than vice versa, with the rate of intermarriage in Los Angeles being about twice the national average (Tucker and Mitchell-Kernan, 1990: 209–218). It used to be, says Monahan, that black male-white female marriage usually involved a female from a low sta-tus background marrying a high status male, and this was explained as an ex-change: racial status for economic status. Tucker and Mitchell-Kernan add very up-to-date information on the characteristics of black intermarriers by gender. Black women who intermarry are: (1) younger, (2) more educated, (3) more likely to have been previously married, and (4) more likely to differ signifi-cantly in age from their spouse than are black women who don't intermarry. On the other hand, intermarrying black males are: (1) more likely to be employed, (2) higher in income, (3) older, and (4) older at the time of their first marriage (Tucker and Mitchell-Kernan; 1990). It is interesting that the information on the males still fits Monahan's generalization about black male intermarriers being higher in status, though his comparison was between the two couple members rather than between intermarriers and non-intermarriers.

While the black male/white female pair is still more prevalent than its op-posite, Staples notes that the ratio is no longer even close to 4/1. And, he argues (as did Monahan earlier), that it takes more than status to explain these changes. We will turn to motives and explanation in the next section.

Do black-white marriages have as many "strikes against them" as their crit-ics would like us to believe? Heer finds a high rate of attrition for racial inter-marriages, but a substantial difference based on which spouse is of which race. "Of marriages involving a white husband and a black wife contracted in the ten years prior to the 1960 Census, only 47 percent were still in existence in 1970 and of those involving a black husband and a white wife only 63 percent (Heer, 1976: 258). Thus, the white male-black female marriage is not only less frequent, it is less likely to last when it does occur. Both, however, are probably even today more likely to divorce than racially homogamous marriages. It is also possible to infer, however, that with all the social pressures against interracial couples their rate of divorce is actually surprisingly low.

Motives for Racial Intermarriage in the United States

What are the motives behind racial intermarriage in the United States, when the norms of both races are so strongly against it? Though seeking motives can sometimes be a fruitless exercise in intuition, several ideas are worth discussing. Staples, for example, explains why there has been an increase in black female/ white male marriage:

> *Many black women are gravitating toward white men because of the shortage of black men and disenchantment with those they do have access to. In a similar vein, some white men are dissatisfied with white women and their increasing vociferous demands for sex-role parity (Staples, 1988: 316).*

Other more general motives for racial intermarriage have been suggested. One is *repudiation*. Cavan sums up this viewpoint well when she asserts that an interracial marriage "indicates either that the person has not been thoroughly integrated into his social group or has withdrawn from it for some reason. His needs are not met there; he seeks elsewhere for contacts, friendship, and marriage" (Cavan, 1969: 206). The individual may feel like a misfit, may have been rejected, and is manifesting a mutual rejection by overstepping the bounds of one of his or her group's strongest norms.

A second motive, akin to and perhaps a part of the first, is *identity* reinforcement. Earlier in the chapter we noted how individuals may establish their identities through their choice of mates. If a part of an individual's identity is a liberal life approach and a concern for dealing with people on a personal rather than a categorical basis, he or she may seek to demonstrate this identity by means of an interracial marriage. It would seem to me nevertheless, that this motive would in all likelihood be coupled with one of the others, rather than be the sole factor in an interracial marriage.

Psychoanalytically oriented writers have suggested *Oedipal fear* as a third motive for racial intermarriage. Racial intermarriage, or marriage across any major social barrier, is a result, they say, of the person's strong attraction to the opposite sex parent; heterogamy, or intermarriage, reinforces the incest taboo, subtly convincing them that they are not in reality trying to marry their own parent. This idea is as difficult to test as it is intriguing.

The fourth motive for racial intermarriage, alluded to earlier in the chapter, is that racial categories are simply *not salient*, or don't matter, to the individual (Musgrove, 1966: 67–68). It seems doubtful, however, that *nonsalience* is currently the basis for many black-white intermarriages in the United States, since race is made salient by societal structures and attitudes in so many ways that it can only rarely be dismissed as inconsequential. A decrease in salience, however, would be a significant move toward universal availability in this area of mate selection. Whether or not a liberalization of attitudes will have this effect in the near future is conjectural, though it is possible that the small increase in racial intermarriage rates since 1960 is accounted for by such so-called non-salient unions. Yet a lot of societal restructuring appears to be necessary before racial intermarriage would become prevalent and before such marriages can be a matter of nonsalience instead of a reaction to something in the individual's life history. At present, the pressures toward racial homogamy—especially in the black community—still seem to greatly outweigh any opposing pressure toward nonsalience and universal availability.

Marital Adjustments

CHAPTER 11 *In the early years of marriage, the habit patterns of a couple are brought together and many problems in early adjustment are faced. These include future orientation, differential growth, in-law relations, and the arrival of a child. In a patriarchal society, women have to make more adjustments than men, and U.S. society still has patriarchal characteristics. Two areas of marital adjustment — finances and sex — are assumed by most observers to hold a uniquely important place in U.S. marriage. We explore the reasons for this assumption and various aspects of these adjustments. A discussion of two other major marital adjustments, those involving power and the division of labor — or deciding and doing — brings the chapter to a close.*

Much of what was said on pairing in Chapters 9 and 10 is applicable to different kinds of pairs: homosexual, cohabiting, and those heading for a legalized marriage. The same is true to a degree of the next three chapters. However, the important distinction has to do with the legalization that defines marriage. Therefore, we will focus on marriage, and will save much of the material on homosexual relationships for later discussion.

SECTION ONE

EARLY MARITAL ADJUSTMENTS

A woman and man have gone out, perhaps have lived together, have narrowed the field of potential mates through various conscious and unconscious means, and have ceremonialized their relationship in marriage. For the majority, Feature 11.1 reminds us, the wedding night is not what it once was.

Feature 11.1 WEDDING NIGHTS CHANGE

Is the thrill gone?

It's a ticklish question: What did you do on your wedding night?

"What's left to do?" laughs a recent bride. . . .

It's the 90s, folks. Brides and grooms seem to do it all before they tie the knot. . . .

So what do they typically do?

"Typically they strip off their clothes, brush their teeth, dive into bed and cuddle and hug. They are relieved of the old-fashioned performance anxieties that used to afflict the wedding night, . . . (Barbara Tober) says.

Laura, 26, and Chris, 27, didn't exactly feel that way. . . .

They came up with a plan.

"We stopped all physical contact a month before the wedding," Laura says.

"We didn't go near each other. Then I moved back to my parents house a week before, so he could come over and court me."

"After the wedding reception at her parents' home, "we took a limo to the hotel, drank champagne, exchanged presents . . . and had an old-fashioned consummation of our vows."

The plan worked, Laura says. "We'd built up so much anticipation that the night turned out very passionate. . . ."

"Wedding Nights Change," Bettijane Levine, *Los Angeles Times*, reprinted in *The Capital Times*, Friday, January 22, 1993.

In view of the separate habits and cultures couple members bring into marriage, they must begin to adjust to the fact that they are now a legal dyad—a marriage—and experimentation leading to the meshing of habit patterns becomes predominant. At first, of course, the euphoria or psychological honeymoon may help the couple rise above tensions and disagreements. However, say Goldscheider and Waite, the "emotional peaks of the honeymoon period need to be routinized and integrated into their ongoing lives. This process takes time and energy and often quite considerable interpersonal skills" (1991: 85). David Reiss writes about the ways in which couples construct their own "reality," including habits or routines. The couple act and make decisions, which helps to produce daily routines and guidelines for subsequent actions and patterns (D. Reiss, 1981: 248).

Not all marital patterns are successful; conflict also emerges. It may appear due to a basic, but heretofore undiscovered, value disagreement—perhaps over politics, or over leisure pursuits, or over the activities that should characterize the wife and woman or the husband and man. Often times, however, the conflict revolves around some seemingly inconsequential aspect of the everyday behavior brought by a couple member into the marriage. It might be a disagreement over the preparation of foods or the time for meals; it might involve bedtime routine or even something as simple as brushing teeth. Or it could involve any of the time, space, and energy concerns mentioned by Kantor and Lehr in Chapter 5. Whatever their bases, such conflicts as occur may produce a blockage of communication or, if accommodations and adjustments are made, may produce a new form of solidarity. Strictly speaking then, cohabitation or not, every new marriage is incompletely defined, just as every new status in life involves undefined elements. Cohabitation may help to define and clarify certain aspects of early marital adjustment, but it cannot resolve all the issues that will arise. During the early months, as routines develop, the marriage itself becomes a problem, or a mutual meeting of internal situations and a joint facing of the external world, or some combination of problem and solution.

The abruptness of the transition to marriage may vary according to experience during dating, with or without cohabitation. It may also vary, according to Ankarloo, by socioeconomic status. Historically, Ankarloo notes, the transition "seemed much more casual in lower strata, partly because independence before marriage was fairly common, but also because of a higher incidence of post marital coresidence with parents" (Ankarloo, 1978: 131). In the 15 years since Ankarloo wrote, the average age at marriage has risen by several years for middle class individuals, meaning that they are more independent at marriage than they were in 1978. Thus, while marriage is definable as an abrupt transition, it can be made less so by various forms of preparation or presocialization.

Early adjustments vary according to the kind of marriage the couple will establish. In Chapter 10 we distinguished the "interactional" from the "parallel" marriage, with the former demanding a greater amount of adjusting. Cancian distinguishes three marriage styles, and the adjustments demanded by each. *Traditional marriage*, based on patriarchy and greater embeddedness of women in the home, requires a certain kind of early adjustment, especially for females.

The *contemporary* pattern, based on independence and limited commitment, often creates a conflict between self-fulfillment and marital bonding. The third, that Cancian says is often ignored, is a *combination* of commitment and support-iveness with self-fulfillment (Cancian, 1987: 8). This may be ignored simply be-cause the balance between habit meshing and independence is so difficult to accomplish. So let us examine some of the adjustments required during the early years of marriage.

Kin and In-laws

Two people headed toward marriage usually spend at least some time with both families and perhaps with other kin as well. Acquaintanceship, however, does not resolve the problems of postmarital adjustment that must be made to kin. A young married person may be emotionally or economically dependent upon parents even after marriage, regardless of residential distance. A certain amount of emotional dependence on parents has been acceptable for a wife after mar-riage, but if a young husband manifests such dependence, it can cause marital problems. Residential location and frequency of contact with parents must be resolved, and the young couple members must reconcile the demands of their two families and kin *networks* for involvement. In an unpublished study of kin-ship in Greensboro, North Carolina, it was apparent that there was an optimal distance to live away from in-laws in order to minimize marital disagreements about interaction with them: about 200 miles. At that distance, you can spend the weekend with them if you wish or avoid it if you wish. In other words, that distance seems to give maximal "fit" between desires and contact. Of course, the extreme case of kin adjustment problems following marriage is when the family was opposed to the marriage and continues to be antagonistic afterward. Kin adjustments are obviously one important aspect of early marital adjustment, and will be discussed further in Chapter 14.

Differential Growth

Since couple members begin marriage with the feeling that the person they chose is very likely the best they can get, marriage must logically begin at the point of maximal fit. "This means," say Troll, Miller, and Atchley, "that any change in either partner is likely to decrease the amount of fit—unless they are lucky enough to change in such ways as to maintain or increase their congru-ence" (Troll et al., 1979: 56). Personalities do not, of course, cease developing and changing when marriage occurs. If two people's dominant tendencies are similar, they may become more alike; if different, they may become more diver-gent. Differential growth, however, is a special and all-too-frequent version of postmarital change. It is best illustrated in this society by the young wife who works while her husband finishes school or graduate studies. All the time she is working, perhaps with one or two children in the home, he is broadening both his knowledge and his horizons as he studies, goes to conferences, and meets oth-ers who are preparing to be professionals. When he takes an occupational posi-tion he discovers that, compared to his female coworkers or graduate students, his wife is intellectually and experientially underdeveloped. The only sensible thing to do, he feels, is to get a new wife, one with whom he can communicate. And his ex-wife finds herself left with the children, as "provincial" as ever, trying to figure out what happened to her husband and to the marriage for which she had worked so hard and sacrificed so much. While this is only one among several possible scenarios for differential growth and early marital breakup, it occurs with sufficient frequency in our patriarchal society to be of concern. Though there are good reasons for marrying at different ages, the issue of differential growth is an argument in favor of later marriage. Ross and Sawhill write:

> *Those who marry young . . . may reduce the time spent searching for appropriate (like-minded) mates, and may also marry at a time when their values and expectations are still undergoing rapid change, thus increasing the risk that these values will later diverge (Ross and Sawhill, 1975: 40).*

Two high school students, in other words, are more likely to experience differential growth than two college students, who are more likely to experience it than two graduate students, who are more likely to experience it than two people "out on the job."

The First Child

Over a generation ago LeMaster wrote about "Parenthood as Crisis" (LeMaster, 1957: 352–355). What he meant was that the upheaval in the lives of couple members when the first child arrives is sufficient to be considered a crisis. A great debate ensued over the term "crisis," but whether the term "adjustment" is more appropriate than "crisis," the fact remains that the coming of the first child is a dramatic event in the life of a couple. Of course, a baby may come to an unmarried woman or to a couple not yet married. However, in this discussion we will focus on the predominant experience of first birth within marriage.

The pregnancy period may give a couple time to discuss parental roles and to plan for the readjustment of household routines, employment, and leisure (Steffensmeier, 1982: 319–344). Deutsch et al. point out the ways in which mothers-to-be seek information during pregnancy (1988: 420–431). And Lamaze and other preparations have involved the father-to-be in the actual birth process to a much greater extent than a generation ago. But the couple can never completely prepare for the transition to parenthood.

The first and most consistent finding is that there is a reversion to more traditional gender roles, no matter how equalitarian a couple's ideology or whether they are pursuing dual careers (McGoldrick, 1989: 212; Charles and Kerr, 1988: 39). An important element in this "reversion" is that "women's involvement in paid work decreased markedly, while their husbands' work involvement tended to remain the same or increase" (Cowan et al., 1991: 85). Waite et al. go into some detail on this issue:

> *The majority of women have jobs prior to pregnancy; most leave these jobs as the pregnancy progresses, so that only one woman in five remains employed in the month that*

the child is born. Some women return to work, but by two years after the birth employ-
ment rates reach only 60 percent of their previous levels. In the absence of parenthood,
the proportion employed would have steadily increased, so that the real employment
deficit due to parenthood exceeds that implied by a comparison of employment before
and after the birth (Waite et al., 1985: 263).

Waite and Desai, examining the National Longitudinal Survey of Youth, report
somewhat different findings: 43 percent of new mothers had returned to work
within three months, and 69 percent within 12 months. Mothers return sooner
if they are in occupations that employ many mothers with small children, while
pregnant women leave later and return earlier if they find their work rewarding
(Desai and Waite, 1991: 551–566).

The other side of the role issue concerns house and child care. Even if there
has been a relatively equal division of such tasks prior to the birth, they immediately become primarily the mother's domain. At this point, says McGoldrick,
"very few couples share household and childcare responsibilities equally"
(1989: 212; also Ruble et al., 1988: 78–87).

So how do these changes affect the couple's adjustment? It seems that a
short (1–2 month) honeymoon period may occur right after the baby's birth,
but this soon gives way to negative effects on the couple members (Miller and
Sillie, 1980: 459–465; Belsky et al., 1983: 79). However, Cowan et al. report that
the decline in satisfaction differs both by gender and by time period:

Women's decline in satisfaction . . . was greater than men's. . . . The negative impact
of these changes was delayed for men; mother's greatest decline in marital satisfaction
occurred from pregnancy to 6 months after birth, whereas fathers reported an even
larger drop between 6 and 18 months postpartum (Cowan et al., 1991: 85).

One key area of adjustment is time: the baby is ignorant of social or clock
time, the result being that the mother may simultaneously be bored and feel that
she lacks time for sleep, leisure, sex—even bathroom time (LaRossa, 1983: 79).
Though the father may increase his time with the baby between the third and
ninth month, the strain on the wife-mother is greater, involving more housework and a feeling of the time constraints noted above. In fact, according to
some writers, becoming a mother requires an even greater role transition—
from wife to wife-mother—than that required from single to married.

Husbands report a change in their wives' sexual responsiveness, so that
this is the key area in which both husbands and wives feel a negative impact of
parenthood (Harriman, 1983: 393). Financial security and psychological pre-
paredness for parenthood aid the father in his adjustment to the pregnancy and
birth of the child (May, 1982: 353–361). The fathers of newborn infants spend
time "socially" with the baby, holding it and playing with it, but are less likely
than mothers to care for the baby's physical needs. In addition, fathers of newborn infants have difficulty with the fact that their wives have less time for
them. This puts the mother in a "double bind." She has to spend more time caring for the baby than her husband does, but he is upset because she is spending
so much time with the baby.

Besides gender and time, other qualifications must be made on the relation between parenthood and marital adjustment. For middle-class women, neither the husband's contribution to childcare nor the ease or difficulty of the infant seemed to affect her self-evaluation the first year after birth. For working-class women, both mattered (Reilly et al., 1987: 295–308). The authors feel that middle-class women simply take longer to fashion their version of the mother role. Working-class women are more likely to question the necessity of moving into the traditional wife-mother role.

The issue of the difficulty or ease of the baby deserves further comment. A crying baby has a negative effect on both parents' self-perceptions, but is reported by fathers as more stressful (Reilly et al., 1987: 304–5; Wilkie and Ames, 1986: 545–550). And to this we might add the finding by Belsky et al. that "what transpires between father and child appears to be more systematically related to the marital relationship than what goes on between mother and child" (Belsky et al., 1991: 495).

Another point concerns the relation of parenthood to marital stability. Waite et al. estimate "that by the time the first child reaches his" or her "second birthday more than 20 percent of the parents would have been divorced or separated if the child had not been born, compared to actual disruption rates of 5–8 percent" (Waite et al., 1985: 850). How long does this "protective" function last? Cowan et al. state that "having a young child functions as a protective factor in preserving the marriage during the early years of childrearing," followed by deterioration in both quantity of time and quality of couple relationship (Cowan et al., 1991: 104). This, however, leaves open the question of deterioration without a child. A study by McHale and Huston compares couples who became parents during the first year of marriage with those who remained childless the first year. They conclude that "many of the changes attributed to parenthood also occur among nonparents" (McHale and Huston, 1985: 409).

One study has connected kin and kin-in-law adjustments with parenthood by looking at the effect of parenthood on mother-daughter and on in-law relations. Lucy Fischer finds that the birth of a child decreases conflict with one's own mother and increases it with one's mother-in-law. The mother-daughter bond is reaffirmed in the birth of a new generation, while contact with the mother-in-law is also increased, but not in an acceptable way. Though both grandmothers give parenting advice, this is perceived as intrusion on the part of the mother-in-law, while it is often solicited from the mother (Fischer, 1983: 187–192).

So what conclusions can we draw from the large numbers of 1980s studies of the transition to parenthood? First, centrifugal and patriarchal forces seem to move couples toward the "husband-breadwinner/wife-homemaker" roles, further embedding the mother in the family. Second, the baby seems to help hold the couple together while also negatively affecting the couple's relationship. Third, factors affecting couple adjustment are social class, the ease or difficulty of the baby, and length of time since the birth. Many new parents, of course, adjust while avoiding the major pitfalls described above. But simply adding a third—helpless—person to the household is sufficient to require a major adjustment on the part of the parents.

Other adjustments are required early in marriage: changing jobs, residential moves, future orientation, and planning. The four most important additional adjustments, however, involve finances, sexuality, decision-making or power, and household labor. These issues will occupy most of the rest of this chapter, but here we will return to the subjects of cohabitation and marital adjustment. Cohabitation has a positive effect on marital adjustment primarily in two areas: sexual adjustment and the meshing of habit patterns. For the other adjustments—kinship, differential growth, the coming of a child—cohabitation is no more beneficial than going out and having serious conversations. Many of the adjustments of early marriage can be discussed and contemplated ahead of time but can only be worked through as they occur. And, as Morton Perlmutter has said, if the cohabitating couple are not seriously working through role adjustments, but are only "playing house," cohabitation is likely to have little, if any, positive effect on early marital adjustment.

Gradual and abrupt transitions continue throughout marriage; they are not resolved at the outset "once and for all." Individuals change jobs and then retire, children leave home, couple members become less physically attractive. Thus, the close of Chapter 13 will deal with the issues of marital satisfaction and happiness as they change over the life cycle of the family.

SECTION TWO

FINANCIAL ADJUSTMENTS IN MARRIAGE

Rainwater once commented concerning the black lower-class family that the "precipitating causes of marital disruption seem to fall mainly into economic or sexual categories" (Rainwater, 1976: 192). A recent study noted that the most consistent predictor of marital quality for blacks is perceived economic adequacy (Clark-Nicolas and Gray-Little, 1991: 645–655). However, one gets the impression from many popular marriage manuals that this is not peculiarly a lower-class or a black phenomenon, but that about half of all marital difficulties are traceable to financial disagreements and the rest to sexual maladjustment. According to Blood and Wolfe's generation-old study, of the eight possible areas of husband-wife disagreement—children, recreation, personality, in-laws, roles, values, sex, and money—*money* causes the greatest number of problems (Blood and Wolfe, 1960: 192).

The importance of economic hardship to marital adjustment is evident in Elder's Depression studies. Working with Jeffrey Liker, Elder finds that heavy income loss led to increased marital disputes about finances. Increasing the husband's personal instability also weakened the marital tie. However, prior experience with income loss was a coping resource for the couple, because they had dealt with the same problem previously (Liker and Elder, 1983: 343–359). Voydanoff et al. report a similar relationship between economic distress and family satisfaction (1988: 545).

Finances are, of course, crucial to the lower-class or poverty family. Hutchison, as reported in Troll, Miller, and Atchley,

> *found that being married made no difference to people whose income was below the poverty line, either in worrying, feeling lonely, or reporting unhappiness or dissatisfaction with their lives. On the other hand, if their income was just above the poverty line, married people were less likely to report these problems than people who were not currently married. Apparently, if one is below the poverty line, not even being married will help (Troll et al., 1979: 55).*

Objective economic conditions influence the husband's hostility to the family as a direct result of "the strain that spouses experienced in trying to meet their perceived needs with inadequate resources" (Conger et al., 1990: 653). In fact, says Chilman, poverty is a leading cause of marital and family instability. Lack of income is related to high unemployment, poor living conditions, and poor health. These conditions give rise to marital distrust, sex segregation, little communication, and authoritarian child-rearing, all of which tend to undermine family stability (Chilman, 1975: 57–58). As for the effect of economic stress on children, Takeuchi et al. find that children from welfare families have higher average levels of depressive symptoms and antisocial and impulsive behavior than other children (Takeuchi et al., 1991: 1031–1041). Economic hardship, however, may bring the family closer together if two conditions are present. If the economic difficulty, such as unemployment, was caused by an *external* source, such as economic depression, rather than internally (for instance, by the father's drinking), and if the family was already *very close*, the hardship may bring them even closer together. Other things being equal, however, the Elder research indicates that strain is a more likely outcome of hardship than togetherness.

Although they are by definition better off financially, higher status families are by no means immune to financial problems and disagreements. The middle-class couple, even if they have the same economic values, may be hard pressed during inflationary times to pay their debts and meet what they may consider to be "basic" expenses, such as helping their offspring get a college education. Financial adjustment, after all, involves the day-to-day explicit and implicit budgeting of family expenditures according to the couple members' expectations regarding how the family should live and what they should have.

Amount of money is not the only economic factor that affects marriage. Who earns the money helps to determine how the money is managed and how other aspects of the marriage work (Smith and Reid, 1986: 47). While more wives are employed and while they are making more money than ever before, there is still a gender gap in earnings when number of working hours and years of experience are controlled (Shelton and Firestone, 1989: 110–111). Yet any earning on the part of the wife requires an adjustment in the marriage, made more difficult if the male holds patriarchal values. Later we will discuss wives' earnings in relation to family power and other issues.

Differing orientations toward money, stereotyped by the husband who hoards and the wife who spends, may derive from the very same economic conditions, such as an economic depression. But why should financial orientations, and the disagreements that arise from divergences in outlook, be as problem-producing as Blood and Wolfe, Rainwater, and others find them to be? At least three factors make money a greater problem in U.S. society than it might otherwise be. First, money and *economic values* are at the heart of the U.S. value system. The standard of living and "things" are crucial elements in the U.S. definition of personal happiness, and personal happiness is, in turn, a focal concern of marriage. The reader may wish to argue that monetary and material values *should not* be central, but it is difficult to contend convincingly that they *are not*. Second, *deferred gratification*, or putting off immediate desires for goals perceived to be of greater value in the future, *can continue for only so long*. In the lower-class family, the personal frustrations that may result from being unable to get ahead in a society that values affluence may be vented against the marital partner. In the middle-class family, a more likely occurrence is that one spouse simply runs out of "deferments" before the other does. One begins, often gradually, to want things now, while the other is still looking to the future. And, of course, the economic system is consciously geared to the fostering of immediate "wants" in individuals and families. There are numerous other ways in which the frustration or deferment of material gratifications may result in marital difficulties. The third factor that increases the probability of conflict regarding finances in the U.S. family is that *it is extremely difficult to talk about and reconcile differences in financial attitudes prior to marriage*. During the pairing process, couples may discuss their financial orientation but, even if they do, it is difficult to foresee how they might react ten years later to the added pressure of an occupation, a home, children, inflation or recession, and perhaps aging parents. This is one of those issues in marriage that requires continuing communication on the part of the spouses if an adequate adjustment is to be maintained.

SECTION THREE

SEXUAL ADJUSTMENT IN MARRIAGE

"My cross-cultural examination of human sexuality," says Ira Reiss, "leads me to conclude that *'the most distinctive social characteristic of sexuality is the high importance in which it is held in virtually all societies'*" (Reiss, 1986: 27). D'Emilio and Freedman report three 19th century patterns of sexuality in the United States:

> *First, both women and men had become more self-conscious about sexuality as a personal choice and not simply a reproductive responsibility. . . . Second, especially within the middle class, sexual desires had become increasingly fused with a romantic quest for emotional intimacy and even spiritual union. . . . Finally, although women and men shared in both the intensification of sexuality as a form of interpersonal intimacy and the separation of sexuality from reproduction, gender made an important difference in the ways they experienced these changes. The separate spheres of the middle class, the emphasis on female purity, the double standard, and women's reproductive role all made*

the transformation of sexuality more problematic for women (D'Emilio and Freed-man, 1988: 84).

In the late 1800s, the major emphasis of enlightened women was not on separating sex from marriage, but on their having more control over marital sexuality (D'Emilio and Freedman, 1988: 154).

The recent discovery of Clelia Mosher's survey of sexuality among women born during the Victorian era is an instructive beginning point for the discussion of sexuality in marriage today. First of all, Mosher found a poor level of understanding of sexual matters on the part of these women at marriage (Mosher, 1980: xiii). Second, she reported (as Ira Reiss notes in his review) that the respondents preferred coitus 2.2 times per month, but engaged in it with their husbands five times a month. This, of course, fits the stereotype of Victorian women having intercourse out of duty to their husbands (Reiss, 1982: 252). Finally, however, Mosher found that more than 75 percent of the women had experienced orgasm, and for more than 33 percent it was a regular occurrence (Mosher, 1980: xiii). Thus, though hardly the initiator of sexual activity, the Victorian woman questioned by Mosher was reasonably likely to be gratified by sex.

According to D'Emilio and Freedman, the two biggest changes in the early 20th century regarding sexuality were "the redefinition of womanhood to include eroticism, and the decline of public reticence about sex" (1988: 233). The notion of sex as pleasure and as a consumable was beginning to catch on in the United States. Yet the biggest change regarding sexuality has to do with the term itself: *sexual adjustment.* Not too many years ago—and in many lower-class families even today—the husband sought sexual gratification, initiated sexual activity, and the wife was expected to provide it. Accompanying this asymmetry was an inhibition and feeling of sinfulness that had pervaded U.S. and British society during the nineteenth century. These historical factors, asymmetry and guilt, form the backdrop against which today's sexual adjustments in marriage must be understood.

A study by Cathy Greenblatt has added substantially to our understanding of sexuality in the early years of marriage. During the first year of marriage, the rates of intercourse ranged from one to 45 times per month, with a mean of 14. These rates declined in the second year, but were still highly correlated with the first year rate. The wide variation in rates is indicative, says Greenblatt, of the fact that there are no norms governing frequency, so that each couple must negotiate its own pattern or habit. "From then on almost everything—children, jobs, commuting, housework, financial worries—that happens to a couple conspires to reduce the degree of sexual interaction, while almost nothing leads to increasing it" (Greenblatt, 1983: 292, 294).

Another study, by Jasso, shows that sexual activity increases for women until almost age 50, while for men it decreases very slightly from age 17 on. Both of these findings fit (though not dramatically) the accepted wisdom regarding men's and women's sexual capabilities over time (Jasso, 1985: 239–240). It was, of course, the research of Masters and Johnson that demonstrated the sexual capabilities of females (1966).

What about expectations, and the relation between sexual adjustment and overall marital adjustment? In Bruce Thomason's study of young, well-educated couples, mutuality of orgasm was thought to be related to marital adjustment. In addition, Thomason reported that both sexual and marital adjustment tended to be better if the spouse was perceived to be sexually attractive, if sexual intercourse was by mutual desire, and if mates were willing and able to have intercourse as often as they wished (Thomason, 1955: 153–163). Lewis and Spanier, in their theoretical summary, state very succinctly: "The greater the sexual compatibility, the more the marital quality" (Lewis and Spanier, 1979: 283).

Such results, when coupled with the influence of Freud and the Kinsey reports, caused some to overcompensate for earlier inhibitions by seeing sexual adjustment as the central fact of marriage, rather than as one element among others. As Margaret Jackson says, in marriage manuals "sexual disharmony was seen as the root cause of all marital disharmony" . . . (Jackson, 1987: 60). However, the overemphasis on sex cannot be totally accounted for by sex research and discussion. Elizabeth Janeway examines two historical factors that have combined to make sex a more important part of life: one is the lessening of ties to nonfamilial individuals and the other is the nonstimulating and artificial nature of the material environment.

> *Our high valuation of sex today is greatly influenced by this physical background: in a world where other bodily satisfactions have lost their sharpness, it remains. But there is a social reason too. The narrowing of the world of physical satisfaction as modern man withdraws from his contact with nature has been paralleled by another phenomenon: . . . The sexual connection, that is, is emphasized by the loss of other social ties just as sexual experience is emphasized by the dwindling of other bodily pleasures (Janeway, 1971: 266–7).*

An immediate problem presented by the conclusions of Kinsey, Thomason, and other researchers is that even when a correlation is found, as between sexual and overall adjustment, one must be cautious about arguing that sexual adjustment is causal. An equally plausible conclusion would be that marital maladjustment results in an unsatisfactory sexual experience, including the inability of the wife to achieve orgasm. Moreover, later researchers have called the correlation itself into question. Feature 11.2 speaks semi-seriously about sex and marriage in noting the divorce of William Masters and Virginia Johnson Masters. Mirra Komarovsky finds that the relation between sexual adjustment and total marital adjustment is low in working-class couples. Many unhappy women have a satisfactory sex life; nevertheless, she finds that, as the wife's educational level increases, so does the relation between sexual and other adjustments (Komarovsky, 1967: 111). John Cuber and Peggy Harroff's study of the marriages of professional and managerial men offers insights into the sexual adjustments of the highly educated. Their study, which included 235 men and 202 women of the upper middle class, indicated that

> *many remain clearly ascetic where sex is concerned. Others are clearly asexual. For still others, sex is overlaid with such strong hostility that an antisexual orientation*

is clear. In sum, we found substantial numbers of men and women who in their present circumstances couldn't care less about anything than they do about sex (Cuber and Harroff, 1965: 172).

Cuber and Harroff, we might note, do not say that these couples might not have a better marriage if they learned to enjoy sex. They simply say that these couples have marriages that are adjusted, that is, are "working." For some of Komarovsky's working-class couples, sex was still so segregated from the rest of marriage as to make the correlation between sex and marital adjustment negligible. For some of Cuber and Harroff's middle-class couples, sex had simply become a matter of mutual nonsalience, with the marriage left to revolve around other aspects of their busy lives. Can the sexually exploitative or asexual marriage be truly well adjusted? Perhaps it is only the expectations and overcompensations born of the post-Victorian era that cause us to consider this impossible.

But what of these expectations? The fact that wives as well as husbands are increasingly expected and expecting to find gratification in the sex act is at the heart of the problem of sexual adjustment today. The notion of mutual orgasm is an issue only when the male is still the initiator and when orgasm is expected only as a result of intercourse (on this, see Gilder, 1987: 12). "Premature ejaculation" is a strange idea that could not mean that the male did so before he was ready; it must mean that he "came" before she was ready. And that can be a problem only when mutuality includes mutual timing. While this may cause the

---

Feature 11.2   SEX GURUS' SPLIT BODES ILL FOR MERE MARRIEDS

What does it mean for married people when even Masters and Johnson, the pioneers of sex research, get divorced?

Does it mean sex isn't enough to sustain a marriage? Does it mean fame and fortune, much less the bonds of matrimony, can't hold two powerful egos intact? . . .

Realizing the effect this divorce would have on America, the director of the Masters and Johnson Institute said the couples's decision was "based on differences in the goals each has for the balance of their lives."

He added: "I'm sure people will say, 'If these two people can't get along, who can?' . . ."

Instead of telling us how sex works, the Masters and Johnson Institute could perform a greater humanitarian service by telling us how to keep our marriages intact.

Joseph F. Pisani, *Greenwich Times*, reprinted in *The Capital Times*, March 3, 1992, B1.

male to question his masculinity or ability to satisfy the female, the "discovery" of the clitoris as the center of female gratification should have freed (1) the female to seek her sexual gratification as aggressively as the male seeks his, (2) a couple from dependence on the male penis, and (3) a couple from any concern with timing. Such freedom, says Susan Lydon, has not always made for variety and mutual pleasure. Rather it has made the bed a "competitive arena, where men and women measure themselves against these mythical rivals, while simultaneously trying to live up to the ecstasies promised them by the marriage manuals and the fantasies of the media" (Lydon, 1972: 170). Thus we have been freed from guilt and asymmetry only to be ensnared in the new trap of "standards of performance." We now feel constrained to "live up" to certain orgasmic goals, both for ourselves and our partners. In fact, says Harris, "we now live under the shadow of a stern moral injunction to make sexual relationships fun" (Harris, 1983: 241).

Even among the middle-aged and elderly, Martha Cleveland notes, there has been a radical shift in sexual expectations. Traditionally it was thought that sex was for young couples, that the elderly were asexual. Now, however, the new norms are a reflection of our culture's frantic search for the fountain of youth and "are actually no more congruent with reality than are the traditional norms" (Cleveland, 1976: 233–240). The elderly must also develop a more balanced perspective on sexuality, instead of expecting too much.

If "I wonder whether I can satisfy her" expresses the male's fear of the emancipated female, "Why don't I enjoy this as much as I should?" is her frequent response. The problem is likely to be that she is still sexually inhibited by her socialization, yet in marriage she is expected—and expects herself—to be able to gain personal satisfaction from sexuality. Even premarital sex, as long as it includes lingering overtones of guilt, will do little to prepare the female for a life of sexual responsiveness. Thus, the combination of overtones of guilt, plus overemphasis on the importance of sex, plus new expectations of mutuality, serves to intensify the problem of sexual adjustment in the contemporary U.S. family and will continue to do so until the attitudinal and behavioral inconsistencies are reconciled, and the expectations are lowered.

The discussion of financial and sexual adjustments will conclude with a proposition regarding the relation between social class and these two adjustments. *In the middle-class marriage sexual adjustment is more problematic than is economic adjustment, while in the working- and especially lower-class marriage, economic adjustment is more problematic than sexual adjustment.* The reasons for assuming that economic adjustments are more problematic in the lower strata are fairly obvious from the discussion of finances. However, there are two reasons for the sexual aspect of the proposition. First, the middle class continues to be more burdened with puritanical guilt feelings about sex and at the same time has incorporated the notion of mutual gratification, while in the lower strata sex is still often defined as strictly a male need. In other words, it is not that lower-class marriages are better adjusted sexually than middle-class marriages but that the issue—adjustment—is simply less likely to arise among the former.

DECIDING AND DOING:
FAMILY POWER AND DIVISION OF LABOR

Studying Family Power

No area of family study is at the same time more intriguing and more fraught with problems than that of power and decision-making—the determination of family outcomes. The problems in this area are the usual twofold bane of social science: *conceptualization* and *measurement*. As David Olson and Carolyn Rabunsky put it, "Although theorists and researchers have shown considerable interest in this concept, it is still lacking in conceptual clarity and valid operational measures" (1972: 232).

What is wrong with the concepts used in the study of family power? "Most investigators," says Constantina Safilios-Rothschild, "have used interchangeably the terms 'family power' or 'power structure' and the terms 'decision making,' 'family authority' and 'influence'" 1970:539). Use of the same term with different meanings and of different terms with the same meaning by writers in this area has made the comparison of their results extremely difficult. As for measurement, Safilios-Rothschild noted in 1970 that most studies of power have been based solely on the responses of wives, and Olson and Rabunsky added that responses do differ, depending on whether the respondent is father, mother, or child. Ten years later, Bokemeier and Monroe report "a continued reliance on individual family members for data on conjugal and/or family level decision making, in spite of the evidence of and warnings about husband-wife response inconsistency (1983: 649). Equally troublesome is the fact that different research methodologies—surveys, laboratory experiments, observation in the home—produce somewhat different pictures of "who has the power." Many authors have simply asserted that what is needed are studies using multiple measuring techniques, so that the biases of the various approaches can be more adequately determined.

But what can be done to clarify the concepts? Some have suggested that the concept *power* be dropped entirely, while others, such as Robert Ryder and Gerald McDonald, feel that it should be used in a strictly interpersonal sense. A has power over B, says Ryder, only if A can lead B to act in keeping with A's intentions, or if A can get B to do something B does not want to do (Ryder, 1972: 40; McDonald, 1980: 842). Power, then, is the overarching interpersonal concept and can be treated as the sum total of the relations among authority, influence, and decision-making. *Authority* is the most easily accessible concept, since it is based on who *ought* to determine outcomes. Much of the information gained from questionnaires pertains to people's ideological views of the way things should work. And Gillespie noted a generation ago that both overt and covert patriarchy keep authority primarily in the hands of males—a point to which we will return later (Gillespie, 1971: 445–458).

Outcomes, however, are not always consistent with authority relations, and the difference between authority and outcome is accounted for by *influence*. Influence may be based on very personal attributes or on acceptance of authority and may therefore either reinforce or undermine the "authority structure." *Decision-making* is the actual event-point in the interplay among influence, authority, and outcome. Yet decision-making is synonymous neither with doing nor with power. The key issue here is the relation between delegating, deciding, and doing. It is obvious that the one who dominates a particular decision may not, in fact, be the one who implements it—that is, actually does the task. Furthermore, it is even possible for the decision to be made by one member of a couple because the other member has delegated the decision-making function or is simply uninterested. This greatly complicates the relationship between decision-making and power, since a decision may be a result of struggle, delegation, or default. In the first case, one can say that the decision-maker has the power; in the latter two cases, greater power appears to lie with the non-decision-maker.

Having noted the various ways to measure family power, and the aspects of it, we should note that Scanzoni and his collaborators have suggested a processual approach that includes the following elements: initiation, response, dynamic episodes, and context—especially past history (Hill and Scanzoni, 1982: 927–941; Scanzoni and Szinovacz, 1980: 60–85). Among the possible responses to initiation are: "Yes," "Yes, but" and "No," with the result being, respectively, consensus, developing agreement, and conflict.

Not only are there measures, aspects, and dynamic properties, but there are different bases for power as well. A useful list of such bases is provided by Bertram Raven, Richard Centers, and Aroldo Rodriguez:

1. Coercive power is based on P's belief that O can and will punish him for noncompliance.
2. Reward power is based on P's expectation that O will do something in return—reward P—if P complies.
3. Expert power stems from P's belief that O has superior knowledge or ability—knows what sort of behavior on P's part will lead P to the best outcome.
4. Legitimate power stems from P's acceptance of a given role structural relationship, believing that O has the right to request compliance in the area and P further feeling obliged to comply.
5. Referent power follows from P's identification with O, or from a desire for such identification. Being part of one unit, P then gets some satisfaction from behaving, feeling, believing, etc., similar to O.
6. Informational power stems from the content of the persuasive communication from O to P—careful and successful explanation of the necessity for change. (O is one person and P is another person) (Raven et al., 1975: 219).

Coercive power, of course, includes the possibility of the use of force, while legitimate power is close to the idea of authority, or who ought to determine the outcome. Saying "Do what I say because I am your husband (or father)," is an attempt to rely on legitimate power. Though there are difficulties in the study of family or marital power, these difficulties are not insurmountable. The foregoing clarifications should help to resolve them and may be useful in presenting the results of the studies already available.

Power and Decision-Making in the U.S. Family

Marital power was a very popular research topic in the 1960s and 1970s, but much less so in the 1980s. One reason may be the difficulties discussed above. Another may be the rethinking of patriarchy and gender that is now occurring as a result of feminist writings.

In the 60s and 70s the assumption was that male authority was giving way to gender equality. This assumption, however, was not necessarily correct. It is quite possible that as male authority lessens, male influence rises, so that his determination of the family's direction is as great or greater than ever before. This was Dair Gillespie's conclusion in the 1970s. Women, Gillespie states, are at a great power disadvantage. Men can prevent their wives, or women in general, from doing things. Baber and Allen, quoting Hare-Mustin, refer to Gillespie's point thus: "Patriarchal marriages are not always characterized by outright oppression, but rather by the preeminence of men's interests and desires and the subordination of women's" (Hare-Mustin, 1991, quoted in Baber and Allen, 1992: 224). Wives take on their husbands' social rank. Women are socialized to play inferior, deferential, receptive social roles. Wives still lack legal power, in terms of such things as the names they bear and control over financial resources, although this situation is changing. Husbands still dominate in determining with whom the couple will associate. In some families the husband still uses physical coercion. Wives get power only when their husbands default, that is, manifest weakness of some sort (Gillespie, 1971).

It is possible to respond that Gillespie is to some extent debating a "straw man," that those being refuted never said that U.S. marriages were now equalitarian, only that they were moving away from institutionalized patriarchy toward equalitarianism. Yet Gillespie's evidence is compelling: while wives may make many decisions and carry out many household tasks, power is still predominantly in the hands of their husbands. Larry Alsbrook even finds that, as communication lessens between married couples, power relations become so polarized as to be almost like those between a dominant group and a minority in society, with the wife resembling the minority (Alsbrook, 1976: 522). From a feminist perspective, Heidi Hartmann notes that the approach to the family that assumes common interests may have been less appropriate than a perspective that views the family as the locus of struggle and conflict (Hartmann, 1981: 366–394; Scanzoni and Polonko, 1980: 31–44). When the wife approximates an equal power relationship, several recent authors have found, it is not only because she is exchanging resources, such as attractiveness or income, for power, but also because the couple adhere to an equalitarian ideology. Equal resources alone—and this idea is consistent with Gillespie's argument—do not result in equal power (Richmond, 1976: 264; Burr et al., 1977: 513). And why is the change toward equality in marriage so slow? Komter notes that, regardless of social class, real change only responds to recognition of stereotyped gender role concepts, and conscious effort to change the stereotype. That is why a verbalized equality may not be translated into couple behavior (Komter, 1989: 187–216).

The workings of power and decision-making in the U.S. family must be specified according to several factors. There is a distinction between perceived and actual decision-making patterns within the home. Both husbands and wives tend to perceive the husband as having the dominant role, with the wife's opinion solicited but the final decision being his. Yet observation of numerous married couples showed that well over half of them were actually equalitarian in their decision-making, coming to decisions together. Few difficulties arise, Scanzoni and Szinovacz find, when both couple members are traditional because the husband's authority is accepted. The same holds true when they are both equalitarian. However, if the husband is traditional and seeks to dominate, while the wife is modern and refuses to "suffer in silence," conflict is likely (Scanzoni and Szinovacz, 1980: 104–116). Some research has found a correlation between social class position and the perceived and actual authority of the male. A generation ago, Goode described these tensions as follows:

> *Lower-class men concede fewer rights* ideologically *than their women in fact obtain, and the more educated men are likely to* concede more rights *ideologically than they in fact grant. One partial resolution of the latter tension is to be found in the frequent assertion from families of professional men that they should not make demands which would interfere with his* work: *He takes precedence as* professional, not *as family head or male; nevertheless, the precedence is his. By contrast, lower-class men demand deference as* men, *as heads of families (Goode, 1963: 21–22).*

On the one hand, the lower-class male claims authority on the basis of traditional or ideological patriarchy (he is "supposed" to be the boss), whereas in actual decision-making the lower-class wife wields substantial authority. This discrepancy between the authority the lower-class husband thinks he should have and the power he actually has may cause considerable marital instability. It may explain why Osmond and Martin found that the intactness of lower-class couples was best accounted for by equalitarian decision-making. In other words, genuine equalitarianism makes for stability in the lower-class marriage (Osmond and Martin, 1978: 328). On the other hand, Goode is saying, the middle-class or educated male ordinarily expresses the *norm* of equalitarianism, but he manages to have more power anyway. At least a partial explanation for the divergence between both perceptions and expectations and actuality is found in Blood and Wolfe's "resource" theory (Blood and Wolfe, 1960). They argued that higher-status husbands have more resources at their disposal—financial and intellectual—than do lower-status husbands. Middle-class wives, even if they are employed, usually contribute a smaller proportion of the total family income. Thus, the higher the family's social and economic position, the greater is the husband's bargaining position, despite the fact that higher-status families have moved further away from traditional patriarchal ideology toward equalitarian expectations. Interestingly enough, Charles Willie and Susan Greenblat find that "the middle-class black family is more equalitarian than any other family type" (Willie and Greenblat, 1978: 691).

Referring back to Raven, Centers, and Rodriguez's six bases for power, we find an expectable class difference. Working- and lower-class couples are higher in the use of coercive, reward, and legitimate power, that is, force, trade-offs, or positional authority, while the middle classes more frequently employed expert or informational power, partly because their members are more verbal and more inclined to use reasoning.[1]

Prior to the 1980s, a second factor complicating the simple change from patriarchy to equalitarian marriage had to do with areas of influence. Blood and Wolfe, and other earlier research found that high-status husbands wielded much influence in the areas of housing, insurance, and wife's employment (Blood and Wolfe, 1960: 33). When you examine closely the list of areas, it is obvious that the husband is dominant in major family decisions. However, questions are being raised about these earlier findings. Mark Rank, studying 278 married couples in Seattle, finds that the greater the husband's resources, the *less* his influence over his wife's employment decision. This seems to fit the "normative equalitarian," instead of the resource, theory (Rank, 1982: 591–604). However, another explanation is that it is the wife's status as much as the husband's that determines decision-making, and that for high status couples negotiation is the key.

How important is a wife's employment to her power? Rallings and Nye put the relation between wife's employment and financial decisions succinctly: "Employment positively affects the power of the wife-mother in financial affairs" (Rallings and Nye, 1979: 212). In addition, the wife makes fewer decisions about routine household matters—and these two findings together are indications that she is spending more time at a job and less time in the home. However, there is disagreement about the total effect of wife's employment on power. Clearly resources and norms are both important, as are the continuing and often covert patriarchal values of society.[2]

This does not mean that an increase in the number of women in the labor force has not had a positive effect on the spread of equalitarian values. Brown, in a study of women's employment and equalitarianism since 1900, reports that the spread of equalitarian values followed by about 14 years the beginning of the rise in women's labor force participation (Brown, 1978: 15). The norm, however, was adopted by couples in which the wife was not working as well as those in which she was. Husband-wife power relations do not remain static over the family's life cycle. One interesting study by Lewis reports that the wife's role in decision-making reaches its zenith during the children's teenage years, and is at its lowest ebb after child-launching and before the husband's retirement. This, of course, is consistent with the fact that the domestic role is crucial during the teenage years, while the husband's breadwinning role is dominant after the child-rearing role has been completed. It is, however, equally noteworthy that after launching, wives want to make more decisions than they made during the preschool years but would prefer to maker *fewer* decisions than they made during the teenage years. A more equalitarian role in decisions, therefore, seems to be what they seek (Lewis, 1972). These are decisions, though, concerning the household, not the "world at large."

To summarize the issue of decision-making and power, it must be repeated that much still remains to be done to clarify the concepts used and to measure adequately what happens. However, from available studies it can be concluded that, despite the fact that in the middle classes companionate or equalitarian ideologies are expressed increasingly, husbands continue to dominate, though not in the African-American middle class. In the middle class, resources, expertise and deference enable them to do so; in the lower class they dominate — when possible — by delegating tasks and decisions to the wife, and/or by asserting traditional male authority. Extensions of the discussion have included consideration of the family life cycle, areas of influence, and women's employment, plus the fact that the manner in which a couple perceive themselves to make decisions and the manner in which they actually do so are frequently very different. Conscious equalitarianism is at present more characteristic of the middle class than of the working and lower classes.

The Division of Labor

Once decisions are made regarding expenditures, child care, or other family matters, they must be implemented. Someone must *do* the various household tasks, handle day-to-day financial matters, and take care of the children. In the stereotypical modern industrial family the man ran the family's productive machinery and supervised the economic division of labor, while the woman cooked, sewed, and cared for the children. With the removal of the economic-productive function from the home, the father could leave the running of the household to his wife and restrict himself to making a living; he could help with heavier, dirtier tasks around the house and play a supportive role in childrearing; or he and his wife could divide the domestic and economic responsibilities equally (see "role-sharing" in Chapter 12). The third has been exceptional, both behaviorally and attitudinally; and a fourth — with the husband as homemaker and the wife as earner — has seldom even been discussed in our male-dominated society. These choices will receive considerable attention in the next chapter, on family roles.

It is noteworthy that the topic of household division of labor received little attention in the 1970s and much in the 1980s — just the opposite of the study of power. One reason for this is that the increase in women's employment has made the issue of household division of labor of interest to both men and women.

The restudy of Middletown (Muncie, Indiana) in 1980 found that women are not usually responsible for disciplining children or for household repairs, but they do share almost equally with their husbands in paying bills. But what interested the researchers was that wives themselves often overestimate their own contributions to these tasks. As in the study of power, men's and women's perceptions may be very different (Condran and Bode, 1982: 424). A consistent finding concerns the effects of women's employment on the division of labor.

Kamo summarizes these well: "The pattern of household division of labor apparently is affected not only by both spouses' monetary contributions, but also by their time availabilities, power relations, and ideologies" (Kamo, 1988: 177).

All of these factors are actually complex in their significance. Of great interest today is the effect of the wife's employment on household labor. Kamo reports the following:

> *On the average, husbands carry 36% of the total domestic work load. . . . For couples in which both spouses work full time outside the home, the husbands' input still averages only 41% and this percentage increases only to 43% when both earn approximately the same amount of money (Kamo, 1988: 194; see also, Coltrane and Ishii-Kuntz, 1992: 43–57).*

Several studies have reported that even this small change toward equality in housework is accounted for not by the husband doing more, but by the wife (and couple) doing less (see Hochschild and Machung, 1989). Donna Berardo et al. make this very clear in their analysis of 1,500 couples. They find that in single-earner couples the wife does 34 of the 42 hours of housework that are done, in dual-earner couples she does 21 of the 33 hours, and in dual-career couples she does 16.6 of the 25 hours of housework done each week (Berardo et al., 1987: 386).

Not only does women's employment ordinarily not equalize amount of time by gender, it does not seem to reallocate the traditional male/female tasks. Blair and Lichter reported that "American males would have to reallocate over 60 percent of their family work time to other tasks before sex equality in the division of labor is achieved" (1991: 91). Employed women, Shelton finds, spend less time on household tasks that require large amounts of time, but the same amount on tasks requiring little bits of time. She suggests that the "small time" tasks may be the ones that are unavoidable, and the employed woman does them anyway, since the man will not. And why, Shelton asks, will men not take an equal hand? She proposes three answers: (1) because their higher wages give them the power to refuse the request to help; (2) because they lack respect for housework duties; (3) because they may increase their own employed work load so as to excuse their lack of helping (Shelton, 1990: 115–135).

Three other interesting findings should be noted. Hilton finds that single-parent families do less household tasks, even food preparation, than two parent families. The greatest discrepancy is in maintenance or repair tasks, which often require significant time commitments (Hilton, 1990: 283–298). Second, the presence of children in the home affects the mother's allocation of time to different tasks, but not the father's. Presumably, the mother simply spends much time caring for the children's needs, while the father does not (Bergen, 1991: 152). Finally, the employed mother does less housework than the unemployed, but she also has less leisure time. Hochschild and Machung call it the "leisure gap," with women cutting back on personal needs, giving up reading, hobbies, television, visits with friends, exercise, and time alone (Hochschild and Machung, 1989: 199).

Before we look at the relation between household division of labor and marital satisfaction, let us note the role of children in household work. Berardo et al. find that the number of hours of housework done by "others" is in the narrow range of 4.6 to 8.1 per week. This, of course, includes that done by both paid help and children, and is hardly a significant amount (Berardo et al., 1987: 386). According to Goldscheider and Waite, the home is still very much a "gender factory." They explain thusly:

> *Daughters, particularly teenage daughters, take a great deal of responsibility for household tasks, while older daughters mostly continue to help, shifting as they mature (and get their driver's license) to tasks outside the household such as grocery shopping and child care, perhaps chauffeuring their younger siblings around. Boys contribute very little to household chores, participating only in yard work and only as teenagers and are mostly exempt from any contribution whatsoever when they reach adulthood (Goldscheider and Waite, 1991: 170).*

To this, Peters adds that, not surprisingly, children in single-parent families do more housework than those in two-parent families (1987: 212). And Hilton and Haldeman, while agreeing that daughters do more than sons, found that children "were less sex segregated in their household task behavior than were parents" (1991: 114).

The final issue to raise regarding division of labor concerns its relation to marital adjustment or satisfaction. Not surprisingly, the congruence of the man's provider-role attitude and domestic role behavior increases his level of marital satisfaction. What this means is that if he sees himself as primary provider he is less happy to take a major hand in the household division of labor (Perry-Jenkins and Crouter, 1990: 136). Furthermore, it seems difficult for husbands and wives to be equally satisfied with the household division of labor (Leslie and Anderson, 1988: 212). Okin notes the greater vulnerability of women to society's continuing inequities. They are socialized for vulnerability, and this is reinforced by "the actual division of labor within almost all current marriages." They are also disadvantaged in the work place by the assumption, says Okin, that workers have wives at home. They are vulnerable to the demands of worker and homemaker, and "their vulnerability peaks if their marriages dissolve and they become single parents" (Okin, 1989: 138). And what about women's perception of this vulnerability and unfairness? Thompson gives us insight into this. The sense of injustice for women is strongly affected by who they compare themselves with:

> *Women would have a stronger sense of injustice about family work if they made between-gender comparisons. Women who compare themselves to their husbands ('I do more than you do') have a stronger sense of entitlement than do women who compare themselves to other women ('I am a superwoman') or compare their husbands to other men ('my husband does more than most'). Women who recognize their wage and family work as necessary work for the good of their families have a better basis on which to make claims on their husbands than do women who see their work as personal need or fail to see it as work (Thompson, 1991: 193).*

Though the wife's employment does reduce the amount of household labor she performs, the dominant gender-role definitions still tend to be: husband primarily breadwinner and secondarily helper around the house, and wife primarily homemaker and secondarily job-holder if both agree. This, however, has already taken us beyond the adjustment issues and into the role concerns of Chapter 12.

SUMMARY OF ADJUSTMENTS

Many adjustments take place early in marriage, only a few of which can be adequately planned for ahead of time. Habit patterns have to be meshed, kin relations have to be balanced, differential growth may occur, and the arrival of a child causes a major readjustment of the couple's lifestyle. Finances are a problem not only for the low status family, but for all families, primarily because of the importance placed upon economics in our society. There has been an increasing tendency, especially in the middle class, toward mutuality and equality in sexuality and decision-making, but many problems of patriarchy and change leave a gap between expectations and reality. The family division of labor continues to keep homemaking more the wife's responsibility than the husband's, even if she is employed outside the home.

Marital Roles

CHAPTER 12

In the course of U.S. history, the role patterns of husbands and wives increasingly came to be defined ideologically as economic and domestic, respectively. The recent liberation movements have emphasized equality both in the economic and familial spheres, but the change has been only as far as neotraditional roles, in which the husband is primarily breadwinner and the wife primarily homemaker, with each helping out in the other's sphere if they both wish it. Patriarchal values and structures have continued to limit change toward true gender equality. Both genders have choices available today, with some options being dual careers, role-sharing, and role reversal—in decreasing order of likelihood.

ROLE DIFFERENTIATION IN THE FAMILY

An important source of change in the family, noted in Chapter 5, is the increasing functional differentiation of modern industrial society, so that economic, political, religious, education, and other institutional functions are less and less embedded within either the nuclear family or the kin group. Talcott Parsons has received more attention recently than he did during the decade from 1975 to 1985, both because he presents a position with which feminist writers find it valuable to debate and because he has some continuing insights. Parsons describes the process of differentiation thus:

> *Differentiation refers to the process by which simple structures are divided into functionally differing components, these components becoming relatively independent of one another, and then recombined into more complex structures in which the functions of the differentiated units are complementary. A key example in the development of industrial society everywhere is the differentiation . . . of the unit of economic production from the kinship household (Parsons, 1962: 103).*

The key word in Parsons' definition is *independent*. His example concerns the way in which the economic-productive role has been removed from the family setting in the modern industrial community.

Parsons' conception of differentiation as it pertains to the family was influenced greatly by his collaboration with Robert Bales, a social psychologist interested in small groups. Bales, in earlier research, had noted that in any small, task-oriented group there tends to evolve a task or *instrumental* leader, whose job it is to lead the way in solving the problem at hand, and a social-emotional or *expressive* leader, who acts to maintain morale and control conflict. By reducing strain, the expressive leader makes a positive contribution to the group's perpetuation and thus to its ability to accomplish its task. The same person, the "great one," may play both the task and social-emotional leadership roles, but more often they are played by two different persons.

Utilizing this perspective drawn from small group research, Parsons' students discovered cross-culturally that the same differentiation of leadership roles occurs within the nuclear family. In the majority of societies, the husband plays the role of instrumental leader, governing the family's economic division of labor, while the wife plays that of the expressive leader. Raymond Adamek has recently mustered data which he feels lend some support to this male/instrumental, female/expressive dichotomy. He finds that in 90 percent of his sample, woman are the major caretakers of infants and youngsters (Adamek, 1982: 1–11). In addition, research has led some to conclude that this sex role distinction is good for family stability. As Aldous, Osmond, and Hicks put it in their summary of the research: "Marital role differentiation, with the husbands performing the occupational role and the wives the family caretaker role, is positively related to marital stability (Aldous, et al., 1979: 242).

Feminist writers, however, have explained that the reason differentiation is related to stability is that patriarchy has been acceptable or normative. And David Cheal argues that "while instrumental and expressive tasks have to be accomplished in a family system, these specialized *tasks* do not have to be performed within specialized roles (Cheal, 1991: 35). The functionists' response has been: "yes, but they are." Quale adds that even Parsons was not as rigid as his disciples have been. She states that Parsons actually says:

> *that there is a strong tendency for nuclear families to organize in that way for convenience, in a society in which men usually and women seldom do productive work outside the home. Indeed, he (Parsons) insists that for full self-development, every man and woman needs to learn how to be both leader and follower, in both instrumental and expressive ways, in both performance-centered . . . and person-centered . . . situations* (Quale, 1988: 51).

From this starting point, Parsons felt he could answer those who observe that the husband has lost power in the family to the wife. In his view what has really happened is that as a result of the removal of the economic producing function from the home to an outside setting, plus the increase in the importance of happiness and emotional satisfactions to family solidarity, the husband plays his major role in the outside world, while the wife's role of social-emotional leadership has become central to the family unit per se. Thus, the husband's role is now almost totally performed in an extrafamilial milieu. The husband has not lost authority; rather, the kind of authority he formerly held within the family cannot now be appropriately exercised because the family no longer engages as a unit in the kind of economic activities over which men exercise authority. The husband formerly ran the economic machinery of the family; the wife continues to run the social-emotional machinery of the family.

This same situation, that is, the differentiation of the husband's economic role from the home, can be interpreted in a different and perhaps more convincing fashion as follows. The removal of the economic-productive function from the home, combined with the male's retention of that function, gave the male *greater* control than ever before over the family unit. As industrialization increased, the position of women declined, for they became increasingly dependent upon male economic provision, and were increasingly captives of the domestic scene. Thus, what Randall Collins calls the private household of the market economy became increasingly male dominated, with the female having to use her sexuality to bargain for income favors (Collins, 1971: 3–21). It is no accident, therefore, that studies of achievement in the industrial United States have ordinarily used male respondents, while studies of the family have actually been studies of women. Changes during the 1970s, however, have begun to blur these clear-cut distinctions.

The theory of industrial role differentiation has been closely linked with another theoretical tradition that says that the sexes are innately different in many ways. Females are born to bear and rear children, the psychoanalytic tradition has argued, and men are born to explore, to compete, and to be independent. "Biology is destiny," and when a woman tries to give up her predestined role she becomes "lost" and confused, no longer knowing who or what she is (Lundberg and Farnham, 1947). George Gilder, forty years later, stated this position concisely: "Women's liberation entails a profound dislocation" (Gilder, 1987: 173). A part of the inherent difference between men and women is related to the idea of "maternal deprivation," or the child's need not just for human contact but for contact with the mother. Boss and Thorne respond to this by saying that "the assumption that mother is all-responsible for the child's well being can cripple women in families" (Boss and Thorne, 1989: 93). Another supposedly inborn difference is the male's need for sexuality, and the female's lack of any such strong need. So goes the psychoanalytic argument that is basic to much of the patriarchal ideology of the U.S. family.

Justification for the industrial world's sexual division of labor does not stop with the idea that it is simply that way but goes on to assume that it *should* be that way. The husband as breadwinner and the wife as homemaker, or the man as task and the woman as social-emotional leader, is good. It is good for the industrial world, since it holds down unemployment and allows the family to follow the breadwinner as *he* pursues job opportunities (see Harris, 1983: 57). While questioning whether it *should* be that way, Rosanna Hertz agrees that "the disruption of the traditional exchange between husbands and wives and the radical break with a 'complementarity of roles' should be enough to subject the marriage to unbearable pressures" (Hertz, 1986: 212). Gender differentiation is good for the family because each member has a complementary role to play, guaranteeing that all the important tasks will be accomplished. And, finally, it is good for the individual since biology is destiny; that is, men and women are doing what they were born to do. Thus, everything hangs together. Harris summarizes this completeness well: this kind of functionalism shows "that an institution must be as it is not only because it 'fits' other institutions, but because it supplies universal human needs" (Harris, 1983: 86). Contradictions or "lack of fit" between two spheres escape this analysis.

The apologists for this sexual division of labor vary greatly. The functionalists, such as Parsons, simply argue that the patriarchal status quo is good for the system. Religious conservatives, like the Mormons, argue that a woman's place is in the home and perceive the familial role as rewarding for women (Hartman and Hartman, 1983: 897–902). Marabel Morgan, in her book *The Total Woman*, stated that a wife must learn to accept her husband by emphasizing his virtues and overlooking his faults; she must admire him and compliment his body; she must adapt to his living schedule and tastes; and she must appreciate and be grateful to him. (In other words, to use McDaniel's terminology, she must be "receptive.") In so doing, Morgan adds, she will be rewarded with nice things (Morgan, 1973). This, of course, is an exchange approach, with the wife exchanging subservience for "goodies." Letha Scanzoni adds that "the loudest voices being heard in today's society are often those of the conservatives who insist on gender role segregation" (Scanzoni, 1988, 134). Finally, in response to critics of sexual differentiation, Harold Christensen has argued that it would be possible for women to gain equality not by taking over men's tasks but by raising the status of homemaking responsibilities and continuing to carry them out (Christensen, 1977: 205–224). A decade later, Kingsley Davis repeated this plea less strongly, urging that "a modified egalitarian system that recognizes a division of labor between husband and wife but minimizes the effect on sex roles by equalizing rewards both at home and in the market place seems the most likely path in the future" (Davis, 1988: 85). Although Christensen claims he is not putting forth a "separate but equal" doctrine, this is how his and Davis's papers read.

So, there is an industrial division of labor that has come to be considered both traditional, or expected, and good: the man is the economic provider and the wife is the homemaker. But Christensen is responding to critics of this division, and it is to those critics that we turn now.

SECTION TWO

THE LIBERATION MOVEMENTS

Women's Liberation

THE *"FEMINIZATION" OF OCCUPATIONS*   In modern industrial society technological advances have reduced the contribution of human strength to societal maintenance to a small proportion of what it has been cross-culturally and historically. Viewed in these terms, technology has resulted, in a sense, in the "feminization" of the occupational structure—not just in its removal from the home. This statement should not be construed to mean that the market no longer favors the male. What it does mean is that there is a great incongruity between the "feminization" of the occupational-economic structure and the male dominance of that structure following the industrial revolution. This makes it much less acceptable for employers to hire and determine salary on the basis of male superiority in handling a particular job. While this may be threatening to the male ego, it has been an open invitation to women to question the former ideology and discriminatory practices that kept them wedded to the home.

The feminization of occupations means several other things besides the reduction in the need for human strength. It means that the expansion of the clerical and service sectors in the 'postindustrial' economy involves tasks previously carried out by females. It also means that college-educated women have increasingly entered traditionally male occupations, such as law and medicine (Gerson, 1985: 213). Finally, it means that, due to various gadgets and devices, fewer household tasks require much strength. And, as Goode states, "as to those that still require strength, most men cannot do them either" (Goode, 1982: 145). These, says Goode, are done by repair specialists.

THE *MODERN WOMEN'S MOVEMENT*   Charlotte Gilman and others raised many of the current feminist issues during the first quarter of the 20th century. However, patriarchal ideology gradually pushed such thinking to the periphery, making the following, described by Ann Ferguson, as the dominant view of women:

In all male dominant systems . . . 'good' women are divided from 'bad' women with re-
gard to their motherhood and sexual roles. Thus, women who are mothers and married
are 'good,' to be distinguished from single 'bad' or 'failed' women who are nonmothers.
Furthermore, 'good' mothers (married) are distinguished from 'bad' mothers (un-
married)" (Ferguson, 1989: 177).

Response to this ideological position regarding women began to gain momentum following World War II. The involvement of Eleanor Roosevelt in the United Nations Commission on the Status of Women and other developments led to an increasing awareness on the part of women of the opportunities they were apparently missing and the burden of subjection under which they were living. As Cheal says,

Feminism is not only an academic school of thought, it is also a broad movement for
change. Supported by a variety of groups and networks, its advocates have made pub-
lic issues out of women's private problems, including domestic violence, childcare and
the financial difficulties of dependent wives (Cheal, 1991: 9).

These concerns came to a head in 1963 with the appearance of Betty Friedan's *The Feminine Mystique* and the report of the Kennedy administration's National Commission on Women (Friedan, 1963). Then in 1966 the National Organization for Women was established, and the modern women's movement had an organizational base. Since then the movement has grown and diversified, and now has a variety of foci.

One set of categories includes feminism-humanism, radical feminism, socialist feminism, and the black women's movement, each with its own constituency and concerns.[1] Women's rights feminism, or the *feminist-humanist* position, represents the early focus of the National Organization for Women. The organization's major concern has been equal opportunity for good, middle-class, high-paying, career-type employment for women. In response to the question "Who is oppressed by whom?" feminist-humanists have answered "Everyone is oppressed by the system of traditional sex roles, men as well as women." The differences between this feminism and the Conservative Right, Cohen and Katzenstein argue, are

not primarily over what children need or whether the family ought to be abolished, but
over the place of men and women in society. Looking past the turmoil, one finds this
common ground: an acceptance of the family as an arrangement that is, at least po-
tentially, productive for the human spirit as well as the body, and a recognition that
all children need stable affectionate care (Cohen and Katzenstein, 1988: 42–43)

A second major position within the modern women's movement is *radical feminism*. The answer to the question "Who is oppressed by whom?" is very straightforward: "Women by men." Men benefit from women's domestic slavery, from their unpaid labor. The opponent in the fight for liberation is the opposite sex. Women must break the chains that bind them in subjection to men, whether those chains be the homemaking role, the rearing of children, or even sexuality. A branch of the Italian women's movement stated this position very clearly:

We affirm all labor hitherto carried out by women, that is: cleaning the house, washing and ironing, sewing, cooking, looking after children, taking care of the old and sick, are forms of labor like any other, which could be carried out equally by men or women and are not of necessity tied to the ghetto of the home (Zaretsky, 1976: 139).

Regarding the "ghetto of the home" concept, Robin Fox makes an important distinction between marriage and motherhood: the former being the legitimate goal of protest, rather than the latter. The women's movement, says Fox, is objecting to

the tyranny of the nuclear family and the ideology of lifelong monogamy. But these are not 'natural,' and it is not clear that they are altogether in the male interest either. What the militant women are objecting to, then, is the role of wife as it has been defined by the nuclear family ideologues. Our analysis tells us that this is quite in order since that role as defined is quite abnormal. For one thing, it robs women of precisely what they are asserting, namely sisterhood. *In starting up their cooperative movements and asserting that as women they have interest to be protected from male exploitation, they are returning to normal (Fox, 1980: 209–210).*

Confusion comes, says Fox, when they think what they are protesting against is motherhood, rather than monogamy. A subgroup within this portion of the women's movement is those who would argue for lesbian freedom from dependence upon the male genitalia for gratification, even as men have never been totally dependent on women for their sexual needs. And, of course, opponents of the movement have attempted to identify this entire position with lesbianism in order to play upon conservative attitudes toward the latter.

Socialist feminism argues that not all men benefit from the industrial capitalist system, only those with high status positions. In other words, high status males oppress low status males and all women. The oppressor is both a class and a sex, and this dual oppression is fostered by the modern capitalist system. Feature 12.1 makes this position very clear. It is not enough, therefore, to overthrow male domination, but class relations must be altered as well by the rising up of all women and of men of the working class.

One group felt left out of most of this until recently: black women. The *black women's* movement was born during the 1970s with the recognition that their problems were not to be solved by the provision of high status jobs or by declaring men and the capitalists to be the enemy. If oppression is by sex, class, and race, the problems are different and the difficulties in effecting change are extremely great. This is the position underlying books like Joyce Ladner's *Tomorrow's Tomorrow* and more recently Pat Collins's *Black Feminist Thought* (Ladner, 1971; Collins, 1990).

Zaretsky distinguishes the last three positions by noting that one of the feminist statements equates women's oppression with oppression within the family, and this, he says, obscures "the special problems of black and brown women, and of industrial working class women" (Zaretsky, 1976: 18).

It is worth noting that each of these positions began a few years later than, and is numerically smaller than, the preceding one. That is, feminist humanism is the oldest and has the broadest base of support, while the most recent and numerically smallest is the black women's movement. This situation is changing, thanks to the work of Collins and others.

A concern that cross-cuts the above categories is reproductive rights. Women's desire to control reproduction confronts patriarchy at one of its most powerful points: fertility and control of children. Linda Gordon notes that reproductive rights "faces the task of finding a program that equally defends women's individual rights to freedom, including sexual freedom, and the dignity of women's need and capacity for nurturance and being nurtured, with or without biological motherhood" (Gordon, 1982: 51).

Another distinction within feminism is divided by Deborah Rhode into "relational" and "individualist." She characterizes them thus:

Feature 12.1   THE MEN WE CARRY IN OUR MINDS

A scholarship enabled me not only to attend college, a rare enough feat in my circle, but even to study in a university meant for the children of the rich. There I met for the first time young men who had assumed from birth that they would lead lives of comfort and power. And for the first time I met women who told me that men were guilty of having kept all the joys and privileges of the earth for themselves. I was baffled. What privileges? What joys? I thought about the maimed, dismal lives of most of the men back home. What had they stolen from the wives and daughters? The right to go five days a week, 12 months a year, for 30 or 40 years to a steel mill or a coal mine? The right to drop bombs and die in war? The right to feel every leak in the roof, every gap in the fence, every cough in the engine as a wound they must mend? The right to feel, when the layoff comes or the plant shuts down, not only afraid but ashamed? . . .

So I was baffled when the women at college accused me and my sex of having cornered the world's pleasures. I think something like my bafflement has been felt by other boys (and by girls as well) who grew up in dirt-poor farm country, in mining country, in black ghettos, in Hispanic barrios, in . . . Third World nations — any place where the fate of men is just as grim and bleak as the fate of women.

When the women I met at college thought about the joys and privileges of men . . . they thought of their fathers who were bankers, physicians, architects, stockbrokers, the big wheels of the big cities . . . . These fathers made the decisions that mattered. They ran the world. . . .

Scott Russell Sanders, "The Men We Carry in Our Minds," *Milkweed Chronicle*, 1984. Reprinted in *Utne Reader*, May-June, 1991, 77.

(1) Relational Feminism—*Emphasizes the family, the couple, or the mother-child dyad as the basic unit of the nation. Physiological differences between the sexes thus become the linchpins for a visionary construction of equitable social differences. The requirements of community, not the needs of the individual, dictate the sociopolitical program.*

(2) Individualist Feminism—*Privileges the individual, virtually without reference to the community or group. Within individualist feminism, womanly qualities or attributes are necessarily downplayed, as are physiological differences (Rhode, 1990: 20).*

Of interest here is that these two orientations, when carried to the extreme, end up as "alpha bias" or "beta bias"—a central debate within feminism. These are well defined by Baber and Allen:

Alpha bias exaggerates the differences between women and men by characterizing them as having essentially opposite natures. Beta bias is the inclination to ignore and minimize differences. Beta bias occurs when the social context and actual differences between women and men are overlooked (Baber and Allen, 1992: 14).

Men's Liberation

A small offshoot of feminist humanism is the men's liberation movement. Born in the realization of their replaceability by females and the recognition that only certain personality potentialities were acceptable for males, this position argues that we are all oppressed by "the system." It is not that no one had expressed such sentiments before, but rather that they had not received organized expression. In fact, according to Zaretsky, in the 1830s and 1840s a domestic manual appeared that decried "that fierce conflict of worldly interests, by which men are so deeply occupied [which compels them] to stifle their best feelings" (Zaretsky, 1976: 52). Why should men have to be independent, competitive, nonemotional, and aggressive if these traits are not natural to them? Wouldn't it be better if an individual, regardless of gender, could be a whole person, or could express a wide range of attributes?

The double bind or "Catch-22" within which the liberated male operates is well described by Maureen Baker and Hans Bakker. Such males get little support in their liberation. Also, unemployed childrearing is still acceptable for the female, but not the male (see "Role Reversal" below). Likewise, there are constraints that prevent male consciousness from even being raised regarding the narrowness and rigidity of traditional "maleness." First, middle-class men do benefit from their traditional dominance. Second, consciousness-raising requires self-disclosure, and this is not made easy for males. Third, men think they don't have the time or energy to spend on consciousness-raising, since they are involved in the "rat-race." Finally, the media continue to reinforce traditional maleness (Baker and Bakker, 1980: 547–561).

Of course, it is hardly surprising that a movement whose aim is to make it possible for members of the dominant sex to take on traditional characteristics of the oppressed sex would make less headway and be met with less enthusiasm than a movement designed to change the conditions of the oppressed.

Where It's At:
Backlash, Neo-Traditionalism, and Role Conflict

BACKLASH   Has U.S. society "bought" the goals of the liberation movements? One school of recent thought argues that there has actually been a backlash against feminist thinking and programming. Susan Faludi, in the book by that title, points out the late-1980s Family Protection Act, which, she says, had one objective: "dismantling nearly every legal achievement of the women's movement" (Faludi, 1991: 236). Not surprisingly, this "dismantling" is even celebrated in magazines such as *Playboy* (see Feature 12.2). According to Goode, backlash in the popular press can be attributed to (1) men who paid lip service to equality finding that they oppose its practical applications, and (2) men and women who never approved of equality finally recognizing it as an actual threat (Goode, 1982: 141).

Some have even claimed that we are now living in the postfeminist era. Okin argues that this claim is due in part to focusing on women who have "made it," and is false regardless of its meaning. It is certainly not true, Okin says, "that feminism has been vanquished, and equally untrue that it is no

---

Feature 12.2 **PLAYBOY EXPOSES HOUSEWIVES
IN A TRIBUTE TO FAMILY VALUES**

Once on the cutting edge of social change, Playboy magazine pays a 10-page tribute in its August issue to Family Values, in the person of 16 American housewives. Every one, it says, busies herself keeping her home tidy and tending to her husband and children when she is not lying around for a passing photographer. . . .

This emphasis on the domestic virtues must not be attributed to mere nostalgia or a Moral Majority-like reaction to feminism. The spread is Playboy's twist on the post-liberation spirit. The choice for today's women . . . is no longer between job and family; with a subsidy here, a tax break there, they can have it all. Playboy, loyal to its chronic cause, adds that men no longer need choose between breakfast and bed. Here is evidence that they can have it all, too . . . .

The subtext is plain and fits into the boyish fantasy that Playboy has been purveying since its beginnings, or Superwoman serving Everyman. In the magazine's imagination, these women have moved beyond indignation at the exploitation of female flesh to celebration of what rouses men. And their husbands have advanced from possessiveness to pride in their wives' glowing attributes. It portends a more sharing society, and Playboy has always been for that . . . .

Walter Goodman, "Playboy exposes housewives in a tribute to Family Values," *New York Times*, reprinted in *Wisconsin State Journal*, August 3, 1992.

longer needed because its aims have been fulfilled. Until there is justice within the family, women will not be able to gain equality in politics, at work, or in any other sphere" (Okin, 1989: 4).

Several writers have argued that the backlash has been mostly verbal, and has merely succeeded in slowing down the process of change, looking worse to those feminists most involved in the efforts for change. Jeanne Fleming, for example, argues that despite active opposition to feminism, "resistance to change in women's rights and roles has not been growing." In fact, says Fleming, from 1975 to 1985 the American public became increasingly favorable to a wide range of women's issues (Fleming, 1988: 63; see also Mason and Lu, 1988: 39–57).

NEO-TRADITIONALISM   A decade ago writers like Elizabeth Janeway were arguing that very little had changed. In 1984 Lloyd Lueptow stated that "evidence of change in women's roles is very limited, as least in comparison with the potential change theoretically possible." The key change is labor force participation of women, with its by-product effects on age at marriage, fertility, and divorce (Lueptow, 1984: 277). Another way of looking at the change is to say, as Ferree does, that women's efforts to "have it all"

> *have only succeeded in locking women as a group ever more tightly in the grip of patriarchy and capitalism. Women who seek to mitigate the strain of participating in two differently organized work systems tend to seek out positions that are structurally marginal to both, such as part-time jobs, occupations that utilize the use-value skills and relationships formed in domestic labor, temporary employment (Ferree, 1987: 299).*

The marginal occupational role for women described by Ferree is one variety of neo-traditional gender roles. Ferree notes that in such marriages husbands and wives average about 60 hours of work a week. However, most of the man's hours are spent on the job, and most of the woman's are spent in homemaking (Ferree, 1991: 178). The term *neo-traditional* means that, although both husband and wife can work if they wish, the husband's work comes first, both in terms of amount earned and in influence on where the family resides. The wife works only to supplement the family income, and she does the majority of housework and child care, while the husband "helps out" (see Greif, 1985: 163 on neo-traditionalism).

There is a second variety of neo-traditionalism that Herma Hill Kay has called, somewhat tongue-in-cheek, the "triple career" family, meaning the wife has two careers — occupation and domestic — while the husband has one. Arlie Hochschild has insightfully labelled this housework following paid work as the *Second Shift*. She has noted the ways in which fatigue, sickness, and emotional exhaustion affect such women, and has commented on how difficult it is to get men to do their share in the home (Hochschild, 1989: 190–200; see also Blumstein and Schwartz, 1983). Neo-traditionalism seems to be the point at which the majority of U.S. couples are currently located on the continuum from breadwinner-homemaker to role sharing (Hochschild calls this "transitional").

ROLE CONFLICT   Have men and women agreed that neotraditionalism is what they want? Apparently not. Several studies over the past 20 years have found women to be more egalitarian than men (Araji, 1977: 318; Scanzoni and

Fox, 1980: 743–756; Covin and Brush, 1991: 393–416; and especially Hochschild, 1989). The fact that women and men disagree attitudinally about gender roles would presumably lead to a substantial amount of conflict. This is in fact what Scanzoni and Szinovacz find: the traditional male/equalitarian female couple find their relationship unsatisfactory and face conflict (1980: 104). However, this point can be broadened to say, as Robert Ort pointed out many years ago, that it is very difficult to play the roles you want to play and that your spouse wants you to play at the same time that your spouse is playing the roles both of you want her/him to play (Ort, 1950: 691–699).

By broadening role incongruity and conflict beyond the egalitarian/traditional axis, we find other points of strain and tension. Googins notes that there are at least four potential work/family conflicts: (1) these responsibilities may simply compete with each other; (2) two or more persons may have roles that do not coordinate with each other; (3) goals and activities may compete with each other; (4) other institutional demands (school, etc.) may also impinge on work and family functioning (Googins, 1991; 6–7). Another of these conflicts is noted by Moen and Dempster-McClain, who find the majority of both employed mothers and fathers saying they would prefer to work fewer hours a week so as to have more family time (1987: 588).

Several additional points regarding role behavior and role preferences have been made by various researchers. McDermid et al. find in a longitudinal study that a group at risk for marital difficulties are those with traditional attitudes who take on more egalitarian roles, presumably in part because the couple needed the wife's employment (MacDermid et al., 1990: 475–486). An interesting study by Perry-Jenkins and Crouter divides men into three provider orientations: main/secondary, coprovider, and reluctant coprovider. They then examine how these preferences are related to housework. Not surprisingly, coprovider husbands who do much housework are much more satisfied than either of the other two groups who help out a lot. In other words, it is again a matter of congruence between desires/attitudes and behavior (Perry-Jenkins and Crouter, 1990: 136–156).

Therefore, since women have moved further toward equalitarian preferences than men, it is an inescapable fact that many neo-traditional women are likely to pair up with traditional men, and many egalitarian women will either find a neo-traditional man or no one at all. By this we do not mean there are no truly egalitarian males, as you will see in the discussion of "role sharing" below.

SECTION THREE

HUSBAND-FATHER ROLE CHOICES

Thus far, the major concerns have been with the liberation movements, especially feminism, and with patriarchy and women's struggle for equality. The U.S. male does, of course, confront several issues that demand resolution. First, as noted above, he is being asked to alter his centuries-long patriarchal attitudes and institutions to accept the legitimate claims of women. Second, he must reconcile his sedentary role with the traditional image of the male as subduer of nature (without, as Feature 12.3 notes, much help from the ever-present media). Third, he (along with his partner) must determine how much of his time and energy to invest in the extrafamilial world and how much he will reserve for the family. Finally, he must reconcile the emerging democratic family ideology with the lingering image of male as patriarch and authority for his children. We will look at some of these issues in this section.

Home Versus Community

Men's life courses, says Morgan, "are not simply in the context of family or household settings but also in relation to a variety of public, occupational, and state settings" (Morgan, 1990: 89). But how do men balance these two settings, especially when most of their rewards come from their extra-familial roles? Pauline Boss studied families of men missing-in-action in Vietnam and also the

Feature 12.3   A TIME FOR MEN TO PULL TOGETHER

Ironically, men's own sense of loss has fed the male mystique. As men become more and more powerless in their own lives, they are given more and more media images of excessive, caricatured masculinity with which to identify. Men look to manufactured macho characters from the Wild West, working-class America, and modern war in the hope of gaining some sense of what it means to be a man. The primary symbols of the male mystique are almost never caring fathers, stewards of the land, or community organizers. Instead, over several decades these aggressively masculine figures have evolved from the Western independent man (John Wayne, Gary Cooper) to the blue-collar macho man (Sly Stallone and Robert DeNiro) and finally to a variety of military and police figures concluding with the violent revelry of *Robocop*.

Modern men are entranced by this simulated masculinity—they experience danger, independence, success, sexuality, idealism, and adventure as voyeurs. Meanwhile, in real life most men lead powerless, subservient lives in the factory or office—frightened of losing their jobs, mortgaged to the gills, and still feeling responsible for supporting their families. Their lauded independence—as well as most of their basic rights—disappear the minute they report for work. The disparity between their real lives and the macho images of masculinity perpetrated by the media confuses and confounds many men.

Andrew Kimball, "A Time for Men to Pull Together," *Utne Reader*, May/June 1991, 70.

families of corporate executives. Based on her research, she has developed a fourfold typology of father involvement in the family. In some families, she says, the father is both physically and psychologically present; that is, he lives there and is involved. In others, he is absent, due to death or divorce. In the families of the missing-in-action and sometimes of divorce, the father may be physically absent but psychologically present. This may be illustrated when the mother says: "Daddy wouldn't like it if you don't drink your milk." The spirit and influence of absent family members may linger for many years after they are physically no longer around, including after death. For our purposes, however, the most important case is that of physical presence but psychological absence; that is, the husband-father who lives there but is simply not available or involved (Boss, 1977: 141–151; Boss et al., 1979: 79–86). This may be a "workaholic" such as a corporate executive father, or a working-class father who doesn't want to be bothered. Though the wife may learn to compensate by being independent and androgynous, the child of the psychologically absent father may face anxiety and have trouble with the development of autonomy.[2] In these cases the father has opted for community rather than home, and much research is currently being done regarding the effects of this choice.

Thus, in an era of institutional differentiation, the male must make a choice: How much of myself shall I invest in my occupation and community and how much in my family?" Psychological absence is but one possible outcome of that choice. Not only does the husband have few guidelines to follow in making the choice, but wives disagree greatly in their expectations for their husbands. If the wife has high expectations for him as a husband and father, his work involvement is more likely to be evaluated negatively. If he (and his wife) opt for less emphasis on breadwinning and more on family, he may still be open to criticism from others who still support the breadwinning ideology. Men, says Marilyn Rueschemeyer, "get mixed messages from their wives. On the one hand, they are asked to spend more time at home; on the other hand, a few wives are quite ambitious for their husbands" (Rueschemeyer, 1981: 47). This is true regardless of whether the wife herself is employed or not. Wives look very positively at "family times," but also are pleased by their husbands' achievements. One popular newspaper columnist opened the issue to a public forum after publishing a letter from a wife who complained bitterly that her husband expended all his energy at work and had none left for her or the children. The results were most instructive. A large number of wives agreed entirely with this complaint, expressing the wish that their husbands would spend a little less time and energy trying to "get ahead" and a little more in meeting their wives' and children's needs. Yet an equally large number argued vehemently that they would rather be married to a successful husband who provided well for his wife and children than to a family man with little ambition.

There is no such thing as a "rule for balance" between work and family; whatever balance there is is a matter for the couple to determine (Osherson and Dill, 1983: 339–346). Recently, Sweet and Bumpass found in the NSFH data that there seemed to be an optimum number of occupational hours that wives preferred their husbands to be doing — regardless of how much they actually were working: 35–40 hours. This means, of course, that some wives wanted their husband to work more, and many wanted them to work less than they currently do.

A poor income or status at work may be compensated for by an enhanced family life. However, Hochschild notes that for some men failing at work or otherwise feeling bad about themselves, avoiding work at home may be a way of balancing the scales with their wives (Hochschild, 1989: 200). This not-too-happy statement leads us to the following conclusion: men have traditionally been expected to put work first. Today, they are expected to be recreational companions, to gratify their wives sexually, and to be confidants and problem solvers for their spouses.[3] Since both roles—work and family—are available, the couple must work out in terms of the husband's personality and abilities and the wife's expectations how he will divide his time and energy resources. Men can keep busy with their occupations and community affairs if they wish. Thus, those who *want* to escape home and family are likely to use the ready-made excuse of extrafamilial demands.

Husband and Father

Not unrelated to the foregoing issue is the question of how the male will perform as husband and father. Does he try to be patriarch, making the key decisions himself and restricting his wife to homemaking and motherhood? Does he reject "women's work" around the house? Does he work around the house grudgingly or willingly? It is not the decline in parental and male authority that is the problem—in fact, that decline may eventually be a solution; the problem is the couple's disagreement over their respective roles or the husband's excessive concern about the position he has presumably lost.

Perhaps the most open issue confronting the male in the home is the definition of the father role. When the father headed the family's economic division of labor in an agrarian society, his responsibilities were clear. But in the modern industrial world what should a father be? Should he be the *adviser and grand inquisitor*, the final authority and high court of appeals? This approach is caricatured in the description of the mother who, having taken all the misbehavior she can stand from her children, finally announces, "Just wait 'til your father gets home." Father is thus expected to walk in the door and spank or scold the child for actions he did not witness. Such a role is acceptable to some fathers because it convinces them that they have not yielded their position as patriarch, despite the fact that they are not at home much of the time.

Should the father be the *everyday Santa Claus*, who wouldn't dare come home from a business trip without "something for the kids"? This pattern is caricatured in the father whose return home is greeted, not by, "We're glad you're home, Dad," but by, "What did you bring us, Dad?" It is a viable approach for many fathers who invest neither time nor energy in their offspring, but who do have money.

Finally, should the father try to be the *buddy and pal*, who can't really appreciate his children until they are big enough to catch a ball or to enjoy camping? This is caricatured in the cartoon that depicts the teenage son's response when his aging and paunchy father enters the room clad in his baseball uniform: "Gee, Dad, I want a father, not a pal!" There are advice-givers and critics to match each of these role choices: A generation ago, Myron Brenton depicted this dilemma as follows:

> *If he concentrates on being a pal to his son, he's evading his role as authority figure. If he has a nurturant bent, some of the psychiatrists call him a motherly father. If he doesn't do any nurturing to speak of, he's accused of distancing himself from his children. If he's the sole disciplinarian, he takes on, in his youngster's eyes, the image of an ogre. If he doesn't discipline them sufficiently, he's a weak father. If he's well off and gives his children all the material advantages he didn't have, he's spoiling them, leaving them unprepared for life's hard knocks. If he's well off but doesn't spoil them the way other fathers in the community do their boys and girls, he gains the reputation of a latter-day Scrooge. . . . And, repeatedly, these accusing voices tell him that he has given up his rightful place as head of the family, as guide and mentor to his children (Brenton, 1966: 135).*

Obviously, for most fathers the performance of the father role includes some combination of these possibilities. However, from our review of socialization in Chapter 8 we can assume that the inquisitor or authority approach may be more a working- or lower-class orientation and the Santa Claus approach primarily an upper-middle-class orientation (see Biblarz, 1992).

Having begun this section with a discussion of psychological father absence, it is important to examine just how involved fathers are in childrearing. According to Michael Lamb, fathers spend 20–25 percent as much time as mothers do in direct interaction with children, with the largest discrepancy being in the area of responsibility for children's needs. Lamb adds that: "even when both mother and father are employed 30 or more hours per week, the amount of responsibility assumed by fathers appears to be negligible, just as it does when mothers are unemployed" (Lamb, 1987: 9). However, Crouter et al. report that there is an important difference between dual-earner and single-earner fathers. Dual-earner fathers are significantly more involved in child care activities that they initiate. However, higher levels of father involvement may be detrimental to the father's marital happiness (Crouter et al., 1987: 431–440). On the other hand, commitment to work does not impact negatively on a father's commitment to parenting. Perhaps this is because the father's satisfaction in work gives him a greater stake in promoting the child's development and maturity (Greenberger and Goldberg, 1989: 22–35). This, however, is not true for mothers. That is, the more mothers are committed to work, the less committed they are to parenting. The authors believe this may be because combining work and parenting is not yet normative for the wife-mother. Finally, fathers are more involved with sons than with daughters, regardless of the age of the child (Lamb, 1987: 9).

Recent sociological and psychological literature also reports the effects of father involvement on the children's development. Ehrensaft and Hochschild agree almost exactly on this point. Says Ehrensaft: "Father's involvement in the care of the children can enhance the child's development of bonding and attachment, with the equation: the more the involvement, the better the outcomes for the child" (Ehrensaft, 1987: 201). Hochschild adds that the more involved the father is, the better developed the child is intellectually and socially (1989: 236). However, two cautions are necessary: first, Ehrensaft notes that even in shared-parenting couples the father feels more separated from the child. He is more capable of setting it aside, while the mother cannot (1987: 67). Furthermore, time involvement is not the only factor influencing child outcomes. Democratic fathering encourages positive child development more than does autocratic fathering.

The critical issue, we should repeat, is that norms or guidelines for husbanding and parenting are so ill-defined that the man is compelled to determine his role behaviors in accordance with his personality and the expectations of his wife.

SECTION FOUR

WIFE-MOTHER ROLE CHOICES

As we noted in Chapters 2 and 3, women have played important economic roles in many societies, while suffering under overt patriarchy (as in traditional China). In the past 150 years, separation of economic production from family has made the homemaking wife-mother role normative, and has subordinated this role to the life and roles of the husband. Now, however, McGoldrick notes the beginnings of a change:

> *Women have always played a central role in families, but the idea that they have a life cycle apart from their roles as wife and mother is relatively recent, and still not widely accepted in our culture. The expectation has been that women would take care of the needs of others, first men, then children, then the elderly. They went from being daughter, to wife, to mother, their status defined by the male in the relationship and their role by their position in the family's life cycle (McGoldrick, 1989: 200).*

The notion of an independent life cycle is still not a reality for most women, and when it is real it is often out of necessity, not choice (e.g., the single mother).

A second general issue regarding women's roles concerns the significance of the term "feminine" or "female." Gill et al. note that because we live in a male-dominated society, "the term 'feminine' seems to connote deference to males, emotionality, and lack of assertiveness, rather than the more positive qualities that facilitate interpersonal interaction" (Gill et al., 1987: 396). Society has a long way to go to focus on the more positive aspects of what has been considered femininity.

Keeping in mind the negative elements in life cycle expectations and in the connotations of feminine, let us examine the role choices available to women today. The interplay between mass education for women, the possibility of occupation and economic independence, and both the expectation and deprecation of homemaking, has intensified the problematic aspects of women's role choices. Is the choice a dichotomous one between working or staying home, and are these equal options? Baber and Monaghan, for example, find that among college women careers are expected, but so is child-bearing. And while they do not expect to subordinate their careers to those of a partner, marriage and fertility expectations seem to be on a separate and qualitatively different plane from other role options (Baber and Monaghan, 1988: 201). In other words, for most of these women home/mother roles were not an option, but an assumption. Lucy Fischer broadens this notion to say that "a daughter's identification with her mother's role as a mother transcends their generic identity as females. . . . The status of women in our society is bound up with their roles as mothers" (Fischer, 1986: 197). However, Myra Strober notes a somewhat different balance for some women in two-earner couples:

> *Women appear to be choosing two-earner families not as a second best alternative but as a preferred life-style. Moreover, for many and perhaps most young families it is childrearing that is added on to work, rather than the other way around: the decision appears increasingly to be whether or not to have a child, rather than whether or not to work (Strober, 1988: 162).*

The complexity of women's role choices goes way beyond the simple dichotomy of employment vs. non-employment. As just noted, some see motherhood as the most basic element in women's roles; others see employment as basic, with other potential roles being adjusted. Gerson, in her book *Hard Choices*, refers to women's choices in the language of the zero-sum game. That is, the trade-offs are such that complete fulfillment is just not possible: "Whether a woman opts for work, motherhood, or some combination of the two, she must accept the costs of what is foregone as well as the benefits of what is chosen. In this sense, . . . work and family commitments are posed as competing, alternative commitments" (Gerson, 1985: 193). Still others have referred to the continuing subordination of women's roles (whatever the combination) to those of men (recall Ferree, 1987: 299). Finally, Crockenberg adds that the psychological benefits of employment vs. homemaking "depend in large part on whether or not the mother feels the role she is in was chosen, rather than a necessity or felt obligation, and on whether household and child care responsibilities are shared to her satisfaction" (Crockenberg, 1988: 109). In other words, the complexities in women's roles at present include which one is subordinated, the difficulty in trying to "have it all," the continuing pre-eminence of male roles and lack of male role sharing, and choice vs. non-choice. Many of these issues will receive further attention below.

However, let us spend a little time expanding on the theme of "psychological benefits." The 1990 Virginia Slims poll finds over half of married women saying that "how much my mate helps around the house" is the variable most closely linked to resentment (Townsend and O'Neill, 1990: 26–32). Keith and Schafer respond that feelings of fairness are less important in women's depression than "general comparisons." Even though the employed wife may feel her work burden is unfair, she may still be less depressed than the homemaker. This, however, is not true for men, for whom inequity is closely related to depression (Keith and Schafer, 1987: 208). In fact, Wethington and Kessler speak directly to this point: prior levels of psychological distress do not explain away their finding that employment benefits women emotionally (Wethington and Kessler, 1989: 527). Barnett et al. add that both job improvement and family roles seem to reduce psychological distress for women. This "role-expansion" explanation is that each role acts as a buffer for difficulties with the other (Barnett et al., 1992: 642). Several studies, beginning with Jessie Bernard's writing of a generation ago and continuing through Faludi's summary, indicate that many "afflictions disproportionately plague married women," the summary being that there are "only two primary causes for female depression: low social status and marriage" (Faludi, 1991: 37). Of course, in conjunction with the other findings, this very likely means that in today's world women most at risk for psychological and psychosomatic difficulties are unemployed homemakers with domineering and unhelpful spouses. But the discussions of role choices and distress have inevitably led us into the issue of employment. So let us focus in more detail on women's employment and the accompanying issues.

Employed Wives:
Consensus, Motives, Social Class, and Wages

In 20th century industrial society, women have increasingly entered the labor market, obtaining jobs and promotions on their own. In 1890, when the labor force of the United States was one-sixth female, few women worked for reasons other than economic necessity. Furthermore, at that time "it was unmarried daughters who composed a majority of the female labor force while today it is mothers and wives" (Mason et al., 1978: 214). Sweet and Bumpass predict that before the year 2000 there will be no difference in the employment rates of men and women (Sweet and Bumpass, 1987: 401). Annemette Sorensen divides married women's employment into four patterns:

1. *conventional,* or those who left the labor force at marriage or first birth, and never returned;
2. *interrupted,* those who left at marriage or first birth and returned after last birth;
3. *double-track,* those who returned to the labor force *before* the birth of the last child; and
4. *unstable,* or unclassifiable, such as those who have been in and out of the labor force several times (Sorensen, 1983: 311–321).

A slightly different and more frequent version of #2 is when the woman returns to the labor force when the last child enters school.

Figure 12.1 shows how dramatically women's labor force participation has changed in the past 50 years. Breadwinner-homemaker married couples have dropped from over two-thirds of all families to 20 percent. At the same time dual-earner couples have risen from under 10 percent to over 40 percent. There is every indication that change will continue in the same direction in the years ahead—as Sweet and Bumpass stated. As for labor force participation of

FIGURE 12.1   THE CHANGING LABOR FORCE PATTERNS OF FAMILIES, 1940–90

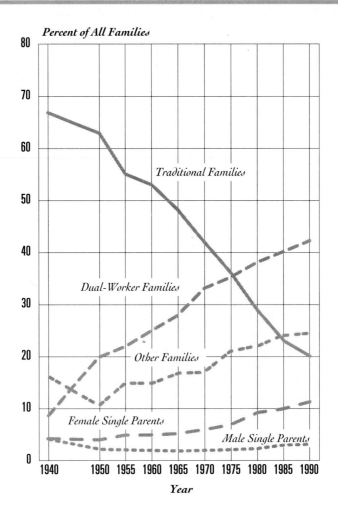

wives/mothers with children, Figure 12.2 reports that in 1985, 49 percent of mothers were employed while the youngest child was one year old or under. This was double the figure for the same mothers in 1970, and even higher than the 47 percent of mothers employed in 1970 when their youngest child was over six (see Tiedje et al., 1990: 63–72 for more on educated employed mothers with a child under one year old).

We will now look at four sets of issues regarding wives' employment and marital relationships—issues that overlap but are analytically separable: (a) role attitudes and consensus; (b) motives, or why the woman is doing what she is doing; (c) social class differences and wife's work status; and (d) women's earnings or wages.

FIGURE 12.2   PERCENT OF MARRIED WOMEN WITH CHILDREN (AND HUSBANDS PRESENT) WHO PARTICIPATE IN THE LABOR FORCE, BY AGE OF YOUNGEST CHILD, 1970–85

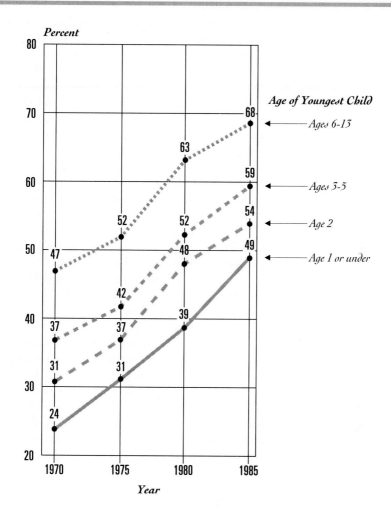

ROLE CONSENSUS   Earlier we stated that gender role congruence is important to marital adjustment. That is, if both spouses are doing what they prefer to be doing and what their spouse prefers them to be doing, adjustment is likely to be good. However, recently several researchers have found that the direction of incongruence also affects adjustment. Not surprisingly, the traditional husband/egalitarian wife couple has the lowest level of marital adjustment. However, "whether or not the wife is in the labor force, both partners report better marriages when the wife's expectations are less traditional (Li and Caldwell, 1987: 106; and Vannoy-Hiller and Philliber, 1989: 115). It is, Vannoy-Hiller and Philliber add, a matter of perception more than reality. The more traditional the wife *believes* her husband's expectations to be, the lower the quality of marriage experienced by both partners.

Thus, both consensus and direction of incongruence affect marital quality. So, apparently, does the wife's attainment and job satisfaction. Hiller and Dyehouse find, in a review of articles on dual-career marriages, that "the higher the occupational status, income, education, and job satisfaction of the wife, the more the husband approves of her working" (Hiller and Dyehouse, 1987: 791). Yet in another paper Vannoy and Philliber state that the more competitive the wife is, the lower the marital quality for both couple members (Vannoy and Philliber, 1992: 387–398). These two findings would seem to mean that the wife should be successful and satisfied but not overly competitive, especially with her husband.

Some authors have reported that husbands of employed wives are simply less satisfied with their lives, even manifesting symptoms of physical illness. Others, like Hiller and Dyehouse above, find women's employment good for their marriages. As in any such debate, it is likely that some husbands adjust well to their wives' employment and others do not. One reason some do not is that, even if the husband expresses a willingness to have his wife work, he may still define her working as threatening or as undermining his dominant role of economic provider. This is particularly true of men with low self-esteem, who simply do not want a "triple-threat" wife who has a career, is a capable home-maker, and is beautiful (Hollender and Schafer, 1981: 1119–1203). Further-more, he may be willing to have her work as long as he does not have to contribute equally to running the household. That is, if she would work 16 hours a day, half on the job and half at home, that would be fine with him. But the effect of such an uneven burden upon the marriage can only be negative.

Of course, consensus is a part of many marriages. However, Hochschild identifies three bases for marital tension: (1) between the husband's idea of what he and his wife should do at home and work, and his wife's idea about that; (2) tension between the desire to live the old-fashioned breadwinner-homemaker life, and the economic realities that make that life impossible; and (3) the tension between the family's need for care and the devaluation of the work required to provide such care—the care once provided by a homemaker (Hochschild, 1989: 204). In other words, tension involves not just disagreement between a couple's role preferences but also the hard realities and demands that life in today's world places on individuals and families.

The complexity of the consensual issue, or husbands' and wives' attitudes, is well summarized in Aldous, Osmond, and Hicks's theoretical review of the literature: "We are left," they say, "with a contradiction."

How do we reconcile this increased marital satisfaction due to women's employment outside the home with our speculation that divorce will become more common as women become less dependent on the salaries of their occupationally preoccupied husbands? The occupational commitment of women's employment, we believe, is the critical variable among the affluent. Professional women are increasingly expecting that family re-sponsibilities will be shared equally between husbands and wives. These women being occupationally committed themselves may better understand the commitment of their husbands. They would not, however, be satisfied in marriages in which busy husbands left them with major family responsibilities (Aldous et al., 1979: 251).

MOTIVES While this topic has already been mentioned briefly, we turn now to a consideration of why the wife is employed outside the home. According to Garfinkel and McLanahan, "the negative consequences of wives' employment are concentrated among couples with traditional values who find it necessary for the wife to work" (1986: 68). But what does it actually mean for a wife to be "employed out of necessity?" The important fact, it would seem, is that she *perceives* her employment to be a necessity rather than a choice. If she perceives and defines it as a necessity, all the negative intimations that her working still arouses regarding her and her husband are heightened, and her marital adjustment suffers.

The psychological benefits of employment depend almost entirely on the mother of a young child feeling that she chose to work, rather than working out of necessity or obligation (Crockenberg, 1988: 109). Motivations for working are one area in which there are racial differences. Eggebeen and Hawkins assume that single and black mothers work out of necessity, and that it is among white women with high-earning husbands that the motive of choice to foster a particular life-style occurs (Eggebeen and Hawkins, 1990: 48–66). However, they studied only white employed wives, while Paula Avioli studied white and black employed and unemployed wives with a child under three years of age. She finds the following: *white employed wives* work because of interest in participating in the labor force; *black employed wives* work out of financial need, and usually work full time; *white housewives* have little attachment to the labor force, and their husbands don't want them to work; *black housewives* have financial need, but cannot find work (Avioli, 1985: 739–745). While this fourfold distinction is clearly an oversimplification, it does raise the issues of race and class—and we will return to the latter.

Two other findings are noteworthy. Ferree comments that noneconomic motivations plus high education seem to be a required combination for an egalitarian relationship (Ferree, 1987: 291). This, however, has been questioned by those who have found black women working out of necessity, while black marriages are egalitarian. Obviously, the roles and motivations of men are equally important. This brings me to Vannoy-Hiller and Philliber's finding that a spouse's motive "to be better than his or her spouse is incompatible with emotional bonds that produce high-quality marriages" (1989: 128). What this means is that working out of necessity or by choice is only part of the issue; the other part is competitiveness vs. supportiveness.

Even the variable choice vs. necessity is more complex than we have made it out to be; after all, mixed motivations are clearly possible. Furthermore, to say that one is working "out of necessity" is actually to describe a particular instance of role dissensus: she prefers to stay home but is forced to work. For, as Jeanne Hafstrom and Marilyn Dunsing report, if many who say they are working out of necessity would work anyway, what is the significance of necessity (Hafstrom and Dunsing, 1965: 409)? In short, much of the discussion of motivation, in terms of its influence on adjustment, can be summarized as follows: the wife stays home or works because she and her husband agree that she should. In such instances adjustment is satisfactory. The wife stays home although her husband wishes she would work. This is perhaps the least frequent option empirically, but it could result in marital maladjustment. Finally—and this is the extension—the wife is employed, but either her husband wants her to stay home or else *she wishes she could stay home*, the result being a substantial likelihood of marital maladjustment.

SOCIAL CLASS   More women than men hold to an egalitarian ideology, and more middle-class than working-class couples hold to an egalitarian ideology. According to Hochschild, "most marriages were either torn by, or a settled compromise between, these two ideals" (Hochschild, 1989: 189). Much of what has been said about working by choice has implicitly referred to middle-class couples. However, Burris finds that working-class women express more satisfaction with full-time mothering than middle-class women do. In addition, working-class couples are less influenced by the male-breadwinner ideology, probably due to material necessity (Burris, 1991: 50–66). Thus, middle-class women are more likely to want to work and, being better off, are more likely to perceive themselves as working by choice.

The greater marital problems caused when the wife in the lower status family works are a direct function of the alternative presented at the end of the discussion of motives. That is, more low status wives work out of necessity, wishing they could stay home (or at least that they had the option of doing so), and more low status wives work whose husbands would prefer, on traditional ideological grounds, that they stay home. It is in the middle-class family that the combination of an equalitarian ideology and choice increases the likelihood that husbands and wife can reach a consensus regarding her role choices based on preference.

WAGES   Even when consensus is reached, several major issues still confront the highly trained married woman today. First, she may believe that she can handle both a career and the primary domestic role, but once into her career, she may find herself making demands on her husband which neither of them had foreseen. "Likewise, liberal husbands who entered marriage with the plan to share housework equally are led—by the demands of their jobs and personalities—to revert to the old pattern" (Matthaei, 1982: 309). In other words, the demands of their occupational roles cause her to change from a neo-traditional to a more equalitarian role preference, while he changes from an equalitarian preference to a neo-traditional, or even traditional, attitude. This change is, of course, a likely source of conflict. Second, even if she and her husband are in agreement, she may find it difficult to pursue a career, rather than simply "hold a job." A problem is *getting started*: there are still many more openings for women in clerical and sales jobs than in the professions and management. Her third problem is that even if she gets started on a career, she may do so at a *lower salary* level and with less possibility of promotion than a male with equal training. Scanzoni et al. make the following comment about occupations and wages:

> *Although inroads have been made in male-dominated occupations and the gap in earnings has decreased among younger, highly educated women, neither the overall gap*

between men's and women's wages nor the overall degree of occupational segregation has changed appreciably (Scanzoni et al., 1989: 190).

Catherine Fillmore adds that in Canada even legislation "has been ineffective in bringing about significant changes in women's wage rates" (Fillmore, 1990: 295). In fact, say Bryant et al., husbands of lower status may receive more income than wives of higher status (Bryant et al., 1988: 513).

But what do the data show about husbands' and wives' relative incomes? How often, in dual-earner couples, does the wife earn as much or more than her husband? In 1981, 16 percent of women in such couples earned more than their husbands, and another 2 percent earned as much (Vannoy-Hiller and Philliber, 1989: 13). This means that in the other 82 percent of dual-earner couples the husband earns more. Several partial explanations for this have been examined, including household labor, hours worked, experience, and motherhood. Shelton and Firestone report the following regarding housework and experience:

> *By estimating predicted earnings for women from their own equation but substituting men's time spent in household labor, we found that only $22.41 or 8.2% of the earnings gap between men and women could be directly attributed to the women's greater participation in household labor. . . . (In addition), women's fewer hours worked per week and fewer years of experience accounted for 21.3% of the earnings gap (Shelton and Firestone, 1989: 110–111).*

As for motherhood, Koreman and Neumark found no direct effects on wages. However, they say this is misleading, since women's lower wages cause them to curtail their labor market involvement, thereby reducing their accumulation of labor market experience and tenure (Koreman and Neumark, 1992: 233–255). Of course, this leaves much of the explanation as continuing public and private patriarchy, or greater reward for males in the marketplace.

A final comment for this section is that while most males are willing for their wives to be employed, they do *not* want them to be *overly committed* to their work. In other words, the highest marital adjustment scores are often reported when both couple members are satisfied with their jobs and the husband is high and the wife low on job salience. Even with consensus, then, the husband may not want his wife's work to "get in the way" of other things. In terms of role consensus, regardless of social class, U.S. couples are still a long way from the goals of either women's or men's liberation.

Wife's Employment, Child Care, and Child Adjustment

In 1985, over 50 percent of mothers with children under six years of age were employed (see Figure 12.2). Belsky and Eggebeen report that fulltime employment of a mother during the first or second year of the child's life is associated with lower child adjustment during the first three years of life (1991: 1083–1110). Several studies have reported possible temporary negative effects on the cognitive development of young sons of working mothers (Michel and Fuhr, 1988: 206). However, greater paternal attention may prevent such problems. As for older children, Haveman et al. report that the positive effects of extra income more than offset the negative effects of mother absence during the teenage years (Haveman et al., 1991: 149). These are a few of the recent findings.

In terms of satisfaction, control, and other aspects of child-rearing, the worst adjustment is found among those nonworking mothers who prefer to work. But do the children not feel deprived when their mother works? Employed mothers may actually spend more time with their children doing what the *children* enjoy than do unemployed mothers; that is, in high quality parent-child interaction. They may even show more love toward their children, either because they are happier working and miss their children, or perhaps because they feel a certain amount of guilt at working in the face of the lingering conventional ideology. An insightful study by David Jorgensen examined leisure contacts between the father and various family members when the mother is employed. He finds that her job cuts down on leisure time spent with her husband but that it increases the leisure activity between father and the children and also that involving the whole family unit. Thus, the "cost" in lost couple leisure activity is balanced by the "benefit" in family leisure (Jorgensen, 1977: 197–208). It would seem to follow from these findings that this is at least a partial explanation for why wife employment is harder on the marital relationship than it is on the children.

No matter how much the mother works, it is best if her hours are relatively regular and if she works from the early months after the baby's birth or else waits until the child starts school. In other words, feelings of maternal (that is, parental) deprivation, which have been of great concern to those arguing against the mother's working, are most apt to appear if the mother starts to work while the child is between ages two and five. And, of course, adequate help in the form of daycare is increasingly important as women's employment rises, and is a topic that only recently has begun to receive the attention it deserves. Daycare includes that provided by centers, by family providers, and by employers. There has been a dramatic increase in the number of children cared for in centers either all day or after school for older children (Hofferth and Phillips, 1987: 567–568). Simultaneously, the numbers of children cared for by home providers has increased. Such providers are almost always mothers themselves, an indication of the continuing secondary status of women's labor force participation (Nelson, 1987: 78–94). Family or home daycare is chosen by (1) those who work non-day shifts, (2) those with lower income, and (3) those with friends or relatives readily available. A slowly growing type of daycare is that provided by employers. In 1987 the Bureau of Labor Statistics reported that only 2 percent of 10,000 business and government organizations sponsored daycare centers for their workers, and another 3 percent covered the expenses of such centers (Aldous, 1990: 355–367). This study also reported that these services were most often found in large companies, in companies where women workers were mostly of childbearing age, and—unfortunately—were available to those who need them least, the professional and managerial staff.

Traditional observers have sought to deter use of daycare, thereby keeping the mother at home, by noting the risk to the child. However, Faludi points out that the risk to children of molestation is almost twice as high at home as in daycare.

Children are far more likely to be beaten, too, at the family hearth, . . . and the phys-
ical abuse at home tends to be of a longer duration, more severe and more traumatic
than any violence children faced in daycare centers (Faludi, 1991: 43).

Faludi adds that 20 years of research have consistently found "that if daycare
has any long-term effect on children, it seems to make them slightly more gre-
garious and independent. Daycare children also appear to be more broad-
minded about sex roles" (1991: 43). In other words, daycare is neither better
nor worse than parent care for a child's development. The determinant is the
quality and stability of the care available in relation to the ability of the parent
or parents to cope with their children.

Another issue regarding children today concerns self-care, or the "latch-
key" phenomenon. Hyman Rodman and his colleagues used a magazine-
distributed questionnaire to look at the self-care arrangements of children
under age 14. While the sample is not generalizable, they did not find strongly
negative effects of self-care on the social or psychological functioning of the
children (Rodman et al., 1985: 413–418; Rodman and Pratto, 1987: 573–578).
Of course, the finding of no difference simply means that the kind of attention
paid to the children by the parents when they are with them is more important
than the specific arrangement for the child when the parent is not there.

Given the qualifications regarding role consensus or dissensus of couple
members, motives for work, and adequacy and stability of help, Marotz-Baden
et al. summarize the effect of the mother's employment on the child as follows:

The current reviews of the literature provide relatively consistent evidence that mater-
nal employment may be related to quality parent-child interactions and role modeling
that stimulates positive aspirations and cognitive skill development. It seems evident
that maternal employment is not the relevant variable. Rather, mother's happiness
with her role, adequate supervision, and sufficient support systems for caring for chil-
dren are more critical. . . . (Marotz-Baden et al., 1979: 5–14).

SECTION FIVE

BEYOND NEOTRADITIONAL ROLES

Though at present the majority of married couples have opted for neo-traditional
roles, and some are still male-breadwinner/female-homemaker, there are other
possible choices. The three most likely to occur, in decreasing order of prevalence, are dual careers, role-sharing, and role reversal.

Dual Careers

The dual-career marriage is different from that simply involving two earners in
that both are committed to occupations in which advancement is possible. Both
couple members are likely to be highly educated, and the wife is not merely sup-
plementing the family income but is involved in a gratifying and demanding

occupation. Two criticisms have been raised regarding the definition of the dual career couple. First, Hiller and Dyehouse note that the literature has confused high job commitment, a psychological variable, with high status occupation, a sociological variable (Hiller and Dyehouse, 1987: 787). It is clearly possible to be highly committed to an occupation such as child care worker or kindergarten teacher, but this is not ordinarily what is meant by "career." A career is a high status occupation which makes possible advancement and which requires a certain amount of commitment. But the occupation, usually professional or managerial, is essential to the concept "career."

The second criticism of the concept "dual career" has been raised by Ferree. Often dual career has been confused with "role sharing," or total equality. It is, however, quite likely that most "dual career" women will in fact be "triple career," in Kay's sense, meaning that they still do the majority of the housework. The dual career model systematically misrepresents women's experiences with paid work and housework by making "career commitment" central. This, says Ferree,

> makes the conflicts women experience seem individual and psychological rather than structural because it compares working-class women, not with working-class men, but with those women in the professions who most closely conform to male professionals in their career orientation and commitment (Ferree, 1987: 291).

Our focus, then, will be on women in high status and demanding occupations, who are highly committed to their work, but who are very likely to still be the primary domestic worker as well.

The advantages of dual careers include the personal psychological payoff of self-realization, the rise in the family's standard of living, the development of independence in the children, and vicarious gratification in each other. The last may be a result of joint work, but more often it is a matter of making suggestions or merely discussing each other's work. Rosanna Hertz expands on this last advantage:

> we might posit that the dissolution of separate spheres ought to give the marital bond a more creative and supportive foundation and encourage those same elements that traditional theories present as essential to marital longevity: intimacy, trust, and nurturance. . . . In short, a dual-career marriage has the potential to be a more rather than less durable relationship than the normative model (Hertz, 1986: 213).

What does it take for a couple to develop dual careers, and what are the problems? Burke and Weir find a particular kind of personality combination in dual-career couples:

> . . . members of dual-career families when compared with members of single-career families are more self-reliant, self-sufficient individuals. And whereas the working wife may be characterized as more self-assertive than housewives, husbands of working wives can be characterized as less assertive and less concerned with power and authority than husbands of housewives (Burke and Weir, 1976: 459).

In fact, it is those couples with the most androgynous personalities that seem to do best in dual career marriages, especially if the wife's occupational attainment is greater than her husband's (Hiller and Philliber, 1982: 57–58).

Occupational attainment, however, is a central problem for the dual-career wife. Married career women have more trouble with advancement because, among other reasons: (a) Husbands still have more control over where to live, so that a woman with an opportunity for career advancement may not accept it if it would mean residential movement for her family (Gilliland, 1979: 345–358; Fortas et al., 1980: 59–65); (b) The husband in the dual-career family is more likely to travel, for example to professional meetings, than his wife; (c) Many career women still feel that housework and childcare are primarily their responsibility—in other words, they still have "triple-career" attitudes, as Ferree noted above (Yogev, 1981: 865–871); and (d) Many career women will interrupt their careers during the preschool years of their children and then try to return to work, resulting in criticism from colleagues and nonadvancement. The career mother, in fact, confronts an interesting double bind: in the view of those around her she is supposed to be caring for her home and children but is supposed to let nothing stand in the way of her career.

An interesting paper by Veronica Thomas reports that for dual career couples work is an important part of their lives, but both black and white dual-career couples "heavily depend upon their marriages for their overall happiness and psychological well-being" (Thomas, 1990: 176). Since marriage is still central, and since so many problems confront the dual-career couple, it is not surprising that marital problems and even divorce are more likely among these couples than among neotraditional and traditional couples (Philliber and Hiller, 1983: 168). Of course, one reason for this is that the couple members are equally capable of surviving economically on their own.

If, however, a couple can overcome the worst elements of patriarchy, can strike some bargains, genuinely appreciate each other's accomplishments, and have the kind of personalities described by Burke and Weir, dual careers are an alternative to neo-traditionalism.[4]

Role-Sharing

"The more the role-sharing," says Lewis and Spanier, "the more the marital quality" (Lewis and Spanier, 1979: 283). Role-sharing does not mean each spouse doing some housework and each making a little money. It does not mean dual careers with the husband still dominant. Role-sharing, as defined by Linda Haas, means that the couple members share equally in economic support of the family, in housework, and in decision-making (Haas, 1980: 289–296; Haas, 1982: 747–760). In their book on *role sharing*, Smith and Reid state their general thesis thus:

> *couples who are attempting to achieve a role-sharing marriage are struggling to define and implement emerging values about marital relationships, values that include equality of opportunity for career development and fairness in division of domestic and parental responsibilities (Smith and Reid, 1986: 3).*

Not surprisingly, women are more likely to favor role sharing than men, and are more likely to be the initiators, suggesting to their husbands that they try it.

Despite being the instigators, Haas finds that the wives have more trouble moving into the area of traditionally male chores and more trouble giving up some of the traditionally female chores. There are several reasons for this. First, more males learn "female" chores (such as cooking) as children than females learn "male" chores, such as tinkering with machinery. Secondly, some of the male household chores, such as wiring, demand more skill than traditionally female jobs like washing clothes and basic cooking. Thirdly, females may have higher standards for housework and may thus find it difficult to tolerate the male's level of household care. The issues of efficiency and standards are insightfully presented in Dave Barry's inimitable style in Feature 12.4. Finally, Haas suggests that it may be primarily a matter of self-confidence: boys are socialized to be more confident than girls, and it takes confidence to tackle new

Feature 12.4 DIRT—A REASON TO BREAK UP

(WARNING: Those of you who detest blatant and unfair—but nonetheless generally true—sexual stereotypes should leave the room at this time.)

OK. The major issue facing a man and woman who decide to live together is: Dirt. I'm serious. Men and women do not feel the same way about dirt at all. Men and women don't even see dirt the same way. Women, for hormonal reasons, can see individual dirt molecules, whereas men tend not to notice them until they join together in clumps large enough to support commercial agriculture. There are exceptions, but over 85 percent of all males are legally classifiable as Cleaning Impaired.

This can lead to serious problems in a relationship. Let's say a couple has decided to divide the housework absolutely even-steven. Now, when it's the woman's turn to clean, say, the bathroom, she will go in there and actually clean it. The man, on the other hand, when it's his turn, will look around and, because he is incapable of seeing the dirt, will figure nothing major is called for so he'll maybe flush the toilet and let it go at that. Then the woman will say: "Why didn't you clean the bathroom? It's filthy!" And the man, whose concept of "filthy" comes from men's rooms in bars where you frequently see bacteria the size of cocker spaniels frisking around, will have no idea what she's talking about.

I have a writer friend, Clint Collins, who once proposed that as a quick "touch-up" measure, you could cut a piece of 2-by-4 the same width as the vacuum cleaner and drag it across the carpet to produce those little parallel tracks, which, as far as Clint could tell, were the major result of vacuuming. (Clint was unaware for the first 10 or 15 years of his marriage that vacuum cleaners had little bags in them. He speculated the dirt went through the electrical cord and into the wall.)

Dave Barry, "Dirt—a Reason to Break Up," *Wisconsin State Journal*, November 2, 1987. From *Dave Barry's Guide to Marriage and/or Sex*.

responsibilities and tasks as an adult and to relinquish other tasks that have been a source of self-esteem.

It required constant vigilance on the part of Haas's role-sharing couples not to fall back into a division of labor based on efficiency, that is, who did a task best or with the most ease (what Rossi and Rossi call the *groove of competencies*) (Rossi and Rossi, 1990: 149). The problem with such efficiency is that it quickly slipped into a male-dominance position, since there were more female chores, and they were so often less skilled and lower status tasks. Besides the wives' problems in giving up old tasks and taking on new ones and the "efficiency-division" problem, other major problems involved what chores to do, whose turn it was to do them, and conflicts between the spouses' jobs and between job and home duties. John DeFrain's study of androgynous couples includes the following list of problems: lack of sufficient job flexibility to accommodate role-sharing, adequate daycare, and — as Haas and Barry noted — different housekeeping standards (DeFrain, 1979: 242). Yet, says Haas, despite all these difficulties, her couples were succeeding fairly well at role-sharing. Why? Because of their commitment to an arrangement they felt had the potential of producing great benefits. These benefits include virtually all the aims of women's and men's liberation: that is, making it possible for both males and females to be "whole" or complete people. And it should not be surprising, in light of the Russian experience referred to in Chapter 3, that more problems arise in trying to equalize the domestic scene than in equalizing the economic provider function.

Role Reversal

In the discussion of women's roles, the choice "to work or not to work" was dealt with at great length; such an issue was not raised in the discussion of men's roles. The reason is obvious: for the vast majority of men it is a foregone conclusion that they will at least try to find a job. Even the liberation movements do not call for the freedom to reverse the traditional roles, only to meet in the middle. However, genuine freedom of choice would have to at least include this as an option, and, if that were the case, it would not be newsworthy when it occurred. But until recently it still made the papers, carrying with it overtones that "there must be something wrong with those people." After all, the stereotypical attitude would go, why would a male voluntarily take on such a role? When you think about it, such a question is another put-down for the homemaking role.

SECTION SIX

CONCLUSION: NONCHANGE AND THE VALUE OF CHOICE

Differences between traditional and neotraditional families have been catalogued in this chapter, and the conclusion is that most U.S. families are neotraditional, with the traditional model still widespread among the working and lower classes. How do these types look when they are placed upon the marital

FIGURE 12.3   MARITAL ROLES IN THE CONTEMPORARY UNITED STATES IN RELATION
TO THE MARITAL ROLE CONTINUUM

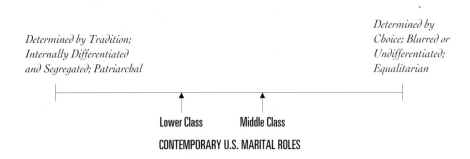

Determined by Tradition;
Internally Differentiated
and Segregated; Patriarchal

Determined by
Choice; Blurred or
Undifferentiated;
Equalitarian

Lower Class   Middle Class
CONTEMPORARY U.S. MARITAL ROLES

role continuum of Chapter 5? (see Figure 12.3.) Unquestionably, the middle-class family is closer to the "choice-blurred-equalitarian" end of the continuum than is either the working- or lower-class family. Yet many middle-class marriages are still quite traditional, and neo-traditional marriages cannot be considered entirely open and choice-based as long as the traditional ideology defines certain options as deviant and unacceptable—an example being the aforementioned husband-homemaker—wife-breadwinner choice.

Is the U.S. family going to stabilize at the point of neo-traditionalism, with perhaps some increase in dual-career families? The answer to this question involves the patriarchy still found in male attitudes and society's structures. Until husbands and society play a larger role in home-related tasks, role behaviors ant attitudes will continue to be inconsistent, and women will continue to be in a double bind. "The ideal goal," Carl Degler states, "would be one in which the values of family and the realization of women's individuality could be reconciled" (Degler, 1980: 473). This chapter has catalogued the difficulties in achieving that reconciliation.

One final comment concerns the vocabulary employed to describe the equalitarian marriage—both in the popular press and in the sociological literature. We have, throughout Chapters 11 and 12, used the language and literature at our disposal: *ambiguities, problems, ill-defined, dilemmas* (see Gerson, 1985: 193; Baber and Monaghan, 1988). Such terms have been loaded with negative connotations. These same historical changes and conditions could be described by the terms freedom, opportunity, emancipation, challenge. In fact, as Letha Scanzoni notes, among conservatives today "innovation, negotiation, freedom to choose how one wants to pattern one's own marriage and family life are considered signs of moral decay" (Scanzoni, 1988: 134). Freedom, as Erich Fromm pointed out, may give rise to fear and anxiety, and the desire to escape back into certainty and—in this case—patriarchy (Fromm, 1941). Even the popular press, dominated by males or by those raised in a male-dominated society, is likely to see male control as desirable.

On the other hand, it is certainly possible that once the contemporary family has escaped its midstream position, abandoning the lingering elements of a traditional patriarchy, the freedom to choose for oneself may result in a heightened fulfillment and development of the unique potentialities of each person and marriage. Oscar and Mary Handlin express it this way:

> *Freedom carries with it obligations—for decisions, for choices, and for unexpected experiences. It threatens routine and order, breeds change, conflict, and insecurity. Yet some men and women seek it in preference to the comfort of unvarying habit, to the certainty of infallible authority, to the peace of a rigid system which admits no questions and holds each individual in place (Handlin and Handlin, 1971: v).*

Regardless of whether one sees increasing freedom as opportunity or problem, one should be cognizant of the subtle value implications of the terms being used to describe the now and future role choices of men and women.

Marriage: Communication and Satisfaction

CHAPTER 13

Much of the adjustment and role behavior information found in Chapters 11 and 12 can be usefully interpreted from a communications perspective. Communication includes both what we say and the way we say it. Some families communicate constantly and totally, while others are much less communicative. Families live by rules that they have developed, and that can be changed either by agreement or by one member breaking them. Communication can lead to conflict, but it can also lead to problem-solving. In the latter part of the chapter we look at sources of marital satisfaction over the life cycle, and types of adjusted marriages.

COMMUNICATION IN THE FAMILY

According to P. Watzlawick and his colleagues, it is impossible *not* to communicate (Watzlawick et al. 1967: 51). Communication is basic to self-disclosure, rapport, and empathy; and we noted that these are essential to mate selection in the United States today. Harold Raush, Ann Greif, and Jane Nugent state the importance of communication thus:

> *When each family must evolve its own destiny, it faces tasks not only of developing its own rules but also of defining how and by whom these rules are made and the conditions for change. A massive burden is thus placed on communication (Raush, 1979: 469).*

Many of the adjustment problems and much of the role behavior discussed in Chapters 11 and 12 can be usefully interpreted from a communications perspective.

Characteristics of Communication

The two major elements in communication are *what* is said and the *way* it is said. Students of communication have called these elements "communication" and "metacommunication," or the "message" and the "metamessage." One element is the verbal communication itself; the other is the way in which it is conveyed. It is possible to say, "Isn't it a beautiful morning?" for example, in many different ways. We can say it enthusiastically and have people agreeing with us. Or we can say it solemnly and have people wonder what is the matter. Or we can say it when the rain is pouring and the wind is gusting to 50 miles per hour, and our listener will know we are being sarcastic. Sarcasm is, then, giving a message that is so inconsistent with agreed-upon understandings and with our metamessage that the listener knows we do not mean it. But think of the number of times we have heard the questions, "Are you being sarcastic?" or "Are you serious?" The reason is that communication is easier when the message and metamessage are consistent or congruent. A husband may say, "What's wrong?" and his wife may reply, "Nothing at all." Yet her metamessage may convey: "Plenty is wrong, but I'm not going to tell *you*." It is quite possible for family members to develop mechanisms of communication that others simply cannot translate, as when a husband taps the floor three times with his heel to let his wife know that it's time to leave a social gathering. Communication is more than words: it includes demeanor, circumstance, facial expression, biases of the listener, and nonverbal cues (on the last, see Nolles, 1987: 149–175).

Watzlawick said: "It is impossible not to communicate," or "One cannot *not* communicate." To this we should, however, respond. "Yet, but it is possible not to translate or to mistranslate." The same message may be translated in very different ways by different listeners. At a party one might say: "It's about time we took the need for daycare seriously, so that women could have the opportunity for equal employment with men." A male hearing the comment might think:

"He's one of those feminists, trying to take away all of our advantages." A female listener might think: "He's a chauvinist; he's in favor of daycare so he won't have to take a hand in caring for children himself." The words were the same, but they were translated two different ways.

A particularly difficult form of communication to deal with is the double bind, the message in which the communicator gives the respondent two opposing commands so that nothing the latter can do is "right." The double bind involves a set of mutually exclusive injunctions. "A typical example," say Raush, Greif, and Nugent "is that of the mother who, having asked her child for a hug, stiffens and withdraws as he approaches and then to the child's subsequent withdrawal responds, 'Don't you love your mother?'" (Raush et al., 1979: 473). Suzanne Retzinger gives the example of David and Colleen to show how the double bind may be used to maintain a conflictful style of communication: "Although David gives the appearance of being sexist, he expressed several times that he would prefer Colleen to be independent, direct, and decisive. But his manner says the opposite; he sabotages this type of behavior when it does occur" (Retzinger, 1991: 115). Other examples of the double bind in the family are such comments and questions as "I need your help," "You fouled it up," "Why aren't you more helpful?" and "Why can't you do it right?" A double bind may occur over time rather than all at once. That is, one message is given at one point in time and the other later.

Reception of a message is very often in terms of what we want to hear. If we are in love, we may interpret positively whatever we hear from our partner; later, we may begin to hear the same person as he or she really is. Most family fights are over the metamessage, not the message, as exemplified by the question, "What did you mean by that?" Or there may be a missing shade of meaning, as might have happened in the old radio show, "The Bickersons":

> *"George, do you love me?"*
> *"Yes, I love you."*
> *"Say it again."*
> *"I love you!"*
> *"You don't say it like you mean it!"*
> *"Oh no, not this again—turn over and go to sleep!"*

Outcomes: Balance, Conflict, and Types of Family Communication

BALANCE   Every family develops an equilibrium of some kind, though it may be healthy or pathological. This equilibrium is developed by means of feedback, as the family members respond positively or negatively to each other's communications. This equilibrium can be based on complementarity or symmetry. In the former case, one family member gives orders and another obeys or one shouts and the other speaks calmly. In symmetry both may shout, or both may give orders, or both may speak softly. The relations between parents and offspring are complementary during the early years, with the parents in command. Later, the offspring may come to dominate, though it is more likely that the generations will arrive at a symmetrical relationship of adult to adult. A difficult family task is to change from complementarity to symmetry, or vice versa. As children grow up and leave home, for example, the parents must learn to stop communicating with them as children and to deal with them symmetrically. Or, if the parents become old and mentally infirm, the offspring may have to make the painful transition to treating them in a complementary and subordinate fashion. Or, when a middle-aged homemaker becomes committed to the goals of women's liberation for herself, she may be faced with the task of convincing her husband to accept a more symmetrical relationship. Raush, Greif, and Nugent argue that the most mature marital relationship involves a complex mixture of complementary and symmetrical communications, with each member of the couple having the opportunity to express a variety of personality facets (Raush et al., 1979: 483).

CONFLICT It would be an oversimplification to assert that open communication leads to marital happiness. Intimacy breeds negative as well as positive communication; communication may be problem-producing instead of solution-producing. The relation between conflict and problem-solving is interesting. Prior to marriage the two are closely related. However, Kelly et al. find that "once couples have been married for a while there is no tendency for couples who have high conflict to make greater efforts at problem-solving (Kelly et al., 1985: 167). And, unfortunately, the absence of positive efforts at problem-solving are associated with later divorce (Buehlman et al., 1992: 295–318).

Conflict, says Retzinger, is dysfunctional when it threatens an equilibrium based on rigidity (Retzinger, 1991: 4–5). In other words, separation gives rise to conflict, more than vice versa. And there are many situations, such as women trying to change men's views on gender roles, that run the risk of confronting such rigidity (see Vannoy-Hiller and Philliber, 1989: 31). But to say that rigidity = conflict = divorce is to ignore the other side of the equation. Conflict, after all, may lead to problem-solving and growth. Samuel Vuchinich notes several ways normal families manage conflict:

> *First, many conflicts (36%) are 'nipped in the bud' through accepting corrections or ignoring oppositional initiations. Second, there are egalitarian conflict-initiation rights that give all family members the right to initiate conflicts. This promotes open communication and allows everyone to feel as though they 'have some clout.' Third, once a conflict is under way, there is a stable probability of continuing the conflict . . . at each successive turn. . . . Fourth, specific social arrangements are used to end about 35% of the conflict episodes. But most conflicts (61%) end in a standoff, which may be the simplest way to get out of conflicts (Vuchinich, 1987: 600).*

Michael Argyle and Adrian Furnham, studying sources of satisfaction and conflict in various kinds of long-term relationships, find that one's relationship with one's spouse provides both the greatest amount of conflict and of satisfaction. They also conclude that a high level of conflict is normal in marriage (Argyle and Furnham, 1983: 481–493). Thus, communication is necessary to family equilibrium, but it may result in conflict, with either positive or negative results, depending, says Retzinger, "on the ability to acknowledge feelings that signal the state of the bond" (Retzinger, 1991: 191). Extreme cases are the couples described by John Cuber and Peggy Harroff, who stay together, but are "conflict-habituated" (1965). The five types of adjusted marriages described by these authors will be discussed at the end of this chapter.

TYPES OF FAMILY COMMUNICATION   Some families avoid communication; others are constantly engaged. In "engaged" families, when a message enters from one member, it immediately zips through to the other side, so that, for example, by the time dinner is over everyone knows that Suzie failed her biology exam. At the other extreme are families where no one tells anyone else anything, the result being isolation within the family. Vannoy-Hiller and Philliber describe this situation thus:

> *We expect people to disclose and to be transparent in families, but there is a great deal of evidence to show that this is not the case. Children do not know parents; parents do not know what their children think or do; husbands and wives are often strangers (Vannoy-Hiller and Philliber, 1989: 80).*

Of course, each family member may have a confidant outside the family, or some people may confide in no one.

Extending the distinction between communicative and uncommunicative families, David Reiss distinguishes three modes by which families process information. First is *collaborative effectiveness*, with the family members pooling information in order to come to a shared solution or conclusion. Second is *isolated independence*, the uncommunicative family in which each family member processes information on his or her own. Third is *closed-in hyperresponsiveness*, which is a high mode of communication, like the first one. However, the communication is about each other, rather than processing the information either individually or together (Reiss, 1981: 55–56). These communicational approaches are part of what Reiss calls the "family paradigm," or its unique set of shared constructs, expectations, and fantasies about its social world.

Individual communication styles have been distinguished as *conventional* (such as cocktail banter and pure sociability), *speculative* (analytic), *controlling* (high, one-way verbalization), and *contactful* (open, self-disclosure) (Hawkins et al., 1980: 585–593). Husbands value the contactful style in their wives, but prefer to use the controlling style for themselves, although their wives prefer for their husbands *not* to use it.

The tendency in the working and lower classes in the recent past has been to avoid much contactful communication, especially by husbands. However, the amount of self-disclosure may not be what matters to marital satisfaction, but simply that the amount of communication is perceived as similar and desirable (Davidson et al., 1983: 93–102). After all, privacy may be what is desired by the working-class husband. However, according to Hawkins et al. there has been a change so that increasingly at present "all couples, regardless of class, espouse a modern ideal of intimacy (respectful confrontation of feelings) in marital communications" (Hawkins et al., 1979: 489). Whether this would hold for families deep in poverty is still questionable.

Besides communication by social class, another distinction in couple communication concerns length of marriage. We noted earlier that Kelly et al. found

married couples making less effort to resolve conflicts than those not yet married. Susan Crohan adds that both black and white couples in the first year of
marriage who use destructive conflict styles are in danger of marital instability
later on (Crohan, 1992: 100). Zietlow and Sillars report very important differences in marital communication and conflict styles over the life course:

> *Generally, retired couples rated marital problems as non-salient and their conversa-
> tions were non-conflictive. However, those among the retired groups who perceived
> salient, unresolved problems in the marriage were extremely conflictive, producing
> chains of reciprocal confrontative statements. Middle-aged couples were also non-
> conflictive and non-committal in their discussions but, unlike the retired couples,'
> middle-aged couples became analytic when marital problems were salient. Young cou-
> ples had a comparatively intense, engagement style of interaction, characterized by al-
> teration between analytic, confrontative and humorous remarks. The results suggest
> that marital communication is shaped by a combination of developmental, life stage,
> and cohort influence (Zietlow and Sillars, 1988: 223).*

They add the comment that "for the elderly in our sample, communication appeared to be a reflection of the relationship, not a tool for adjusting it" (Zietlow
and Sillars, 1988: 243).

It is possible for there to be avoidance and engagement within the same
family. The parents may communicate intimately with each other, and their offspring with each other, but there may be almost no intimate messages shared
across the generations. Or the males may talk and the females confide, but with
almost no sharing across gender. Or one family member may be isolated, while
the others communicate openly and freely, often about the isolated person. Paul
Rosenblatt and Sandra Titus studied in some detail the need of families for both
togetherness and apartness. Because of the intimacy and togetherness norm
noted by Hawkins, Weisberg, and Ray above, it may be extremely difficult for
family members to admit that they need communicational distance as well. A
compelling togetherness norm, say Rosenblatt and Titus, is that family members should take at least some meals together. Family members may overcome
this norm by restricting interaction while eating by watching television, reading
or, in the case of the parents, by focusing on the children (Rosenblatt and Titus,
1976: 367–380). The issue of communication avoidance and engagement in the
family is almost synonymous with that of privacy in colonial and postcolonial
America, discussed in Chapter 4.

Rules, Rule Change, and Deviance

"When a set of people interact over a period of time, they come to share expectations about the way in which *each other* will behave" (Harris, 1983: 33). These
shared expectations are the family rules, and they cover everything from the habit
patterns of Chapter 11 to who is allowed to shout and under what conditions.
When all the rules are known and all the family members are abiding by them, the
family is in equilibrium. "Knowing" the rules does not mean that they have ever
been verbalized, much less that they are written down somewhere. What it means
is that they are part of the family's "construction of reality" (Reiss, 1981: 181).

Why are rules required? Because no system, including the family, can operate without shared understandings, without shared definitions of how to behave and how not to behave.

It is possible—even necessary—for a family to change its rules from time to time. Then the rules may change from *implicit* to *explicit*, or *expressed*. If a husband loses his job, for example, it may not be possible for the family to continue the same standard of living as before; therefore, they may have a family conference at which the issue is how to cut back expenses. Or a wife may say: "I think we should open up our marriage, so that we can respond to other people sexually." If the husband says: "I've been thinking about the same thing. Let's try it and continue to communicate about our feelings," what they have agreed to do is to try to change the rules. Rules and rule change have been called *first-order structure* and *first-order change*. The crucial question about first-order change is, "Has there been communication so that everyone in the system knows where everyone else is?" Constant communication is necessary as a system attempts first-order change.

But suppose the husband in the above example says: "No! I don't want you involved with other men." The wife has two options: she can operate by the old rules, or she can deviate from the couple's rules without her husband's agreement. If she does the latter, she has introduced behavior to the family that is not covered by its rules. With such a change, called *second-order change*, the couple members do not know where they are going or even how to communicate about it. For that matter, should they even try to communicate about it?

Another reason why such deviance is so difficult for a family to handle is that it is almost impossible for the person causing the problem to also be the solution. So, for example, in the case of the discovery of an extramarital sexual affair, how can the spouse who deviated, or who caused the problem, also play the problem-solving role that he or she may have played for many years for the offended spouse? Or, for example, a teenager may deviate from parental expectations and rules, with the result that the parents may feel that they have only two options: first, they try to force their offspring back in line with their rules, which seldom works, or second, they decide that their rules were not that important anyway, which is hard to admit.

Second-order change almost always tests family commitments and flexibility. The family flounders, trying to determine how to reinstate the rules or what new rules to instate. Second-order change, or deviance, is one of the cases where open communication may not necessarily result in a happier or better adjusted marriage, though it may. It is clearly easier to effect change by discussing and changing the rules in advance. However, if a couple or family are capable of working through a second-order change, it may result in growth and a deepening of a marriage, rather than in chaos and disorganization. Issues of crisis and disorganization will arise again in Chapter 16.

Miscellaneous Conclusions on Communication

Based upon the concepts and family types of the preceding discussion is the following series of axioms or conclusions regarding family communication.

TRANSMISSION   The communication style of the family one is raised in is carried through life by the individual. Avoiding or engaged, complementary or symmetrical, hyperresponsive or collaborative, the style of your family of orientation is likely to become your style. If you try to change it, you will fail unless you understand the underlying dynamics. Much of the responsibility for breakup during the first few years of marriage may lie in the inability of the newly married couple to integrate two very different communication and rule patterns. Prior to marriage such differences may seem humorous or inconsequential; after marriage they may result in conflict and disintegration.

COUPLES DON'T EXIST; MARRIED INDIVIDUALS DO   Because of the difficulties of avoidance, metacommunication, and translation, spouses may in fact be involved in very different marriages. A husband may be perfectly satisfied every week to spend five days at home and the weekend with his mother 50 miles away and may think his wife is satisfied with the arrangement. His wife, however, may be very upset about his tie to his absent mother's apron strings and may be attempting to convey it in subtle ways. Because of transmission and translation problems, two people seldom share the same marriage. After all he is married to her, and she to him. There is a needed caution regarding the notion that the family constructs a shared reality: shared, yes, but also uniquely viewed through the eyes of each family member.

THINKING, FEELING, ACTING, AND SENSING   Western societies, such as that of the United States, tend to emphasize "thinking" and "acting" types of communication. We attempt to be or we think we are rational in our communication patterns. Higher status Western families tend to be more oriented in this direction than other groups. And European societies differ in the extent to which negative emotional expression is seen as an acceptable, even desirable, part of family life. Eastern religions and philosophies try to strike more of a balance between all four bases for communication and relationship. There are also gender differences in these four, as we shall see.

GENDER DIFFERENCES IN COMMUNICATION   Women have traditionally been permitted a wider range of metamessages, since they have not been taken as seriously. However, women have also been more hemmed in by demands (or rules) than men. That is, they have been more individually embedded in their families. Tannen notes that there has been no parallel stereotype to the "henpecked husband," since it has been acceptable for husbands to be overbearing (Tannen, 1990: 152). She adds that women being labelled as nags "may result from the interplay of men's and women's styles, whereby many women are inclined to do what is asked of them and many men are inclined to resist even the slightest hint that anyone, especially a woman, is telling them what to do" (Tannen, 1990: 31). In addition, the wife has been more involved in family maintenance than the husband, which is one reason for her greater degree of self-disclosure and support behavior (Rusbult, 1987: 223).

On another point, in heterosexual groups, women tend to ask questions and men answer them. Having answers for everything, incidentally, is one of the expectations or demands from which Warren Farrell and the liberationists are concerned with freeing men (Farrell, 1975). There are, says Morton Perlmutter, three messages that are basic to human communication: "When you . . .";

"I feel . . ."; "I want . . . ." Thus we might say, "When you (drum your fingers), I feel (nervous); I want you (to stop)." Traditionally the sexes have differed in their use of these three messages. Women have stopped with the first two, leaving it up to the men to solve the problem. The man, on the other hand, has simply said: "I want you to stop," and has left it up to her to figure out what she is doing that he doesn't like. Men have especially avoided the second: "I feel." After all, men are not supposed to "feel." These gender differences in communication patterns, though overstated and changing, are one area in which the liberation movements have already had some effect, though there is still much sexism in conflict communication. Whether that effect will increase in the future remains to be seen.[1]

Communication, in conclusion, can help resolve marital and family difficulties, or it can result in conflict. But regardless of the outcome, it seems virtually impossible, as Watzlawick says, *not* to communicate. It may even be, as Perlmutter claims, that the *only* phenomena in relationships, including family relationships, are communicational.

SECTION TWO

MARITAL HAPPINESS AND SATISFACTION

Marital satisfaction is another of those areas, like family power, that is as difficult to deal with as it is important. And, like the study of power, it suffers from both conceptual and measurement problems. Methodologically, the question has been raised of whether several important studies of satisfactions and tensions were in fact examining positive and negative feelings instead. Conceptually, the terms adjustment, satisfaction, quality, happiness, and stability have been employed synonymously at times and divergently at other times. When specific, divergent meanings have been attached to them, stability has been restricted to whether the marriage is together or broken up, adjustment has referred to the processes of accommodation and adaptation referred to in Chapter 11, and happiness and satisfaction have been distinguished only by the former being a little more intense and less rational than the latter. We will restrict ourselves to notions of satisfaction and happiness, using them interchangeably, and will use only a few references to adjustment until the end of the chapter. The foci will be employment and children in relation to satisfaction, gender differences in marital satisfaction, and changing satisfaction over the marital life cycle.

Employment and Marital Satisfaction

For men, marital satisfaction is found less often among the extremely successful and the extremely unsuccessful; it is also found less often among those highly satisfied with their jobs and those highly dissatisfied. In other words, an average amount of job success and satisfaction is related to the highest level of marital satisfaction, according to Aldous, Osmond, and Hicks (1979: 244, 248). Perhaps the most successful and the least successful are more likely to get static from spouse and family, one for being too work-involved and the other for not being involved enough (recall the discussion of husband role choices in Chapter 12). It is, furthermore, the intrinsic characteristics of work, such as enjoying it and finding it meaningful, that are related to marital satisfaction, not extrinsic benefits, such as income and status. Although the issue is somewhat different for women, due to the neo-traditional role situation in which the U.S. family finds itself, they also have a curvilinear pattern, with part-time employed women being more satisfied with their marriages than either the full-time employed or the unemployed. Perhaps, again, a higher proportion of part-time employed women feel they have control over their work situation, making it possible to balance it with the demands and privileges of the family. An interesting study by Patricia Freudiger reports that both employed and previously employed wives find their greatest life satisfaction in their marriages, not in their current or previous jobs. However, for those women who have never been employed since marriage, what matters most to their satisfaction is the financial provision and occupational prestige of their husbands (Freudiger, 1983: 216–217). However, the housewife's emphasis on her husband's job may place a strain on him. The key word for both sexes regarding work and marital satisfaction seems to be *balance*, emphasizing neither work nor family unduly.

Children and Marital Satisfaction

As noted in Chapter 7, children are an economic burden today, but they are still highly valued. In the research, however, there is disagreement as to whether couple satisfaction is greater when the children are very young than when they are teenagers, or vice versa. But, in general, couples currently raising children are less satisfied with their marriages than either those who had never had children or those whose children had left home (Glenn and McLanahan, 1982: 63–72). Crnic and Greenberg's study of mothers with very young children shows that hassles between mother and child may have general effects, "with potential for creating or perpetuating parental distress, family dysfunction, and disruption in children's development" (Crnic and Greenberg, 1990: 1635). Furthermore, according to Abbott and Brody, wives with two male children report lower levels of marital cohesion and satisfaction than either mothers of daughters or childless wives. Their plausible explanation is that young boys are simply more demanding temperamentally and behaviorally than girls (Abbott and Brody, 1985: 77–84).

At the end of the child-rearing period, Elizabeth Harkins found a slight negative effect on parental well-being as the last child departed from home. This disappeared within two years following the event. The effect was more negative if the children did not leave home at the expected time (Harkins, 1978: 549; Targ, 1979: 465–471). Thus, if children left before the end of high school or stayed for several years after that, it was more negative for the marriage than their leaving at the expected time.

Finally, in their book *Families in Later Life*, Troll, Miller, and Atchley claim that parents should

> *feel rather expansive and in high spirits before they have children, more constricted and pinched during the time they are raising the children and educating them, freer again once the children can be more self-supporting . . . (Troll et al., 1979: 44).*

As Umberson and Gove put it, the benefits of parenting depends on the child achieving and maintaining independence from the parents (Umberson and Gove 1989: 440–462). The overall effect of children, especially older children, on marital happiness and satisfaction seems to be negative, though the picture is not altogether clear.

Gender, Marriage, and the Life Cycle

The issue of children and marital satisfaction has already introduced a life cycle approach. General life satisfaction and happiness increases for men over the life cycle, according to an interesting older study by Joseph Harry. The source of satisfaction, however, changes as the man passes through the different stages. Young married men define happiness in terms of their relationship with their spouse. With preschool children in the home, men redefined the bases for happiness to include familial elements, especially the young children. Fathers of teenagers define happiness in terms of leisure and excitement, with the latter being the key term. This may, of course, be an attempt to recapture the youth that they see mirrored in their own teenagers. Finally, when the children are gone, the element of excitement again becomes negligible, with marital and extrafamilial involvements primary (Harry, 1976: 289–296). Harry's two most intriguing findings are: first, the importance of excitement in the life of the man in his mid-forties with teenage offspring, and second, the fact that, except in cases of widowerhood or divorce, men's general happiness seems to rise over the life cycle. The "mid-life crisis" issue cannot be passed over by simply stating the word "excitement." A study by Cohen, for example, indicates that middle-aged males are concerned about their physical deterioration, their unfulfilled aspirations, and their changing family roles (Cohen, 1979: 465–471). Yet for most males the result seems to be a "mellowing out," rather than a serious upset or dissatisfaction. In a more recent study, women were also found to have mid-life identity concerns, which may lead both to distance from their children and to marital disenchantment (Steinberg and Silverberg, 1987: 751–760). Unlike Harry, they find the husband's mid-life concerns reflected in marital unhappiness. As for the "empty-nest" period, there is general agreement that marital happiness is greater than at any time since before the children were born. White and Edwards state that emptying the nest is associated with significant improvement in marital happiness (1990: 235–242).

Research on gender differences in satisfaction over the life cycle is contradictory. Mary Alice Beyer and Robert Whitehurst compare men's and women's satisfaction, confirming Harry's findings for men. Their study suggests a basic trend: men and women experience such different modes of adaptation that there is an essential reversal of positive and negative meaning for the two sexes. Men seem to experience negative effects early in marriage, while women begin marriage more positively. As the middle years approach, according to Beyer and Whitehurst, this situation reverses itself with men becoming more positive in their marital experience and women more negative as length of marriage increases. Chadwick, Albrecht, and Kunz report an interesting and somewhat parallel finding: the longer a couple are married, the greater the husband's willingness to marry the same person again. But this is not true for wives (Beyer and Whitehurst, 1976: 109–120; Chadwick et al., 1976: 439). Recall that, according to Bernard, marriage is a "sick" state of affairs for women.

In other words, the supposed curvilinear pattern over the life cycle may be a result of not separating by gender, since both sexes seem to be fairly low in satisfaction when the children are in school but living at home. But the women seem to have "started high," dropped down, and leveled off, while the men started lower, and in later life gained in satisfaction. Yet in all this, one is reminded of the discussion of complementary needs in mate selection, which was singularly inconclusive. When these dissenting results are combined with the complaints about the methodology of life-cycle studies, the weight of evidence is in Beyer and Whitehurst's direction, but not very strongly.

SECTION THREE

FIVE TYPES OF ADJUSTED MARRIAGES

In recent years there have been several excellent categorizations of different types of marriages, especially the Circumplex Model developed by David Olson and others. However, the categories that best fit the discussion of communication earlier in this chapter are found in Cuber and Harroff's generation-old study of *The Significant Americans*. They asked how many of their married respondents had ever contemplated divorce, and from their sample, they chose only the 107 men and 104 women who answered "Never." These 211 were then divided into five categories of adjusted or functioning marriages. Here are their five types.

PASSIVE-CONGENIAL   In passive-congenial marriages there is no spark or excitement. It has always been that way. The couple members are realistic and accepting of the lack of vitality in their marriages, never having expected anything else. They also find it acceptable because many of the friends' marriages are the same way. Such a matter-of-fact marriage can give the individual independence, security, and the freedom, time, and energy to spend on other things. Said a very busy and committed physician:

I don't know why everyone seems to make so much about men and women and marriage. Of course, I'm married and if anything happened to my wife, I'd get married again. I think it's the proper way to live. It's convenient, orderly, and solves a lot of problems. But there are other things in life. . . . I'll bet if you talked to my wife you wouldn't get any of that "trapped housewife" stuff from her either. Now that the children are grown, she finds a lot of useful and necessary work to do in this community. She works as hard as I do (Cuber and Harroff, 1965: 54).

\CONFLICT-HABITUATED   Couple members in conflict-habituated marriages fight about everything. Sometimes such a pattern has developed in the course of the marriage, while other times it can be traced back to the pre-marital period. The couple members argue about politics, about where their children should go to college, about finances, about sex, and about what they did and didn't say. The tension and conflict are controlled, in the sense that each knows how the game is to be played. As one of the offspring was quoted as saying, "Dad and Mom are at it again." These are not couples, remember, that are contemplating divorce; they are married and expect to remain so.

Some psychiatrists have gone so far as to suggest that it is precisely the deep need to do psychological battle with one another which constitutes the cohesive factor insuring continuity of the marriage. . . . And it can, and does for some, last for a whole lifetime (Cuber and Harroff, 1965: 46).

Earlier in the chapter we spoke of "engaged" and "avoiding" couples; these couples are very definitely engaged. They may, furthermore, be operating by the rules or the first-order structure. In fact, their running conflict may be what brings stability, even satisfaction to their marriage (see Feature 13.1). But to say that they have an "adjusted" marriage does not mean they cannot imagine anything better (Argyle and Farnham, 1983: 481–493). It just means that their conflict has become a habitual part of their marriage.

\DEVITALIZED   Devitalized marriages are extremely common. They are marriages that "have seen better days." As the term indicates, the marriage used to be exciting and vital, but now it is not. In fact, at present it is hardly distinguishable from the passive-congenial; the main difference is that these people have memories of the way it was. Some couple members are bitter and wish it could be better. But, again, they console themselves with the judgment that "marriage is like this—except for a few oddballs and pretenders who claim otherwise" (Cuber and Harroff, 1965: 50). That is, they assume that most other people's marriages are like theirs. A not-inconsequential number of the passive-congenial and devitalized do not just have a poor sex life, they have no sex life at all. Living in a post-Freudian day when sexuality is assumed to be important to *any* kind of life satisfaction, it is difficult for us to imagine couples living in adjusted but asexual marriages.

\VITAL   Vital marriages are not predicated as much on shared activities as on simply enjoying each other's company. A vital couple will attempt to avoid conflict, but when it occurs it will be over an important, not trivial issue, and it will be settled as quickly as possible. One man described his vital marriage thus:

I cheerfully, and that's putting it mildly, passed up two good promotions because one of them would have required some travelling and the other would have taken evenings and weekend time—and that's when Pat and I live. The hours with her (after twenty-two years of marriage) are what I live for. You should meet her. . . (Cuber and Harroff, 1965: 55).

Members of a vital couple do not monopolize each other's time; they simply enjoy the time they do spend together and orient much of their lives around that focal point. And, as another study of vital marriages has found, these couple members have strong egos and high needs for sex and intimacy (Ammons and Stinnett, 1980: 37–42).

\ *TOTAL*   The total marriage is a multifaceted, vital relationship. It is, say Cuber and Harroff, quite rare, and usually people in such marriages know that theirs is exceptional. The authors state: "We occasionally found relationships so total that all aspects of life were mutually shared and enthusiastically participated in" (Cuber and Harroff, 1965: 59). Neither spouse in the total marriage

Feature 13.1   HERMAN

HERMAN®

"There's nothing on TV. D'you want to have an argument?"

Unger, Universal Press Syndicate, *Badger Herald*, November 7, 1985, 22.

has a private existence. This, like the conflict-habituated marriage, is predicated upon a high level of communicational "engagement." As we said, communication can result in intimacy and empathy or conflict or some of both.

All these types of marriages, Cuber and Harroff claim, are adjusted; they are not degrees of adjustment. There may, of course, be movement from one category to another over the life cycle. Also, it is possible for members of the same couple to be in two different kinds of marriages, based on their own perceptions and experiences of the marriage. In addition, the same phenomenon may have a different significance in different types of marriages: a sexual affair, for example, may occur in order to cause trouble in the conflict-habituated, to escape boredom in the passive-congenial, to capture what has been lost in the devitalized, or may be a response to freedom and emancipation, perhaps with the spouse condoning it, in the vital.

It is worth noting in closing that couples whose marriages are considered adjusted today may reach the "breaking point" tomorrow, whether the marriage is conflict-habituated, devitalized, or even vital. After all, you may get tired of fighting, or someone more vital or exciting may come along. Even open communication and living by the rules do not solve all married couples' problems. Chapters 16 and 17 will examine crises and divorce as important contemporary issues in the U.S. family. But first we will look at kinship and aging.

Kinship Relationships

***

CHAPTER 14

Kinship units in certain societies, such as the Afghan,
serve economic, political, religious, and other institutional functions.
Additional functions performed by the larger kin units in some
societies include: property-holding and inheritance, housing, need-
obligation, and affective or emotional ties. There is, however, no sim-
ple, linear removal of these functions as one moves from Durkheim's
"mechanically solidary" society to the "organically solidary" modern
industrial state. Yet, compared to the Afghans, the kinship units of
the United States are less central to society's operation, fulfilling a
primary affective function and a secondary need-obligation function,
and performing idiosyncratically in the areas of inheritance and
housing. In this chapter the significance of kin terms, the relative as

a person, and the meanings of "distance" with respect to kin are also considered. The last portion of the chapter is given to a characterization of relationships among the following kin: parents and adult offspring, adult siblings, secondary kin, and in-laws, with attention to kinkeeping, and to gender and ethnic differences.

Maturing individuals in modern industrial society ordinarily live with one or two parents, brothers, and sisters. They are also likely to be acquainted with aunts, uncles, cousins, and grandparents, with whom they do not live but who nevertheless are considered important because of their status as kinfolk or relatives. Upon reaching adulthood and marrying, they do not terminate their relationships with their families of orientation, that is, parents and siblings, but these, too, become a part of the kin network—the "kin of orientation." It is this network, involving parents and adult offspring, siblings, grandparents, aunts and uncles, as well as in-laws, that concerns us in this chapter. The very fact that kin outside the individual's nuclear family have received little attention since the early chapters of this volume should indicate to the reader something of the author's perspective on the importance of kin in the United States. But in order to understand U.S. kinship we shall once again resort to cross-cultural and historical comparisons.

SECTION ONE

KIN FUNCTIONS IN CROSS-CULTURAL PERSPECTIVE

In such societies as traditional Afghan, institutions and individuals alike are embedded within the larger kin unit, so that most of the activities and interactions that occur are based upon kin ties of one sort or another. David Schneider characterizes the difference between kinship in such societies and kinship in Western societies today:

> The kinship systems of modern, western societies are relatively differentiated as compared with the kinship systems found in many primitive and peasant societies. By "differentiated" I mean simply that kinship is clearly and sharply distinguished from all other kinds of social institutions and relationships. In many primitive and peasant societies a large number of kinds of institutions are organized and built as parts of the kinship system itself. Thus the major social units of the society may be kin groups — lineages perhaps. These same kin groups may be property-owning units, the political units, the religious units, and so on. Thus, whatever a man does in such a society he does as a kinsman of one kind or another[1] [Schneider, 1968: v]

The institutionally embedded Afghans, for example, have no political institutions beyond the village council, which consists of the elders in the various family units. These same elders perform the major religious rituals on behalf of their kin. Even the economic division of labor is coterminous with the kin networks, there being no separate market functionaries.

One major variation described in Chapter 5 is that between institutional embeddedness within the kin network and institutional embeddedness within the nuclear family. It was noted that classical Chinese society differed from Afghan society in being characterized by a small number of powerful, institutionally and individually embedded patrilineages with the majority of nonaffluent kin networks separated into nuclear families. The description of colonial America showed the major institutional functions somewhat embedded in nuclear families, but not in kin networks. Finally, a crucial change that took place between colonial times and the present was seen to be the increasing differentiation of institutional functions from the nuclear family—the larger kin group having already lost most of its institutional significance before the colonial period.

Patriarchy exists in both kin-based societies and those in which the small nuclear family is normative. However, there are some major gender differences between the two. Warner et al. note that wives have more power in nuclear family societies than in extended kin societies, because the wife is more essential and less replaceable in the former (Warner et al., 1986: 121–128). This, however, is somewhat offset when she is restricted to the domestic sphere and is thus dependent on the husband financially. Also, women gradually played an increasingly central kin role as industry and economic life were differentiated (became less embedded) from the kin network. Oliker describes this change thus:

> *Histories of the daily lives of women and men in early industrial society suggest that bonds among female kin and neighbors were less affected by encroaching industry than were bonds among males. Indeed, as women continued to exchange child care, sick care, domestic production, and kinship ritual, kinship bonds remained critical through the vicissitudes of daily family survival. Even though the man's new provider role required less daily exchange among kin, the woman's domestic responsibilities continued to rely on—indeed, in periods of market contraction, relied increasingly on—nonmarket exchange among friends and kin (Oliker, 1989: 23).*

There are some functions that kin groups have performed in some societies, whose change cannot be traced in a linear fashion. These functions include:

♦ property-holding and inheritance;
♦ housing and maintenance of residential proximity;
♦ obligation, or helping in time of need; and
♦ affection, emotional ties, or primary relationships (Adams, 1968–9: 55).

The first of these, *inheritance*, is clearly a kin function in societies with corporate lineages. In fact, as Harris says, "if the property concerned is a farm whose economic viability depends on its *size*, then, in order to inherit, the children of the owner of that farm will have to stay together to work on it" (Harris, 1983: 21).

But in both the small hunting and gathering band and in colonial America, the property-holding unit through which inheritance was controlled was the nuclear family represented by its male head, whose socially determined prerogative may be to pass the inheritance to one offspring or to divide it among all. The lineal systems discussed in Chapter 2 are, of course, still present in an attenuated form in the United States. Inheritance in the lineages passes to the children—sons in the patrilineage and daughters in the matrilineage. In the United States, however, the dominant kinship model, called the Standard American by Farber, is characterized by the spouse's being given priority over the children (Farber, 1981: 57).

A change which has taken place since colonial days is that the wife can hold property separately from her husband and can distribute it to her offspring separately if she so desires. Furthermore, there are not only differences *between* societies in the stress on inheritance and the control of property, but also differences by status *within* societies. In U.S. society, Farber has noted, high status groups have much to gain by working out mutually beneficial marriage alliances and by stressing not only the economic family estate but what he calls the "symbolic family estate." Inheritance, then, includes both property and "name," or significant ancestry, and these forms of inheritance serve to separate or differentiate those of higher status from the rest of society (Farber, 1971: 6, 115). (For more on U.S. inheritance, see Rosenfield's *To Heir Is Human*, 1993.)

The *housing-residential proximity* function, which is in reality two functions, is most difficult to place on a change continuum. For one thing, household sharing may assume various forms. In one society, the form may be the "longhouse," in which the men live apart from the women and children. In another it may be a joint family of brothers and their wives and children. In a third, aged parents may live with one of their married offspring. Furthermore, although the norms of certain societies include household sharing, residence may actually be proximate rather than shared—with the kin group functioning as a unit. Finally, housing may be temporarily shared with kin in virtually any society, including that of the contemporary United States. Beck and Beck call this the "intermittent extended family," occurring as one or more family members pass through a transition or crisis (Beck and Beck, 1989: 147–168). Thus, if the issue is simply kin proximity, one might argue that there is a progressive change toward greater dispersion from the small, undifferentiated society to the modern industrial society. But if the issue is stated as the provision by kin of housing for one another, this is about as likely in rural-to-urban migrant groups in the United States as it is in the Hindu joint family in India. The difference is that, in the former case, the relatives with whom one *should* share residence are not specified, and permanent sharing is not expected.

The *obligatory* function, based on the expectation that one will help kin under certain circumstances, varies greatly. In one society, the strongest obligation may be to the mother's brother; in another, to the grandfather; in still another, to one's own parents. Also, the obligations range from warrior allegiance and a proper burial to financial assistance or simply keeping in touch. In the

United States, according to the Rossis, the "obligation to provide financial aid moves in a more restricted network than the obligation to provide comfort" (Rossi and Rossi, 1990: 207). A good example of the kind of help kin may provide in U.S. society is job recruitment and migration. That is, employees tell kin about opportunities where they work, or help them migrate to where work is available (Grieco, 1982: 701–707). The strongest sense of obligation in contemporary U.S. kinship seems to be between aging parents and their adult offspring, but even this is mitigated by the equally powerful societal value of nuclear family independence and self-sufficiency.

Unlike the U.S. upper class, in which the inheritance-differentiated function is still strong, the working and lower classes are characterized by proximity and strong obligation. "Domestic aspects of kinship," says Farber, "are those which emerge in the course of living together. . . . The domestic level predominates in the lower class and represents the use of kindred as an aggregate by a population at the mercy of economic uncertainties" (Farber, 1971: 114–115).

The final function, providing affectional or *emotional* ties for the individual, operates as a matter of choice in most kinship systems. Though each society has an expectation that certain kin will provide such ties, the actual strength of affectional relationships is extremely varied. In societies in which institutions are embedded in the kin network, so that one kin line has jural and economic power over the individual, his or her closest ties are often with members of the other line. For example, in some patrilineal societies, the individual's closest feelings are toward members of her or his mother's kin group. Perhaps the most outstanding examples in U.S. kinship of the blocking of affect by functional ties are those instances when sons and their father work in the same business and, as a result, seek leisure interaction and emotional gratifications elsewhere among their kin. Farber goes so far as to say that modern society actually discourages nonbureaucratic personal commitments, such as kinship "(a) by emphasizing personal freedom in nonwork affairs and (b) by defining traditional family and kinship institutions as coercive, as ineffective loci of socialization, and as interfering with self-realization . . ." (Farber, 1981: 16). Jarrett adds that affection is simply not necessary for kin obligation to be carried out. The "affection myth" may need to be dispelled, "so that caregiving is done from motives of kinship obligations which, historically, have formed the basis for family aid" (Jarrett, 1985: 5).

David Popenoe notes that some scholars have argued that kin ties in Western societies have strengthened again since World War II. However, he says, it is very important to distinguish between three meanings of the term 'kinship ties':

1. the extent to which extended kinship obligations and rights take precedence (have control) over their conjugal and nonkinship counterparts;
2. the extent of interdependence among nuclear families within kinship networks; and
3. the number of people encompassed in a person's web of kinship obligations and rights (Popenoe, 1988: 47).

Clearly, says Popenoe, the first cannot be said to have strengthened recently. Litwak and Kulis have actually attempted to determine how close people must live to kin in order to deliver various services, since technology does negate some of the separating effects of distance (Litwak and Kulis, 1987: 660).

One can say in conclusion that the greatest difference in kinship between, for example, Afghan society and contemporary U.S. society is the removal of institutional functions so that the kin network in and of itself seldom performs economic-productive, political, religious, or educational functions. Apart from that change, however, it is difficult to summarize briefly the changes in the specific functions performed by kin in different societies. It is best perhaps to stop with the assertion that, in the contemporary United States, kin perform a general affective function, a particular obligatory function, and operate differentially by class in the areas of inheritance and housing. Yet this type of summarization only hints at many crucial issues that must be confronted before kinship in the United States can be adequately characterized.

SECTION TWO

SOME ISSUES IN KINSHIP ANALYSIS

According to Farber four kinship models are definable worldwide, but the two that are most applicable to U.S. society are the *Standard*, noted above, and the *Parentela* order. The former emphasizes ancestry, and the latter descent (as in the lineage systems). The former seems most appropriate to a society that emphasizes social and residential mobility with its focus on family *history*, while the latter is better suited to a stable, perhaps agriculture-based society with its emphasis on inheritance and *density*. Though the Standard is widespread behaviorally, Farber finds it a point of concern that it is the other model that is in general use in American family law (1981: 50, 57). Farber's distinctions will be useful at various points in the discussion of U.S. kinship.

Of the many issues regarding kinship that could be reviewed in a book on the family, there are five that seem most essential to understanding kin relations in the United States. These include the significance of *kin terms*, the idea of the *relative as a person*, the meaning of kin *"distance,"* and the issues of kin *unimportance* and nuclear family *isolation* in urban-industrial society.

Kin Terms

For many years, the significance of kin terms was debated in the literature on kinship. Do the terms used—such as *mother's brother, parallel cousin,* or *aunt*—have direct behavioral connotations, so that the compilation and comparison of terminological systems can be used to symbolize the kinship systems of different societies? Or are the terms psychologically grounded cultural constructs only indirectly related, at best, to behavioral patterns? Or are the terms anachronistic survivals only partially correlated with actual kinship norms, behaviors, and roles in a given society? Lewis Henry Morgan, says Fox, "saw in the study of terminology the royal road to the understanding of kinship systems" (Fox, 1967: 240). Fred Eggan states bluntly that "the verbal behavior symbolizes the socially defined relationships" (Eggan, 1950: 295). Radcliffe-Brown shows that Choctaw and Omaha kin terms are as reasonable for their kinship systems as are our terms for our system. Likewise, Rodger Davies points out that the kin-based Syrian Arabs employ terms that distinguish among five generations (Radcliffe-Brown, 1941: 31; Davies, 1949: 249). This stress on the sociological significance of terminology is epitomized in Murdock's book *Social Structure*, in which various types of kinship systems are classified and distinguished from one another primarily on the basis of terms (Murdock, 1949).

On the other side of the question are such scholars as A. L. Kroeber, who claimed that kinship terms reflect psychology, not sociology. In fact, says Kroeber, kinship systems are "linguistic patterns of logic, and their uncritical and unrestrained use as if they were uncontaminated reflectors of past or present institutions" is unsound and dangerous (Kroeber, 1951: 172, 181). And, as Fox notes, Bronislaw Malinowski had little use for the study of kin terms, arguing that the study of norms and actual relationships would be more productive (Fox, 1967: 240).

While the debate has not been completely resolved, it seems that Fox's conclusion is valid. Kinship systems, he says, are many-sided, and terminology may not reflect every side. What a system of terms may tell us

> *is* how the people themselves *see their world of kin. Who do they distinguish from whom and on what basis? It is often the case that they regard a certain distinction as crucial which has no meaning for us in terms of our analysis of the system of groups, alliances, etc. (Fox, 1967: 243). [Italics in original.]*

There is, then, a correlation between terminology and behavior, but it is simply not perfect.

A part of the discussion of kin terms has concerned the European-U.S. system and its peculiarities. Fox, for example, points out that in this system "the terms for members of the nuclear family (father, mother, son, daughter, brother, sister) are *not used for anyone outside the family*. This is very different "from the terminological systems of societies in which the nuclear family receives little or no stress" (Fox 1967: 258). Among the Papago Indians of southern Arizona and northern Mexico, for example, "all cousins of every degree, on both sides, are called brothers and sisters," although the Papago can, if need be, use words that mean a "near brother" (one's own) and a "far brother" (a cousin) (Underhill, 1965: 150). The European-American terminological system (which Murdock classifies with the "Eskimo") manifests both the bilateral nature of our kin relations—that is, our normatively equal relation to both mother's and father's kin—and the special importance attached to members of the nuclear family.

> *Mother may be called "mother," "mom," "ma," "mummy," "mamma," by her first name, nickname, diminutive, "old woman," and a variety of other less commonly used designations.*

Father may be called "father," "pop," "pa," "dad," "daddy," by his first name, diminutive, "old man," "boss," and a variety of less commonly used designations. Uncles may be addressed or referred to as uncle-plus-first name, first name alone, or uncle alone. Similarly for aunts (Schneider and Homans, 1955: 1195).

Schneider and Homans then proceed to report the relationship between terms and behavior. Among their findings are the following:

1. On the assumption that parental terms can be ranged on a continuum from most formal, *father* and *mother,* to least formal, first name only, there is a tendency for both sexes to become relatively more formal with their same-sex parent.
2. Use of the terms *father* and *mother* for one's parents symbolizes a more formal and less close relationship with them.
3. Females use a wider variety of terms for their parents than do males for theirs.
4. The tendency is "for more first-name-alone designations to be applied to aunts and uncles on the mother's side than on the father's."
5. Males are more likely than females to address aunts and uncles by first name alone. In cases of either strong positive or strong negative sentiment the formal terms *aunt* and *uncle* are dropped and first name only is used (Schneider and Homans, 1955).

Since Schneider and Homans' article appeared, attempts at replication have verified only findings 3, 4, and 5. Hagstrom and Hadden interpret these findings to mean that females are generally more involved in kinship and that people tend to be somewhat closer to maternal kin. Hagstrom and Hadden also found that, with the exception of females and their fathers' siblings, aunt and uncle terminology and sentiment is unilinear rather than curvilinear; that is, the closer one feels to an aunt or uncle the more likely one is to use first name only (Hagstrom and Hadden, 1965: 324–332).

That there may be more than one kinship system in the United States is made clear by Farber in his reconciliation of the views of Ward Goodenough and Schneider on terminology. Goodenough, after working with a New England sample, reported that *affines* (kin-by-marriage) as well as blood kin are considered to be relatives. However, first cousins "have no ascribed lifelong obligations other than a show of cordiality" (Goodenough, 1965: 281). Schneider, on the other hand, having investigated kin terms in the Midwest, concluded that kinship is primarily a matter of blood ties. Thus, the first cousin is in the inner circle of kin, while affines are not truly kin at all (Schneider, 1965: 292–294). Moreover, he finds that terminological distinctions exist that express the structural distinctions he is reporting.

Farber's response is that they are both right. There is the old New England kinship system, with its emphasis upon marriage as linking two kin groups, and there is the Midwestern type, with its emphasis upon blood kin. He goes on to conclude that in present-day U.S. society the former is more prevalent in higher status groups, the latter in lower status groups. Suppose, then, one felt close to one's parents-in-law. This would probably be expressed at the higher statuses, says Farber, by the use of the terms *mother* and *father* and at the lower statuses by the use of their first names—to indicate that they are friends, not kin. Farber further generalizes this distinction to speak to the issue raised by Hagstrom and Hadden: in high status families affection is generally expressed by using the appropriate kin term; in low status families, by using first names (Farber, 1971: 44–52).

In addition to cross-cultural comparisons and analysis of the significance of kin terms in the United States, the study of kin terms includes the naming of children. In a sample of 384 primarily middle-class women in the Chicago area, Alice Rossi noted that between 1920 and 1950 there was a tendency away from naming offspring for mother's mother and father's father and toward naming them for mother's father and especially father's mother (Rossi, 1965: 512). This, she feels, may indicate a greater equalitarianism within the family and the lessening role segregation between males and females and between maternal and paternal kin.

Rossi's article has, of course, only scratched the surface of what might be discovered from a study of names and naming. In fact, as can be seen from the sources used in this discussion, little has been done recently—though much could be done—in the analysis of kinship terms in a single society such as the United States. Farber's discoveries are a step in the right direction.

The Relative as a Person

The kinship network does not consist of terminological distinctions or of roles and functions, but of people. These people have various personalities, behave in various ways, and view their social worlds from various perspectives. The kinship component of a relationship gives it an enduring quality, as distinct from the contingent solidarity of friendship; but, within this difference, the unique character of a kin relationship results from the involvement of kinfolk with one another. There are, as Schneider points out, "Famous Relatives" who hold a particularly honored place among their kin (Schneider, 1968: 67). Whether dead or alive, they are referred to with pride. Or a cousin with whom one enjoys doing things may be described as "more a friend than a relative," the implication of the expression being that the term *cousin* ordinarily connotes little affection or interaction, while this particular cousin is of greater significance than that. On the other side of this coin are the friends one refers to as "Uncle Roald" and "Aunt Maurine," though they are actually not relatives at all. The kin terms indicate a relationship that is based on more than the fleeting interests and activities of the typical friendship and is enduring and intimate to a degree usually present in relationships with certain kin.

It is very likely that the fuzziness of kinship designations in the United States, and the flexibility with which kin ties are interpreted by specific people, are related to the great emphasis that is placed on personal achievement rather than on ascription. This emphasis is related both to the restricted terminological system referred to above and to the great variability in the actual relations between people holding the same structural positions within the kinship system, such as mother-son or uncle-niece. This variability is made clearer by examining the three meanings of "distance" in kinship, especially as these pertain to U.S. kin relations.

Kin "Distance"

Distance, says Schneider, means three things in U.S. kinship. First, it signifies *genealogical* distance, so that we may speak of a second cousin as being a more distant kinsman than an uncle. Some have tried to delineate the various circles of relatives in U.S. society according to genealogical distance. Thus, the inner circle of relatives includes only those from Ego's families of procreation and orientation—parents and children, brothers and sisters. The outer circle of relatives includes those from Ego's parents' family or orientation, including aunts, uncles, and grandparents. Finally, beyond this outer circle are cousins, great aunts, and so on. The respondents in Rossi and Rossi's study actually put the following numerical ranking on obligation to categories of relatives:

> *What mattered most for obligation level was not a specific* type *of kinperson, but the degree of relatedness of ego to the various kintypes. Grandparents, grandchildren, and siblings—all related to ego through* one *connecting link—evoked comparable levels of felt obligation (between 6 and 7 on a 10-point scale); aunts and uncles, nieces and nephews—related to ego through* two *connecting links—showed similar levels of obligation (between 4 and 5 on the scale); while the lowest obligation level was to cousins—related through a minimum of* three *connecting links (a mean of 3.2 on the scale) (Rossi and Rossi, 1990: 491).*

In analyses of this kind, only Goodenough has fixed the position of affinal relatives, such as in-laws or aunts and uncles by marriage.

The terms *closeness* and *distance* immediately elicit a second interpretation that Schneider calls *socioemotional* distance. Feelings toward kin may or may not be governed by genealogical distance. In fact, Johnson claims that people "most often use the subjective notions of closeness and distance rather than genealogical distance to identify their relatives" (Johnson, 1988: 166). Emotional closeness is governed as much by the interactions and experiences shared or not shared with certain relatives as by genealogical distance. On this point, Kath Weston notes the way in which discourse and culture have "denied lesbians and gays access to kinship" by treating them as outcasts (Weston, 1991: 21).

This matter of "sharing or not sharing" takes us to the third type of distance that pertains to kinship: *physical* or residential distance. Intense interaction clearly requires proximity, and proximity in U.S. society is broadly related to genealogical closeness. However, the association among the three types of closeness or distance is far from perfect. Proximity is simply not a sufficient condition for intimacy or socioemotional closeness. Parents, on the one hand, are considered intimate relatives even when not physically accessible. Aunts, uncles, and cousins, on the other hand, may be quite proximate, yet not be objects of great affection or frequent interaction. Schneider puts the same point thus: "A person who is genealogically close may be physically distant and neutral on the socioemotional dimension. Or a person may be close socioemotionally and physically but distant genealogically" (Schneider, 1968: 73). The same functional character of U.S. kinship that gives rise to a terminological system stressing the nuclear family and that allows for fuzzy boundaries and idiosyncratic personal relationships within the kin network also makes for a relatively low correlation among the three types of closeness or distance in U.S. kinship. But what, precisely, is the "functional" character of U.S. kinship?

Unimportance, Isolation, and Consistency

Fifty years ago, Parsons wrote an article on kinship in the United States in which he made three major points. First, compared with kinship in many other societies, kinship in the United States is relatively unimportant to the ongoing of the society. With the parceling out of institutional functions to other settings, that is, institutional differentiation, the kinship network has little role to play in societal maintenance, particularly compared with the role it played in the past (and which it still plays in some cultures). Second, the normal household unit is the nuclear, conjugal family, living "in a home segregated from those of both pairs of parents (if living) and . . . economically independent of both. In a very large proportion of cases the geographical separation is considerable" (Parsons, 1943: 27). Third, this isolated, open, bilateral kinship system with nuclear household units is most "functional" for, or best suited to, the U.S. occupational system and urban living. It makes residential mobility in pursuit of occupational opportunities much easier than if one's corporate kin group have to be carried along on each move.

This article and its conclusions have been a favorite target of kinship researchers since the 1950s. Among other things, these researchers discovered that adult offspring are more likely to live close to their parents and other kin than "considerably separated" from them. Cancian, reviewing much of the research, states that 60 percent of Americans visit a relative at least once a week, with the parent-adult offspring bond being especially strong. Noting that Parsons was writing about the middle class, specifically excluding farmers, matrifocal lower-class families, and the upper class, several researchers found that even among middle-class families the separation from kin is not likely to be great.

Even more important, researchers noted that the kin network does "function" in several ways: providing affectional ties, help when needed, and even supports for or deterrents to residential mobility. The functionality of the kin network, demonstrated in study after study, led Sussman to conclude that

> the evidence on the viability of an existing kinship structure carrying on extensive activities among kin is so convincing that we find it unnecessary to continue further descriptive work in order to establish the existence of the kin network in modern urban society (Sussman, 1965: 63).

Some lower-class individuals and families may be isolated, and some highly residentially and socially mobile middle-class families may pay little attention to kin, though Darroch notes that in the nineteenth century families migrated along kin lines (Darroch, 1981: 257–277). Richard Osborn and J. Ivan Williams report that "younger people and people of high social status not only move more frequently but their moves are more likely to result in reduced propinquity" (Osborn and Williams, 1976: 205). This means two things: first, higher status families tend to follow the job market, regardless of the location of kin, and second, young marrieds are moving away from their families, though later in life they may close the residential distance again.

The pattern is for working-class people to have a cluster of kin close at hand, and for high status individuals to be very much concerned about their kin links—the symbolic family estate. It is worth noting at this point that at present both the domestic and the symbolic estate function can be found among the black population of the United States. For example, Parish et al. find that young black mothers are more likely to live near kin and to receive child-care assistance from them than whites (Parish et al., 1991: 203–215). And Robert Taylor finds that "familial relationships, proximity to relatives, and family contact all play a crucial role in the informal social support networks of blacks" (Taylor, 1986: 74). These bonds include both residential distance and affective closeness. In addition, one aspect of the increasing ethnic solidarity of the African-American community is what Alex Haley calls the search for "roots." In Farber's terms, these roots are the black individual's symbolic family estate.

Therefore, although Parsons claimed that kinship is relatively unimportant in U.S. society and that this is consistent with the economic-industrial structure of this society, his critics responded: yes, but nuclear families are not isolated, kin networks do function, and many of their functions are perfectly consistent with the economic structure of the society. Where kinship and economics seem at odds is ordinarily when kin relations and the economic-productive function are linked directly, as in a family-run business. Twenty years after the original article, Parsons sought to reemphasize his comparative perspective, while at the same time acknowledging the findings of his critics. The view of the "isolated nuclear family" and that of its critics, Parsons' claims

> *are not contradictory but complementary. The concept of isolation applies in the first instance to kinship structure as seen in the perspective of anthropological studies in that field. In this context our system represents an extreme type, which is well described by that term. It does not, however, follow that all relations to kin outside the nuclear family are broken. Indeed, the very psychological importance for the individual of the nuclear family in which he was born and brought up would make any such conception impossible (Parsons, 1965: 35).*

Gary Lee calls the isolation of the nuclear family in the United States a "relative" matter, meaning that it is isolated compared to most other times and places (Lee, 1980: 924).

Thus, it may be concluded that neither institutions nor individuals are as embedded in the kin networks of the United States as they have been in many other societies. This is not to say, however, that kinship performs no functions in the United States. Nor is it to say that its performance of certain functions is inconsistent with the achievement-based institutions of that society. Nor, finally, is it to say that the absence of individual embeddedness in a household and solidarity sense means that kin are isolated from one another, either interactionally or emotionally. It does mean that the volitional element, the flexibility and variety that come with choice, is heightened in U.S. kinship. It also means that generalizations about kin are risky, and that when they are based simply on "the kin network" they are clearly overgeneralizations. Likewise, when the generalizations are about "the family" and kin they are also incorrect, since females are much more embedded in the kin network than are males, as we will see in the discussion of parents and offspring below. One must, instead, speak of the relations between specific categories of kin—parents and offspring, siblings, in-laws, and so on—as in Section Three.

SECTION THREE

CATEGORIES OF U.S. KIN AND THEIR CHARACTERISTICS

Adults and their Parents

In 1970 I wrote that "the relations between young adults and their aging parents are ordinarily the closest kin tie attitudinally and residentially (Adams, 1971: 177). The relations between parents and adult offspring can be characterized by the phrase *positive concern*. This positive, or active, concern is manifested in several ways. First, there is extremely frequent contact between these intergenerational kin. When they live close to one another, weekly or more frequent contact is the rule. However, "to bridge the distances separating the residences of parents and children takes both time and money," and communication by telephone or travel cannot be as frequent as in cases of proximity (Rossi and Rossi, 1990: 387; Fischer, 1982: 370–372). The gender difference is pointed out by the Rossis, who find that distance represents

> the *major factor affecting the frequency of interaction between mothers and adult children in all parent-child dyads. . . . In contact with fathers, however, the quality of the relationship has even more of an influence than sheer opportunity as indexed by geographic distance (Rossi and Rossi, 1990: 387).*

A second manifestation of positive concern between adult offspring and their parents is the strong affectional tie, which, according to the Rossis, increases over the adult years regardless of who rates it. However, as in the case of residential distance, this varies from family to family and by gender. Of the four possible parent-offspring relationships—mother-daughter, mother-son, father-daughter, father-son—the closest, both affectionally and interactionally, is that between mother and daughter. We will say more about this bond later.

The third aspect of positive concern is obligation, which includes both being "on call" and regular forms of aid. The help pattern, say the Rossis, "tends to be reciprocal in nature for two or more decades, when children are in their mid-twenties to mid-forties and parents in their mid-forties to mid-sixties" (Rossi and Rossi, 1990: 498). At the beginning of that period of time, most of the aid flows downward, from parents to children, while later it flows both ways. Finally, if the parents live long enough, it may flow mostly from offspring to parents. And "women kin evoke more obligation than men, especially if they are unmarried or widowed" (Rossi and Rossi, 1990: 206). This, then, is the nature of positive concern between parents and adult offspring.

Several qualifications must be mentioned regarding this contact-affection-obligation configuration. First, the obligatory element does not stand in the way of affectional closeness unless it becomes the primary factor in continued contact. An example of such a situation is the young adult male who has few interests in common with his widowed mother, but is obliged to help her anyway (Adams, 1968: 50–59). The issue of "interests in common" raises a second qualification: the Rossis note that they were unprepared "to find that dissensus in core values (religion, politics, general outlook on life) would depress the emotional closeness of parents and adult children" (Rossi and Rossi, 1990: 361). The third qualification is that obligation to aging parents may be greatly affected by a divorce, especially earlier in the offspring's life. It would not be surprising that all aspects of relationship with the non-custodial parent are affected by a divorce while the child is still at home. In fact, when the offspring is an adult a divorce on the part of either generation may have a weakening effect on the parent-adult offspring relationship. The final qualification is that social mobility, meaning the movement of the offspring to a different occupational level, "influences feelings and perceptions but not behavior." That is, mobility is related to neither visiting nor aid, except when a son has been downwardly mobile (Kulis, 1987: 429–430).

The mother-daughter bond is one of, as Lucy Fischer puts it, "linked lives" (Fischer, 1986). This linking, says Fischer, is not merely one of forced labor due to patriarchy. It is one predicated on the "kinkeeping" function performed by women in this society. It is also a result of what Willmott and Young a generation ago called "female role convergence." Based on the traditional norm of women as mothers and wives, this argument simply said that while men assume a variety of occupations, mothers and daughters are more likely to assume the same role in adulthood (Willmott and Young, 1960: 84). While liberation is changing this, the fact remains that the motherhood role (not marriage) coupled with that of kinkeeper links women more strongly than men in the kin network.

Additional specifics of mother-daughter relations include the fact that adult daughters are the principal caregivers for the elderly, one result being a feeling of strain and constraint (Brody, 1985: 26: Roff et al., 1986: 364). Jill Suitor finds that when a married daughter returns to school this meets with the approval of a well-educated mother, but with disapproval by a less-educated mother. The reasons for this seem to be that the more educated mother holds more liberal gender role attitudes, and the daughter's further education will make her's and her mother's education closer together (Suitor, 1987: 441–442).

However, while the mother-daughter relationship is the closest, we should re-peat that all four parent-offspring relationships tend to be closer than relation-ships between any other two relatives in U.S. kin networks. Most of the exceptions to this are found among siblings.

Adult Sibling Relations

In the Parentela Order, with its emphasis upon lineage, the tie between grand-parents and grandchildren tends to be the second most intense, after the parent-child. However, in the Standard American model siblings take precedence (Barber, 1981: 46). The terms that seem to summarize best the relations be-tween adult siblings are *interest* and *comparison/identification*. Interest simply means a general feeling that one should keep up with one's siblings, keep posted on their activities, but that except in extreme circumstances there is no need for contact to be as frequent or mutual aid to be as great as is that with parents. In fact, apart from the exchange of babysitting between proximate sisters, the sharing of financial or other forms of aid between siblings is likely to become a bone of contention or even a basis for alienation. Interest, then, is just that: the individual is "interested" in how brothers and sisters are getting along.

This notion of sibling rivalry has been a topic of discussion for some time in the socialization literature. It must now be added that when brothers and sisters leave home such rivalry does not end, but is transformed into *comparison* or *identification*. In a success- and achievement-oriented society, with substantial emphasis on individualism within the family, brothers and sisters are the com-parative reference group par excellence. That is, the question "How am I doing?" can well be answered by noting how one's achievements compare with those of one's siblings. Siblings, unlike friends, are "givens" in the individual's social network. We cannot (as we can with friends) drop them if we become dissatisfied with them. And when the kin of orientation (adult offspring and their parents) get together, conversation is likely to turn—sometimes subtly, sometimes openly—to how well brother George or sister Susan is doing profes-sionally or to how their marriages are going. There can be considerable emo-tional alienation between brothers whose occupations diverge greatly in prestige. In the other sibling comparisons, a prestige divergence generally results in a one-way, or unreciprocated, identification. That is, the lower status sibling ex-presses affection for (and sometimes jealousy of) and wants to be like the higher status sibling, but the feelings are not reciprocated. This, then, is one point at which the economic success values of the society impinge upon and help to determine the social psychology of kin involvement. It is noteworthy, however, that such variations in feeling are not very evident in the area of in-teraction. Females especially seem to have little control over the frequency of their contact with siblings and are thus unable, due to obligation, to bring that frequency into line with their feelings. This is, of course, another indication of the greater obligatory burden that females bear in kinship relations.

Recently Ann Goetting has summarized the work of Ciccirelli, Lamb and Sutton-Smith, and others on sibling relations across the life cycle (see Cicirelli,

1985, 177–214; Lamb and Sutton-Smith, 1982). Her summary of adult sibling relations includes the issues of interest and comparison described above, but goes further. The relations between *young adult* siblings, says Goetting, include the following: (1) companionship; (2) emotional support; (3) cooperation in care for the elderly; and (4) aid and services (Goetting, 1986: 703–714). The relations between siblings in *old age* include (1) and (4) from the previous list, but (2) is reminiscence or shared memory, and (3) is the resolution of rivalry. Several comments on her list are in order. First, it is possible that care for the elderly may be a matter of strain and even bitter disagreement rather than cooperation, though the latter is clearly the goal. Second, aid occurs when there is proximity, but even then not as often as between them and their parents. Third, the resolution of rivalry means laying to rest whatever remnants exist of the comparison noted above.

Some pairs of brothers and sisters evolve activity patterns that make them extremely close friends in adulthood. "Best friend" status for a sibling is, however, the exception rather than the rule. And activity-based relationships are even less prevalent between secondary kin, such as cousins.

Secondary Kinship

Secondary kin are all those relatives who were not at some time in the past a part of Ego's family or orientation: aunts, uncles, cousins, grandparents, and so on. The best terms to use in describing the contacts between such kin in U.S. society are *circumstantial* and *incidental*. Secondary kin relations seldom involve frequent contact, common interests, mutual aid, or strong affectional and obligatory concern. Yearly contact—the Christmas card, for example, or perhaps kin reunion at holidays or during a vacation—frequently suffices. The incidental nature of such kin relations may be seen in those instances in which an aunt and uncle drop in while one is visiting parents or in which one goes to see a cousin while on a trip home for the purpose of visiting parents and siblings. The circumstantial side of secondary kin contact is well depicted in the "wakes and weddings" relatives of whom Schneider speaks. These are kin brought together by such circumstances as the marriage or death of a mutual kinsman (Schneider, 1968: 70). Interestingly enough, Rosenblatt et al. find that, in general, kin visits involving "family trouble" (death, illness, etc.) are characterized by less tension and a greater feeling that the visit was "a good one" (Rosenblatt et al., 1981: 403–409).

The notion of incidental and circumstantial contact is opposed to that of intentional or volitional contact, and fits quite well the character of most secondary kin in the United States. In the Greensboro study, a few respondents were troubled by the weakness of secondary kin ties. The wife of a clerk explained: "It is distressing that distance is pulling families apart so. Seeing relatives was very important when I was young, and I miss it now. It bothers me that my children don't know their cousins and play with them like I did" (Adams, 1968: 161). However, a much greater proportion of respondents made this sort of comment: "My parents and sister mean a lot to me, but I simply don't have time to spend keeping up with a lot of kinsfolk that don't mean anything to me anyway." Or even more pointedly: "I have an aunt and one cousin besides my mother and brothers that mean a lot to me. As for the others—phooey!"

It should be noted that in the United States there are two prime exceptions to circumstantiality. One is grandparents of the young adult, who the Rossis placed in the second circle of kin along with siblings, as being connected through one link. In fact, such aging grandparents, along with females, form the hub of kin activity and involvement. Cherlin and Furstenberg's important study of grandparents in the United States distinguishes three styles of grandparenting: 55 percent of their respondents are companionate, 29 percent are remote, and 16 percent are involved (Cherlin and Furstenberg, 1986: 70, 77). The companionate is simply frequent enough contact, but without either services or much parenting behavior. The ones who are most likely to indicate a lot less time than they would like are, of course, the remote. For the "involved" role (that is, parenting and services) to be played, three conditions are necessary: proximity, being younger, and need (such as a divorce) (Cherlin and Furstenberg, 1986: 205).

An important point in their study is that grandparents feel that a lot has been gained since they were grandchildren: warmth, understanding, and love. These grandparents feel that the more unstable family life is, the greater the supportive role needed from grandparents. However, Cherlin and Furstenberg note that the increasing strength of the grandparent-grandchild relationship is overstated by their respondents. After all, the harsh reality of death rates fifty years ago meant that one-fourth of the current grandparents never knew a grandparent themselves (Cherlin and Furstenberg, 1986: 47, 48).

Other research has found that grandparents—especially in the higher social classes—often pass monetary gifts to younger generations (Caplow, 1982: 382–392). Also, grandfathers may be particularly helpful to the single mother with a small child (Gershenson, 1983: 596). But by the time the young person reaches adulthood and marries, some grandparents are no longer alive.

One further point: earlier we spoke of the "kinkeeping" function often performed by women. This role is often played by a grandmother, who is the hub of kin activity; in fact, her death frequently means the fragmenting of the kin network. Another potential kinkeeper is an elderly lifelong single woman (Allen and Pickett, 1987: 517–526). Still another is a sibling, who takes over when the grandmother dies (Rosenthal, 1985: 965–974). But the fact that it is women rather than men, and older rather than younger, who most often do the "work" of kin contact, a central figure is likely to be grandmother—as long as she is alive. Women play this kinkeeping role, we should add, for several reasons. One is their greater embeddedness in the family through socialization. Another is male avoidance of the task, an indication of the delegatory power we noted in Chapter 11.

The second exception to circumstantiality is the activity and mutual concern of the secondary kin of many ethnic groups. The Rossis note the obligation to secondary kin among Irish and blacks, who had close childhood relations especially to aunts and uncles (Rossi and Rossi, 1990: 246). The activities that indicate the closeness — originally means for insuring mutual survival — are now more likely to be means for achieving individual success. Leichter and Mitchell report a phenomenon that was somewhat prevalent among the Jewish families they studied in New York City:

> *Family circles and cousin clubs may also support occupational achievement by giving instrumental help as an organization: the group's loan fund may help to support children's education, or special collections may be taken up when there is particular need on the part of one member (Leichter and Mitchell, 1967: 156).*

Such secondary kin support has not automatically disappeared as the various ethnic groups have been incorporated into the dominant structures of U.S. society. Yet these exceptions do not alter the overriding generalization that, even in the lower and working classes, secondary kin ordinarily play a relatively minor role in the individual's social network.

In-Law Relations

The discussion of in-laws, the relatives one gains by marriage, requires that several distinctions be made. First, it should be — but is not always — made clear whether one is referring to the spouses' relations with their in-laws or with the influence of the in-laws upon relations between the spouses. This section will attempt to deal with both. Second, investigations of in-law relationships should distinguish between specific in-laws, such as the husband's mother and the wife's mother, sisters-in-law, and so on. Such specification is as necessary here as it is in the discussion of blood kin. Third, the focus of in-law studies should be not only on the roots of trouble or conflict — which is the case for most such studies — but also on the conditions that make for satisfactory relationships. Both are discussed below.

According to Goetting, in-law relationships are, for the most part, without intensity. The reasons for this include: (1) the partial replacement of kin functions by formal organizations; (2) the increase in individualistic over familistic values; (3) geographic mobility; and (4) feminism, which may serve to weaken ties between women and their in-laws, especially if the in-laws are more conservative (Goetting, 1990: 67–90).

This last point reminds us that in her classic article on sex roles, Komarovsky hypothesized that as a result of the female's close ties to her parents, in-law trouble would more often involve the husband and wife's parents than the wife and husband's parents (Komarovsky, 1950: 508–516). Several later studies also found substantial conflict between the husband and the wife's parents. Yet, despite these studies, the majority of studies since Komarovsky's hypothesis was formulated have found in-law troubles to be generally more frequent between the wife and the husband's mother. This is the case in spite of the tendency of married couples to interact somewhat more often with the wife's parents than with the husband's.

The factors that give rise to in-law conflict or peace have not all been specified, but several have been tentatively isolated. Older women have less in-law trouble than *younger* ones. The presence of offspring in the home is likely to improve relations, particularly between the two mothers. Thus, the fact that younger marrieds appear to have more in-law troubles than older marrieds can be explained partially by the independence struggle that is completed during the early years of marriage and partially by in-law stresses that result from the birth of the grandchild. Fischer puts this very succinctly: "The birth of the child increases the importance of both the mother-daughter and the mother-in-law daughter-in-law bonds, while accentuating the asymmetry between these relationships" (Fischer, 1983: 192).

The second and third necessary, but not sufficient, conditions for in-law trouble are *proximity* and *dependence*. There is simply less likely to be trouble with in-laws when they are at a distance than when they are close by and interaction is frequent. Dependence, though not entirely separate from age and proximity, is a third factor. Young adult wives are more likely to be somewhat emotionally dependent on their parents than are husbands on theirs, but the latter situation, when it occurs, is more likely to cause trouble between his wife and his parents.

Several researchers have found that after marriage the husband's allegiance may actually transfer to his wife's family (Goetting, 1990: 67–90). But treating a daughter- or, more often, son-in-law as family or as one's own offspring is not the only mechanism for avoiding in-law conflict, especially with the mother-in-law. The myth of mother-in-law trouble has itself caused many women to resolve *not* to be that way, but to do everything possible not to meddle. Even gender equality may have helped to smooth out in-law relations, and to improve their quality in recent years.

A generation ago, Judson and Mary Landis found a close relation between marital happiness and good in-law relations (Landis and Landis, 1963: 331–335). But as noted often in this volume, a simple relationship may be causatively interpreted only with great caution. Although it is easy to jump to the conclusion that in-law trouble causes marital difficulties, an equally plausible interpretation would be that marital difficulties disrupt the relations of couples with other members of their social network — including in-laws — as well. Still, however one explains it, there is a relationship between in-law trouble and marital conflict.

A final point on the asymmetry in in-laws relations comes from the Rossis. We believe, they say,

> though we cannot cite any supportive evidence, that parents tend to feel more comfortable and 'at home' literally and figuratively with their daughter and their daughter's spouse than with their sons and daughters-in-law, precisely because women largely determine the cuisine, childrearing values, and social activities of a household (Rossi and Rossi, 1990: 360).

And, again, feeling comfortable is a likely conflict reducer.

Conclusions

The least disrupted marriages, in terms of kin relationships, are those in which there are children and in which the couple live at least four or five hours away from the two sets of close kin and manifest little emotional dependence upon kin, so that their attention is focused on their own family of procreation rather than on their kin of orientation or other relatives. Such a conclusion assumes, though, that a great amount of value is placed upon simply avoiding conflict, with the positive functions of kinship involvement considered insignificant. However, the literature on kinship in the United States seems to show that most people disagree with Barrington Moore's assertion that kinship is nothing more than a barbaric "obligation to give affection as a duty to a particular set of persons on account of the accident of birth (Moore, 1958: 163). Despite the emphasis society places on individualism and independence—which makes the relations of couples with their parents, in-laws, and other kin tenuous at times—most people seem to prefer the sense of identity, emotional support, visiting, and emergency help that genealogically close kin provide, rather than the independence and isolation that might be achieved in a totally individualized society.

Compared with those of other societies, cross-culturally and historically, kinship ties in the United States appear insignificant and weak. There is little institutional embeddedness in the kin network, and individual embeddedness in terms of solidarity exists more among women and only with the kin of orientation in most middle-class and some working- and lower-class families. But U.S. kin ties do have a form of viability that is positively valued by most Americans. Whether kin ties *should* "wither away" for the sake of other, more individualistic, values, as Moore believes they should, is a question the reader may decide.

Aging and the Family
in the United States

CHAPTER 15

For married couples in the United States aging usually involves the relinquishing of two key roles—the parental and the occupational. Aging requires numerous decisions and a substantial reorientation of activity patterns. The discussion of aging in this chapter has four major foci: the theory of disengagement, socialization into old age, the issue of age grading and the social network, and marriage. Widowhood is discussed, and in the concluding section a brief comparison is drawn between old age and adolescence.

Throughout the history of mankind, aging has always meant losing hair, friends, illusions, and strength; and dealing with senescent or senile fellows has always been a problem for families and communities. However, in most known cultures, some sorts of compensation to their inevitable losses and decrements had been devised and were available to the aging individuals. The aged have indeed very often been considered more wise, influential, and honored people. We have within a few decades almost ruined such a conception of life. In the same time we have made old age a common and lengthier experience, and made it a period of isolation, anguish, boredom, and uselessness (Philbert, 1965: 5).

This depiction of the honored elderly of the past, Peter Laslett feels, is based on a somewhat faulty historical stereotype. Not all the elderly, only those of high status, were, to use Michel Philbert's words, considered wise, influential, and honored (Laslett, 1977). Yet, despite this appropriate historical caution, John Demos generalizes as follows about old age in the past:

If old age is a social problem now, what was it in former times? Surely, much has changed. The numbers have changed, for one thing. . . . Social factors have changed as well. Retirement . . . is now the critical marker of the aging process; there was no precise pre-modern equivalent . . . . If old age is difficult now, probably it was less so then. When the elderly were fewer, perhaps they were more valued—even 'venerated.' When they were not retired, they may have felt themselves to be more useful and capable. Pre-modern old people probably were better off than their present-day counterparts, as to social and economic position, but they seem to have paid a price for this, in various forms of psychological disadvantage (Demos, 1986: 15).

This chapter, therefore, examines a period in the life of individuals that has decreased in usefulness, if not in honor, as it has increased in prevalence in U.S. society. Longevity is currently 71 years for men and 78 years for women in a society that emphasizes the achievements of the young adult years and the glories of youth. In fact, the proportion of the U.S. population aged 65 and over was 4 percent in 1900 and 11 percent in 1977. Projections are that by 2000 A.D. it will be 13 percent, and that by 2020 the percent will be 14–17, about 43 million people (Shanas and Sussman, 1981: 226).

A further breakdown of the elderly in the United States shows that "3/4 of elderly men and 2/5 of elderly women still maintain their own household with their spouse." Another one-eighth and one-third of men and women, respectively, live alone or in non-family households. "The 22 million elderly households in the United States in 1980 constituted over 1/4 of all households" (Sweet and Bumpass, 1987: 332–333). As for the "old-old," or those over 85, seven out of 10 are women, about 5 percent are still employed, and the average household income is about $20,000; only about 15 percent are poor (Longino, 1986: 38–42). (For some myths about the elderly, see Feature 15.1.)

What is happening to these ever-increasing numbers of aged? Are they adjusting easily or with difficulty to this stage of the life cycle? And what are the requisites for adjustment? According to one important theory, adjustment to old age is effected by the process of *disengagement.*

SECTION ONE

DISENGAGEMENT THEORY AND ITS CRITICS

Disengagement theory was first set forth by Elaine Cumming, Lois Dean, and David Newell in a 1960 *Sociometry* article and was developed further in *Growing Old: The Process of Disengagement*, a book by Cumming and William Henry, published in 1961. The study on which the theory is based involved 279 old people in the Kansas City area, ranging from working class to upper middle class (Cumming et al., 1960; Cumming and Henry, 1961). Very simply, disengagement is treated as a universal theory of the reduction of one's life space and of the change to a positive orientation toward death in old age.

At the heart of disengagement is the forfeiting of the individual's major life role: for the woman this ordinarily means (to Cumming and Henry) the parental role; for the man, the occupational role. "On the whole men make an abrupt

---

Feature 15.1 **MYTHS ABOUT THE ELDERLY**

A sure way to become unpopular is to write something even mildly critical of older Americans. A recent column of mine—entitled "The Elderly Aren't Needy"—provoked an avalanche of angry letters . . . . The general thrust is that I'm either misguided or loathsome. "One reader wrote: "I hope you never reach 65." Another branded me "an alien life form hatched from a rock."

What I said is that old age by itself doesn't make someone needy. There are many needy older Americans. But most of the elderly are relatively healthy and, like most other Americans, neither fabulously wealthy nor desperately poor . . . .

Another false argument for ignoring Social Security is that it's a pension. Many angry readers wrote, in effect: "I contributed for 40 years, and now I'm taking out what's mine." Not so . . . . Social Security is a welfare program: today's taxpayers pay today's beneficiaries. It's a great program that's created huge social benefits, but it's still welfare . . . .

In my earlier column, I suggested that social-security benefits should be taxed like ordinary income. Most social-security income is now tax-exempt. As a result, tax burdens of younger, lower-income workers are raised to provide tax relief for older, higher-income Americans . . . .

Robert J. Samuelson, "Myths About the Elderly," *Newsweek*, April 18, 1988: 57.

transition from the engaged to the disengaged state, but it is soon resolved; women have a smoother passage, which lasts longer" (Cumming and Henry, 1961: 159). A concomitant of the role loss at the launching of offspring and at retirement is the "decreased interaction between the aging person and others in the social systems he belongs to . . . . His withdrawal may be accompanied from the outset by an increased preoccupation with himself" (Cumming and Henry, 1961: 14). There are changes, say Cumming and Henry, in the number of people with whom the aged person interacts and in the amount of interaction. There are qualitative changes in interaction commensurate with decreased involvement. And there are changes in personality that cause decreased interpersonal involvement and result in increased preoccupation with self. Preoccupation with self includes facing the inevitability of death. Any demoralization that results from the combination of role loss, withdrawal, and facing death, Cumming and Henry feel, is only temporary. Older people eventually come to appreciate the disengaged state and to orient positively to it (Cumming, 1963: 142). One reason for this positive orientation, pointed out by Deutscher in his discussion of the postparental period, is that old age is

> *a time of new freedoms: freedom from the economic responsibilities of children; freedom to be mobile (geographically); freedom from housework and other chores. And, finally, freedom to be one's self for the first time since the children came along (Deutscher, 1962: 524).*

Thus, disengagement theory is, according to its proponents, a cross-culturally applicable theory that includes a generally positive orientation on the part of the aged to the loss of their major roles, to their withdrawal from the social world, and to their increasing preoccupation with self and death.

Criticism of disengagement theory has been both direct and indirect. The best example of direct criticism is a volume edited by Arnold Rose and Warren Peterson, *Older People and Their Social World*. Using the concept of "aging group consciousness," the editors assert that

> *aging group conscious persons have not become disengaged from social roles as a result of aging and retirement. Rather, for most of them, aging and retirement have opened up new roles, because of the increase of leisure time and because of their aging group consciousness (Rose and Peterson, 1965: 26).*

In order to criticize disengagement theory, Rose and Peterson begin by describing it as follows:

> *The Cumming and Henry theory of disengagement is that the society and the individual prepare* in advance *for the ultimate "disengagement" of incurable, incapacitating disease and death by an* inevitable, gradual, and mutually satisfying process of *disengagement . . . . Cumming and Henry say that the values in American culture of competitive achievement and of future orientation make this society especially negative toward aging and hence encourage disengagement. But the process itself must be understood to be inevitable and universal, according to the theory, and not limited to any one group in a society or any one society (Rose and Peterson, 1965: 360, 361).*

The most direct criticisms made by Rose and Peterson are that the theory of disengagement is neither cross-culturally applicable nor universally applicable even in the United States and that the process of disengagement is not necessarily viewed positively when it does occur. In other words, they question (1) whether it occurs, and, if so, (2) whether it is positive. The U.S. culture and economic system at one time created conditions that led to the disengagement of large numbers of the aged. Although disengagement may make for a sense of freedom (as Deutscher claims), Rose and Peterson cite evidence provided by Robert Havighurst and his associates

> *that the engaged elderly, rather than the disengaged, are the ones who generally, although not always, are happiest and have the greatest expressed life satisfaction (Rose and Peterson, 1965: 363).*

Recently, Joan Aldous and others have described the positive nature of the lives of the engaged elderly and near-elderly, especially the well-off and physically healthy (Aldous, 1987: 227–234).

Retreat, disintegration, devastation, threat, desolation —these are some of the terms used by various authors to describe negatively the transition into old age. Disengagement, according to Ethel Shanas, is based on bereavement. "The kind of theory we need is one that suggests not the image of erosion but, rather, that of sudden, if partial, disintegration and patched-up reconstruction" (Shanas, 1968: 285).

How, then did Cumming and her associates arrive at the conclusion that aging and disengagement are actually considered of positive value? This conclusion resulted in part from the fact they primarily sampled healthy people. Once old persons find themselves staying well and outliving their peers, their satisfaction increases as they compare themselves with others. They are grateful to be alive and well, disengaged or not. Frances Hellebrandt agrees with this interpretation of the healthy affluent elderly: they are upbeat and optimistic about the rest of their lives until serious health problems set them back (Hellebrandt, 1980: 404–417). A more subtle reason for the theory is that it draws the functionalist conclusion that "What is, must be," or, to change it slightly, "What is, is good."

If the theory of disengagement is not only *not* cross-culturally valid, but unable even to account of old age in U.S. society, how might it be corrected or expanded? For one thing, disengagement is psychologically continuous and gradual; early social attitudes are manifested behaviorally in the way one reacts to the departure of children and retirement. Robert Atchley has turned this fact into what he calls a *continuity theory* of normal aging. This theory notes that strategies used are tied to past experience as much as possible (Atchley, 1989: 183–190). While hardly a complete theory, it does point out that non-change is every bit as important to the elderly as disengaging from major life roles. Likewise, David Ekardt speaks of the "busy ethic," that requires an individual to have positive goals for retirement, not just the avoidance of work (Ekardt, 1986: 239–244).

On the other hand, a positive orientation toward disengagement is found among those dissatisfied with their earlier life. For example, the socially active woman who wishes she could escape the entertaining and other responsibilities demanded by her husband's occupation may be positively oriented toward disengagement for many years before she can manifest this attitude in her behavior. Or the woman or man who finds no meaning in her or his occupation may be oriented positively toward disengagement virtually throughout their work career. Many working-class people are more accepting of aging than are middle-class people. Aging, yes, but not necessarily retirement. Troll, for example, points out that the retired working-class husband who spends much time with household chores, as many do, may find them demeaning. Seeing them as "woman's work," the ex-manual laborer who has few outside interests in old age may react negatively rather than positively toward disengagement from his work role (Troll, 1971: 198). Thus, in terms of roles, there may actually be three categories of elderly persons in U.S. society: (a) the positively oriented disengaged, who may have experienced "anticipatory disengagement" for many years prior to old age; (b) the negatively oriented disengaged, who, in relinquishing their dominant life roles, give up a highly valued part of their lives or who find old age to be a period of domestic entrapment, sickness, bereavement, and loneliness, rather than one of freedom. These, says John Sill, are the elderly who are increasingly aware of their finitude (Sill, 1980: 457–462); (c) The aged who do not become disengaged at all. The self-employed male or female who never retires exemplifies the still-engaged aged. The repeal of compulsory retirement and the improved health of the elderly has meant that the number of still-engaged elderly is growing rapidly, while the two categories of disengagement begin later and later in life. Gunhild Hagestad is one of the recent writers who has sought to dissociate old age from images of decline, senility, and dependency, and to identify the positive, expansive aspects of an aging society (Hagestad, 1987: 417–422).

Thus far, we have referred to the critics who have questioned the cross-cultural applicability of disengagement theory and who, while admitting that many U.S. aged become disengaged from their major life roles, have noted that some react positively and some negatively to disengagement. A further criticism of the theory concerns the issue of withdrawal from the social network. While many of the aged do become cut off from other people and preoccupied with themselves, two other patterns also occur. One, noted in the previous chapter, is found when the elderly play a central role in the kin network. Troll et al. describe this as follows:

> *Older people sometimes disengage from their roles outside their families, but they rarely disengage from their involvements inside their families. They disengage into rather than from their families. As their worlds shrink, their spouses, children and grandchildren, and even their siblings and other relatives become more important to them (Troll et al., 1979: 6).*

"If they have them," we might add. This pyramidal kinship structure, characterized by substantial contact with children and grandchildren, nephews and nieces, and other kin, is more prevalent among working-class aged.

The other alternative to disengagement by the elderly from the social network is aging-group consciousness (Rose and Peterson, 1965; Rosow, 1967).

Many elderly are neither isolated nor are they involved in a network of kin of descending generations. Rather, they are age-segregated and in frequent contact with other elderly. It is debated whether such age-segregation is good or bad for the elderly, though there is no question that widow's clubs in local churches and other manifestations of age-grouping are not always accompanied by low morale or feelings of family neglect. In any case, the main point is that many elderly people do not simply withdraw from social contact but either continue (and even intensify) their contacts with kin and friends or else become active in groups whose members are aware of their common age bond.

The various criticisms of disengagement theory were brought together by Arlie Hochschild, who argues that Cumming and Henry's theory is unfalsifiable; counterevidence, Hochschild says, is virtually impossible. The engaged or active elderly are considered to be "unsuccessful disengagers," or else off in their timing, or simply exceptions. Furthermore, by not separating disengagement into its constituent parts, such as psychological, social, material, and family, and by not concerning themselves with the meaning of the process for the elderly themselves, Cumming and Henry have reduced a highly complex and variable process to a unitary, universal, positive stage of life (Hochschild, 1975: 553–569).

Cumming and Henry have identified an important aspect of aging in the United States: the relinquishing of the crucial parental and occupational roles in old age. This role loss, however, may be viewed positively or negatively by the individual, and it may or may not be accompanied by a withdrawal from social interaction, a reduction of one's life space, and a preoccupation with self. The debate regarding disengagement theory is reminiscent of the "isolated nuclear family" debate discussed in Chapter 14. Parsons said that kin are less functional in industrial society, and his critics responded: "But they *do* function." Cumming and her associates say that the aged are functionally unimportant, and their critics answer: "Yes, but they *do* things." More importantly, increasing longevity and the change away from compulsory retirement make old age a much more multifaceted phenomenon than it was just a few years ago. Old age for the 65- and for the 85-year-old are very different conditions, as it is for the healthy or declining and for the retired or employed. And the variety of responses to old age in the United States makes highly questionable a theory claiming that disengagement is a universal, positive fact of old age and that old age invariably includes role loss, social withdrawal, and preoccupation with death. The responses to aging are the result of a series of decisions, particularly with respect to retirement, that must be made as old age is reached.

SOCIALIZATION: THE DECISIONS OF THE ELDERLY

How difficult are the adjustments to aging? They are most certainly made more difficult than they would otherwise be by the fact that roles and norms, or expectations concerning what the aged should do and be, are so poorly spelled out.

The departure of children and retirement from one's occupation are the kinds of life changes that demand substantial reorientation on the part of individuals and married couples. The greatest amount of difficulty is likely to be experienced by two types of persons: the wife who has poured body and soul into her children, with few outside interests except those that furthered her children's development, and the husband whose entire commitment has been to his occupation. While each of these occurs less and less frequently, they still deserve some comment. The domestic-parental mother can very easily shrivel up mentally and even physically when her children achieve independence and she finds herself still "attached to her absent children's apron strings." The children's very independence may drain the meaning from her life, if it was sustained by nurturing them. McGoldrick expresses the other side of this problem thus:

> *For some women, the period just after launching their children may be a time of special stress, since they often feel very much behind in the skills to deal with the outside world. Just when the children no longer need them and they are beginning to be defined by the male world as too old to be desirable, they must venture outward (McGoldrick, 1989: 217).*

Of course, the increase in women's employment reduces the probability of this "empty-nest syndrome." The question now is whether mothers (or fathers) prepare any better today for post-parenthood than they did in the recent past.

Likewise, many a man has died only a few months after retirement. If the entire significance of a man's life was wrapped up in working and earning, the physical and psychological adjustment necessitated by retirement may be too much for him. However, as retirement ceases to be compulsory, the work-oriented male is more and more likely to continue to work by choice—thus reducing the phenomenon just noted. But the family-oriented woman and the job-oriented man who have no alternative values and interests to fall back on are likely to be poorly prepared for *positive disengagement* from their major life roles.

The hyper-domestic woman and the hyper-occupational man are, however, but a small portion of the picture of old age. *Economics* and *health* have much to say about how the elderly adjust to that stage of life. Health is a major variable affecting not only individual life satisfaction (positive or negative disengagement), but kin interaction, residence, and even finances (Streib and Beck, 1980: 937–956). Kelley, for example, notes how illness or deterioration affects a marriage: "It is obvious that a severe illness and disability of either spouse create extreme shifts toward unequal dependence. The affected spouse loses in terms of ability to provide rewards for the partner and gains in terms of needs that it is often the partner's lot to satisfy" (Kelley, 1981: 292). Aside from the general deterioration that goes with aging, several factors seem to reduce health problems. These include employment, religion, marriage or a close adult relationships, social support, and higher status (Coleman et al., 1987: 761; Koenig et al., 1988; Anson, 1989: 185; Cantor, 1991: 337-346).

What are the statistics on retirement? Sweet and Bumpass report that three-fifths of men and one-third of women between 60 and 64 were employed in 1980. This was reduced by half between ages 65 and 69, and to almost zero for both genders by age 80 (Sweet and Bumpass, 1987: 333). Longino disagrees with the last figure, stating that about 6 percent of those over 85 are still working (Longino, 1986: 38–42). In the past decade these figures have risen, but not dramatically. Income in retirement, on the average, declines over 50 percent. The irony of Social Security, say Streib and Beck, is that it enables the elderly to live independently but in poverty (Streib and Beck, 1980). Medicaid, Medicare, and Social Security are all partial determinants of the life chances of the elderly (Clark and Menefee, 1981: 132–137), and with the aging of the population, some worry that the Social Security system may eventually "go broke."

Gibson notes the difference between black and white retirees. She speaks of the unretired-retired black, who does not have work but does not consider him or herself retired (Gibson, 1987: 697). This, of course, is the old age equivalent of the earlier black problem of unemployment. Recently Szinovacz and others have done important research on the retirement of women in comparison to men. She reports that a woman's retirement occurs in relation to other life events more often than does a man's. A family member's illness, for example, may trigger a woman's retirement. However, Szinovacz also notes that a partial explanation may be a woman's greater tendency to recall relevant events—perhaps as a result of some of the socialization and role differences noted in Chapters 8 and 12 (Szinovacz and Washo, 1992: 191–196).

In the problematic atmosphere of retirement and economics, negotiation and decision-making are central to the life of the elderly. According to Scanzoni and Szinovacz:

> *One major transition in later life, namely the retirement of one or both spouses, requires them to engage in a series of decision-making processes which often go far beyond retirement planning itself. The changes brought about by this event often lead to the reopening of previously agreed upon issues. . . .*
>
> *If for no other reason, ongoing changes in women's and men's sex role preferences as well as changes in their employment and retirement patterns, suggest that as cohorts of persons keep on passing into the senior life-span stage, they can expect continual increases in the frequencies of explicit decisioning, conflicts, and negotiation (Scanzoni and Scinovacz, 1980: 254).*

What are some of the decisions the elderly must make? First they must make *residential* decisions. These include deciding whether to stay in the home in which they reared their children or whether to change residence completely. Change of residence may mean deciding whether to move into an apartment, a mobile home, or a smaller house in the same community (perhaps closer to the business district and public transportation); whether to move to a retirement, or age-segregated community; or whether to move to a community in which their children or other kin reside. Although it is a highly visible phenomenon, the rate of migration to sunbelt areas by retirees is only five percent that of nonretirees moving to those areas, and involves, for the most part, high-status people from cold climates (Chevan and Fischer, 1979: 1365–1380; Longino and Lipman, 1981: 169–177). Martha Riche simply states that the elderly tend to stay right where they are when they retire, though not necessarily in the same house.

She distinguishes residence by age, with retirement communities targeting those age 60–74 who are married, in good health, and active. Congregate care communities are for those 75–84 who do not need nursing care, but do need some help. Many of these are widows. Then there are the continuing care communities for those who need round-the-clock care (Riche, 1986: 50–56).

Secondly the elderly must make decisions about *activities*. They may continue to pursue the same activities as before or take up new ones. They may join new organizations—perhaps age-graded groups, such as golden age clubs—or continue their current affiliations with religious and other groups, or simply drop many old activities and organizations. Several researchers have noted the importance of the church to the social integration of the black elderly (Taylor and Chatters, 1986: 637–642; Johnson and Barer, 1990: 726–733).

A third set of decisions, related to the two already introduced has to do with their *social networks*. How should they relate in terms of proximity and contact to age companions, children, and other friends and kin? Should they simply disengage from most social contacts?

The final set of decisions concerns *marital relations* (if, of course, the marriage is still intact). In which activities should the aged couple participate jointly, and in which as individuals? How should household responsibilities be divided, now that the husband or both couple members no longer go off to work each morning? These last two decision areas—social network relations and marital relations in old age—have been the objects of substantial research, and are complex and important enough to require a more intensive look.

SECTION THREE

THE SOCIAL NETWORK AND AGE SEGREGATION

The social networks of the elderly consist of *kin*, who are primarily children and others of the descending generation, and *non-kin*, who are mostly part of their own generation.

Kin Relations of the Elderly

Families mean "responsibility, especially toward the very young and very old. People believe that families are the group of first and last resort" (Fogel et al., 1981: xix). While that may be true, Shanas and Sussman point out that there are also some fairly negative myths about old people and their families in the Western world: "First, that older people are alienated from their children; second, that older people, particularly those living alone, are isolated; and third, that families are unwilling or unable to care for their frail elderly members" (Shanas and Sussman, 1981: 218). These myths, says Shanas, are just that: they are incorrect. In fact, the elderly are likely to keep in touch with whatever kin they have. This may mean considerable contact with their own aging brothers and sisters, as noted in Chapter 14, but more often the focus is on children and grandchildren. Separate-but-near is the rule of residence in old age.

"Most old parents," Troll, Miller, and Atchley add, "prefer to live alone, though they live near and see their children frequently . . . . They do not tend to live in the same household unless either parents or children are in such poor health that they cannot take care of themselves or unless financial circumstances make it necessary" (Troll et al., 1979: 104, 106).

A great deal of aid flows between parents and their adult offspring, as noted in Chapter 14. Two models have been proposed to account for the direction of flow. The *reciprocal*, or role reversal, model contends that when the children are getting settled into adulthood, their parents help them, but later on, as the parents move into old age, the flow of aid reverses, moving from the middle-aged offspring to their elderly parents. The *serial*, or linear model, contends that each generation continuously passes resources along to its descendants (Cheal, 1983: 805–813). Not surprisingly, there is some evidence in support of each model. David Cheal finds that both status and deterioration must be taken into consideration. The high-status elderly are overseers of an important symbolic and economic family estate. "Since earnings peak late for men in high-level occupational groups," says Valerie Oppenheimer, "such couples (or one survivor, at least) should enter old age with a much greater economic advantage than other socioeconomic groups" (Oppenheimer, 1981: 60). In fact, those who have accumulated a substantial estate may not ever have to be dependent on their offspring for economic survival, resulting in serial aid at the high socioeconomic levels. However, little accumulation means reciprocal aid in old age. One qualification on serial aid among the affluent is also in order. If they live long enough and deteriorate slowly enough, a substantial estate may be used up, resulting in reciprocal aid for them as well. The very wealthy, of course, are least likely to face this. The role reversal that makes the less affluent elderly dependent on their adult offspring, with no authority base to offset their dependence, may be a real psychological threat to the elderly. Dependence on adult offspring may not only be alienative, it may even result in "elder abuse," an occurrence only now receiving attention and concern (Pedrick-Cornell and Gelles, 1982: 457–465; Doublas, 1983: 395–402; see also Scharlach, 1987: 627–631 on role strain between mothers and adult daughters). But the dominant theme is solidarity between the generations, and much recent research has explicated the caregiving role of daughters and its effect on the quality of the relationship from both the daughter's and the parent's standpoint (Walker et al., 1990: 51–56; Moss et al., 1985: 134–140; Brody et al., 1989: 529–538). Relations between the elderly and their offspring might be summarized by saying that they are based more on friendship than authority; two variations on that theme are that (1) the elderly may be family resources for their adult offspring who are going through major life changes and stresses (Greenberg and Becker, 1988: 786–791), or (2) instances of serious dependence by the aged on their offspring may cause various manifestations of intergenerational strain.

Some complications in the kin relations of the elderly deserve mention. First, gender differences are such that men are more likely to still be living with a spouse. However, divorce has left a substantial number of elderly men alone, and being alone is more likely to mean loneliness for men than for women. What Spitze and Miner say for elderly black men holds for white as well: For the "subgroup of black men who are not currently married, who live alone, and who are also less involved with both children and the church, their needs for both contact and assistance may be unmet" (Spitze and Miner, 1992: 218). We will say more about marriage and gender in the next section.

A second issue concerns the small families and voluntary childlessness that are increasingly prevalent in U.S. society. Few or no children means that the elderly will have little support from or contact with the descending generation. It also means they will have fewer elderly siblings as well. Christine Bachrach says that "Childlessness is associated with a relatively high probability of isolation for those in poor health and those with working-class backgrounds, but not for those with few health problems or nonmanual backgrounds" (Bachrach, 1980: 636; see also Ikels, 1988; and Rempel, 1985, on the childless elderly). Again, health and economics make the difference. If the small family and increased longevity continue to be prevalent in this society, the elderly will be thrown increasingly on the resources of friends, community, and perhaps religious organizations (on religion as a coping strategy for the elderly, see Koenig et al., 1988: 303-310).

The mention of community resources raises the issue of *institutionalization*. About six percent of the elderly are in institutional settings at present, though over 20 percent spend some time in institutions prior to death. In fact, one-fourth of the women and one-sixth of the men over age 85 are living in institutions (Sweet and Bumpass, 1987: 332). There are, of course, minimal care institutions for the able elderly, medium care facilities, and care communities that provide guaranteed shelter and health care for those in continuous need (see Riche, 1986: 50–56). The closer relation between offspring and their institutionalized parents, reported by many of the former, may in large part be explained by the freeing of the offspring from a major burden of care just prior to institutionalization. Only a small fraction report the kind of "dumping" and neglect on the part of offspring that is often played upon in the popular press (Smith and Bengtson, 1979: 438–447).

The next issue involves the adaptation of older gay and lesbian adults. Quam and Whitford interviewed 80 elderly homosexuals at a conference, and found the same issues as those confronting other elderly, plus the added factor:

> *The areas of concern for aging gay men and lesbian women are primarily the same ones as for most aging adults — loneliness, health, and income. However, the aging gay men and lesbian women find another layer of concerns for the future. Respondents wrote movingly of fears of rejection by adult children and grandchildren when as a parent or grandparent they came out in their family (Quam and Whitford, 1992: 373).*

The role of grandparent is, of course, intertwined with the intergenerational issues just discussed. However, there is no need to repeat what was said about grandparenting in Chapter 14. We will simply note that in working- and lower-class families, the aging parents are apt to provide important friendship relations for their descendants, but the likelihood that they will be dependent on their adult offspring strains the friendship to some extent. In the middle class, the elderly are less likely to be dependent and more apt to control an inheritance, but are also more likely to be residentially separated from their offspring, thereby reducing the friendship role. In sum, then, children do not assure less loneliness, or a more positive disengagement toward death (Keith, 1983: 403–409). Whatever role the aged play in the lives of their children and other kin is ordinarily based on social-emotional centrality, but this role is often tenuous because the aged are simply not defined as necessary by their descending kin.

Non-Kin and Age-Grading

As a result of their devaluation by society in general and their "surplus" character in the eyes of kin, the elderly tend increasingly to become a subsociety, with a few distinctive cultural elements. Those forming subsocieties are most often found either in retirement communities or in central cities.

A constraint on assimilation into an elderly peer group is a person's marital status. Some subcommunities of elderly consist of widows, especially in big cities, while retirement communities often involve couples. Thus, one of the bases for a residential or activity decision in old age may very well be the death of one's spouse, which may require the seeking out of age companions whose marital status is the same as one's own. One image of the age-segregated elderly is as poverty-stricken and clustered together in central city ghettoes. Fred Pampel and Harvey Choldin have examined this generalization and come to the following conclusions.

> *Previous conceptions of the aged as highly segregated in inner city ghettoes are exaggerated. Although age-segregation is moderate, and distance from the central business district is related to percent 65+, the aged are dispersed throughout the city and are not concentrated in undesirable city blocks with low value housing, high density and high crowding. Thus, while there are certainly older persons segregated in poor housing near the central city, they are not typical according to our data. The aged population is heterogeneous and older persons are not as poor and ill-housed as the stereotypes have suggested (Pampel and Choldin, 1978: 1136).*

Several authors stated a generation ago that the age-graded elderly feel a greater sense of integration into society than do those elderly who depend for social contact on the descending generation. Recently, Gary Lee has confirmed this with a large sample of respondents in the state of Washington: "the strongest predictor of marital satisfaction . . . here is frequency of interaction with friends, and this effect is positive . . ." (Lee, 1988: 780). As noted earlier, one source of interaction with friends is religion, with church groups and activities being central to the lives of many elderly, especially black Americans. Another element in non-kin interaction is dating or going out, and Bulcroft and O'Connor recently talked with 35 persons over 60 about such relationships. Their findings are that

> *older persons place greater emphasis on the companionate nature of the relationships, rather than accentuating the passionate aspects of later life dating; . . . the dating partner typically provides an emotional and sexual outlet which cannot be attributed to (others) . . . . (W)hile older women derive increased prestige from dating, older men stress the importance of dating as a means for self-disclosure. Dating is indeed a hedge against loneliness in later life (Bulcroft and O'Connor, 1986: 397).*

One night stands and multiple partners were almost never reported.

The middle-class elderly fit the picture of the ideally age-segregated more closely than do the working- and lower-class aged. Their kin tend to be more scattered than are those of the blue-collar aged, and they have more friends. While those friends are also more scattered, the middle-class aged have a greater number of options open to them in terms of socialization into old age, due to their generally greater economic resources and their more cosmopolitan life orientations. This, however, does not necessarily mean a smoother transition into old age for middle-class persons, because they are more likely to have a strong positive orientation toward the major life roles which they must give up, and therefore to be negatively oriented toward retirement and disengagement.

SECTION FOUR

MARRIED AND WIDOWED ELDERLY

The shift of focus away from children in the empty nest years and the incorporation of the husband *into* the home are the tasks that give married life among the U.S. elderly its particular character. In the mid-1980s, three-fourths of elderly men and two-fifths of elderly women were maintaining their own households with their spouse (Sweet and Bumpass, 1987: 332). Themes that emerge from the literature on the elderly are: an increase in conventionality, greater marital satisfaction, a decrease in passion, a restructuring of housework, and concern with health.

Conventionality (and conservatism) are questionable, but Caspi et al. do find that elderly couples change in the same direction over the course of their marriage (Caspi et al., 1992: 281–291). The elderly are not unhappy with their lot. Having disengaged *into* the family, they may report their marriages happier than before. (Of course, some of this is because the unhappiest are no longer married; recall Chapter 13). Marital satisfaction is, in turn, related positively to morale among the elderly, though especially for women. Lee feels that the importance of his finding is that the husband in old age simply responds favorably to having a spouse, while the wife responds to the *quality* of the relationship with her husband (Lee, 1978: 136, 137). Old age, then, if coupled with marriage and reasonable health, is not a time of disenchantment with life, but of comparative satisfaction.

While some have noted a general tapering off of sexual activity in old age, Simone de Beauvoir has asserted that negativism concerning the aged is often expressed in terms of their sexuality (Morgan, 1975: 197). It is perhaps this societal negativism, not any lack of physiological capability, that causes sexuality to diminish in old age. However, it may also be a loss of erotic interest, as William Griffitt points out.

> *While the monotony of lengthy sexual relationships may well lead many aged men and women to lose erotic interest in and responsiveness to their aging partners, other observations suggest that some older men and women not only become erotically unresponsive to their marital partners, but also actually begin to react with sexual aversion to what they perceive as increasingly unattractive features of appearance (Griffitt, 1981: 310).*

The work of Masters and Johnson has made it clear that sexual responsiveness, like all other bodily processes, is slower among the elderly, but that factor does not mean that it is not both desirable and possible (Masters and Johnson, 1968). (See Feature 15.2.)

In turning to household responsibilities, our major concern will be with the effect of the husband's retirement. Research on household work during retirement is important for several reasons, says Lorraine Dorfman: (1) loss of occupational role may mean more involvement in home activities and in hobbies or

---

Feature 15.2 **SEX AND THE SENIOR CITIZEN**

. . . despite increasing scientific evidence to the contrary, our culture continues to foster the belief that by the time one is in his or her 60s, sex is neither necessary nor possible. Or if it *does* occur, it is somehow not quite normal. Not that it certainly isn't nice for the old folks to be indulging in it.

Some older people fear the ridicule or censure of younger persons if they show signs of still being interested in sex. Children and even grandchildren disapprove, make them feel guilty. . . .

We may be slowly acclimating ourselves to the idea that there is sexuality after 65, but we are still a long way from actively helping older people to express it fully, or to deal with their feelings about it . . . .

Clearly, there is more to sexuality after 65 than just the act of sex. For the man, there is the satisfaction of feeling still masculine; for the woman, still feminine; for both, still being wanted and needed. There is the comforting warmth of physical nearness, the pleasure of companionship. There is the rewarding emotional intimacy of shared joys. . . .

Norman M. Lobsenz, "Sex and the Senior Citizen," *The New York Times Magazine*, 20 January, 1974, pp. 54–55, 70–71.

other leisure; (2) division of labor may also express power relationships; (3) much can be learned about couple patterns over the life course by studying retirement (Dorfman, 1992: 159–173). Men do become more involved in housework than formerly, but the tasks they do are stereotypically masculine ones, such as burning trash, fixing faucets, or administrative ones like paying bills (Keith and Brubaker, 1979: 497–502). The typical division of household tasks is apparent even in retirement. Elizabeth Hill and Lorraine Dorfman, therefore, suggest "that it would be advantageous for the husband to learn to participate in household tasks earlier in the life cycle, since his participation is correlated with satisfaction of the wife when retirement occurs (Hill and Dorfman, 1982: 199). An interesting summary comment comes from Rexroat and Shehan:

> *While husbands spend very little time in housework, they are more likely to increase their time in household labor during periods of low or no occupational involvement, that is, early in their employment careers and after retirement. Wives, on the other hand, spend less time in housework before and after childrearing (Rexroat and Shehan, 1987: 747).*

Men become more reflective and mellow and less aggressive in old age, while women become more assertive. Cooper and Gutmann state it thus: "post-empty nest women are more free to express some of the masculine qualities of assertion, aggression, and executive capacity which they had had to repress in the service of parenthood" (1987: 352). Moreover, they say, a more administrative feminine role works toward bridging the gender gap. It may not be that women have more "power" in the sense of our earlier discussion, but simply that role sharing is more likely than when children are in the home. And role sharing—involving more housework by the man and more decision-making by the woman—seems to make for a closer relationship. Timothy Brubaker states that "for most married . . . elderly persons, spouses provide extraordinary companionship and support throughout the later years" (Brubaker, 1990: 962). Thus, the issue of power among elderly couples has not been resolved by research, but companionship and role sharing certainly seem more prevalent among the elderly. And, as Robert Atchley says, "a solid marriage is a central part of 'the good life' for married older people, and reactions of married people to various life events are conditioned by the fact that these changes occur in the context of a couple . . . (Atchley, 1992: 146).

To conclude, we have found sexual activity reduced but important, retirement to have changed both spouse's roles, and power relations not completely understood. Is it safe to state that old age is a good time for married couples? The marital satisfaction literature responds with a guarded "yes." But it is also true that whatever the couple's "social construction" has become, it is likely to be even more so in old age. A conflict habituated couple will have more time for conflict. A passive-congenial couple may be just as passive. And, says Zube, another possible trajectory is that the elderly husband expects more from family life, while the elderly wife looks outside the family for interests.

> *Differing trajectories of men and their wives can place them on a collision course. Resentments can flare when the wife seeks expression outside the home at a time when the*

TABLE 15.1   FOUR WAYS IN WHICH THE AGED MAY RELATE TO THEIR SPOUSES AND
TO THEIR SOCIAL NETWORKS

	MARRIAGE (Cohesion)	SOCIAL NETWORK (Ties)
Types		
I	High	Close-knit
II	High	Loose-knit
III	Low	Close-knit
IV	Low	Loose-knit

✦   Type I—The adjustment of an aged couple may be characterized by high cohesion to each other and by close ties to their social networks. Such a couple finds meaning in shared activities and in continued contacts with persons outside the home, including friends and kin. Many of the couple's former role adjustments are maintained as they move together through their various joint activities, as well as separately within their individual networks.

✦   Type II—The aged couple's adjustment may combine high marital cohesion with a loose bond to extrafamilial persons. This is the prototype of what the popular press calls "togetherness." The couple share not only goals—a bond that may have characterized their earlier lives—but activities as well. This is a likely pattern for striving and successful couples who were too busy during their adult careers to develop strong ties to other persons.

✦   Type III—There is low couple cohesion in conjunction with close ties to members of the social network. This relationship is exemplified by the old man who spends most of his time with his cronies while his wife is busy with her clubs. The peer group reasserts itself, perhaps as marital disenchantment gives rise to a kind of mutual avoidance. Network relations may involve kin instead of friends; this type of adjustment in old age is most apt to be found among those couples who have experienced the greatest amount of role segregation or differentiation during their adult lives, that is, working- and lower-class couples.

✦   Type IV—The low-cohesion couple is loosely tied to the social network. This situation is especially troublesome for the retired male, whom it compels to find hobbies, such as the basement workshop or the garden, with which to occupy himself during his declining years. The wife, under these circumstances, may vigorously pursue every speck of dust in the home, and may think of her husband as in the way. The couple live together but are not really together.

husband seeks increased mutuality and affection and even dependency within the confines of the home (Zube, 1982: 155).

In other words, then, the heightened importance of the relationship itself in old age ordinarily has a positive effect, but may instead give rise to new role conflicts.

Marital Cohesion and Network Ties

Socialization into old age includes decisions about residence, activity, the social network, and couple relations. Thompson and Streib, in a classic article on "Meaningful Activity in a Family Context," summarize much of the foregoing discussion by means of a useful fourfold typology (see Table 15.1). This typology, focusing on the social network and marital relations, has been specified by other writers, but not replaced (Thompson and Streib, 1961: 177–211).

In which of the four types is the desolation of one spouse likely to be the greatest at the death of the other? A Type II spouse, whose activity patterns in old age have involved doing things with his or her spouse, is obviously going to be profoundly affected by such a loss. However, substantial desolation also occurs when a member of a Type IV couple dies. For, while the old age of Type IV couples may have been spent in conflict or avoidance, their habit patterns are almost as interwoven as are those of Type II couples. Thus the bereavement of the surviving spouse, regardless of the specific character of the husband-wife bond, is greatest in those instances in which the individual lacks a close social network to "absorb" them. Essex and Nam add that the quality of social contact is more important than the quantity, though they are unable to say whether family or friends are more important to emotional well-being (Essex and Nam, 1987: 104). Several have reported that the spouse's death is more devastating for a male than for a female in our society, an important reason for this being the elderly male's more restricted social world. Women maintain closer family contacts than men, as we noted in Chapter 14, and their friendships, though fewer, are more intimate. Edward Powers and Gordon Bultena describe this distinction clearly:

> . . . *the social worlds of aged men and women are distinct in many ways. Men have more frequent social contact but limit their interaction to family and friends. Men are less likely than women to have intimate friends and are less likely to replace lost friends. Women have a diverse social world and* many have intimate ties outside the immediate family. *It is somewhat ironic that the last years of men's lives should be so precarious in a society that has been largely oriented toward the privileged position of men [Italics added.]* (Powers and Bultena, 1976: 746).

The desolation of the surviving spouse, it should be added, can also be mitigated by remarriage. At present, the elderly widower is more likely to remarry than is the elderly widow, partly because of the low ratio of men to women at this stage of life. However, the older the widow or widower, the less likely they are to remarry (Smith et al., 1991: 361-374). Widowers are not only more likely to remarry than widows, remarriage is more important to their well-being. In fact, Vannoy-Hiller and Philliber report, "research shows that married men are healthier and live longer than single men, but that the reverse is true for women" (1989: 28). Remarriage will be discussed more generally in the last part of Chapter 17.

Widowhood

The population of elderly women who are healthy, nonpoor, educated, widowed, and unemployed is growing. By the year 2000 there will be an estimated 19 million of them. The work of Helena Lopata and others has provided much information about the lives of widows in the United States. Though there may be some contact with kin, widows do not have the kind of kin support they seem to need. David Morgan interviewed 39 widows and found that 40 percent of all mentions of social contact were negative, with family relations more problematic than non-family (Morgan, 1989: 101-107). One reason for this is that friends are "achieved" or chosen, and similar in age, while children and grandchildren are "ascribed," or given, very different in age, and contain an obligatory element. An interesting sub-issue is whether employed daughters are less able to provide care for their aging widowed mothers. According to Brody and Schoonover the answer is "no." They state that "the noninstitutionalized dependent elderly are not suffering neglect due to increased work-force participation of their daughters" (Brody and Schoonover, 1986: 380). Widows and other elderly are more likely to live alone than with a relative or friend. However, there is a big difference by race, with white women much more likely to live alone. Choi's explanation is most interesting in light of the discussion in Chapter 6:

> these findings lead to the speculation that non-white elderly women may not cherish privacy and independence so much as the duty to maintain family cohesiveness and that they see the stresses of loneliness as much less bearable than the stresses of multi-generational family life (Choi, 1991: 504).

The significance of these findings would seem to be that while autonomy is desired by the elderly, when one's spouse dies, lack of embeddedness in a larger network can leave the widow or widower in a difficult situation. Even one's own children seem incapable of completely solving the "support" problem of the widow (though this is more true for whites than for blacks). Rather, it seems to require a peer group, such as a widow's club, or remarriage—or at least a heterosexual companion. In the previous section we commented on the dating relationships of elderly widows and widowers. Let us now briefly mention cohabitation among the elderly. There are signs that point to an increasing willingness of older people to experiment with alternative lifestyles after their children have been launched and when their spouses are no longer alive. Cohabitation between single elderly, both for companionship and to maintain Social Security payments, and greater freedom, has been reported by researchers and the mass media. Such experimentation, often in retirement communities, may have been learned from the younger generation and may thus be an example of reverse socialization. It is as yet too early to tell whether unconventionality will become increasingly prevalent among the elderly, but it is an issue that deserves further research attention.

A word about the economic position of widows is in order. In a review of the literature, Carolyn Balkwell finds a 50 percent drop in income for widows, resulting in economic hardship (Balkwell, 1981: 117–127). About 20 percent of older women live at or below the income level determined to be adequate by the Social Security Administration, but the figure is 50 percent for the widowed elderly (Minkler and Stone, 17). Older minority women are the poorest segment of American society. Zick and Smith add that widows and widowers do not necessarily become poor all at once; the decline in economic well-being continues for several years (Zick and Smith, 1986: 674). According to Morgan, it is not inability to handle financial matters that makes for widows' financial troubles: "having had primary or shared responsibility for finances during marriage made no significant difference in the likelihood of being poor or of a decline in the standard of living . . . (Morgan, 1986: 667).

Throughout we have been speaking of the widowed elderly, which is understandable in view of the dramatic reduction in premature deaths in this century. However, it is noteworthy that when *all* widows are considered, 61.5 percent are employed compared to 44 percent of all married women (Morgan, 1980: 581–587). Maxi Szinovacz and her colleagues have found that formerly married (including widowed) women retire later than married, and almost one in ten do not plan to retire at all (Morgan, 1992: 124). Though it may appear as if women seek employment when their husbands die, Leslie Morgan finds that these widows were already working when their husbands were living. It would seem that they have originally gone to work as a reaction to the husband's serious illness or disability or else have been working already. But more research is needed to confirm this explanation.

SECTION FIVE

OLD AGE AND ADOLESCENCE: A COMPARISON

By now in this chapter it should be apparent that, even without the inevitabilities of sickness and death, old age is a period of uncertainty and change in the United States, with few positive compensations. Even the reasonably satisfactory marital adjustments found among the aged are to some extent achieved "by default," by giving up other major life roles. And, of course, the many elderly who no longer have marital partners, though generally forced to give up their major life roles, cannot avail themselves of this compensating satisfaction. According to Leo Simmons, writing forty years ago,

> *while we have made much ado over the discovery of adolescence as a unique stage in life experiences, and recognized it as quite different from adulthood, we are continuing — mistakenly — to regard aging as little more than a somewhat discredited extension of mid-adulthood. . . .*
>
> *There are some quite justifiable reasons to assume that a shift from mid-life to old age can be as significant a change as that from adolescence to adulthood, and the range of variations in the successful fruition of life in old age may really be much wider than it is for youth (Simmons, 1952: 51).*

If one looks back over this chapter, at least three points of similarity between old age and adolescence in the United States become apparent. First, the multiple decisions that the aged must make parallel the multiple decisions of the adolescent and demonstrate that a vast amount of *socialization* takes place during both adolescence and old age. Granted, the decisions of adolescence are concerned with the *engagement* process, or the assumption of one's major life roles, while those of old age are related to *disengagement*, or their relinquishment, but the choices are numerous during both periods. Second, both the adolescent and the elderly person are presented with *unclear role options*. The question "How should the adolescent behave?" posed in Chapter 8 may appropriately be applied to the aged as well. For, in U.S. society, the behavioral expectations for both young people and old people are not clear-cut, but are—within limits—up to individual decision. As long as adolescents and the aged stay out of the way, they may determine their own social behaviors. This condition, "staying out of the way," brings us to the final similarity between the elderly and the adolescents. In some ways both groups have the character of minorities, or at least of *subsocieties*. They are increasingly age-segregated; they have little social power as a group; and they are tolerated as long as they keep to themselves—although this is something of an overstatement. One response to minority status is the "Gray Panther" organization, a national organization concerned with the social and economic plight of the elderly. Even among the working classes, the aged are decreasingly individually embedded in their kin networks. An important reason for treating adolescents and the aged as subsocieties appears to be economic: both categories are encouraged to stay out of the occupational market—the adolescents by postponing their entry, the aged by hastening their departure—so that unemployment rates may be kept to a minimum.

Despite these similarities, old age is generally a more pessimistic and negative period than adolescence, for adolescents have their adult futures to look forward to, while the elderly must find pleasure in leisure activity and comfort in thoughts of the past, looking forward to decline and death. Some of the aged may find satisfaction in leisure and "a job well done," as disengagement theory says they should, but many others in the United States simply cannot make their peace with this period of ill-defined choices, separation, and loss.

Stress, Crisis, and Violence in the Family

CHAPTER 16

Family life involves both pattern and change. Thus far we have concentrated primarily on the patterns that develop and persist in the modern family. In this chapter the foci of attention are the acts, events, and processes—such as violence, unemployment, child birth, and alcoholism—that require some form of major adjustment on the part of the family. An attempt is made to develop a framework for distinguishing among various changes and challenges that confront families and for summarizing the conditions that determine different family responses. Family violence is then discussed in some detail, including marital, child, elder, and courtship.

Life in the family is not just many years of habit and routine. Nor is it many years of love and harmony—though the rhetoric and ideology of family emphasize such positives. Although some married people may complain that "nothing exciting ever happens," the fact is transition and change are as central to family experience as are continuity and pattern. The normative transitions of parenthood, the departure of children, physical decline, and death are expected and inevitable; in addition, most families face unexpected challenges or stressors.

U.S. society is characterized by patriarchal elements, including the norm of male authority in much of the population. The institutions are less embedded in the family than ever before, so that individuals (especially males) leave home to work and return home with expectations of rest and sustenance. Family members are still intensely embedded in small nuclear families, and the combination of lingering patriarchy, institutional differentiation, and family intensity results in various stresses, even violence.

The literature on expected and unexpected acts, events, and processes as they relate to families is voluminous. It includes studies of infidelity, illegitimacy, unemployment, physical and mental illness, alcoholism, violence, divorce, and death. (Chapter 17 will deal with the last two as well as remarriage following divorce.) The terms used to describe family responses to these stressors are numerous and often vague. They include: trouble, problem, crisis, stress, strain, deviance, disorganization, breakdown, maladjustment, and disintegration, and their opposites, such as organization, adaptation, coping, and integration. The family, says Feature 16.1, is both the cause and cure for stress.

The three key terms are stressor, crisis, and more recently strain. In much of the early literature, stress and crisis were used almost interchangeably. However, these three concepts are now distinguished as follows: *stressors* are stimuli to which the family (or individual) must respond. *Strain* is a condition of felt tension or objective difficulty (Olson et al., 1988: 19). A *crisis* is when things are out of control, or when the rules are not working. Strain and crisis are both responses to stimuli, with the latter being somewhat more intense or dramatic. One form of strain is "role strain," in which—due to some stressor such as childbirth or unemployment—family roles no longer work as they did in the past. And, as we noted in Chapter 13, deviance is when a family member changes the rules just for themselves, with a likely result being strain or crisis.

Important as clarity of terminology is, our foci will be: (a) family stressor or stimuli variations, (b) factors affecting the family's response, (c) processes through which families go in reacting to stressors, and (d) family violence as a stressor.

SECTION ONE

FAMILY STRESSOR VARIATIONS

Normative and Non-Normative

"Stressors may be divided into normative (expected, scheduled) or non-normative (unexpected)" (McCubbin et al., 1980: 856–858). Typical *normative stressors* are those that happen to virtually everyone who has a family, such as the transition to parenthood, child launching, retirement, widowhood, residential movement, and occupational change. *Non-normative stressors* or events include unemployment, violence, alcoholism, mental illness, various types of disasters, an extramarital affair, and physical disability. The second type of stressor is more likely to result in a crisis or disorganization than the first, because they are unexpected. In fact, in some ways the terms "expected-unexpected" capture better the real significance of this distinction. A death in old age is expected, but a premature death is not. The birth of a child is expected, but not the birth of a handicapped or retarded child. Thus, normative events must be defined not only as "happening to everyone," but as happening at certain times and with certain outcomes, and if the timing or outcome varies it must be considered unexpected, or non-normative.

Many good accounts of normative stressors are appearing in the literature such as the transition to parenthood, boundary changes, and changes in household composition (Boss, 1980: 445–450; Menaghan, 1983: 371–386; Cowan et al., 1991: 79–109). Elizabeth Menaghan's study of household transitions finds that

Feature 16.1 FAMILY: BOTH CAUSE OF AND CURE FOR STRESS

Durham, N.H—A new and more complex view of the powerful effects of stress on the nation's families has emerged from a gathering of scholars here. The researchers also offered new insights on the family's paradoxical role in both causing and relieving stress, and underscored the importance of the family in social scientists' attempts to understand how stress affects individuals. . . .

In categorizing the causes of family stress, some sources are primary, Dr. Pearlin said, conditions generated within the family. Among many kinds of primary stress, he cited "scheduled life events," eventful changes rooted in the life cycle such as marriage, childbirth or the aging or death of parents or spouses. . . .

Other research pointed to "male-biased assumptions," about stress, as Grace Baruch termed them. "Stress is seen as an ailment that can be caught at work and not at home," said Dr. Baruch, program director of the Wellesley College Center for Research on Women. "The home has been seen as a sanctuary and a haven, while work has been viewed as a high-stress environment."

However, studies have underscored "the stressfulness of family life itself," she said, adding that for both women and men, work can buffer family stress, especially enjoyable work. . . .

Glenn Collins, "Family: Both Cause of and Cure for Stress," *New York Times*, Style, Monday, June 9, 1986.

four years after the transition little effect of starting school, leaving home, or later births is discernible (Menaghan, 1983). These, of course, are normative events, and Burr has pointed out one reason why they are not crisis-producing, but may not even have long-term effects. When an event is expected, says Burr, the individual or the family can engage in anticipatory socialization, or pre-learning. This can in turn ease the transition and result in a lower level of disorganization or crisis (Burr, 1973: 125).

External Versus Internal Origin

A stressor may originate outside the family or within it. The family's response to an *external stressor*—a natural disaster, a depression, or a war—may either be disorganization or increased solidarity, depending on its internal resources. However, the likelihood of crisis is greater with an *internal stressor*, an event that originates within the family. For example, compare the family that loses its belongings in a flood with the family whose resources are gambled away by the husband. Or compare the family in which the husband, like millions of others, loses his job in a depression with the family in which the husband loses his job because of excessive drinking. One study finds individuals are less threatened today by job loss because they view it "as less their own responsibility" (Thomas et al., 1980: 517–524). Or compare the family disrupted by war with the family disrupted by the husband's desertion. In each of these paired instances, the latter eventuality is more likely to cause family difficulty because the blame cannot be placed outside the family. In other words, internal blame adds to the stress. Donald Hansen states that "if an individual family member or family unit is faulted for experiencing a particular problem, the blame itself will be additionally stressful" (Hansen, 1988: 148). Even in a SIDS death, parents concerned with attributing blame are more distressed rather than less (Downey et al., 1990: 939). Therefore, placing blame is stress-producing, and blaming a family member is particularly so.

Temporary Versus Permanent

Some stressors are "one shot deals" or *temporary stressors*, while others are *permanent stressors*. An illness is ordinarily temporary, but it may result in a permanent disability. The terms used synonymously with temporary and permanent in discussing illness are *acute* and *chronic*. Hansen states that chronic stressors, such as the presence of a severely handicapped family member or one with a terminal illness, generally are harder to assess than the more striking disjunctive events such as divorce and unemployment" (Hansen, 1988: 150). They are not just harder to assess, but to deal with, because the temporary situation may be treated that way, while a chronic condition requires new rules and adjustments. Unemployment is less stressful if it occurs less often, because it can be treated as an acute, rather than chronic, condition (see Voydanoff and Donnelly, 1988: 98). The various natural disasters are ordinarily acute, since a flood or tornado usually strikes only once. Divorce may be seen as a temporary or acute stressor depending on the lateness of the break. McAdoo and Peters have noted that race itself is a permanent stressor for many black parents (McAdoo, 1982: 487–488; Peters and Massey, 1983: 193–215).

Voluntary Versus Involuntary

The *voluntary/involuntary* stressors are similar to but not the same as the internal/external stressors. Death is a good example of the difference: clearly an internal stressor, it can be either involuntary in the case of a natural death, or voluntary in the case of suicide. A physical illness is ordinarily involuntary, but there may be a voluntary element if the individual did not take proper precautions to prevent the illness. Diane Vaughan makes an interesting and pertinent point about divorce. In most divorces, she says, there is an initiator. For the initiator, the divorce is a voluntary stressor, for the partner it is not. This is but one reason the divorce is less stressful for the initiator, or for the one who wants out (Vaughan, 1986: 189). Most forms of deviant behavior, such as a sexual affair or juvenile delinquency, are volitional or voluntary, while most forms of chronic physical and mental problems are involuntary.

When the temporary/permanent and voluntary/involuntary distinctions are combined, the results appear to be as shown in Figure 16.1. This is an oversimplification, or a median tendency, because divorce may not be permanent and unemployment may be permanent. Furthermore, one of the stressors, such as alcoholism, may result in another, such as violence or unemployment. But this introduces the issue of compounding.

Clustering of stressors increases the chances that a crisis will result. This *compounding* applies especially to normative stressors. Thus, the individual who graduates from college, marries, and moves to a new city all at the same time is more likely to find the implicit rules for life and relationships not working. Furthermore, non-normative stressors may also compound, as one gives rise to another. For example, the infidelity of one spouse may contribute to the alcoholism of the other with divorce as the eventual outcome of the compounding.

In sum, stressor variations include whether the stressor is normative or non-normative (expected or unexpected), has an external or internal origin, is temporary or permanent (acute/chronic), is voluntary or involuntary, and finally whether it is compounded or clustered with other stressors, or occurs alone.

Lest we treat stressors as if they are not gender-differentiated, a study by Whiffen and Gottlieb is worth mentioning. They found the following gender distinction:

> *when husbands were distressed, both they and their wives reported more depressive symptoms, more life stress, and more maladaptive coping. In contrast, when wives were maritally distressed, the effects were restricted to their own functioning; their husbands' responses and functioning did not differ from those of the husbands of non-distressed wives. These findings were interpreted as consistent with the assertion that women are more vulnerable than are men to life stress, and especially to stressors involving disturbances in their social field (Whiffen and Gottlieb, 1989: 327).*

In the context of our guiding concepts, another way to say it is that women are still more personally embedded in families than men, with a disturbance in that sphere causing them more distress than it does men.

FIGURE 16.1   VOLUNTARY/INVOLUNTARY AND TEMPORARY/PERMANENT STRESSORS

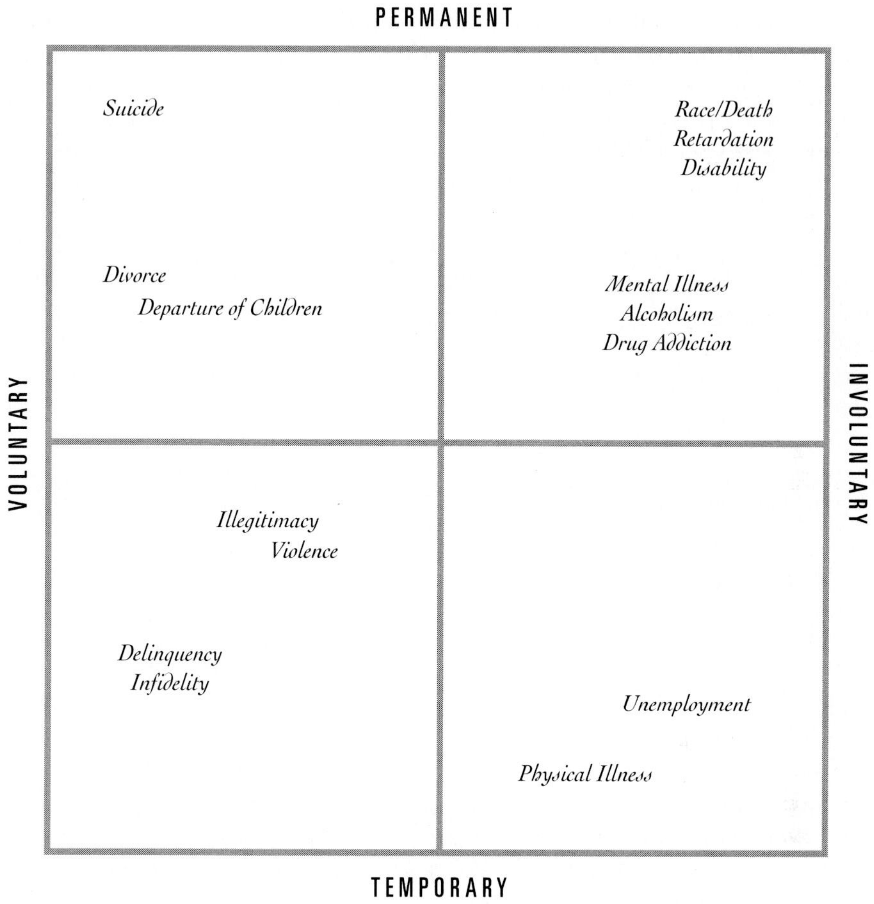

PERMANENT

VOLUNTARY		INVOLUNTARY
Suicide		Race/Death Retardation Disability
Divorce Departure of Children		Mental Illness Alcoholism Drug Addiction
Illegitimacy Violence		
Delinquency Infidelity		
		Unemployment
		Physical Illness

TEMPORARY

SECTION TWO

FAMILY RESPONSE FACTORS

Definition, or Perception, of the Stressor

Here is a variable closely related to some of those already discussed. For example, when a family is able to define an external event as threatening to many people, it may be easier to ride it out. However, the condition under which this variable is best distinguished from the others is one in which a particular event, circumstance, or process is simply not defined as a stressor. When a family does not define the birth of a child out of wedlock as deviant behavior, or as a stressor, any crisis that results will not be from disgrace or internal strain but will be because of ostracism from those people in society who define the behavior as deviant (Moen and Howery, 1988: 148).

David Reiss talks at length about the way family perceptions determine outcomes. Some families, he says, perceive a problem as something "out there," which the family together must solve. Others perceive a problem as a stimulus whereby each individual may demonstrate independence and mastery. Still other families perceive a problem as a stimulus to the family to demonstrate its togetherness (Reiss, 1981: 69–70). Each of these responses is due to a different perception and definition of problems by families. Lyn Wikler points out that whether having a mentally retarded child results in a family crisis is very much a function of the family's perception of the situation as a stressor (Wikler, 1981: 282–283). Likewise, Paul Power notes that if a chronically ill husband/father is defined as being incapable, the family's crisis response is greater (Power, 1979: 616–621). Finally, a husband's unemployment is less likely to be defined as a stressor today than in previous generations precisely because society's definition of the providing role is not as clear-cut and one-sided as it once was (Thomas et al., 1980). Thus, perception is a factor that is as important as it is hard to measure. If a family defines a situation as a stressor, as deserving of a crisis, then the family's response is much more likely to be just that: a crisis.[1]

Coping 1: Family Organization and Adaptability

Two factors—family organization and family and social network—are of prime importance to the family's vulnerability or invulnerability according to Reiss: "The first is the family's level of organization at the time of the stress." (Reiss, 1981: 186) Thirty-five years ago this "level of organization" factor was described by Reuben Hill, who noted that it is

> *possible to explain the different reactions of crisis-proof and crisis-prone families to sharp decreases in income during the Depression by these twin factors of integration and adaptability, with a restudy [by Angell] suggesting the greater importance of family adaptability (Hill, 1958: 144).*

Thus, the family with mutual role expectations, common goals, flexibility, and a sense of satisfaction in family experience is more adequately organized and less vulnerable to stressor events than are other families. Hamilton McCubbin et al. also write in their review article about adaptability and cohesiveness (or the closeness of bonding) as positive factors in dealing with stressors (McCubbin et al.. 1980: 858). An example of how such factors work is found in Liker and Elder's research on marriage in the Depression: families that started out with weak marriages and unstable men were greatly affected by income loss (Liker and Elder, 1983: 343–359).

The importance of flexibility or adaptability is noted by Elaine Blechman: "Although at first glance multiproblem families appear chaotic and unpredictable, their infrequent engagement in transitions suggests a rigid, inflexible, and static system" (Blechman, 1991: 226). In other words, problems or stressors require adjustment and rule change, and by definition inflexible families have trouble making the necessary adjustments. Lavee, Olson, and McCubbin add that flexibility interacts with cohesion or connectedness to affect strain. A highly connected and inflexible family is susceptible to strain as a result of a stressor. But so is a separated (or loosely connected) and flexible family, since in this instance each family member may "flex" or adjust in a different manner from the others (Olson et al., 1988: 41; Lavee and Olson, 1991: 786–798).

While such variables are unquestionably important to family stability, there are two problems in their use as predictors of family response. First, they are somewhat *tautological* in their relation to the stressor events. For example, the family in which a member deviates from expectations can be said to have weak mutual expectations. Likewise, the family that is unable to adapt to the birth of a retarded child obviously lacks flexibility. In other words, the variable that is said to help the family withstand stress may also be considered part of the stressor syndrome itself. Second—and this is really inseparable from the first problem—such internal variables are almost inherently post hoc. How can it be determined whether a family is organized and adaptable until it has confronted an event that tests its organization and adaptability?

Although difficult to use in a predictive fashion, David Klein and Reuben Hill break down flexibility and adaptability into several components related to problem-solving. They find, for example, that the complexity of information processed by a family, when coupled with a great amount of communication, creativity, and conflict, is related to effective problem-solving (Klein and Hill, 1979: 527). Despite the difficulty in using family organization predictively, it is obviously important in families' responses to stressors.

Coping 2: Family and Social Network

The second factor which David Reiss sees as important to the family's vulnerability or invulnerability is "the quality of its ties with its social environment" (Reiss, 1981: 1986). The family that is embedded in a strong, supportive network of kin and friends is better able to absorb the shock of a stressor. In fact, among the less privileged in society, Sandro Segre finds an integrative kinship structure as leading to stability in family life, and Noel Cazenave and Murray Straus add that such embeddedness even reduces the likelihood of violence in the family (Segre, 1975: 131–136; Cazenave and Straus, 1979: 280–300).

Researchers have found that, even when the family is not highly embedded in its kin network, it may call upon kin for assistance in times of external threat. Furthermore, though the network may not reduce the stressor itself, it is important "in promoting recovery from . . . crisis experienced in the family as a result of life changes, thereby contributing to the family's regenerative power" (McCubbin et al., 1980: 864). When the kin-network embedded family, the large nuclear family, the small nuclear family, and the individualistic family are compared, the small nuclear family appears to be most vulnerable to stressor events originating within the family unit itself. The intensity of emotional ties and the strength of mutual expectations in the small family make it quite likely that both deviant behavior and family breakup will severely test its coping ability.

An interesting study of strains affecting women distinguishes the effects of social support from spouse, relatives and friends. Strong support from one's spouse reduces the strain of marital, parental, and financial difficulties. Support from a relative reduces marital and financial strain, and friend support helps primarily with marital strain (Ladewig et al., 1990: 36–47). These results are not surprising: one's spouse is most helpful in dealing with one's parents, and relatives are more likely to help financially than are friends. The point is that all members of the social network are not equally available in all situations requiring social support.

Two final qualifications are in order. First, particular kinds of stressors, such as serious difficulties between the spouses, may result in the social network's "choosing up sides" and exacerbating the difficulties instead of cushioning and reducing the stress. Secondly, the most individualized family, in which commitment to the family itself is minimal and commitment to self is maximal, might be little troubled by a stressor even when there is no supportive network. However, the fact remains that there are apparently few families in which an individualized laissez-faire attitude regarding member behavior is so extreme that the family has *no* implicit rules or mutual expectations whatsoever.

Coping 3: Personal, Material and Community Resources

The personal resources that make it easier to cope with a stressor include education, health, intellectual ability, communicative ability, and the ability to be intimate. Material resources are just that: money. Clearly, certain stressors are directly reduced in their effects by these resources. Good health aids the elderly in coping with role and interpersonal loss. Communicative ability makes it possible for families to work together through deviance and interpersonal difficulties. And wealth will tide the family over unemployment or other economic setbacks (Kessler and Essex, 1982: 484–507; Elder and Liker, 1982: 241–269). Likewise, availability of community agencies, such as social workers or insurance, can ease the effects of a stressor. So coping with stress is not just a matter of the family's organization and network, it is also a function of the resources — personal and material — contained in the family,[2] and those available in the community.

Accumulation

Earlier we noted that stressors may become compounded: one leading to another. Appropriate here is the fact that previous experience with stress is predictive of successful coping. In other words, if you have dealt with stressors before, you should be more likely to do it again. Thus accumulation of stress and accumulation of coping experience are, in fact, two different things. However, even the positive effect of coping experience must be questioned on two grounds. First, McCubbin and Patterson note that coping itself may be a potential stressor: the person who "copes" by drinking may cause the family hardship. Or the family that copes with inflation by cutting back on health care may face the stress of illness (McCubbin and Patterson, 1982: 26–47). In addition, there may be a "straw that breaks the camel's back." That is, the family copes with one stressor after another, appears strong, but one final stressor causes personal and family disorganization (Imig, 1981: 367–371).

We have catalogued the stressors and the likely familial responses to them and have outlined the conditions under which a family is apt to be more or less susceptible to crisis and disorganization. Given the variables that influence the *intensity* of family response, the *greatest threat* to the family is likely to result from the following combination of factors: a small, nonkin-embedded, *nuclear family* lacking *flexibility* confronts an *unexpected, internal* challenge that it *defines* as a *stressor*. The *least threat*, or greatest resilience, is likely to characterize the *adaptable, kin-embedded* family that faces an *expected* event, an *external* challenge, or a *situation not defined as crisis-provoking*. This section has pointed out that stimuli and responses involve a complex set of factors; the following section will place these into the processual frameworks of Hill and Farber, and those who have specified their processes.

SECTION THREE

FRAMEWORKS FOR ANALYZING THE PROCESS OF FAMILY RESPONSE TO STRESSORS

Several authors have developed frameworks to deal with the processes of family reaction to various stimuli. Some of these frameworks have been derived from research on a specific problem. For example, E. Wight Bakke described the stages of the family's response to unemployment during the Depression as follows:

- ✦ momentum stability
- ✦ unstable equilibrium
- ✦ disorganization
- ✦ experimental readjustment
- ✦ permanent readjustment.

Likewise, Joan Jackson traces the family's reaction to alcoholism through denial, admission, attempts to eliminate the problem, strain and disorganization, exclusion of the alcoholic, and reorganization of the family (Bakke, 1949; Jackson, 1962).

Other frameworks, however, are not problem-specific, but are general descriptions of the process of family adjustment to crisis. According to Reuben Hill, following Earl Koos, the parts of the process are: "crisis-disorganization-recovery-reorganization" (See Figure 16.2). Hill discusses the conditions that enable some families to react to a stressor without disorganization (Hill, 1949: 139–150). Hill's process is based on the following formula: ABC = X. A is the stressor, B is the family's resources, C is perception, and X is the amount of crisis.

FIGURE 16.2   HILL'S "ROLLER-COASTER PROFILE" OF FAMILY REACTION TO A CRISIS-PROVOKING EVENT

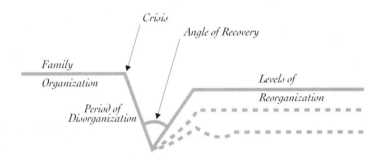

SOURCE: Reuben Hill, **Families Under Stress** (New York: Harper and Brothers, 1949), p.14; and Earl Lomon Koos, **Families in Trouble** (Morningside Heights, N.Y.: King's Crown, 1946), pp. 108-11.

To be more mathematically accurate, we might say that A − B + C = X; that is, the resources lessen the amount of stress, while stressors and the perception of them increase the amount of crisis.

McCubbin and his associates have qualified and clarified the ABC = X process, showing that the actual process is much more complex. Calling it "double ABC = X," they note that adaptation to a stressor, for example, a rule change, is a stressor itself. There is, in fact, a pile-up that occurs as family life progresses:

> It appears that the family struggles not only with the transitional crisis situation itself but with an accumulation of demands that stem from current as well as previous, unresolved family life changes. . . . This pile-up of demands negatively influences the level of adaptation (Lavee et al., 1985: 822).

They add that, of course, the negative effect of pile-up is buffered by certain resources, as we noted earlier.

Another complexity in the ABC = X model comes from Alexis Walker, who notes that besides process and pile-up, there are different analytic levels: individual, dyad, social network, and society. Walker's concern is that the entire context be taken into consideration, not just individual or family reactions and adjustments (Walker, 1985: 827-837). As is so often true in social science, a simple and elegant model, such as Hill's, is found to require a more complex understanding.

Farber wrote a generation ago about the lengthy process of family adaptation and reorganization following a stressor. He labels this the "crisis process," though it is more accurately the "family adjustment, or reorganization, process" (Farber, 1964: 403–406). Changes that affect one family member, says Farber, affect the others as well. Drawing upon Bakke, Jackson, and others who have described family response to specific stressors, Farber defines the stages of family adjustment to crisis as follows: The first stage is an attempt to handle the challenge within existing role structures—combining the ideas of denial and momentum stability.

A part of the rationale behind this approach is the hope that the condition is temporary and that restoration will soon occur. If the situation is not righted, the second stage, facing the problem, is reached—the result being a test of former family commitments. In the third stage, the problem becomes public and extrafamilial ties are altered, often by intense involvement with an outside expert or professional. Reiss likewise speaks of the involvement of outsiders in producing the "crisis construct" (Reiss, 1981: 190). The fourth stage is role reorientation, or, using the term in Sprey's sense, reorganization. That is, a new set of mutual expectations is developed and accepted by the family members. To use Reiss' language, the new rules now become implicit. Yen Peterson has pointed out how this operates in the case of a physical disability. If the person is not totally disabled, the situation remains ambiguous longer (Petersen, 1979: 47–51). However, if the person is totally disabled, the role—while dramatically altered—may at least be more clearly redefined. The fifth and final stage of the family's adjustment to crisis is "freezing out," or the removal of the crisis-causing individual from the home so that the family unit can get on with the business of passing on its culture.

Although Farber's crisis process furnishes excellent conceptual tools with which to tackle the vast literature on family response, it has limitations in applicability that become apparent as one attempts to relate it to the various acts, events, and processes mentioned at the beginning of this chapter. Many crises never advance beyond stage one; that is, the crisis is temporary and the family is reconstituted in pretty much its precrisis state. Stages two and three may well occur in reverse order, with a problem becoming public knowledge while the family continues to deny its existence. In fact, being confronted by a member of one's social network may trigger the family's admission that "we've got a problem," Finally, "freezing out" may differ in two ways from Farber's view of it as the last stage of the crisis process. In some instances, such as the launching of an offspring or the death of a family member, freezing out may be the *first* stage of the process, followed by admission of the crisis and reorganization. In other instances, instead of the *individual* being frozen out of the family unit, the *behavior* may be frozen out and the individual reinstated. A good illustration of this is when a middle-class family discovers that a daughter is premaritally pregnant and sends her to a home for unwed mothers. After the child is born and adopted, the young woman returns home from her "Mediterranean cruise," often with the proviso that she never discuss her "illegitimate" child. In this instance, it is the behavior, not the individual, that has been frozen out of the family unit. And the individual may confront psychological difficulties later.

Farber's crisis process does not, therefore, apply equally or in the same way to all the types of stressors that may confront the family. For that reason, we will reintroduce some of the temporary/permanent and voluntary/involuntary factors referred to earlier to clarify how Farber's process actually works. (See Table 16.1). A voluntary-temporary stressor, which would include most forms of deviant behavior, may simply be frozen out of the family's thoughts and lives and the individual reinstated on the assumption that the behavior will never be repeated. This would apply as well to the sorts of family conflict mentioned in Chapters 11 and

TABLE 16.1   MOST LIKELY FAMILY RESPONSES TO STRESSORS

Type of Stressor (with example)	Responses
Voluntary-Temporary (illegitimacy)	Freeze out behavior → reinstate person (if behavior persists, other stressors may follow)
Involuntary-Temporary (unemployment)	Ignore or deny or else admit → temporarily reorganize → reinstate family role structure
Voluntary-Permanent (divorce)	Reorganize
Involuntary-Permanent	Admit → freeze out person → reorganize (death; admit → reorganize)

13. For example, one way a married couple may resolve constant disagreements about family finances is to make a basic decision about the distribution of income each month and subsequently "freeze out" that area of life from family communication. If, however, a voluntary-temporary stressor, such as infidelity, persists or becomes chronic, the result may be disorganization in the sense of a confusion of expectations, a loss of consensus on "the rules of the game."

An involuntary-temporary stressor, such as unemployment, is apt to be met first with the assumption that it will soon be over and therefore requires no family adjustment except a tightening of the family budget. If the situation is not immediately remedied, the family may admit its predicament, may adjust temporarily (perhaps by means of unemployment compensation), and may subsequently reinstate the former family role structure when the husband is once again employed.

Two permanent types of stressors ordinarily involve a freezing out of the individual. In divorce and the departure of children, the freezing out is voluntary and requires the reorganization of the remaining family members. The involuntary forms of permanent stress include death, which requires admission and reorganization, and retardation and mental illness, which are often responded to by eventually recognizing the problem, freezing out (or institutionalizing) the person, and reorganizing the family.

This section has examined stressors, response factors, and the processes whereby families adjust or reorganize. The next section will focus on one major area of family stress today—family violence.

SECTION FOUR

FAMILY VIOLENCE

The family in the modern industrial world, we said in Chapter 5, is expected to meet the individual's need to be loved, understood, and treated as a whole person, and the ideology of the happy family encourages people to get married and stay married. Yet meeting such social-emotional needs is a heavy burden for any small group to bear, and the happy family ideology is hard to live up to. Yet, as Miller says, "the assumption of family harmony continues on undiminished; the rhetorics of safe home and violent street remain in an important sense more real than the empirical 'realities' they seem to hide" (Miller, 1990: 283). Family violence, frequent as it is, is treated as either an unusual occurrence or else—at the other extreme—as normative, or as discipline instead of violence.

Thus it is that many married couples today, unable to meet the needs for love and understanding, feel free to break ties and try someone else. Divorce, however, is not always a prompt and automatic response to unmet needs. In many families there is an interim period between a failure to meet social-emotional needs and divorce, during which much conflict may occur, some of it violent. In other families there is no divorce, only the verbal and physical expression of dissatisfaction. Until recently we preferred to ignore the fact that violence is almost as typical of families as is love, and even professionals, working with or studying the family, shared this outlook. It is noteworthy that from 1939 to 1969 not a single article on violence appeared in the *Journal of Marriage and the Family*, while today it is one of the three or four most frequent foci of attention in that journal. At the turn of this century, mention of family violence was met with the standard response that only a crazy person would beat loved ones. Now there are psychiatric, social-psychological, and sociological theories to account for family violence.[3] Among the numerous theories, we will briefly present five.

1. *Resource* theory contends that the more resources a person can deploy, the less need she/he will have for violence. Violence is a last resort for the person with few resources.

2. *Systems* theory, well explicated in Giles-Sims' book, argues that violence is a system product, perpetuated by positive feedback and retarded by negative feedback within the family system (Giles-Sims, 1983).

3. *Ecological* theory relates family violence to the environment and cultural supports. If the family's milieu condones violence, this will foster it. Likewise, a mismatch of parent and child or family to neighborhood and community can lead to violence.

4. *Economic* theory says that violence and abuse arise out of socially structured stress—low income, unemployment, poverty, perhaps illness.

5. *Patriarchal* theory contends that historically male dominance was supported by any means, including violence, which was simply part of the society's norms (Gelles, 1985: 347–367).[4]

Today, patriarchal theory has been expanded by feminism's critique of all the institutions of society, especially the household. While many of feminism's concerns have been with women and children, its analysis has begun "to take a more critical look at the position of men in families. This became especially sharpened around the issues of domestic violence and, more recently, child sexual abuse, where the overwhelming proportion of perpetrators are male" (Morgan, 1990: 69).

Likewise, patriarchal theory has been combined with resource theory to emphasize not just authority (patriarchy), but power (resources). Gelles and Straus put it thus:

> *The greater the inequality, the more one person makes all the decisions and has all the power, the greater the risk of violence. Power, power confrontations, and perceived threats to domination, in fact, are underlying issues in almost all acts of family violence (Gelles and Straus, 1988: 82).*

How prevalent is violence in the U.S. family? That, of course, depends on how it is defined. A distinction is often made between abuse and violence, with violence referring to all forms of physical aggression, while abuse refers to aggression that causes injury and also to nonphysical acts of maltreatment that cause harm. In other words, this distinction is between the perpetrator and the outcome and also between physical and all forms of harm. But it must be noted that these definitions are not always adhered to, and abuse and violence are employed almost synonymously in much of the literature.

Definition is only part of the problem. Does the rapid increase in the literature about violence mean that there is more violence, or simply that it is defined more negatively and, thus, as a problem deserving of attention? Most observers assume the latter. Yet, with all the attention today, there very likely continues to be underreporting, including class and racial biases that go into its discovery or hiddenness. In fact, a word about racial differences might be in order at this point. Gelles and Straus report that black families do not have higher overall rates of violence than do whites, though the former are under more stress continually (1988: 86). Elsewhere, Gelles and his colleagues report a decrease in the rate of violence toward black women, but an increase in violence toward black children, since 1975 (Hampton et al., 1989: 969, 977). But categories of violence will be dealt with below.

So with all the definitional, statistical, and reporting difficulties, we will nevertheless use the best estimates to be found in the literature as we examine violence in various family relationships, starting with spouses.[5]

Spouse Abuse

Fights between family members are the largest single category of police calls; and Feature 16.2 notes some of the recent statistics.

It is, furthermore, the physically stronger members of the family who are likely to abuse the weaker members. This means that the two most prevalent forms of serious family violence are wife-beating and child abuse. A specific factor that contributes to wife abuse, W.J. Goode believes, is the unwillingness of human beings to terminate a conflict by either submission or escape. In fact, "Fighting conversation" between intimates, says Goode, "being so unsatisfactory because it exposes still more disagreements and hostility as it progresses, does not easily lend itself to a safe completion" (Goode, 1971: 632).

Although the husband is the main perpetrator of couple violence, it may go the other way. An interesting debate has revolved around the issue of gender symmetry in spouse violence. Using the Conflict Tactics Scale (CTS), Straus and Gelles conclude that in both 1975 and 1985 women were about as violent as men (Straus and Gelles, 1986: 470). The reasons for women's violence against their husbands (and children) are listed as follows by Flynn (adapting from Straus):

First, attacks by husbands often lead to retaliatory violence by wives. Continued experiences as a victim may also lead women to imitate the violent actions of their husbands. Second, the "implicit cultural norms which make the marriage license also a hitting license are accepted to about the same degree by women as by men" (Straus, 1980: 702). Third, both men and women receive training in use of violence through exposure to violence in childhood. Fourth, women's greater responsibility for child care result in more use of physical punishment and more child abuse by women. . . . Fifth, the sexual inequality in marriage creates a high degree of frustration for women (Flynn, 1990: 196).

While Straus admits that husbands are more likely to do severe damage than are wives, and may more often be actors instead of reactors (see Saunders,

Feature 16.2 WIFE BEATING, THE SILENT CRIME

There is nothing new about wife beating. It has always happened, everywhere. Often it is accepted as a natural if regrettable part of woman's status as her husband's property. Throughout history unlucky women have been subjected to the whims and brutality of their husbands. The colloquial phrase "rule of thumb" is supposedly derived from the ancient right of a husband to discipline his wife with a rod "no thicker than his thumb." In the U.S. the statistics reflect no unprecedented epidemic of domestic violence, but only a quite recent effort to collect figures—often inexact, but startling even when allowances are made for error—on what has always existed:

+ Nearly 6 million wives will be abused by their husbands in any one year.
+ Some 2,000 to 4,000 women are beaten to death annually.
+ The nation's police spend one-third of their time responding to domestic-violence calls.
+ Battery is the single major cause of injury to women, more significant than auto accidents, rapes or muggings.

What is new is that in the U.S. wife beating is no longer widely accepted as an inevitable and private matter.

Maureen Dowd, "Wife Beating: the Silent Crime," *Time*, September 5, 1983: 23.

1988: 95, on this), the strongest criticism comes from an article entitled "The Myth of Sexual Symmetry in Marital Violence." In this paper Dobash et al. note the problems with the CTS, including the fact that "play" hitting may be counted as violence. In addition, they note that men are larger and are socialized to use violence to get what they want more often than are women (Dobash et al., 1992: 83–84).

A study by Kersti Yllo deals with prevalence, but helps to raise the issue of cause as well. Yllo uses the United States as the unit of analysis, and divides the states according to the status of women as measured by education, employment, political involvement, and laws passed in their favor. The level of violence against women was highest in those states where their status is lowest, but almost as high in the states where their status is highest. Violence of wives against husbands, on the other hand, simply becomes more frequent as the women's status becomes higher (Yllo, 1983: 67–86). Thus, in the high-wife-status states, the level of violence between spouses is comparable, while in the low-wife-status states the level of violence against wives is double that against husbands.

How does Yllo's study relate to cause or theory? The wife-beater and his family setting have been described by some as patriarchal and by others as reactions to women's liberation. The patriarch may, as noted earlier, feel the necessity of "disciplining" his wife, while the husband who feels threatened by women's societal advances and new-found assertiveness may resort to violence to compensate for his perceived loss of control. Yllo's results simply say both are true: the "boss" is more likely to resort to violence, but so is the threatened male. But not surprisingly in the more equalitarian setting, the wife may also express her assertiveness by means of violence (on this, see Hornung et al., 1981: 675–692).

While violence is in the family histories of most wife-beaters, it is also in the history of most beaten wives. In other words, women who observed violence when growing up are likely to experience it in their marriages. In addition, her subjective dependency on her husband is related to minor acts of violence, while her objective (economic) dependency on him is related to severe violence (Kalmuss and Straus, 1982: 277–286). This does not, of course, mean that dependency causes abuse, but rather that it increases the likelihood that the wife will *tolerate* it. But the outcomes will be discussed below.

The issue of minor acts versus severe violence leads us to a consideration of patterns. Follingstad et al. find five major categories or patterns: (1) high frequency, severe, long-term; (2) low frequency and mild, short-term, the women begin fairly assertive; (3) medium frequency and severity, but getting worse over time, minimizes the man's responsibility: (4) medium frequency, no increase over time; (5) high frequency at outset, but decreasing over time — most likely to use a shelter (Follingstad et al., 1991: 187–204).

What triggers wife abuse? According to Jean Giles-Sims, a life transition (or normative stressor) is very often the triggering factor in severe violence. Most often in the study, the trigger was a residential move, but it could also accompany a pregnancy — which, of course, is a time when the wife is most defenseless and dependent. However, Gelles' research does not find pregnant women more likely to be victimized than non-pregnant women of the same age. Rather, younger wives are more likely to be both pregnant and abused. However, he did find that pregnant women reported abuse to be focused on the abdomen, and in some cases increasing in frequency or severity (Gelles, 1988: 845). In Giles-Sims study, almost all the women had forgiven the first incident, but as a pattern became established, fewer and fewer were willing to forgive and forget (Giles-Sims, 1983: 59). The more frequent and severe the violence, the more likely the wife will seek outside intervention. However, there are substantial impediments to getting protection and cooperation from the police and courts. David Ford notes that:

> *Police officers disliked domestic runs for several reasons. They knew domestics were unpredictable and dangerous; they were called upon to assume the role of counsellor, for which they had no professional training; and they did not have legal authority to act freely. . . . And of course some officers shared community sentiments tending to support wife-battery (Ford, 1983: 465–466; see also Berk and Newton, 1985: 253–262).*

Likewise, women received different information on their rights, and similar cases were treated differently by the courts. This very often resulted in the wife being back in the home with an angry and embarrassed husband. Once she leaves to seek help, perhaps at a shelter for battered women, what are her alternatives? According to Berk et al., two likely outcomes of time in a shelter are either a change in the marriage or a move toward breakup for those women who are already taking control of their lives, or retaliation by the husband against those women who simply return home (Berk et al., 1986: 481).

Thus, she may return home with no change, or return with a major restructuring of the "family paradigm," though this tends to be rare. Or she can leave. The women who stay tend to be married longer, be unemployed, and to say they still love their husbands, while those who leave have the opposite characteristics (Strube and Barbour, 1983: 785–793). And, besides love, why do women stay? Because "he's not always that way," because they hope to change him, because they are dependent or have "learned helplessness" (Launius and Lindquist, 1988: 307–318), because of fear, or because they have learned to accommodate. Deborah Tannen speaks to this last point:

> *The most extreme example I have encountered of the conviction that accommodation is the best way to achieve domestic harmony came from a woman who talked to me about her very early marriage to a man so violent that she feared for the lives of her children and herself. In explaining to me why she had tolerated his beatings, she said that her husband had had a difficult childhood, deprived of love, and she felt she could heal his wounds—and those of their relationship—by providing him unconditional love (Tannen, 1990: 185).*

Returning to race and class issues in spouse violence, Stets notes that blacks are likely to move from verbal to physical violence, though this may actually be a class difference (Stets, 1990:501–514). In fact, according to Lockhart and White, it is class and not race that accounts for black-white differences. Lower-class marriages seem to experience more spouse violence, and blacks have lower socio-economic status than whites (Lockhart and White, 1989: 421–436); Lockhart, 1987; 603–610).

Another issue in spouse abuse concerns marital rape. In traditional English law and elsewhere the husband had legal right to his wife's body for sexual purposes. This doctrine is still accepted in the United States, with only a few instances of legal punishment of husbands who have sexually abused their wives. States are now beginning to limit the husband's immunity from rape laws, but given the continuing sentiment in favor of husband control over his wife's body and the difficulty in prosecuting rape cases in general, much change remains to be carried out in this area before wives will have much real protection against forced sex within marriage (Freeman, 1981: 1–29).

Children in the homes of battered wives are a particularly important and understudied issue. One study finds that wives change their behavior toward their children when the husband is present, and the amount of stress the mother is experiencing is a powerful predictor of child behavior problems (Holden and Ritchie, 1991: 311–327). Hilton reports that the children of more than half of a small sample of abused women have been direct witnesses to the abuse. These mothers are concerned about intergenerational transmission of violence to their children (Hilton: 1992: 77–86). Christopoulos et al. add that in their sample of shelter women and their children, the daughters were more likely than the sons to experience psychological difficulties (Christopoulos, 1987: 617). The overall effect of spouse abuse on children in the home is clearly negative, and this brings us to actual abuse of the children.

Child Abuse

Michael Martin and James Walters use the term *abuse* as an umbrella, covering all forms of child maltreatment. The types of child abuse include: abandonment, physical abuse (regardless of intent), emotional abuse, neglect (withholding basic needs) and sexual abuse (Martin and Walters, 1982: 267–276; Gordon, 1979-1980: 115–145). According to a 1980 report from the American Humane Society, emotional abuse and neglect occur half as often as cases of physical abuse, and physical abuse occurs less than half as often as physical and educational neglect (American Humane Society, 1981). If estimates for spouses are low, those for children may be more skewed, due to the stigma attached and to the fact that the abused child is less likely to seek help than is the abused

TABLE 16.2   TYPES OF CHILD ABUSE AND RELATED FACTORS

Type of Abuse	Related Factors
Abandonment	Promiscuity or alcoholism of the mother
Physical abuse	Parent-child conflict, with nonbiologically related person in the household
Emotional abuse	Child's emotional and intellectual inadequacies
Neglect	Parental intellectual inadequacies, and financial problems
Sexual abuse	Promiscuity or alcoholism of the father

spouse, and may even be too young to verbalize. Medical reports by doctors, in the case of serious injury, are a major source of information.

Silber finds that non-abusing families are more able to verbally negotiate, a possible factor in reducing the likelihood of abuse (Silber, 1990: 368–384). However, the factor most often mentioned as contributing to child abuse is the parent's own socialization for violence and the inadequacy of the parent's childhood. According to Goode, the abuser typically received little love or tenderness and frequently was abused as a child, and thus as a parent he or she combines a high level of demand with a great desire for response. Essentially, such parents

> *approach the task of child care with the wish to do something for the child, a deep need for the child to fill their own lacks, to salve their own hurt self-esteem, to give them love, and a harsh demand that the child behave in a certain way. Failing that, the child demonstrates thereby his lack of respect, love, affection, goodness, and so on (Goode, 1971: 634).*

Rand Conger et al. agree on the importance of the parent's own childhood, but add two qualifications:

> *The data suggest that a combination of particular childhood experiences together with rapid life changes may be an influence on the occurrence of child abuse. . . . Also clear, however, is the fact that over half (53%) of the abusive parents do not report a history of being abused (Conger et al., 1979: 73).*

The parent's background is important, but many parents with inadequate childhoods do *not* become abusers, and life changes or transitions are again mentioned as an accompanying condition to abuse.

Younger parents are more prone to abuse than older ones, and—recalling the discussion of the social network as a coping mechanism—isolated parents are more likely to be abusive than those tied closely to a social network (Cazenave and Straus, 1979). One of the most insightful attempts to deal with causation is found in Martin and Walters' paper in which they distinguished five types of abuse. Each of these, they feel, is linked to a different set of preconditions (see Table 16.2) (Martin and Walters, 1982).

The context or situation itself is, of course, not unrelated to child abuse. Very often the housewife who feels trapped, who is frustrated at being an unemployed mother, or who has unplanned children (Zuravin, 1991), is apt to feel most threatened when the child does not respond as she desires. Likewise, the young or unsuccessful husband may respond to occupational frustration with child abuse. Lee Bowker et al. speak at some length about the relations between various forms of nuclear family abuse:

> *The link between wife beating and child abuse may be related to the power inequality between husband and wife as well as that between parents and children. Children in a family often become their father's victims at the same time that he is abusing their mother. . . . children frequently witnessed wife beating incidents between their parents. Moore coined the phrase "yo-yo" children to label how children are often used as pawns*

in arguments by parents who are unable to discuss any rational solution to their difficulties (Bowker et al., 1988: 159).

The triggering mechanism for child abuse may be the child's failure to comply with parental insistence that he or she stop crying. While the crying may have a perfectly legitimate physical basis, the vulnerable parent construes it to mean that the child lacks self-control or is willful, unresponsive, and bad. This discussion of causes, while suggestive, is incomplete. Gelles, for example, finds that of the 19 traits of child abusers reported by various investigators, there is agreement on only 4, with the other 15 being unique to the particular writer (Gelles, 1976: 139).

The effects of child abuse are suggested in several recent researches. Dean et al. find that maltreated children are less likely to make up stories about kindness in peer and parent-child relations than are non-abused children (Dean et al., 1986: 617-626). And another study finds, in keeping with earlier research, that abused children are more aggressive and less compliant than nonabused. Also, abused children were more likely to accompany their noncompliance with anger and verbal refusal (Trickett and Kuczynski, 1986: 115–123). Thus, the results of abuse are not compliance and docility, but anger and later difficulties in social relationships.

Other Abusive Intimate Relations

Spouses abuse each other, and parents sometimes abuse their children. What about *brothers and sisters*? Sometimes an infant is injured by an older but still young sibling. This may be a result of jealousy, or simply a lack of understanding the consequences of their acts. Older siblings, such as teenagers, may have more serious conflicts, however. What do adolescent siblings fight about? Three possibilities are *funny looks* and other negative metacommunications, *responsibilities* ("It's your turn"), and most important, *space* ("Get out of my room"). One study concludes that sibling violence is the strongest predictor of future violent behavior on the part of the perpetrator (Gully et al., 1981: 333–337).

Another form of abuse that is "coming out of the closet" is *elder* abuse. Though estimates do not yet exist, this type of abuse is generally acknowledged to be quite prevalent, especially when neglect is included on the list of types. Possible causes include the strain of care and its costs. Richard Douglass concludes from his research that:

The most common causes of neglect and abuse appear to include the consequences of adult caretakers becoming overtaxed by the requirements of caring for a frail and dependent adult. Physical, economic or emotional limitations can reduce the adequate recognition of the needs of an older person and prevent the caregiver from being responsive to those needs. The burden of caring, without occasional relief, can lead to despair, anger, resentment, or violence among some caretakers. A family that is already at the brink of crisis for any reason will only be more quickly thrown into a disastrous chain of events when a frail and dependent parent presents unexpected problems and demands on the family's physical, emotional, and financial resources (Douglass, 1983: 401).

There are commonalities between elder and child abuse in that both of the abused are in a dependent situation, both produce stress in the caregiver, and neither are able to represent themselves politically—with dependency being the key (Faulkner, 1982: 69–91; Pillemer, 1985: 146–158). The next few years will see an increase in our information on both abuse and neglect of the elderly.

A variation on the theme of elder abuse is adolescent violence against parents. Recently Agnew and Huguley reported that

> *rates of parent assault bear little or no relationship to a) the sex of the adolescent, b) socioeconomic status, c) family structure, and d) the size of the adolescent. Males become somewhat less likely to hit mothers and more likely to hit fathers as they age, while females become more likely to hit both mothers and fathers as they age. . . . mothers are more often hit than fathers (Agnew and Huguley, 1989: 710).*

Courtship violence is another form of intimate abuse. James Makepeace's research indicates that 61.5 percent of his sample of college students knew someone who had been involved in courtship violence. However, in one of his studies he found that 21 percent had had at least one direct personal experience, while in his other study 14 percent of males and 9 percent of females reported having employed some form of interpersonal violence against a dating partner (Makepeace, 1981: 97–102; Makepeace, 1983: 101–109). More recently, Thompson reports from 350 undergraduates that over one-fourth of both men and women have been targets or perpetrators of physical aggression, with little difference by gender (Thompson, 1991: 261–278). He finds that both men *and* women who have a history of physical aggression rate themselves higher on masculinity than those who do not (Thompson, 1991: 273). Another study adds that males under stress and who have social ties with abusive peers are more likely to be abusive in dating relationships (DeKeseredy, 1990: 236–243).

Bernard and Bernard find that 74 percent of abusive males had experienced violence in their families of orientation, while only 32 percent of nonabusive adolescents had come from homes in which violence was manifested (Bernard and Bernard, 1983: 283–286). Many others have found connections between family and courtship violence (Roscoe and Benaske, 1985; Breslin et al., 1990; Thompson, 1986; DeMaris, 1990).

What were the immediate causes or "triggers" for violence? Makepeace reports three: jealousy, disagreements over drinking behavior, and anger over sexual denial. Every specific type of violent behavior was more prevalent among males than females, and Makepeace finds that women are unlikely to marry men who have abused them during courtship (Makepeace, 1983).

In tying this to marriage, Roscoe and Benaske argue that "to understand domestic violence it may be more advantageous to study courtship violence than violence in the family of origin" (1985: 424). It is also instructive that several studies report violence beginning right after marriage—perhaps as an outgrowth of earlier restraint. That is, the violent male who lost an earlier partner due to violence may "restrain himself" the next time until after marriage. But this is speculation.

SECTION FIVE

A BRIEF CONCLUSION

This chapter has reviewed the variations in stimuli or stressors, and the factors that help to determine the family's reaction, including perception and various coping mechanisms. Then Hill's and Farber's family processes for dealing with the effects of stressors were examined, along with the corrections to them. The final section has focused on one major area of family maladjustment—that caused by violence. Looking at both prevalence and causes, we have reviewed the great advances that have been made in knowledge about spouse and child abuse, and have noted the new interest in sibling, elder, and courtship violence. The complexities of causation are obvious, but a start has been made in understanding the negative side of family embeddedness and intimacy, and the continuing effects of patriarchy.

Stressors may be met with adaptation, with reorganization, with breakup of the marriage, and eventually by death. Chapter 17 will focus on marital breakup as well as the phenomenon of remarriage.

Divorce, Death, And Remarriage

CHAPTER 17

Divorce is seen by some in the United States today as a problem, and by others as a solution. It is currently more frequent than at any other time in our history, and is indicative of less institutional and individual embeddedness. There are numerous predictors or causes of divorce. The legal process includes the grounds, alimony and child support, and property division, with much change or reform going on in each of these areas. Post-divorce adjustment involves the emotional and material adjustments of the divorcees, and the short- and long-term responses of children. Marital breakup by premature death occurs less frequently than earlier in our history. One response to either divorce or death is remarriage, and much research is currently being done on both the marital relations resulting from a remarriage and the step-relations produced thereby.

Dr. and Mrs. Alexander Goodman
have the honor of announcing
the divorce of their daughter
Barbara Jane
from
Ronald Melvin what's his name
in the year of our Lord
nineteen hundred and seventy
Superior Court
Los Angeles, California (Lewis, 1983)

A brief legend from nineteenth-century India may also serve to introduce one of the two most frequently investigated U.S. family topics at the present time — divorce:

> *In the first year of the reign of King Julief, two thousand married couples were sepa-*
> *rated, by the magistrates, with their own consent. The emperor was so indignant, on*
> *learning these particulars, that he abolished the privilege of divorce. In the course of*
> *the following year, the number of marriages in Agra was less than before by three*
> *thousand; the number of adulteries was greater by seven thousand; three hundred*
> *women were burned alive for poisoning their husbands; seventy-five men were burned*
> *for the murder of their wives; and the quantity of furniture broken and destroyed, in*
> *the interior of private families, amounted to the value of three millions of rupees. The*
> *emperor reestablished the privilege of divorce (Blake, 1962: 80–81).*

A divorce announcement and a legend about the privilege of divorce: these are indicative of a frequent, though still painful, aspect of contemporary family life. However, many commentators still feel that making divorce easy is just another compromise with the "weaknesses of the flesh." To these writers, the rate of divorce in the United States is another sign of the imminent collapse of both the family system and the society. Is the increase in the divorce rate during the twentieth century necessarily a sign of moral degeneration? While the increase may be so interpreted, other writers have argued precisely the opposite. For example, Henry Foster states that "sexual dissatisfaction in marriage today is more apt to lead to divorce and remarriage than to the acquisition of a mistress or a visit to a prostitute. In this sense, it may be argued, divorce promotes public morality" (Foster, 1969: 142).

The long–term trend in divorce rates, "not just in the United States, where the rates are the highest in the world, but in other industrial and industrializing nations," has been upward for at least a century (Phillips, 1988).[1] And, as both Quale and Goode note, divorce is and has been widespread in many different kinds of societies (Quale, 1988: 118; Goode, 1993, *passim*). In the U.S. in earlier centuries, says Kitson, "even when there were more pressing forces such as economics and family ties holding couples together, long marriage was a rarity" (Kitson, 1992: 16). The reason is that death ended marriages that today might be ended in divorce.

The increase in the divorce rate clearly exemplifies the reduction in both institutional and individual embeddedness. As the various functions have moved out of the family, there are less reasons to keep any given marriage together. And as families have become more tenuous and less functionally central to society, individuals, especially women, have become less surrounded by or embedded in them. But does the increase in the divorce rate also indicate either a breakdown in the U.S. marriage system or a decrease in its popularity? To some extent the answer to the second is now "yes." Though a part of it is a delay in marriage, it is somewhat less popular than it was a generation ago. However, much of the explanation lies in a greater unwillingness to be unhappily married. Coupled with cohabitation, treating marriage as a conditional contract has begun to affect the popularity of marriage, but so far only marginally. What the higher divorce rate unquestionably means is that a lessened social stigma is attached to divorce than was the case a generation earlier; divorce has become more acceptable as a "cultural alternative" or as a solution to an intolerable marriage.

The effect of divorce upon the marriage and family system of the United States, O'Neill claims, justifies neither the expectations of the liberals, who thought it would act as a safety valve and solve all the internal inconsistencies in our family system, nor the fears of the conservatives, who believed that the availability of divorce would signal the disintegration of the family as we know it. What has happened is that what was once a legal and moral problem has increasingly become a clinical one. But that makes it sound too much like the issue is settled. Halem writes clearly about the current ambivalence:

> The scientific terminology and statistical data suggested a clinical presentation of divorce and marital breakdown, but once again the language of the sciences only masked a moralistic message. These researchers, like their predecessors, were stating that the fate of children and by extension of society rested with the preservation of the traditional . . . family.
>
> Even as they avowed their neutrality, many researchers initiated their studies and analyzed their findings on the basis of preconceptions of deviance. . . .
>
> On the one hand, clinical theories on divorce justified the elimination of adversary proceedings. . . . On the other hand, scientific data came to be viewed by many as a strong defense for anti-divorce measures. . . . Somewhere along the way the prevention of individual alienation and maladjustment became inextricably confused with the preservation of marriages (Halem, 1980: 193, 230).

So here we have the issues of patriarchy, individualism, and the family once again. The preservation of marriages runs counter to the increasing economic independence of women, and can be viewed as an attempt to keep women tied into a dependent and subordinate status. And individualism uses divorce as a solution to an individual problem—namely, an unhappy marriage. Historically and cross-culturally the male ordinarily had the right to initiate divorce, not the female. Shere Hite reports (and somewhat exaggerates) a dramatic change:

> It is most often women who are deciding on and asking for divorces. . . . Most women say they tried for several years to improve their relationship before deciding to leave. And most, contrary to expectations, ask for and get divorces, not because the man is being "unfaithful," and not because of "poor sex," but because of their loneliness and emotional isolation within the marriage (Hite, 1987: 459).

Thus, whether one evaluates divorce as problem or solution depends on whether one values the permanent family or the individual more. However, even this is oversimplified because a divorce may solve some individual problems and produce others, or it may solve one person's problems and simultaneously cause problems for other people, such as spouse or children.

From moral to clinical issue, from family problem to individual solution, Lenore Weitzman has catalogued some of the factors in the "normalization" of divorce:

> *First, the social stigma attached to divorce is declining and divorce is increasingly seen as a normal event. Second, increased alternatives to a present marriage are available today, either through remarriage or in remaining single. Third, women's increased labor force participation and independent earnings mean that they have more options, especially economic options, for a viable existence outside their present marriage. And fourth, the rising standard of expectations for marital happiness makes it difficult for both men and women to justify remaining in an unsatisfactory marriage (Weitzman, 1981: 145–146).*

Normalization, alternatives, rising women's status, and expectations of marital happiness are some of the major themes that will arise time and again in this chapter. The important point here is that divorce is one of those family issues around which the familist-individualist and patriarchal-equalitarian debates revolve.

Thinking About Divorce

Before we examine the rates, causes, and effects of divorce in some detail, a few words are in order regarding the recent studies of contemplating, or thinking about divorce. Several years ago, Levinger developed a useful framework for dealing with divorce as an exchange process, a framework which was adapted to the discussion of mate selection in Chapter 10. Divorce, said Levinger, is a result of the interplay between attractions, barriers, and alternative attractions. If the attractions to the current mate are great, the likelihood of divorce is lessened. If the attractions are negligible, but the barriers to getting out are great, that also binds one to the current marriage. However, if the alternatives — another person or perhaps a life goal — are great, the likelihood of breakup increases. Attractions + barriers – alternative attractions = likelihood of staying married (Levinger, 1965: 19–28). Becker's work on the family from an economic perspective also argues that marriages dissolve when the utility from staying married falls below that expected from getting a divorce (Becker, 1981: 234f).

While these approaches may capture the essence of the process, many specifics are obviously missing. Joan Huber and Glenna Spitze, for example, find that, in general, women think about divorce more than men. This, of course, is consistent with Hite's finding, reported above, that women more often decide to divorce. And though income is not related to thinking about divorce, women's employment experience is related to *both* partners' thinking about it. In addition, having a child under six years of age is related to the man thinking about it less, but not the woman, while the longer the couple are married, the less *both* think about it (Huber and Spitze, 1980: 75–89).

Booth and White found that thinking about divorce was more likely during the first ten years of marriage, and also when both spouses are employed (Booth and White, 1980: 605–616). In a later study they added further information regarding early divorce, using Levinger's terminology: "because barriers are few and alternatives high, people in short marriages get divorced even when their marriages are not very unhappy . . . marital happiness has a stronger impact on divorce in longer duration marriages" (White and Booth, 1991: 18).

The most recent and complete treatments of thinking about divorce are found in works by Vaughan, Kayser, and Kitson (Vaughan, 1986; Kayser, 1993; Kitson, 1992). Kitson notes, at some length, that

> *individuals contemplating divorce do attempt to weigh the negatives and positives of their marriages and the alternatives available. They assess costs such as the importance of a number of reasons for hesitancy in the divorce decision—the partner's ages, the length of the marriage, their responsibility for children, and the need to make preparation for living on one's own. They also assess marital rewards such as family income, the extent to which the spouse has lived up to expectations for marital roles, the personal growth and freedom the marriage has allowed, and the availability of alternative partners (Kitson, 1992: 109).*

Lest this discussion make thinking about divorce seem too objective and rational, let us add a quote from Douglas and Atwell's book:

> *Rather than being swept off a cliff into an abyss of despair, . . . most love partnerships gone awry stumble along from one minicrisis to growing minicrisis; and it is not clear to those stumbling around in the dark, clashing in the "fogs of marital discord," until things are pretty bad indeed that they are careening downward (Douglas and Atwell, 1988: 229).*

According to Diane Vaughan and Karen Kayser, the end of love and uncoupling "can be reversed, halted, or delayed—or accelerated—by the actions of the two people involved," very much like the mate selection process or Farber's crisis process described in Chapter 16 (Vaughan, 1986: 9; Kayser, 1993). One way to handle marital trouble is by trying to alter the rules, either unilaterally or with the other person's consent (recall the discussion of rule change and deviance in Chapter 13; Vaughan, 1986: 18).

A problem with some of the earlier studies is that the dependent variable is simply having thought about divorce, and one might do that even if he or she were not married. Thus, Booth et al. produce a Marital Instability Scale that includes whether the couple have seriously suggested divorce in the past three years, whether they have discussed it with a close friend, discussed consulting an attorney, and whether the thought has simply crossed their minds (Booth et al., 1983: 387–394). This seems more complete than simply thinking about it, and is clearly an *instability scale*. It intentionally leaves out those couples who have bad marriages but who, for whatever reason, have not and will not consider divorce. This would, of course, require a *maladjustment scale* instead.

Edwards and Sanders have produced a "Coming Apart" Model, which begins with Levinger and ends up being almost the mirror image of the mate selection process of Chapter 10. Involving background heterogeneity, lower marital congruity (or similarity), attractions—barriers—alternatives, and lower commitment, the Coming-Apart Model captures much of what previous writers have said about contemplating, and then carrying out, a divorce (Edwards and Saunders, 1981: 379–389).

PREVALENCE OF DIVORCE IN THE UNITED STATES

The classic work on the prevalence of divorce in the United States is Paul Jacobson's *American Marriage and Divorce*. Jacobson traces the rate of divorce per 1,000 existing marriages from 1860 to 1956 (Jacobson, 1959). Combining his data with the government's *Monthly Vital Statistics* reports since 1956, Figure 17.1 plots the rate of divorce from 1860 to the present by 5-year intervals. The two high points in U.S. divorce rates occurred between 1946 and 1950 and from 1970 to the present. The rate climbed every year from 1966 to 1976, being exactly double in 1976 what it had been ten years earlier. And, Colleen Johnson adds, while not predicting the future, "the divorce rate did stabilize at a high level in the early 1980s, at the same time the high remarriage rate began declining" (Johnson, 1988: 62). In fact, from 1988 to 1992 the rate actually declined ever so slightly (*Monthly Vital Statistics*, 1993).

Just how high is the U.S. divorce rate at present? According to Furstenberg, it is higher than in any other developed nation by a considerable margin (1990). The usual estimate is that about one in two U.S. marriages are now ending in divorce, but Martin and Bumpass claim that taking into account some underreporting, "about two-thirds of all first marriages are likely to end in separation or divorce" (Martin and Bumpass, 1989: 37).

Two issues concerning prevalence deserve some attention. The first is the quasi-leveling of the rate in the late 1970s. One reason for this is that divorce rates have always gone up during postwar periods, as couples come back together. The post-Vietnam period is hard to delimit, but it was clearly during the early 1970s. Second, the age structure of the population itself is important to the rate of divorce. In Chapter 7, the baby-boom period of 1946–1960 was described. And earlier in this chapter we referred to the fact that most divorces occur during the first few years after marriage. The large baby-boom cohort passed through its twenties during the 1965–75 period. This means that during that decade these people passed through the typical age of marriage and also the high-risk period for divorce. Thus it is possible that a part of the rise from 1965 to 1975 was simply a function of the age of our population, and that the leveling off is in fact an indication of a high, but fairly constant, rate in the future.

An important study by A. Wade Smith and June Meitz divides married people into four cohorts—First World War, Depression, Second World War, and Vietnam—in order to compare divorce rates. They find that the rate for the Second World War cohort (born between 1924 and 1937) is the highest, followed by the Depression cohort. What is important, however, is that the old-

FIGURE 17.1   DIVORCE RATE PER 1,000 MARRIAGES IN THE UNITED STATES BETWEEN 1860 AND 1980 BY FIVE-YEAR INTERVALS

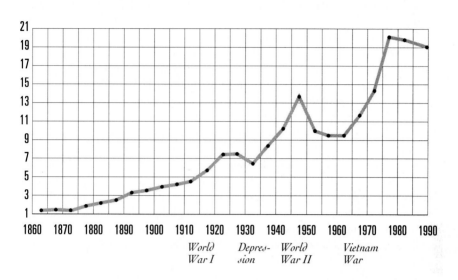

SOURCE: *Computed from annual rates, by permission of the author, from Paul H. Jacobson,* **American Marriage and Divorce,** *Copyright © 1959 (Rinehart & Co., Inc.), Xerox Corp. Book Publications, OP 31,413, Ann Arbor; p. 90 table, 42; and* **Monthly Vital Statistics** *(Rockville, Md.: U.S. Department of Health, Education, and Welfare), selected yearly and monthly reports, especially 28 February 1974, 15 March 1979, and 16 February 1995.*

est and youngest cohorts have the lowest rates, and the youngest is primarily *baby-boom adults* (Smith and Meitz, 1983: 616). This means that while the rate of divorce was going up in the 1960s and early 1970s, this is not completely accounted for by "baby boomers," but also by older couples divorcing at a higher rate than every before. More important, a conservative trend seems apparent among the young marrieds, but to propose a drop in the divorce rate in the immediate future would assume no other important changes in U.S. society that might contribute to keeping the rate high, or even raising it. As the discussion of no-fault divorce and alternatives to monogamy will demonstrate, such a conservative assumption may not be warranted.

A longstanding assumption has been that divorce rates rise with prosperity and decline during economic downturns. Scott South looks at business cycles while controlling for the steady rise in the divorce rate, and finds that "the divorce rate tends to rise during periods of economic contraction and fall (or at least rise more slowly) during periods of economic expansion" (South, 1985: 38). However, he concludes not that the previous research was wrong, but that today the context is different. There are both motivations and opportunities to divorce, and South states that these may not be highly correlated:

> *Prosperity raises the opportunity to divorce by making divorce more affordable but reduces the desire to divorce by putting less financial stress on marriages. Economic*

contraction, on the other hand, decreases the affordability of divorce but probably increases the desire to divorce by raising levels of stress and tension (South, 1985: 38).

It is also instructive to relate the divorce rate to death and desertion. While the divorce rate has risen in 100 years from 1 to 20 per 1,000 marriages, the death rate has declined substantially during the same period. It might seem reasonable to argue that one explanation for the increase in divorce is that couples whose unhappy marriages would have been terminated by death 100 years ago live long enough today to terminate them by divorce. The problem with this explanation is that more than half of today's divorces occur during the first eight years of marriage; thus, the explanation is partial at best.

A second explanation for a portion of the increase in divorce has to do with desertions. Prior to 1900 desertion and heading west was the common way for husbands to escape an intolerable marriage. Rubin Todres's research on "runaway wives" indicates that desertion should no longer be thought of as the "poor man's divorce"; Todres's respondents were neither poor nor men (Todres, 1978: 17–21). Today, the divorce rate is only slightly higher than the desertion rate, so the rise in the divorce rate is not simply due to an increased tendency to legalize separations. It seems most probable that legalization accounts for about half of the increase in divorces since the mid–1800s.

Let us look at divorce rates by other variables, beginning with (a) *Women's employment:* interdependency and male domination, based on the gendered division of labor, has been weakened. Women's participation in the labor force has made them increasingly economically independent. While it is unlikely that women would say that holding a job caused their divorce, the fact is that their employment is an enabling factor (Furstenberg, 1990: 381; Beer, 1989: 4; Goode, 1993: 8). (b) *Income:* The divorce rate is negatively related to family income, but positively related to the wife's earnings (Norton, 1983; Price-Bonham and Balswick, 1980: 960–962). What this means of course is that the situation mostly likely to result in divorce is when family income is low, but the wife earns more than her husband. (c) *Education:* Education is inversely or negatively related to divorce, meaning that the more education one has the less likely they will divorce. However, even though the marriages of those with college degrees are particularly stable, the relationship is not entirely linear. Women with graduate degrees have a higher divorce rate than those with undergraduate degrees (Castro and Bumpass, 1989: 42). (d) *Race:* Marriages of black women are much less stable than those of white women. "After 10 years, less than 20% of the first marriages of white women have been dissolved compared to over 40% of the first marriages of black women. For second marriages, the respective figures are 22% and 37%" (Teachman, 1986: 588). One reason black divorce rates are higher is that certain social characteristics put them at higher risk. "They have a higher rate of urbanization, greater independence of women, earlier age at marriage, earlier fertility, a higher education and income levels for the wife and lower income status for the husband" (Staples, 1990: 288). Also, black women are likely to be separated longer before divorcing than are white women (Wineberg, 1990: 110). (e) *Age:* Younger, especially teenage, marriages are fragile, and the younger the couple, the more likely they are to break up (Norton,

1983; Bumpass et al., 1991: 27f). Early marriage and divorce will be discussed more fully in the next section. (f) *Children:* The presence of children in a marriage reduces the likelihood of divorce, but not as much as it once did. Heaton reports that marriage dissolution rates for couples with one child are 74% as high as for childless couples, with the rate being 63% for two-child marriages and 56% after the third child (Heaton, 1990: 55–63). However, this effect lessens as the youngest child becomes older, so that in the long run children have only a modest stabilizing effect (Heaton, 1990; Waite and Lillard, 1991: 930–953; Rankin and Manaker, 1985: 43–52). Finally, Goode argues that when other variables are controlled, the presence of children now accounts for virtually none of the difference in marital stability (Goode, 1993: 33–34).

Other factors besides children reduce the likelihood of divorce. One, of course, is belief that marriage is a long-term commitment. And one place where this belief is found is in certain religious groups. Commitment is also related to what some researchers call "social integration," including church membership, close friends, and residential stability (Lauer and Lauer, 1986: 382; Booth et al., 1991: 207–224; Breault and Kposowa, 1987: 549; Shelton, 1987: 827).

Reconciliation

Before turning to why people divorce, a word is in order regarding why some couples reconcile, or why the divorce process is sometimes terminated. One of the major sources concerning couples who reconcile is Karen Kayser's new book *When Love Dies* (1993). She describes the process whereby some couples rekindle their love, often through conscious efforts, including counselling. In addition, Bumpass et al. found that spells of separation followed by reconciliation are extremely common, with 40 percent of couples who first separated between 1970 and 1984 reconciling at least once (Bumpass et al., 1991: 27). However, at the time of their interview only 40 percent of the separated and reconciled couples were still together. At a later stage, Kitson found that divorce petitions were more likely to be withdrawn "if the husband filed for the divorce, if fewer legal grounds were used for the divorce, if the spouses were similar in age, and if they had few or no minor children" (Kitson, 1992: 39). In other words, children may not keep marriages together when divorce is first contemplated. More research on reconciliation is still needed.

SECTION TWO

WHY DO PEOPLE DIVORCE?

When we focus on the causes of divorce, we find two types of variables discussed in the literature. The first are the indirect causes for the kinds of sociocultural categorical differences presented above. The second are the direct causes, or the answers given by people seeking divorce to specific questions about why they want a divorce.

Socioeconomics: Income, Education, Occupation

Recently it has been argued that the lower a family's income and education, the more likely a divorce will occur. A partial explanation for this is that low-status families are more susceptible to many of the stressors discussed above, including alcoholism and unemployment; possible outcomes of such stressors are disorganization and crisis, and eventually divorce. However, when Morgan distinguishes separations that end in divorce from those that are never legalized, the finding is that those with higher incomes are somewhat more likely to go through the process of legal divorce (Morgan, 1988: 496). In addition, welfare has been investigated as a factor in low-status divorces, and "young marriages disproportionately involve persons from lower- or working-class backgrounds" (Bartz and Winch, 1981: 298). (Welfare and early marriage will be treated below as separate causal factors.)

One further socioeconomic issue runs counter to the above. We noted that high income for women is related to divorce, and when coupled with the foregoing, it looks like marriage is weakened when the wife's status is higher than her husband's. The causal aspects of this fact seem to be twofold: the threatened male ego and the wife's economic independence. Many males, steeped in the traditional bread-winning ideology, simply cannot cope with an economically successful wife and may become alienated from the marriage. Even more important, the wife who earns does not have to put up with an unsatisfactory marriage. Ahrons and Rodgers succinctly state the "women's issues" that have loosened the marriage bond:

> *As women become more independent economically, their need for marriage as their source of economic support lessens. As they strive for more equality in society, their need for marriage as a source of status also lessens. Finally, when women may choose to have sexual relations without fear of pregnancy and societal scorn, their need for marriage (for) sexual satisfaction is reduced as well (Ahrons and Rodgers, 1987: 14–15).*

(For more on women's employment and divorce, see Greenstein, 1990: 657–676).

In the discussion of spouse abuse it was noted that dependent women are more likely to stay and take it. This is the other side of that coin: independent women will leave. In fact, this raises an interesting and more general issue: marriage was traditionally based upon mutual dependence between two incomplete people who completed each other in marriage. That mutual need, as we noted in Chapters 4 and 5, kept them together, almost without regard to how they felt about each other and the marriage. What is the new "glue" for the marriage of two independent, self-sufficient people? The answer is: we have not yet figured that out. In other words, self-sufficiency + marital maladjustment = divorce. So not all socioeconomic variables are inversely related to divorce: women's earnings are the exception.

Welfare

Conservatives have often argued against welfare by saying that welfare weakens marriage. Bahr finds some confirmation for this in the fact that for both blacks and whites—but especially for whites—those on welfare dissolved their marriages at a higher rate than those not on welfare, even when other relevant socioeconomic variables are controlled (Bahr, 1979). However, Thomas Draper argues with the proposition that welfare causes marital instability. If anything, he feels, causality runs the other direction: "If there is a causal relationship, the only one supported by the present analysis is that divorce and separation cause women to go on welfare, perhaps as a means of keeping the rest of the family together" (Draper, 1981: 298). The various income maintenance studies have also left the question of causal relation between public assistance and marital stability very much open to question.

Early and Late Marriages

The instability of teenage marriages is true at all status levels and is thus not strictly a low-status phenomenon. Nor is it true for certain cohorts but not for others. For example, Smith and Meitz found that early marriers are 12 percent more likely to divorce in each of the four cohorts: First World War, Depression, Second World War, and Vietnam (Smith and Meitz, 1983). But why are youthful marriages on the whole less likely to last? One possible reason is that early marriers have less stable personalities, or simply different personalities from those marrying at the typical time. However, Rockwell et al. find no significant personality differences between early and typical marriers. They do find differences between the divorced and the still-married, with the divorced being more assertive and nonconformist, but these differences might hold for those marrying at any age (Rockwell, et al., 1979: 399–404).

Much of the instability in early marriages is accounted for by the socioeconomic factors already noted. Teenaged marriers have less education, lower status occupations, and earn less income than later marriers (Kiernan, 1986: 35–54; Teti et al., 1987: 499). There are, however, three other partial answers as to why youthful marriages are less stable:

1. divergence, or differential growth
2. marriage as an escape,
3. premarital pregnancy.

Some have claimed that in a society that stresses both personal choice of a mate and deferred adulthood, young people are not psychologically and intellectually prepared to make sound mate choices. Quale calls this the maturity factor in marital role stress. While this assumption can easily be questioned by noting the way in which improved diet and the mass media help young people mature (physically and mentally) earlier than ever before, the fact remains that the earlier a couple marry the greater the likelihood is that there will be a *divergence* in their careers, interests, and personalities during the first few years of their marriage and that it will therefore end in divorce.

A second possible explanation for breakup of early marriages is that they are often as much an *escape from* something as a *commitment to* something. Young people who find themselves increasingly unable to put up with stifling or unhappy homes may see marriage as an opportunity to escape and, therefore, may not allow sufficient time for unstable or unworkable dating relationships to run their course and dissolve. One way of escaping from home is to force parental acceptance of a marriage by means of a *premarital pregnancy*. This is the reason most often mentioned for the greater instability of youthful marriages, though many have found that, by itself, premarital pregnancy accounts for only a small portion of the variation. Why should marriages involving a pregnancy be less stable? Premarital pregnancy disrupts the courtship process and does not allow for the elimination of relationships that would have been abandoned if allowed to run their course.

As we noted in Chapter 10, both early and late marriages may have strikes against them. A late marriage may be within a limited field of eligible people, so that the risk of incompatibility and dissimilarity is increased. Interestingly enough, Booth and Edwards find that late marriages (or those begun later than the typical time) are less stable. The reasons for this they find to be dissatisfaction due to (a) lack of agreement with mates, and (b) lack of companionship (Booth and Edwards, 1985: 67–75). In other words, in early and late marriages the working of choice is short-circuited.

Generational Transmission

Another partial cause of divorce is parental divorce. As in other areas of life, children learn from their parents' example. It is not that children of divorced people make poorer mate choices; but that these children learn from their parents that divorce is all right. In fact in recent studies, children of divorced parents rate divorce more favorably than others do, but "desensitization" may not be the correct term; divorce is seen as an appropriate solution to a bad marriage. If it was good enough for their parents, it is a possibility for them as well if "worse comes to worst" in their own marriages. Numerous researchers have found signs of such transmission (Perlman and Fehr, 1987: 21; Glenn and Kramer, 1987: 811).

On the other hand, many young people say that their parents' divorce was so painful for them that they will go to great lengths in their own marriages to avoid it. However, if one has seen not only parents but others using divorce as the solution to a bad marriage, they may abandon their good intentions if their own marriage goes bad. The divorce rate, after all, measures how willing people are to put up with unhappiness and dissatisfaction (Quale, 1988: 204).

Direct Reasons

This brings us to the direct causes or reasons for divorce mentioned by divorced and divorcing persons.

A generation ago George Levinger divided his sample of 600 Cleveland applicants for divorce into lower status and middle status groups, and reported the following differences by gender and socioeconomic status in reasons given for desiring a divorce:

Lower-status wives were considerably more likely than middle-status wives to complain about financial problems, physical abuse and drinking. Middle-class wives were significantly more prone to complain about lack of love, infidelity and excessive demands. Middle-class husbands paralleled the wives in their significantly greater concern with lack of love; on the other hand, they were significantly less likely than lower-class husbands to complain of the wife's infidelity (Levinger, 1966: 806).

The difference is that lower status marriages (and, therefore, complaints) are focused in the areas of physiological needs for food and safety or protection, while higher status marriages tend to take these matters for granted and are thus more concerned about forms of emotional and psychological expression.

More recently, the emphasis has been on gender differences in reasons for divorce. Maureen Baker finds increasing numbers of women leaving a marriage because of domestic violence (Baker, 1984). This, of course, does not necessarily indicate more violence, but rather more willingness on the part of women to leave. Finlay et al. find that women with non-traditional sex-role attitudes and men with traditional attitudes are increasingly likely to divorce, adding that divorce itself has a radicalizing effect on women (Finlay et al., 1985: 642). The liberal female-traditional male combination is a problem in role inconsistency, as we noted in Chapter 12. Kitson adds that liberal attitudes are positively related to divorce, although, she says, "it is difficult to determine whether their liberal attitudes contributed to the divorce decisions or whether their experiences in going through divorce broadened their attitudes" (Kitson, 1992: 76). Feature 17.1, by Jane Brody, describes conditions giving rise to divorce, according to several researchers.

W. J. Goode writes that there are five types of factors that have some weight in the decision to divorce: (1) precipitating factors, (2) predisposing factors, (3) range of alternatives, (4) social pressures, and (5) the individual's norms and values (Goode, 1993: 8). The precipitating factor might be falling in love with someone else, while a predisposing factor could be having argued for years. The range of alternatives, of course, includes a woman who works full-time having an economic alternative. Social pressure could include that to remain married (e.g., social integration), while norms and values include the liberal attitude just noted.

In an article on divorce mediation, Kenneth Kressel et al. distinguished four types of couples going through the divorce process. These types are neither sociocultural categories, nor are they based on direct reasons given for the divorce. They are, rather, portraits of the couple relationships at the time of divorce, and present a useful conclusion to the discussion of divorce causes. The four types are:

1. *Enmeshed:* Couples have lots of conflict, communication, and ambivalence over the divorce.
2. *Autistic:* Couples have little communication or conflict, but still much anxiety and ambivalence over the divorce. In this type of divorce, resolution or settlement is very difficult.

3. *Direct*: Couples have frequent and open communication, with conflict and disagreement and moderate ambivalence.
4. *Disengaged*: Couples have low ambivalence, low conflict, and low communication, due to lack of interest rather than anxiety. These people simply don't care much about the divorce, each other, or the settlement (Kressel et al., 1980: 101–116).

It is possible to relate these four types to the categorical differences noted earlier: for example, the enmeshed are usually upper-middle-class couples and the autistic are usually working-class. Remember the distinction in Chapter 10 between interactional and parallel marriages.

Feature 17.1   To Predict Divorce. . . .

Though a "failing grade" on any one dimension may not doom a marriage, poor scores in several areas were associated with strains. These are the dimensions assessed:

Affection toward the spouse.
Negativity toward the spouse, which included vagueness about what attracted them to their spouse and how much they disagreed, and the negative feelings they expressed about each other.
Expansiveness, or how expressive each partner was. . . .
"We-ness" versus separateness, or how much the spouses saw themselves as part of a team as opposed to emphasizing their independence.
Gender stereotypes, or how much like "traditional" men and women the spouses were in their emotional expressions and responses and their roles in the family.
Volatility, or intensity of their feelings toward each other when dealing with conflict.
Chaos, a couple's feeling that they had little control. . . .
Glorifying the struggle, or acknowledgement that there were hard times in the marriage but pride at having gotten through them.
Marital disappointment and disillusionment.

Among the couples who divorced, the husbands were likely to be "low in fondness, low in we-ness, low in expansiveness, while also being high in negativity and marital disappointment," the researchers said. For the wife, important predictors of divorce included being low in togetherness and high in marital disappointment.

Jane Brody, "To Predict Divorce, Ask 125 Questions," *New York Times*, August 11, 1992, B6–7.

LEGAL ASPECTS OF DIVORCE

Though divorce is used today as a solution to an unhappy marriage, it should be obvious from the typology presented above that, though it is ordinarily a response to stressors in the marriage, divorce is a stressor itself. One of the focal points of that stress has been the divorce process, including its legal aspects. Divorce laws differ from state to state and are changing rapidly. This section will examine legal grounds, especially no-fault divorce, economic settlement—including property division, alimony and support—and custody.

Legal Grounds for Divorce

Through the early twentieth century the "big three" grounds for divorce were desertion, adultery, and cruelty, with the latter gradually making inroads within the legal system into the first two. By the 1950s, according to Jacobson, some 60 percent of divorces were granted on the basis of cruelty, often mental cruelty (Jacobson, 1959: 121). The history of divorce law until the 1970s was one of plaintiff and defendant, of establishing fault, of collusion and perjury. If anything, this adversarial proceeding served to increase the stress of an already painful process. Love was increasingly the central fact of marriage, but its cessation was not a legal ground for divorce. The rare contested divorce is the best illustration of the negative aspects of our legal divorce history. Wrote Michael Wheeler in 1974:

> *If the parties are still on good enough terms to work out an acceptable agreement on division of property and custody of children, they ordinarily will have no trouble getting a divorce on the basis of cruelty or some similar ground. But if the husband and wife have lost all respect for each other, if they want to use the courts to punish their spouse, if the divorce is contested, then there is a good chance the divorce will be denied (Wheeler, 1974: 17).*

The first major attempt to correct the inconsistencies in U.S. divorce laws was the 1970 California law abolishing divorce. Replacing divorce with "dissolution," the

> *legislature did far more than create a new name for termination of marriage. It also eliminated all fault-related grounds, such as adultery and extreme cruelty, and in their place substituted a no-fault standard, 'irreconcilable differences,' which have caused the irremediable breakdown of the marriage (Wheeler, 1974: 19).*

During the decade of the 1970s, no-fault divorce spread "like wildfire," so that by 1980 only Illinois and South Dakota still limited divorce to the fault-based grounds and no states do today. In the past few years attention has turned to evaluating the effects of no-fault on rates and outcomes. When the California statute was passed, many argued that the rate would rise dramatically, as people found it easier to obtain a divorce. However, Ruth Dixon and Lenore Weitzman find that in California the rate was essentially unaffected. Though the rate went from 4.1 per 1,000 marriages in 1969 to 5.6 in 1970, they claim that it was not a real rise in rate, but an acceleration of the process, following a delay the previous year. In other words, in 1969 people were waiting until the new statute took effect, while in 1970 the shortened residence requirement resulted in divorces being completed that would ordinarily have carried over until 1971 (Dixon and Weitzman, 1980: 299). Harvey Sepler reports that in 87 percent of the states no-fault has had no effect on the divorce rate (Sepler, 1981). With no effect on the rate, what *have* the effects been? In California, the effects include less court time taken up with divorce, a reduction in the time from initial filing to final decree — from a year down to six months — less acrimony between the couple, more husbands filing for divorce, little change in custody of children, and a little more equity in property divisions (Dixon and Weitzman, 1980: 300–302). Charles Welch and Sharon Price-Bonham, comparing no-fault in California, Georgia, and Washington, find alimony payments to the wife less frequent under no-fault, while the amount of child support paid to the custodial parent stayed the same, when inflation was accounted for (Welch and Price-Bonham, 1983: 411–418).

The change in legal grounds for divorce is consistent with cessation of love and companionship as central reasons for divorce. Ahrons and Rodgers put it thus: "If a major, perhaps the key, reason for marriage today is love, companionship, and emotional support, then a key justification for terminating the marriage becomes the failure of marriage to meet these objectives. Thus, the 'incompatibility' grounds for divorce became more commonly cited . . ." (Ahrons and Rodgers, 1987: 15). Furstenberg states that gradually "the standard shifted from one which required couples to remain married even if they were not in love to one which virtually demanded divorce unless they remained in love" (Furstenberg, 1990: 380). While an overstatement, Furstenberg's comments indicate that no-fault has been a central part of the change from a moral-legal "problem" definition of divorce to a clinical definition. The legal reforms include changes in alimony, support, and custody, and will be more substantially treated below. But first a word about divorce mediation.

Divorce Mediation

One portion of the clinical approach to divorce is mediation. By making husband and wife into legal adversaries, the traditional divorce process escalated anger and distrust. Under no-fault, some couples are still unable to agree on the division of assets and on custody. Kitson states that mediation "is increasingly being mandated for such couples, and courts are being required to establish mediation services" (Kitson, 1992: 351). Mediation ideally begins before the divorce, and continues through the post-divorce adjustment period. Mediation works well in those cases where there is still sufficient trust and communication between the couple that they will disclose honestly their assets and avoid any attempts at revenge. However, a nasty divorce will still be a nasty divorce despite mediation, because it is up to the parties themselves to cooperate and "work through" the divorce (Winks, 1980–81: 615–653). It is, in other words, a good concept which works as well as the divorcing parties allow it to work. The advantages, when it works as designed, are lower costs, a better or more equitable settlement, and a reduction in post-divorce animosity.

Alimony and Support

Alimony has traditionally been "wife support." This is because of the law on property division at divorce, which was traditionally based on the idea that it belongs to whomever earned it. Under separate property, as Weitzman describes it, "a spouse retains all the property he or she brought into the marriage, and all the property he or she earns or inherits during the course of the marriage (Weitzman, 1981: 72). The inevitable result in the separate-property states is to leave the wives working without pay on their husbands' farms, or in the home, with no assets whatsoever to call their own should the marriage dissolve. How then could a woman financially survive post-divorce—without a job and without property to call her own? It is by means of alimony, or a court-adjudicated determination of how much money the husband has to give the wife on a regular basis. In many cases the settlements are quite generous, but the difficulty both psychologically and materially of being financially obligated to a man one is no longer married to is obvious. The longer the couple has been married, the longer the alimony is likely to be in effect, since it takes women longer to become employed and self-sufficient the longer they have been dependent on their husbands.

Several additional points need to be made. First, despite the substantial alimony payments made by wealthy men, the typical woman is financially worse off after the divorce. Second, society is increasingly working toward legal methods for helping divorced women train for self-sufficiency, including payments for her schooling and child care, rather than directing alimony at her perpetual dependence. Third, hand-in-hand with no-fault divorce has been the adoption in state after state of a "community" property statute to replace the former separate-property law. Community property means that the divorcing parties control the assets that they brought into the marriage, but anything accumulated during the marriage is divided equally, regardless of who earned it. This means that there has been a decline in alimony payments, as equal division has replaced it. It also means that when alimony is paid, the courts are more likely to limit the time period for the payments, so as to encourage the ex-wife to become independent (McGraw et al., 1980–81). Fourth and finally, alimony is not always awarded from husband to wife. Though occurring infrequently, if the ex-wife has more income or more assets, the court may order her to pay support to her ex-husband. For example, a woman with a good-paying job in a public school system had a husband who was infrequently employed. They had a house and took care of his mother. The divorce settlement required the ex-wife and their teenaged sons to move into an apartment while the husband was awarded the house, was given responsibility for his mother, and received $500 a month alimony from his ex-wife. As employment equalizes between men and women, such settlements should occur more frequently. There are, however, still a few states in which payments from wife to husband are not legal. This means, as Oster points out, that in those states "women are not able to induce their husbands to invest in them by the promise of future alimony payments. This is surely an unintended and perverse result" (Oster, 1987: 86). Feminists, says Goode, have argued for the continuation of alimony for (1) older home-makers; (2) middle-aged women who need further training, or have a "marriage-induced disability;" and (3) women with custody (Goode, 1993: 342).

This, then, leads from spouse support (alimony) to the other form of sup-port, that involving children. Child support awards seem not to have been af-fected by no-fault, but the big problem has been and is enforcement. Garfinkel and McLanahan note that only 60 percent of those eligible for child support are awarded it by the courts, only half of these receive the full amount, and 30 per-cent receive nothing (Garfinkel and McLanahan, 1986: 25). It has been all too easy for the noncustodial parent, having been ordered to pay support, to escape to another state. After all, the final punishment for delinquent payments is jail, and this *guarantees* the inability to pay. Many states have sought ways to im-prove enforcement, including mandatory wage deductions, which many men's groups oppose. In 1984, however, Congress passed legislation which gave the courts authority to garnish wages to ensure payment of child support, and the states have begun using this means of enforcement if employers will cooperate.

Recent concern with child support has focused on the fact that the contin-uing responsibility for parenting should be incorporated (Schaeffer, 1990: 178–180). Wright and Price note that this is, in fact, crucial. That is, when the quality of the ex-spouse's relationship is fairly good, the payment of child sup-port awards is more likely (Wright and Price, 1986: 87). And Nichols-Casebolt argues that even if more child support were ordered by the courts and a higher percent of that ordered by the courts were paid, the non-custodial parent would still be better off financially than the custodial (Nichols-Casebolt, 1986: 879).

Once property and support settlements are made by the courts, is that the end of the litigation process? Not in actuality. Halem notes what in fact occurs, and why:

> *Because the decision is often considered unsatisfactory by at least one party, because judicial enforcement, to say the least, is inadequate, and because a legal ruling may do little to resolve interpersonal problems between the spouses, the initial judgment may be challenged again and again in court on the basis of "new evidence," "changed cir-cumstances," or failure to comply with court orders (Halem, 1982: 50).*

The final decree is often not final at all, particularly when the settlement in-volves child custody.

Child Custody

In patrilineages, which have been the cross-culturally dominant norm, the hus-band's family has received custody of children when a marriage splits. How-ever, Goode makes an interesting point about the distinction between child custody and child care cross-culturally:

To put it bluntly, East or West, men have never been willing to take on the daily tasks of child-care. They wanted—and perhaps still want—to have custody as long as they did not have to take care of the children . . . as long as the women in their extended kin . . . would accept the burden. Moreover, since the importance of lineage continues to decline, even the ideological value of custody decreases (Goode, 1993: 278).

In the urban, industrial U.S. tradition the husband was awarded the property and the wife was awarded the children. This is not surprising in view of the stereotypical "husband-breadwinner, wife-homemaker/mother" distinction. Although the property settlement aspect of divorce is changing rapidly in many states, custody determination is changing more slowly. Weitzman explains clearly what is happening:

While most statutes have put the wife on an equal footing with the husband, and have instructed the courts to award custody in the best interest of the child, judges typically have held that it is in the child's best interest not to be separated from the mother—unless she has been shown to be unfit (Weitzman, 1981: 101).

The wife still has custody more often than not (Seltzer, 1990), but she is not compensated for the child-care duties she must perform, since support is based strictly on economic issues. One writer argued that the determination of custody by a lawyer overemphasizes the economic dimension. He feels that a social worker would be more capable of determining the best emotional and developmental interest of the child because the child's needs are clearly not only economic (Kirschner, 1978–79: 275–296).

An interesting study of 55 divorcing couples found that the parents agree on the importance of various criteria, such as quality of life for the child, in determining custody. Not surprisingly, however, couples "did not agree on the extent to which each criterion favored one or the other to have custody. Parents rated themselves as more suitable to have custody than they were perceived by their partner" (Lowery, 1985: 241). This, of course, is a basis for the custody struggles that sometimes occur. So what are the reasons why the 600,000 single fathers reported by Greif in 1983 got custody? According to his study of 1,136 of these fathers, the most important reasons are: mutual agreement—36 percent, children picked him—26 percent, and 21 percent—he offered a more secure home, wife couldn't handle the children, he won the custody battle, and the wife deserted. Winning a court battle is noteworthy, since only a few years earlier the husband almost never won a contested custody (Greif, 1985: 38, 41). A study of custody among hispanic, white, and intermarried couples produced several important findings. First, there were no differences between white and hispanic couples in terms of father-child contact after divorce. Second, fathers in intermarried couples had a higher level of participation with the children, regardless of which spouse was of which ethnic group. Gray concludes that the reasons for this are either (1) the father is concerned about losing the children into another ethnic group, or (2) he is more anxious to maintain the children's contact with his kin, or both (Gray, 1992: 55–68).

One result of concern for the child's best interest, coupled with more amiable divorces, has been joint-custody determinations. In 1980 nine states had specific joint-custody language in their statutes, ten years later more than double that number. Joint custody may or may not mean equal time with both parents. What it does mean is that both parents still have equal responsibility for decisions concerning the child's welfare. The court will not award joint custody unless the parents agree to it, and in order to agree to it, they must trust each other as parents. The attempt is made to equalize time spent with each parent as much as possible, and to give the child a similar environment with each parent. The primary advantage in joint custody is that the child does not "lose" one parent, as in the more typical divorce. In other words, the child is taught that both mother and father still love him or her and want to be a parent; they simply do not want to be married to each other. Two recent studies show, however, that joint custody falls far short of the ideal. Kline et al. report that overall children adjust no better in joint than in single-custody arrangements. The key factor is how the parents relate to each other (Kline et al., 1989: 430–438). Likewise, Coysh et al. in the same study find that joint custody is not even indicative of the ex-spouses' relation to each other (Coysh, 1989: 52–71). Other complications arise when one parent decides to relocate, or when one parent remarries, especially if this parent and the new spouse decide they would like to adopt the child. But joint custody, even with all the difficulties to be ironed out, is another attempt to lessen the crisis-causing aspects of divorce for all the parties involved.

No-fault divorce, community property, child-support enforcement, joint custody: all these are obvious attempts to lessen the trauma of divorce, and to treat it more as a solution than as a problem. Yet the reform of divorce laws is still in progress, and not every observer is convinced that we have completed the transition from the moral approach to divorce to the clinical. Writes Halem:

> *The law had not become the healing agent that the reformers envisioned. Divorce had become easier to obtain and perhaps a less traumatizing experience, but the welfare and interests of adults and children were not appreciably safeguarded. Maybe the whole idea of making the divorce process a therapeutic proceeding was simply an impossible dream. The clinical conception of divorce imposed a burden on the legal system that it was not equipped to assume (Halem, 1980: 155).*

While Halem writes in the past tense, she is referring to present reality. Yet it is quite possible that the legal system did not and does not intend to make divorce purely therapeutic. We are still too ambivalent in our society about individualism and familism, especially about freedom and equality for women, and thus about divorce as problem or solution, to move completely to the therapeutic view of divorce. An example of the finale to a therapeutic approach is the couple who mailed invitations to their divorce celebration: "Archibald and Veronica cordially invite you to come and help us celebrate our divorce." This is far from the typical practice and a long way from opening the back door to marriage as easily and comfortably as we open the front door. Less traumatic the process most certainly is, but not without stress.

POST-DIVORCE ADJUSTMENTS

Kitson defines adjustment as "being relatively free of symptoms of psychological disturbance, having a sense of self-esteem, and having put the marriage and former partner in enough perspective that one's identity is no longer tied to being married or to the former partner (Kitson, 1992: 20). The stages (or issues) in divorce adjustment are (1) legal, (2) social, (3) economic, (4) parental, and (5) psychological (Kitson, 1992: 5–7).

In a manner very similar to Farber's crisis process in Chapter 16, Constance Ahrons describe divorce as a five-stage process:

1. *individual cognition:* couple realizes their marriage is lousy;
2. *family metacognition*: couple discusses their problems openly with others;
3. *separation*: the couple separate;
4. *reorganization*: new roles and adjustments are made;
5. *redefinition*: new family redefines its relations to each other and to society.

Some of this is psychological, much is economic, social, and structural. Wallerstein and Blakeslee give a slightly different three-stage version of this process (see Wallerstein and Blakeslee, 1989: 8f).

Let us examine the different issues raised by Kitson, beginning with (5) the emotional divorce. Divorcing couples ordinarily have not worked through all their pre-divorce problems. Vaughan notes that initiating legal proceedings is simply formal confirmation of the relationship's demise (Vaughan, 1986: 173). Douglas and Atwell describe the post-divorce problem thusly:

> *Most people who have been in love separate and divorce long before they have fully unbonded and must go through a prolonged mourning process when they break up and divorce. Each individual's mourning process will be somewhat unique, depending on the particular insecurities and securities, the particular emotions, morals and cognitions, and the situations involved (Douglas and Atwell, 1988: 267).*

More specifically, Menaghan finds that difficulties with psychological well-being do not reflect pre-existing difficulties but rather the "negative life conditions that follow divorce" (Menaghan, 1985: 295). And when long-lasting marriages break up, a person's very identity may be threatened. These feelings, and the internal conflicts they arouse, are not amenable to a quick fix or short recuperation (Wallerstein and Blakeslee, 1989: 6). Divorce is seldom a totally mutual decision, and the initiator of the divorce is usually more accepting of it (Thompson and Spanier, 1983: 103–114; see also Vaughan, 1986 and Kayser, 1993). Doherty et al. add that men have lower psychological well-being prior to the divorce, but it does not get any worse, while women's adjustment gets progressively worse in the early months after the divorce. This leads us to other elements in post-divorce adjustment.

Social adjustment, Kitson's (2), differs by gender. According to the men in White and Bloom's study, the major problem is loneliness, including missing the constant contact with children from the marriage. Having a sexual involvement with someone new is favorable to post-divorce adjustment, while continuing to be sexually involved with one's ex-wife is negatively related to adjustment (White and Bloom, 1981: 349–360). Acock and Hurlbert find that social networks resume their premarital characteristics, meaning that women have an advantage (1990: 245–264), due to their greater embeddedness even today in family and social network than men. However, Gerstel qualifies this by finding that men more easily develop casual ties (Gerstel, 1988: 343). For a woman, the primary problem is not ordinarily a matter of loneliness. Fairly quickly she becomes involved closely with friends, family of orientation, or a new man—and each of these cushions the loss of her spouse (McLanahan, 1983: 347–357). A study by McLanahan et al. gives much insight into the post-divorce social adjustments of women, and McLanahan also notes that the stresses associated with being a single mother become much less frequent within two years after divorce (McLanahan et al., 1981: 601–612). In other words, women's kin-friend-family networks re-emerge more quickly, while men seek new acquaintances—but these do not completely solve problems of loneliness for the latter.

The major post-divorce adjustment problem for women is (3) economics. Despite attempts to balance economic settlements between men and women, women were actually doing worse after divorce economically in the 1980s than in the 1970s (Kitson, 1992: 220). Gerner et al. find that women's mean income dropped by one-third the year before divorce, and Albrecht finds two-thirds of his female respondents reporting lower incomes after divorce, while one-fourth of his ex-husbands actually report more income (Gerner, 1990: 7–22; Albrecht, 1980: 67). A part of women's economic problems is the limitations of the labor market, due both to lack of training and to lack of opportunities. Goode adds that it is simply not enough to facilitate payments to ex-wives, there must be full participation of women in the work force, including both education and child care (Grella, 1990: 53; Goode, 1993: 341). The negative economic effect on women is even greater if she has custody of the children, meaning that about 90 percent of the children of divorce are also affected economically (Weitzman, 1988: 246; see also Arendell, 1990: 479–480).

As for post-divorce couple relations, marriages often still end with acrimony. Ahrons reports four kinds of post-divorce relationships: "Perfect Pals, Cooperative Colleagues, Angry Associates, and Fiery Foes" (Ahrons and Rodgers, 1987: 114–115). The first are very rare, involving continued friendship and co-parenting. According to Ambert and Hobart, contact of all kinds is infrequent, though more frequent when there are children. However, the more children the less contact (Ambert, 1988: 327; Hobart, 1990: 81–97). Besides the large number of "Angry" and "Fiery" divorcees, Ahrons and Rodgers note a potential fifth type, which is as unusual as the Pals; this they call the "Dissolved Duos." These ordinarily result from residential movement and distance, and involve no contact at all (Ahrons and Rodgers, 1987: 121).

Let us close the discussion of post-divorce adjustments for the ex-spouses with some good recent summaries of women's and men's adjustments, or gender differences. For women, says Johnson, the aftermath of divorce is as follows: women have economic problems (only 14 percent of women have household incomes over $20,000, while 54 percent of the men do); and women need more child care (Johnson, 1988: 86–87). On the other hand, women are absorbed into their social network, and have less housework to do. As for men, Greif describes the ones who do well after divorce as follows: they (1) are financially comfortable, (2) were involved in housework and childcare during the marriage, (3) they attribute the breakup to both couple members, (4) they are satisfied with childcare arrangements, and with their ex-wife's care of the child. They have regular contact with their children, and sought sole custody (regardless of whether they got it) (Greif, 1985: 151). So positive experience with the children is good, as is financial comfort. But loneliness is an ongoing post-divorce problem for men. A final gender difference is noted by Tannen: When women indicated

> *they had gained freedom by divorce, they meant that they had gained "independence and autonomy." It was a relief for them not to have to worry about how their husbands would react to what they did, and not have to be "responsive to a disgruntled spouse." When men mentioned freedom as a benefit of divorce, they meant freedom from obligation—the relief of feeling "less confined," "less claustrophobic," and having "fewer responsibilities" (Tannen, 1990: 41).*

Children's Adjustments

Divorces increasingly involve couples with children. In 1948, only 42 percent of divorcing couples had children under 18, while by 1962 it reached 60 percent and involved 537,000 children. Since then the percent has risen slightly and the number of children of divorce has reached a million. One result of the increasing prevalence of divorce among couples with children has been an outpouring of research on post-divorce child adjustment; however, not all the findings are consistent. Following is a review of some of what is known.

Wallerstein and Blakeslee's book *Second Chances* notes that the experience of divorce

> *is entirely different for parents and children. As a parent puts his or her life together in post divorce years, they say, children will inevitably improve. But it does not follow that a happy or happier adult will necessarily become a better parent. The "trickle down" theory is not relevant to parent-child relationships (Wallerstein and Blakeslee, 1989: 10).*

What are some of the issues children face? Wallerstein and Blakeslee list several: (1) children are profoundly concerned not only for themselves, but for their parents' welfare; (2) children of all ages feel rejected when their parents divorce; (3) children are angry with their parents for violating the unwritten rule—that parents are supposed to sacrifice for their children, not the other way around; (4) children feel intense loneliness; (5) loyalty conflicts may cause them to change from one parent to the other and back; (6) many children feel guilty, feeling it is their job to mend their parents' marriage (Wallerstein and Blakeslee, 1989: 12–13).

Though Wallerstein and Blakeslee caution about the lack of trickle-down, it is true that child stress is less when the parents are getting along, and when they support each other's efforts at parenting (Johnston, 1990: 405, 413; Tschann et al., 1989: 431). A divorce may effect both children's health (Mauldon, 1990; Johnston, 1990) and school performance. In fact, Mauldon states that there is a 50 percent increase in risk of illness for children after their parents' divorce. One of the personality issues about which there is disagreement in the literature is self-esteem (Raschke and Raschke, 1979; Cooper et al., 1983). However, Raphael et al. find in Australia that adolescents do have lower self-esteem (Raphael et al., 1990: 698).

This brings us to adolescents and divorce. Economic difficulties have some negative impact on the adjustments of adolescents, but so does the character of their parents' relationship (Abelsohn and Sayman, 1991). These authors report that the two extreme versions of parent relationships—enmeshed (or overly engaged) and disengaged—are more negative for adolescents' social adjustments than the various moderate degrees of ex-spouse involvements with each other. Some of the adolescent issues that have been researched are high school experience, delinquency, and substance abuse. Astone and McLanahan found adolescents from divorces having less supervision over their school work, and this in turn was related to increased truancy and negativism toward school. However, looking at many variables they conclude (as did Clark in Chapter 6) "that family income and the number of adults in the household are not the only factors that affect how well students navigate the schooling process" (Astone and McLanahan, 1991: 319).

Matsueda and Heimer report that attachment to parents indirectly affects the inclination to delinquency, but the broken home *directly* affects this attachment and definitions favorable to delinquency (Matsueda and Heimer, 1987: 835). Likewise, Doherty and Needle report more substance use by adolescents whose parents are divorced (1991: 328–337). This, however, is more true of boys than girls, while the girls have lower self-esteem. Hetherington adds that noncompliant, aggressive behavior is more likely to be found in boys two to three years after a divorce (Hetherington, 1991: 168).

So what about long-term effects of divorce on offspring? Some have assumed that after a few years the negative effects of divorce virtually disappear, but the recent research does not show this. Furstenberg states in his summary article that "evidence is surfacing to suggest that the long term effects of marital disruption may have been underestimated" (Furstenberg, 1990: 393). One view of long-term effects is found in Feature 17.2. Glenn and Kramer add that one reason long-term negative effects are not large is that people from intact families do not uniformly escape the negative effects of family life (1985: 905–912). Another study reports that adult daughters of divorced parents expect more years of participation in the labor force and are more likely to believe in the positive effects of quality child care on their children (Schroeder et al., 1992: 273–292). And, finally, children of divorce are still somewhat more likely to go through a divorce themselves—perhaps because they have seen their parents use it as a problem-solving mechanism, or perhaps because some of those whose parents did not divorce are part of a sub-culture that still believes in marital permanence.

As for the relationship between children and their divorced parents, White et al. find that divorce does not weaken the child's attachment to the custodial parent, except in cases where ex-spouse conflict is great (1985: 19). Ambert reports that custodial fathers, more than mothers, think they are appreciated more by their children after a divorce. Perhaps the rarity of father custody means that only special father-child relationships are rewarded with custody (Ambert, 1982: 73–86).

But what about the idea of joint custody and of co-parenting? Furstenberg and Nord argue that "coparenting among formerly married couples is more of a myth than a reality in all but a tiny fraction of families" (1985: 903). Seltzer, and Bianchi and Seltzer, report what they call a surprisingly low level of contact between children and the absent parent—ordinarily the father. However, black fathers have a somewhat higher probability of visiting and sharing in child-rearing decisions (Seltzer, 1991: 79–101; Bianchi and Seltzer, 1986: 42–47). Mott qualifies this by noting some difficulties in defining when a father is "really

Feature 17.2 CHILDREN AFTER DIVORCE

In these two girls we saw a pattern that we documented in 66 percent of the young women in our study between the ages of 19 and 23; half of them were seriously derailed by it. The sleeper effect occurs at a time when these young women are making decisions with long-term implications for their lives. Faced with issues of commitment, love and sex in an adult context, they are aware that the game is serious. If they tie with the wrong man, have children too soon, or choose harmful life styles, the effects can be tragic. Overcome by fears and anxieties, they begin to make connections between these feelings and their parents' divorce:

"I'm so afraid I'll marry someone like my dad."

"How can you believe in commitment when anyone can change his mind anytime?"

"I am in awe of people who stay together."

We can no longer say—as most experts have held in recent years—that girls are generally less troubled by the divorce experience than boys. Our study strongly indicates, for the first time, that girls experience serious effects of divorce at the time they are entering young adulthood. Perhaps the risk for girls and boys is equalized over the long term.

Judith Wallerstein, "Children After Divorce: Wounds That Don't Heal," *The New York Times Magazine*, January 22, 1989: 21).

gone" (Mott, 1990: 499–517). Thus, despite divorce-law reform, the breakup of marriage usually drives a deep wedge between children and their fathers.

Kitson summarizes well why divorce will continue to be distressing, or stressful, despite legal reforms: (1) with marriage still idealized, there will be a sense of *failure*; (2) having chosen a partner poorly makes one feel like a *fool*; (3) even if divorce is becoming "normal," many normal life events cause stress (see Chapter 16); (4) divorce still occurs with *acrimony*; (5) divorce often includes *ambivalence*—"maybe we could have worked things out;" (6) divorce is not just a loss of a person, but of lifestyle, status, even family and friends; (7) divorce means many other changes: residence, work, child responsibility, etc. (Kitson, 1992: 347). Individuals are still embedded in their families, so breaking ties is painful. Unlike the effect premature death has on the family (discussed in the following section), the divorcee still exists after the divorce, and may disappear from the life of the ex-spouse and children—with the accompanying sense of loss, or may continue to make life miserable for the other ex-spouse and children.

SECTION FIVE

DEATH AND FAMILY

Even in the 1960s, approximately two marriages were terminated by death for every one that ended in divorce. However, if statistical analysis is restricted to those marriages *prematurely* terminated by death, the ratio is much smaller. Chapter 15 discussed the adjustment of the remaining spouse to the death of a spouse in old age. This section will examine premature marital breakup by death. In an article on death and the family, Uhlenberg asks how declining mortality has affected the family at the four life-cycle stages. (a) To *children* it means deeper parent-child bonds because more children survive, a decline in the probability of orphanhood, and an increasing likelihood that a child will know his or her grandparents; (b) To *young adults* it means—despite the rise in the divorce rate—an increase in the stability of marriage, with the median length of marriage now being 25 years; (c) To the *middle aged* it means the appearance of an empty-nest stage, although the nest is being filled with elderly parents; and (d) To the *elderly* it means more people will reach old age, and the length of time spent as a widow has increased from 3.8 years in 1900 to 9.7 years in 1976. Widowhood used to be followed by remarriage because it happened earlier in adulthood, while today it is usually followed by the death of the remaining spouse because it takes place in old age (Uhlenberg, 1980: 313–320).

Traditionally, the response to death has been supportive of the bereaved in two ways. First, the institutionalized death ritual seeks to help the individual face the fact of death. This is extremely important in working through the grief process. The child who is allowed to retain fantasies about the eventual return of a deceased father may be in for serious mental difficulties. Granted, there has been a substantial furor in recent years over whether the removal of the critically ill from the home and current U.S. funeral practices are helpful or harmful to the individual in facing and admitting the death of a loved one. Nevertheless, the unmistakable finality of death is one of the points of greatest distinction between death and divorce: "We are divorced now" indicates considerably less closure than "He is dead now"; as Bohannon puts it, in divorce she becomes your "ex-wife," not your "non-wife." This distinction is particularly obvious when the ex-spouse remains nearby and interacts from time to time with the children. In other words, working through the bereavement caused by divorce is more difficult than working through the bereavement caused by death. However, a study by Gove and Shin finds that the psychology of well-being of the individual experiencing a premature death is worse than the older person experiencing widowhood (Gove and Shin, 1989: 141).

A second difference between the responses to death and divorce is that friends and kin rally to the support of the individual bereaved by death. Both material and emotional support may be forthcoming in the event of death, although, as Lopata reports for her urban widows, the support may not always be long-lasting. In fact, Smith and Zick find that 33 percent of their originally non-poor sample experienced at least one year of poverty after widowhood. However, "longer marriages serve to insulate survivors from extreme poverty" (Smith and Zick, 1986: 629). In any case, alienation from one's social network is more likely following divorce than following a premature death.

There are also differences between death and divorce in relations with the community and larger society. Religious ceremonies are available to the widowed, while divorce may be accompanied by religious criticism—even ostracism. In addition, the divorced may confront emotional stress due to the necessity of dealing with the legal system. Feature 17.3 shows how businesses may even deal differently with the widowed and the divorced.

Feature 17.3 **GOING IT ALONE**

I went into a store one time and I was looking at some beds for my son. I spoke to the salesman and he asked me, "Is this going to be cash or charge?" I said, "Well, I don't know yet," because I was thinking of starting some credit of my own. And he said, "Well, what does your husband do?" And I said, "I'm divorced." And he said, very cold, very distant, "Oh, well, I'm terribly sorry. Are you working?" I went back the next day and I got another salesman. And the same thing, "What does your husband do?" And I said, "I lost my husband six months ago." "Well," he says, "I'm sure we can work something out." Boy I got all the sympathy in the world.

Robert S. Weiss, *Going It Alone: The Family Life and Social Situation of the Single Parent.* New York: Basic Books, 10–11.

A fourth aspect of the resolution of premature death in a family is that a long period of institutionalized mourning is not expected following the death of a young parent. Instead, the remarriage of the remaining parent or spouse is accepted within a reasonably short period of time following the bereavement. This is, of course, the point of greatest similarity between responses to death and divorce.

The death of a young child or parent is less common and, therefore, likely to be more traumatic than was the case in the past. The trauma may be greater in those instances in which the support of friends and kin is largely verbal and short-lived. Ideally, however, society has devised a basic resolution consisting of assistance to the individual in facing or admitting the loss; support from one's social network; and, in the case of the death of a young adult, renewed courtship and remarriage for the remaining spouse.

Section Six

REMARRIAGE AND STEP-RELATIONSHIPS

Remarriage following divorce is common — almost "normal." What are not normal or institutionalized are the complex relationships that result from remarriage (Cherlin, 1978). In this section we will discuss both its frequency and its complexities. Beer finds that 83 percent of divorced men and 76 percent of divorced women remarry (Beer, 1989: 7). Remarriage in the past ordinarily followed a death, and occurred because the family division of labor depended on adults of both genders performing different tasks, as we noted in Chapter 5 (Ihinger-Tallman and Pasley, 1987: 16). Today it is a result of love and the desire for companionship, and, in the case of some women, the continuing need for economic support.

There are some 10 million U.S. couples in which at least one spouse has been previously married. Of these, only the wife was previously divorced in 30 percent, compared to the husband and both having been divorced in 35 percent each (Cherlin and McCarthy, 1985: 22–30). And given the current remarriage rates, "it is also projected that approximately 25–30 percent of American children will live for some period of time in a remarried household" (Ahrons and Rodgers, 1987: 154) — and some project this figure even higher.

Looking at age, education, the presence of children, and race, the following differences in remarriage are found. Women who married the first time after age 22, or who divorced in mid-life, are less likely to remarry than other women. Young childless women are most likely to remarry, while those with several children are least likely to remarry — but, ironically, most likely to need it. Highly educated women are less likely to remarry than less educated, according to Glick and Lin (1986: 737). However, Smock disagrees, finding that if number of children are controlled, remarriage rates do not differ by age for white women, and are positively related for black women. And overall, rates of remarriage for blacks are one-fourth those of white non-hispanics (Ahrons and Rodgers, 1987: 184; Glick and Lin, 1986; Bumpass et al., 1990; Smock, 1990: 467). Thus, men—especially widowed and older men—are more likely to remarry than women, as are whites and women without children.

Ann Goetting has written about the six stations in (or issues in) adjusting to a remarriage:

1. *emotional*—the new attraction;
2. *psychic*—redefining yourself as a member of a new couple;
3. *community*—changing social relationships, including giving up single friends and linking up with new friends who are a result of the new marriage;
4. *parental*—working out relationships with own children and stepchildren.
5. *economic*—working through the problems of who supports whom and who pays for what. Barbara Fishman calls this the merging of "two disparate economies into a cooperative financial organization which will be different from anything . . . previously experienced" (Fishman, 1983: 361).
6. *legal*—financial and legal aspects of responsibility to current and former spouse and children" (Goetting, 1982: 213–222).

Kenneth Walker and Lillian Messinger state that the greatest differences between first families and reconstituted ones have to do with boundaries and roles. The boundaries of the reconstituted family are more ambiguous (to use Pauline Boss' term) or more permeable. They are less well-defined, because ex-spouses and stepchildren are constantly flowing in and out. In addition, roles have to be achieved, rather than being ascribed. The stepmother must "win" the love of her stepchildren, it is not automatic "because she is Mother" (Walker and Messinger, 1979; 185–192). The ill-defined nature of relationships in reconstituted families is the focus of Cherlin's attention, and he points out that we do not yet have even an adequate vocabulary for describing the complex family and kin relations that result from second and subsequent marriages (Cherlin, 1978: 643–645).

Husband-Wife Relations

One of the newest issues in remarriage concerns the pairing up process itself. Of course, much is the same as that for first "pairings," as discussed in Chapter 10. However, in a study of 105 couples with children, Ganong and Coleman found that the primary way they prepared was by cohabiting (59 percent). Many of these couples also used either counseling or reading materials, or both. In addition, the majority discussed dealing with children from the previous marriage. Other topics of discussion were finances, the previous marriage, doubts, and careers (Ganong and Coleman, 1989: 28–33). Besides cohabitation, O'Flaherty and Eells find that those who married quickly the first time also did so the second time. However, older males are more likely to shorten the process the second time (O'Flaherty and Eells, 1988: 499, 505). In a very thorough article on the effect of the pairing up process on previous relationships, Rodgers and Conrad report the fact that courtship may enhance the divorcee's sense of self-esteem, which may in turn positively affect relations with children. In contrast, it may also bring with it stressors not present in one's first pairing process. Ambivalence about whether the new partner will make a good parent for one's children is but one of the stressors. The authors make it clear that more research is needed to clarify the relation between courtship for remarriage and the various other factors in the divorcee's life (Rodgers and Conrad, 1986: 767–775).

In a study of general happiness, remarried people expressed greater happiness than divorced people, and also indicated their current marriage is better than their first (Albrecht, 1979). However, when the remarried are compared not with their own first marriages (which dissolved) but with other first married, the former report slightly lower levels of marital quality, satisfaction, and happiness (Ihinger-Tallman, 1988: 25–48). White reports that remarried women are more likely than men to report an unhappy second marriage. She argues that economic need pushes many women into a second marriage, while for men it is more likely to be a "pull" based on attraction (White, 1979: 869–876).

The age of a remarried mother's children seems not to affect marital adjustment, but mothers of preschoolers have a higher general level of psychological distress—a result, presumably, of dealing with the needs of a new relationship and those of very young children (Kurdek, 1990: 81–85). Another study shows that remarital quality is affected by division of labor, relation to the children, and also to the former spouse (Guisinger et al., 1989: 454; Hobart and Brown, 1988). These findings are indicative of the complexities of remarried relationships.

Overall, remarriages are somewhat more fragile than first marriages. Goldscheider and Waite state that the divorce and remarriage experience "leads to *less* sharing between husbands and wives in their new marriages, decreasing the likelihood that they will build close bonds as they make their new home together" (1991: 122). This, says Larson, includes less intimacy and lower levels of conflict resolution (1987: 327). Whyte adds that remarriages are more "brittle" than first marriages, with the divorce rate being 7–10 percent higher in remarriages (Whyte, 1990: 255). While this difference may be lessening as divorce and remarriage become ever more prevalent, perhaps the smallness of the difference is what is noteworthy. Given the complexities and uncertainties of remarriage, the smallness of the difference is probably indicative of how hard the remarried work at their new relationships. Let us look at some of these complexities.

Stepparent-Stepchild Relations

The Cinderella fairy tale is an exaggeration of stepparent-stepchild relations, but negative stereotypes do exist—especially about stepmothers (Fine, 1986: 541). Due to the fact that biological parents exist elsewhere, families resulting from remarriage face issues that are quite different from those in first marriages. Crosbie-Burnett et al. summarize these issues as follows: (1) the stepparent and stepchild begin their relationship when the child is partly grown; (2) the step-parent is a newcomer to an ongoing family; (3) stepparents and stepchildren have continuing bonds to family members outside the household; (4) role definitions for stepparenting are unclear, or uninstitutionalized; (5) there are even unclear incest taboos between stepparents and stepchildren and between step-siblings (Crosbie-Burnett, 1988: 302).

An important distinction is whether the family involves a stepmother or stepfather. Obviously, given the predominance of mother custody, most remarriages involve a stepfather and biological mother to the children. Several researchers have found that the stepfather relation tends to be more positive than the stepmother, and also that the custodial father relation to his own children is very positive. Reasons for the more positive nature of both step- and biological father relationships are easy to understand. For one thing, the mother-children relationship is ordinarily close psychologically, and thus it is difficult for step-mothers to give their stepchildren space, that is, to not push themselves on the children. The other side of this coin is that stepfathers tend to be ineffective in controlling or monitoring their stepchildren's activities (Hetherington, 1991: 170). And, of course, it is a rare father who receives custody, so his closeness to his children is expectable. And this very closeness may to some extent drive a wedge between these children and their stepmothers (Santrock and Sitterle, 1987: 290; Hobart, 1987; 274; Sauer and Fine, 1988: 434; Ambert, 1986: 795–804). Ambert notes that the stepparent role may involve live-in or visiting stepchildren, and for most stepmothers the husband's children are not live-in, which is a great help to the stepmother's relation with them. In other words, the most difficult structural situation is where the father has custody and the step-mother tries to relate to his children. Ahrons and Rodgers state that the problem of the stepparent is not knowing whether to act as a substitute or as an additional parent (1987: 166). Another obvious problem stems from the absent parent influencing his or her children against the stepparent.

Focusing on the issue of the stepparent pushing him or herself on the child, Sharon and James Turnbull note that the stepparent often has unrealistically high or idealized expectations for the relationship with the stepchild. Problems which bother the stepparent sound

> *identical to those that arise, without undue trauma, in the daily lives of all parents. But the issues, however mundane, are imbued with extra meanings for the stepparent who is striving for perfection (Turnbull and Turnbull, 1983: 227–230).*

The Turnbulls then suggest neutral territory, flexibility, and enforcing limits; allowing an outlet for feelings about the natural parent; expecting ambivalence, patience, allowing the child to take a major responsibility for relationship development; and, finally, maintaining the primacy of the marriage relationship.

An interesting issue concerns the effect on various steprelationships of the remarried couple producing children. In 1975, Duberman reported that "our" children perform a bridging function for "his" and "hers" (Duberman, 1975: 105–112). Recently, in a study of 105 Midwestern families, Ganong and Coleman reported "no significant differences between families with mutual children and those without" (1988: 687). Further research with a larger sample might help to resolve this question.

Looking at the same relationships from the stepchild's perspective, Lutz finds that the stepchild is less stressed if they lost the natural parent by divorce rather than by death (Lutz, 1983: 367–375). This means that, while for adults the existence of an ex-spouse is negative, for the child is it better for the biological parent to still exist. Not surprisingly, a class of college students thought that stepparents had less obligation to be supportive and helpful than do biological parents. The variety of expectations about stepparent behavior indicates the ill-defined (or non-institutionalized) nature of expectations (Schwebel et al., 1991: 43). Adolescent girls have more trouble interacting with their stepfathers than do boys, even when the stepfathers make sustained efforts to develop good relationships (Vuchinich et al., 1991: 618–626). In fact, in general cross-sex steprelations are more problematic than same-sex.

The negative aspects of stepparent-stepchild relations are well summarized by White and Booth:

> *parents with stepchildren more often would enjoy living away from their children, perceive their children as causing them problems, are dissatisfied with their spouse's relationship to their children, think their marriage has a negative effect on their relationship with their own children, and wish they had never remarried (White and Booth, 1985: 697).*

White and Booth even find that stepparents "launch" their teenagers, or move them out of the home, faster than do first-married couples. Stating our conclusions more broadly, we might generalize by saying that these relationships are better the younger the children are, the longer marriage has existed, and the better the relationship between the remarried couple themselves. And as this phenomenon becomes more and more prevalent, norms may develop to determine privacy and intimacy, love and distance, discipline and leniency.

Stepsiblings and Other Relationships

Not surprisingly, if the remarried couple have a good marriage, and if they relate well to their stepchildren, the stepchildren—or stepsiblings—relate well to each other. MacKinnon states this as follows: "the quality of the other relationships in the family are important predictors of sibling interactions" (1988: 474). From another angle, Ihinger-Tallman notes that a divorce may intensify sibling bonds, and those bonds may result in distance between biological siblings and stepsiblings after a remarriage. In fact, the author says, those attachments and distances may be critical factors in the success or failure of the new marriage (Ihinger-Tallman, 1987: 178).

In Chapter 14 we talked about adult relations between siblings, noting that "comparison" is the adult version of sibling rivalry. Beer comments that with stepsiblings "there is a perception that it is 'us' and 'them,' there is no instant love between stepsiblings" (Beer, 1989: 32). The three recurring stepsibling tensions are: (1) equality is not enough—the feeling of a scarcity of parental love; (2) invaders and landlords—space, who lives where, who was there first, and so forth; and (3) Santa Claus syndrome—gifts to one child and not to another (Beer, 1989: 44).

What about other kin and friends? According to Duberman, they are just curious about how life is going for the remarried. Very often after a remarriage an ex-spouse will keep in touch with and remain close to ex-in-laws, even though the relationship with the spouse/offspring is over. There is, of course, no actual term for an ex-in-law, and it is not altogether clear whether closeness to the ex-spouse's relatives is good or bad for adjustment in the current marriage.

William Beer summarizes the differences between stepfamilies and other families in the following manner:

1. the structure of the stepfamily is more complex.
2. the stepfamily is in process, changing more rapidly.
3. stepfamilies are 'meta-families,' including large numbers of people with ill-defined roles.
4. roles and relationships are undefined; no accepted expectations.
5. laws about stepfamilies are confused, reflecting the social confusion.
6. stepfamilies are "ready-made," while nuclear families form over time.
7. myths of instant love or recreated families may impede the formation of cohesion (Beer, 1989). We should add that the myth of the wicked stepparent may also have an effect on cohesion.

Earlier, Cherlin wrote about many of these factors, saying that the lack of institutionalization and its concomitant difficulties can be seen in language, the legal system, and in other customs. The remarried do not even have an accepted terminology for new parent or child, and misunderstandings arise concerning who calls whom what. Legally, our society is not clear on financial, sexual, and other responsibilities and prohibitions of remarriage. And other practices, such as discipline of the children, are almost totally void of customary guidelines.

Yet remarriages are currently not dramatically less stable than first marriages, and Duberman is convinced that reconstituted families may be heading for even greater stability in the future. This is not only because of increased numbers and their consequent increasing institutionalization but because normality or typicality are the goals they are striving so hard to attain (Duberman, 1975: 137).

SECTION SEVEN

CONCLUSIONS

In a totally nonindividually-embedded or individualistic society and family system, deviance would cause no family crisis, and divorce would cause relatively little stress. Married people would simply "go their way." But the U.S. family is characterized by strong bonds and frequently by strong norms as well. Divorce is therefore not pursued as nonchalantly as the pessimists and conservatives of the early twentieth century predicted it would be.

At present there is a clear-cut value disagreement about divorce. Those who feel the individual should be embedded in the nuclear family and serve its needs assert that to lessen the strains of divorce by simplifying the laws and institutionalizing emotional support for the divorcee is to invite more divorces. The strains, it is argued, are "functional" for keeping down the rate of divorce. The individualistically oriented, on the other hand, feel that divorce is a valuable safety valve for the U.S. family system, and should be made as personally painless as possible. It would even be possible to construct rituals that would aid in post-divorce adjustment, as Feature 17.4 demonstrates. Regardless of one's value position, there are signs that continuing changes in the law are the wave of the future—but when or how (or whether) the other strains will be reduced is highly problematic.

The concern today for personhood, individual happiness, and psychological needs has already resulted in dramatic changes in divorce norms and laws;

Feature 17.4 BRIDES ASIDE,
HOW ABOUT DIVORCE SHOWER?

The invitation read, "Come to a shower." The gifts included a set a dishes, flatwear, crystal glasses and an electric juicer—perfect presents for a bride.

But the guest of honor was a man, and the party was a divorce shower.

When Andy Hoffmann split with his wife 18 months ago after two years of marriage, he lost the china, the silverware, the pots and pans, the towels and sheets, the stereo, even the bed frame.

Since then Hoffmann, 28, a Manhattan attorney, has eaten a lot of takeout food directly from the cardboard containers. He's borrowed towels from his health club. And his mattress and box spring sit on the floor in his one-bedroom apartment on East 27th Street.

Friends who heard that his cupboards were bare decided he shouldn't have to wait to get remarried to eat off real plates again. So they threw him a divorce shower to celebrate his new freedom and help him set up house as a bachelor . . . .

Hoffmann sat in his living room on a recent Friday night surrounded by 30 friends and ripped the wrappings off his presents. "I'm not too good at this," he said as he struggled to open a large red box. "My wife opened all our wedding gifts."

"Brides Aside, How About Divorce Shower?" *Wisconsin State Journal*, November 21, 1985, C2.

one could almost say that, along with industrial and sexual revolutions has come the divorce revolution. This same concern has also given rise to large numbers of reconstituted families. In addition, many people—old as well as young—are either advocating or experimenting with alternatives to the traditional family. Each of these alternatives is meant to solve some problem or inconsistency in the small nuclear family unit and is aimed at meeting the needs of individuals. These are the subject of Chapter 18.

Alternative Family Styles

CHAPTER 18

The prevalence and accept-ability of cohabitation is such that we included it in the discussion of pairing up in Chapter 9. However, it is still more often a pre- or post-marriage than a non-marriage. Childless marriage, gender role changes, reinventing marriage, extramarital sex, commuter marriage, and open marriage are changes that could be incorporated without changing the structure, but only changing the content of what takes place in marriage. Alternatives to traditional marriage are singlehood, single parenthood, marriage contracts, communes, homosexuality, and perhaps polygyny after 60. Most widespread today are cohabitation, singlehood, and single parenthood, with gender role changes becoming normative, and extramarital sex and homosexuality fairly prevalent but not normative.

The "Year of the Family"—1980—was to be celebrated by a White House Conference on the subject. Yet preparations included changing the conference to one on "families" rather than "the family." The fact of diversity, say the Bergers, has been made into a *norm* of diversity (Berger and Berger, 1983: 59, 63). According to Maxine Baca-Zinn, feminists have challenged the male-breadwinner—female-homemaker ideology, attempting to give equal weight to a variety of living arrangements, including "nonmarital cohabitation, single-parent households, extended kinship units and expanded households, dual-worker families, commuter marriages, gay and lesbian households, and collectives" (Baca-Zinn, 1991: 121). These are some of the varieties we will discuss in this chapter. However, Scanzoni et al. caution that simply changing the word "family" to "families" and reviewing the research on alternatives (as we will be doing) does not explicitly challenge the rest of the symbol system of traditional families, as found in the writings of functionalists and conservatives (Scanzoni et al., 1989, 38). If, for example, we were to change the focus to intimate relations, and ignore legalization, the research questions and insights generated might be different. While we have done some of this in speaking of "pairing up" in Chapters 9 and 10, and in noting the continued prevalence of patriarchy, the fact is we have also continued to speak of "the family" and "alternatives." In other words, due to the normative dominance of a particular kind of family, we have followed the outline of the "family life cycle" from fertility to death, while indicating that the behavioral variety within this pattern is great. All this means is that "family" and variations are not yet equally valued or equally normative in this society.

When alternative family styles are introduced, it is likely that either cohabitation or singlehood will come to mind. There is, however, a wide range of variations and proposals for experiments that would fit under this heading. These experiments and proposals can be divided into three major types. First, certain alternatives, such as cohabitation, are mainly *outside* and *parallel to* monogamous marriage, and are not an immediate threat to the traditional family because the majority engaging in them still plan to be, or have been, married. Second, there are alternatives, such as further change in gender roles, that could be *incorporated* into the monogamous nuclear family without changing its structure, only the content of what takes place there. Third, there are alternatives *to*, or mutually exclusive from, the traditional family. These are the ways of organizing life, such as singlehood or living in communes and others noted by Baca-Zinn above, that are engaged in instead of the monogamous nuclear family, but not simultaneously with it. The following sections will examine each of these types in some detail.

SECTION ONE

PARALLEL ALTERNATIVES

The alternatives that are outside and parallel to the family are primarily concerned with the premarital period, though in some cases the postmarital. *Cohabitation*, or the nonlegalized heterosexual domestic unit, is the prime example.

You will recall that we discussed cohabitation thoroughly in Chapter 9, stating that it is now both prevalent and acceptable enough to be considered part of the pairing up process. Yet it should be mentioned again here simply in order to note that it is neither done by everyone, nor is it totally normative; rather, it is in mid-stream between being an alternative and being numerically dominant and accepted.

Cohabitation is treated as a parallel alternative because it still occurs primarily before or after marriage, not instead of it. Most of the discussion in Chapter 9 had to do with premarital cohabitating. But Sweet and Bumpass report that in "1980 over 800,000 formerly married women under age 60 were cohabitating," with the highest percent being between ages 20 and 29 (Sweet and Bumpass, 1987: 261). What is not known is how many of these 800,000 finally married the person they were living with. Yet it is generally believed that the number of *never*-marrying cohabitors is on the increase, and that this is a trend that is likely to continue.

Another expression of the parallel alternative is Havelock Ellis' century-old idea of the "trial marriage," and Margaret Mead's *individualized* or nonparental marriage (Ellis, 1936; Mead, 1970: 75–84). The individualized marriage is a contract that would allow for experimentation prior to the conventional child-rearing marriage but would entail more commitment than cohabitation. So as long as living together takes place either before or after a traditional marriage, it cannot be considered a non-marriage, but a parallel alternative. Section 3 will say more about singlehood as a permanent lifestyle, but we turn now to the "Incorporable Alternatives."

SECTION TWO

INCORPORABLE ALTERNATIVES

Voluntary Childlessness

One alternative or variety that can be incorporated into traditional legalized marriages is *childlessness*. This is somewhat close to Mead's nonparental contract, except that it takes place in a typical marriage. Callan and the Matthews have researched involuntary childlessness, finding that while this requires an adjustment of identity, it is also related to a loving marriage—perhaps because of sharing the trials and frustrations of infertility (Callan, 1987: 847; Matthews and Matthews, 1986: 641).

Voluntary childlessness (VC) is an interesting phenomenon, having been studied by Jean Veevers in the 1970s, and by Elaine Campbell and others recently (Veevers, 1973: 356–365; Veevers, 1974); Campbell, 1985). Like nonmarital cohabitation, this is a behavior that is increasing rapidly, and Googins argues that 40 percent of women baby boomers (those born 1946–1960) may remain childless, compared with 20 percent of their mothers' generation (Googins,

1991: 21). While this estimate may be somewhat high, it is noteworthy that approximately half of the childless are so by choice. Without mutual agreement by a couple, VC cannot occur. Some couples have determined to be childless from early in their lives; however, most become VCs after a period of postponement. According to Campbell, the "decision to remain childless stems from one of two basic positions. Individuals are motivated either to *avoiding the penalties of parenthood* or to *protecting the rewards of childlessness*" (Campbell, 1985: 137). And what are the rewards: pursuing careers, fulfilling ambitions, maintaining a way of life, and sustaining a standard of living. Much of this concerns freedom, which the critics define as selfishness (see Feature 18.1).

Who are the VCs? They are high status in every way: educationally, occupationally, and in terms of income. They have roughly one-fifth more money to spend than couples with children, and this extra income is generated more by the wife than by the husband (Bloom and Bennett, 1986: 54–55). They have satisfying marriages that are excellent examples of Bernard's "interactional" or best-friend marriage (Chapter 10). In Victor Callan's study, they describe themselves as: intelligent, practical, individualistic, self-fulfilled, well-adjusted,

---

Feature 18.1   **CHILDLESS HAVE MORE CHOICES**

. . . Selfishness is just another myth that people who choose childlessness must deal with, says Childless by Choice's Carin Smith. Some others:

"Nobody's going to take care of us when we're old."
"Who's going to take the photos (you've collected) when you die?"
"How are you going to be immortal?"
Smith is eager to offer a rebuttal . . . .
"Immortality? . . . We looked at what are the other ways, besides making more bodies."

Another myth, says ChildFree Network's Leslie Lafayette, is that childless people regret their decision when they get old. "People would think that, but I have a large data base; we have people of all ages. I have seen very little regret from people who haven't had children. I've seen more from people who have. That's really sad."

"Regrets? Not really," says John Barklage, 60, of Cincinnati, who belongs to Childless by Choice. "People say when we reach retirement, children will come help us out. I know quite a few who haven't," says the retired civil servant. Like many other child-free people, Barklage doesn't dislike kids; he volunteers his time with the Boy Scouts. . . ."

Martin F. Kohn, "Childless Have More Choices," *Wisconsin State Journal*, November 14, 1993, 1G, 4G. From Knight-Ridder Newspapers.

nonconforming, and concerned (Callan, 1983: 87–96). VC couples are more likely to hold an equalitarian ideology, even when compared with others of the same status. Wineberg, however, finds that among whites VC marriages are more likely to separate. This should not be surprising, since children are not present to hold together a weakened couple relationship. Blacks, especially high status blacks, are even more likely to be VCs than high status whites (Boyd, 1989: 331). Remembering that the trials of parenting is a major motive for being VC, a higher rate of black VCs should be expected, given the added burdens blacks face in raising children in this society.

Here, then, is an illustration of the giving up of one aspect of familism — parenthood — in favor of both marriage and individualism. And, as women become more occupationally and economically liberated, this choice will become more frequent.

Change in Gender Roles

Discussion of the voluntarily childless leads us to a more general treatment of changing gender roles. While this was the topic of Chapter 12, it is worth pointing out that we are far from gender equality, either in society or in the family. Most of reality for women, say Scanzoni et al., "ranges from the wife's withdrawal from the labor force to an attachment to paid labor that is *secondary* to the needs and interests of her husband and children" (Scanzoni et al., 1989: 16). Those are the two roles that we have called in this book traditional and neo-traditional. What is yet to become normative is a full-time, year-round attachment of women to the labor force (Smith and Reid, 1986: 24). How important is women's employment to gender equality? Hertz argues that "concerns with 'equity' between husbands and wives rarely precede the construction of the dual-career marriage. Rather, those concerns commonly *follow* investments in two careers" (Hertz, 1987: 421).

Dual careers, or women's occupational commitment, has several corollaries. One of these is split-shift parenting, in which the couple are both full-time workers and full-time caregivers (McEnroe, 1991: 50–52). This is made possible by 24-hour supermarkets and other round-the-clock services. An alternative to this is day care, which so far has been either unavailable to many, or available but expensive. Changes in women's employment opportunities have far outrun increases in employer-sponsored or other forms of day care. In fact, Christensen claims that "of the approximately 13 million children under the age of 13 who are in need of childcare services, over 7 million are known to have them, leaving over 5 million children in this country without any known childcare arrangements" (Christensen, 1987: 483).

But the point is clear: changes are possible that would make for genuine gender equality. Males and females could be freed from traditional sex role definitions, resulting in both role sharing and role reversal. The androgynous society, say Joy and Howard Osofsky, will be a society with no stereotypic sex role differentiation. They do not mean that males and females will behave in exactly the same way; rather, the hereditary differences and differences in socially acquired interests of individuals will be given full freedom of expression. Couples may live in accordance with traditional sex roles, but such a lifestyle will be by choice (Osofsky and Osofsky, 1972: 411-418). The truly androgynous and equalitarian alternative would require considerable social engineering, but Ferguson closes her book with a powerful statement of this incorporable alternative:

> *feminist counterculture family forms, since they can be democratic rather than authoritarian, can provide all of us with an alternative to . . . capitalist and patriarchal sex/affective production. These forms can provide women with alternative power bases through which to challenge male dominance at the same time as they provide male allies with a way to create more equalitarian relations between themselves, women, and children (Ferguson, 1989: 187).*

Reinvented Marriage; Extended Networks

As an incorporable alternative that might improve marriage, Sidney Jourard has proposed the *reinvented marriage*. Jourard feels that multiple arrangements within the same marriage might help keep interest alive, and "devitalization" from setting in. Perhaps the couple—even while on good terms—should live apart for awhile just to rekindle their desire for and interest in each other. That this is not a new idea can be seen from a 1927 article by Samuel Hopkins Adams about a sabbatical year from marriage (see Feature 18.2). From time to time, says Jourard, the children might be sent away, to facilitate the recapture of the "honeymoon feeling" (Jourard, 1970: 47–49). This, incidentally, should not be held off until the children are grown and gone—by that time it may be too late! Taken by itself, reinvented marriage is, of course, hardly a panacea for marital difficulties, but taken in conjunction with role freedom and other alternatives, it could have a salutary effect.

The resurrection of the *intimate network* has been proposed by a number of writers. It is not sufficient, they feel, to refurbish the marriage itself. What is needed are other intimate individuals with whom to share the nuclear family's excessive emotional load. Frederick Stoller, for example, believes that it would be possible to intensify compatible neighborhood ties, so that sharing could take place in all areas but sex. One of the great lacks of the contemporary family, he feels, is people with whom to communicate more than surface concerns (Stoller, 1970: 145–160). The privacy of the nuclear family is also a disadvantage, making for the violence and frustration discussed in Chapter 16. This, then, would be a pseudo-kin network consisting of neighbors and friends. A similar proposal by Sylvia Clavan and Ethel Vatter calls for linking a nuclear family with an elderly couple in a pseudograndparental relationship. This "affiliated family" unit would meet the needs of children for contact with the elderly, of adults for communication and the sharing of responsibilities, and of the aged for meaningful interaction with a family unit (Clavan and Vatter, 1972: 499–504). Some religious groups have been trying to implement this suggestion—with some success.

Extramarital Sex

Another alternative for possible incorporation into the existing marital family structure is *extramarital sex (EMS)*. One theologian, for example, argued in the 1970s that it might be possible to redefine marriage not in terms of sexual exclusiveness, but in terms of dialogue or communication—for, after all, language is distinctively human, sexual intercourse is not (Hobbs, 1970: 39). It should be said at the beginning of this discussion, however, that there are few signs that such a change and incorporation is taking place. Unlike premarital sexuality, extramarital intercourse is hardly more acceptable normatively than it was one or two centuries ago (Seiss, 1981: 271–283). It happens, but guilt and secretiveness are still present; few couples have an agreed-upon sexually open marriage.

The topic of EMS was extremely popular in the 1970s, but by a decade ago it had almost disappeared from the literature on intimacy and family. How prevalent is it at present? Estimates from the 1970s for this "closet" phenomenon

Feature 18.2   A SABBATICAL YEAR FOR MARRIAGE

My modest suggestion is merely a palliative, a preservative. It is the simple, old, and well-tested expedient of a vacation at stated intervals, such as all colleges and many progressive business institutions now include in their regime, a sort of sabbatical year, or month, or fortnight. Conceive of a state of society wherein the marriage agreement should contain without public scandal, a clause to the effect: "In and after the second year of the joint life of the contracting parties, they shall, circumstances permitting, separate for a period of not less than __ weeks nor more than __ months, during which time each shall honestly endeavor to reconstitute his or her own individuality."

Timorously, I venture the theory that 90 percent of the trouble with matrimony lies in its being too close a corporation. Certainly it is the closest corporation known to society, modern or ancient. In none other do I discover any such undertaking as is tacitly read into the compact by so many love-blinded absolutists, to wit: "I hereby agree to live with this man (or woman) day in and day out, to share his quarters, his meals, his amusements, his vacations, his goings-out and his comings-in, world-without-let-up, Amen."

This mutual slavery would seem to derive from a belief that by the sacrifice of two individualities a joint-personality can be achieved, a theory more in consonance with medieval alchemy than with modern habit. Small wonder that so many marriages fail to survive the deadly compression. . . .

ranged from one-third to two-thirds of married people. Maykovich claims that whatever increase there has been is accounted for by educated, middle-class women (Maykovich, 1976: 695). In speaking of the future, Murstein agrees, saying that the increase in EMS has gone hand-in-hand with the increase in the status of women. Equality and androgyny, says Murstein, have made women "more desirable as companions both intra- and extramaritally" (Murstein, 1984: 82).

People engage in extramarital sex for a variety of reasons. Some are simply "emancipated"; that is, they believe it is all right and they act upon that belief. In fact, according to the Ziskins, there are several different kinds of extramarital sex contracts that married couples have built into their marriages. These include the swinging contract, independent, partial living apart, and the one-way contract (not surprisingly, usually the man's "way.") According to the Ziskins, open and honest communication is absolutely essential to the comarital sex contract; agreements must be reached concerning proper and improper times, off-limits people, and whether to talk to each other about specific affairs or not

Why not give to marriage a set vacation once in so often? The ever-startled moralist will scent depravity. The more timid among woman-kind, a rapidly vanishing tribe, may suspect . . . the Other woman, lurking somewhere in the background. But these are mere vestigial survivals of the ancient and puritanical conviction of sin in the other fellow, on the theory that the logical alternative to monotony is infidelity. There is nothing repugnant to morality in this proposal; and it might well keep life from wearing threadbare. . . .

For the sabbatical vacation no claim is advanced other than that it might give marriage in general a better chance of survival. Granted that it would definitely end a number of unions. Darby would never come back from that fishing trip, or Joan would next be heard of from a round-the-world-in-two-years tour; these are fragile combinations. We may fairly ask whether they were worth preserving in any case. Would not an equal or greater number of imperilled but still salvable unions be saved? The leave-of-absence would keep a happy fellowship keen and vivified; it might well, by affording surcease of friction, render a maladjusted combination endurable, and so durable. At worst, if the temporary separation became permanent, it is better that a marriage end by a clean severance than be slowly stifled to death through years of intolerable contact. . . . Why not let in a breath of fresh air?

Samuel Hopkins Adams, "A Sabbatical Year for Marriage," *Reader's Digest*, January, 1928, 573–574. Condensed from *Harper's Magazine*, December, 1927.

(Ziskin and Ziskin, 1973: 35). The number of couples capable of such open communication and such a contract is very small.

A second reason for extramarital sex is marital maladjustment. Edwards and Booth relate extramarital sex to marital sexuality thus: "Specifically, it appears that the more severe the marital strain—a salient aspect of the context considered—the lower the frequency of marital coitus; and as the latter becomes more infrequent, the more likely is extramarital involvement to occur (Edwards and Booth, 1976). Other well-known reasons for engaging in extramarital affairs include feelings of sexual inadequacy, self-doubts or ego weaknesses of various kinds, the search for excitement, and a reaction to failures of various kinds.

Sexual affairs are either short-term or long-term, fleeting or regular. The fleeting affair may be with a prostitute, a stranger, or an acquaintance, the last being the least frequent type. Prostitution is currently diminishing, while sexual contact with a stranger—which is most likely to occur when the individuals involved are away from home—is now more prevalent. A fleeting affair with a person one already knows can be particularly troublesome, affecting either the marriage, or the mutual relationship between the acquaintances, or both.

Long-term extramarital affairs are also primarily of three kinds—the sexual liaison, the "other wife," and spouse swapping or group sex (Bell and Gordon, 1972). The sexual liaison may be based on a special meeting time and place and lasts for varying periods of time. When one speaks of "having an affair" this is usually what is meant. Having a second wife is a much less frequent phenomenon and involves supporting two different domestic units, usually with only one based on a legal marriage. In some instances each "wife" knows about the other, while in others only the nonlegal spouse knows that there are two households. The third type of long-term extramarital sex contact—and the one that received the most attention in the 1970s—was spouse swapping, or swinging. The effects of swinging were reported by some to be an increase in closeness between the spouses, but others found jealousy an ever-present possibility. The discovery of one's hang-ups and the inability to live up to one's fantasies were two other negative possibilities. The fraction of the U.S. population that engaged in swinging was at least as small as those who have the kind of EMS contract advocated by the Ziskins, and the threat of AIDS has in all likelihood reduced it even further.

There are those, like the Ziskins, who advocate extramarital sex contracts for the emotionally mature. There are others, especially most of the official moral leaders of society, who strongly oppose sexuality outside of wedlock. It is noteworthy that the college students sampled by Leslie Strong still saw sexual exclusiveness as a highly valued marital expectation (Strong, 1978).

We have discussed extramarital sex under the heading "incorporable alternatives" not because we think it should become acceptable, but only because it *could*. At present, however, as seen in Chapter 13, when an extramarital affair occurs and becomes known it is likely to be deviance and result in the disorganization, and sometimes breakup, of the marriage.

Commuter Marriage

As you may recall from Chapters 2 and 3, one of the central characteristics of marriage and family is co-residence, or the sharing of a common household. An incorporable alternative from which co-residence is missing is *commuter marriage*. Ordinarily a response to two careers requiring separate living locations, commuter marriage is an attempt to keep marriage alive, while not letting it stand in the way of individual goals. It is, in other words, a way for individualism and familism to co-exist, but with familism decidedly in the background. Harriet Gross and Naomi Gerstel have researched commuter marriage, and they find it to be a practice of high-status couples. Often they are young couples with no children, and in such cases separate residence causes little difficulty as long as they can get together frequently on weekends and holidays, and as long as they perceive it as temporary (which it may or may not be). For older couples, especially those with children, the adjustment may be more traumatic. The husband feels a real sense of loss, with the wife not around to do "neotraditional" domestic chores. The wife feels a sense of freedom and independence, but when there are children the burden borders on that of the divorced mother. Guilt and resentment show up in various ways, but this is one method—albeit a "lopsided" one in favor of the career—of adjusting occupational and marital demands. It is not widespread at present, but could become more so as women become increasingly committed to careers (Gerstel and Gross, 1984; see also Groves and Horm-Wingerd, 1991: 212–217).

Open Marriage

An alternative that encompasses many of the proposals that could be incorporated into marriage is what Nena and George O'Neil call *"open marriage."* This means seeing marriage as an open system, in which the couple members do not lose their separate identities, but rather work together to accomplish both personal and interpersonal growth. David Reiss calls it "boundary openness," and focuses his definition on the freedom with which a family allows people and information to enter it and shape its development. The closed family, says Reiss, cling to each other in novel situations (Reiss, 1981: 332). According to the O'Neills, in a closed marriage the couple members tend to cling to each other in all kinds of situations, not just novel ones (O'Neill and O'Neill, 1972).

Younger couples are characterized by somewhat more openness in their marriages than older couples, and there is a slight relationship between openness and better marital adjustment. The growth the O'Neills speak of may occur through all sorts of nonconformity to traditional ways, including the gender role freedom and sexual freedom referred to above. As an open system, then, marriage must be based on mutual commitment, but not of the exclusive sort that can make, and has made, marriage a prison for many people (Wachowiak and Brass, 1980: 57–62). It is apparent that open marriage and the other alternatives discussed in this section are all oriented in some way toward increasing personhood or individual fulfillment, while continuing a certain amount of embeddedness of the individual in the nuclear family. But there are also alternatives that question the nuclear family directly—its structure as well as its traditional content.

SECTION THREE

ALTERNATIVES TO THE FAMILY

Singlehood

The traditional societal value placed on marriage is such that the never-married *single* individual is likely to be accused, according to Stein, of one or more of the following:

> *If singlehood is discussed at all, it is generally in terms of singles as being hostile toward marriage or toward persons of the opposite sex; as being homosexual; as fixating on parents; as unattractive, or as having physical or financial obstacles to finding a mate; as unwilling to assume responsibility, or afraid of involvement; as unable to do well in the dating/mating game or having unrealistic criteria for finding a mate; as perceiving marriage as a threat to a career or as being in geographical, educational, or occupational isolation. The possibility that some people might actually choose to be single because they want to be, because they feel it would contribute to their growth and well-being to remain so, is simply not believed possible (Stein, 1976: 4).*

Ferguson contrasts traditional views of women in an interesting way: "women who are mothers and married are 'good,' to be distinguished from single 'bad' or 'failed' women who are non-mothers," and from 'bad' mothers who are unmarried (Ferguson, 1989: 177). There are actually, according to Cargan, two stereotypes of the single adult: the loner, and the "swinger," or someone enjoying lots of nonexclusive sex. However, Cargan finds, loneliness is not a function of being single but of having been previously married, so it does not hold for the never-married. And fewer and fewer singles deserve the label "swinger," as defined above. In other words, neither stereotype actually fits any large portion of the people we are now discussing.

In 1971 in the United States, there were 41 million single adults over age 18, and by 1975 the figure was 47 million. Of these, some 30 million had never been married, while the rest were separated, widowed, or divorced. Googins adds that single-person households increased by 89 percent between 1970 and 1982 (Googins, 1991: 20). The growth in singlehood—as distinct from postponement of marriage—is due to more education and employment for women, and the increasing ease of having a social life as a single. It is impossible to know, we should add, how many never-married persons are confirmed singles and how many are simply postponing marriage. The pressures to marry are still very great, and many of the singles clubs are in reality dating and mating organizations. As Stein puts it: "One of the major products being sold to singles is marriage" (Stein, 1976: 37).

Though singlehood (with or without cohabitation) is a choice that is somewhat easier today than in the recent past, one study from the 1980s shows the single female to still be at a disadvantage (Loewenstein et al., 1981: 1127–1141). Single women in this study mention loneliness, financial strain, and no mate, kids, or sex as their major problems. However, these women also see positive advantages to being single, and are satisfied with life if they have their health, friends, and work. In fact, the authors conclude, about the same percentage of single women are dissatisfied with life as would be found in a random sample of the national population. Stein lists the strong pulls for remaining single as: "freedom, enjoyment, opportunities to meet people and develop friendships, economic independence, more and better sexual experiences, and personal development" (Stein, 1976: 71).

Singlehood, then, is still temporary for most people, rather than a matter of permanent choice. The married still look upon the single with a mixture of jealousy and pity, says Stein, an obvious reaction to the two stereotypes of swinging and loneliness referred to above. As an alternative to the family, singlehood is in the process of cultural emergence, but is not yet an equally legitimized or normative alternative alongside marriage.

Single Parenthood

The above concerned unattached, never-married singles, not *single persons with children*. The latter, however, have received much more attention than the former, and we have already discussed their adjustments and those of their children in Chapter 17 and elsewhere. So a brief mention here will suffice. Garfinkel and McLanahan estimated in the mid-1980s that half of U.S. children would spend part of their childhood in a family headed by their mother (1986: 1). Five years later Googins estimated that the percent is almost 60 (1991: 22). Between 1950 and 1980 the number of female-headed families increased more than threefold for whites and sixfold for blacks. In 1960 only one in 12 U.S. children lived in a household headed by a woman; by 1990 it was close to one in four (Garfinkel and McLanahan, 1986: 1). Increasing numbers of these units are formed by the never-married, but the majority still involve the separated, deserted, and divorced. Jan Trost has argued that the parent *without* custody of the children should also be considered a single-parent family, since he or she is still a parent, although the children live elsewhere (Trost, 1980: 129–138). The noncustodial parent does, of course, continue — at least ideally — to have an interest in the children's welfare, and may even take a hand in providing for their economic needs. But most of the research and writing on single parents pertains to those whose children live with them, and that will be the focus here.

One category of single mothers that has been virtually ignored is those who are so by choice. While this has increased in the last 20 years, it is still not treated as a viable option, even in studies dealing with women's reproductive rights. Single mothers always face some stress-producing legal and economic prejudices. However as Potter and Knaub point out, "the inflexibility of defining the family in other than traditional terms impacts societal attitudes, thereby compounding the negative impact on single mothers by choice" (Potter and Knaub, 1988: 247). Ehrensaft qualifies this by noting that the "stigma of unwed mother and the child born out of wedlock, although still present, has diminished significantly, making it easier for a woman, if she chooses, to pursue the option of the fatherless family" (Ehrensaft, 1987: 5).

The disadvantageous position of the single-mother family was referred to earlier. Here we will simply note that single parents are more depressed and have more problems with their children than do either first-married or remarried mothers (Fine et al., 1986: 400). One important reason for this is that in objective terms they are worse off. Norton and Glick describe this as follows:

> By most objective measurements, the vast majority of these families hold a disadvantageous position in society relative to other family groups. They are characterized by a higher rate of poverty, a higher percentage of minority representation, relatively low education, and a high rate of mobility. In short, as a group, they generally have little equity or stature in American society and constitute a group with unusually pressing social and economic needs (Norton and Glick, 1986: 16).

Several recent studies of single fathers demonstrate the concern that these men have for their children. They reduce outside activities and organizational memberships and spend a great deal of time overseeing their children's development (Orthner and Lewis, 1979: 27–47). Barbara Risman adds that "when males take full responsibility for child care, when they meet expectations usually confined to females, they develop intimate and affectionate relationships with their children (Risman, 1986: 101).

How do the children of single parents (usually mothers) do in adulthood? They tend to have somewhat greater levels of marital instability and of depression, with much but not all of this accounted for by their economic hardships earlier in life (Amato, 1991: 543–556; Mueller and Cooper, 1986: 175).

If there is pressure on the single individual to marry, there is even more pressure on the single parent, though finding a mate may be more difficult for the man or woman encumbered with children. In the 1980s, support for the single parent appeared in the form of a bimonthly paper, *The Single Parent News*, published in Santa Monica, California. However, while an increasing proportion of the U.S. population live as singles or single parents, remaining single still runs counter to the dominant nuclear family ideology.

Nonlegalized Marriage

Several redefinitions, not of the content of the marriage relationship, but of the *legal form of marriage* itself, have been proposed. Marriage could be redefined as a nonlegal voluntary association that lasts "for as long as we both shall love." Margaret Mead, as we have already mentioned, has proposed that a distinction be made between "individualized" and "parental" marriages, each of which would be bound by a different set of legal and cultural obligations. A third way of redefining marriage is by means of the marriage contract, a method studied by Marvin Sussman, Lenore Weitzman, and others. The contract may be renewable annually, or every three years, or may run until one signatory wants out. In any case the marriage contract ordinarily tries to build in a great amount of equality and usually involves a definable period, after which the signatories must agree to continue. Weitzman feels that such contracts will help to structure partnership and equalization of rights and responsibilities into intimate relationships. There is still some difficulty in making such contracts legally binding, since many states do not recognize them, but this has not kept them from proliferating (Weitzman, 1981).

Polygyny After Sixty

An interesting proposal advanced by Victor Kassel suggests that longevity differences between the sexes in U.S. society make *polygyny*, that is, one man and several wives, a logical alternative *after the age of 60* (Kassel, 1970: 137–144). This, he asserts, would solve some problems of the aged (discussed in Chapter 15)—loneliness, desolation at the loss of a spouse, being forgotten by a youth-oriented society.

Communes

During the 1970s, the best known alternative to the family was the *commune*. Communes have flourished during and after every wartime period in U.S. history, but have tended to die out within a short period of time, leaving only the hardiest and most meaningful. And as the prevalence of communes has diminished, so has the appearance of new literature on the subject. However, this way of organizing life is still important enough to deserve attention in this section.

Communes range from the religious community with sexual exclusiveness to forms of group marriage. Some communes are primarily economic, with property held in common but with the responsibility for other aspects of life left to nuclear family units, which often include children. Other communes are political, their chief aim being some sort of revolutionary orientation, with other aspects of life subsidiary to that aim. Still others are noncreedal, their members' major concern being experience—perhaps with drugs, perhaps with sex—or the desire for intimacy and communication. Many of these experiential communes, epitomized by the urban communes of the late 1960s, last but a short time. In fact, the average life of the urban commune is two years; the individual in it can be expected to stay for eight months (Rothchild and Wolf, 1976; Jaffe and Kanter, 1976: 169–192; Cornfield, 1981: 115–126).

There is a great variety of communes and an equally great variety of reasons why people join them. Stein lists some of the reasons:

Some join for primarily economic reasons: it is cheaper to live with others than to live alone. For others, communes offer greater order and regularity than did their earlier, more chaotic lives. For most, it is a need for support and for friendships among people who care in a world they see as mostly non-caring. For some it is a way to leave home, to get away from parents, and to live in a more stimulating and interesting environment. For almost all, it represents some sort of break with the past and a search for a viable alternative to things they had tried but did not like. It is also exploratory for many—a way of trying out a new life-style merely for the sake of the new experience.

For some, it is a way to live with a lover; for others, it represents a way to live in the single state in the company of others. It is a search for like-minded people. For some, it is primarily a search for companionship; for others, it is a search for community (Stein, 1976: 94).

One of the most interesting forms of commune is the rural or urban commune in which children are being raised. According to Rossi, "communally reared children, far from being liberated, are often neglected, joyless creatures" (Rossi, 1977: 25). Commune parents, say Rothchild and Wolf, do not care as much what their children do, as how they behave while doing it. The commune child is to be straight, or honest and open, in dealing with people. The commune child is neither taught to feel guilty, nor is he or she overprotected from the environment. "So you have the paradox of children who are not individually spared from death, sex, freak-outs, or pain, living in a world that collectively protects them from the bad vibes of America." Rothchild and Wolf compare the child raised in the commune with one raised in middle-class America. "Commune parents wanted a kind of emotional goodness for their children—which they gave them at the cost of the self-centered drive that leads to great personal achievement. We couldn't see famous writers or scientists coming out of that generation of ragamuffins." We could not, they say, give our egos and minds to our middle-class children "without handing them a lot of that attendant ugliness that communes had stamped out" (Rothchild and Wolf, 1976: 204, 207).

Many communes fail to find what they are seeking. Sometimes they fail because their members have compounded each other's problems. Sometimes they fail because their members try only to get but have nothing to give, the result often being, as in swinging, that the women are exploited by the men. Sometimes the opposition of neighbors causes communes founded on weak commitment to fly apart. Sometimes communes fail because they lack a vision, a goal larger than themselves, to live and strive for. In an interesting recent research Aidala interviewed 635 former commune members. Her findings are that (1) ex-commune members are less likely to be married and more likely to live in multi-adult households; (2) they see the possibility of collective living in the future; (3) "attitudes show continuity of ideological criticism of traditional life styles and a commitment to emotional openness and negotiated role relations within the family." Their final conclusion is that "communal experimentation was both a manifestation of and a contributor to the larger process of family change" (Aidala, 1989: 311).

The commune movement of the late sixties and early seventies has subsided. The commune ideal, however, has not died; only the superficial experiments have failed to survive. The promise of the ideal-type commune continues to give rise to new experiments, and there are enough successes to give proponents of the commune alternative continued hope.

Closely linked to the commune is *group* and *multilateral marriage*. Group marriage, say Larry and Joan Constantine, is primarily a living arrangement, while multilateral marriage is a family arrangement (Constantine and Constantine, 1971). The multilateral marriage can include three-person marriages (of which the Constantines found only 35 examples), while group marriage classically means at least two of each sex. Group marriage, Ellis feels, can combine the advantages of swinging with those of the intimate communication network (Ellis, 1973: 81–86). Of course, in most states such units still lack the kind of legal acceptance that would change them from isolated experiments to an accepted alternative.

Homosexuality

One of the alternatives to the family that has had the greatest difficulty escaping stigma has been *homosexuality*. Largely as a result of organizing for their civil rights, homosexuals have found themselves at least part way "out of the closet." Yet even legally the battles for the rights of homosexuals are hardly over. David Rosen has found that the New York Court of Appeals defined the term "family" as applying to gay couples who had lived together for ten years. However, the term "spouse" did not apply to a gay partner, and the term "parent" was not applied to a lesbian partner, who was denied visitation rights to a child she had formerly parented with the biological mother (Rosen, 1991: 29–44). The legal fight for custody has still been a losing battle for many homosexuals, who have been defined as unfit parents simply as a result of their sexual orientation. Even with the strides made before the law, the gay/lesbian community still finds itself at a disadvantage in being defended or in having its rights upheld. On the plus side for homosexuals is the fact that some companies are now instituting insurance and other policies that apply strictly to the needs of the informal—as distinct from the legally married—household.

Almost a century ago, Havelock Ellis attempted to remove the stigma from homosexuality, arguing that it was a hereditary condition, "as natural for its practitioners as heterosexual relations were for the majority" (Ellis, in D'Emilio and Freedman, 1988: 224). The medical, or illness, model of the 19th century was challenged by Ellis' hereditary model, but by the 1920s Freudianism had swung the pendulum back again. For almost 50 years, homosexuality was treated for the most part as a moral and medical issue. But with the new feminism of the 1960s and 1970s came a linking of patriarchy with heterosexuality. Charlotte Bunch wrote:

> *The Lesbian rejects male sexual/political domination; she defies his world, his social organization, his ideology, and his definition of her as inferior. Lesbianism puts women first while the society declares the male supreme. Lesbianism . . . threatens male supremacy at its core (Bunch, 1975: 93).*

A logical conclusion implied is that to end male supremacy women must be lesbians. Male critics have, in turn, tried to identify all of radical feminism with lesbianism, as we noted in Chapter 12.

Arguing for the normality of homosexuality in human societies, Ira Reiss notes insightfully the conditions under which such a preference is expressed through behavior. According to Reiss, in patriarchal societies, the more rigid the male gender role, the greater the likelihood of male homosexual behavior. He adds that there are problems with heterosexuality that may push one toward homosexuality, but in a gender-flexible and sexually permissive society there are also pulls to experiment. "Such experimentation will produce the impression of greater homosexuality, but it may not establish any increase in homosexual *preference*—just an increased acceptance of homosexual *behavior*" (Reiss, 1986: 160–161).

Kath Weston's important book *Families We Choose* makes a valuable distinction between homosexual units as "families" rather than as alternatives to the family. Granted, they are not marital units by the traditional definition, and thus they fit in this section of the chapter, but Weston points out the ways in which gay and lesbian couples attempt to incorporate kin, friends, even children, into their lives. Of course, one reason why their families are chosen is because they are often rejected by blood kin, meaning that "family building" must be done by the homosexual couple from among those who are accepting of their orientation (Weston, 1991).

The issue of acceptance has been raised in much of the recent research. Strommen points out that much of the stigma is based on the idea that homosexuality is "unnatural" because it cannot result in reproduction. Thus, the notion that homosexuality is incompatible with children and child-rearing is one reason for the idea, noted above, that homosexuals do not live in families (Strommen, 1990: 11–12). That, of course, is what Weston's book seeks to redefine. As for stigma, Lieblich and Freidman find that women have made more progress than men in accepting alternatives to the monogamous nuclear family. They argue that this is because society exerts more pressure on men than on women to conform. I would argue that even more important is that patriarchy itself makes it to men's advantage to defend the status quo, and to oppose alternatives—they simply have more to lose. And Feature 18.3 proposes a third explanation for men's fear of homosexuality in men. As for lesbians, some have argued that the stigma they face is even greater, due to the historically greater

---

Feature 18.3 WHY ARE GAY MEN SO FEARED?

Gay men are the victims of insults, prejudice, abuse, violence, sometimes murder. Why are gay men hated by so many other men? Some maintain that homosexuality is unnatural or a threat to the family. But celibacy is also unnatural, yet nuns and priests are not regularly attacked. . . .

Men are particularly prone to use anger and violence against those they think are undermining their masculinity. And it is here that we can find at least some of the roots of homophobia and gay-bashing. . . .

Those societies that are best able to accept homosexuals are also societies that are able to accept assertive women and gentle men, and they tend to be less prone to the violence produced by hypermasculinity.

Dennis Altman, "Why Are Gay Men So Feared?" *Utne Reader*, May/June, 1991, 75. Excerpted from *The New Internationalist*, November, 1989.

linking of women to parenting. McGoldrick notes some of the problems creating difficulty for lesbian women, including the lack of 'marker events' like marriage and the parenting issue just referred to (McGoldrick, 1989: 22). The best treatment to date of the struggles and needs of lesbian women is found in Baber and Allen's book *Women and Families* (1992).

The issue of social support, referred to by Weston, is discussed by Kurdek. He finds that gays and lesbians are supported by friends, who of course are chosen, more than by kin (Kurdek, 1988: 509). Not surprisingly, social support helps the psychological adjustment of homosexuals. Expanding on the issue of adjustment, Zacks et al. find that lesbian couples are higher on measures of cohesion and adaptability than are heterosexual couples. This makes sense when you think about the adaptability required to deal with society's stigmatizing, and the couple cohesion required to survive in an often hostile environment (Zacks et al., 1988: 471–484). Kurdek's research finds that lesbian and gay couples separate when dissatisfaction is high and emotional ties weaken, since there are few legal entanglements. He also finds lesbian couples to have a better relationship quality than gays, a result of the gender differences noted above (Kurdek, 1992: 139; Kurdek, 1989: 54–55). Some studies have discussed the relationship between gay fathers and their children, again seeking to remove some of the phobias of the larger society regarding homosexuality. Homosexual fathers do not have "sexual desires" toward their sons, nor do they have a disproportionately large number of gay offspring (Bozett, 1980: 173–179). But Gottman has noted the difficulty children have if they learn about their father's homosexuality only during a custody dispute at divorce. It is not that their parents' homosexuality affects their children, but rather that honesty and trust are essential (Gottman, 1990: 191).

Another point concerns homosexuality among ethnic minority families. Morales reports that "coming out" jeopardizes both family and ethnic relationships, leaving these groups even more uprooted than members of the dominant white society (Morales, 1990: 233). In other words, minority and homosexual status confront these people with "triple jeopardy"—stigma from family, ethnic group, and the larger society.

The continual necessity in the literature to try to "normalize" and justify the attitudes and behaviors of homosexuals is an indication of how far this alternative is from being equally accepted alongside the monogamous nuclear family, though change is in that direction.

SECTION FOUR

SUMMARY AND CONCLUSIONS

Alternative family styles were classified into three major categories: those that parallel the nuclear family, those incorporable into it, and those opposed to it. Some of these are currently being tried by large numbers of people, others are

TABLE 18.1   TYPES OF ALTERNATIVES AND THEIR EXPERIMENTAL PREVALENCE TODAY

Type of Alternative	Widespread Acceptance	Fairly Widespread Experimentation	Little Experimentation— Mostly Proposed	Only Proposed
Parallel	cohabitation*	—	—	individualized or nonchild
Incorporable	—	sex role change extramarital sex voluntary childless	commuter marriage network open marriage contracts	reinvented
Alternatives to	single single parent	commune homosexuality	group marriage	polygyny after 60

*This has been treated as close to being normative.

being experimented with by a few, while others are only being talked about. Table 18.1 summarizes the types of alternatives and their experimental prevalence. From a long list of possible marital and family forms, Strong's college students selected four in which they would be most willing to participate. These were: "the egalitarian marriage, the traditional sex role segregated marriage, the five-year evaluation and renewal of the marriage relationship and prolonged cohabitation (Strong, 1978: 501). Other possibilities, such as serial monogamy and single parenthood, they did not consider to be intentional, while still others, such as extramarital sex, they considered undesirable and unadvisable. Which of these various alternatives are most likely to become equally legitimated alongside the nuclear family? That question cannot be answered until we have summarized our generalizations concerning the U.S. family.

The Family: Today and Tomorrow

CHAPTER 19

As noted in Chapter 1, some feel the family is reasonably stable, while the majority of observers see it as in trouble, if not disintegrating. In the United States, the family relates to a variety of other institutions, and has a variety of inconsistent elements. The key issue underlying most of the family system's characteristics and changes is the struggle between individualistic and familistic values. What sorts of changes are likely to take place in the future? The family could outlast the various alternatives or it could be destroyed by them. Some alternatives, such as staying single and gender role changes, are already becoming legitimated alongside the monogamous nuclear family.

THE FAMILY TODAY

The first step in peering into the future would seem to be to review where we are. Much of the world is attempting to resolve gender role issues, or is trying to loosen the ties that bind them to the lineage, or is seeking freedom in mate selection. At the same time, the family in this country is characterized by happiness and unhappiness. It is the cradle of love and violence (Collier et al., 1982). It evokes feelings of unity and continuity as well as struggles to be free. A large proportion of the U.S. population is marrying and having children, but many are also getting divorced or experimenting with alternatives. It is this intimate institution, with its functions and inconsistencies, that must now be reviewed.

There are fewer and fewer observers who would argue, as Bane did in the 1970s, that the family as traditionally defined is doing all right. Rather, those who argue against concern do so on the basis of the argument that the functions of childbearing and childrearing, intimacy, status placement, and so on, are still being met—though less frequently by the monogamous nuclear family. We begin this chapter by examining briefly functions in relation to other institutions, and follow that with a discussion of inconsistencies.

Functions and Other Institutions

We have seen repeatedly that the family in the United States seeks to perform the important function of providing *affective* or primary relationship ties for its members. In the middle-class family, those ties are likely to be quite intense within the nuclear family but not to extend very far out into the kin network, while in the families of the working and lower classes, the burden of love and understanding is more often shared by other kin as well. The same holds for the direction-giving function played by the family in *socialization*: much socialization takes place outside the U.S. home, but it is in the nuclear family that individuals acquire their attitudes and cultural orientation, reinforced or contradicted by extrafamilial influences. Lower- and working-class children are somewhat more likely than are middle-class children to be influenced considerably by other members of the social network as well as by parents and siblings. Thus, affection and direction, or strong bonds and norms, are produced by family experience and may be viewed as important aspects of the family's functioning in contemporary U.S. society. However, it is noteworthy that in the past decade even affection and socialization needs have been met apart from the monogamous nuclear family: by homosexual units, by single parents, and so on.

The *economic* system and values of U.S. society are also related in a crucial way to the nuclear family. This unit seldom operates as a productive segment of the economy, but it does serve as a basic *consumer* of the goods of the market. Thus, it is not unexpected that the larger society would stress simultaneously the easing of divorce restrictions and the desirability of marriage and a family, for "the family is a major consumer." The high rates of divorce and marriage are quite consistent with the needs of the U.S. economic system and the materialistic values fostered thereby.

There is more, however, to economics and family than family-as-consumer. The continuing rise in women's employment has caused child-care, provided by businesses or funded by government, to become a major issue (Campbell, 1985: 143). In a provocative way, Edelman notes that our national rhetoric indicates "that it is proper for government to subsidize three-martini corporate lunches but improper for government to subsidize child care to help millions of poor working mothers escape welfare" (Edelman, 1987: 37). Edelman states very clearly the way national economic *policy* has increased the gap between rich and poor in U.S. society, leaving the poor—especially poor children—to hunger, abuse, and death.

While such policy has widened the rich/poor gap, other commentators note the way the *legal* system is changing to take into account family varieties and alternatives. In predicting the future, Kirkendall states that this legal flexibility, just beginning at present, will be dominant by the year 2020. Perhaps in areas such as homosexual or single parenting, the U.S. government and legal system will increasingly respect "the exercise of positive and responsible decision making" (Kirkendall, 1984: 264). Even now, say Scanzoni et al., family law needs increasingly to think of legal status as a variable, not as a norm surrounded by deviants (Scanzoni et al., 1989: 94). A long-standing argument has been whether the law leads or follows social change. In the case of families, it is clear that the latter is more often the case.

Two other institutions deserve mention in relation to family life. The *media* are the subject of debate much like that regarding the law. Television watching is, without doubt, a dominant aspect of most families' lives, having changed the character of what families do together. More importantly, the immediacy of television and movies in individuals' and families' lives is such that the issue of whether the media "cause" certain behaviors seems urgent. The morality of the media is an issue that will continue to be a focus of research attention. As for *religion*, U.S. families range from being anti-religious, through a-religious, to being highly involved in religious institutions and guided by such beliefs. Discussions of the family's loss of functions have often focused on institutional religion as having both removed it from family life and having compartmentalized religious behavior from the rest of life. In a specialized society, even religion is a segment of life for many people. This is why we can speak of the increase in secularization and at the same time note the fact that church membership is higher today than it was in colonial days. Certain religious values are at the very heart of the debate about the morality or immorality of the various alternatives to the monogamous nuclear family. (For more on religion and family, one good source is Thomas, *The Religion and Family Connection*: 1988.)

The *varieties* of U.S. families were the specific subject of Chapter 6, and differences between middle-, working-, and lower-class families in the United States have been referred to in virtually every chapter. The racial and ethnic subsocieties primarily mirror the culture of the other families in the society that are of the same socioeconomic level. There is, however, some cultural distinctiveness based on differences in traditions and treatment by the larger society. In the case of the black family this distinctiveness is based on survival mechanisms, such as extended kin ties, against prejudice, discrimination and poverty, as well as current stress on ethnicity. Another kind of variety is based not on family cultures, but on the individuals involved in the household. This would include reconstituted families, single-parent families, single individuals, three-generation households, and others. As we have said, there is no such thing as *the* U.S. family.

Inconsistencies

In the course of time, the various parts of any given social system do not change at the same rate of speed or with the same degree of completeness. The result is that the same subsystem, such as the U.S. family, is simultaneously characterized by interrelations with the larger society and by inconsistencies and fragmentary changes. Such *inconsistencies* or contradictions, to use Cheal's term (Cheal, 1991: 23), may be extracted from the preceding chapters, and include the following:

+ The rhetoric of family harmony and the reality of family behavior. Leslie Miller writes at length about this problem, showing the way in which the rhetoric causes us to treat violence in families as a surprising and unusual event (Miller, 1990). A good example of the resulting distortion of perception is the general belief that day care is more risky for children than is parental care, even though the vast majority of violence against children occurs in families.

+ The U.S. family, particularly its middle-class variety, is currently walking a difficult line between stress on ego struggle and on conformity; parents teach their children to adapt and to assert their uniqueness but also to comply with the strong family norms referred to above. That is, the family's attempt to transmit its culture to its offspring is somewhat inconsistent with the heterogeneous nature of the norms that the growing individual is likely to confront by the time he or she reaches adulthood. This is the socialization focus on the current struggle between individualism and nuclear family individual embeddedness.

+ An inconsistency in working-class socialization is found in the father's attempt to assert traditional absolute male authority, when he lacks the resources or societal support to make his authority acceptable. Another inconsistent element in socialization is the earlier maturation of young people, coupled with their being kept out of adult roles longer than ever. An exception to this inconsistency is, however, another inconsistency: between early parenthood and society's negativism toward it.

✦ In marriage, there is role choice without sexual equality. This is a partial change, and it is quite possible that having the door halfway open
is more tension-producing than having it either shut or open. C. C.
Harris notes that Parsons' form of functionalism assumed that women
would not be employed outside the home, thereby restricting them to
their "domain" (Harris, 1983: 57). The inconsistency or strain is particularly great for women who have been socialized for success and
also to be the major home and child keepers (Quale, 1988: 308). And
the problem is intensified by the fact that many women are more oriented toward role sharing than are the men they will pair up with.

✦ In kinship relations, the norms of independence from parents and filial obligation to them often run at cross-purposes, serving to increase
the ambivalence of such cross-generational kin toward one another.
Daniel Smith believes, incidentally, that the independence/obligation
ambivalence may eventually be settled by complete apartness. We
have moved, he says, from living with to living near, and it is possible
that we are headed for living completely apart (Smith, 1981).

✦ Divorce laws and expectations are still extremely inconsistent and
fragmented. In some cases, the no-fault ground for divorce is out of
keeping with the reasons; in other cases it is fairly close. As divorce
becomes more prevalent, the strain and pain surrounding it continues,
and methods and structures for coping with divorce remain underdeveloped. Likewise, remarriage after divorce has far outrun the institutionalization of step-relationships, or even the terminology used to either describe or live it.

✦ The family is both *isolated* from the larger society and *impinged upon* by
it. Perhaps the distinction between the family as a "haven" and as not
a haven, but harassed, is one between *is*-ness and *ought*-ness. As noted
above, the family seeks to perform the affective function, and for
some it does, and seeks to raise its children to maturity, but for many
it has been made weak and incapable by the encroachment of outsiders. But this brings us back to socialization again.

✦ A most intriguing inconsistency is that between sexual freedom and
the threat of AIDS. Some have argued that AIDS fears have reduced
sexual activity among teenagers (see Feature 19.1). Others argue that
it has not reduced the frequency of intercourse, but the number of
partners (Ku et al., 1992: 100–106). Factual information about AIDS
has been hard to collect, but is now on the increase. Crandall and
Coleman report that those diagnosed as having AIDS are likely to say
they have received more social support since the diagnosis than that
they have received less. Yet the stigma is also present (Crandall and
Coleman, 1992: 163–177). Over half of Anderson et al.'s high school
students report having had instruction about AIDS, but Ku et al. find
that education about how to resist intercourse is more influential in
reducing sexual activity than instruction either about contraception or

AIDS (Ku et al., 1992: 104). Noting the problem with education as the panacea, Bowser et al. state that it is much more important to address the underlying social and psychological conditions that encourage sexual behavior (Bowser et al., 1990; see also Morales, 1990: 233–234). Our major point, however, is that sexual freedom and the AIDs threat are incompatible.

✦ To repeat a point from the previous section, an important inconsistency is that between "the family" as norm and varieties of behavior. The contradiction, says Cheal, "between the idealization of the 'one' and the social construction of 'the many' is found not only in society but in books by so-called experts on "the family" (Cheal, 1991).

These are, of course, far from all the inconsistencies present in U.S. families. It seems that the resolution of at least some of them will aid the individual in her or his interpersonal and intrapersonal adjustments.

Five Continua

In Chapter 5, five continua were presented upon which the characteristics of the U.S. family might be located. These continua pertain to mate selection, socialization, marital roles, institutional embeddedness, and individual embeddedness. Each of the continua is, of course, a complex of variables; locating the contemporary U.S. family upon the continua is accomplished only by reducing its variations to a single set of dimensions. Thus, heeding the proper cautions regarding oversimplification, these continua may be profitably employed to summarize many of the findings reported in the preceding pages (see Figure 19.1).

Feature 19.1   AIDS FEARS REVERSE RISE IN TEEN SEX

Concern about AIDS may be putting the brakes on two decades of rising sexual activity among teenagers, government surveys show.

Fewer teens had sex with fewer partners in 1991 than in 1989, the Federal Centers for Disease Control and Prevention in Atlanta reported.

During the same period, more teens got AIDs education at school and talked about AIDS at home, CDC said.

"We're cautiously optimistic that young people may be beginning to reduce their risk of HIV infection," said researcher Lloyd Kolbe. "But we're going to need several more years of data to show whether this is a long-term trend."

Kim Painter, "AIDS fears reverse rise in teen sex," *USA Today*, November 21–23, 1992, p. 1.

FIGURE 19.1 A Tentative Location of the Contemporary U.S. Family on Five Ideal-Typical Continua Concerning the Family and Its Characteristics

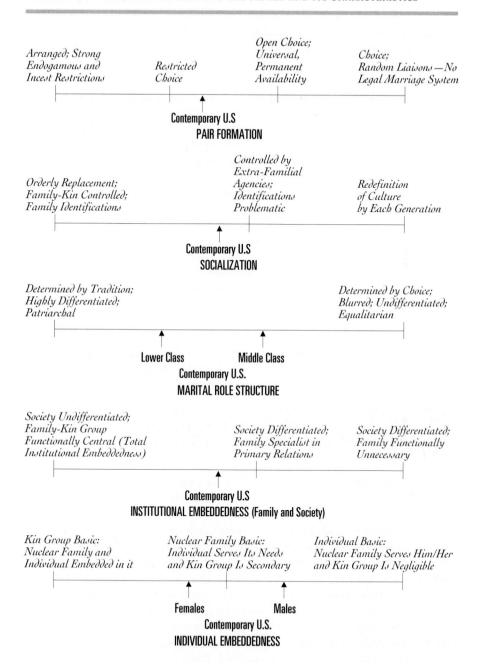

1. *Mate choices* in the United States are based on personal desires, but are restricted considerably by propinquity and the salient family values concerning such issues as religion and race.

2. *Socialization*: the individual is influenced by both familial and extrafamilial socializing agents, with the direction-giving influence of parents still substantial.

3. *Marital roles*: there is modified role choice in marriage, which we have called neotraditionalism. Certain options are available to both sexes, though aspects of the old patriarchy and the economic-familial division of labor by sex are still operative in the working and lower classes and subtly operative in the middle class.

4. *Institutional embeddedness*: other institutions have become highly differentiated from the kin group and the nuclear family. The latter still specializes in primary relations, socialization, and economic consumption, and sometimes in recreation and religion.

5. Nuclear family *individual embeddedness* and individualism are currently vying for ascendancy in U.S. society, with the movement clearly toward individualism. However, men have been less embedded in their families than women, so the question is actually "should women have the same freedoms and opportunities that have been available to men, and, if so, how and how soon?"

The issue of individual embeddedness, or familism versus individualism, must be expanded at this point because it seems to be the key to understanding most of the characteristics of, and change in, the U.S family at present. Scanzoni et al. describe the "increasing pervasiveness of *individualism* thus:

> *Aside from conservative religionists, increasing numbers of Americans are unwilling to sacrifice personal interests for the sake of preserving particular structures. One result of these trends is that the institution of the family is evolving into varieties of adult and child living arrangements (Scanzoni et al., 1989: 34).*

Norval Glenn adds to this that the goal of "having a happy marriage" (an individualistic goal) ranked higher in the quality of life survey than either "being married" or "being married to the same person for life" (Glenn, 1992: 30–37).

Gender differences regarding this issue begin with the fact that while many of the supports for structural patriarchy have been weakened or, according to Morgan, crumbled, this "has not necessarily meant the weakening of male power," though it may be "more diffusely distributed" (Morgan, 1990: 76). Francoeur, writing regarding the year 2020, notes that in 1980 the family was still deeply rooted in patriarchal values, but movement is toward "intentional families," focusing on persons and the growth qualities of their relations (Francoeur, 1984: 203). In an insightful discussion, Hite adds that it is not just that women want "out," or to be less embedded. Rather, she says, women "say *men* should learn the 'traditional values' of emotional support, connection, and nurturing"—meaning they should become *more* embedded in their families or intimate relationships (Hite, 1987: 739).

Nena O'Neill, who with her husband George created a stir in 1972 with the publication of *Open Marriage*, embodies in her own work the struggle between familism and individualism. Her 1972 book was a call for individualistic values to be incorporated into marriage. In 1977, she published a book entitled *The Marriage Premise*, in which she states that marriage rests on five foundation stones:

✦ Primariness of each partner to the other, each being the other's most important person.

✦ Intimacy—not only physical intimacy but the way we open and reveal ourselves to the person we marry.

✦ Connections and the network of family—the ties created by a marriage to other families, past and future.

✦ Continuity—the sense of building a history together over a span of time; and the way we come in time to know one another so deeply.

✦ Responsibility to the commitment we make when we marry—to our partner, to ourselves and to the family we create (O'Neill, 1977).

O'Neill's last three principles are, of course, concerned with individual embeddedness, that is, with the embeddedness of the individual in family, in kinship, and in generations past and present. She must be aware that these principles, especially the last three, run counter to the increasingly prevalent mood of the time—a mood that spawns tenuous connections, ignores continuity, and rejects responsibility. Any principle that smacks of commitment to relationship for the sake of relationship itself, rather than for "what I can get out of it," is likely to be on the defensive today.

Individualism is central to the issues of this book: for example, divorce, sex role choice, and gratification. But is it the wave of the future? If so, does it mean the destruction of the family?

SECTION TWO

THE FAMILY TOMORROW

During the 1930s and 1940s, Carle Zimmerman, Pitirim A. Sorokin, and others analyzed the changes that had occurred in the U.S. family since the nineteenth century and concluded that its future was one of *disintegration*. Zimmerman summarized such predictions in 1949:

> *The influence of these gradual developments during several centuries, and the recent upheavals, have given us a plethora of unusual family behavior in recent years. Some persons see these changes as "progress," or the breaking through toward a new and more interesting family system. Others, including the writer, look upon it as a polarization of values typical of the breakdown of a family system. . . .*

> *We must look upon the present confusion of family values as the beginning of vi-olent breaking up of a system. The mores or social forces present when it rose to power now no longer exist. Negative polarization is here because the crisis is at hand (Zim-merman, 1949: 200–201).[1]*

Just as some authors describe today's marital role choices as "problems," "predicaments," or "dilemmas," so these authors were convinced that changes in the nineteenth and twentieth centuries were negative in their import and sig-naled the disintegration of the family—and perhaps society as we know it.

In the mid-1940s, Ernest Burgess and Harvey Locke responded to these dire predictions by asserting that the U.S. family was not disintegrating, but was *reorganizing* with characteristics that approximate the companionship fam-ily. "Family reorganization," the authors claimed,

> *may be considered in its two aspects: (1) the checking of tendencies to disorganization in the individual family and its reshaping through the redefining of attitudes and val-ues of the husband and wife and parents and children; and (2) the development in so-ciety of a new conception of the family which its members individually and collectively attempt to realize (Burgess and Locke, 1945).*

The family would stabilize, they felt, within 20 to 30 years, due to education, more security in the economy, and a slowing down of immigration and popula-tion increase. This meant that stability would be reached between 1965 and 1975. In addition, Burgess and Locke saw certain trends of the early 1940s as continuing in the future, among them:

1. declining birthrate and smaller-sized families;
2. increase in the proportion married among those of marriageable age;
3. lowering of the age at marriage, coincident with family life education;
4. increase in the employment of all women, including married women;
5. decline in the family's historic functions in favor of emotional func-tions, such as happiness and companionship.

Speaking of marriage, Harris calls the Burgess-Locke change "from institution to companionship" de-institutionalization. By this he means that:

> *if marriage is a prerequisite of neither mating, co-residence, nor child-rearing, and does not regulate sexual access, it ceases to be in any sense the institution of marriage and simply becomes a type of relationship available to mates should they happen to choose it (Harris, 1983: 209).*

For some 50 years the twin themes of reorganization and disintegration (or "decline," to use Popenoe's term, 1988: 809) have been part of the ideological debate regarding the family. Since the 1960s, however, several authors have again taken up the themes of projection and prediction, based on current statis-tical trends and on an informed survey of societal changes and their significance for the family. One of the more insightful projections was that of Robert Parke and Paul Glick, working with 1960 census data. They agreed with Burgess and Locke's projection of the proportion married and continued it into the future;

they found the age at marriage *increasing* and projected this too; and they found family size small and likely to remain at or about the current level. In addition, they projected other trends, such as the following:

> *Over and above any general decline in mortality, the declines in the difference between the ages of the husband and wife will reduce the frequency of widowhood and increase the proportion of couples who survive jointly to retirement age.*
>
> *. . . Declines in the relative frequency of divorce and separation should result to the extent that there are reductions in poverty and general improvements in the socioeconomic status of the population (Parke and Glick, 1967: 256).*

Ten years after Parke and Glick predicted the above trends, Man Singh Das and Panos Bardis projected the following worldwide trends:

1. equalitarian family relations, with less sex segregation and less subjugation of women;
2. more individualism and independence;
3. greater institutional differentiation—or less embeddedness of institutions in the family;
4. urban life increasingly dominant;
5. more birth control and family planning;
6. more social mobility;
7. more marital disruption;
8. more neglect of the elderly;
9. more formal education for children; and
10. more government influence on family activities (Das and Bardis, 1978: 419).

While their projections pertained to Asia, many have already happened or are happening in the United States, and the list contains few surprises. Another decade later, Arthur Norton made predictions regarding families and children in the year 2000. Two new predictions were that the rate of never marrying will continue to rise, something that was happening in the 1980s, and that the rate of divorce might drop somewhat, a slight change in this direction having been noted in Chapter 17 (Norton, 1987: 6–9).

While the projection of trends performs a useful service for researchers studying the family, more exciting and debatable predictions result from taking a holistic perspective. For example, in his book *The Third Wave*, Alvin Toffler views the computer as the wave of today and tomorrow, and predicts the "electronic cottage." By this he means that the productive function may return to the home and be centered in the home computer and the home communication network. Though not exactly a return to the family farm, it will bring families back into close daily contact with each other (Toffler, 1980: 224–242). You may or may not agree with his prediction, but it is thought-provoking.

How hard is it to predict the future? Glick, who projected trends 20 years earlier, notes some of the problems, in referring to divorce and remarriage: future trends *are not easy to predict with confidence, partly because the levels of the rates appear to have approached either a turning point toward higher levels or to have entered a period of relative stability. Moreover, as is usually the situation, some potential developments are likely to raise the levels while others are likely to lower them (Glick and Lin, 1986: 744).*

Goode notes the same uncertainties, while adding the likelihood of unforeseen variables: While all change curves eventually flatten out, the fact is:

An expanding population of animals or plants does not simply, out of its wisdom, decide to reduce its growth. Instead, predators, disease, and starvation do that for them. And so for great empires: they declined because they were forced to do so, not because their leaders chose to live a simple traditional life.

Thus, although I have no doubt that the curves will eventually fall away from their precipitous upward movement, I do not now see what variables will come into play to make them do so (Goode, 1993: 335).

With these appropriate cautions, let us ask how the monogamous nuclear family (MNF) institution will relate to other family or intimate lifestyles. The best available data suggest three answers.

The first answer is: *the "family" will outlast the alternatives.* Uhlenberg reminds us that in "speculating on the family of the future, one should not ignore the remarkable stability and adaptability of the American family during the past century of vast change" (Uhlenberg, 1978: 95). The family will swallow up or absorb whichever of the first two types of alternatives, that is, those within and those parallel, that seem workable. They will be added, as have cohabitation and gender role changes, as the safety valves the family needs to retrench itself in a day of rapid change. This point is reminiscent of the turn-of-the-century debate concerning divorce. At the beginning of the twentieth century the radicals were saying that an increase in the flexibility of divorce laws would increase the divorce rate, thereby destroying the Victorian family—and that's good. The conservatives, concurrently, were saying that increasing the flexibility of divorce laws would increase the divorce rate and thereby destroy the family—and that's bad. Both agreed on the outcome; they simply disagreed in their value positions. The fact is that both were wrong. Divorce merely became the safety valve that the family system needed at that time to "weed out the bad bets."[2]

In addition, the family will outlast the third group of alternatives as long as they are just protests among a few disenchanted. As Rick Margolis and Joyce Gardener point out, communes are often formed by young people whose needs for understanding, love, and intimacy were unfulfilled within their nuclear families. They are seeking to resurrect a larger pseudo-kin network in the hopes of meeting those needs. It is no wonder that many such communes, consisting of young people who have brought their problems and bad experiences together in the new network, should fail grandly in a brief period. Furthermore, people will still be drawn to parenting and will need intimacy, and the best place to find both is in the monogamous nuclear family. Also, the family will outlast the alternatives as long as policymakers, lawmakers, moral leaders, and the helping professions continue to define the MNF as of intrinsic value and as worthy of perpetuation. Such is likely to be a dominant orientation into the foreseeable future. In fact, say the Bergers, given freedom to choose between various forms, the majority will opt for the traditional monogamous family, which they call the "bourgeois" family. It is "the people's choice" because it still works best (Berger and Berger, 1983: 208–209). Finally, as long as we are afraid of freedom and are comfortable in our life patterns, change will come slowly and painfully, if at all. Erich Fromm reminded us years ago how we escape from freedom, and Jourard put it this way more recently:

> Not *to capitalize on our increased release from economic necessity,* not *to "play" creatively with such existential forms as marriage, family life, schooling, leisure pursuits, etc., is a kind of madness, a dread of, and escape from, freedom and the terror it engenders.* . . . *Not to legitimize such experimentation and exploration is to make life in our society unlivable for an increasing proportion of the population [Italics in original]* (Jourard, 1970: 46).

Thus, these arguments would say that the MNF will incorporate some alternatives as safety valves and will outlive those that are but fleeting attempts to solve individual difficulties. It will outlast them because most people will continue to prefer it as the best of all possible intimate worlds.

Yet in Jourard's statement we already have the seed for a second answer to the question: Will the family survive the alternatives? This answer is: *yes, the MNF will continue to exist, but it will be alongside a series of increasingly legitimated alternatives.* Jourard implies that many people have found our family form unlivable or impossible. In other words, several of the alternatives are not just the "protests of a few disenchanted." If there is one value demonstrated by U.S. society over its long history, it is instrumentalism. That is, we are concerned with what works, or what functions best to solve our problems. And while the Bergers argue that for most people the "bourgeois" family works best, not everyone agrees. Becker, for example, argues thus:

> *Many deplore individualism and lament the passing of the traditional family, but my analysis implies that individualism replaces familialism because many family functions in traditional societies are more effectively handled by markets and other organizations of modern societies (Becker, 1981: 244).*

Although he speaks as if the struggle between individual and family values were completed, his point is valid. Many changes have occurred because the monogamous nuclear family did *not* work best in all circumstances. As internal pressures build within our family system, increasing numbers of persons will begin to look for viable alternatives. And here is where today's movements, whether singlehood or feminism with its multiple goals, will provide increasingly legitimated alternatives. The reason is that the overarching value in our society is more and more the individual and his or her self-actualization. As concern for individual happiness becomes increasingly dominant, so will a multiplicity of alternatives be needed to allow for the self-fulfillment of a great variety of individual personalities. Economic, legal, and familial values will give ground grudgingly, but the individual and her or his needs and wants in U.S.

society cannot be denied. And that such change toward freedom of choice is occurring also cannot be denied (see D'Emilio and Freedman, 1988: 359; Scanzoni and Marsiglio, 1991: 130).

This, then, leads to the threshold of a third possible answer to the question: Will the MNF survive the alternatives? This answer is: *no, the family as a legalized institution cannot stay alive in the face of the alternatives*. It is, slowly but surely, on the way out. Such an answer grows, as did the previous answer, out of the instrumental perspective, that is, what works best equals "the good." However, to arrive at this conclusion, a third factor must be added to the family's strains and to the alternatives' propaganda and practice. That factor is the bio-technological advances now taking place in various laboratories. In 1950 and again in 1960, Nimkoff reviewed some of these advances in terms of their possible effects upon families. Improvements in contraception, artificial insemination, incubator birth (in which, after conception, the fetus resides outside the human body), control over the sex of the child, and work with hormones—all have implications for contemporary life (Nimkoff, 1962: 121–127). Gilder notes that the three technical approaches about which most is known and that are likely to have the most far-reaching implication are "in-vitro or test-tube fertilization; extracorporeal gestation (the artificial womb); and cloning, the exact reproduction or 'xeroxing' of particular genotypes" (Gilder, 1987: 180). Portner and Etkin add that other technological advances have affected work and family life: the computer revolution, robotics, the potential colonization of space, and advances affecting life expectancy (Portner and Etkin, 1984: 212–214).

The debate rages regarding the freezing of ova and fetuses: if preservation of the ovum were perfected, reproduction outside the human body would become possible. And if it were found, further, that incubator fetuses were able to avoid birth defects and were more uniformly able to maximize the positive hereditary features of the two parents, then instrumental values might lead increasing numbers of people to a new view of what works best.

Granted, at this time it is difficult for many people to try to imagine society without our legalized form of monogamy. Yet this is reminiscent of the history of anesthesia in the 1800s. Anesthesia was usable medically for some thirty years—a generation—before it was accepted socially or ethically. From the pulpit and elsewhere people were reminded by devout clerics that women were meant to give birth in pain and that to eliminate such pain artificially was immoral. It took a generation for an equally devout, but scientifically enlightened, cleric to discover the verse in Genesis that said: "And God caused a deep sleep to fall upon Adam, and he removed one of his ribs, and from it he made woman" (Genesis 2:21). From that moment on, the *"oughtness"* battle was won. Our values may not be prepared when discoveries are made, but this third answer to our question makes four assumptions:

1. the family does have internal strains;
2. alternatives exist that work for many people;
3. science does not take a vacation; and
4. people's values eventually catch up with and incorporate scientific advances.

On these assumptions it is possible to argue that somewhere out in the dim future the MNF will cease to exist. But that is all right, because by then we will no longer value it or see it as necessary any more than we currently value or see as necessary the feudal system or the notion that the earth is the center of the universe.

So there you have it, three answers to the question: Will the family survive the alternative lifestyles? It is the relative weight you assign to such factors as society's supports for today's family, the alternatives as reactions against it, our fear of freedom, the propaganda of the alternatives, instrumental and individual values, and scientific advances that will determine your own conclusions about the family's future.

Personally, I feel that while there is evidence for the first and third answers to the question, I would close by selecting the second answer for the foreseeable future. We do not like to choose, but we must increasingly do so; many are uncomfortable with freedom, but we will increasingly exercise it. Our choices will gradually lead to the legitimation of certain of the alternatives alongside legalized monogamy. Which of the alternatives are most likely to become fully accepted: singlehood and cohabitation, single parenthood, gender role sharing, voluntary childlessness, homosexuality? All these are consistent with the increasingly individualistic values of the day and can be seen as forms or content of "families." What about the commune or pseudo-kin network? These are not likely to become widespread because they seek to recapture commitment to a larger group, while the course of history has led toward ever more constricted commitments. The nuclear family may remain the numerically dominant type if, even in a day of many choices, the majority feel it is the best arrangement for them. Barring some unforeseen calamity, the future is one of alternative styles of intimate life, whether or not we call them "families." (Clanton, 1984: 44).

FOOTNOTES

2.1   For a parallel but somewhat divergent treatment of family structural variations, see Meyer F. Nimkoff, *Comparative Family Systems* (Boston: Houghton Mifflin, 1965), chapter 2. Perhaps the most insightful introduction to cross-cultural differences in family and kinship is J. Robin Fox's *Kinship and Marriage* (Baltimore: Penguin, 1967). Fox points out clearly how *unimportant* marriage is in many societies compared to various blood kin ties. In this chapter we have treated marriage as more central than it actually is cross-culturally, because most Western readers have grown up in a marriage-centered and nuclear family-centered system. The interested reader may, however, want to move on to a book such as Fox's.

2.2   Further discussion of incest taboos, joking relations, and avoidance may be found in Murdock, *Social Structure*, especially 273–276, 292–303. On "role inertia" as an explanation for incest taboos, see William R. Catton, "What's in a Name? The Case for Role Inertia," *Journal of Marriage and the Family, 31* (1969): 15–18.

2.3   In *The Red Lamp of Incest* and in *Kinship and Marriage,* Fox distinguishes quite carefully and consistently between *incest* taboos, or sexual restrictions, and *endogamy* prohibitions, or restrictions on mating (marriage). We have not drawn this distinction quite so carefully in the preceding explanation, since the discussion is predicated on the interwoven nature of sexual attractions and mating prescriptions.

3.1   For an extended treatment of the process of weakening the intermediate structures of family, kinship, and religion, so that in modern society the individual lies more open to state control, see Robert A. Nisbet, *Community and Power,* New York: Oxford University Press, 1962 ed.

3.2   A good treatment of Soviet family law from 1917 to 1945 is found in Becky L. Glass and Margaret K. Stolee, "Family Law in Soviet Russia, 1917–1945," *Journal of Marriage and the Family, 49* (1987): 893–902.

4.1   Peter Laslett, cofounder of the Cambridge Group for the History of Population and Social Structure, has been a key figure in the "new family history"; see Laslett, *The World We Have Lost* (New York: Scribner's, 1965); Laslett and Richard Wall, eds., *Household and Family in Past Time* (New York: Cambridge University Press, 1972); Laslett, *Family Life and Illicit Love in Earlier Generations: Essays in Historical Sociology* (New York: Cambridge University Press, 1977). Another is Lawrence Stone, *The Family, Sex and Marriage in England, 1500–1800* (New York: Harper and Row, 1977). A major source for historical materials is the *Journal of Family History,* edited by Tamara Hareven.

4.2   For more on this, see Morton M. Hunt, *The Natural History of Love* (New York: Knopf, 1959). Literary illustrations can be found in Alfred Lord Tennyson's *Idylls of the King* (Boston: Ticknor and Fields, 1859).

4.3   We must admit that the date used to indicate the close of the colonial period—1800—is more arbitrary than most. Other possibilities were 1776, the year in which the colonial period ended politically, and 1850, by which year the industrial revolution was in full swing in the United States. The year 1800 is merely a compromise, indicating the beginning of a new century and incipient industrialization, though marking no specific event and no specific break with the past.

4.4   Washington Irving, *The Legend of Sleepy Hollow* (London: MacMillan, 1920). For other literature, see the footnotes to Herman R. Lantz, et al., "Pre-Industrial Patterns in the Colonial Family in America: A Content Analysis of Colonial Magazines," *American Sociological Review, 33* (1968): 413–426.

4.5   On legal aspects of American family history, see Steven Mintz, "Regulating the American Family," *Journal of Family History, 14* (1989): 387–408.

4.6   These figures make clear just how deceiving longevity can be. Longevity is, of course, an av-
        erage. But when we hear that in some countries the figures are 46 for men and 49 for women
        we may assume that about age 50 both sexes are "dropping like flies." However, it is more
        likely that large numbers are simply not surviving early childhood. After all, if a 2-year-old
        and an 80-year-old both die, the average is 41. In other words, a pattern of early and late
        deaths means that the *average* age at death is not necessarily the *typical* age at death.

4.7   On this, the McNalls comment: "There are few reliable statistics on the number of marriages
        that were dissolved, however, because . . . a husband or wife often left without obtaining a
        divorce" (McNall and McNall, 1983: 20).

4.8.   Of crucial importance is still William J. Goode, *World Revolution and Family Patterns* (New
        York: Free Press, 1963). Other sources are: Barbara Laslett, "The Family as a Public and
        Private Institution: A Historical Perspective," *Journal of Marriage and the Family*, (1973):
        480–492; John Modell, Frank F. Furstenberg, Jr., and Theodore Hershberg, "Social
        Change and Transitions to Adulthood in Historical Perspective," *Journal of Family History*,
        (1976): 7–32; Tamara Hareven, *Family Time and Industrial Time* (Cambridge: Cambridge Uni-
        versity Press, 1982).

4.9   One of the most generally agreed-upon observations is that the father, and parents generally,
        have lost *formal* authority over their offspring since the mid-eighteenth century. Richard
        Sennett, for example, reports that in mid-19th century Chicago many middle-class fathers
        were stagnant occupationally; and since they could not convey an image of strength to their
        sons, the mothers took on that role (Sennett, 1970: 154). Another source on this issue is
        Henretta, 1973: 202. As he puts it: "Patriarchy had given way to parental solicitude and aid."

4.10   C. C. Harris notes that Lawrence Stone speaks of individualism as "a growing introspection"
        and as "a demand for personal autonomy." Harris then states that 44 pages later Stone talks
        of individualism as the rise of the concept that each person is unique (Stone, 1977: 223–224,
        268; in Harris, 1983: 146–148). We will use it in all three ways from time to time, but will
        focus on the issue of personal autonomy.

4.11   This subject should more accurately be introduced when changes in the family's relations
        with the external world are treated, but is raised here to prepare the reader for the "internal"
        issue of husband-wife roles in marriage.

4.12   Today's father role options are well spelled out in Lamb, 1987: 5. See Chapter 12.

4.13   On this, see Morris Zelditch, Jr., "Cross-Cultural Analysis of Family Structure," in Chris-
        tensen, ed., *Handbook of Marriage and the Family* (Chicago: Rand McNally, 1964): 492–497;
        and Marie Withers Osmond, "Cross-Societal Family Research: A Macro-Sociological
        Overview of the Seventies," *Journal of Marriage and the Family*, 42 (1980): 995–1016.

5.1   It is noteworthy that, based on his perception of a more similar physical strength on the part
        of men and women in the past, Durkheim concludes that men and women have become *more*
        differentiated and specialized over time. This may be correct. However, he was writing in
        the Victorian era and missed the fact that similar strength did not necessarily mean similar
        duties within the family.

5.2   Sources that postulate a curvilinear pattern of nuclear family dominance in the band, corpo-
        rate kin group dominance in agricultural and pastoral societies, and nuclear family domi-
        nance again in the industrial state are M. F. Nimkoff and Russell Middleton, "Types of
        Family and Types of Economy," *American Journal of Sociology*, 66 (1960): 225; and Rae Lesser
        Blumberg and Robert Winch, "Societal Complexity and Familial Complexity: Evidence for
        the Curvilinear Hypothesis," *American Journal of Sociology*, 77 (1972): 888–919.

5.3   Note that the six types depicted in Figure 5-1 should not be considered as a unilineal con-
        tinuum through which all societies must pass in the process of change. Note furthermore
        that the types describe society from the family's perspective. The same individual plays mul-
        tiple roles, but the issue here is whether they are played as a member of the family and
        within the family setting or in separate locations and at specific times. The interwoven fab-
        ric of life in society is not captured by Figure 5.1.

5.4   While teaching in East Africa, I had the experience of trying to "warn" my students of the
        perils of nuclear familism and of capitalist over-development, only to be met with the re-
        sponse: "We want to learn for ourselves; we would like to have your 'problems' for a while."

5.5   By "positive identification" is meant the attempt to model one's behavior after that of another person. The process of identification is both complex and important, and will be referred to in greater detail in Chapter 8.

5.6   Robert Winch and Rae Lesser Blumberg, "Societal Complexity and Familiar Organization," in Winch and Louis Wolf Goodman, eds., *Selected Studies in Marriage and the Family*, (New York: Holt, Rinehart, and Winston, 1968 ed.); and Murray Straus, "Family Organization and Problem Solving Ability in Relation to Societal Modernization." These authors use the word *function* very clearly and well to mean "tasks performed." Kin networks, as Straus puts it, "vary tremendously in the number and importance of the functions they perform."

6.1   See Ingoldsby (1991: 57–62) for an interesting cultural explanation of familism and machismo.

6.2   For a good review of Asian-American family characteristics, see Wilkinson, 1987: 183–210.

6.3   There is disagreement in the black community regarding the appropriateness of "black" versus "African-American." We will, therefore, use the two terms synonymously and interchangeably.

6.4   The sheer amount of recent research makes African-American families one of the three or four most studied topics in this book.

6.5   The word *faded* is used advisedly at this point. Did the African heritage disappear entirely, or did certain seeds, such as the strong kin unit, survive into the modern period? This issue will be discussed further.

6.6   Interesting recent discussions of the Frazier-Herskovitz debate are found in Willie, 1988: 222–223, and in Walker (1988: 102–103).

6.7   On marital stability, see Steckel, 1980: 406–421. For a discussion of gender roles, see White (1983: 248–261).

6.8   The issue of home ownership is used by O'Hare to assess the metropolitan areas which are "best for blacks." He finds that the Southern cities are better for black home ownership, while the rest of the country is better for income. His conclusion is that the economic situation is not the total picture of quality of life for African-Americans (O'Hare, 1986: 26–33).

7.1   It would be well at this point to distinguish fertility from fecundity. In demographic terms, *fertility* means the actual number of live births a mother has; *fecundity* means the capability of producing children. The fecund period is that period following puberty during which the female is capable of producing children.

7.2   On this, see Ryder, 1970; Weiner, 1983: 279–291. On timing of births, see Koo et al., 1987: 281–293.

7.3   On nonmarital births by age of women, see Maris A. Vinovskis, "An 'Epidemic' of Adolescent Pregnancy? Some Historical Considerations," *Journal of Family History*, 6: 205–230.

7.4   On communication between couples in deciding to sterilize, see Bean et al., 1983: 395–403. On communication regarding abortion, see Plutzer and Ryan, 1987: 183–189; and Smith and Kronauge, 1990: 585–598).

8.1   For a brief discussion of these theories, see Flake-Hobson et al., 1980: 155–162. For a lengthier discussion, see Deutsch and Krauss, 1965: chapters 4–6.

8.2   An interesting study of family identification in the nineteenth century is Horn, 1983: 367–382.

8.3   Of course, part of the reason for the self-concept problem, or "identity crisis," that is so much talked about today is simply an increased emphasis in 20th-century America on introspection and self-awareness. That is, any crisis is at least partially a result of affluence, of having the time and energy to pose the question "Who am I?"

9.1   The works of Bronislaw Malinowski were often read by the culture-bound public of Great Britain more for titillation than for information. But good examples of anthropological works dealing with sex are Malinowski, *The Sexual Life of Savages*, and Malinowski, *Sex and Repression in Savage Society*.

9.2   As noted in Chapter 2, Robin Fox insightfully states: "There is no need to institute laws to promote sexual promiscuity. But any restrictions on sexual proclivities need social sanctions" (Fox, *The Red Lamp of Incest*, 205).

9.3   For a review of studies before 1960, see Ehrmann, 1959: 33–34. For the 1960s and 1970s, see Reiss and Miller, 1979: 57–100. The stream of studies, we should add, continues into the 1990s, and the more recent of them will be quoted in the pages ahead.

9.4   Premarital intercourse is an example of a *cumulative* statistic, that is, one that can only get larger. Once having engaged in sexual activity, you can never again not have. Such statistics are best studied, therefore, at the end of the period in which the observor is interested. Fertility and "ever-married" should also be studied after the time in question is over. For fertility, that is when the fecund period is finished, and for marriage it is when one can no longer get married—meaning after death, since one can marry for the first time at any age.

10.1   William J. Goode draws this conclusion in his article "The Theoretical Importance of Love" (1959: 38–47). A good compilation of views on attraction and love is found in Murstein, 1971.

10.2   An article by Liston and Salts notes that love was the number one "selection value" for both Malaysian and U.S. university students (Liston and Salts, 1988: 361–369).

10.3   Much of the organization and some content of the following section is drawn from Adams, 1979: 259–267.

11.1   On economics in the U.S. value system, see Shepard B. Clough, *Basic Values of Western Civilization.* (New York: Columbia University Press, 1960): 15; and Robin M. Williams, Jr., *American Society: A Sociological Interpretation.* (New York: Knopf, 1960 ed.), Chapters 10–14.

11.2   A most interesting recent study of influence tactics and sexual orientation is Howard et al., "Sex, Power, and Influence Tactics in Intimate Relationships," *Journal of Personality and Social Psychology,* 51: 102–109.

11.3   On careers, gender role orientation, and perceived equity in relation to power, see Sexton and Perlman, "Couples' Career Orientation, Gender Role Orientation, and Perceived Equity as Determinants of Marital Power," *Journal of Marriage and the Family, 51:* 933–941.

12.1   I want to thank Kathy Blee for this four-fold organizational scheme.

12.2   See Patricia Voydanoff, "Work Roles as Stressors in Corporate Families," *Family Relations,* 29: 489–494; Paul Ammons, Josie Nelson, and John Wodarski, "Surviving Corporate Moves," *Family Relations,* (1982): 207–212; J. Roland Fleck et al., "Father Psychological Absence and Heterosexual Behavior, Personal Adjustment and Sex-Typing in Adolescent Girls," *Adolescence: 15:* 847–860; Raymond J. Sauer, "Absentee Father Syndrome," *The Family Coordinator, 28:* 245–249.

12.3   On these three emerging male roles, see F. Ivan Nye and Felix Berardo, *The Family: Its Structure and Interaction.* (New York: MacMillan, 1973): 252–255.

12.4   In Chapter 18 we will look at those couples who are married, but who do not let their marriage stand in the way of career advancement. They simply solve the residential mobility problem by living apart in a "commuter marriage."

13.1   For more on gender differences in communication, see Barbara B. White, "Gender Differences in Marital Communication Patterns," *Family Process,* 28: 89–106.

13.2   The life cycle, while a useful heuristic device, has been questioned as explaining anything once the length of marriage and the presence or absence of children are controlled. On this, see Steven L. Nock, "The Family Life Cycle," *Journal of Marriage and the Family, 41:* 15–26.

16.1   A classic article by Earl Lomon Koos and Donald Fulcomer speaks of such combinations. It is referred to in Hill, 1958: 145.

16.2   For more on "appraisal of the situation" as a stress-buffering factor, see Lavee et al., 1987: 857–873.

16.3   An excellent and comprehensive symposium on family coping strategies is Moch et al., 1987: 113–125.

16.4   Some excellent review articles of violence literature and theories are: Gelles, 1980; Breines and Gordon, 1983: 490–531; Gelles, 1985: 347–367.

16.5   Gelles, 1985, reviews several other theories. In another country, when I discussed wife-battering as a family problem in the United States, I was told: "No, it is not a problem. It is a solution to a problem; the problem is uppity women."

17.1   For a thorough and fascinating account of the history of divorce in the United States, see Riley, 1993.

19.1   For more on diagnoses of the family's disintegration, see Zimmerman, 1947; and Sorokin, 1937.

19.2   The best source on divorce at the turn of the century, and the ideological debate surrounding it, is O'Neill, 1967.

REFERENCES

Abbott, D. A., & Brody, G. H. (1985). The Relation of Child Age, Gender, and Number of Children to the Marital Adjustment of Wives. *Journal of Marriage and the Family, 47,* 77–84.

Abelsohn, D. and Sayman, G. S. (1991). Adolescent Adjustment to Parental Divorce: An Investigation from the Perspective of Basic Dimensions of Structural Family Therapy Theory. *Family Process, 30,* 177–192.

Aberle, D. F., Cohen, A. K., Davis, K., Levy, Jr., M. J., & Sutton, F. X. (1950). "The Functional Prerequisites of a Society," *Ethics, 60,* 100–111.

Abrahamsen, A. F., Morrison, P. A., & Waite, L. J. (1988). Teenagers Willing to Consider Single Parenthood: Who is at Greater Risk? *Family Planning Perspectives, 20,* 13–18.

Acock, A. C., & Bengtson, V. L. (1980). Socialization and Attribution Processes: Actual Versus Perceived Similarity Among Parents and Youth. *Journal of Marriage and the Family, 42,* 501–515.

Acock, A. C., & Hurlbert, J. S. (1990). "Social Network Analysis: A Structural Perspective for Family Studies," *Journal of Social and Personal Relationships, 7,* 245–264.

Adamek, P. J. (1982). Testing the Family Role Complementarity Model. *Journal of Comparative Family Studies, 13,* 1–11.

Adams, B. N. (1968a). *Kinship in an Urban Setting.* Chicago: Markham.

Adams, B. N. (1968b). The Middle Class Adult and His Widowed or Still-Married Mother. *Social Problems, 16,* 50–59.

Adams, B. N. (1968–1969). Kinship Systems and Adaptation to Modernization. *Studies in Comparative International Development, 4.*

Adams, B. N. (1971). Isolation, Function, and Beyond: American Kinship in the 1960s. in Broderick, (ed.), *A Decade of Family Research and Action.* Minneapolis: National Council on Family Relations.

Adams, B. N. (1979). Mate Selection in the United States: A Theoretical Summarization. in Burr et al., (Eds.), *Contemporary Theories About the Family Volume I.* New York: Free Press.

Adams, B. N., & Mburugu, E. (1994). Kikuyu Bridewealth and Polygyny Today. *Journal of Comparative Family Studies.*

Adams, B. N., & Steinmetz, S. (1993). Family Theory and Methods in the Classics. in P. Boss, W. Doherty, R. LaRossa, W. Schumm, S. Steinmetz, (Eds.), *Handbook of Family Theory and Methods* (pp. 71–94). New York: Plenum.

Agassi, J. B. (1991). Theories of Gender Inequality: Lessons from the Israeli Kibbutz. in Lorber and Farrell, (Eds.), *The Social Construction of Gender.* Newbury Park, CA.: Sage.

Agnew, R., & Huguley, S. (1989). Adolescent Violence Toward Parents. *Journal of Marriage and the Family, 51,* 699–711.

Ahrons, C. R., & Rodgers, R. H. (1987). *Divorced Families: A Multidisciplinary View.* New York: W. W. Norton.

Aidala, A. A. (1989). Communes and Changing Family Norms: Marriage and Life-Style Choice Among Former Members of Communal Groups. *Journal of Family Issues, 10,* 311–338.

Albrecht, S. L. (1979). Correlates of Marital Happiness Among the Remarried. *Journal of Marriage and the Family, 41,* 857–866.

Albrecht, S. L. (1980). Reactions and Adjustments to Divorce: Differences in the Experiences of Males and Females. *Family Relations, 29.*

Aldous, J. (1987). New Views on the Family Life of the Elderly and the Near-Elderly. *Journal of Marriage and the Family, 49,* 227–234.

Aldous, J. (1990). Specification and Speculation Concerning the Politics of Workplace Family Policies. *Journal of Family Issues, 11,* 355–367.

Aldous, J., Osmond, M. W., & Hicks, M. W. (1979). Men's Work and Men's Families. in Burr et al., (Eds.), *Contemporary Theories About the Family, Volume I.* New York: Free Press.

Allen, K. R. (1989). *Single Women/Family Ties — Life Histories of Older Women.* Newbury Park, CA.: Sage.

Allen, K. R., & Pickett, R. (1987). Forgotten Streams in the Family Life Course: Utilization of Qualitative Retrospective Interviews in the Analysis of Lifelong Single Women's Family Careers. *Journal of Marriage and the Family, 49,* 517–526.

Alsbrook, L. (1976). Marital Communication and Sexism. *Social Casework, 57.*

Alwin, D. F. (1988). From Obedience to Autonomy: Changes in Traits Desired in Children, 1924–1978. *Public Opinion Quarterly, 52,* 33–52.

Alwin, D. F. (1989). Social Stratification, Conditions of Work, and Parental Socialization Values. in Eisenberg et al., (Eds.), *Social and Moral Values.* Hillsdale, N.J., Erlbaum.

Amato, P. R. (1991). Parental Absence During Childhood and Depression in Later Life. *Sociological Quarterly, 32,* 543–556.

Amato, P. R., & Zuo, J. (1992). Rural Poverty, Urban Poverty, and Psychological Well Being. *Sociological Quarterly, 33,* 229–240.

Ambert, A. (1982). Differences in Children's Behavior Toward Custodial Mothers and Custodial Fathers. *Journal of Marriage and the Family, 44,* 73–86.

Ambert, A. (1986). Being a Stepparent: Live-In and Visiting Stepchildren. *Journal of Marriage and the Family, 48,* 795–804.

Ambert, A. (1988). Relationships Between Ex-Spouses: Individual and Dyadic Perspectives. *Journal of Social and Personal Relationships, 5,* 327–346.

American Humane Association (1981). *National Analysis of Official Neglect and Abuse Reporting, 1980.* Denver.

Ammons, P., Nelson, J., & Wodarski, J. (1982). Surviving Corporate Moves: Sources of Stress and Adaption Among Corporate Executive Families. *Family Relations, 1982,* 207–212.

Ammons, P., & Stinnett, N. (1980). The Vital Marriage: A Closer Look. *Family Relations, 29,* 37–42.

Anderson, J. E., Kann, L., Holtzman, D., Arday, S., Truman, B., & Kolbe, L. (1990). HIV/AIDS Knowledge and Sexual Behavior Among High School Students. *Family Planning Perspectives, 22,* 252–255.

Ankarloo, B. (1978). Marriage and Family Formation. in T. K. Hareven (Ed.), *Transitions: The Family and the Life Course in Historical Perspective.* New York: Academic.

Anson, O. (1989). Marital Status and Women's Health Revisited: The Importance of a Proximate Adult. *Journal of Marriage and the Family, 51,* 185–194.

Araji, S. K. (1977). Husbands' and Wives' Attitude-Behavior Congruence on Family Roles. *Journal of Marriage and the Family, 39.*

Arendell, T. Divorce: A Women's Issue. in Christopher Carlson (Ed.), *Perspectives on the Family: History, Class and Feminism* (pp. 479–495). Belmont, CA.: Wadsworth.

Argyle, M., & Furnham, A. (1983). Sources of Satisfaction and Conflict in Long-Term Relationships. *Journal of Marriage and the Family, 45,* 481–493.

Aries, P. (1977). The Family and the City. *Daedalus.* (Spring).

Astone, N. M., & McLanahan, S. S. (1991). Family Structure, Parental Practices and High School Completion. *American Sociological Review, 56,* 309–320.

Atchley, R. C. (1989). A Continuity Theory of Normal Aging. *Gerontologist, 29,* 183–190.

Atchley, R. C. (1992). Retirement and Marital Satisfaction. in Szinovacz et al., eds., *Families and Retirement.* Newbury Park, CA.: Sage, 145–158.

Atkinson, L. E., Lincoln, R., & Forrest, J. D. (1986). The Next Contraceptive Revolution. *Family Planning Perspectives, 18,* 19–26.

Atkinson, M. P., & Glass, B. L. (1985). Marital Age Heterogamy and Homogamy, 1900 to 1980. *Journal of Marriage and the Family, 47,* 685–691.

Avioli, P. S. (1985). The Labor-Force Participation of Married Mothers of Infants. *Journal of Marriage and the Family, 47,* 739–745.

Baber, K. M., & Monaghan, P. (1988). College Women's Career and Motherhood Expectations: New Options, Old Dilemmas. *Sex Roles, 19,* 189–203.

Baber, K. M., & Allen, K. R. (1992). *Women and Families: Feminist Reconstructions.* New York: Guilford.

Baca-Zinn, M. (1991). Family, Feminism, and Race in America. in J. Lorber & S. A. Farrell (Eds.), *The Social Construction of Gender* (pp. 119–133). Newbury Park, CA: Sage (also in *Gender and Society,* 1990, *4,* 68–82).

Bachrach, C. A. (1980). Childlessness and Social Isolation Among the Elderly. *Journal of Marriage and the Family, 42,* 627–637.

Bahr, S. J. (1979). The Effects of Welfare on Marital Stability and Remarriage. *Journal of Marriage and the Family, 41,* 553–560.

Baker, M. (1984). His and Her Divorce Research: New Theoretical Directions in Canadian and American Research. *Journal of Comparative Family Studies, 15.*

Baker, M. & Bakker, J. I. H. (1980). The Double-Bind of the Middle Class Male: Men's Liberation and the Male Sex Role. *Journal of Comparative Family Studies, 11,* 547–561.

Bakke, E. W. (1949). *Citizens Without Work.* New Haven: Yale University Press.

Balkwell, C. (1981). Transition to Widowhood: A Review of the Literature. *Family Relations, 30,* 117–127.

Bane, M. J. (1976). *Here To Stay: American Families in the Twentieth Century.* New York: Basic Books.

Banks, J. A. (1981). *Victorian Values: Secularism and the Size of Families.* London: Routledge and Kegan Paul.

Barnett, R. C., Marshall, N. L., & Singer, J. D. (1992). Job Experiences Over Time, Multiple Roles, and Women's Mental Health: A Longitudinal Study. *Journal of Personality and Social Psychology, 62,* 634–644.

Barth, F. (1954). Father's Brother's Daughter's Marriage in Kurdistan. *Southwestern Journal of Anthropology, 10,* 167–169.

Bartz, K. W., & Nye, F. I. (1981). Early Marriage: A Propositional Formulation. *Journal of Marriage and the Family, 43.*

Baumrind, D. (1991). Effective Parenting During the Early Adolescent Transition. in Cowan and Hetherington (Eds.), *Family Transitions* (pp. 111–163). New Jersey: Lawrence Erlbaum.

Bean, F. D., Clark, M. P., Swicegood, G., & Williams, D. (1983). Husband-Wife Communication, Wife's Employment, and the Decision for Male or Female Sterilization. *Journal of Marriage and the Family, 45,* 395–403.

Becerra, R. (1988). The Mexican American Family. in Mindel et al. (Eds.), *Ethnic Families in America* (pp. 141–172). New York: Elsevier.

Beck, P. W. (1978–79). Nontraditional Lifestyles and the Law. *Journal of Family Law, 17,* 685–702.

Beck, R. W., & Beck, S. H. (1989). The Incidence of Extended Household Among Middle-Aged Black and White Women: Estimates from a 15-year Panel Study. *Journal of Family Issues, 10,* 147–168.

Becker, G. S. (1981). *A Treatise on the Family.* Cambridge, MA: Harvard University Press.

Beer, W. R. (1989). *Strangers in the House: the World of Stepsiblings and Half-Siblings.* New Brunswick, N.J.: Transaction Books.

Bell, R. R., & Coughey, K. (1980). Premarital Sexual Experience Among College Females, 1958, 1968, 1978. *Family Relations, 29,* 353–357.

Bell, R. R., & Gordon, M. (1972). *The Social Dimension of Human Sexuality.* Boston: Little, Brown.

Bell, Y. R., Bonie, C. L., & Baldwin, J. A. (1990). Afrocentric Cultural Consciousness and African-American Male-Female Relationships. *Journal of Black Studies, 21,* 162–189.

Belsky, J., & Eggebeen, D. (1991). Early and Extensive Maternal Employment and Young Children's Socioemotional Development: Children of the National Longitudinal Survey of Youth. *Journal of Marriage and the Family, 53,* 1083–1110.

Belsky, J., Spanier, G. B., & Rovine, M. (1983). Stability and Change in Marriage Across the Transition to Parenthood. *Journal of Marriage and the Family, 45.*

Belsky, J., Youngblade, L., Rovine, M., & Volling, B. (1991). Patterns of Marital Change and Parent-Child Interaction. *Journal of Marriage and the Family, 53,* 487–498.

Bengtson, V. L., & Kuypers, J. A. (1971). Generational Differences and the Generational Stake. *Aging and Human Development, 2,* 249–260.

Bennett, N. G., Bloom, D. E., & Blanc, A. K. (1988). Commitment and the Modern Union: Assessing the Link Between Premarital Cohabitation and Subsequent Marital Stability. *American Sociological Review, 53,* 127–138.

Bennett, S. K., & Elder, G. H., Jr. (1980). Women's Work in the Family Economy: A Study of Depression Hardship in Women's Lives. *Journal of Family History, 4,* 422–431.

Berardo, D. H., Shehan, C. L., & Leslie, G. R. (1987). A Residue of Tradition: Jobs, Careers, and Spouses' Time in Housework. *Journal of Marriage and the Family, 49,* 381–390.

Bergen, E. (1991). The Economic Context of Labor Allocation: Implications for Gender Stratification. *Journal of Family Issues, 12,* 140–157.

Berger, B., & Berger, P. L. (1983). *The War Over the Family: Capturing the Middle Ground.* Garden City, N.J.: Doubleday Anchor.

Berhner, L. K. (1973). Recent Research on the History of the Family in Western Europe. *Journal of Marriage and the Family, 35,* 395–405.

Berk, R. A., & Newton, P. J. (1985). Does Arrest Really Deter Wife Battery? An Effort to Replicate the Findings of the Minneapolis Spouse Abuse Experiment, *American Sociological Review, 50,* 253–262.

Berk, R. A., Newton, P. J., & Berk, S. F. (1986). What a Difference a Day Makes: An Empirical Study of the Impact of Shelters for Battered Women. *Journal of Marriage and the Family, 48,* 481–490.

Bernard, J. (1964). The Adjustment of Married Mates. in H. Christensen (Ed.), *Handbook of Marriage and the Family.* Chicago: Rand McNally.

Bernard, J. (1966). *Marriage and Family Among Negroes.* Englewood Cliffs, N.J.: Prentice-Hall.

Bernard, J. (1971). The Paradox of the Happy Family. in V. Gornick and B. Moran (Eds.), *Woman in a Sexist Society.* New York: Mentor.

Bernard, M. L., & Bernard, J. L. (1983). Violent Intimacy: The Family as a Model for Love Relationships. *Family Relations, 32,* 283–286.

Beyer, M. A., & Whitehurst, R. N. (1976). Value Changes and Length of Marriage: Some Correlates of Consonance and Dissonance. *International Journal of Sociology of the Family, 6,* 109–120.

Bianchi, S. M., & Seltzer, J. A. (1986). Life Without Father. *American Demographics, 8,* 42–47.

Biblarz, T. J. (1992). *Social Class and the American Family: Differences in Values and Behaviors.* Unpublished manuscript.

Biddle, B. J., Bank, B. J., & Marlin, M. M. (1980). Parental and Peer Influence on Adolescents. *Social Forces, 58,* 1057–1079.

Biernat, M., & Wortman, C. B. (1991). Sharing of Home Responsibilities Between Professionally Employed Women and Their Husbands. *Journal of Personality and Social Psychology, 60,* 844–860.

Billingsley, A. (1968). *Black Families in White America.* Englewood Cliffs, N.J.: Prentice-Hall.

Bims, H. (1974). The Black Family: A Proud Reappraisal. *Ebony,* (March), 125.

Blair, S. L., & Lichter, D. T. (1991). Measuring the Division of Household Labor: Gender Segregation of Housework Among American Couples. *Journal of Family Issues, 12,* 91–113.

Blake, N. M. (1982). *The Road to Reno: A History of Divorce.* New York: MacMillan.

Blau, P. M., Blum, T. C., & Schwartz, J. E. (1982). Heterogeneity and Intermarriage. *American Sociological Review, 27,* 45–62.

Blechman, E. A. (1991). Effective Communication: Enabling Multiproblem Families to Change. *Family Transitions* (pp. 219–244). New Jersey: Erlbaum.

Blood, R. O., Jr., & Wolfe, D. M. (1960). *Husbands and Wives.* New York: Free Press.

Bloom, D. E., & Bennett, N. G. (1986). Childless Couples. *American Demographics, 8,* 22–25, 54–55.

Bloom, L. Z. (1976). Its All for Your Own Good: Parent-Child Relationships in Popular American Child-Rearing Literature, 1820–1970. *Journal of Popular Culture, 10.*

Blumberg, P. M., & Paul, P. W. (1975). Continuities and Discontinuities in Upper-Class Marriages. *Journal of Marriage and the Family, 37.*

Blumberg, R. L., & Winch, R. F. (1972). Societal Complexity and Familial Complexity: Evidence for the Curvilinear Hypothesis. *American Journal of Sociology, 77,* 888–919.

Blumstein, P., & Schwartz, P. (1983). *American Couples: Money, Work, Sex.* New York: William Morrow.

Bokemeier, J., & Monroe, P. (1983). Continued Reliance on One Respondent in Family Decision-Making Studies: A Content Analysis. *Journal of Marriage and the Family, 45.*

Bolton, C. (1961). Mate Selection as the Development of a Relationship. *Marriage and Family Living, 23,* 234–240.

Booth, A., & Edwards, J. N. (1985). Age at Marriage and Marital Instability. *Journal of Marriage and the Family, 47,* 67–75.

Booth, A., Edwards, J. N., & Johnson, D. R. (1991). Social Integration and Divorce. *Social Forces, 70,* 207–224.

Booth, A., Johnson, D., & Edwards, J. N. (1983). "Measuring Marital Instability." *Journal of Marriage and the Family, 45,* 387–394.

Booth, A., & White, L. (1980). Thinking About Divorce, *Journal of Marriage and the Family, 42,* 605–616.

Boss, P. (1977). A Clarification of the Concept of Psychological Father Presence in Families Experiencing Ambiguity of Boundary. *Journal of Marriage and the Family, 39,* 141–151.

Boss, P. G. (1980). Normative Family Stress: Family Boundary Changes Across the Life-Span. *Family Relations, 29,* 445–450.

Boss, P. G., & Gurko, T. A. (1993). The Relationships of Men and Women in Marriage, in Maddock et al. (Eds.), *Perestroika and Family Life: Post-U.S.S.R. and U.S. Perspectives.* New York: Guilford.

Boss, P., McCubbin, H. I., and Lester, G. (1979). The Corporate Executive Wife's Coping Pattern in Response to Routine Husband-Father Absence: Implications for Family Stress Theory. *Family Process, 18,* 79–86.

Boss, P., & Thorne, B. (1989). Family Sociology and Family Therapy: A Feminist Link. in McGoldrick, Anderson, and Walsh (Eds.), *Women in Families.* New York: Norton.

Bossard, J. H. S. (1932). Residential Propinquity as a Factor in Mate Selection. *American Journal of Sociology, 38,* 219–224.

Bowen, G. L. (1983). The Evolution of Soviet Family Policy: Female Liberation Versus Social Cohesion. *Journal of Comparative Family Studies, 14,* 299–313.

Bowker, L. H., Arbitell, M., & McFerron, J. R. (1988). On the Relationship Between Wife Beating and Child Abuse. in Yllo and Bograd (Eds.), *Feminist Perspectives on Wife Abuse.* Newbury Park, CA: Sage.

Bowlby, J. (1969). *Attachment and Loss—Volume I: Attachment.* New York: Basic Books.

Bowman, P. J. (1988). Postindustrial Displacement and Family Role Strains: Challenges to the Black Family. in Voydanoff and Majka (Eds.), *Families and Economic Distress: Coping Strategies and Social Policy.* Newbury Park, CA.: Sage.

Bowser, B. P., Fullilove, M. T., & Fullilove, R. E. (1990). African-American Youth and AIDS High Risk Behavior—the Social Context and Barriers to Prevention. *Youth and Society, 22,* 54–66.

Boyd. R. L. (1989). Minority Status and Childlessness. *Sociological Inquiry, 59,* 331–342.

Bozett, F. W. (1980). Gay Fathers: How and Why They Disclose Their Homosexuality to Their Children. *Family Relations, 29,* 173–179.

Breault, K. D., & Kposowa, A. J. (1987). Explaining Divorce in the United States: A Study of 3,111 Counties, 1980. *Journal of Marriage and the Family, 49,* 549–558.

Breines, W., & Gordon, L. (1983). The New Scholarship on Family Violence. *Signs, 8,* 490–531.

Brenton, M. (1966). *The American Male.* New York: Coward-McCann.

Breslin, F. C., Riggs, D. S., O'Leary, K. D., & Arias, I. (1990). Family Precursors: Expected and Actual Consequences of Dating Aggression. *Journal of Interpersonal Violence, 5,* 247–258.

Brim, O. G., Jr., & Wheeler, S. (1966). *Socialization After Childhood: Two Essays.* New York: Wiley.

Brodbar-Nemzer, J. Y. (1988). The Contemporary Jewish Family. in D. L. Thomas (Ed.), *The Religion and Family Connection: Social Science Perspectives.* Provo, UT: Brigham Young University.

Broderick, C. B. (1971). Beyond the Five Conceptual Frameworks: A Decade of Development in Family Theory. *Journal of Marriage and the Family, 33.*

Broderick, C. B. (1984). *Marriage and the Family.* Englewood Cliffs, N.J.: Prentice-Hall.

Brody, E. M. (1985). Parent Care as a Normative Family Stress. *Gerontologist, 25,* 19–29.

Brody, E. M., Hoffman, C., Kleban, M. H., Schoonover, C. B. (1989). Caregiving Daughters

and Their Local Siblings: Perceptions, Strains, and Interactions. *Gerontologist, 29,* 529–538.

Brody, E. M., & Schoonover, C. B. (1986). Patterns of Parent-Care When Adult Daughters Work and When They Do Not. *Gerontologist, 26,* 372–381.

Broman, C. L., Neighbors, H. W., & Jackson, J. S. (1988). Racial Group Identification Among Black Adults. *Social Forces, 67,* 146–158.

Brown, B. (1979). Parents' Discipline of Children in Public Places. *The Family Coordinator, 28,* 67–71.

Brown, B. W. (1978). Wife-Employment and the Emergence of Egalitarian Marital Role Prescriptions: 1900–1974. *Journal of Comparative Family Studies, 9.*

Brubaker, T. H. (1990). Families in Later Life: A Burgeoning Research Area. *Journal of Marriage and the Family, 52,* 959–981.

Brym, R. J., Gillespie, M. W., & Gillis, A. R. (1985). Anomie, Opportunity, and the Density of Ethnic Ties: Another View of Jewish Outmarriage in Canada. *Canadian Review of Sociology and Anthropology, 22,* 102–112.

Bryant, E. S., VanderMey, B. J., & Burgess, N. J. (1988). Coemployed Spouses: Differences, Strategies, and Discrimination. *Journal of Family Issues, 9,* 496–517.

Buehlman, K. T., Gottman, J. M., & Katz, L. F. (1992). How a Couple Views Their Past Predicts Their Future: Predicting Divorce from an Oral History Interview. *Journal of Family Psychology, 5,* 295–318.

Bulcroft, K., & O'Connor, M. (1986). The Importance of Dating Relationships on Quality of Life for Older Persons. *Family Relations, 55,* 397–401.

Bumpass, L. (1979). Fertility and Family Planning. in Romney et al. (Eds.), *Gynecology and Obstetrics: The Health Care of Women* (pp. 374–386). New York: McGraw-Hill.

Bumpass, L. (1987). The Risk of an Unwanted Birth: The Changing Context of Contraceptive Sterilization in the U.S. *Population Studies, 41,* 347–363.

Bumpass, L. L., Martin, T. C., & Sweet, J. A. (1991). The Impact of Family Background and Early Marital Factors on Marital Disruption. *Journal of Family Issues, 12,* 22–42.

Bumpass, L., & McLanahan, S. (1989). Unmarried Motherhood: Recent Trends, Composition, and Black-White Differences. *Demography, 216,* 279–286.

Bumpass, L. L., & Sweet, J. (1989). National Estimates of Cohabitation. *Demography, 26,* 615–625.

Bumpass, L. L., Sweet, J. A., & Cherlin, A. (1991). The Role of Cohabitation in Declining Rates of Marriage. *Journal of Marriage and the Family, 55,* 913–927.

Bumpass, L., Sweet, J., & Martin, T. C. (1990). Changing Patterns of Remarriage. *Journal of Marriage and the Family, 52,* 747–756.

Burgess, E., & Locke, H. (1945). *The Family: From Institution to Companionship.* New York: American.

Burke, R. J., & Weir, T. (1976). Some Personality Differences Between Members of One-Career and Two-Career Families. *Journal of Marriage and the Family, 38.*

Burr, W. R. (1973). *Theory Construction and the Sociology of the Family.* New York: Wiley.

Burr, W., Ahern, L., & Knowles, E. M. (1977). An Empirical Test of Rodman's Theory of Resources in Cultural Context. *Journal of Marriage and the Family, 39*.

Burr, W. R., & Leigh, G. K. (1983). Famology: A New Discipline. *Journal of Marriage and the Family, 45*, 467–480.

Burr, W. R., Hill, R., Nye, F. I., & Reiss, I. (1979). *Contemporary Theories About the Family, Volumes 1 and 2*. New York: Free Press.

Burris, B. H. (1991). Employed Mothers: The Impact of Class and Marital Status on the Prioritizing of Family and Work. *Social Science Quarterly, 72*, 50–66.

Bushman, R. L. (1981). Family Security in the Transition from Farm to City, 1750–1850. *Journal of Family History, 6*, 238–256.

Calhoun, A. W. (1945). *A Social History of the American Family, Volume 1*. New York: Barnes and Noble.

Callan, V. J. (1983). The Voluntary Childless and Their Perceptions of Parenthood and Childlessness. *Journal of Comparative Family Studies, 14*, 87–96.

Callan, V. J. (1987). The Personal and Marital Adjustment of Mothers and of Voluntarily and Involuntarily Childless Wives. *Journal of Marriage and the Family, 49*, 847–856.

Callan, V. J., & Noller, P. (1986). Perceptions of Communicative Relationships in Families with Adolescents. *Journal of Marriage and the Family, 48*, 813–820.

Campbell, E. (1985). *The Childless Marriage: An Exploratory Study of Couples Who Do Not Want Children*. London: Tavistock.

Cancian, F. M. (1987). *Love in America — Gender and Self-Development*. Cambridge: Cambridge University Press.

Cantor, M. H. (1991). Family and Community: Changing Roles in an Aging Society. *Gerontologist, 31*, 337–346.

Caplan, P. (1987). *The Cultural Construction of Sexuality*. London: Tavistock.

Caplow, T. (1982). Christmas Gifts and Kin Networks. *American Sociological Review, 47*, 383–392.

Caplow, T., Bahr, H. M., Chadwick, B. A., Hill, R., & Williamson, M. H. (1982). *Middletown's Families: Fifty Years of Change and Continuity*. Minneapolis: University of Minnesota Press.

Cargan, L. (1981). Singles: An Examination of Two Stereotypes. *Family Relations, 30*, 377–385.

Caspi, A., & Herbener, E. S. (1990). Continuity and Change: Assortative Mating and the Consistency of Personality in Adulthood. *Journal of Personality and Social Psychology, 58*, 250–258.

Caspi, A., Ozer, D. J., & Herbener, E. S. (1992). Shared Experiences and the Similarity of Personalities: A Longitudinal Study of Married Couples. *Journal of Personality and Social Psychology, 62*, 281–291.

Cassidy, M. L., & Lee, G. R. (1989). The Study of Polyandry: A Critique and Synthesis. *Journal of Comparative Family Studies*. (Spring), 1–9.

Cate, R. M., & Koval, J. E. (1983). Heterosexual Relationship Development: Is It Really a Sequential Process? *Adolescence, 18*, 507–514.

Catton, W. R. (1964). A Comparison of Mathematical Models for the Effect of Residential Propinquity on Mate Selection. *American Sociology Review, 29*.

Catton, W. R. (1969). What's in a Name? The Case for Role Inertia. *Journal of Marriage and the Family. 31*, 15–18.

Cavan, R. S. (1964). Subcultural Variations and Mobility. in H. T. Chistensen (Ed.), *Handbook of Marriage and the Family*. Chicago: Rand McNally.

Cavan, R. S. (1969). *The American Family*. New York: Crowell.

Cazenave, N. A., & Straus, M. A. (1979). Race, Class, Network Embeddedness and Family Violence: A Search for Parent Support Systems. *Journal of Comparative Family Studies, 10*, 280–300.

Center on Budget and Policy Priorities. (1986). Falling Behind — A Report on How Blacks Have Fared Under Reagan. *Journal of Black Studies, 17*, 148–172.

Chadwick, B. A., Albrecht, S. L., & Kunz, P. R. (1976). Marital and Family Role Satisfaction. *Journal of Marriage and the Family, 38*, 431–440.

Chalifous, J-J. (1980). Secondary Marriage and Levels of Seniority Among the Abisi (PITI) Nigeria. *Journal of Comparative Family Studies, 11*, 325–334.

Charles, N., & Kerr, M. (1988). *Women, Food, and Families*. Manchester, Eng.: Manchester University Press.

Cheal, D. (1991). *Family and the State of Theory*. Toronto: University of Toronto Press.

Cheal, D. J. (1983). Intergenerational Family Transfers. *Journal of Marriage and the Family, 45*, 805–813.

Cherlin, A. (1978). Remarriage as an Incomplete Institution. *American Journal of Sociology, 84*.

Cherlin, A. (1980). Postponing Marriage: The Influence of Young Women's Work Expectations. *Journal of Marriage and the Family, 42*, 355–365.

Cherlin, A. (1981). *Marriage Divorce Remarriage*. Cambridge, MA: Harvard University Press.

Cherlin, A., & Celebuski, C. (1983). Are Jewish Families Different? Some Evidence from the General Social Survey. *Journal of Marriage and the Family, 45*, 903–910.

Cherlin, A. J., & Furstenberg, F. F. (1986). *The New American Grandparent*. New York: Basic Books.

Cherlin, A., & McCarthy, J. (1985). Remarried Couple Households: Data from the June 1980 Current Population Survey. *Journal of Marriage and the Family, 47*, 23–30.

Chevan, A., & Fischer, L. R. (1979). Retirement and Interstate Migration. *Social Forces, 57*, 1365–1380.

Chilman, C. S. (1975). Families in Poverty in the Early 1970s: Rates, Associated Factors, Some Implications. *Journal of Marriage and the Family, 37*.

Choi, N. G. (1991). Racial Determinants of Living Arrangements of Widowed and Divorced Elderly Women. *Gerontologist, 31*, 496–504.

Christensen, H. T. (1964). *Handbook of Marriage and the Family*. Chicago: Rand McNally.

Christensen, H. T. (1977). Relationship Between Differentiation and Equality in the Sex Role Structure: Conceptual Models and Suggested Research. in Lenero-Otero (Ed.), *Beyond the Nuclear Family Model* (pp. 205–224). Beverly Hills, CA: Sage.

Christensen, J. B. (1954). *Double Descent Among the Fanti*. New Haven, CT.: Human Relations Area Files.

Christensen, K. E. (1987). Women, Families, and Home-Based Employment. in Gerstel & Gross

(Eds.), *Families and Work* (pp. 478–490). Philadelphia: Temple University Press.

Christopoulos, C., Cohn, D. A., Shaw, D. S., Joyce, S., Sullivan-Hanson, J., Kraft, S. P., & Emery, R. E. (1987). Children of Abused Women: I. Adjustment at Time of Shelter Residence. *Journal of Marriage and the Family, 49,* 611–619.

Chudacoff, H. P., & Hareven, T. K. (1979). From the Empty Nest to Family Dissolution: Life Course Transitions into Old Age. *Journal of Family History, 4,* 69–83.

Cicirelli, V. G. (1985). Sibling Relationships Throughout the Life Cycle. in L. L'Abate (Ed.), *The Handbook of Family Psychology and Therapy* (pp. 177–214). Homewood, IL: Dorsey.

Clanton, G. (1984). Social Forces and the Changing Family. in Kirkendall & Gravatt (Eds.), *Marriage and the Family in the Year 2020* (pp. 13–46). Buffalo: Prometheus.

Clark, R. M. (1983). *Family Life and School Achievement: Why Poor Black Children Succeed or Fail.* Chicago: University of Chicago Press.

Clark, R. L., & Menefee, J. A. (1981). Federal Expenditures for the Elderly: Past and Future. *The Gerontologist, 21,* 132–137.

Clark-Nicolas, P., & Gray-Little, B. (1991). Effect of Economic Resources on Marital Quality in Black Married Couples. *Journal of Marriage and the Family, 53,* 645–655.

Clarke, J. (1978). Sex Differences and Its Future. *Journal of Comparative Family Studies, 9.*

Clavan, S., & Vatter, E. (1972). The Affiliated Family: A Continued Analysis. *Family Life Coordinator, 21,* 499–504.

Cleveland, M. (1976). Sex in Marriage: At 40 and Beyond. *The Family Coordinator, 25,* 233–240.

Coale, A. (1989). Marriage and Childbearing in China since 1940. *Social Forces, 67,* 833–850.

Cohen, J. F. (1979). Male Roles in Mid-Life. *The Family Coordinator, 28,* 465–471.

Coleman, E. R. (1973). Medieval Marriage Characteristics: A Neglected Factor in the History of Medieval Serfdom. in Rabb & Rotberg (Eds.), *The Family in History.* New York: Harper and Row.

Coleman, L. M., Antonucci, T. C., Adelmann, P. K., & Crohan, S. E. (1987). Social Roles in the Lives of Middle-Aged and Older Black Women. *Journal of Marriage and the Family, 49,* 761–771.

Collier, J., Rosaldo, M. Z., & Yanagisako, S. (1982). Is There a Family? New Anthropological Views. in B. Thorne & M. Yalom (Eds.), *Rethinking the Family: Some Feminist Questions* (pp. 25–39). New York: Longman.

Collins, P. H. (1990). *Black Feminist Thought: Knowledge, Consciousness, and the Politics of Empowerment.* Boston: Unwin, Hyman.

Collins, R. (1971). A Conflict Theory of Sexual Stratification. *Social Problems, 19,* 3–21.

Coltrane, S., & Ishii-Kuntz, M. (1992). Men's Housework: A Life Course Perspective. *Journal of Marriage and the Family, 54,* 43–57.

Comte, A. (1842). *The Positive Philosophy.* New York: Peter Eckler, 1875.

Condran, J. G., & Bode, J. G. (1982). Rashomon, Working Wives, and Family Division of Labor: Middleton, 1980. *Journal of Marriage and the Family, 44.*

Conger, R. D., Elder, G. H. Jr., Lorenz, F. O., Conger, K. J., Simons, R. L., Whitbeck, L. B., Huck, S., & Melby, J. N. (1990). Linking Economic Hardship to Marital Quality and Instability. *Journal of Marriage and the Family, 52,* 643–656.

Constantine, L. L., & Constantine, J. M. (1971). Group and Multilateral Marriage: Definitional Notes, Glossary, and Annotated Bibliography. *Family Process, 10,* 157–176.

Cooney, R. S., Rogler, L. H., & Schroeder, E. (1981). Puerto Rican Fertility: An Examination of Social Characteristics, Assimilation, and Minority Status Variables. *Social Forces, 59,* 1094–1113.

Cooper, J. E., Holman, J., & Braithwaite, V. A. (1983). Self-Esteem and Family Cohesion: The Child's Perspective and Adjustment. *Journal of Marriage and the Family, 45,* 153–159.

Cooper, K. L., & Gutmann, D. (1987). Gender Identity and Ego Mastery Style in Middle-Aged, Pre- and Post-Empty-Nest Women. *Gerontologist, 27,* 347–352.

Cooper, K., Chassin, L., & Zeiss, A. (1985). The Relation of Sex-Role Self-Concept and Sex-Role Attitudes to the Marital Satisfaction and Personal Adjustment of Dual-Worker Couples with Pre-School Children. *Sex Roles, 12,* 227–241.

Cornfield, N. (1981). The Success of Urban Communes. *Journal of Marriage and the Family, 45,* 115–126.

Cott, N. F. (1976). Eighteenth Century Family and Social Life Revealed in Massachusetts Divorce Records. *Journal of Social History, 10.*

Covin, T. J., & Brush, C. C. (1991). An Examination of Male and Female Attitudes Toward Career and Family Issues. *Sex Roles, 25,* 393–416.

Cowan, C. P., Cowan, P. A., Heming, G., & Miller, N. B. (1991). Becoming A Family: Marriage, Parenting, and Child Development. in Cowan & Hetherington (Eds.), *Family Transitions* (pp. 79–109). New Jersey: Erlbaum.

Coysh, W. S., Johnston, J. R., Tschann, J. M., Wallerstein, J. S., & Kline, M. (1989). Parental Postdivorce Adjustment In Joint and Sole Physical Custody Families. *Journal of Family Issues, 10,* 52–71.

Crandall, C. S., & Coleman, R. (1992). AIDS-Related Stigmatization and the Disruption of Social Relationships. *Journal of Social and Personal Relationships, 9,* 163–177.

Crnic, K. A., & Greenberg, M. T. (1990). Minor Parenting Stresses with Young Children. *Child Development, 61,* 1628–1637.

Crockenberg, S. B. (1988). Stress and Role Satisfaction Experienced by Employed and Nonemployed Mothers with Young Children. *Lifestyles, 9,* 97–109.

Crohan, S. E. (1992). Marital Happiness and Spousal Consensus on Beliefs about Marital Conflict: A Longitudinal Investigation. *Journal of Social and Personal Relationships, 9,* 89–102.

Cromwell, R. E., & Olson, D. H. (1975). *Power in Families.* New York: Wiley.

Crosbie-Burnett, M., Skyles, A., & Becker-Haven, J. (1988). Exploring Stepfamilies from a Feminist Perspective. in Dornbusch & Strober (Eds.), *Feminism, Children, and the New Families* (pp. 297–326). New York: Guilford.

Cuber, J. F., & Harroff, P. B. (1965). *The Significant Americans: A Study of Sexual Behavior among the Affluent.* New York: Appleton-Century-Crofts.

Cumming, E. (1963). Further Thoughts on the Theory of Disengagement. *International Social Science Journal, 15,* 377–393.

Cumming, E., Dean, L. R., & Newell, D. S. (1960). Disengagement: A Tentative Theory of Aging. *Sociometry, 23.*

Cumming, E., & Henry, W. (1961). *Growing Old: The Process of Disengagement.* New York: Basic Books.

Dahlin, M. (1980). Perspective on the Family Life of the Elderly in 1900. *The Gerontologist, 20.*

Darroch, A. G. (1981). Migrants in the Nineteenth Century: Fugitives or Families in Motion. *Journal of Family History, 6,* 257–277.

Darwin, C. (1871). The Descent of Man. In *Great Books of the Western World, Volume 49.* Chicago: Encyclopedia Britannica, 1971.

Darwin, C. (1859). *Origin of the Species in the Process of Natural Selection.* London: Murray.

Davidson, B., Balswick, J., & Haverston, C. (1983). Affective Self-Disclosure and Marital Adjustment: A Test of Equity Theory. *Journal of Marriage and the Family, 45,* 93–102.

Davies, M., & Kandel, D. B. (1980). Parental and Peer Influences on Adolescents' Educational Plans: Some Further Evidence. *American Journal of Sociology, 87.*

Davies, R. P. (1949). Syrian Arabic Kinship Terms. *Southwestern Journal of Anthropology, 5.*

Davis, K. (1949). *Human Society.* New York: MacMillan.

Davis, K. (1988). Wives and Work: A Theory of the Sex-Role Revolution and Its Consequences. in Dornbusch & Strober (Eds.), *Feminism, Children, and the New Families* (pp. 67–86). New York: Guilford.

Davis, R. A. (1989). Teenage Pregnancy: A Theoretical Analysis of a Social Problem. *Adolescence, 24,* 19–28.

Deal, J. W., & Wampler, M. S. (1986). Dating Violence: The Primacy of Previous Experience. *Journal of Social and Personal Relationships, 3,* 457–471.

Dean, A. L., Malik, M. M., Richards, W., & Stringer, S. A. (1986). Effects of Parental Maltreatment on Children's Conceptions of Interpersonal Relationships. *Developmental Psychology, 22,* 617–626.

deChesnay, M. (1986). Jamaican Family Structure: The Paradox of Normalcy. *Family Process, 25,* 293–300.

DeFrain, J. (1979). Androgynous Parents Tell Who They Are and What They Need. *The Family Coordinator, 28.*

Degler, C. (1980). *At Odds: Women and the Family in America from the Revolution to the Present.* New York: Oxford University Press.

DeKeseredy, W. S. (1990). Woman Abuse in Dating Relationships: The Contribution of Male Peer Support. *Sociological Inquiry, 60,* 236–243.

Delamater, J., & MacCorquodale, P. (1979). *Premarital Sexuality: Attitudes, Relationships, Behavior.* Madison, WI: University of Wisconsin Press.

DeMaris, A. (1987). The Efficacy of Spouse Abuse Model in Accounting for Courtship Violence. *Journal of Family Issues, 8,* 291–305.

DeMaris, A. (1990). The Dynamics of Generational Transfer in Courtship Violence: A Bi-racial Exploration. *Journal of Marriage and the Family, 52,* 219–231.

DeMaris, A., & Rao, K. V. (1992). Premarital Cohabitation and Subsequent Marital Stability in the United States: A Reassessment. *Journal of Marriage and the Family, 54,* 178–190.

D'Emilio, J., & Freedman, E. B. (1988). *Intimate Matters: A History of Sexuality in America.* New York: Harper and Row.

Demo, D. H. (1992). Parent-Child Relations: Assessing Recent Changes. *Journal of Marriage and the Family, 54,* 104–117.

Demo, D. H., Small, S. A., & Savin-Williams, R. C. (1987). Family Relations and the Self-Esteem of Adolescents and Their Parents. *Journal of Marriage and the Family, 49,* 705–715.

Demos, J. (1970). *A Little Commonwealth: Family Life in Plymouth Colony.* New York: Oxford University Press.

Demos, J. (1973). Development Perspectives on the History of Childhood. in Rabb & Rotberg (Eds.), *The Family in History* (pp. 127–139). New York: Harper Torchbooks.

Demos, J. (1986). *Past, Present, and Personal: The Family and the Life Course in American History.* New York: Oxford University Press.

Desai, S., & Waite, L. J. (1991). Women's Employment During Pregnancy and After the First Birth: Occupational Characteristics and Work Commitment. *American Sociological Review, 56,* 551–566.

Detzner, D. F., & Sinelnikov, A. B. (1993). Intergenerational Relations in Soviet and American Families. in Maddock et al., (Eds.), *Perestroika and Family Life: Post-U.S.S.R. and U.S. Perspectives.* New York: Guilford.

Deutsch, F. M., Ruble, D. N., Fleming, A., Brooks-Gunn, J., & Stangor, C. (1988). Information-Seeking and Maternal Self-Definition During the Transition to Motherhood. *Journal of Personality and Social Psychology, 55,* 420–431.

Deutsch, M., & Krauss, R. M. (1965). *Theories in Social Psychology.* New York: Basic Books.

Deutscher, I. (1962). Socialization for Postparental Life. in Arnold Rose (Ed.), *Human Behavior and Social Processes.* Boston: Houghton-Mifflin.

"Digest". (1991). Concern Over AIDS Changed Sexual Behavior Among One Third of Unmarried U.S. Women. *Family Planning Perspectives, 23,* 234–235.

Dill, B. T. (1979). The Dialectics of Black Womanhood. *Signs, 4,* 543–555.

Dixon, R. B., & Weitzman, L. J. (1980). Evaluating the Impact of No-Fault Divorce in California. *Family Relations, 29.*

Dobash, R. P., Dobash, R. E., Wilson, M., & Daly, M. (1992). The Myth of Sexual Symmetry in Marital Violence. *Social Problems, 39,* 71–91.

Doherty, W. J., & Needle, R. H. (1991). Psychological Divorce and Substance Use Among Adolescents Before and After a Parental Divorce. *Child Development, 62,* 328–337.

Doherty, W. J., Su, S., & Needle, R. (1989). Marital Disruption and Psychological Well-Being. *Journal of Family Issues, 10,* 72–85.

Dorfman, L. T. (1992). Couples in Retirement: Division of Household Work. in Szinovacz et al., (Eds.), *Families and Retirement* (pp. 159–173). Newbury Park, CA: Sage.

Douglas, J. D., & Atwell, F. C. (1988). *Love, Sex, and Intimacy.* Newbury Park, CA: Sage.

Douglass, R. L. (1983). Domestic Neglect and Abuse of the Elderly: Implications for Research and Service. *Family Relations, 32,* 395–402.

Downey, G., Silver, R. C., & Wortman, C. B. (1990). Reconsidering the Attribution-Adjustment Relation Following a Major Negative Event: Coping with the Loss of a Child. *Journal of Personality and Social Psychology, 59,* 925–940.

Draper, T. W. (1981). On the Relationship Between Welfare and Marital Stability: A Research Note. *Journal of Marriage and the Family, 43.*

Draper, T. W., & A. C. Marcos (Eds.). (1990). *Family Variables: Conceptualization, Measurement, and Use.* Newbury Park, CA: Sage.

Duberman, L. (1975). *The Reconstituted Family: A Study of Remarried Couples and Their Children.* Chicago: Nelson-Hall.

DuBois, D. L., Felner, R. D., Brand, S., Adan, A. M., & Evans, E. G. (1992). A Prospective Study of Life Stress, Social Support, and Adaptation in Early Adolescence. *Child Development, 63,* 542–557.

Durkheim, E. (1893). *The Division of Labor in Society.* New York: Free Press, 1964 ed.

Durkheim, E. (1885). Review of A. Schaeffle, *Bau und Leben des Socialem Korpers: Erste Band.* in *Revue Philosophique, 19,* 84–101.

Early, F. H. (1982). The French-Canadian Family Economy and Standard-of-Living in Lowell, Massachusetts, 1870. *Journal of Family History, 7,* 180–199.

Eckland, B. K. (1968). Theories of Mate Selection. *Eugenics Quarterly, 15.*

Edelman, M. W. (1987). *Families in Peril: An Agenda for Social Change.* Cambridge, MA: Harvard University Press.

Edwards, J. N., & Booth, A. (1976). Sexual Behavior In and Out of Marriage: An Assessment of Correlates. *Journal of Marriage and the Family, 58.*

Edwards, J., & Saunders, J. M. (1981). Coming Apart: A Model of the Marital Dissolution Decision. *Journal of Marriage and the Family, 43,* 379–389.

Eggan, F. (1950). *Social Organization of the Western Pueblos.* Chicago: University of Chicago Press.

Eggebeen, D. J., Crockett, L. J., & Hawkins, A. J. (1990). Patterns of Adult Male Coresidence Among Young Children of Adolescent Mothers. *Family Planning Perspectives, 22,* 219–223.

Eggebeen, D. J., & Hawkins, A. J. (1990). Economic Need and Wives' Employment. *Journal of Family of Issues, 11,* 48–66.

Eggebeen, D. J., & Lichter, D. T. (1991). Race, Family Structure, and Changing Poverty among American Children. *American Sociological Review, 56,* 801–817.

Ehrensaft, D. (1987). *Parenting Together: Men and Women Sharing the Care of Their Children.* New York: MacMillan.

Ehrmann, W. (1959). *Premarital Dating Behavior.* New York: Holt, Rinehart, and Winston.

Ekardt, D. J. (1986). The Busy Ethic: Moral Continuity Between Work and Retirement. *Gerontologist, 26,* 239–244.

Ekechi, F. K. (1976). African Polygamy and Western Christian Ethnocentrism. *Journal of African Studies, 3.*

Elder, G. H. (1974). *Children of the Great Depression.* Chicago: University of Chicago Press.

Elder, G. H., Jr. (1978). Family History and the Life Course. in T. K. Hareven (Eds.), *Transitions: The Family and the Life Course Historical Perspective.* New York: Academic.

Elder, G. H., & Liker, J. (1982). Hard Times in Women's Lives: Historical Influences Across Forty Years. *American Journal of Sociology, 88,* 241–269.

Elkins, S. M. (1963). *Slavery: A Problem in American Institutional and Intellectual Life.* New York: Grosset and Dunlap.

Ellis, A. (1973). Group Marriage: A Possible Alternative? in Streib (Ed.), *The Changing Family* (pp. 81–86). Reading, MA.: Addison-Wesley.

Ellis, H. (1936). *Studies in the Psychology of Sex.* New York: Random House.

Engels, F. (1942). *The Origin of the Family, Private Property, and the State.* New York: International.

Enright, R. D., Lapsley, D. K., Drivas, A. E., Fehr, L. A. (1980). Parental Influences on the Development of Adolescent Autonomy and Identity. *Journal of Youth and Adolescence, 9,* 529–545.

Entwisle, D. R., & Doering, S. (1988). The Emergent Father Role. *Sex Roles, 18,* 119–141.

Erickson, J. A., Yancey, W. L., & Ericksen, E. P. (1979). The Division of Family Roles. *Journal of Marriage and the Family, 41.*

Erlanger, H. (1974). Class and Punishment in Child-rearing. *American Sociological Review, 40.*

Essex, M. J., & Nam, S. (1987). Marital Status and Loneliness Among Older Women: The Differential Importance of Close Family and Friends. *Journal of Marriage and the Family, 49,* 93–106.

Evans, E. D., Rutberg, J., Sather, C., & Turner, C. (1991). Content Analysis of Contemporary Teen Magazines for Adolescent Families. *Youth and Society, 23,* 99–120.

Faludi, S. (1991). *Backlash.* New York: Crown.

Faragher, J. (1976). Old Women and Old Men in Seventeenth-Century Wethersfield, Conn. *Women's Studies, 4.*

Farber, B. (1964). *Family: Organization and Interaction.* San Francisco: Chandler.

Farber, B. (1971). *Kinship and Class: A Midwestern Study.* New York: Basic Books.

Farber, B. (1981). *Conceptions of Kinship.* New York: Elsevier North Holland.

Farber, N. (1990). The Significance of Race and Class in Marital Decisions among Unmarried Adolescent Mothers. *Social Problems, 37,* 51–63.

Farber, S. M., Mustacchi, P., & Wilson, R. H. L. (1965). *Man and Civilization: The Family's Search For Survival.* New York: McGraw-Hill.

Farrell, W. (1975). *The Liberated Male.* New York: Bantam Books.

Faulkner, L. R. (1982). Mandating the Reporting of Suspected Cases of Elder Abuse: An Inappropriate, Ineffective, and Ageist Response to the Abuse of Older Adults. *Family Law Quarterly, 16,* 69–91.

Featherhead, N. T. (1985). Masculinity, Femininity, Self-Esteem, and Subclinical Depression. *Sex Roles, 12,* 491–500.

Feltey, K. M., Ainslie, J. J., & Geib, A. (1991). Sexual Coercion Attitudes Among High School Students: The Influence of Gender and Rape Education. *Youth and Society, 23,* 229–250.

Ferguson, A. (1989). *Blood at the Root: Motherhood, Sexuality, and Male Dominance.* London: Pandora.

Ferree, M. M. (1987). Family and Job for Working Class Women: Gender and Class Systems Seen From Below. in Gerstel & Gross (Eds.), *Families and Work* (pp. 289–301). Philadelphia: Temple University Press.

Ferree, M. M. (1991). The Gender Division of Labor in Two-Earner Marriages. *Journal of Family Issues, 12,* 158–180.

Fiese, B. H. (1992). Dimensions of Family Rituals Across Two Generations: Relation to Adolescent Identity. *Family Process, 31,* 151–162.

Fillmore, C. J. (1990). Gender Differences in Earnings: A Re-Analysis and Prognosis for Canadian Women. *The Canadian Journal of Sociology, 15,* 275–299.

Fine, M. A. (1986) Perceptions of Stepparents: Variations in Stereotypes as a Function of Current Family Structure. *Journal of Marriage and the Family, 48,* 537–543.

Fine, M. A., Donnelly, B. W., & Voydanoff, P. (1986). Adjustment and Satisfaction of Parents: A Comparison of Intact, Single-Parent, and Stepparent Families. *Journal of Family Issues, 7,* 391–404.

Fine, M. A., McKenry, P. C., Donnelly, B. W., & Voydanoff, P. (1992). Perceived Adjustment of Parents and Children: Variations by Family Structure, Race and Gender. *Journal of Marriage and the Family, 54,* 118–127.

Finlay, B., Starnes, C. E., & Alvarez, F. B. (1985). Recent Changes in Sex-Role Ideology Among Divorced Men and Women: Some Possible Causes and Implications. *Sex Roles, 12,* 637–653.

Fischer, C. S. (1982). The Dispersion of Kinship Ties in Modern Society: Contemporary Data and Historical Speculation. *Journal of Family History, 7.*

Fischer, L. R. (1983). Mothers and Mothers-in-law. *Journal of Marriage and the Family, 45,* 187–192.

Fischer, L. R. (1986). *Linked Lives: Adult Daughters and Their Mothers.* New York: Harper and Row.

Fisher, W. A., & Khotin, L. (1977). Soviet Family Research. *Journal of Marriage and the Family, 39.*

Fishman, B. (1983). The Economic Behavior of Stepfamilies. *Family Relations, 32.*

Flaherty, D. (1972). *Privacy in Colonial New England.* Charlottesville, VA: University of Virginia Press.

Flake-Hobson, C., & Skeen, P., & Robinson, B. E. (1980). Review of Theories and Research Concerning Sex-Role Development and Androgyny with Suggestions for Teachers. *Family Relations, 29,* 155–162.

Fleck, J. R., Fuller, C. C., Malin, S. Z., & Miller, D. H. (1980). Father Psychological Absence and Heterosexual Behavior, Personal Adjustment and Sex-Typing in Adolescent Girls. *Adolescence, 15,* 847–860.

Flynn, C. P. (1990). Relationship Violence By Women: Issues and Implications. *Family Relations, 39,* 194–198.

Fogel, R., & Engerman, S. (1974). *Time on the Cross.* Boston: Little, Brown.

Fogel, R. W., Hatfield, E., Kiesler, S. B., & Shanas, E. (1981). *Aging: Stability and Change in the Family.* New York: Academic.

Follingstad, D. R., Laughlin, J. E., Polek, D. S., Rutledge, L. L., & Hause, E. S. (1991). Identification of Patterns of Wife Abuse. *Journal of Interpersonal Violence, 6,* 187–204.

Ford, D. S. (1983). Wife-Battery and Criminal Justice: A Study of Victim Decision Making. *Family Relations, 32.*

Foster, H. H., Jr. (1969). The Future of Family Law. *The Annals, 383.*

Foster, M. A., Wallston, B. S., & Berger, M. (1980) Feminist Orientation and Job-Seeking Behavior Among Dual-Career Couples. *Sex Roles, 6,* 59–65.

Fox, B. J. (1988). Conceptualizing Patriarchy. *Canadian Review of Sociology and Anthropology, 25,* 163–181.

Fox, R. (1962). Sibling Incest. *British Journal of Sociology, 13.*

Fox, R. (1967). *Kinship and Marriage.* Baltimore: Penguin.

Fox, R. (1980). *The Red Lamp of Incest.* New York: E. P. Dutton.

Francoeur, R. T. (1984). Moral Concepts in the Year 2020 — The Individual, the Family, and Society. and Transformations in Human Reproduction. in Kirkendall & Gravatt (Eds.), *Marriage and the Family in the Year 2020* (pp. 183–204; 89–105). Buffalo: Prometheus.

Frazier, E. F. (1957). *Black Bourgeoisie.* Chicago: University of Chicago Press.

Freedman, M. (1961–62). The Family in China, Past and Present. *Pacific Affairs, 34,* 323–336.

Freeman, M. D. A. (1981). But If You Can't Rape Your Wife, Who(m) Can You Rape? The Marital Rape Exemption Re-Examined. *Family Law Quarterly, 15,* 1–29.

Freud, S. (1920). *A General Introduction to Psychoanalysis.* New York: Liveright.

Freudiger, P. (1983). Life Satisfaction Among Three Categories of Married Women. *Journal of Marriage and the Family, 45.*

Friedan, B. (1963). *The Feminine Mystique.* New York: Dell.

Fromm, E. (1941). *Escape from Freedom.* New York: Rinehart.

Furstenberg, F. F., Jr. (1990). Divorce and the American Family. *Annual Review of Sociology, 16,* 379–403.

Furstenberg, F. F., Jr., & Nord, C. W. (1985). Parenting Apart: Patterns of Childrearing After Marital Disruption. *Journal of Marriage and the Family, 47,* 893–904.

Furstenberg, F. F., Jr., Hershberg, T., & Modell, J. (1975). The Origins of the Female-Headed Black Family: The Impact of the Urban Experience. *Journal of Interdisciplinary History, 6.*

Furstenberg, F. F., Jr., Levine, J. A., & Brooks-Gunn, J. (1990). The Children of Teenage Mothers: Patterns of Early Childbearing in Two Generations. *Family Planning Perspectives, 22,* 54–61.

Furstenberg, F. F., Jr., Morgan, S. P., Moore, K. A., & Peterson, J. L. (1987). Race Differences in the Timing of Adolescent Intercourse. *American Sociology Review, 52,* 511–518.

Galambos, N. L., & Silbereisen, R. K. (1987). Income Changes, Parental Life Outlook, and Adolescent Expectations for Job Success. *Journal of Marriage and the Family, 49,* 141–149.

Ganong, L. H., & Coleman, M. (1987). Effects of Children on Parental Sex-Role Orientation. *Journal of Family Issues, 8,* 278–290.

Ganong, L. L., & Coleman, M. (1988). Do Mutual Children Cement Bonds in Stepfamilies. *Journal of Marriage and the Family, 50,* 687–698.

Ganong, L. H., & Coleman, M. (1989). Preparing for Remarriage: Anticipating the Issues, Seeking Solutions. *Family Relations, 58,* 28–33.

Garbarino, J., & Ebata, A. (1983). The Significance of Ethnic and Cultural Differences in Child Maltreatment. *Journal of Marriage and the Family, 45,* 773–783.

Gardner, S. (1990). Images of Family Over the Family Life Cycle. *The Sociological Quarterly, 31,* 77–92.

Garfinkel, I., & McLanahan, S. S. (1986). *Single Mothers and Their Children.* Washington: Urban Institute.

Gargiulo, J., Attie, I., Brooks-Gunn, J., & Warren, M. P. (1987). Girls' Dating Behavior as a Function of Social Context and Maturation. *Developmental Psychology, 23,* 730–737.

Gately, D. W., & Schwebel, A. I. (1991). The Challenge Model of Children's Adjustment to Parental Divorce: Explaining Favorable Post Divorce Outcomes in Children. *Journal of Family Psychology, 5,* 60–81.

Geboy, M. J. (1981). Who's Listening to the 'Experts'? The Use of Child Care Materials by Parents. *Family Relations, 39,* 205–210.

Geiger, H. K. (1968). *The Family in Soviet Russia.* Cambridge, MA: Harvard University Press.

Gelles, R. J. (1976). Demythologizing Child Abuse. *The Family Coordinator, 25.*

Gelles, R. J. (1980). Violence in the Family: A Review of Research in the Seventies. *Journal of Marriage and the Family, 42.*

Gelles, R. J. (1985). Family Violence. *Annual Review of Sociology, 11,* 347–367.

Gelles, R. J. (1988). Violence and Pregnancy: Are Pregnant Women at Greater Risk of Abuse? *Journal of Marriage and the Family, 50,* 841–847.

Gelles, R. J., & Straus, M. A. (1988). *Intimate Violence: the Causes and Consequences of Abuse in the American Family.* New York: Simon and Schuster.

Gerner, J. L., Montalto, C. P., & Bryant, W. K. (1990). Work Patterns and Marital Status Change. *Lifestyles, 11,* 7–22.

Gershenson, H. P. (1983). Redefining Fatherhood in Families with White Adolescent Mothers. *Journal of Marriage and the Family, 45.*

Gerson, K. (1985). *Hard Choices: How Women Decide About Work, Career, and Motherhood.* Los Angeles: University of California Press.

Gerstel, N. (1988). Divorce Gender and Social Integration. *Gender and Society, 2,* 343–367.

Gerstel, N., & Gross, H. (1984). *Commuter Marriage.* New York: Guilford.

Gerstel, N., & Gross, H. E. (1987). *Families and Work.* Philadelphia: Temple University Press.

Gibson, R. C. (1987). Reconceptualizing Retirement for Black Americans. *Gerontologist, 27,* 691–698.

Gilder, G. (1987). *Men and Marriage.* Gretna, LA: Pelican.

Giles-Sims, J. (1983). *Wife-Battering: A Systems Theory Approach.* New York: Guilford.

Giles-Sims, J. (1985). A Longitudinal Study of Battered Children of Battered Wives. *Family Relations, 54,* 205–210.

Gill, S., Stockard, J., Johnson, M., & Williams, S. (1987). Measuring Gender Differences: The Expressive Dimension and Critique of Androgyny Scales. *Sex Roles, 17,* 375–400.

Gillespie, D. L. (1971). Who Has the Power? The Marital Struggle. *Journal of Marriage and the Family, 33,* 445–458.

Gilliland, N. C. (1979). The Problem of Geographic Mobility for Dual-Career Families. *Journal of Comparative Family Studies, 10,* 345–358.

Glasco, L. A. (1975). The Life Cycles and Household Structure of American Ethnic Groups: Irish, Germans, and Native-Born Whites in Buffalo, N.Y., 1855. *Journal of Urban History, 3.*

Glass, B. L., & Stolee, M. K. (1987). Family Law in Soviet Russia, 1917–1945. *Journal of Marriage and the Family, 49,* 893–902.

Glass, J., Bengtson, V. L., & Dunham, C. (1986). Attitude Similarity in Three Generation Families: Socialization, Status Inheritance or Reciprocal Influence. *American Sociological Review, 51,* 685–698.

Glenn, N. D. (1982). Interreligious Marriage in the United States: Patterns and Recent Trends. *Journal of Marriage and the Family, 44,* 555–566.

Glenn, N. D. (1991). The Recent Trend in Marital Success in the United States. *Journal of Marriage and the Family, 53,* 261–270.

Glenn, N. D. (1992). What Does Family Mean? *American Demographics, 14,* 30–37.

Glenn, N. D., & Kramer, K. B. (1985). The Psychological Well-Being of Adult Children of Divorce. *Journal of Marriage and the Family, 47,* 905–912.

Glenn, N. D., & McLanahan, S. (1982). Children and Marital Happiness: A Further Specification of the Relationship. *Journal of Marriage and the Family, 44,* 63–72.

Glick, P. C., & Sung-Ling Lin. (1986). Recent Changes in Divorce and Remarriage. *Journal of Marriage and the Family, 48,* 737–747.

Glick, P. C., & Spanier, G. (1980). Married and Unmarried Cohabitation in the United States. *Journal of Marriage and the Family, 42.*

Goetting, A. (1986). The Developmental Tasks of Siblingship Over the Life Cycle. *Journal of Marriage and the Family, 48,* 703–714.

Goetting, A. (1990). Patterns of Support Among In-Laws in the United States: a Review of Research. *Journal of Family Issues, 11,* 67–90.

Goetting, A. (1982). The Six Stations of Remarriage: Developmental Tasks of Remarriage After Divorce. *Family Relations, 31,* 213–222.

Gold, R. B., & Daley, D. (1991). Public Funding of Contraceptive, Sterilization, and Abortion Services, Fiscal Year 1990. *Family Planning Perspectives, 23,* 204–211.

Goldscheider, F. K., & Goldscheider, C. (1991). The Intergenerational Flow of Income: Family Structure and the Status of Black Americans. *Journal of Marriage and the Family, 53,* 499–508.

Goldscheider, F. K., & Waite, L. J. (1987). Nest-Leaving Patterns and the Transition to Marriage for Young Men and Women. *Journal of Marriage and the Family, 49,* 507–516.

Goldscheider, F. K., & Waite, L. J. (1991). *New Families, No Families.* Berkeley: University of California Press.

Goode, W. J. (1956). *After Divorce.* New York: Free Press.

Goode, W. J. (1959). The Theoretical Importance of Love. *American Sociological Review, 24,* 38–47.

Goode, W. J. (1963). *World Revolution and Family Patterns.* New York: Free Press.

Goode, W. J. (1971). Force and Violence in the Family. *Journal of Marriage and the Family, 33.*

Goode, W. J. (1993). *World Changes in Divorce Patterns.* New Haven: Yale University Press.

Goodenough. W. H. (1965). Yankee Kinship Terminology: A Problem in Componential Analysis. *American Anthropologist, 67.*

Goodwin, R. (1990). Sex Differences Among Partner Preferences: Are the Sexes Really Very Similar? *Sex Roles, 23,* 501–513.

Googins, B. K. (1991). *Work/Family Conflicts: Private Lives—Public Responses.* New York: Auburn House.

Gordon, Marianna (1979–80). Child Maltreatment: An Overview of Current Approaches. *Journal of Family Law, 18,* 115–145.

Gordon, Michael (1981). Was Waller Ever Right? The Rating and Dating Complex Reconsidered. *Journal of Marriage and the Family, 43,* 67–76.

Gorer, G. (1964). *The American People: A Study in National Character.* New York: Norton.

Gottman, J. S. (1990). Children of Gay and Lesbian Parents. in Bozett & Sussman (Eds.), *Homosexuality and Family Relations* (pp. 177–196). New York: Haworth.

Gough, E. K. (1959). The Nayars and the Definition of Marriage. *Journal of the Royal Anthropological Institute, 89* (Pt 1.).

Gove, W. R., Briggs, C., & Hughes, M. (1990). The Effect of Marriage on the Well-Being of Adults: A Theoretical Analysis. *Journal of Family Issues, 11,* 4–35.

Gove, W. R., & Hee-Choon Shin. (1989). The Psychological Well-Being of Divorced Men and Widowed Men and Women, *Journal of Family Issues, 10,* 122–144.

Graham, J. Q., Jr. (1983). Family and Fertility in Rural Ohio: Wood County, Ohio, in 1968, *Journal of Family History, 8,* 262–278.

Gray, K. D. (1992). Fathers' Participation in Child Custody Arrangements among Hispanic, Non-Hispanic White, and Intermarried Families. *Journal of Comparative Family Studies, 23,* 55–68.

Greenberg, J. S., & Bedecker, M. (1988). Aging Parents as Family Resources. *Gerontologist, 26,* 786–791.

Greenberger, E., & Goldberg, W. A., (1989). Work, Parenting, and the Socialization of Children. *Developmental Psychology, 25,* 22–35.

Greenblatt, C. S. (1983). The Salience of Sexuality in the Early Years of Marriage. *Journal of Marriage and the Family, 45.*

Greenstein, T. N. (1985). Occupation and Divorce. *Journal of Family Issues, 6,* 347–357.

Greenstein, T. N. (1990). Marital Disruption and the Employment of Married Women. *Journal of Marriage and the Family, 52,* 657–676.

Greif, G. L. (1985). *Single Fathers.* Lexington, MA: Lexington.

Grella, C. E. (1990). Irreconcilable Differences: Women Defining Class After Divorce and Downward Mobility. *Gender and Society, 4,* 41–55.

Greven, P. J., Jr. (1970). *Four Generations: Population, Land, and Family in Colonial Andover, Massachusetts.* Ithaca, NY: Cornell University Press.

Grieco, M. S. (1982). Family Structure and Industrial Employment: The Role of Information and Migration. *Journal of Marriage and the Family, 44,* 701–707.

Griffitt, W. (1981). Sexual Intimacy in Aging Marital Partners. in Vogel et al. (Eds.), *Aging.* New York: Academic.

Grindstaff, C. F., Balakrishnan, T. R., & Dewitt, D. J. (1991). Educational Attainment, Age at First Birth, and Lifetime Fertility: An Analysis of Canadian Fertility Survey Data. *Canadian Review of Sociology and Anthropology, 28,* 324–339.

Grinnell, G. B. (1923). *The Cheyenne Indians: Their History and Ways of Life* (2 Volumes). New Haven: Yale University Press.

Groves, M. M., & Horm-Wingerd, D. M. (1991). Commuter Marriages: Personal, Family and Career Issues. *Sociology and Social Research, 75,* 212–217.

Guisinger, S., Cowan, P. A., & Schuldberg, D. (1989). Changing Parent and Spouse Relations in the First Years of Remarriage of Divorced Fathers. *Journal of Marriage and the Family, 51,* 445–456.

Gully, K. J., Dengerink, H. A., Pepping, M., & Bergstrom, D. (1981). Research Note: Sibling Contribution to Violent Behavior. *Journal of Marriage and the Family, 43,* 333–337.

Gurak, D. T., & Fitzpatrick, J. P. (1982). Intermarriage Among Hispanic Ethnic Groups in New York City. *American Journal of Sociology, 87,* 921–934.

Gutman, H. G. (1975). Persistent Myths About the Afro-American Family. *Journal of Interdisciplinary History, 6.*

Guttman, J., Rosenberg, M., & Hertz-Lazarowitz, R. L. (1989). Children of Divorce and Their Intimate Relationships With Parents and Peers. *Youth and Society, 21,* 85–104.

Gwartney-Gibbs, P. A. (1986). The Institutionalization of Premarital Cohabitation: Estimates from Marriage License Applications, 1970 and 1980. *Journal of Marriage and the Family, 48,* 423–434.

Haas, L. (1980). Role-Sharing Couples: A Study of Egalitarian Marriages. *Family Relations, 29,* 289–296.

Haas, L. (1982). Determinants of Role Sharing Behavior: A Case Study of Egalitarian Couples. *Sex Roles, 8,* 747–760.

Habakkuk, H. J. (1955). Family Structure and Economic Change in Nineteenth-Century Europe. *The Journal of Economic History, 15,* 1–12.

Hafstrom, J. L., & Dunsing, M. M. (1965). A Comparison of Economic Choices in One-Earner and Two-Earner Families. *Journal of Marriage and the Family, 27.*

Hagestad, G. O. (1987). Able Elderly in the Family Context: Changes, Chances, and Challenges. *Gerontologist, 27,* 417–422.

Hagstrom, W. O., & Hadden, J. K. (1965). Sentiment and Kinship Terminology in American Society. *Journal of Marriage and the Family, 27,* 324–332.

Halem, L. C. (1980). *Divorce Reform: Changing Legal and Social Perspectives.* New York: Free Press.

Halem, L. C. (1982). *Separated and Divorced Women.* Westport: Greenwood.

Haley, A. (1974). *Roots.* Garden City, NY: Doubleday.

Hampton, R. L., Gelles, R. J., & Harrop, J. W. (1989). Is Violence in Black Families Increasing? A Comparison of 1975 and 1985 Survey Rates. *Journal of Marriage and the Family, 51,* 969–980.

Handlin, O. (1941). *Boston's Immigrants.* Cambridge, MA: Harvard University Press.

Handlin, O. (1951). *The Uprooted.* Boston: Little, Brown.

Handlin, O., & Handlin, M. F. (1971). *Facing Life: Youth and the Family in American History.* Boston: Little, Brown.

Hanifi, M. J. (1978). The Family in Afghanistan. in Das & Bardis (Eds.), *The Family in Asia.* New Delhi: Vikas.

Hanson, S. L., Myers, D. E., & Ginsburg, A. L. (1987). The Role of Responsibility and Knowledge in Reducing Teenage Out-of-Wedlock Childbearing. *Journal of Marriage and the Family, 49,* 241–256.

Hardesty, C., & Bokemeier, J. (1989). Finding Time and Making Do: Distribution of Household Labor in Nonmetropolitan Marriages. *Journal of Marriage and the Family, 51,* 253–267.

Hareven, T. K. (1971). *Anonymous Americans: Explorations in Nineteenth Century Social History.* Englewood Cliffs, NJ: Prentice-Hall.

Hareven, T. K. (1977). Family Time and Historical Time. *Daedalus* (Spring).

Hareven, T. K. (1978). *Transitions: The Family and the Life Course in Historical Perspective.* New York: Academic.

Hareven, T. (1982). *Family Time and Industrial Time.* Cambridge, Eng.: University of Cambridge Press.

Harkins, E. B. (1978). Effects of Empty Nest Transition on Self-Report of Psychological and Physical Well-Being. *Journal of Marriage and the Family, 40.*

Harriman, L. C. (1983). Personal and Marital Changes Accompany Parenthood. *Family Relations, 32.*

Harris, R. J. (1980). An Examination of the Effects of Ethnicity, Socioeconomic Status and Generation on Familism and Sex Role Orientations. *Journal of Comparative Family Studies, 11,* 173–193.

Harris, W. (1976). Work and the Family in Black Atlanta, 1880. *Journal of Social History, 9,* 319–330.

Harry, J. (1976). Evolving Sources of Happiness for Men Over the Life Cycle: A Structural Analysis. *Journal of Marriage and the Family, 38,* 289–296.

Hartman, M., & Hartman, H. (1983). Sex-Role Attitudes of Mormons vs. Non-Mormons in Utah. *Journal of Marriage and the Family, 45,* 897–902.

Hartmann, H. I. (1981). The Family as the Locus of Gender, Class, and Political Struggle: The Example of Housework. *Signs, 6,* 366–394.

Haurin, R. J., & Mott, F. L. (1990). Adolescent Sexual Activity in the Family Context: The Impact of Older Siblings. *Demography, 27,* 537–557.

Haveman, R., Wolfe, B., & Spaulding, J. (1991). Childhood Events and Circumstances Influencing High School Completion. *Demography, 28,* 133–157.

Hawkins, A. J., & Eggebeen, D. J. (1991). Are Fathers Fungible? Patterns of Coresident Adult Men in Maritally Disrupted Families and Young Children's Well Being. *Journal of Marriage and the Family, 53,* 958–972.

Hawkins, J. L., Weisberg, C., & Ray, D. L. (1979). Marital Communication Style and Social Class. in Burr et al. (Eds.), *Contemporary Theories About the Family, Volume I.* New York: Free Press.

Hawkins, J. L., Weisberg, C., & Ray, D. L. (1980). Spouse Differences in Communication Style: Preference, Perception, Behavior. *Journal of Marriage and the Family, 42,* 585–593.

Hayghe, H. V. (1986). Rise in Mothers' Labor Force Activity Includes Those with Infants. *Monthly Labor Review.* Washington, D.C.: Bureau of Labor Statistics, U.S. Department of Labor, 109 (2).

Hayghe, H. V. (1990). Family Members in the Work Force. *Monthly Labor Review.* Washington, D.C.: Bureau of Labor Statistics, U.S. Department of Labor, 113 (3).

Heaton, T. B. (1990). Marital Stability Throughout the Child-Rearing Years. *Demography, 27,* 55–63.

Heer, D. M. (1966). Negro-White Marriage in the United States. *Journal of Marriage and the Family, 28.*

Heer, D. M. (1974). The Prevalence of Black-White Marriage in the United States, 1960 and 1970. *Journal of Marriage and the Family, 36,* 246–258.

Hellebrandt, F. A. (1980). Aging Among the Advantaged: A New Look at the Stereotype of the Elderly. *The Gerontologist, 20,* 404–417.

Hendrick, S. S., & Hendrick, C. (1992). *Liking, Loving and Relating.* Pacific Grove, CA.: Brooks/ Cole.

Henretta, J. A. (1973). The Morphology of New England Society in the Colonial Period. in Rabb & Rotberg (Eds.), *The Family in History.* New York: Harper and Row.

Henry, J. (1963). *Culture Against Man.* New York: Random House.

Herberg, W. (1960). *Protestant-Catholic-Jew.* Garden City, NY: Doubleday.

Herlihy, D. (1983). The Making of the Medieval Family: Symmetry, Structure, and Sentiment. *Journal of Family History, 8.*

Herold, E. S. (1979). Variables Influencing the Dating Adjustment of University Students. *Journal of Youth and Adolescence, 8,* 73–79.

Herold, E. S., & Goodwin, M. S. (1981). Premarital Sexual Guilt and Contraceptive Attitudes and Behavior. *Family Relations, 30.*

Herskovitz, M. J. (1941). *The Myth of the Negro Past.* New York: Harper and Brothers.

Hertz, R. (1986). *More Equal Than Others: Women and Men in Dual-Career Marriages.* Berkeley: University of California Press.

Hertz, R. (1987). Three Careers: His, Hers, and Theirs. in Gerstel & Gross (Eds.), *Families and Work* (pp. 408–421). Philadelphia: Temple University Press.

Hill, C. T., Rubin, Z., & Peplau, L. A. (1976). Breakup Before Marriage: The End of 103 Affairs. *Journal of Social Issues, 32.*

Hill, E. A., & Dorfman, L. T. (1982). Reaction of Housewives to the Retirement of Their Husbands. *Family Relations, 31.*

Hill, R. (1958). Generic Features of Families Under Stress. *Social Casework, 39.*

Hill, W., & Scanzoni, J. (1982). An Approach for Assessing Marital Decision-Making Processes. *Journal of Marriage and the Family, 44,* 927–941.

Hiller, D. V., & Dyehouse, J. (1987). A Case for Banishing "Dual-Career Marriages" from the Research Literature. *Journal of Marriage and the Family, 49,* 787–795.

Hiller, D. V., & Philliber, W. W. (1982). Predicting Marital and Career Success Among Dual-Worker Couples. *Journal of Marriage and the Family, 44.*

Hiller, D. V., & Philliber, W. W. (1986). Determinants of Social Class Identification for Dual-Earner Couples. *Journal of Marriage and the Family, 48,* 583–587.

Hilton, J. M. (1990). Differences in Allocation of Family Time Spent on Household Tasks Among Single-Parent, One-Earner, and Two-Earner Families. *Lifestyles, 11,* 283–298.

Hilton, J. M., & Haldeman, V. A. (1991). Gender Differences in the Performance of Household Tasks by Adults and Children in Single-Parent and Two-Parent, Two-Earner Families. *Journal of Family Issues, 12,* 114–130.

Hilton, N. Z. (1992). Battered Women's Concerns About Their Children Witnessing Wife Assault. *Journal of Interpersonal Violence, 7,* 77–86.

Himmelhoch, J., & Fava, S. F. (1955). *Sexual Behavior in American Society.* New York: Norton.

Hite, S. (1987). *Women and Love—A Cultural Revolution in Progress.* New York: Alfred E. Knopf.

Hobart, C. (1987). Parent-Child Relations in Remarried Families. *Journal of Family Issues, 8,* 259–277.

Hobart, C. (1990). Relationships Between the Formerly Married. *Journal of Comparative Family Studies, 21,* 81–97.

Hobart, C. (1992). How They Handle It: Young Canadians, Sex, and AIDS. *Youth and Society, 23,* 411–433.

Hobbs, E. C. (1970). An Alternative Model From a Theological Perspective. in Otto (Ed.), *The Family in Search of a Future.* New York: Appleton-Century-Crofts.

Hochschild, A. R. (1975). Disengagement Theory: A Critique and Proposal. *American Sociological Review, 40,* 553–569.

Hochschild, A., with Machung, A. (1989). *The Second Shift.* New York: Avon.

Hoelter, J., & Harper, L. (1987). Structural and Interpersonal Family Influences on Adolescent Self-Conception. *Journal of Marriage and the Family, 49,* 129–139.

Hofferth, S. L. (1983). Childbearing Decision Making and Family Well-Being: A Dynamic, Sequential Model. *American Sociological Review, 48,* 533–545.

Hofferth, S. L. (1985). Updating Children's Life Course. *Journal of Marriage and the Family, 47,* 93–115.

Hofferth, S. L., & Phillips, D. A. (1987). Child Care in the United States, 1970 to 1995. *Journal of Marriage and the Family, 49,* 559–571.

Hoffman, L. W. (1972). Early Childhood Experiences and Women's Achievement Motives. *Journal of Social Issues, 28.*

Holden, G. W., & Ritchie, K. L. (1991) Linking Extreme Marital Discord, Child Rearing, and Child Behavior Problems: Evidence from Battered Women. *Child Development, 62,* 311–327.

Hollander, J., & Shafer, L. (1981). Males Acceptance of Female Career Roles. *Sex Roles, 7,* 1189–1203.

Holman, T. B., & Burr, W. R. (1980). Beyond the Beyond: The Growth of Family Theories in the 1970s. *Journal of Marriage and the Family, 42.*

Horn, M. (1983). "Sisters Worthy of Respect": Family Dynamics and Women's Roles in the Blackwell Family. *Journal of Family History, 8,* 367–382.

Hornung, C. A., McCullough, B. C., & Taichi Sugimoto. (1981). Status Relationships in Marriage: Risk Factors in Spouse Abuse. *Journal of Marriage and the Family, 43,* 675–692.

Howard, J. A., Blumstein, P., & Schwartz, P. (1986). Sex, Power, and Influence Tactics in Intimate Relationships. *Journal of Personality and Social Psychology, 51,* 102–109.

Huang-Hickrod, L. J., & Leonard, W. M., II. (1980). A Quasi-Longitudinal Study of Students' Attitudes Toward Cohabitation. *International Journal of Sociology of the Family, 10,* 281–300.

Huber, J., & Spitze, G. (1980). Considering Divorce: An Expansion of Becker's Theory of Marital Instability. *American Journal of Sociology, 86,* 75–89.

Hunt, M. M. (1959). *The Natural History of Love.* New York: Knopf.

Huttman, E. (1991). A Research Note on the Dreams and Aspirations of Black Families. *Journal of Comparative Family Studies, 22,* 147–158.

Ikels, C. (1988). Delayed Reciprocity and the Support Networks of the Childless Elderly. *Journal of Comparative Family Studies, 19.*

Imig, D. R. (1981). Accumulated Stress of Life Changes and Interpersonal Effectiveness in the Family. *Family Relations, 30,* 367–371.

Ingoldsby, B. B. (1991). The Latin American Family: Familism Vs. Machismo. *Journal of Comparative Family Studies, 22,* 57–62.

Irving, W. (1920). *The Legend of Sleepy Hollow.* London: MacMillan.

Jackson, J. K. (1962). Alcoholism and the Family. in Pitman & Snyder (Eds.), *Society, Culture, and Drinking Patterns.* New York: Wiley.

Jacobsen, R. B., & Bigner, J. J. (1991). Black Versus White Single Parents and the Value of Children. *Journal of Black Studies, 21,* 302–312.

Jacobson, P. H. (1959). *American Marriage and Divorce.* New York: Rinehart and Company.

Jaffe, D. F., & Kanter, R. M. (1976). Couple Strains in Communal Households: A Four-Factor Model of Separation Process. *Journal of Social Issues, 32,* 169–192.

Jaffee, F., & Dryfoos, J. (1976). Fertility Control Services for Adolescents: Access and Utilization, *Family Planning Perspectives, 8.*

Janeway, E. (1971). *Man's World, Woman's Place: A Study of Social Mythology.* New York: Dell.

Jaramillo, P. T., & Zapata, J. T. (1987). Roles and Alliances within Mexican-American and Anglo Families. *Journal of Marriage and the Family, 49,* 727–735.

Jarrett, W. H. (1985). Caregiving Within Kinship Systems: Is Affection Really Necessary? *Gerontologists, 25,* 5–10.

Jasso, G. (1985). Marital Coital Frequency and the Passage of Time: Estimating and Separate Effects of Spouses' Ages and Marital Duration, Birth and Marriage Cohorts, and Period Influences. *American Sociological Review, 50,* 224–241.

Johnson, C. L. (1988). *Ex Familia—Grandparents, Parents, and Children Adjust to Divorce.* New Brunswick, NJ: Rutgers University Press.

Johnson, C. L., & Barer, B. M. (1990). Families and Networks Among Older Inner-City Blacks. *Gerontologist, 50,* 726–733.

Johnson, J. H. (1986). *Life Events as Stressors in Childhood and Adolescence.* Newbury Park, CA: Sage.

Johnston, J. R. (1990). Role Diffusion and Role Reversal: Structural Variation in Divorced Families and Children's Functioning. *Family Relations, 39,* 405–413.

Jones, E., Forrest, J. D., Goldman, N., Henshaw, S. K., Lincoln, R., Rosoff, J., Westoff, C., & Wulf, D. (1985). Teenage Pregnancy in Developed Countries: Determinants and Policy Implications. *Family Planning Perspectives, 17,* 53–63.

Jorgensen, D. E. (1977). The Effects of Social Position, and Wife/Mother Employment on Family Leisure Time: A Study of Fathers. *International Journal of Sociology of the Family, 7,* 197–208.

Jorgenson, S. R., King, S. L., & Torrey, B. A. (1980). Dyadic and Social Network Influences on Adolescent Exposure to Pregnancy Risk. *Journal of Marriage and the Family, 42,* 141–155.

Jourard, S. M. (1970). Reinventing Marriage: The Perspective of a Psychologist. in Otto (Ed.), *The Family in Search of a Future.* New York: Appleton-Century-Crofts.

Juster, S. M., & Vinovskis, M. A. (1987). Changing Perspectives on the American Family in the Past. *Annual Review of Sociology, 13,* 193–216.

Kagan, J. (1977). The Child in the Family. *Daedalus* (Spring).

Kahn, J. R., & London, K. A. (1991). Premarital Sex and the Risk of Divorce. *Journal of Marriage and the Family, 53,* 845–855.

Kalmuss, D. S., & Straus, M. A. (1982). Wife's Marital Dependency and Wife Abuse. *Journal of Marriage and the Family, 44,* 277–286.

Kamo, Yoshinori. (1988). Determinants of Household Division of Labor: Resources, Power, and Ideology. *Journal of Family Issues, 9,* 177–200.

Kantor, D., & Lehr, W. (1975). *Inside the Family: Toward a Theory of Family Process.* New York: Harper and Row.

Kassell, V. (1970). Polygyny After Sixty. in Otto (Ed.), *The Family in Search of a Future* (pp. 137–144). New York: Appleton-Century-Crofts.

Katsche, P. (1983). Household and Family in Hispanic Northern New Mexico. *Journal of Comparative Family Studies, 14,* 151–165.

Katz, A. M., & Hill, R. (1958). Residential Propinquity and Marital Selection: A Review of Theory, Method, and Fact. *Marriage and Family Living, 20,* 27–35.

Keith, P. M. (1983). A Comparison of the Resources of Parents and Childless Men and Women in Very Old Age. *Family Relations, 32,* 403–409.

Keith, P. M., & Brubaker, T. H. (1979). Male Household Roles in Later Life: A Look at Masculinity and Marital Relationships. *The Family Coordinator, 28,* 497–502.

Keith, P. M., & Schafer, R. B. (1987). Relative Deprivation, Equity/Inequity, and Psychological Well-Being: Men and Women in One- and Two-Job Families. *Journal of Family Issues, 8,* 199–211.

Keller, S. (1991). The American Upper Class Family: Precarious Claims on the Future. *Journal of Comparative Family Studies, 22,* 159–182.

Kelley, H. H. (1981). Marriage Relationships and Aging. in Vogel et al. (Eds.), *Aging.* New York: Academic.

Kelly, C., Huston, T., & Cate, R. M. (1985). Premarital Relationship Correlates of the Erosion of Satisfaction in Marriage. *Journal of Social and Personal Relationships, 2,* 167–178.

Kelly, C., & Goodwin, G. C. (1983). Adolescents' Perceptions of Three Styles of Parental Control. *Adolescence, 18,* 567–571.

Kerckhoff, A. (1974). The Social Context of Interpersonal Attraction. In Huston, (Ed.), *Foundations of Interpersonal Attraction.* New York: Academic.

Kerckhoff, A., & Davis, K. E. (1962). Value Consensus and Need Complementarity in Mate Selection. *American Sociological Review, 27,* 295–303.

Kessler, R. C., & Essex, M. (1982). Marital Status and Depression: The Importance of Coping Resources. *Social Forces, 61,* 484–507.

Kett, J. F. (1973). Adolescence and Youth in Nineteenth-Century America. in Rabb & Rotberg (Eds.), *The Family in History.* New York: Harper and Row.

Kharchev, A. G. (1964). *Brak i sem'ia v SSSR.* Moscow: Oypt sotsiologicheskogo issledovaniia.

Kiecolt, K. J., & Acock, A. C. (1988). The Long-term Effects of Family Structure on Gender-Role Attitudes. *Journal of Marriage and the Family, 50,* 709–717.

Kiernan, K. E. (1986). Teenage Marriage and Marital Breakdown: A Longitudinal Study. *Population Studies, 40,* 35–54.

Kikumura, A., & Kitano, H. H. L. (1973). Interracial Marriage: A Picture of the Japanese-Americans. *Journal of Social Issues, 29,* 67–81.

Kinsey, A. C., et al. (1948). *Sexual Behavior in the Human Male.* Philadelphia: Saunders.

Kinsey, A. C., et al. (1953). *Sexual Behavior in the Human Female.* Philadelphia: Saunders.

Kirkendall, L. A. (1984). Family Options, Governments, and the Social Milieu: Viewed from the Twenty-First Century. in Kirkendall & Gravatt (Eds.), *Marriage and the Family in the Year 2020* (pp. 247–267). Buffalo: Prometheus.

Kirkendall, L. A., & Gravatt, A. E. (Eds.). (1984). *Marriage and the Family in the Year 2020.* Buffalo: Prometheus.

Kirshner, S. G. (1978–79). Child Custody Determination—A Better Way! *Journal of Family Law, 17,* 275–296.

Kitson, G. C., Babri, K. B., & Roach, M. J. (1985). Who Divorces and Why. *Journal of Family Issues, 6,* 255–293.

Kitson, G., with Holmes, W. (1992). *Portrait of Divorce: Adjustment to Marital Breakdown.* New York: Guilford.

Klein, D. M., & Hill, R. (1979). Determinants of Family Problem-Solving Effectiveness. in Burr et al. (Eds.), *Contemporary Theories About the Family, Volume I.* New York: Free Press.

Klein, D. M., & Jurich, J. A. (1993). Metatheory and Family Studies. in P. Boss et al. (Eds.), *Sourcebook of Family Theories and Methods.* New York: Plenum.

Klein, H. (1990). Adolescence, Youth and Young Adulthood—Rethinking Current Conceptualizations of Life Stage. *Youth and Society, 21,* 446–471.

Kline, M., Tschann, J. M., Johnston, J. R., & Wallerstein, J. S. (1989). Children's Adjustments in Joint and Sole Physical Custody Families. *Developmental Psychology, 25,* 430–438.

Kline, M., Johnston, J. R., & Tschann, J. M. (1991). The Long Shadow of Marital Conflict:

A Model of Children's Post-divorce Adjustment. *Journal of Marriage and the Family, 55,* 297–309.

Knox, D. (1980). Trends in Marriage and the Family—the 1980s. *Family Relations, 29,* 145–150.

Knox, D., & Wilson, K. (1981). Dating Behaviors of University Students. *Family Relations, 39,* 255–258.

Koenig, H. G., George, L. K., & Siegler, I. C. (1988). The Use of Religion and Other Emotion-Regulating Coping Strategies Among Older Adults. *Gerontologist, 28,* 303–310.

Kolbe, R., & LaVoie, J. C. (1981). Sex-Role Stereotyping in Preschool Children's Picture Books. *Social Psychology Quarterly, 44,* 369–374.

Komarovsky, M. (1950). Functional Analysis of Sex Roles. *American Sociological Review, 15,* 508–516.

Komarovsky, M. (1967). *Blue-Collar Marriage.* New York: Random House, Vintage Books.

Komter, A. (1989). Hidden Power in Marriage. *Gender and Society, 3,* 187–216.

Koo, H. P., Suchindran, C. M., & Griffith, J. D. (1987). The Completion of Childbearing: Change and Variation in Timing. *Journal of Marriage and the Family, 49,* 281–293.

Korenman, S., & Neumark, D. (1992). Marriage, Motherhood, and Wages. *The Journal of Human Resources, 27,* 233–255.

Korman, S. K. (1983). Nontraditional Dating Behavior: Date-Initiation and Date Expense-Sharing Among Feminists and Non-Feminists. *Family Relations, 52.*

Koyle, P. F. C., Olsen, J., Jensen, L. C., & Cundick, B. (1989). Comparison of Sexual Behaviors Among Adolescents Having an Early, Middle, and Late First Intercourse Experience. *Youth and Society, 20,* 461–476.

Krain, M. (1977). A Definition of Dyadic Boundaries and an Empirical Study of Boundary Establishment in Courtship. *International Journal of Sociology of the Family, 7.*

Krause, N. (1987). Stress in Racial Differences in Self-Reported Health Among the Elderly. *Gerontologist, 27,* 72–76.

Kresser, K., Jaffee, N., Tuchman, B., Watson, C., & Deutsch, M. (1980). A Typology of Divorcing Couples: Implications for Mediation and the Divorce Process. *Family Process, 19,* 101–116.

Kroeber, A. L. (1952). *The Nature of Culture.* Chicago: University of Chicago Press.

Krokoff, L. J., Gottman, J. M., & Roy, A. K. (1988). Blue-Collar and White-Collar Marital Interaction and Communication Orientation. *Journal of Social and Personal Relationships, 5,* 201–221.

Ku, L. C., Sonenstein, F. N., & Pleck, J. H. (1992). The Association of AIDS Education and Sex Education with Sexual Behavior and Condom Use Among Teenage Men. *Family Planning Perspectives, 24,* 100–106.

Kulik, J. A., & Harackiewicz, J. (1979). Opposite-Sex Interpersonal Attraction as a Function of the Sex-Roles of the Perceiver and the Perceived. *Sex Roles, 5,* 443–452.

Kulis, S. (1987). Socially Mobile Daughters and Sons of the Elderly: Mobility Effects Within the Family Revisited. *Journal of Marriage and the Family, 49,* 421–433.

Kurdek, L. A. (1988). Perceived Social Support in Gays and Lesbians Cohabiting Relationships. *Journal of Personality and Social Psychology, 54,* 504–509.

Kurdek, L. A. (1989). Relationship Quality in Gay and Lesbian Cohabiting Couples: A One Year Follow-Up Study. *Journal of Social and Personal Relationships, 6,* 39–59.

Kurdek, L. A. (1990). Effects of Child Age on the Marital Quality and Psychological Distress of Newly Married Mothers and Stepfathers. *Journal of Marriage and the Family, 52,* 81–85.

Kurdek, L. A. (1991). Marital Stability and Changes in Marital Quality in Newly Wed Couples: A Test of the Contextual Model. *Journal of Social and Personal Relationships, 8,* 27–48.

Kurdek, L. A. (1992). Relationship Stability and Relationship Satisfaction in Cohabiting Gay and Lesbian Couples: A Prospective Longitudinal Test of the Contextual and Interdependence Models. *Journal of Social and Personal Relationships, 9,* 125–142.

Kushner, P. I. (1956). O Nekotorykh protsessakh priozkhodiashchikh v sovremennoi Kolkhoznoi sem'e. *Sovetskaia Etnographia, 3.*

Ladewig, B. H., McGee, G. W., & Nevill, W. (1990). Life Strains and Depression Affect Among Women: Moderating Effects of Social Support. *Journal of Family Issues, 11,* 36–47.

Ladner, J. A. (1971). *Tomorrow's Tomorrow: The Black Woman.* Garden City, NJ: Doubleday.

Laidig, G. L., Schutjer, W. A., & Stokes, G. S. (1981). Agricultural Variation and Human Fertility in Antebellum Pennsylvania. *Journal of Family History, 6,* 195–204.

Laing, R. D. (1969). *Self and Others.* New York: Pantheon.

Laing, R. D. (1971). *The Politics of the Family and Other Essays.* New York: Pantheon.

Laing, R. D., & Esterson, A. (1964). *Sanity, Madness, and the Family.* London: Tavistock.

Lamb, M. (1987). Introduction: the Emergent American Father, in Lamb (Ed.), *The Father's Role—Cross-Cultural Perspectives* (pp. 1–18). Hillsdale, NJ: Erlbaum.

Lamb, M., & Sutton-Smith, B. (1982). *Sibling Relationships: Their Nature and Significance Across the Life Span.* Hillsdale, NJ: Erlbaum.

Landale, N. S. (1989). Opportunity, Movement and Marriage: U.S. Farm Sons at the Turn of the Century. *Journal of Family History, 14,* 365–386.

Landale, N. S., & Tolnay, S. E. (1991). Group Differences in Economic Opportunity and the Timing of Marriage: Blacks and Whites in the Rural South, 1910. *American Sociological Review, 56,* 33–45.

Landis, J. T., & Landis, M. G. (1963). *Building a Successful Marriage.* Englewood Cliffs, NJ: Prentice-Hall.

Lantz, H., & O'Hara, M. (1977). The Jewish Family in Early America. *International Journal of Sociology of the Family, 7.*

Lantz, H. R., Schmitt, R. L., & Herman, R. (1973). The Preindustrial Family in America: A Further Examination of Early Magazines. *American Journal of Sociology, 79.*

LaRossa, R. (1983). The Transition to Parenthood and the Social Reality of Time. *Journal of Marriage and the Family, 45.*

Larson, J. H. (1987). A Comparison of Intimacy in First-Married and Remarried Couples. *Journal of Family Issues, 8,* 319–331.

Larson, L. E., & Munro, B. (1990). Religious Intermarriage in Canada in the 1980s. *Journal of Comparative Family Studies, 21,* 239–250.

Larson, R. W. (1983). Adolescents' Daily Experience With Family and Friends: Contrasting Opportunity Systems. *Journal of Marriage and the Family, 45,* 739–750.

Lasch, C. (1977). *Haven in a Heartless World: The Family Besieged.* New York: Basic Books.

Laska, S. B., & Micklin, M. (1981). Modernization, the Family, and Work Socialization: A Comparative Study of U.S. and Colombian Youth. *Journal of Comparative Family Studies, 12,* 187–204.

Laslett, B. (1973). The Family as a Public and Private Institution: A Historical Perspective. *Journal of Marriage and the Family, 35,* 480–492.

Laslett, P. (1965). *The World We Have Lost.* New York: Scribner's.

Laslett, P. (1973). Age at Menarche in Europe Since the Eighteenth Century. in Rabb & Rotberg (Eds.), *The Family in History.* New York: Harper and Row.

Laslett, P. (1977). *Family Life and Illicit Love in Earlier Generations: Essays on Historical Sociology.* New York: Cambridge University Press.

Laslett, P., & Wall, R., Eds. (1972). *Household and Family in Past Time.* New York: Cambridge University Press.

Lauer, R. H., & Lauer, J. C. (1986). Factors in Long-Term Marriages. *Journal of Family Issues, 7,* 382–390.

Launius, M. H., & Lindquist, C. U. (1988). Learned Helplessness, External Locus of Control, and Passivity in Battered Women. *Journal of Interpersonal Violence, 3,* 307–318.

Lavee, Y., McCubbin, H. I., & Olson, D. H. (1987). The Effect of Stressful Life Events and Transitions on Family Functioning and Well-Being. *Journal of Marriage and the Family, 49,* 857–873.

Lavee, Y., McCubbin, H. I., & Patterson, J. M. (1985). The Double ABCX Model of Family Stress and Adaptation: An Empirical Test by Analysis of Structural Equations with Latent Variables. *Journal of Marriage and the Family, 47,* 811–825.

Lavee, Y., & Olson, D. H. (1991). Family Types and Response to Stress. *Journal of Marriage and the Family, 53,* 786–798.

Layard, J. (1942). *Stone Men of Malekula.* London: Chatto and Windus.

Lazar, R. J. (1978). Asian Family and Society—A Theoretical Overview. in Das & Bardis (Eds.), *The Family in Asia.* New Delhi: Vikas.

Lee, G. (1978). Marriage and Morale in Later Life. *Journal of Marriage and the Family, 40.*

Lee, G. R. (1979). Marital Structure and Economic Systems. *Journal of Marriage and the Family, 41,* 701–713.

Lee, G. R. (1980). Kinship in the Seventies: A Decade Review of Research and Theory. *Journal of Marriage and the Family, 42.*

Lee, G. R. (1988). Marital Satisfaction in Later Life: The Effects on Nonmarital Roles. *Journal of Marriage and the Family, 50,* 775–783.

Lee, G. R., & Stone, L. H. (1980). Mate-Selection Systems and Criteria: Variation According to Family Structure. *Journal of Marriage and the Family, 42,* 319–326.

Lee, G. R., & Whitbeck, L. B. (1990). Economic Systems and Rates of Polygyny. *Journal of Comparative Family Studies, 21,* 13–25.

Leichter, H. J., & Mitchell, W. E. (1967). *Kinship and Casework.* New York: Russell Sage Foundation.

LeMaster, E. E. (1957). Parenthood as Crisis. *Marriage and Family Living, 19,* 352–355.

LeMaster, E. E. (1974). *Parents in Modern America.* Homewood, IL.: Dorsey.

Lerner, G. (1986). *The Creation of Patriarchy.* Oxford, Eng.: Oxford University Press.

Leslie, L. A., & Anderson, E. A. (1988). Men's and Women's Participation in Domestic Roles: Impact on Quality of Life and Marital Adjustment. *Journal of Family Psychology, 2,* 212–226.

Leslie, L. A., Huston, T. L., & Johnson, M. P. (1986). Parental Reactions to Dating Relationships: Do They Make a Difference? *Journal of Marriage and the Family, 48,* 57–66.

Levinger, G. (1965). Marital Cohesiveness and Dissolution: An Integrative Review. *Journal of Marriage and the Family, 27,* 19–28.

Levinger, G. (1966). Sources of Marital Dissatisfaction Among Applicants for Divorce. *American Journal of Orthopsychiatry, 32,* 803–807.

Levinger, G., Senn, D. J., & Jorgensen, B. W. (1970). Progress Toward Permanence in Courtship: A Test of the Kerckhoff-Davis Hypothesis. *Sociometry, 33,* 427–443.

Lewis, P. H. (1983). Innovative Divorce Rituals: Their Psycho-Social Functions. *Journal of Divorce, 6,* 71–81.

Lewis, R. A. (1972). Satisfaction with Conjugal Power over the Family Life Cycle. (Paper delivered at the National Council on Family Relations meetings, October 31).

Lewis, R. (1973). A Longitudinal Test of a Developmental Framework for Premarital Dyadic Formation. *Journal of Marriage and the Family, 35,* 16–25.

Lewis, R. A., & Spanier, G. B. (1979). Theorizing about the Quality and Stability of Marriage. in Burr et al. (Eds.), *Contemporary Theories About the Family, Volume 1.* New York: Free Press.

Li, J. T., & Caldwell, R. A. (1987). Magnitude and Directional Effects of Marital Sex-Role Incongruence on Marital Adjustment. *Journal of Family Issues, 8,* 97–110.

Lichter, D. T. (1990). Delayed Marriage, Marital Homogamy, and the Mate Selection Process Among White Females. *Social Science Quarterly, 71,* 802–811.

Lichter, D. T., LeClere, F. B., & McLaughlin, D. K. (1991). Local Marriage Markets and the Marital Behavior of Black and White Women. *American Journal of Sociology, 96,* 843–867.

Lieblich, A., Friedman, G. (1985). Attitudes Toward Male and Female Homosexuality and Sex Role Stereotypes in Israeli and American Students. *Sex Roles, 12,* 561–570.

Liker, J. K., & Elder, G. H., Jr. (1983). Economic Hardship and Marital Relations in the 1930s. *American Sociological Review, 48,* 343–359.

Liston, A., & Salts, C. J. (1988). Mate Selection Values: A Comparison of Malaysian and U.S. Students. *Journal of Comparative Family Studies, 19,* 361–369.

Litwak, E., & Kulis, S. (1987). Technology, Proximity, and Measures of Kin Support. *Journal of Marriage and the Family, 49,* 649–661.

Lo, C. C., & Globetti, G. (1991). Parents Noticing Teenage Drinking: Evidence from College Freshmen. *Sociology and Social Research, 76*, 20–29.

Lockhart, L. L. (1987). A Reexamination of the Effects of Race and Social Class on the Incidence of Marital Violence: A Search for Reliable Differences. *Journal of Marriage and the Family, 49*, 603–610.

Lockhart, L., & White, B. W. (1989). Understanding Marital Violence in the Black Community. *Journal of Interpersonal Violence, 4*, 421–436.

Locksley, A. (1982). Social Class and Marital Attitudes and Behavior. *Journal of Marriage and the Family, 44*.

Loewenstein, S. F., Bloch, N. E., Campion, J., Epstein, J. S., Gale, P., & Salvatore, M. (1981). A Study of Satisfactions and Stresses of Single Women in Midlife. *Sex Roles, 7*, 1127–1141.

Longino, C. F., Jr. (1986). A State by State Look at the Oldest Americans. *American Demographics, 8*, 38–42.

Longino, C. F., Jr., & Lipman, A. (1981). Married and Spouseless Men and Women in Planned Retirement Communities: Support Network Differentials. *Journal of Marriage and the Family, 43*, 169–177.

Lowery, C. R. (1985). Child Custody in Divorce: Parents' Decisions and Perceptions. *Family Relations, 34*, 241–249.

Lowie, R. (1920). *Primitive Society*. New York: Boni and Liveright.

Lueptow, L. B. (1980). Social Change and Sex Role Change in Adolescent Orientations Toward Life, Work, and Achievement: 1964–1975. *Social Psychology Quarterly, 43*, 48–59.

Lueptow, L. B. (1984). *Adolescent Sex Roles and Social Change*. New York: Columbia University Press.

Lundberg, F., & Farnham, M. (1947). *Modern Woman: the Lost Sex*. New York: Harper and Row.

Lune, K. E., & Gwartney-Gibbs, P. A. (1985). Violence in the Context of Dating and Sex. *Journal of Family Issues, 6*, 45–59.

Lutz, P. (1983). The Stepfamily: An Adolescent Perspective. *Family Relations, 32*, 367–375.

Lydon, S. (1972). The Politics of Orgasm. in Bell & Gordon (Eds.), *The Social Dimension of Human Sexuality*. Boston: Little, Brown.

MacDermid, S. M., Huston, T. L., & McHale, S. M. (1990). Changes in Marriage Associated with the Transition to Parenthood: Individual Differences as a Function of Sex-Role Attitudes and Changes in the Division of Household Labor. *Journal of Marriage and the Family, 52*, 475–486.

MacKinnon, C. E. (1988). Influences on Sibling Relations in Families With Married and Divorced Parents: Family Form or Family Quality? *Journal of Family Issues, 9*, 469–477.

Macklin, E. (1980). Nontraditional Family Forms: A Decade of Research. *Journal of Marriage and the Family, 42*, 905–923.

Maddock, J. W., Hogan, J. M., Antonov, A. I., & Matskovsky, M. S., Eds. (1993) *Perestroika and Family Life: Post-U.S.S.R. and U.S. Perspectives*. New York: Guilford.

Maddock, J. W., & Kon, I. S. (1993). Sexuality and Family Life. in Maddock et al. (Eds.), *Perestroika and Family Life*. New York: Guilford.

Major, B. (1979). Sex Role Orientation and Fear of Success: Clarifying an Unclear Relationship. *Sex Roles, 5*, 63–70.

Makepeace, J. M. (1981). Courtship Violence Among College Students. *Family Relations, 30*, 97–102.

Makepeace, J. M. (1983). Life Events Stress and Courtship Violence. *Family Relations, 32*, 101–109.

Malinowski, B. (1927). *Sex and Repression in Savage Society*. London: Routledge and Kegan Paul.

Malinowski, B. (1929). *The Sexual Life of Savages in Northwestern Melanesia*. New York: Liveright.

Mare, R. D. (1991). Five Decades of Educational Assortative Mating. *American Sociological Review, 56*, 15–32.

Markowski, E. M., & Johnston, M. J. (1980). Behavior, Temperament, Perceived Temperament and Idealization of Cohabiting Couples Who Married. *International Journal of Sociology of the Family, 10*, 115–125.

Marotz-Baden, R., Adams, G. R., Bueche, N., Munro, B., & Munro, G. (1979). Family Form or Family Process: Reconsidering the Deficit Family Model Approach. *The Family Coordinator, 28*, 5–14.

Martin, M. J., & Walters, J. (1982). Familial Correlates of Selected Types of Child Abuse and Neglect. *Journal of Marriage and the Family, 44*, 267–276.

Martin, T. C., & Bumpass, L. L. (1989). Recent Trends in Marital Demography. *Demography, 26*, 37–51.

Mason, K. O., & Yu-Hsia Lu. (1988). Attitudes Toward Women's Familial Role: Changes in the United States, 1977–1985. *Gender and Society, 2*, 39–57.

Mason, K. O., Vinovskis, M. A., & Hareven, T. (1978). Women's Work and the Life Course in Essex Co., Mass., 1880. in Hareven (Ed.), *Transitions*. New York: Academic.

Masters, W. H., & Johnson, V. E. (1966). *Human Sexual Response*. New York: Bantam.

Maticka-Tyndale, E. (1991). Modification of Sexual Activities in the Era of AIDS: A Trend Analysis of Adolescent Sexual Activities. *Youth and Society, 23*, 31–49.

Matsueda, R. L., & Heimer, K. (1987). Race, Family Structure and Delinquency: A Test of Differential Association and Social Control Theories. *American Sociological Review, 52*, 826–840.

Matthaei, J. (1982). *An Economic History of Women in America*. New York: Schocken.

Matthews, R., & Matthews, A. M. (1986). Infertility and Involuntary Childlessness: The Transition to Nonparenthood. *Journal of Marriage and the Family, 48*, 641–649.

Mauldon, J. (1990). The Effect of Marital Disruption on Children's Health. *Demography, 27*, 431–446.

May, K. A. (1982). Factors Contributing to First-Time Fathers' Readiness for Fatherhood: An Exploratory Study. *Family Relations, 31*, 353–361.

Maykovich, M. K. (1976). Attitudes Versus Behavior in Extramarital Sexual Relations. *Journal of Marriage and the Family, 58*.

Mayolin, L. (1989). Gender and the Prerogatives of Dating and Marriage: An Experimental Assessment of a Sample of College Students. *Sex Roles, 20*, 91–102.

McAdoo, H. P. (1978). Factors Related to Stability in Upwardly Mobile Black Families. *Journal of Marriage and the Family, 40*.

McAdoo, H. P. (1982). Stress Absorbing Systems in Black Families. *Family Relations, 31.*

McCracken, G. (1983). The Exchange of Children in Tudor England: An Anthropological Phenomenon in Historical Context. *Journal of Family History, 8,* 303–313.

McCubbin, H. I., Joy, C. B., Cauble, A. E., Comeau, J. K., Patterson, J. M., & Needle, R. H. (1980). Family Stress and Coping: A Decade Review. *Journal of Marriage and the Family, 42.*

McCubbin, H. I., & Patterson, J. M., (1982). Family Adaptation to Crisis. in McCubbin et al. (Eds.), *Family Stress, Coping, and Social Support* (pp. 26–47). Springfield, IL.: Charles C. Thomas.

McDaniel, C. O. (1969). Dating Roles and Reasons for Dating. *Journal of Marriage and the Family, 31.*

McDonald, G. W. (1981). Structural Exchange and Marital Interaction. *Journal of Marriage and the Family, 43,* 825–839.

McEnroe, J. (1991). Split-Shift Parenting. *American Demographics, 13,* 50–52.

McGoldrick, M. (1989). "Women through the Family Life Cycle. in McGoldrick et al. (Eds.), *Women in Families* (pp. 200–226). New York: Norton.

McGraw, R. E., Sterin, G. J., & Davis, J. M. (1981–82). A Case Study in Divorce Law Reform and Its Aftermath. *Journal of Family Law, 20,* 443–487.

McHale, S. M., & Huston, T. L. (1985). The Effect of the Transition to Parenthood on the Marriage Relationship. *Journal of Family Issues, 6,* 409–433.

McLanahan, S. (1983). Family Structure and Stress: A Longitudinal Comparison of Two-Parent and Female-Headed Families, *Journal of Marriage and the Family, 45,* 347–357.

McLanahan, S., Wedemeyer, N. V., & Adelberg, T. (1981). Network Structure, Social Support, and Psychological Well-Being in the Single-Parent Family. *Journal of Marriage and the Family, 43,* 601–612.

McLaughlin, S. D., & Micklin, M. (1983). The Timing of the First Birth and Changes in Personal Efficacy. *Journal of Marriage and the Family, 45,* 47–55.

McLaughlin, V. Y. (1973). Patterns of Work and Family Organization: Buffalo's Italians. in Rabb & Rotberg (Eds.), *The Family in History.* New York: Harper and Row.

McLoyd, V. C. (1990). The Impact of Economic Hardship on Black Families and Children: Psychological Distress, Parenting and Socio-Emotional Development. *Child Development, 61,* 311–346.

McNall, S. G., & McNall, S. A. (1983). *Plains Families: Exploring Sociology Through Social History.* New York: St. Martin's.

Mead, M. (1950). *Sex and Temperament.* New York: New American Library, Mentor Books.

Mead, M. (1958). Adolescence in Primitive and Modern Society. in Maccoby et al. (Eds.), *Readings in Social Psychology.* New York: Henry Holt.

Mead, M. (1970). Marriage in Two Steps. in Otto (Ed.), *The Family in Search of a Future* (pp. 75–84). New York: Appleton-Century-Crofts.

Menaghan, E. (1983). Marital Stress and Family Transitions: A Panel Analysis. *Journal of Marriage and the Family, 45,* 371–386.

Menaghan, E. G. (1985). Depressive Affect and Subsequent Divorce. *Journal of Family Issues, 6,* 295–306.

Mill, J. S. (1859). On Liberty. In *Great Books of the Western World, Volume 43.* Chicago: Encyclopedia Britannica (1971).

Miller, B. C., & Heaton, T. B. (1991). Age at First Intercourse and the Timing of Marriage and Childbirth. *Journal of Marriage and the Family, 53,* 719–732.

Miller, B. C., & Sollie, D. L. (1980). Normal Stresses During the Transition to Parenthood. *Family Relations, 29,* 459–465.

Miller, L. J. (1990). Violent Families and the Rhetoric of Harmony. *British Journal of Sociology, 41,* 263–288.

Miller, Z. L. (1968). *Boss Cox's Cincinnati: Urban Politics in the Progressive Era.* New York: Oxford University Press.

Minkler, M., & Stone, R. (1985). The Feminization of Poverty and Older Women. *Gerontologist, 25,* 351–357.

Mintz, S. (1989). Regulating the American Family. *Journal of Family History, 14,* 387–408.

Mirande, A. (1979). A Reinterpretation of Male Dominance in the Chicano Family. *The Family Coordinator, 28.*

Mischel, H. N. & Fuhr, R. (1988). Maternal Employment: Its Psychological Effects on Children and Their Families. in Dornbusch & Strober (Eds.), *Feminism, Children, and the New Families* (pp. 191–211). New York: Guilford.

Mitterauer, M., & Sieder, R. (1982). *The European Family: Patriarchy to Partnership from the Middle Ages to the Present.* Chicago: University of Chicago Press.

Moch, L. P., Folbre, N., Smith, D. S., Cornell, L. L., & Tilly, L. A. (1987). Family Strategy: A Dialogue. *Historical Methods, 20,* 113–125.

Modell, J. (1980). Normative Aspects of American Marriage Timing Since World War II. *Journal of Family History, 5,* 210–234.

Modell, J., Furstenberg, F. F., Jr., & Hershberg, T. (1976). Social Change and Transitions to Adulthood in Historical Perspective. *Journal of Family History, 7–32.*

Moen, P., & Dempster-McClain, D. I. (1987). Employed Parents: Role Strain, Work Time, and Preferences for Working Less. *Journal of Marriage and the Family, 49,* 579–590.

Moen, P., & Howery, C. B. (1988). The Significance of Time in the Study of Families Under Stress. in Klein & Aldous (Eds.), *Social Stress and Family Development* (pp. 131–156). New York: Guilford.

Monahan, T. P. (1976). An Overview of Statistics on Interracial Marriage in the United States with Data on its Extent from 1963–1970. *Journal of Marriage and the Family, 38,* 223–231.

Montgomery, J., & Fewer, W. (1988). *Family Systems and Beyond.* New York: Human Sciences Press.

Monthly Vital Statistics Report (1993). Births, Marriages, Divorces, and Deaths for September 1992. Washington, D.C.: National Center for Health Statistics (February 16).

Moore, B. (1958). *Political Power and Social Theory.* Cambridge, MA: Harvard University Press.

Moore, D. (1987). Parent-Adolescent Separation: The Construction of Adulthood by Late Adolescents. *Developmental Psychology, 23,* 298–307.

Moore, K. A., Peterson, J. L., & Furstenberg, F. F. (1986). Parental Attitudes and the Occurrence of Early Sexual Activity. *Journal of Marriage and the Family, 48,* 777–782.

Morales, E. S. (1990). Ethnic Minority Families and Minority Gays and Lesbians. in Bozett & Sussman (Eds.), *Homosexuality and Family Relations* (pp. 217–239). New York: Haworth.

Morgan, D. (1989). Adjusting to Widowhood: Do Social Networks Really Make It Easier? *Gerontologist, 29,* 101–107.

Morgan, D. H. J. (1975). *Social Theory and the Family.* London: Routledge and Kegan Paul.

Morgan, D. H. J. (1990). Issues of Critical Sociological Theory: Men in Families. in Sprey (Ed.), *Fashioning Family Theory: New Approaches* (pp. 67–106). Newbury Park, CA.: Sage.

Morgan, L. A. (1980). Work in Widowhood: A Viable Option? *Gerontologist, 20,* 581–587.

Morgan, L. A. (1986). The Financial Experience of Widowed Women: Evidence from the LRHS. *Gerontologist, 26,* 663–668.

Morgan, L. A. (1988). Outcomes of Marital Separation: A Longitudinal Test of Predictors. *Journal of Marriage and the Family, 50,* 493–498.

Morgan, L. A. (1992). Marital Status and Retirement Plans: Do Widowhood and Divorce Make a Difference? in Szinovacz et al. (Eds.), *Families and Retirement* (pp. 114–128). Newbury Park, CA: Sage.

Morgan, M. (1973). *The Total Woman.* New York: Pocket Books.

Morgan, M., & Golden, H. H. (1979). Immigrant Families in an Industrial City: A Study of Households in Holyoke, in 1880. *Journal of Family History, 4,* 59–68.

Mosher, C. D. (1980). *The Mosher Survey.* New York: Arno.

Mosher, W. D. (1987). Infertility: Why Business is Booming. *American Demographics, 9,* 42–43.

Moss, M. S., Moss, S. Z., & Moles, E. L. (1985). The Quality of Relationships Between Elderly Parents and Their Out-of-Town Children. *Gerontologist, 25,* 134–140.

Mott, F. L. (1990). When is a Father Really Gone? Parental-Child Contact in Father-Absent Homes. *Demography 27,* 499–517.

Moynihan, D. P. (1965). *The Negro Family: The Case for National Action.* Washington: Department of Labor.

Mueller, D. P., & Cooper, P. W. (1986). Children of Single Parent Families: How They Fare as Young Adults. *Family Relations, 35,* 169–175.

Murdock, G. P. (1949). *Social Structure.* New York: MacMillan.

Murdock, G. P. (1957). World Ethnographic Sample. *American Anthropologist, 59.*

Murstein, B. I. (1961). The Complementary Needs Hypothesis in Newlyweds and Middle-Aged Married Couples. *Journal of Abnormal and Social Psychology, 63,* 194–197.

Murstein, B. I. (1967). *Who Will Marry Whom?* New York: Springer.

Murstein, B. I. (1971). *Theories of Attraction and Love.* New York: Springer.

Murstein, B. I. (1974). Clarification of Obfuscation on Conjugation: A Reply to a Criticism of the SVR Theory of Marital Choice. *Journal of Marriage and the Family, 36,* 231–234.

Murstein, B. I. (1980). Mate Selection in the 1970s. *Journal of Marriage and the Family, 42,* 777–792.

Murstein, B. I. (1984). "Mate" Selection in the Year 2020. in Kirkendall & Gravatt (Eds.), *Marriage and the Family in the Year 2020* (pp. 73–88). Buffalo: Prometheus.

Musgrove, F. (1966). *The Family, Education, and Society.* London: Routledge and Kegan Paul.

Myricks, N. (1980). Palimony: The Impact of Marvin vs. Marvin. *Family Relations, 29,* 210–215.

Napier, A. Y. (1971). The Marriage of Families: Cross-Generational Complementarity. *Family Process, 9,* 373–395.

Nelson, C., & Keith, J. (1990). Comparisons of Female and Male Early Adolescent Sex Role Attitude and Behavior Development. *Adolescence, 25,* 183–204.

Nelson, M. K. (1987). Providing Family Day Care: An Analysis of Home-Based Work. *Social Problems, 35,* 78–94.

Newcomb, M. D. (1986). Cohabitation, Marriage, and Divorce among Adolescents and Young Adults. *Journal of Social and Personal Relationships, 3,* 473–494.

Newcomb, P. R. (1979). Cohabitation in America. *Journal of Marriage and the Family, 41,* 597–603.

Nichols-Casebolt, A. (1986). The Economic Impact of Child Support Reform on the Poverty Status of Custodial and Noncustodial Families. *Journal of Marriage and the Family, 48,* 875–880.

Nimkoff, M. F. (1962). Biological Discoveries and the Future of the Family. *Social Forces, 41,* 121–127.

Nimkoff, M. F. (1965). *Comparative Family Systems.* Boston: Houghton Mifflin.

Nimkoff, M. F., & Middleton, R. (1960). Types of Family and Types of Economy. *American Journal of Sociology, 66.*

Nisbet, R. A. (1962). *Community and Power.* New York: Oxford University Press.

Nock, S. L. (1979). The Family Life Cycle: Empirical or Conceptual Tool? *Journal of Marriage and the Family, 41,* 15–26.

Nock, S. L. (1987). The Symbolic Meaning of Childbearing. *Journal of Family Issues, 8,* 373–393.

Norton, A. J. (1983). Family Life Cycle: 1980. *Journal of Marriage and the Family, 45.*

Norton, A. J. (1987). Families and Children in the Year 2000. *Children Today, 16,* 6–9.

Norton, A. J., & Glick, P. C. (1986). One Parent Families: A Social and Economic Profile. *Family Relations, 35,* 9–16.

Notes and Queries on Anthropology (6th ed). (1951). London: Routledge and Kegan Paul.

Nsamenang, A. B. (1987). A West African Perspective, in M. Lamb (Ed.), *The Father's Role—Cross Cultural Perspectives.* Hillsdale, N.J.: Erlbaum.

Nye, F. I. (1978). Is Choice and Exchange Theory the Key? *Journal of Marriage and the Family, 40.*

Nye, F. I. (1980). Family Mini Theories as Special Instances of Choice and Exchange Theory. *Journal of Marriage and the Family, 42,* 479–489.

Nye, F. I., & Berardo, F. (1973). *The Family: Its Structure and Interaction.* New York: MacMillan.

O'Flaherty, K. M., & Eells, L. W. (1988). Courtship Behavior of the Remarried. *Journal of Marriage and the Family, 50,* 499–506.

Ogburn, W. F. (1933). The Family and Its Functions. in W. F. Ogburn (Ed.), *Recent Social Trends* (ch. 13). New York: McGraw-Hill.

O'Hare, W. (1986a). The Eight Myths of Poverty. *American Demographics, 8,* 22–25.

O'Hare, W. (1986b). The Best Metro for Blacks. *American Demographics, 8,* 26–33.

O'Hare, W. (1990a). A New Look at Asian Americans. *American Demographics, 12,* 26–31.

O'Hare, W. (1990b). The Rise of Hispanic Affluence. *American Demographics, 12,* 40–43.

Okin, S. M. (1989). *Justice, Gender, and the Family.* New York: Basic Books.

Oliker, S. J. (1989). *Best Friends and Marriage: Exchange Among Women.* Berkeley: University of California Press.

Olson, D. H., Lavee, Y., & McCubbin, H. I. (1988). Types of Families and Family Response to Stress Across the Family Life Cycle. in Klein & Aldous (Eds.), *Social Stress and Family Development* (pp. 16–43). New York: Guilford.

Olson, D. H., & Matskovsky, M. S. (1993). Soviet and American Families: A Comparative Overview. in Maddock et al. (Eds.), *Perestroika and Family Life.* New York: Guilford.

Olson, D. H., & Rabunsky, C. M. (1972). Validity of Four Measures of Family Power. *Journal of Marriage and the Family, 34.*

O'Neill, N. (1977). *The Marriage Premise.* New York: Evans.

O'Neill, N., & O'Neill, G. (1972). *Open Marriage.* New York: M. Evans.

O'Neill, W. L. (1967). *Divorce in the Progressive Era.* New Haven: Yale University Press.

Oppenheimer, V. K. (1981). The Changing Nature of Life Cycle Squeezes: Implications for the Socioeconomic Position of the Elderly. in Fogel et al. (Eds.), *Aging.* New York: Academic.

Ort, R. S. (1950). A Study of Role-Conflicts as Related to Happiness in Marriage. *Journal of Abnormal and Social Psychology, 45,* 691–699.

Orthner, D. K., and Lewis, K. (1979). Evidence of Single-Father Competence in Childrearing. *Family Law Quarterly, 13,* 27–47.

Osborn, R. W., & Williams, J. I. (1976). Determining Patterns of Exchange and Expanded Family Relationships. *International Journal of Sociology of the Family, 6.*

Osherson, S., & Dill, D. (1983). Varying Work and Family Choices: Their Impact on Men's Work Satisfaction. *Journal of Marriage and the Family, 45,* 339–346.

Osmond, M. W. (1980). Cross-Societal Family Research: A Macro-Sociological Overview of the Seventies. *Journal of Marriage and the Family, 42,* 995–1016.

Osmond, M. W., & Martin, P. Y. (1978). A Contingency Model of Marital Organization of Low Income Families. *Journal of Marriage and the Family, 40.*

Osofsky, J. D., & Osofsky, H. J. (1972). Androgyny as a Life Style. *Family Life Coordinator, 21,* 411–418.

Oster, S. M. (1987). A Note on the Determinants of Alimony. *Journal of Marriage and the Family, 49,* 81–86.

Otto, L. (1979). Antecedents and Consequences of Marital Timing. in Burr et al. (Eds.), *Contemporary Theories About the Family, Volume I.* New York: Free Press.

Pampel, F. C., & Choldin, H. M. (1978). Urban Location and Segregation of the Aged: A Block-Level Analysis. *Social Forces, 56.*

Parish, W. L., Lingxin Hao, & Hogan, D. P. (1991). Family Support Networks, Welfare and Work Among Young Mothers. *Journal of Marriage and the Family, 53,* 203–215.

Parish, W. L., Jr., & Schwartz, M. (1972). Household Complexity in Nineteenth Century France. *American Sociological Review, 37.*

Parke, R., Jr., & Glick, P. C. (1967). Prospective Changes in Marriage and the Family. *Journal of Marriage and the Family, 29.*

Parsons, T. (1943). The Kinship System of the Contemporary United States. *American Anthropologist, 45,* 22–38.

Parsons, T. (1949). The Social Structure of the Family. in R. N. Anshen (Ed.), *The Family: Its Function and Destiny.* New York: Harper.

Parsons, T. (1954). The Incest Taboo in Relation to Social Structure and the Socialization of the Child. *British Journal of Sociology, 5.*

Parsons, T. (1955). The American Family: Its Relation to Personality and the Social Structure. in T. Parsons & R. F. Bales (Eds.), *Family, Socialization, and Interaction Process.* New York: Free Press.

Parsons, T. (1962). Youth in the Context of American Society. *Daedalus* (Winter).

Parsons, T. (1965). The Normal American Family. in Farber et al. (Eds.), *Man and Civilization.* New York: McGraw-Hill.

Pedrick-Cornell, C., & Gelles, R. J. (1982). Elder Abuse: The Status of Current Knowledge. *Family Relations, 31,* 457–465.

Perlman, D., & Fehr, B. (1987). The Development of Intimate Relationships. in Perlman & Duck (Eds.), *Intimate Relationships: Development, Dynamics, and Deterioration.* Newbury Park, CA: Sage.

Perry-Jenkins, M., & Crouter, A. C. (1990). Men's Provider-Role Attitudes: Implications for Household Work and Marital Satisfaction. *Journal of Family Issues, 11,* 136–156.

Peters, J. M. (1987). Time Used for Household Work: A Study of School-Age Children from Single-Parent, Two-Parent, One-Earner, and Two-Earner Families. *Journal of Family Issues, 8,* 212–225.

Peters, J. F. (1985). Adolescents as Socialization Agents to Parents. *Adolescence, 20,* 921–933.

Peters, M. F. (1988). Parenting in Black Families with Young Children: A Historical Perspective. in H. P. McAdoo (Ed.), *Black Families* (pp. 228–241). Newbury Park, CA: Sage.

Peters, M. F., & Massey, G. (1983). Mundane Extreme Environmental Stress in Family Stress Theories: the Case of Black Families in White America. *Marriage and Family Review, 6,* 193–218.

Peterson, Y. (1979). The Impact of Physical Disability on Marital Adjustment: A Literature Review. *The Family Coordinator, 28,* 47–51.

Philbert, M. A. J. (1965). The Emergence of Social Gerontology. *Journal of Social Issues, 21.*

Philliber, W. W., & Hiller, D. V. (1983). Relative Occupational Attainments of Spouses and Later Changes in Marriage and Wife's Work Experience. *Journal of Marriage and the Family, 45.*

Phillips, R. (1988). *Putting Asunder: A History of Divorce in Western Societies.* Cambridge, Eng.: Cambridge University Press.

Phinney, V. G., Jensen, L. C., Olsen, J. A., & Cundick, B. (1990). The Relationship Between Early Development and Psychosexual Behaviors in Adolescent Females. *Adolescence, 25,* 321–332.

Pillemar, K. (1985). The Dangers of Dependency: New Findings on Domestic Violence Against the Elderly. *Social Problems, 33,* 146–158.

Plutzer, E., & Ryan, B. (1987). Notifying Husbands about an Abortion: An Empirical Look at Constitutional and Policy Dilemmas. *Sociology and Social Research, 71,* 183–189.

Popenoe, D. (1987). Beyond the Nuclear Family: A Statistical Portrait of the Changing Family in Sweden. *Journal of Marriage and the Family, 49,* 173–183.

Popenoe, D. (1988). *Disturbing the Nest: Family Change and Decline in Modern Society.* New York: Aldine de Gruyter.

Potter, A. E., & Knaub, P. K. (1988). Single Motherhood By Choice: A Parenting Alternative. *Lifestyles, 9,* 240–249.

Powell-Griner, E., & Trent, K. (1987). Sociodemographic Determinants of Abortion in the United States. *Demography, 24,* 553–561.

Power, P. (1979). The Chronically Ill Husband and Father: His Role in the Family. *The Family Coordinator, 28,* 616–621.

Powers, E. A., & Bultena, G. L. (1976). Sex Differences in Intimate Friendships of Old Age. *Journal of Marriage and the Family, 38.*

Prager, K. J., & Bailey, J. M. (1985). Androgyny, Ego Development, and Psychosocial Crisis Resolution. *Sex Roles, 13,* 525–536.

Presser, H. B. (1986). Shift Work among American Women and Child Care. *Journal of Marriage and the Family, 48,* 551–563.

Price-Bonham, S., & Balswick, J. O. (1980). The Noninstitutions: Divorce, Desertion, and Remarriage. *Journal of Marriage and the Family, 42.*

Quale, G. R. (1988). *A History of Marriage Systems.* Westport, CT: Greenwood.

Quam, J. K., & Whitford, G. S. (1992). Adaptation and Age-Related Expectations of Older Gay and Lesbian Adults. *Gerontologist, 32,* 367–374.

Rabb, T. K., & Rotberg, R. I. (Eds.). (1973). *The Family in History: Interdisciplinary Essays.* New York: Harper and Row.

Radcliffe-Brown, A. R. (1941). The Study of Kinship Systems. *Journal of the Royal Anthropological Institute, 71.*

Rainwater, L. (1966). Crucible of Identity: The Negro Lower-Class Family. *Daedalus* (Winter).

Rallings, E. M., & Nye, F. I. (1979). Wife-Mother Employment, Family and Society. in W. Burr et al. (Eds.), *Contemporary Theories about the Family, Volume I.* New York: Free Press.

Rank, M. R. (1982). Determinants of Conjugal Influences in Wives' Employment Decision Making. *Journal of Marriage and the Family, 44,* 591–604.

Rank, M. R. (1987). The Formation and Dissolution of Marriages in the Welfare Population. *Journal of Marriage and the Family, 49,* 15–20.

Rank, M. R. (1989). Fertility Among Women on Welfare: Incidence and Determinants. *American Sociological Review, 54,* 296–304.

Rankin, R. P., & Manaker, J. S. (1985). The Duration of Marriage in a Divorcing Population: The Impact of Children. *Journal of Marriage and the Family, 47,* 43–52.

Raphael, B., Cubis, J., Dunne, M., Lewin, T., & Kelly, B. (1990). The Impact of Parents Loss on Adolescents' Psychological Characteristics. *Adolescence, 25,* 689–700.

Rapoport, T. (1988). Socialization Patterns in the Family, the School, and the Youth Movement. *Youth and Society, 20,* 159–179.

Raschke, H. J., & Raschke, V. J. (1979). Family Conflict and Children's Self-Concepts: A Comparison of Intact and Single-Parent Families. *Journal of Marriage and the Family, 41,* 367–374.

Raush, H. L., Greif, A. C., & Nugent, J. (1979). Communication in Couples and Families. in Burr et al. (Eds.), *Contemporary Theories about the Family, Volume I.* New York: Free Press.

Raven, B. H., Centers, R., & Rodriguez, A. (1975). The Bases of Conjugal Power. in Cromwell & Olson (Eds.), *Power in Families.* New York: Wiley.

Reilly, T. W., Entwisle, D. R., & Doering, S. G. (1987). Socialization into Parenthood: A Longitudinal Study of the Development of Self-Evaluations. *Journal of Marriage and the Family, 49,* 295–308.

Reiss, D. (1981). *The Family's Construction of Reality.* Cambridge, MA: Harvard University Press.

Reiss, I. L. (1965). The Universality of the Family: A Conceptual Analysis. *Journal of Marriage and the Family, 27.*

Reiss, I. L. (1967). *The Social Context of Premarital Sexual Permissiveness.* New York: Holt, Rinehart, and Winston.

Reiss, I. (1981). Some Observations on Ideology and Sexuality in America. *Journal of Marriage and the Family, 43,* 271–283.

Reiss, I. (1982). [Review of *The Mosher Survey*] *Journal of Marriage and the Family, 44,* 252.

Reiss, I. L. (1986). *Journey into Sexuality: An Exploratory Voyage.* Englewood Cliffs, NJ: Prentice-Hall.

Reiss, I., & Miller, B. (1979). Heterosexual Permissiveness: A Theoretical Analysis. in Burr et al. (Eds.), *Contemporary Theories About the Family, Volume I.* New York: Free Press.

Rempel, J. (1985). Childless Elderly: What Are They Missing? *Journal of Marriage and the Family, 47,* 343–348.

Retzinger, S. M. (1991). *Violent Emotions: Shame and Rage in Marital Quarrels.* Beverly Hills: Sage.

Rexroat, C., & Shehan, C. (1987). The Family Life Cycle and Spouses' Time in Housework. *Journal of Marriage and the Family, 49,* 737–750.

Rhode, D. L. (1990). *Theoretical Perspectives on Sexual Difference.* New Haven, CT: Yale University Press.

Riche, M. F. (1986). Retirement's Lifestyle Pioneers, *American Demographics, 8,* 50–56.

Riche, M. F. (1987). Mysterious Young Adults. *American Demographics, 9,* 38–43.

Riche, M. F. (1990). The Boomerang Age. *American Demographics, 12,* 24–30.

Richmond, M. L. (1976). Beyond Resource Theory: Another Look at Factors Enabling Women to Affect Family Interaction. *Journal of Marriage and the Family, 38.*

Riesman, D., Glazer, N., & Denney, R. (1950). *The Lonely Crowd.* New Haven, CT: Yale University Press.

Riggs, D. S., O'Leary, K. D., & Breslin, F. C. (1990). Multiple Correlates of Physical Aggression in Dating Couples. *Journal of Interpersonal Violence, 5,* 61–73.

Riley, G. (1993). *Divorce: An American Tradition.* New York: Oxford University Press.

Rischin, M. (1962). *The Promised City: New York's Jews, 1870–1914.* Cambridge, MA: Harvard University Press.

Risman, B. J. (1986). Can Men "Mother"? Life As a Single Father. *Family Relations, 35,* 95–102.

Risman, B. J., Hill, C. T., Rubin, Z., & Peplau, L. A. (1981). Living Together in College: Implications for Courtship. *Journal of Marriage and the Family, 43,* 77–83.

Robinson, I. E., & Jedlicka, D. (1982). Change in Sexual Attitudes and Behavior of College Students from 1965 to 1980: A Research Note. *Journal of Marriage and the Family, 44,* 237–240.

Rockwell, R. C., Elder, G. H., Jr., & Ross, D. J. (1979). Psychological Patterns in Marital Timing and Divorce. *Social Psychological Quarterly, 42,* 399–404.

Rodgers, R. H., & Conrad, L. M. (1986). Courtship for Remarriage: Influences on Family Reorganization After Divorce. *Journal of Marriage and the Family, 48,* 767–775.

Rodman, H., & Pratto, D. J. (1987). Child's Age and Mother's Employment in Relation to Greater Use of Self-Care Arrangements for Children. *Journal of Marriage and the Family, 49,* 573–578.

Rodman, H., Pratto, D. J., & Nelson, R. S. (1985). Child Care Arrangements and Children's Functioning: A Comparison of Self-Care and Adult-Care Children. *Developmental Psychology, 21,* 413–418.

Roff, L. L., Klemmeck, D. L. (1986). Norms for Employed Daughters' and Sons' Behavior Toward Frail Older Parents. *Sex Roles, 14,* 363–368.

Rohner, R. P. (1986). *The Warmth Dimension.* Beverly Hills: Sage.

Roscoe, B., & Benaske, N. (1985). Courtship Violence Experienced by Abused Wives: Similarities in Patterns of Abuse. *Family Relations, 34,* 419–424.

Roscoe, B., Diana, M. S., & Brooks, R. H., II. (1987). Early, Middle, and Late Adolescents' Views on Dating and Factors Influencing Partner Selection. *Adolescence, 85,* 60–68.

Roscoe, B., & Kruger, T. L. (1990). AIDS: Late Adolescents' Knowledge and Its Influence on Sexual Behavior. *Adolescence, 25,* 39–48.

Rose, A. M., & Peterson, W. A., Eds. (1965). *Older People and Their Social World.* Philadelphia: Davis.

Rosen, D. M. (1991). What Is a Family? Nature, Culture, and the Law. *Marriage and Family Review, 17,* 29–44.

Rosenblatt, P. C., & Titus, S. L. (1976). Together and Apart in the Family. *Humanitas, 12,* 367–380.

Rosenblatt, P. C., Johnson, P. A., & Anderson, R. M. (1981). When Out-of-Town Relatives Visit. *Family Relations, 30,* 403–409.

Rosenfeld, H. (1958). Process of Structural Change Within the Arab Village Extended Family. *American Anthropologist, 60,* 1127–1139.

Rosenfeld, J. P. (1979). *The Legacy of Aging.* Norwood, N.J.: Ablex.

Rosenthal, C. J. (1985). Kinkeeping in the Familial Division of Labor. *Journal of Marriage and the Family, 47,* 965–974.

Rosow, I. (1967). *Social Integration of the Aged.* New York: Free Press.

Ross, H. L., & Sawhill, I. V. (1975). *Time of Transition: The Growth of Families Headed by Women.* Washington, D.C.: The Urban Institute.

Rossi, A. S. (1965). Naming Children in Middle Class Families. *American Sociological Review, 30.*

Rossi, A. S. (1977). A Biosocial Perspective On Parenting. *Daedalus* (Spring).

Rossi, A. S., & Rossi, P. H. (1990). *Of Human Bonding: Parent-Child Relations Across the Life Course.* New York: Aldine de Gruyter.

Rothchild, J., & Wolf, S. (1976). *The Children of the Counterculture.* Garden City, NY: Doubleday.

Rothman, D. J. (1973). Documents in Search of a Historian: Toward a History of Childhood and Youth in America. in Rabb & Rotberg (Eds.), *The Family in History* (pp. 181–189). New York: Harper Torchbooks.

Rousseau, J. J. (1755). *Discourse on the Origin of Inequality; Discourse on Political Economy.* in *Great Books of the Western World, Volume 38.* Chicago: Encyclopedia Britannica (1971).

Rubin, Z. (1973). *Liking and Loving.* New York: Holt, Rinehart, and Winston.

Rubin, Z., Hill, C. T., Peplau, L. A., & Dunkel-Schetter, C. (1980). Self-Disclosure in Dating Couples, Sex Roles and the Ethic of Openness. *Journal of Marriage and the Family, 42,* 305–317.

Rubin, Z., Peplau, L. A., & Hill, C. T. (1981). Loving and Leaving: Sex Differences in Romantic Attachments. *Sex Roles, 7,* 821–835.

Ruble, D. N., Fleming, A. S., Hackel, L. S., & Stangor, C. (1988). Changes in the Marital Relationship During the Transition to First Time Motherhood: Effects of Violated Expectations Concerning Division of Household Labor. *Journal of Personality and Social Psychology, 55,* 78–87.

Rueschemeyer, M. (1981). *Professional Work and Marriage: An East-West Comparison.* New York: St. Martin's.

Rusbult, C. E. (1987). Responses to Dissatisfaction in Close Relationships: The Exit — Voice — Loyalty — Neglect Model. in Perlman & Duck (Eds.), *Intimate Relationships* (pp. 209–237). Newbury Park, CA: Sage.

Rusbult, C. E., Johnson, D. J., & Marow, G. D. (1986). Impact of Couple Patterns of Problem Solving on Distress and Non-distress in Dating Relationships. *Journal of Personality and Social Psychology, 50,* 744–753.

Russell, D. E. H. (1986). *The Secret Trauma — Incest in the Lives of Girls and Women.* New York: Basic Books.

Ryder, N. B. (1970). The Emergence of a Modern Fertility Pattern: United States, 1917–1966. in Behrman et al. (Eds.), *Fertility and Family Planning.* Ann Arbor: University of Michigan Press.

Ryder, R. G. (1972). What Is Power?: Definitional Considerations and Some Research Implications. *Science and Psychoanalysis, 20.*

Sacks, M. P. (1977). Unchanging Times: A Comparison of the Everyday Life of Soviet Working Men and Women Between 1923–1966. *Journal of Marriage and the Family, 39.*

Safilios-Rothschild, C. (1970). The Study of Family Power Structure: A Review 1960–1969. *Journal of Marriage and the Family, 32.*

St. John, C., & Rowe, D. (1990). Adolescent Background and Fertility Norms: Implications for Racial Differences in Early Childbearing. *Social Science Quarterly, 71,* 152–162.

Santrock, J. W., & Sitterle, K. A. (1987). Parent-Child Relationships in Stepmother Families. in Pasley and Ihinger-Tallman (Eds.), *Remarriage and Stepparenting* (pp. 273–299). New York: Guilford.

Sather, K. (1989). Sixteenth and Seventeenth Century Child-Rearing: A Matter of Discipline. *Journal of Social History, 22,* 735–743.

Sauer, L. E., & Fine, M. A. (1988). Parent-Child Relationships in Stepparent Families. *Journal of Family Psychology, 1,* 434–451.

Sauer, R. J. (1979). Absentee Father Syndrome. *The Family Coordinator, 28,* 245–249.

Saunders, D. G. (1988). Wife Abuse, Husband Abuse, or Mutual Combat? in Yllo and Bograd (Eds.), *Feminist Perspectives on Wife Abuse.* Newbury Park, CA: Sage.

Sawhill, I. V. (1977). Economic Perspectives on the Family. *Daedalus* (Spring).

Scanzoni, J., & Fox, G. L. (1980). Sex Roles, Family, and Society: The Seventies and Beyond. *Journal of Marriage and the Family, 42,* 743–756.

Scanzoni, J., & Marsiglio, W. (1991). Wider Families as Primary Relationships. *Marriage and Family Review, 17,* 117–133.

Scanzoni, J., & Polonko, K. (1980). A Conceptual Approach to Explicit Marital Negotiation. *Journal of Marriage and the Family, 42,* 31–44.

Scanzoni, J., Polonko, K., Teachman, J., & Thompson, L. (1989). *The Sexual Bond: Rethinking Families and Close Relationships.* Newbury Park, CA: Sage.

Scanzoni, J., & Szinovacz, M. (1980). *Family Decision-Making: A Developmental Sex Role Model.* Beverly Hills: Sage.

Schaeffer, N. C. (1990). Principles of Justice in Judgments About Child Support. *Social Forces, 69,* 157–180.

Schafer, R. B., & Keith, P. M. (1980). Equity and Depression Among Married Couples. *Social Psychology Quarterly, 43,* 430–435.

Scharlach, A. E. (1987). Role Strain in Mother-Daughter Relationships in Later Life. *Gerontologist, 27,* 627–631.

Schelsky, H. (1954). The Family in Germany, *Marriage and Family Living, 16.*

Schneider, D. M. (1965). American Kin Terms for Kinsmen: A Critique of Goodenough's Componential Analysis of Yankee Kinship Terminology. *American Anthropologist, 67,* 292–294.

Schneider, D. M. (1968). *American Kinship: A Cultural Account.* Englewood Cliffs, NJ: Prentice-Hall.

Schneider, D. M., Homans, G. C. (1955). Kinship Terminology and the American Kinship System. *American Anthropologist, 57.*

Schoen, R. (1992). First Unions and the Stability of First Marriages. *Journal of Marriage and the Family, 54,* 281–284.

Schoen, R., & Cohen, L. E. (1980). Ethnic Endogamy Among Mexican American Grooms: A Reanalysis of Generational and Occupational Effects. *American Journal of Sociology, 86.*

Schoen, R., & Kluegel, J. P. (1988). The Widening Gap in Black and White Marriage Rates: The Impact of Population Composition and Differential Marriage Propensities. *American Sociological Review, 53,* 895–907.

Schroeder, K. A., Blood, L. L., & Maluso, D. (1992). An Intergenerational Analysis of Expectations for Women's Career and Family Roles. *Sex Roles, 26,* 273–292.

Schuby, T. D. (1975). Class, Power, Kinship and Social Cohesion: A Case Study of a Local Elite. *Sociological Focus, 8,* 243–255.

Schultz, M. (1990). Divorce Patterns in 19th Century New England. *Journal of Family History, 15,* 101–115.

Schwartz, J. S. (1979). Women Under Socialism: Role Definitions of Soviet Women. *Social Forces, 58,* 67–88.

Schwebel, A. I., Fine, M. A., & Renner, M. A. (1991). A Study of Perceptions of the Stepparent Role. *Journal of Family Issues, 12,* 43–57.

Scott, J. W., & Perry, R. (1990). Do Black Family Headship Structures Make a Difference in Teenage Pregnancy? A Comparison of One-Parent and Two-Parent Families. *Sociological Focus, 23,* 1–16.

Sebald, H. (1986). Adolescents' Shifting Orientation Toward Parents and Peers: A Curvilinear Trend Over Recent Decades. *Journal of Marriage and the Family, 48,* 5–13.

Segre, S. (1975). Family Stability, Social Classes and Values in Traditional and Industrial Societies. *Journal of Marriage and the Family, 37,* 431–436.

Seltzer, J. A. (1990). Legal and Physical Custody Arrangements in Recent Divorces. *Social Science Quarterly, 71,* 250–263.

Seltzer, J. A. (1991). Relationships Between Fathers and Children Who Live Apart: The Father's Role After Separation. *Journal of Marriage and the Family, 53,* 79–101.

Sena-Rivera, J. (1979). Extended Kinship in the United States: Competing Models and the Case of La Familia Chicana. *Journal of Marriage and the Family, 41.*

Sepler, H. J. (1981). Measuring the Effects of No-Fault Divorce Laws Across the Fifty States: Quantifying a Zeitgeist. *Family Law Quarterly, 15,* 65–102.

Seward, R. R. (1973). The Colonial Family in America: Toward a Socio-Historical Restoration of Its Structure. *Journal of Marriage and the Family, 35,* 58–70.

Seward, R. R. (1974). Family Size in the United States: An Exploratory Study of Trends. *Kansas Journal of Sociology, 10,* 119–136.

Sexton, C. S., & Perlman, D. S. (1989). Couples' Career Orientation, Gender Role Orientation, and Perceived Equity as Determinants of Marital Power. *Journal of Marriage and the Family, 51,* 933–941.

Shah, F., & Zelnik, M. (1981). Parent and Peer Influence on Sexual Behavior, Contraceptive Use, and Pregnancy Experience of Young Women. *Journal of Marriage and the Family, 43,* 339–348.

Shanas, E. (1968). *Old People in Three Industrial Societies*. New York: Atherton.

Shanas, E., & Sussman, M. (1981). The Family in Later Life: Social Structure and Social Policy. in Fogel et al. (Eds.), *Aging: Stability and Change in the Family*. New York: Academic.

Shelton, B. A. (1987). Variations in Divorce Rates by Community Size: A Test of the Social Integration Explanation. *Journal of Marriage and the Family, 49*, 827–832.

Shelton, B. A. (1990). The Distribution of Household Tasks: Does Wife's Employment Make a Difference? *Journal of Family Issues, 11*, 115–135.

Shelton, B. A., & Firestone, J. (1989). Household Labor and the Gender Gap in Earnings. *Gender and Society, 3*, 105–112.

Shibutani, T., & Kian M. Kwan. (1965). *Ethnic Stratification*. New York: MacMillan.

Shifflett, C. A. (1975). The Household Composition of Rural Black Families: Louisa County, Virginia, 1880. *Journal of Interdisciplinary History, 6*, 240–245.

Shimkin, D., Shimkin, E. M., & Frate, D. A., Eds. (1978). *The Extended Family in Black Societies* (pp. 3–170). The Hague: Mouton Publishers.

Shlapentokh, V. (1991). The Soviet Family in the Period of the Decay of Socialism. *Journal of Comparative Family Studies, 22*, 267–279.

Shorter, E. (1973). Illegitimacy, Sexual Revolution, and Social Change in Modern Europe. in Rabb & Rotberg (Eds.), *The Family in History*.

Shorter, E. (1975). *The Making of the Modern Family*. New York: Basic Books.

Signorielli, N. (1991). Adolescents and Ambivalence Toward Marriage: A Cultivation Analysis. *Youth and Society, 23*, 121–149.

Silber, S. (1990). Conflict Negotiation in Child Abusing and Nonabusing Families. *Journal of Family Psychology, 3*, 368–384.

Sill, J. S. (1980). Disengagement Reconsidered: Awareness of Finitude. *The Gerontologist, 20*, 457–462.

Silverberg, S. B., & Steinberg, L. (1990). Psychological Well-Being of Parents with Early Adolescent Children. *Developmental Psychology, 26*, 658–666.

Simmons, L. W. (1952). Social Participation of the Aged in Different Cultures. *The Annals, 279*.

Simon, J., & Gagnon, W. (1968). *Youth Cultures and Aspects of the Socialization Process: College Study Marginal Book*. Bloomington, IN: Institute for Sex Research.

Simpson, J. A., Rholes, W. S., & Nelligan, J. S. (1992). Support Seeking and Support Giving Within Couples in an Anxiety Provoking Situation: The Role of Attachment Styles. *Journal of Personality and Social Psychology, 62*, 434–446.

Sindberg, R. M., Roberts, A. E., & McClain, D. (1972). Mate Selection Factors in Computer Matched Marriages. *Journal of Marriage and the Family, 34*.

Singh, B. K. (1980). Trends in Attitudes Toward Premarital Sexual Relations. *Journal of Marriage and the Family, 42*, 387–393.

Skipper, J. K., & Nass, G. (1966). Dating Behavior: A Framework for Analysis and an Illustration. *Journal of Marriage and the Family, 28*, 412–420.

Smith, A. W., & Meitz, J. E. G. (1983). Cohorts, Education, and the Decline in Disrupted Marriages. *Journal of Marriage and the Family, 45*.

Smith, A. D., & Reid, W. J. (1986). *Role-Sharing Marriage*. New York: Columbia University Press.

Smith, D. S. (1979). Life Course, Norms, and the Family System of Older Americans in 1900. *Journal of Family History, 4*, 285–298.

Smith, D. S. (1980). The Long Cycle in American Illegitimacy and Prenuptial Pregnancy. in Laslett et al. (Eds.), *Bastardy and Its Comparative History*. Cambridge, MA: Harvard University Press.

Smith, H. W., & Kronauge, C. (1990). The Politics of Abortion: Husband Notification Legislation, Self-Disclosure, and Marital Bargaining. *The Sociological Quarterly, 31*, 585–598.

Smith, J. E., & Kunz, P. R. (1976). Polygyny and Fertility in Nineteenth Century America. *Population Studies, 30*.

Smith, K. R., & Zick, C. D. (1986). The Incidence of Poverty Among the Recently Widowed: Mediating Factors in the Life Course. *Journal of Marriage and the Family, 48*, 619–630.

Smith, K. R., Zick, C. D., & Duncan, G. J. (1991). Remarriage Patterns Among Recent Widows and Widowers. *Demography, 28*, 361–374.

Smith, K. F., & Bengtson, V. (1979). Positive Consequences of Institutionalization: Solidarity Between Elderly Parents and Their Middle-Aged Children. *The Gerontologist, 19*, 438–447.

Smith, M. D., & Fisher, L. J. (1982). Sex Role Attitudes and Social Class: A Reanalysis and Clarification. *Journal of Comparative Family Studies, 13*, 77–88.

Smith, T. E. (1981). Adolescent Agreement with Perceived Maternal and Paternal Educational Goals. *Journal of Marriage and the Family, 43*, 85–93.

Smith-Rosenberg, C. (1975). The Female World of Love and Ritual. *Signs, 1*, 1–29.

Smock, P. J. (1990). Remarriage Patterns of Black and White Women: Reassessing the Role of Educational Attainment. *Demography, 27*, 467–473.

Snyder, E. C. (1971). Attitudes: A Study of Homogamy and Marital Selectivity. *Journal of Marriage and the Family, 26*, 373–395.

Sorensen, A. (1983). Women's Employment Patterns After Marriage. *Journal of Marriage and the Family, 45*, 311–321.

Sorokin, P. A. (1937). *Social and Culture Dynamics, 4 Volumes*. New York: American.

South, S. J. (1985). "Economic Conditions and the Divorce Rate. *Journal of Marriage and the Family, 47*, 31–41.

South, S. J. (1991). Sociodemographic Differentials in Mate Selection Preferences. *Journal of Marriage and the Family, 53*, 928–940.

South, S. J., & Lloyd, K. M. (1992). Marriage Markets and Nonmarital Fertility in the United States. *Demography, 29*, 247–264.

Spanier, G. (1983). Married and Unmarried Cohabitation in the United States: 1980. *Journal of Marriage and the Family, 42*.

Spencer, H. (1893). *The Principles of Ethics, Volume 2*. Indianapolis: Library Classics (1978).

Spickard, J. V. (1988). Families and Religion: An Anthropological Typology. in Thomas (Ed.), *The Religion and Family Connection* (pp. 324–342). Provo: Brigham Young University.

Spitze, G., & Miner, S. (1992). Gender Differences in Adult Child Contact Among Black Elderly Parents. *Gerontologist, 32,* 213–218.

Spurlock, J. (1988). Free Love Network in America: 1850–1860. *Journal of Social History, 21,* 765–779.

Squier, D. A., & Quadagno, J. S. (1988). The Italian American Family. in Mindel et al. (Eds.), *Ethnic Families in America* (pp. 109–137). New York: Elsevier.

Stacey, J. (1983). *Patriarchy and Socialist Revolution in China.* Berkeley: University of California Press.

Stacey, J. (1990). *Brave New Families: Stories of Domestic Upheaval in Late Twentieth Century America.* New York: Basic Books.

Stack, S. (1988). The Effect of Domestic/Religious Individualism on Suicide. in Thomas (Ed.), *The Religion and Family Connection: Social Science Perspectives.* Provo, UT: Brigham Young Press.

Stahl, A. (1991). Parents' Attitudes Toward the Death of Infants in the Traditional Jewish-Oriental Family. *Journal of Comparative Family Studies, 22,* 75–83.

Staples, R. (1987). Social Structure and Black Family Life: an Analysis of Current Trends. *Journal of Black Studies, 17,* 267–286.

Staples, R. (1988). The Black American Family. in Mindel et al. (Eds.), *Ethnic Families in America* (pp. 303–324). New York: Elsevier.

Staples, R. (1990). Changes in Black Family Structure: The Conflict Between Family Ideology and Structural Conditions. in Carlson (Ed.), *Perspectives on Family History, Class, and Feminism* (pp. 281–294). Belmont, CA: Wadsworth.

Staples, R., & Mirande, A. (1980). Racial and Cultural Variations Among American Families: A Decennial Review of the Literature on Minority Families. *Journal of Marriage and the Family, 42.*

Steckel, R. H. (1980). Slave Marriage and the Family. *Journal of Family History, 5,* 406–421.

Steffensmeier, R. H. (1982). A Role Model of the Transition to Parenthood. *Journal of Marriage and the Family, 44,* 319–334.

Stein, P. (1976). *Single.* Englewood Cliffs, NJ: Prentice-Hall.

Steinberg, L., & Silverberg, S. B. (1987). Influences on Marital Satisfaction During the Middle Stages of the Family Life Cycle. *Journal of Marriage and the Family, 49,* 751–760.

Steinmetz, S. K. (1979). Disciplinary Techniques and Their Relationship to Aggressiveness, Dependency, and Conscience. in Burr et al. (Eds.), *Contemporary Theories About the Family, Volume I.* New York: Basic Books.

Stephen, T. D. (1985). Fixed-Sequence and Circular Causal Models of Relationships Development: Divergent Views on the Role of Communication in Intimacy. *Journal of Marriage and the Family, 47,* 955–963.

Stephens, W. N. (1963). *The Family in Cross-Cultural Perspective.* New York: Holt, Rinehart and Winston.

Stets, J. E. (1990). Verbal and Physical Aggression in Marriage. *Journal of Marriage and the Family, 52,* 501–514.

Stets, J. E., & Pirog-Good, M. A. (1990). Interpersonal Control and Courtship Aggression. *Journal of Social and Personal Relationships, 7,* 371–394.

Stiles, H. R. (1934). *Bundling: Its Origin, Progress and Decline in America.* New York: Book Collectors Association.

Stoller, F. H. (1970). The Intimate Network of Families as a New Structure. in Otto (Ed.), *The Family in Search of a Future* (pp. 145–160). New York: Appleton-Century-Crofts.

Stone, L. (1977). *The Family, Sex and Marriage in England, 1500–1800.* New York: Harper and Row.

Straus, M. (1971). Familial Organization and Problem Solving Ability in Relation to Societal Modernization. *Journal of Comparative Family Studies, 3,* 70–83.

Straus, M. A. (1971). Some Social Antecedents of Physical Punishment: A Linkage Theory Interpretation. *Journal of Marriage and the Family, 33.*

Straus, M. A. (1980). Victims and Aggressors in Marital Violence. *American Behavioral Scientist, 23,* 681–704.

Straus, M. A., & Gelles, R. J. (1986). Societal Change and Change in Family Violence from 1975 to 1985 As Revealed By Two National Surveys. *Journal of Marriage and the Family, 48,* 465–479.

Strauss, A. (1946). The Ideal and the Chosen Mate. *American Journal of Sociology, 52,* 204–210.

Streib, G. F., & Beck, R. W. (1980). Older Family: A Decade Review. *Journal of Marriage and the Family, 42,* 937–956.

Strober, M. H. (1988). Two-Earner Families. in Dornbusch and Strober (Eds), *Feminism, Children, and the New Families* (pp. 161–190). New York: Guilford.

Strong, B. (1973). Toward a History of the Experiential Family: Sex and Incest in the Nineteenth Century Family. *Journal of Marriage and the Family, 35.*

Strube, M. J., & Barbour, L. S. (1983). The Decision to Leave An Abusive Relationship: Economic Dependence and Psychological Commitment. *Journal of Marriage and the Family, 45,* 785–793.

Suitor, J. J. (1987). Mother-Daughter Relations When Married Daughter Returns to School: Effects of Status Similarity. *Journal of Marriage and the Family, 49,* 435–444.

Surra, C. A. (1990). Research and Theory on Mate Selection and Premarital Relationships in the 1980s. *Journal of Marriage and the Family, 52,* 844–865.

Sussman, M. B. (1965). Relationships of Adult Children with Their Parents in the United States. in Shanas and Streib (Eds.), *Social Structure and the Family.* Englewood Cliffs, NJ: Prentice-Hall.

Swafford, M. (1978). Sex Differences in Soviet Earnings, *American Sociological Review, 42.*

Sweet, J. A., & Bumpass, L. L. (1987). *American Families and Households.* New York: Russell Sage.

Szinovacz, M., & Washo, C. (1992). Gender Differences in Exposure to Life Events and Adaptation to Retirement. *Journal of Gerontology, 47,* 191–196.

Takeuchi, D. T., Williams, D. R., & Adair, R. K. (1991). Economic Distress in the Family and Children's Emotional and Behavioral Problems. *Journal of Marriage and the Family, 53,* 1031–1041.

Tannen, D. (1990). *You Just Don't Understand: Women and Men in Conversation.* New York: William Morrow.

Targ, D. B. (1979). Toward a Reassessment of Women's Experience at Middle Age. *The Family Coordinator, 28,* 465–471.

Taylor, R. J. (1986). Receipt of Support from Family among Black Americans: Demographic and Familial Differences. *Journal of Marriage and the Family, 48,* 67–77.

Taylor, R. J., & Chatters, L. M. (1986). Church-Based Informal Support Among Elderly Blacks. *Gerontologist, 26,* 637–642.

Teachman, J. D. (1986). First and Second Marital Dissolution: a Decomposition Exercise for Whites and Blacks. *The Sociological Quarterly, 27,* 571–590.

Teachman, J. D., & Polonko, K. A. (1990). Cohabitation and Marital Stability in the U.S. *Social Forces, 69,* 207–220.

Teachman, J. D., & Schollaert, P. T. (1991). Direct and Indirect Effects of Religion on Birth Timing: A Decomposition Exercise Using Discrete-Time Hazard-Rate Models. *Sociological Quarterly, 32,* 151–159.

Tennyson, A., Lord. (1859). *Idylls of the King.* Boston: Ticknor and Fields.

Teti, D. M., Lamb, M. E., & Elster, A. B. (1987). Long-Range Socioeconomic and Marital Consequences of Adolescent Marriage in Three Cohorts of Adult Males. *Journal of Marriage and the Family, 49,* 499–506.

Thibaut, J., & Kelley, H. (1959). *The Social Psychology of Groups.* New York: Wiley.

Thomas, D. L. (1988). *The Religion and Family Connection: Social Science Perspectives.* Provo, UT: Brigham Young University Press.

Thomas, D. L., & Weigert, A. J. (1971). Socialization and Adolescent Conformity to Significant Others: A Cross-National Analysis. *American Sociological Review, 36.*

Thomas, L. E., McCabe, E., & Berry, J. E. (1980). Unemployment and Family Stress: A Reassessment. *Family Relations, 29,* 517–524.

Thomas, V. G. (1990). Determinants of Global Life Happiness and Marital Happiness in Dual-Career Black Couples. *Family Relations, 39,* 174–178.

Thomason, B. (1955). Marital Sexual Behavior and Total Marital Adjustment: A Research Report. in Himmelhoch & Fava (Eds.), *Sexual Behavior in American Society.* New York: Norton.

Thompson, E. H., Jr. (1991). The Maleness of Violence in Dating Relationships: An Appraisal of Stereotypes. *Sex Roles, 24,* 261–278.

Thompson, K. (1980). A Comparison of Black and White Adolescents' Beliefs About Having Children. *Journal of Marriage and the Family, 42.*

Thompson, L. (1991). Family Work: Women's Sense of Fairness. *Journal of Family Issues, 12,* 181–196.

Thompson, L., & Spanier, G. B. (1983). The End of Marriage and Acceptance of Marriage Termination. *Journal of Marriage and the Family, 45,* 103–114.

Thompson, W. E., & Streib, G. F. (1961). Meaningful Activity in a Family Context. in Robert W. Kleemeier (Ed.), *Aging and Leisure: A Research Perspective into the Meaningful Use of Leisure Time* (pp. 177–211). New York: Oxford University Press.

Thompson, W. E. (1986). Courtship Violence — Toward a Conceptual Understanding. *Youth and Society, 18,* 162–176.

Thomson, E., & Colella, U. (1992). Cohabitation and Marital Stability: Quality or Commitment? *Journal of Marriage and the Family, 54,* 259–267.

Thorne, B., with Yalom, M. (1982). *Rethinking the Family: Some Feminist Questions.* New York: Longman.

Thornton, A. (1988). Cohabitation and Marriage in the 1980s. *Demography, 25,* 497–508.

Thornton, A. (1990). The Courtship Process and Adolescent Sexuality. *Journal of Family Issues, 11,* 239–273.

Thornton, A., & Camburn, D. (1987). The Influence of the Family on Premarital Sexual Attitudes and Behavior. *Demography, 24,* 323–340.

Tiedje, L. B., Wortman, C. B., Downey, G., Emmons, C., Biernat, M., & Lang, E. (1990). Women with Multiple Roles: Role-Compatibility Perceptions, Satisfaction, and Mental Health. *Journal of Marriage and the Family, 52,* 63–72.

Tienda, M., & Angel, R. (1982). Headship and Household Composition Among Blacks, Hispanics, and Other Whites. *Social Forces, 61,* 508–531.

Tietze, C. (1977). The Effect of Legalization of Abortion on Population Growth and Public Health. *Family Planning Perspectives, 9.*

Tinker, J. N. (1973). Intermarriage and Ethnic Boundaries: The Japanese-American Case. *Journal of Social Issues, 29,* 49–66.

Todres, R. (1978). Runaway Wives: An Increasing North-American Phenomenon. *The Family Coordinator, 27,* 17–21.

Toffler, A. (1980). *The Third Wave.* New York: William Morrow.

Tolman, A. E., Diekmann, K. A., & McCartney, K. (1989). Social Connectedness and Mothering: Effects of Maternal Employment and Maternal Absence. *Journal of Personality and Social Psychology, 56,* 942–949.

Tolnay, S. E. (1983). Fertility of Southern Black Farmers in 1900: Evidence and Speculation. *Journal of Family History, 8,* 314–332.

Townsend, B., & O'Neil, K. (1990). American Women Get Mad. *American Demographics, 12,* 26–32.

Trickett, P. K., & Kuczynski, L. (1986). Children's Misbehaviors and Parental Discipline Strategies in Abusive and Non-Abusive Families. *Developmental Psychology, 22,* 115–123.

Troll, L. A. (1971). The Family of Later Life: A Decade Review. in Broderick (Ed.), *A Decade Review of Family Research and Action.* Minneapolis: National Council on Family Relations.

Troll, L. (1987). Gender Differences in Cross-Generation Networks. *Sex Roles, 17,* 751–766.

Troll, L., & Bengtson, V. (1979). Generations in the Family. in Burr et al. (Eds.), *Contemporary Theories about the Family, Volume I.* New York: Free Press.

Troll, L. A., Miller, S. J., & Atchley, R. C. (1979). *Families in Later Life.* Belmont, CA: Wadsworth.

Trost, J. (1980). The Concept of One-Parent Family. *Journal of Comparative Family Studies, 11,* 129–138.

Trost, J. (ed.). (1980). *The Family in Change.* Vesteras, Sweden: International Library.

Tschann, J., Johnston, J. R., & Kline, M. (1989). Family Process and Children's Functioning During Divorce. *Journal of Marriage and the Family, 51,* 431–444.

Tucker, M. B., & Mitchell-Kernan, C. (1990). New Trends in Black American Interracial Marriage: the Social Structural Context. *Journal of Marriage and the Family, 52,* 209–218.

Tucker, M. B., & Taylor, R. J. (1989). Demographic Correlates of Relationship Status Among Black Americans. *Journal of Marriage and the Family, 51,* 655–665.

Turnbull, S. K., & Turnbull, J. M. (1983). To Dream the Impossible Dream: An Agenda for Stepparents. *Family Relations, 32,* 227–230.

Udry, J. R. (1963). Complementarity in Mate Selection: A Perceptual Approach. *Marriage and Family Living, 25,* 281–289.

Udry, J. R. (1965). The Influence of the Ideal Mate Image on Mate Selection and Mate Perception. *Journal of Marriage and the Family, 27,* 477–482.

Uhlenberg, P. (1978). Changing Configurations of the Life Course. in T. K. Hareven (Ed.), *Transitions: The Family and the Life Course in Historical Perspective.* New York: Academic.

Uhlenberg, P. (1980). Death and the Family. *Journal of Family History, 5,* 313–320.

Umberson, D., & Gove, W. R. (1989). Parenthood and Psychological Well-Being: Theory, Measurement and Stage in the Family Life Course. *Journal of Family Issues, 10,* 440–462.

Upchurch, D. M., & McCarthy, J. (1990). The Timing of First Birth and High School Completion. *American Sociological Review, 55,* 224–234.

Urlanis, B. (1971). Babushka v sem'e. *Literaturnaya gazeta,* March 3: 11.

Vannoy, D. (1991). Social Differentiation, Contemporary Marriage, and Human Development. *Journal of Family Issues, 12,* 251–267.

Vannoy, D., & Philliber, W. W. (1992). Wife's Employment and Quality of Marriage. *Journal of Marriage and the Family, 54,* 387-398.

Vannoy-Hiller, D., & Philliber, W. W. (1989). *Equal Partners: Successful Women in Marriage.* Newbury Park, CA: Sage.

Vaughan, D. (1986). *Uncoupling: Turning Points in Intimate Relationships.* New York: Oxford University Press.

Veevers, J. E. (1973). Voluntary Childless Wives. *Sociology and Social Research, 57,* 356–365.

Veevers, J. E. (1974). The Moral Careers of Voluntarily Childless Wives. in S. Wakil (Ed.), *Marriage and the Family in Canada: A Reader.* Toronto: Copp-Clark.

Vinovskis, M. A. (1981). An "Epidemic" of Adolescent Pregnancy? Some Historical Considerations. *Journal of Family History, 6,* 205–230.

Vosburgh, M. G., & Juliani, R. N. (1990). Contrasts in Ethnic Family Patterns: The Irish and the Italians. *Journal of Comparative Family Studies, 21,* 269–286.

Voydanoff, P. (1980). Work Roles as Stressors in Corporate Families, *Family Relations, 29.*

Voydanoff, P., & Donnelly, B. W. (1988). Economic Distress, Family Coping, and Quality of Family Life. in Voydanoff & Majka (Eds.), *Families and*

Economic Distress (pp. 97–116). Newbury Park, CA: Sage.

Voydanoff, P., Donnelly, B. W., & Fine, M. A. (1988). Economic Distress, Social Integration, and Family Satisfaction. *Journal of Family Issues, 9,* 545–564.

Vuchinich, S. (1987). Starting and Stopping Spontaneous Family Conflicts. *Journal of Marriage and the Family, 49,* 591–601.

Vuchinich, S., Hetherington, E. M., Vuchinich, R. A., & Clingempeel, W. G. (1991). Parent-Child Interaction and Gender Differences in Early Adolescents' Adaptation to Stepfamilies. *Developmental Psychology, 27,* 618–626.

Wachowiak, D., & Bragg, H. (1980). Open Marriage and Marital Adjustment. *Journal of Marriage and the Family, 42,* 57–62.

Waite, L. J., Haggstrom, G. W., & Kanouse, D. E. (1985a). Changes in the Employment Activities of New Parents. *American Sociological Review, 50,* 263–272.

Waite, L. J., Haggstrom, G. W., & Kanouse, D. E. (1985b). The Consequences of Parenthood for the Marital Stability of Young Adults. *American Sociological Review, 50,* 850–857.

Waite, L. J., & Lillard, L. A. (1991). Children and Marital Disruption, *American Journal of Sociology, 96,* 930–953.

Waldrop, J. (1990). Shades of Black. *American Demographics, 12,* 30–34.

Walker, A. J. (1985). Reconceptualizing Family Stress. *Journal of Marriage and the Family, 47,* 827–837.

Walker, A. J., Pratt, C. C., Hwa-Yong Shin, & Jones, L. L. (1990). Motives for Parental Caregiving and Relationship Quality. *Family Relations, 39,* 51–56.

Walker, H. A. (1988). Black-White Differences in Marriage and Family Patterns. in Dornbusch & Strober (Eds.), *Feminism, Children, and the New Families.* New York: Guilford.

Walker, K. N., & Messinger, L. (1979). Remarriage After Divorce: Dissolution and Reconstruction of Family Boundaries. *Family Process, 18,* 185–192.

Wall, R. (1989). Leaving Home and Living Alone: An Historical Perspective. *Population Studies, 43,* 369–389.

Waller, W. (1937). The Rating and Dating Complex. *American Sociological Review, 2,* 727–734.

Waller, W., & Hill, R. (1951). *The Family: A Dynamic Interpretation.* New York: Holt, Rinehart, and Winston.

Wallerstein, J. S., & Blakeslee, S. (1989). *Second Chances: Men, Women, and Children a Decade After Divorce.* New York: Ticknor and Fields.

Walster, E., & Walster, G. W. (1978). *A New Look at Love.* Reading, MA: Addison-Wesley.

Walters, J., & Stinnett, N. (1971). Parent-Child Relationships: A Decade Review of Research. in Broderick (Ed.), *A Decade Review of Research and Action.* Minneapolis: National Council on Family Relations.

Walters, L. (1982). Are Families Different from Other Groups? *Journal of Marriage and the Family, 44,* 341–350.

Ware, H. (1979). Polygyny: Women's Views in a Transitional Society, Nigeria 1975. *Journal of Marriage and the Family, 41.*

Warner, R. L., Lee, G. R., & Lee, J. (1986). Social Organization, Spousal Resources, and Marital Power: A Cross-Cultural Study. *Journal of Marriage and the Family, 48,* 121–128.

Watson, J. B. (1928). *Psychological Care of Infant and Child.* New York: W. W. Norton.

Watson, R. E. L. (1983). Premarital Cohabitation vs. Traditional Courtship: Their Effects on Subsequent Marital Adjustment. *Family Relations, 32,* 139–147.

Watzlawick, P., Beavin, J. H., & Jackson, D. D. (1967). *Pragmatics of Human Communication: A Study of Interactional Patterns, Pathologies, and Paradoxes.* New York: Norton.

Weigert, A. J., & Thomas, D. L. (1971). Family as a Conditional Universe. *Journal of Marriage and the Family, 33,* 188–194.

Weiner, N. F. (1983). Baby Bust and Baby Boom: A Study of Family Size in a Group of Chicago Faculty Wives Born 1900–1934. *Journal of Family History, 8,* 279–291.

Weiss, R. S. (1979). *Going It Alone: The Family Life and Social Situation of the Single Parent.* New York: Basic Books.

Weitzman, L. J. (1972). Sex-Role Socialization in Picture Books for Preschool Children. *American Journal of Sociology, 77,* 1125–1150.

Weitzman, L. J. (1981). *The Marriage Contract: Spouses, Lovers, and the Law.* New York: Free Press.

Weitzman, L. J. (1988). Women and Children Last: The Social and Economic Consequences of Divorce Reform Laws. Dornbusch and Strober (Eds.), *Feminism, Children and the New Families* (pp. 212–248). New York: Guilford.

Welch, C. E., & Price-Bonham, S. (1983). A Decade of No-Fault Divorce Revisited: California, Georgia, and Washington. *Journal of Marriage and the Family, 45,* 411–418.

Wells, R. V. (1992). The Population of England's Colonies in America: Old English or New Americans? *Population Studies, 46,* 85–102.

Wente, A. S., & Cockenberg, S. B. (1976). Transition to Fatherhood: Lamaze Preparation, Adjustment Difficulty and the Husband-Wife Relationship. *The Family Coordinator, 25.*

Werner, P. D., & LaRussa, G. W. (1985). Persistence and Change in Sex-Role Stereotypes. *Sex Roles, 12,* 1089–1100.

Westermarck, E. (1926). *A Short History of Marriage.* New York: MacMillan.

Westoff, C. F., & Ryder, N. B. (1977). *The Contraceptive Revolution.* Princeton, NJ: Princeton University Press.

Wetherell, C. (1981). Slave Kinship: A Case Study of the South Carolina Good Hope Plantation, 1835–1856. *Journal of Family History, 6,* 294–308.

Wethington, E., & Kessler, R. C. (1989). Employment, Parental Responsibility, and Psychological Distress: A Longitudinal Study of Married Women. *Journal of Family Issues, 10,* 527–546.

Wheeler, M. (1974). *No-Fault Divorce.* Boston: Beacon.

Whiffen, V. E. & Gottlieb, I. H. (1989). Stress and Coping in Maritally Distressed and Nondistressed Couples. *Journal of Social and Personal Relationships, 6,* 327–344.

White, B. B. (1989). Gender Differences in Marital Communication Patterns. *Family Process, 28,* 89–106.

White, D. G. (1983). Female Slaves: Sex Roles and Status in the Antebellum Plantation South. *Journal of Family History, 8,* 248–261.

White, L. K. (1979). Sex Differentials in the Effect of Remarriage on Global Happiness. *Journal of Marriage and the Family, 41,* 869–876.

White, L. K., & Booth, A. (1985). The Quality and Stability of Remarriages: the Role of Stepchildren. *American Sociological Review, 50,* 689–698.

White, L. K., & Booth, A. (1991). Divorce Over the Life Course: The Role of Marital Happiness. *Journal of Family Issues, 12,* 5–21.

White, L. K., Brinkerhoff, D. B., & Booth, A. (1985). The Effect of Marital Disruption on Child's Attachment to Parents. *Journal of Family Issues, 6,* 5–22.

White, L., & Edwards, J. N. (1990). Emptying the Nest and Parental Well-Being: An Analysis of National Panel Data. *American Sociological Review, 55,* 235–242.

White, S. W., & Bloom, B. L. (1981). Factors Related to the Adjustment of Divorcing Men. *Family Relations, 30,* 349–360.

Whyte, M. K. (1990). *Dating, Mating, and Marriage.* New York: Aldine de Gruyter.

Wikler, L. (1981). Chronic Stresses of Families of Mentally Retarded Children. *Family Relations, 59,* 281–288.

Wilcox, J., & Golden, H. H. (1982). Prolific Immigrants and Dwindling Natives?: Fertility Patterns in Western Massachusetts, 1850–1880. *Journal of Family History, 7,* 265–288.

Wilkie, C. F., & Ames, E. W. (1986). The Relationship of Infant Crying to Parental Stress in the Transition to Parenthood. *Journal of Marriage and the Family, 48,* 545–550.

Wilkinson, D. (1987). Ethnicity. in Sussman & Steinmetz (Eds.), *Handbook of Marriage and the Family.* New York: Plenum.

Williams, J. A., Jr., Bean, F. D., & Curtis, R. L., Jr. (1970). The Impact of Parental Constraints on the Development of Behavior Disorders. *Social Forces, 49,* 283–291.

Williams, J. D., & Jacoby, A. P. (1989). The Effects of Premarital Heterosexual and Homosexual Experience on Dating and Marriage Desirability. *Journal of Marriage and the Family, 51,* 489–497.

Williams, L. B. (1991). Determinants of Unintended Childbearing Among Ever-Married Women in the United States 1973–1988. *Family Planning Perspectives, 23,* 212–215.

Williams, N. (1990). *The Mexican American Family: Tradition and Change.* New York: General Hall.

Willie, C. V. (1988). *A New Look at Black Families.* Dix Hills, NY: General Hall.

Willie, C. V., & Greenblatt, S. L. (1978). Four "Classic" Studies of Power Relationships in Black Families: A Review and Look to the Future. *Journal of Marriage and the Family, 40.*

Willmott, P., & Young, M. (1960). *Family and Class in a London Suburb.* London: Routledge and Kegan Paul.

Wilson, S. M., & Medora, N. P. (1990). Gender Comparisons of College Students' Attitudes Toward Sexual Behavior. *Adolescence, 25,* 615–627.

Winch, R. F. (1958). *Mate-Selection: A Study of Complementary Needs.* New York: Harper and Brothers.

Winch, R. F. (1962). *Identification and Its Familial Determinants.* Indianapolis: Bobbs-Merrill.

Winch, R. F. (1967). Another Look at the Theory of Complementary Needs in Mate Selection. *Journal of Marriage and the Family, 29,* 756–762.

Winch, R. F. (1979). Toward a Model of Familial Organization. in W. Burr, R. Hill, F. I. Nye, & I. Reiss (Eds.), *Contemporary Theories about the Family, Volume I.* New York: Free Press.

Winch, R., & Blumberg, R. L. (1968). Societal Complexity and Familial Organization. in Winch & Goodman (Eds.), *Selected Studies in Marriage and the Family.* New York: Holt, Rinehart, and Winston.

Wineberg, H. (1990a). Delayed Childbearing, Childlessness, and Marital Disruption. *Journal of Comparative Family Studies, 21,* 99–111.

Wineberg, H. (1990b). Variations in Fertility by Marital Status and Marriage Order. *Family Planning Perspectives, 22,* 256–260.

Winks, P. L. (1980–81). Divorce Mediation: A Nonadversary Procedure for the No-Fault Divorce. *Journal of Family Law, 19,* 615–653.

Wojtkiewicz, R. A., McLanahan, S., & Garfinkel, I. (1990). The Growth of Families Headed By Women: 1950–1980. *Demography, 27,* 19–30.

Wolfenstein, M. (1953). Trends in Infant Care. *American Journal of Orthopsychiatry, 23,* 120–130.

Woolsey, S. H. (1977). Pied Piper Politics and the Child Care Debate. *Daedalus* (Spring).

Wright, D. W., & Price, S. (1986). Court-Ordered Child Support Payment: The Effect of the Former-Spouse Relationship on Compliance. *Journal of Marriage and the Family, 48,* 869–874.

Wright, P. H., & Keple, T. (1981). Friends and Parents of a Sample of High School Juniors: An Exploratory Study of Relationship Intensity and Interpersonal Rewards. *Journal of Marriage and the Family, 43,* 559–570.

Ybarra, L. (1982). When Wives Work: The Impact on the Chicano Family. *Journal of Marriage and the Family, 44,* 169–178.

Yllo, K. (1983). Sexual Equality and Violence Against Wives in American States. *Journal of Comparative Family Studies, 14,* 67–86.

Yogev, S. (1981). Do Professional Women Have Egalitarian Marital Relationships? *Journal of Marriage and the Family, 43,* 865–871.

Young, F. W. (1967). Incest Taboos and Social Solidarity. *American Journal of Sociology, 72,* 589–600.

Zacks, E., Green, R., & Marrow, J. (1988). Comparing Lesbian and Heterosexual Couples on the Circumplex Model: An Initial Investigation. *Family Process, 27,* 471–484.

Zaretsky, E. (1976). *Capitalism, the Family, and Personal Life.* New York: Harper and Row.

Zelditch, M. (1955). Role Differentiation in the Nuclear Family: A Comparative Study. in Parsons and Bales (Eds.), *Family, Socialization, and Interaction Process.* New York: Free Press.

Zelditch, M., Jr. (1964). Cross-Cultural Analysis of Family Structure. in Christensen (Ed.), *Handbook of Marriage and the Family* (pp. 492–497).

Zelnik, M., Kantner, J. F., & Ford, K. (1981). *Sex and Pregnancy in Adolescence.* Beverly Hills: Sage.

Zick, C. D., & Smith, K. R. (1986). Immediate and Delayed Effects of Widowhood on Poverty: Patterns from the 1970s. *Gerontologist, 26,* 669–675.

Zietlow, P. H., & Sillars, A. L. (1988). Life-Stage Differences in Communication During Marital Conflicts. *Journal of Social and Personal Relationships, 5,* 223–245.

Zimmerman, C. C. (1947). *Family Civilization.* New York: Harper and Brothers.

Zimmerman, C. C. (1949). *The Family of Tomorrow.* New York: Harper and Brothers.

Ziskin, J., & Ziskin, M. (1973). *The Extra-Marital Sex Contract.* Los Angeles: Nash.

Zube, M. (1982). Changing Behavior and Outlook of Aging Men and Women: Implications for Marriage in the Middle and Later Years. *Family Relations, 31,* 147–156.

Zuravin, S. J. (1991). Unplanned Childbearing and Family Size: Their Relationship to Child Neglect and Abuse. *Family Planning Perspectives, 23,* 155–161.

INDEX OF NAMES

INDEX OF SUBJECTS